D0267111

KEYGuide

On the Move

The Sights

What to Do

Walks and Tours

Eating and Staying

Planning

Maps

KEYGuide

# The AA KEYGuide Paris

# Contents


## Understanding Paris 4–10

## Living Paris 11–22
Food in Paris 12–13
Style in Paris 14–15
Culture and Design 16–17
Entertainment in Paris 18–19
The River Seine 20–21
Romance in Paris 22

## The Story of Paris 23–40
250BC–AD1000: The Beginnings 24–25
1000–1450: Medieval Paris 26–27
1450–1640: Royal Authority 28–29
1640–1789: Life at Versailles 30–31
1789–1799: The Revolution 32–33
1799–1815: Napoleon's Paris 34–35
1815–1900: 19th-Century Turmoil 36–37
1900–2000: The 20th Century 38–39
From 2000: 21st-Century Paris 40

## On the Move 41–64
Arriving 42–46
By Air 42–43
By Train 44–45
By Car or Long-Distance Bus 46
Getting Around 47–59
Introduction and Tickets 47–48
Paris Métro 49–53
Buses 54–55
RER and Other Train Lines 56–57
Taxis and the Batobus 58
Walking, Bicycling, In-line Skating 59
Driving 60–61
Visitors with a Disability 62
Leaving Paris 63–64

## The Sights 65–170
Sights Locator Maps 66–69
Sightseeing Areas 70–75
A–Z of Sights 76–170

## What to Do 171–222
Shopping 172–192
Shopping Locator Maps 172–175
Shopping Introduction 176
Shopping Areas 177–181
Shopping Directory 182–192
Chain Stores 190–191
Performance 193–208
Performance Introduction 193
Performance Locator Maps 194–197
Performance 198–208
Nightlife 209–215
Sports and Activities 216–220
Children's Paris 221
Festivals and Events 222


**KEY TO SYMBOLS**

- Map reference
- Address
- Telephone number
- Opening times
- Admission prices
- Métro station
- Bus number
- Train station
- Ferry/boat
- Driving directions
- Tourist office
- Tours
- Guidebook
- Restaurant
- Café
- Shop
- Lavatories
- Number of rooms
- Parking
- No smoking
- Air conditioning
- Swimming pool
- Gym
- Other useful information

## Out and About 223–248

Walks 224–233
River Trip 234–235
Excursions 236–247
City Tours 248

## Eating 249–278

Locator Maps 250–253
Eating Out in Paris 254–259
A–Z of Restaurants 260–277
Chain Restaurants 278

## Staying 279–294

Locator Maps 280–283
Staying in Paris 284
A–Z of Hotels 285–293
Chain Hotels 294

## Planning 295–316

Before You Go 296–297
Practicalities 298–299
Money Matters 300–301
Health 302–303
Communication 304–305
Finding Help 305–306
Media 306–307
Opening Times and Tickets 307–308
Tourist Offices 308–309
Films and Books 309
Websites 310
Words and Phrases 311–316

## Maps

Sightseeing and Shopping Areas Inside Front Cover
City Locator 4
Greater Paris 6–7
Airport Locator 42
Métro 52–53
Train Station Locator 57
Sights Locator 66–69
Sightseeing Areas 70–75
Champs-Élysées 79
Parc de la Villette 147
Shopping Locator 172–175
Shopping Areas 177–181
Performance Locator 194–197
Walks 224–233
River Trip 234–235
Excursions 236
Versailles 247
Eating Locator 250–253
Staying Locator 280–283
Street Atlas 317–333
Métro Inside Back Cover

## Indexes

Street Index 334–340
Index 341–347

Credits 348–350

# UNDERSTANDING PARIS

**Paris is a seductive capital, legendary for its cuisine, fashion, art collections and architectural beauty. It is a vibrant international city and the heart of France's political, economic, social and cultural life. Although it is thoroughly modern, reminders of the past are vital to the tourism economy and the government strictly enforces building codes and protects historic monuments. So change comes in smaller ways—in fashions, food styles and shop façades. Parisians are still as willing to take to the streets in protest as they were during the Revolution, although they can also demonstrate a strong conservative, conformist streak. The city is making a concerted effort to help visitors feel welcome and Parisians are friendlier and more helpful than they are sometimes reputed to be.**

**FINDING YOUR WAY AROUND**

Paris has no shortage of must-see sights, but if you spend your visit dashing between the Eiffel Tower, Notre-Dame, the Louvre and Sacré-Cœur you'll miss out on the essence of the city. The secret to glimpsing Paris's heart is to enjoy the humble pleasures as well as the world-famous landmarks. Make time to people-watch in a café in St-Germain-des-Prés, relax in the peaceful Jardin du Palais Royal or shop for cheese at one of the local markets.

The Métro is a good way of getting around, with stops by all the key sights, but to really get to know the layout of the city, you can't beat walking between the *quartiers* (districts). Try wandering from St-Germain-des-Prés, through the Latin Quarter, to the Île de la Cité, or from Bastille to Le Marais and across to the Centre Georges Pompidou.

In addition to its *quartiers*, identified by name, Paris is broken into *arrondissements*, numbered 1 to 20. These spiral out in a clockwise direction from the Louvre. You can usually tell which *arrondissement* your destination is in by looking at the last two digits of the postal code.

Paris is split in two by the curving River Seine, with the northern section called the Right Bank and the smaller southern part called the Left Bank. Thirty-six bridges connect the two sides. Northeast of the Latin Quarter, two islands sit in the middle of the Seine: the historic Île de la Cité and the tiny Île St-Louis.

**THE ECONOMY**

Paris and the rest of the Île-de-France region are the economic powerhouse of France, accounting for 30 per cent of French GDP. The Île de France has a population of 11 million and is home to more than 650,000 companies, while Paris has just over two million residents and 250,000 companies. Tourism is one of its major economic strengths—Paris attracted more than 28 million visitors in 2002. Other key sectors are financial services, information technology, digital imaging, fashion, design and creative industries. The good news for visitors and residents alike is that it is not an overly expensive city—a 2002 study of cost of living in 144 cities ranked Paris in 74th place. But as in many other countries, France's economy suffered from the after-effects of September 11: Economic growth slowed to 1.2 per cent in 2002. The unemployment rate has been creeping up and was at 9.3 per cent in March 2003.

## PARIS'S DISTRICTS AT A GLANCE

**Latin Quarter** (Left Bank, east): Paris's heart of learning since the Middle Ages, packed with churches, medieval alleyways and the beautiful Jardin du Luxembourg.
**St-Germain-des-Prés** (Left Bank, central): Bordering the Latin Quarter and packed with cafés and bookshops.
**Montparnasse** (Left Bank, south): Dominated by the giant Tour Montparnasse.
**Chaillot** (Right Bank, west): Its focal point is the Palais de Chaillot, with its wonderful views across the Seine to the Eiffel Tower.
**Champs-Élysées** (Right Bank, west-central): Paris's most famous avenue is packed with shops, cinemas and cafés, and crowned by the Arc de Triomphe.
**Faubourg St-Honoré** (Right Bank, north of Champs-Élysées): The place to head for haute couture.

*The flower market, Île de la Cité*

*Cabaret at Montmartre*

*Enjoying a drink on the Île St-Louis*

**Les Halles** (Right Bank, central): Once the hub of market life, Les Halles now has a vast modern shopping complex, as well as Paris's most confusing Métro station.
**Le Marais** (Right Bank, east-central): Trendy cafés, shops and avant-garde art galleries. The Centre Georges Pompidou sits on its western border.
**Bastille** (Right Bank, east): Once the launch pad to the Revolution, now a fashionable nightspot, close to Le Marais.
**Île de la Cité** (on the Seine): This hectic island is the birthplace of Paris, and home to Notre-Dame, the Conciergerie and Sainte-Chapelle.
**Île St-Louis** (on the Seine): Smaller and quieter than its more famous cousin, the Île de la Cité.
**Pigalle** (Right Bank, south of Montmartre): The red-light district.
**Montmartre** (Right Bank, far north): This former village, on a hill overlooking the city, has two of Paris's most famous landmarks—Sacré-Cœur and, on the Pigalle border, the Moulin Rouge.

### POLITICS

Paris is the undisputed heart of national power, although the government of President Jacques Chirac and Prime Minister Jean-Pierre Raffarin has been making some moves to decentralize and devolve power to the regions. In the 2002 presidential elections, the unthinkable almost happened as anti-immigration sentiments and voter apathy allowed the candidate of the far-right National Front, Jean-Marie Le Pen, to defeat the then Prime Minister Lionel Jospin and enter the second round of elections. This rude awakening brought voters out to re-elect Chirac by a huge majority of almost 82 per cent.

Paris is run by the popular Socialist mayor Bertrand Delanoë, who is working on the greening of the city. He has angered motorists by closing the highway running along the Seine's Right Bank to traffic in the summer, turning part of it into Paris Plage, an urban beach and pleasure park.

### LANGUAGE AND SOCIETY

French is spoken by the entire population of France, although the country has some regional dialects. Most children study English, and many Parisians make the effort to speak it to visitors. The French are extremely proud of their language, however, and make a concerted effort to protect it from anglicization by coining French replacements for such words as Walkman (*balladeur*) and email (*mèl*).

Paris is a multicultural city, with large communities of people of North African, African, Vietnamese, Chinese and other origins. Like most major cities, it is undergoing gentrification, with families and people on lower incomes pushed out to the suburbs as property prices rise in the central districts.

Crime rates have increased in recent years, but Paris is still a fairly safe city for visitors, as long as they take reasonable precautions to protect their belongings from pickpockets.

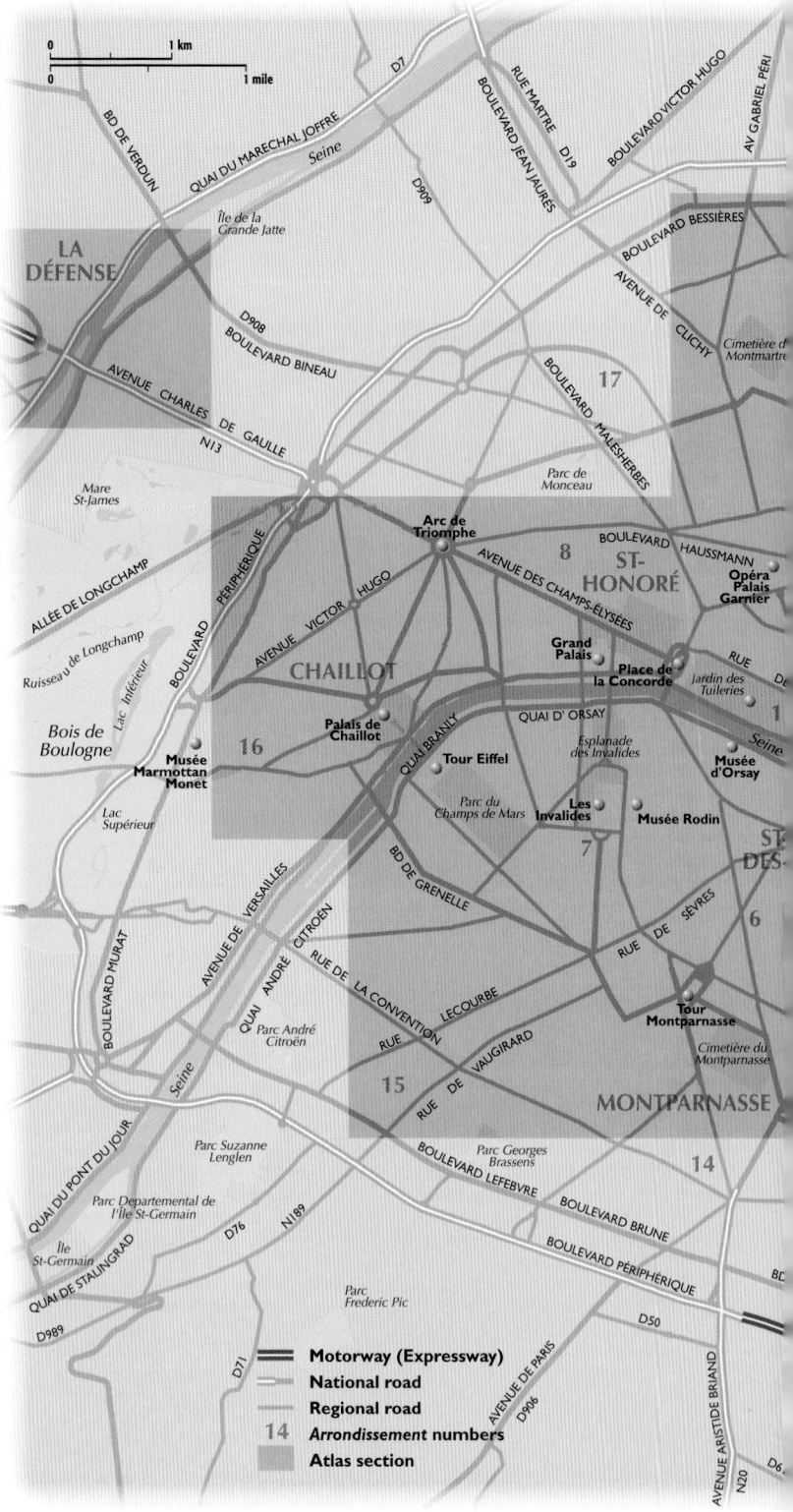
0
1 km
0
1 mile
BD DE VERDUN
QUAI DU MARECHAL JOFFRE
Seine
D7
D909
RUE MARTYRE
D19
BOULEVARD JEAN JAURES
BOULEVARD VICTOR HUGO
AV GABRIEL PERI
Île de la Grande Jatte
LA DÉFENSE
BOULEVARD BESSIÈRES
AVENUE DE CLICHY
Cimetière de Montmartre
D908
BOULEVARD BINEAU
AVENUE CHARLES DE GAULLE
N13
17
BOULEVARD MALESHERBES
Parc de Monceau
Mare St-James
Arc de Triomphe
BOULEVARD HAUSSMANN
8
ST-HONORÉ
Opéra Palais Garnier
ALLÉE DE LONGCHAMP
BOULEVARD PÉRIPHÉRIQUE
AVENUE VICTOR HUGO
AVENUE DES CHAMPS-ÉLYSÉES
Ruisseau de Longchamp
Lac Intérieur
CHAILLOT
Grand Palais
Place de la Concorde
RUE
Jardin des Tuileries
1
Bois de Boulogne
Palais de Chaillot
QUAI D' ORSAY
16
QUAI BRANLY
Tour Eiffel
Esplanade des Invalides
Seine
Musée d'Orsay
Musée Marmottan Monet
Lac Supérieur
Parc du Champs de Mars
Les Invalides
Musée Rodin
7
ST-DES-
BD DE GRENELLE
AVENUE DE VERSAILLES
6
RUE DE SÈVRES
BOULEVARD MURAT
QUAI ANDRÉ CITROEN
RUE DE LA CONVENTION
LECOURBE
Tour Montparnasse
Parc André Citroën
RUE
Cimetière du Montparnasse
Seine
15
RUE DE VAUGIRARD
MONTPARNASSE
Parc Suzanne Lenglen
Parc Georges Brassens
14
BOULEVARD LEFEBVRE
QUAI DU PONT DU JOUR
Parc Departemental de l'Île St-Germain
D76
N189
BOULEVARD BRUNE
Île St-Germain
BOULEVARD PÉRIPHÉRIQUE
QUAI DE STALINGRAD
Parc Frederic Pic
D989
D50
D71
Motorway (Expressway)
National road
Regional road
14 Arrondissement numbers
Atlas section
AVENUE DE PARIS
D906
AVENUE ARISTIDE BRIAND
N20

SEINE-ST-DENIS
Cimetière Parisien de Pantin-Bobigny
Cimetière Parisien de St-Ouen
AVENUE MICHELET
AUTOROUTE DU NORD
E19
N1
AV DU PRÉSIDENT WILSON
Canal St-Denis
D114
AVENUE JEAN JAURÈS
D31
BOULEVARD PÉRIPHÉRIQUE
BOULEVARD NEY
Canal de l'Ourcq
RUE ORDENER
AVENUE JEAN LOLIVE
N3
Parc de la Villette
AVENUE DE FLANDRE
MONTMARTRE
18
Sacré-Cœur
Bassin de la Villette
19
Parc de la Butte Rouge
D117
PIGALLE
BOULEVARD LA FAYETTE
Canal St-Martin
Parc des Buttes Chaumont
9
RUE
10
RUE DE BELLEVILLE
BOULEVARD MORTIER
BD DE SÉBASTOPOL
MAGENTA
Parc de Belleville
2
RÉPUBLIQUE
20
AV DE LA RÉPUBLIQUE
Jardin du Palais Royal
LES HALLES
3
Musée des Arts Décoratifs
Musée d'Art et d'Histoire du Judaïsme
Musée Picasso
Cimetière du Père-Lachaise
RIVOLI
Centre Georges Pompidou
Musée du Louvre
LE MARAIS
BOULEVARD VOLTAIRE
PARIS
Musée Carnavalet
Sainte-Chapelle
Conciergerie
Île de la Cité
4
11
N302
Places des Vosges
GERMAIN PRÉS
Notre-Dame
Musée National du Moyen Âge
Île St-Louis
BASTILLE
BOULEVARD ST-MICHEL
RUE ST-JACQUES
Jardin du Luxembourg
Panthéon
Institut du Monde Arabe
BOULEVARD DIDEROT
12
QUARTIER LATIN
Jardin des Plantes
QUAI D'AUSTERLITZ
La Mosquée
Muséum National d'Histoire Naturelle
5
Parc de Bercy
BOULEVARD ARAGO
BD VINCENT AURIOL
BERCY
N6
QUAI DE BERCY
Lac Daumesnil
BOULEVARD PONIATOWSKI
Île de Bercy
Île de Reuilly
13
TOLBIAC
RUE DE
AVENUE D'ITALIE
AVENUE DE CHOISY
Bois de Vincennes
Seine
D50B
Parc Montsouris
BOULEVARD MASSÉNA
JOURDAN
QUAI DES CARRIÈRES
Parc Kellerman
E50
AUTOROUTE DU SOLEIL
E15
D127
AUTOROUTE DU SOLEIL
AVENUE DE VERDUN
D54B
D124
D55
VAL-DE-MARNE
D38

# THE BEST OF PARIS

## BEST MUSEUMS AND GALLERIES

**Centre Georges Pompidou** (see pages 82–86): It's not to everyone's taste, but this eye-catching venue holds a vast collection of modern art.

**Musée Carnavalet** (see pages 114–115): Paris's history is brought to life with lavish re-creations of period rooms, memorabilia from the Revolution and prehistoric finds.

**Musée du Louvre** (see pages 118–123): One of the world's most famous art galleries—but you'll have to fight your way through crowds to see the *Mona Lisa*.

**Musée National du Moyen Âge—Thermes de Cluny** (see pages 128–129): Don't be put off by the mouthful of a title—this 15th-century mansion is home to a fascinating collection of medieval art, religious items and day-to-day objects.

**Musée d'Orsay** (see pages 130–134): This former station hosts a stunning collection of Impressionist paintings, and a lot more besides.

**Musée Picasso** (see page 135): Paintings, sculptures and drawings by the great 20th-century artist, in the beautiful Hôtel Salé.

**Musée Rodin** (see page 136): This wins a mention as much for its idyllic surroundings as its art. Auguste Rodin's mesmerizing sculptures are dotted around a soothing garden.

*The wonderful station clock at the Musée d'Orsay (above)*

Le Penseur *(left) takes a pause for thought at the Musée Rodin*

## BEST LANDMARKS

**Arc de Triomphe** (see pages 76–79): The focal point for some of France's most prestigious celebrations.

**Grande Arche** (see page 94): It's not yet as famous as the other landmarks mentioned here, but this colossal marble-clad arch symbolizes Paris's eye to the future.

**Notre-Dame** (see pages 137–141): France's most visited religious building, with wonderful views from its towers.

**Sacré-Cœur** (see pages 154–157): This glistening basilica crowns Montmartre's hill.

**Tour Eiffel** (see pages 164–169): Test your nerves on the third level, 280m (896ft) above ground.

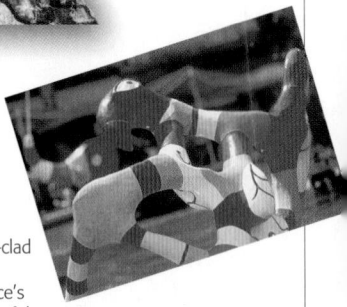

*A lively character from the Stravinsky Fountain, near the Centre Georges Pompidou*

*The Arc de Triomphe (left), commissioned by Napoleon*

## BEST VIEWS

All the landmarks mentioned above give unbeatable views, but the following are also worth a photo stop:

**Palais de Chaillot** (see page 143): Go to the central terrace for wonderful views across the Seine to the Eiffel Tower.

**Panthéon** (see page 144): You can see the Eiffel Tower from the front steps, but for the best panoramas, climb the 206 steps to the circular colonnade.

**Parc de la Turlure** (see page 226): A small, out-of-the-way park in Montmartre with lovely views over Paris and an unusual view of the northern side of Sacré-Cœur.

**La Samaritaine** (see page 192): There are great views across the Seine to the Left Bank from the rooftop 10th floor of Magasin 2 (open April to end October).

**Tour Montparnasse** (see page 170): Take the lift to the 59th-floor terrace for vertigo-inducing views across the city.

**Place de la Concorde** (see page 148): Look northwest along the Champs-Élysées to the Arc de Triomphe, southeast through the Jardin des Tuileries, and southwest across the Seine to the Palais Bourbon.

*Le Ciel de Paris restaurant, on the 56th floor of Tour Montparnasse*

## BEST PLACES TO SHOP

**Agnès B** (see page 185): Chic Parisian fashion.
**Antik Batik** (see page 186): Ethnic-chic.
**Fauchon** (see page 184): The best of French food—at a price.
**Marché aux Puces de St-Ouen** (see page 107): Browse through this vast flea market and you may strike it lucky and find a worthwhile antique.
**Shakespeare and Company** (see page 182): A famous American bookshop alongside the Seine.
**Vanessa Bruno** (see page 187): Casual-chic fashion.

*You can shop for almost anything in Paris*

## BEST PLACES TO STAY

**L'Hotel** (see page 286): Oscar Wilde spent his last days at this deluxe four-star hotel.
**Hôtel Duc de St-Simon** (see page 288): In a beautifully decorated 18th-century mansion near the boulevard St-Germain.
**Hôtel Square** (see page 292): An urban-chic four-star hotel close to the Eiffel Tower.
**Pavillon de la Reine** (see page 292): Louis XIII's wife once lived in this 17th-century residence, on the place des Vosges.
**Ritz** (see page 293): The ultimate in elegance and luxury, former guests include Coco Chanel and Ernest Hemingway.
**Terrass Hotel** (see page 293): There are stunning views from some of the rooms at this four-star hotel in Montmartre.

## BEST PLACES TO EAT

**La Coupole** (see page 266): An art deco brasserie once frequented by Pablo Picasso.
**Georges** (see page 268): Wonderful views and nouvelle cuisine on the top floor of the Centre Georges Pompidou.
**Guy Savoy** (see page 269): A gastronomic temple, close to the Champs-Élysées.
**Market** (see page 270): Contemporary venue with a raw bar and fusion food.
**La Tour d'Argent** (see page 276): Chic interior, great views and exquisite French cuisine.

*Dining at the Brasserie La Lorraine (above), near the Arc de Triomphe. Les Deux Magots (below) is one of Paris's most famous café-bars*

## BEST CAFÉS AND SALONS DE THÉ

**Café Beaubourg** (see page 213): A trendy café near the Centre Georges Pompidou.
**Café de Flore** (see page 213): Follow in the footsteps of Jean-Paul Sartre.
**Les Deux Magots** (see page 211): Hemingway was a frequent visitor to this café-bar in St-Germain-des-Prés.
**Jean-Paul Hévin** (see page 270): Some of Paris's tastiest chocolate.
**Muscade** (see page 271): Enjoy traditional afternoon tea in the grounds of the Palais Royal.

*Clubbing*

## BEST BARS AND CLUBS

**Les Bains** (see page 214): Dance until 6am at this club.
**Café de l'Industrie** (see page 210): A stylish bar in the trendy Bastille area.
**Fourmi** (see page 211): This bar, with its retro interior, is popular with arty types.
**New Régine's Club** (see page 215): A popular restaurant-club, near the Champs-Élysées.
**VIP Room** (see page 215): Popular with the beautiful and the moneyed.

*(From left to right) paintings of Paris; gazing up at the Eiffel Tower; street musicians in Montmartre*

## TOP 15 EXPERIENCES

**Get a bird's eye view of Paris at night** by climbing the Eiffel Tower (see pages 164–169) or the Arc de Triomphe (see pages 76–79).

**Sit in a café in St-Germain-des-Prés** and watch the world go by, or find a bench in the animated Jardin du Luxembourg or Jardin des Tuileries.

**Take a boat trip along the Seine**—it's a cliché but it really is a great way to appreciate the city's major landmarks (see pages 234–235).

**Visit place des Vosges** (see page 150) on a Sunday afternoon, when the cafés are packed with Parisians relaxing to the sounds of street musicians.

**Take advantage of late-opening nights at the Louvre** (Mondays and Wednesdays) and Musée d'Orsay (Thursdays), when there are fewer people.

**Indulge in some retail therapy** in one of the fashion capitals of the world. See pages 177–181 for some of the top shopping areas.

**Stroll along the Champs-Élysées**, Paris's most famous avenue.

**Take the Métro out to Montmartre** for a taste of village life and wonderful views of the city.

**Visit Notre-Dame cathedral** just before a service is due to start.

**Haggle at one of the city's markets** (see page 192), where you can buy anything from cheese and olives to furniture and chandeliers.

**Leave your Métro *carnet* behind for an afternoon and take a wander**—it's the best way to get to know the layout of the city (see pages 224–233 for some suggestions).

**Treat yourself to a meal in one of Paris's top restaurants**—if your credit card is up to it.

**See a performance at the prestigious Opéra Palais Garnier or the striking Opéra Bastille**, or experience the glitz of a show at the famous Moulin Rouge.

**Escape the city** and enjoy some fresher air in the leafy Bois de Vincennes or Bois de Boulogne (see pages 236–237).

**Stroll through the elegant 19th-century shopping arcades known as Les Galeries** (see page 93).

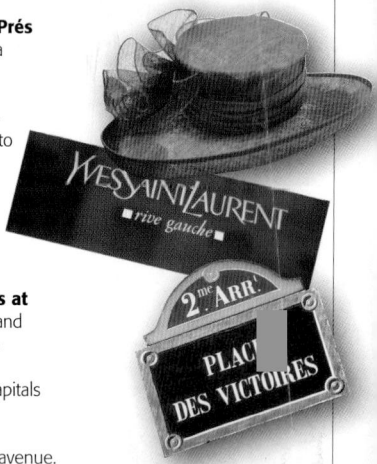


*The Moulin Rouge (below)*

*Walking the dog in the Bois de Vincennes (above).*
*Antiques stands at Bastille (left)*

# Living Paris


Food in Paris 12–13
Style in Paris 14–15
Culture and Design 16–17
Entertainment in Paris 18–19
The River Seine 20–21
Romance in Paris 22

This luxury foodstore (left), in place de la Madeleine, has been selling mustard since 1747

An informal lunch in the Jardin du Palais Royal (left) and truffle recipes for a more sophisticated meal (top right)

# Food in Paris

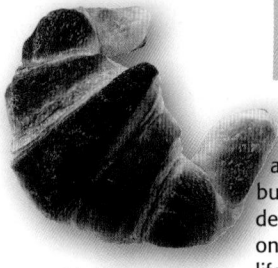

A traditional croissant

Since Paris no longer has a monarchy, it would be easy to assume the class system is dead and buried. Wrong. In this city, one is defined by the table one chooses. No one eats for mere sustenance—food is a lifestyle statement, an evening's entertainment and a way of life. At the sharp end, new chefs flit in and out of vogue with the changing of the seasons. Each September's newspaper reviews can determine the fortunes of a fashionable restaurant as surely as a drama critic's pen assures the life or death of a new musical on Broadway. However, the chic eateries are but the tip of a gastronomic iceberg. Regional restaurants reflect the diversity of French cuisine, with special dishes from Auvergne and Alsace, the Loire and Provence, offering French out-of-towners a taste of home and Parisians a hint of what lies beyond the city. Café culture has an equally wide following, with the smart crowd sipping designer coffees on terraces outside the more fashionable museums and blue-collar Parisians chatting in slang at the zinc counters of their local bars.

**Le Train Bleu**

High above the 21st-century fleet of TGV high-speed trains at Gare de Lyon nestles a relic from travel's golden age. Le Train Bleu is a Belle-Époque station brasserie of the type that elsewhere on Europe's flagship railway system has been demolished to make room for high-tech efficiency and cutting-edge design. The restaurant featured in the 1972 film *Travels with My Aunt* and on news broadcasts when President Mitterrand famously entertained Margaret Thatcher there. Ornate mirrors, chandeliers and paintings have been lovingly restored to match the moustachioed waiters, with their starched ankle-length aprons. Service is as unhurried as ever, and it would not be unusual to spend longer over lunch than on the three-hour journey to the south of France.

A mouth-watering dessert (below) from Gérard Mulot's patisserie

Enjoying a meal in the Restaurant du Jour (above)
The elegant Train Bleu (below) is not your average station diner

## No ice cream please, it's summer!

When the best ice cream store in town is closed, you can be sure that winter is long gone and summer has arrived. One of the great ironies of Paris is that from around mid-July until the end of August, the Maison Berthillon, on the Île St-Louis, shuts up shop, since true Parisians spend the height of summer on the coast. Likewise, the owners have resisted franchising the Berthillon name, so for the remaining months of the year, queues extend round the block as staff take their time preparing delicate scoops of home-made *glaces* and sorbets.

Celebrated chef Alain Ducasse (left)

## Café Psycho

France is famous for its *cafés philo*—philosopher hang-outs where students debate the meaning of life over endless pastis and coffee in imitation of the absinthe-swilling thinkers of old. Paris still has many haunts for would-be Sartres and Jungones. But a new generation has swapped role-models, replacing latter day Descartes with France's answer to Jerry Springer. In a *café psycho*, souls are bared as drinkers offer up their personal problems for group discussion, therapy and entertainment. Psychologists chair and mediate the meeting, while fellow punters chip in with their views. Lively afternoon sessions are held at the Flèche d'Or, a converted railway station on the inner *ceinture* loop in northeast Paris.

## Shut your eyes and enjoy the taste

In the 1990s, when interior decoration began to upstage the food in some of the hippest restaurants, there were mutterings that style was in danger of eclipsing the substance of cuisine. Then, a novel and itinerant dining concept hit town: eating in pitch darkness. Itinerant, since the restaurant not only had no name, but could not even give an address—the sensory-teasing experience would spring up in one unlikely location after another, disappearing for months, even years, before emerging afresh. The idea was simple. Visitors would be escorted by blind waiters into a dining room with no light or windows. Deprived of sight, diners relied on other senses to judge the meal. And so a witty assault on food fads evolved into a reappraisal of priorities.

## Le fast food

After decades of barely concealed hostility, Paris is learning to love *le fast food*. Or at any rate *Le Marks & Spencer sandwich*. When the Paris branch of this British institution closed in 2001 (to Prime Ministerial protest), there came an unlikely rescuer, France's most decorated chef Alain Ducasse, who reinvented the deli sandwich bar with the opening of BE Boulangépicier, his upscale interpretation of the deli. Here, eat-in customers enjoy their meals standing up. What next? Trend-watchers suggest Yatoo Patoo machines—vending machines that offer a full meal—springing up in the unlikeliest corners. The name means Everything Everywhere (*il y a tout partout*)!

Browse in the boutiques in Galerie Vivienne (top, right) or at an exclusive store on the place Vendôme (right)

# *Style in* Paris

Parisian style takes a lot of effort or none at all. It is the expensively coutured mannequin walking her identically attired and tinted dog along the Champs-Élysées. Then again, it is also the scruffy unshaven student with his upturned collar and dangling cigarette, flirting with the pretty girl outside a Métro station.

Paris loves style, in that it celebrates those who are happy with and proud of their own image. Parisian style is as much about lifestyle as the packaging. It is not enough simply to wear the right clothes, you must wear them in the right places, be it a sophisticated bar in the 8th *arrondissement* or a hang-out for poets in the Bastille district. Just as new designers emerge with each fashion week, so up-and-coming streets stake their claim on the consumer map: People shopping for traditional art and antiques choose the galleries by the Louvre and Musée d'Orsay; those on the cutting edge prefer the racier art showrooms around the quai d'Austerlitz; the truly self-confident set their own trends with finds from the fleamarkets.

### Haute couture for less

Every well-tailored Parisian knows the avenue Matignon, but they may not be so ready to admit familiarity with the rue de la Pompe. After all, it would be folly to confess to having spent a mere fraction of the showroom price on a genuine Moschino or Versace original. Nevertheless, the canny good dresser will brave the hordes picking their paths through the racks at the seven Réciproque stores in the road in order to snatch up Lacroix and Dior. Since celebrities rarely wear an outfit twice after it has been photographed by the paparazzi, so Réciproque buys them to resell. To deter thieves, Chanel suits have their prized buttons removed, to be sewn back on once the transaction is complete!

### Open secrets of the Left Bank

The nearest the art and antiques dealers of the Left Bank get to shouting about their wares is during the Cinq Jours de l'Objet Extraordinaire, in late spring. The Carré Rive Gauche is an association of galleries on the tributaries of the rue du Bac and rue de Lille. For five days in early summer, the dealers choose to flaunt their most prized possessions. Each shop selects one special item to promote. To celebrate this uncharacteristic sharing of buried treasure, red carpets suddenly appear outside and abundant floral displays grace the doorways. In recent years, visitors have been invited to admire Venetian chandeliers long hidden away in a Sicilian palazzo, Egyptian textiles and rare Beauvais tapestries.

Police officers have joined the in-line skating craze

Even the buses are telling you to go shopping (below)

## It's a girl thing

No matter how expensive the hotel or how hard you push the credit card, as a casual visitor to Paris you can usually just look on in envy at the assurance of the true society *Parisienne*. But now you have the chance to join the ladies who lunch, women who shop and glamorous patrons of the arts. For a price, women staying at the Hôtel Meurice are paired with a chic local girlfriend for the day and taken out on the town. They can visit Left Bank artists' studios for a private view, stop off for a bite to eat and a gossip at the latest see-and-be-seen restaurant, or go shopping with the girls, touring the boutiques of up-and-coming fashion designers.

## Choccy couture

Since the opening of the Carrousel du Louvre, the catwalk has rarely been free from the popping of flashbulbs and the scrutiny of the fickle arbiters of style. But between the seasonal prêt-à-porter shows and Paris Fashion Week, there is one event where all the critics agree that every item of clothing is good enough to eat. Edible couture is the highlight of the autumn *Salon du Chocolat*, with a catwalk show combining the talents and skills of the finest chocolatiers with the city's more daring designers. Despite the irony of painting whisper-thin supermodels in calorie-laden treats, the event appeals to those who like their style off the shoulder as much as on the tip of the tongue.

## In the fast lane

The Champs-Élysées is packed with traffic even in the small hours, but once a month the famous avenue closes to cars. To benefit, pack your in-line skates. Pari-Roller is the social event of the week, as tens of thousands gather near Montparnasse station on Friday evening. At 10pm the crowd becomes a parade and sets off to explore the city. Strictly for experienced skaters, the route varies each week. Itineraries are posted on the website before the event. Once a month, two hours after the skaters have left the starting point, they turn into place Charles-de-Gaulle for the high-speed descent down the Champs-Élysées.

**Catwalk couture by Jean-Charles de Castelbajac and Jean-Paul Gaultier (right)**

Contemporary meets classic: the Institut du Monde Arabe (far right) and the Louvre through the glass pyramid (top)

# Culture and Design

The futuristic Géode at Parc de la Villette (above)

For a city that is so proud of its artistic and architectural heritage, Paris is surprisingly open to new and challenging ideas. Somehow, the integration of the classic and the avant garde is irresistibly successful. One of the most controversial encounters between old and new was I.M. Pei's Pyramid in the courtyard of the Louvre. Some people were appalled at the idea of setting such an uncompromisingly modern structure within the arms of the palace. Yet the brilliant play of light and water not only revived the museum, but focused attention on the beauty of the original building. Likewise, the 1970s Centre Georges Pompidou stands next to the 16th-century church of St-Merri, and, on the Left Bank, the shadows of the 1980s Institut du Monde Arabe mingle with those of Notre-Dame, on the Île de la Cité. The same refreshing attitude marks out the city's cultural life. Where else are you as likely to see a Katharine Hepburn film as an Eddie Murphy flick? As varied a crowd will pack a church for an evening of Vivaldi as will join a jam session by street musicians.

**The film that saved the station**

When Orson Welles came to Europe to film Franz Kafka's *The Trial*, he saved a Paris landmark from demolition. Having just learned that the production had run out of money and could no longer afford expensive Yugoslav locations, he looked across the river from his room in the Hôtel Meurice and saw two full moons—the twin rose windows of the abandoned Gare d'Orsay. He was inspired to film the rest of the movie inside the imposing railway station, so Orsay became a cathedral and even a court of law. The station had a happier ending than the movie, since filming delayed demolition and gave protesters time to lobby the Ministry of Culture to convert the terminus into one of the world's great museums.

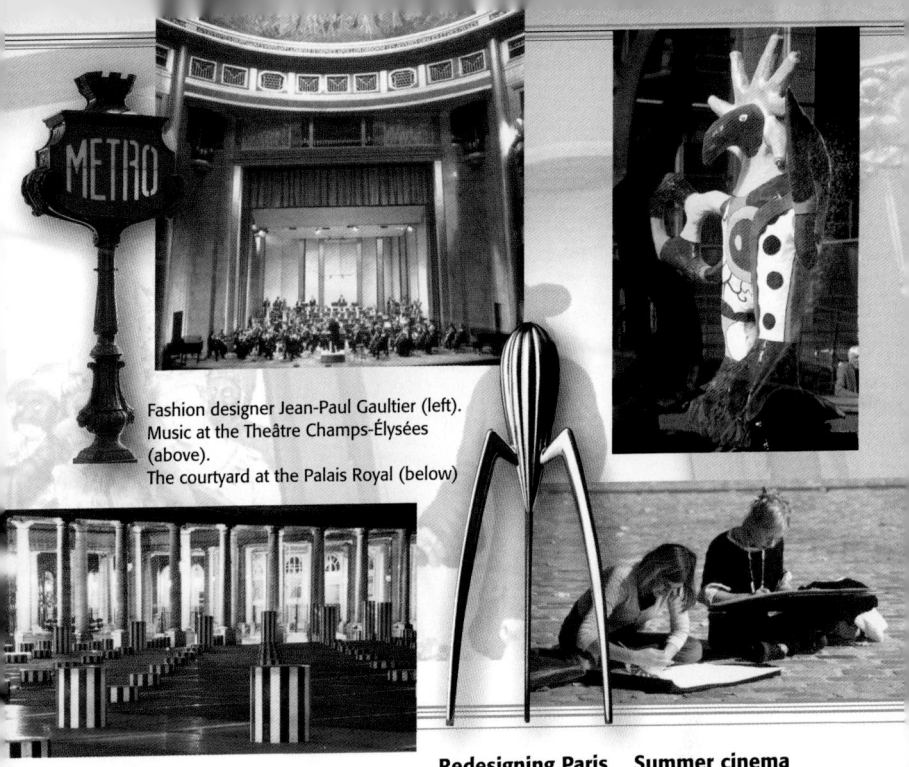


Fashion designer Jean-Paul Gaultier (left).
Music at the Theâtre Champs-Élysées (above).
The courtyard at the Palais Royal (below)

## Bigger than the big screen

No matter how huge the blockbuster, there is one cinema in Paris that can always be relied upon to upstage the action on screen. Le Grand Rex, on the boulevard Poissonnière, is the last of the world's extravagant picture palaces of the 1930s still operating as a mainstream cinema. A Mediterranean night sky adorns the interior of the spectacular domed building, and an arched art deco stage once hosted lavish shows. You can rent an audioguide for a fabulous high-tech walk backstage, through and above the screen, where you'll face a life-size King Kong that escapes its tethers and terrorizes chorus girls waiting in the wings. Eventually, you'll become the unsuspecting star of a film première, performing on the big screen alongside the movie greats.

## Monsieur Shakespeare's first night

Shakespeare is big in Paris. His plays pack out commercial theatres and the Bois de Boulogne has a garden planted with flowers, herbs and trees mentioned in his works. But one play had to wait until 1999 before receiving its Parisian première—the jingoistic *Henry V*, in which English bowmen decimate the French army at the Battle of Agincourt. In fact, outside the village itself, Agincourt remains relatively unknown in France. Director Jean-Luc Benoît risked opening his Avignon festival production in the capital, managing to blame the defeat of the French army on an inept and weak monarchy. The choice of venue was laden with ironies—La Cartoucherie, a former French army arsenal, is in the grounds of the Château de Vincennes, where the victorious Henry V died in 1422.

## Redesigning Paris

He was the man who changed the face of café society, with the influential and much missed Café Costes. Philippe Starck first came to the public's attention when he was commissioned to strip François Mitterrand's presidential apartments at the Élysée Palace of their stuffy imperial furnishings and replace them with the bare minimum. Today, Starck's designs are the sign that you have arrived in a city where style is more important than budget. Nightclubs and bars that have undergone the Philippe Starck treatment are strictly reserved for the beautiful people—the door policy at Les Bains Douches night club, which Starck designed in the 1970s, is still strictly observed. Weekenders coming from London can imbibe the Starck chic before reaching town, in Eurostar trains freshly revitalized by the designer.

## Summer cinema

Summer is the season of cinema in the open air—and in the most unlikely places. From mid-July until the end of August huge screens are erected on the lawns of the Parc de La Villette for the annual Cinéma en Plein Air. Specializing in original-language movies with French subtitles, this is the big event of the picnic season. For the last fortnight of the event, the entire city takes part in Cinéma au Clair de Lune, a series of moonlight screenings in appropriate locations. Previous festivals have seen *Le Fabuleux Destin d'Amélie Poulain* in the streets of Montmartre, the 1947 version of *Les Misérables* outside Victor Hugo's home on place des Vosges, seafaring yarns on the canal banks and major pastoral idylls in the outlying parks.

**Philippe Starck's juice squeezer (above, inset). Part of the zany Stravinsky Fountain (above, top)**

Filming the 1957 movie *Funny Face* (below), with Audrey Hepburn and Fred Astaire

French actress Juliette Binoche (left), star of *Chocolat* (2000) and *The English Patient* (1996)

# *Entertainment in* Paris

Paris comes with a musical soundtrack. Any place that has inspired so many classic love songs is bound to lure musicians from all corners. On the Métro at all hours, outside packed restaurants at noon and in shop doorways by night, itinerant musicians play popular tunes. The music reaches its crescendo on the Fête de la Musique on 21 June, with live bands and orchestras in the main railway stations and huge stages erected in public squares for a night of free concerts.

Music cuts across society, no more so than at the end of the Gay Pride celebrations in June, when party animals of all persuasions dance on the banks of the Seine as the celebrations end with the several thousand strong dawn chorus of *La Vie en Rose*.

Indoor entertainment ranges from productions at the concert halls and the two opera houses to feathered and sequinned showgirl performances. Between the two extremes is a drama scene as varied as that in the West End or Broadway. Many English-language productions are also staged.

As still as stone—a mime artist in Montmartre

**The fabulous Paris of Amélie**

Jean-Pierre Jeunet's cinematic vision *Le Fabuleux Destin d'Amélie Poulain* (2001) re-established Paris as a city for smooching. Keen to capture for themselves a hint of the romance, visitors eagerly scout locations from the film's most memorable moments. Much of the movie was shot around Montmartre, where the Métro station and streets are just as bustling and picturesque in real life as on screen. The actual café and shops featured in the film are on rue des Trois Frères. Other key scenes took place at the Gare de l'Est and Gare du Nord, behind which lies Amélie's hideaway, the Canal St-Martin. The funfair, where actress Audrey Tautou and actor Mathieu Kassowitz ride the ghost train is the Foire du Trône, in the Bois de Vincennes, a fair which takes place every April and May.

The Opéra Palais Garnier (below) was once the largest venue of its kind in the world

Paris's entertainment scene ranges from partying at Club Med World (above) to listening to a brass band in the Jardin du Luxembourg (left, top)—not forgetting the famous Moulin Rouge (left)

## Cabaret on the hill

Just as Baz Luhrmann's sensational 2001 film *Moulin Rouge* dazzled audiences, so the sails of the famous red windmill still dominate the entertainment strip between Pigalle and Clichy, at the foot of Montmartre's hill. Yet beyond the glitz of today's touristy *Moulin* lie many less lavish, but still authentic, cabaret shows. Rue des Martyrs is home to rumbustuous musical entertainment every night. Michou, with his outrageous glasses and sharp suits, still presents Paris's most famous drag revue. Across the road is the rival drag show at Madame Arthur, while more conventional cancan can be seen at the fabulously brash La Nouvelle Eve, at 25 rue Fontaine. For a glimpse of the former haunt of penniless artists, climb Montmartre's hill to Au Lapin Agile, at 22 rue des Saules.

## Stars in their natural habitat

The gossip columns will have you believe that movie stars always hang out at the Buddha Bar and Man Ray. In truth, celluloid legends who call Paris home tend to be seen in the streets around their houses and apartments. Icon Catherine Deneuve likes to shop and sip on the Left Bank–not around the postcard vendors of St-Michel, but the quieter streets beyond the boulevard St-Germain. Le Bon Marché is the department store where you are most likely to bump into a French film star doing the weekly shop. Opposite the shop is the Hotel Lutétia, where Miss Deneuve may be seen granting an interview to journalists from *Madame Figaro* or *Marie Claire*.

## Dancing by the bridge of songs

Films sell Paris as a place where lovers burst into song and dance at the drop of a shoulder strap. The most danced under, over and on bridge in the city is Le Pont Neuf. This was the backdrop for Gene Kelly to sweep Leslie Caron off her feet to the strains of George Gershwin's *Our Love is here to Stay* in *An American in Paris* (1951). Woody Allen paid homage to that scene when he re-created the moment, with the help of Goldie Hawn in *Everyone Says I Love You* (1996). The location shared top billing in *Les Amants du Pont Neuf* (1991) and was the spot where Jeanne Moreau dived into the Seine in François Truffaut's *Jules et Jim* (1962). Romance also blossomed for Audrey Hepburn and Fred Astaire in *Funny Face* (1957).

## Of petticoats and safety pins

These days the whir and blur of bright petticoats of the cancan are as much a part of Paris sightseeing as the Eiffel Tower and Louvre. But, it was not always so socially acceptable. Banned as licentious, the cancan was performed, without underwear, beyond the city limits by prostitutes when it arrived in Paris in the first half of the 19th century. When dance halls gained respectability, performers were obliged to put on suitable undergarments before going onstage. Some performers continued to indulge in a little private enterprise by tearing their knickers, and so, at the Moulin Rouge, Monsieur Durocher sat in the wings to check girls were properly dressed before going on stage. If he discovered a negligent tear, he would repair the garment with safety pins.

The Palais de Justice (below left) and Notre-Dame (right) are among the many historic buildings lining the Seine

# The River Seine

To say that a river runs through Paris is to do the Seine a disservice. It would be fairer to acknowledge that Paris runs along the river. Originally the entire city was surrounded by the Seine, when the Romans founded Lutetia on the Île de la Cité.

Principal sites are strung along the river banks. From April to October a water shuttle—the Batobus—stops at many of them, from the Eiffel Tower in the west, to the Bibliothèque Nationale de France–Site François Mitterrand in the east. Year round, *bateaux mouches* dinner cruises glide past the illuminated buildings and bridges for those who prefer to sightsee from their table. But to discover the true spirit of the riverside and all its contrasts, try to explore the *quais* on foot. There are floating nightclubs by quai François Mauriac on Saturday nights, fire-brigade cadets practising hose technique on the quai Voltaire on Sunday mornings and the St-Michel *bouquinistes* selling old books and vintage postcards.

**Kindness is its own reward**

There is a sign above the door of the rickety American bookstore across the water from Notre-Dame, in the Latin Quarter, that reads 'Be not inhospitable to strangers, lest they be angels in disguise'. Shakespeare and Company is a strange and delightful sanctuary, where new and second-hand volumes stacked on the floor or arranged on shelves are pushed aside to store a blanket here and a sleeping bag there. Visiting writers and artists are welcome to sleep among the paper-backs. When fire ravaged part of the old building, many such strangers worked tirelessly to repay hospitality to angels in disguise.

**Party time**

It is the ultimate Parisian dilemma: Do you stay in town and be seen at all the key openings, private views and fashion shows, or get away from the city and indulge in the blend of beach, barbecue and sheer self-indulgence that is a holiday in the sun? Since many Parisians love to travel, but hate to leave home, Paris has a special resort on the banks of the Seine (pictured above). Saving locals the trouble of going to Mauritius and Martinique, Club Med World has the requisite bamboo umbrellas, pitchers of fruit punch and sun-kissed barmen making cocktails. Robbie Williams and Britney Spears have joined locals dancing in the converted Bercy wine warehouse for a one-night holiday.

Taking it easy by the river (left)

Browsing in the Shakespeare and Company bookshop (below)

A poster in the Galerie Documents, on the rue de la Seine (right)

Pegasus guards Pont Alexandre III (below)

## Liberty

The allée des Cygnes is the Seine's lesser known island. By night it is a popular lovers' rendezvous, but what raises eyebrows on the passing pleasure boats is the sight of the Statue of Liberty by the Pont de Grenelle, facing west to New York. This miniature version of Auguste Bartholdi's famous work is a reminder that the original was a gift from France. Paris is dotted with souvenirs of Bartholdi's giant creations, with another incarnation of Liberty's head peeking out from the bushes of the Jardin du Luxembourg. At place Denfert-Rochereau stands Gustave Eiffel's copper copy of Bartholdi's remarkable Lion of Belfort. The original is sculpted into the famous fortifications of the city of Belfort, in eastern France.

## When the pool floats again

When the banks of the Seine are transformed into Paris Plage, the summer sunbathing beach, true Parisians are appreciative but unimpressed. They recall a former floating swimming pool, Piscine Deligny, built in 1840 and moored at quai Voltaire. Constructed from timbers from the *Dorade*, the ship which brought Napoleon's ashes to Paris, the lido was balanced on 14 pontoons and had 340 changing cabins. After a facelift in 1954, beautiful people continued to flaunt perfect tans and improbable waistlines from the terrace by day, while by night the pool hosted fabulous soirées for the in-crowd. In July 1993 the party finally ended when one of the pontoons moved and the legendary pool was swallowed up by the Seine in less than an hour. Mayor Bertrand Delanoë has pledged to restore the Deligny for the 21st century.

## Down by the riverside

An eclectic collection of boats is moored along the eastern section of the Seine. In the ungainly shadow of the Bibliothèque Nationale de France, the Chinese junk and light-boats become Paris's floating nightclub district, where the young and charmed take to the decks to dance until dawn. Waterside partying is the latest thing. Or is it? Farther along the quay-sides, just beyond the Bois de Vincennes, is Joinville-le-Pont, where the Seine meets the River Marne. Here blue-collar Parisians have been dancing at the water's edge for generations. Real *guinguette* bars, where the grandparents of today's party animals romanced by the light of the moon, still have accordionists who play the songs of Edith Piaf and you can dance to the strains of java, tango and waltz.

The Eiffel Tower at night—the city's ultimate romantic view

There's no getting away from romance, even among the skyscrapers of La Défense district (above)

The Pont des Arts (right) is one of Paris's most romantic bridges

# *Romance in* Paris

Blame it on the love songs and movie clinches, but Paris is a city of romance. The legendary tolerance and celebration of passion in a city that blends intimacy and anonymity lends a frisson to any encounter. Couples celebrating a silver wedding still find the buzz of an affair to remember. Romantic locations abound, from the Pont des Arts footbridge across the Seine (good for watching sunsets) to the temple of love perched on top of a cliff in the Parc des Buttes-Chaumont. This is accentuated by the sheer range of restaurants designed for 'sweet nothings' to be whispered across a candlelit table.
A literary heritage illuminated by tragic lovers and grand passions also helps to fuel present-day relationships. But Parisian romance is not just about candlelit dinners and sunset-watching on bridges: There is little to match the magic of breakfasting on onion soup in a Les Halles bistro after a night on the town, then walking home hand-in-hand through the flower market.

### *Je t'aime*

Incurable romantic Frédéric Baron asked visitors to Montmartre to write down 'I love you' in their own language in the 1990s. He collected more than a thousand *billets-doux* (love letters), which were transcribed by calligrapher Claire Kito and transformed into a mural of tiles and broken hearts by artist Daniel Boulogne. This wall, Le Mur des Je t'Aime, stands in the Jean Rictus garden on place des Abbesses. Here, holiday romances are sealed by young lovers sharing their innermost thoughts in languages such as Esperanto, Basque and Navajo. The garden has cult status among lovers and serial wooers alike, and the wall has a website, where lovers can perfect their pronunciation in order to melt hearts in situ at dusk *(www.lesjetaime.com)*.

### Outkissing Rodin

Auguste Rodin's *The Kiss* is immortalized in stone in his former home on the rue de Varenne, now the Musée Rodin. Visitors wishing to preserve their own French kiss should make their way past an even more popular museum. A few steps beyond the Centre Georges Pompidou is the tiny passage Molière. Here, artist Brigitte Massouiter will take a life cast of the lips of your loved one and provide you with a permanent reminder of your Parisian passion in plaster or bronze. She made her name through casting babies' hands and feet as mother's day gifts. But her workshop has become a magnet to romantics seeking to commemorate *grands amours* with frozen kisses. The studio is open on Friday and Saturday afternoons.

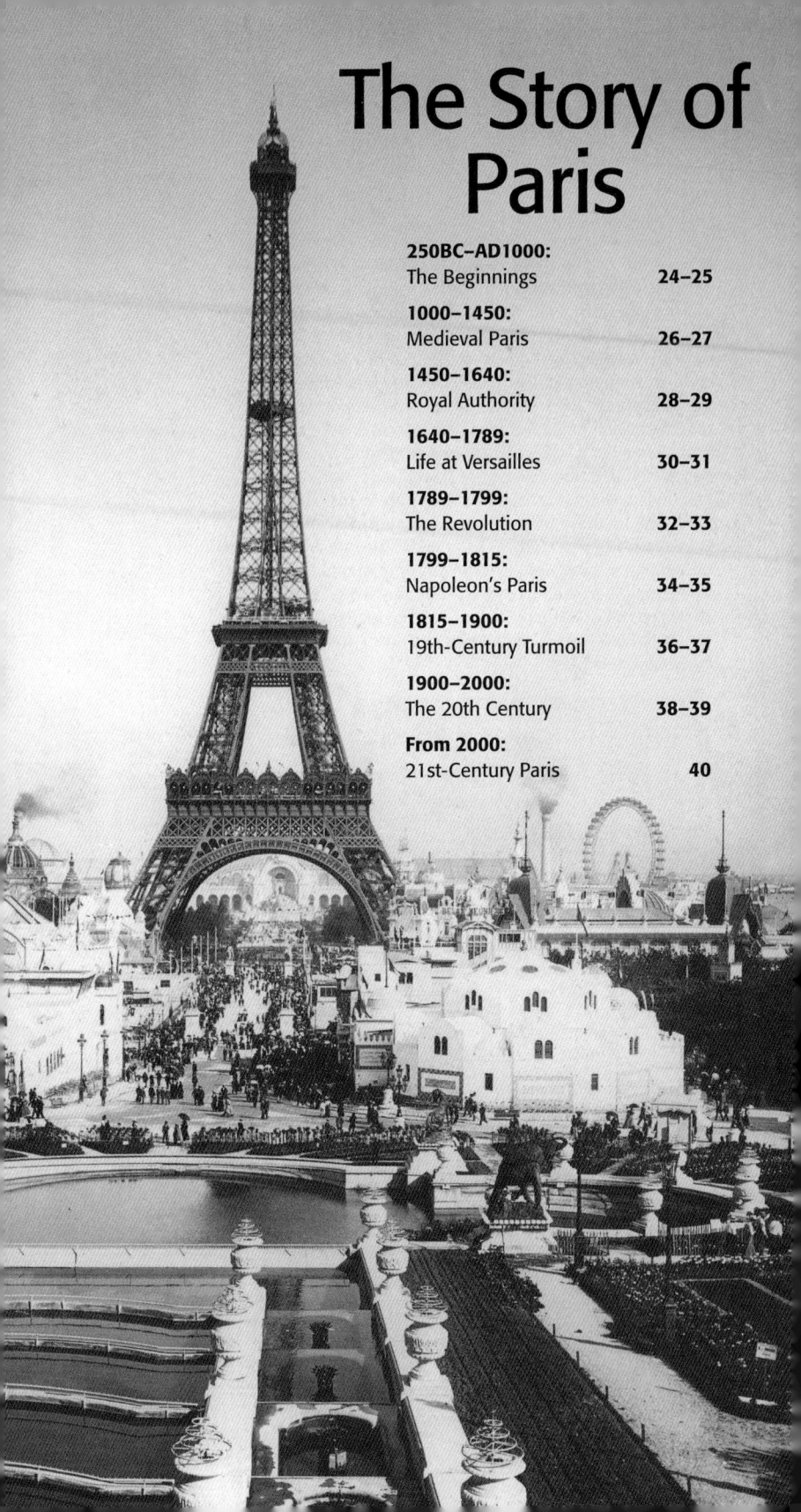

# The Story of Paris


**250BC–AD1000:**
The Beginnings 24–25

**1000–1450:**
Medieval Paris 26–27

**1450–1640:**
Royal Authority 28–29

**1640–1789:**
Life at Versailles 30–31

**1789–1799:**
The Revolution 32–33

**1799–1815:**
Napoleon's Paris 34–35

**1815–1900:**
19th-Century Turmoil 36–37

**1900–2000:**
The 20th Century 38–39

**From 2000:**
21st-Century Paris 40

# *The Beginnings*

Paris began on the Île de la Cité, an island in the middle of the river Seine, when a peaceful Celtic tribe known as the Parisii set up camp there in around 250BC. The Romans began moving up from southern France in about 52BC, after making what is now Provence into a colony in 118BC. They sometimes met tough resistance from Celtic tribes, who united under Vercingetorix to confront them. But the Celts were crushed and all the lands from Belgium to the Mediterranean, and from the Atlantic to the Alps, were renamed Gaul by the Romans. The principal Gallic city was Lyon, while Paris, known as Lutetia, remained a northern backwater. With the collapse of Roman rule in the 5th century AD, Germanic tribes invaded from across the Rhine. Chief among those who settled in northern Gaul were the Franks, who based themselves at Paris. They grew immensely powerful and extended the Frankish empire until, under Charlemagne in the 8th century AD, the Franks controlled all of Roman Gaul. In AD987, Hugues Capet, the Count of Paris, was crowned king of France and made Paris his capital.

**Lutetia**

The Roman town grew, spreading onto the Left Bank of the Seine. It had a theatre, a forum (public square) and a 10,000-seat arena for circuses and popular entertainments such as pitting humans against animals. The Romans also built luxurious public baths, where people met to wash, have a massage, gossip and engage in wrestling contests. On the island, still occupied mainly by Parisii, the Romans built a temple to Jupiter. Then disaster struck. In the 3rd century AD, ferocious warrior tribes from Germany attacked the town and destroyed it before being defeated themselves. The town was triumphantly rebuilt, enlarged, modernized and renamed Paris. The Barbarians' fate was to be the latest entertainment in the arena.

These baths (left), in what is now the Latin Quarter, were the hub of social life in Gallo-Roman Paris

Julius Caesar (above) ordered his troops to take Paris in 52BC

Charlemagne enters Paris (below)

## *250BC*

## St. Denis

St. Denis, the patron saint of France, was born in Italy and was one of seven bishops sent by the Pope to convert Gaul to Catholicism in AD250. Denis became the first bishop of Paris and was so good at converting the populace that the Romans had him killed. He was beheaded at Montmartre (Martyr's Hill) and, according to legend, the indefatigable Denis picked up his own head and carried on walking. It is more likely that his body was thrown into the Seine and later rescued by followers, who built the Basilica of St-Denis on the spot. And where did the legend come from? St. Denis was always depicted with his head in his hands and in the medieval mind image and reality became one.

## St. Geneviève

St. Geneviève, patroness of Paris, was a forceful woman who won through despite the misogyny of the times. She even saved Paris from Atilla the Hun. Born in Nanterre in AD422, it is said that St. Germain of Auxerre caught the look in her eye when she was seven and suggested she dedicate her life to God. She did so, eating only twice a week and having frequent visions. The Bishop of Paris appointed Geneviève Mother Superior to the nuns of Paris and her inspiration and energy helped the Parisians when Atilla's armies approached the city in AD451. She told the citizens to trust in God and to repent of their sins. When they did, the Huns turned away and galloped on to Châlons-en-Champagne.

## Clovis, Chief of the Franks

Geneviève's spiritual powers did not work against the next wave of invaders. With Roman power collapsing, it was impossible for the inhabitants of Paris to fight off warrior tribes like the Franks. With their powerful leader Clovis at their head, the Franks swept into Paris and took control. Clovis based himself in the offices of the expelled Roman governor on the Île de la Cité, and commanded his troops as they fought other tribes for more territory. Geneviève visited Clovis, preached to him, and eventually converted the warrior king to Christianity. A changed man, Clovis built an abbey where in death he and his queen Clotilde could be buried alongside saintly Geneviève.

## Charlemagne

The power of the Franks culminated in the rise of a majestic yet simple leader, Charlemagne, or Carolus Magnus (Charles the Great). He was hero of poetry, song and legend and grandson of Carolus Martel (Charles The Hammer), who had triumphed over the Moorish forces invading from the south. Charlemagne directed an indomitable army into every corner of Gaul and much of Germany and Italy, carving out a vast kingdom. Throughout his dominion, Charlemagne imposed a devout Christianity and the pursuit of learning. In AD800, the Pope crowned him the first Holy Roman Emperor. Charlemagne the Frank had proved beyond doubt that Gaul was now France.

This bust, decorating the 17th-century Hôtel Libéral Bruant, in the Marais, harks back to earlier times

Hugues Capet, King of France in the 10th century

St. Geneviève (below, left), the patron saint of Paris

The Celtic leader Vercingetorix (below)

# AD1000

# *Medieval* Paris

The growing importance of Paris in medieval times had much to do with the city's position on the river Seine. The institutions of church and government stood on the Île de la Cité, while much of the population lived in simple homes on the Left Bank. Many were skilled craftsmen, while others continued to farm the land. Important religious sites, notably at St-Denis and St-Germain, attracted large commercial fairs that brought in thousands of traders and visitors. Everything was dominated by the church—its beliefs and authority were beyond question. Those who did disagree with the church risked their lives and at the end of the 12th century, Jews all over France were rounded up and slaughtered. However, the church was also the chief provider of education and medical care to the poor and was the guiding hand behind the greatest engineering project in medieval Paris: the draining of the marshes of the islands and the Right Bank. When this was done, the city really began to grow.

**Notre-Dame**

One of the greatest of European cathedrals, Notre-Dame dates from1163 and took almost two hundred years to complete. It is a symbol of Paris but was not always treated respectfully. The Revolutionaries desecrated it in the 18th century and turned it into a Temple of Reason, even decapitating the statues in the Gallery of Kings. Victor Hugo, Romantic creator of a mythic Paris, restored it to the public imagination in 1831 with his novel *Notre-Dame de Paris*. Rebuilding soon followed and, like Quasimodo, the Parisians discovered that 'the cathedral was not only company [for them]...it was the universe, nay, more, it was Nature itself.'

Charles VII (left) liberated Paris from the English in 1437

Notre-Dame (left) remains one of France's most important religious sites

Sainte-Chapelle (below) was built by Louis IX to house holy relics

## *1000*

Queen Isabella, wife of Charles VI, arrives in Paris in the 14th century

## Abélard and Héloïse

Peter Abélard, a much admired 12th-century scholar, taught philosophy at the university in Paris. Héloïse, the niece of Canon Fulbert of Notre-Dame, was one of his students. The two fell madly in love and would meet secretly in Héloïse's uncle's house. When Héloïse became pregnant, she fled to Abélard's family home in Brittany and he pledged to marry her. But the enraged Fulbert had Abélard castrated. Héloïse became a nun and Abélard entered a monastery, yet their letters show a torment of love that continued until Abélard's death in 1142. Héloïse lived for another 21 years, and was buried in his grave. The tragic lovers were moved to Père Lachaise cemetery in the 19th century.

## Louis IX and the Crown of Thorns

Louis IX was an enthusiastic buyer of holy relics, acquiring the staff of Moses, a portion of the True Cross and Jesus's swaddling clothes. His greatest prize was the Crown of Thorns, which he bought from the Emperor of Constantinople in the 13th century. The emperor was anxious for French aid and Louis eager for the prestige this crown would give his own claim to the throne. The crown cost more than three times as much as Sainte-Chapelle, the chapel Louis built to house it. Sainte-Chapelle is famed for its beauty, particularly its towering stained-glass windows. The Crown of Thorns is still in Paris, in Notre-Dame.

## The Sorbonne

Robert de Sorbon founded this college of the University of Paris in 1257. The fellows gave free lectures and lived in a closed community, although without religious vows. Robert de Sorbon was a respected professor and preacher, but was also a natural administrator. He drew up a list of regulations for the fellows, which included a dress code (no scandalous clothing) and guidelines for returning library books. Even eating and drinking in private rooms were frowned upon. Robert didn't care to have secrets bandied about, so guests, especially women, were discouraged. Robert seemed to know what caused real trouble however, when he decided that 'No fellow shall have a key to the kitchen'.

## King of France and England

Ten-year-old Henry VI of England was crowned King of France in Notre-Dame on 14 December 1431, although true French kings were always crowned in Reims. Joan of Arc wrote a wonderfully rude letter to Henry, warning 'go home…or beware of the Maid and all the damage you will suffer'. She had attempted to expel the English from France in 1429 and to help Charles VII be crowned King of France in Reims. He did not support Joan in her attack on Paris, although she might have taken it if he had. Henry VI did not enjoy his crown for long—by 1453 the French had driven the English from everywhere except the northern port of Calais.

The tragic lovers Abélard and Héloïse

Henri VI of England was crowned king of France in 1431

1450

The Sorbonne was founded in the 13th century; its chapel (left) dates from the 17th century

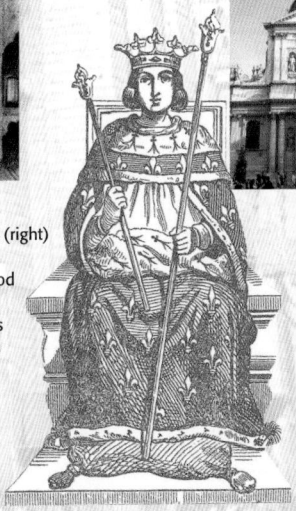

Louis IX (right) gained sainthood in 1297, 27 years after his death

Joan of Arc (below) fought against the English in the early 15th century

# *Royal* Authority

Paris took several decades to recover from the Hundred Years War against England (mid-14th to mid-15th century), the Black Death (1348) and the decadence of the royal court. But by the end of the 15th century, the city had made a fresh start. It eagerly embraced the ideas and the artistic flair of the Italian Renaissance, giving a French character to the new architecture, and was proud of its role as the capital of the reunited French nation. King François I (*R.*1515–1547) most embodied the new world of the French Renaissance. A devotee of Italian art, he invited Leonardo da Vinci to live at the royal palace in Amboise. The artist accepted, bringing the *Mona Lisa* with him, which the king used as the cornerstone of his art collection. In 1528, François announced his intention to move to the Louvre and commissioned significant rebuilding of the palace. More fine buildings followed under the Protestant Henri IV, crowned king in 1589. He converted to Catholicism in 1593 in a bid to stop the Wars of Religion that swept through France in the latter half of the 16th century. He was assassinated in 1610 and was succeeded by his son, Louis XIII.

**François Villon**

François Villon, born in 1431, was one of the greatest of French poets, but he has a bitter connection to Paris. He graduated from the University of Paris and was destined for a career in Law or the Church, but he became restless and spent time in taverns mixing with thieves. In 1455 he killed a priest in a drunken quarrel. After this, he wandered the country, spending time in and out of prison until he was banished in 1463 and was never heard of again. Villon's poetry is vigorous and haunting, but without self-pity. It is fashionable to view him as the country's first cultural rebel, although he is actually a mystery.

François I commissioned a sumptuous rebuilding of the chateau at Fontainebleau (left) in the 16th century

François Villon

Leonardo da Vinci shows the *Mona Lisa* to François I (below)

*1450*

This painting, by Rosso de Rossi, is from the Galerie de François I, at Fontainebleau

## Fit for a King

Even for a king, François I was larger than life. He adored Renaissance style—he grew up at the Loire chateau of Amboise, probably the first French building redesigned on Italianate lines—and on becoming king he invited Leonardo da Vinci to live at Amboise. François moved ceaselessly from chateau to chateau, and had two more magnificent palaces built, at Fontainebleau and Chambord. Eventually, he decided to move to the Louvre, taking his art collection with him. He ordered the palace to be completely rebuilt, but died soon after work began. He left his mark on many buildings in Paris in the form of the salamander and the letter F, his way of saying 'François was here'.

## The Massacre of St. Bartholomew's Day

The brutal murder of thousands of Protestants in Paris on 24 August 1572 is one of the most shocking events in French history. France was riven by wars between Protestants and Catholics but the marriage of King Charles IX's sister, the Catholic Marguerite de Valois, to the Protestant Henri de Navarre (the future Henri IV) was meant to bring the two sides together. The opposite occurred when the king, pressed by his mother, Catherine de Medici, ordered the massacre of Protestant nobles gathered at the Louvre to celebrate the wedding. Three thousand people died in Paris and many more throughout France. Civil war raged throughout the country for more than 20 years.

## The Medici Cycle

Between 1622 and 1625, Rubens painted 21 murals on the life of Marie de Medici, Louis XIII's mother, for her palace in Paris. Marie, second wife of Henri IV, was bad-tempered, ugly and dangerous, so Rubens needed all his diplomatic skills to deal with her. The paintings, he explained carefully, are allegories of how one should look rather than how one does look. In immense baroque extravaganzas, a beautiful Marie is shown arriving in France, getting married and governing the country accompanied by a flock of gods. This propaganda has little to do with reality, as even her husband said she was the biggest troublemaker he had ever known, and her son banished her from France. Ironically, she died in Cologne in a house once occupied by Rubens.

## L'Académie Française

Cardinal Richelieu, chief minister to Louis XIII, formed the Académie Française in 1635 and it still exists today. There are 40 members and only death creates a vacancy. Each member is presented with a richly decorated sword and is addressed as *monsieur*, which rankles with the women academicians. Richelieu, busy creating a centralized government, wanted the Académie to act as a ministry to legislate on the French language. In 1638 the academicians began work on their dictionary—it took them a long time. One wit, on hearing they had reached the letter F, loudly hoped to live until they got to G. In 1694, a mere 58 years after starting, their dictionary was published and has been updated regularly ever since.

King François I, despotic and capricious, yet also a refined Renaissance gentleman

The brilliant but hypochondriac Richelieu, chief minister to Louis XIII

1640

Catherine de Medici (right), wife of Henri II

François I chose the Louvre (below) as his new home

A scene (above) from the Wars of Religion, which raged for years in France

# *Life at* Versailles

Louis XIII died in 1643, when his son, Louis XIV, was only five years old. The new king's mother, Anne of Austria, and Cardinal Mazarin governed while he was a child but in 1661 Louis shocked the Court by announcing he would rule on his own. His authority was absolute and his egotism, extravagance and unrealistic expansionism dominated every aspect of life in Paris and the rest of France. He moved the Court to Versailles and adopted a golden sun as his symbol because, in his opinion, he radiated light over the whole nation. While the Sun King's reign represents the apotheosis of French monarchy, his lavish lifestyle and ceaseless wars led to the political isolation of France, financial problems and extreme social injustice. Much of the vitality of the Great King's reign was extinguished long before his death in 1715. The removal of the five-year-old Louis XV (*R.* 1715–1774) to the Tuileries palace by the regent launched a renewal for the capital. The Court and nobility returned to Paris to throw themselves into a life devoted to pleasure. Though the Court returned to Versailles in 1724, the palace would never again be the focus of French life. By the middle of the reign of Louis XVI (*R.* 1774–1793) and his beautiful, frivolous, unpopular Queen, Marie-Antoinette, the polite reformist mood of the earlier half of the century had turned into a flood of sedition.

This statue of Louis XIV (left) stands at place des Victoires

### The Building of Versailles

When Louis XIV ordered Versailles to be built in 1661, 30,000 workers were hired. Leading architect Louis Le Vau, interior designer Charles Le Brun and landscape architect André Le Nôtre were commissioned to provide a royal home of unprecedented grandeur, in classical style. The king required vast formal gardens full of statuary and fountains and a sumptuous interior adorned with Europe's finest craftsmanship. Work continued up to Louis XIV's death in 1715, with no expense spared. While draining the grounds, thousands of workers died from marsh fever, but were quickly replaced. Mature trees from all over France were replanted here and a whole new town was built alongside the palace. The Royal Court moved into Versailles in 1671.

*1640*

A lavish bedroom at Versailles

## Behind the Throne

Great minds were at work behind the Sun King. At first, Louis XIV's affairs were run by Chief Minister Cardinal Mazarin, who closely followed the footsteps of his predecessor, Cardinal Richelieu. After Mazarin's death in 1661, the king sought advice on all matters of state from Jean-Baptiste Colbert, a brilliant but unassuming politician, son of a cloth merchant. Colbert arranged the downfall of the Superintendant of Finance and took over as finance minister himself. He increased tax revenues, imposed tariffs to protect French commerce, built new canals, revived ailing industries and enabled the navy to protect French merchant shipping. But Colbert's efforts were undermined by the king's continuous search for personal glory.

## Lady of Letters

With the Court tucked away at Versailles, intellectual life in Paris flourished—and women presided over it. In 1676 the writer Madame de Sévigné spent a day at Versailles, gambling, lolling about in boats on the canal and having supper at midnight. But it was not for her. She decided to stay away and wrote the great series of letters to her daughter that give a picture of life in 17th-century Paris. In the 18th century other ladies held literary *salons* where writers Voltaire and Diderot could discuss the *Encyclopédie*, the great intellectual work of the century. This freedom provided the background to the Revolution, as 'the Church, the Law and the Government' was questioned. Versailles was unaware of any of it.

## *Ce Pays Ci*

Versailles gradually drifted like a balloon away from the vibrancy of Paris. Courtiers called Versailles *Ce Pays Ci* (this country), walked differently, developed their own argot and lived by hundreds of meaningless rules (Dukes kneeled on crooked cushions in church, the Royal Princes on straight ones). The Parisian bourgeoisie visited Versailles but could never be a part of it. So when Jeanne Poisson, a beautiful Parisian bourgeoise, caught Louis XV's eye, direct contact with the king was not officially allowed. The problem was resolved when she was made Marquise de Pompadour. She left Paris for Versailles and became the royal mistress.

## The women of Paris speak

The working-class women of Paris were a tough breed, and members of the Court never knew how they would be received when they ventured from Versailles. Madame de Pompadour, a Parisienne herself, found her carriage splattered in mud and Louis XV built a road round the city to avoid their insults, delivered in the slang of the market women and fishwives, *poissard*. This was an anarchic mix of fractured words and chaotic grammar, ideal for ridicule. Marie-Antoinette invited the fishwives of Paris to Versailles in 1777 to teach her friends *poissard* for their amateur dramatics. In 1789 the women sang a *poissard* song inviting the Court to choke on molten gold since they loved it so much.

The 18th-century writer Voltaire

The Princess de Lamballe (left), Marie-Antoinette's closest friend

Madame de Pompadour, mistress to Louis XV

1789

The Court left Paris and moved to Versailles (left) during Louis XIV's reign

Marie-Antoinette, wife of the hapless Louis XVI

The opulent Hall of Mirrors

# *The* Revolution

The Fronde rebellion (1648–1652) had given just a hint of what was to come and anger simmered beneath the surface of life in Paris. The power of the monarchy and the decadent privileges of the aristocracy contrasted sharply with the poverty of working people, and the growing industrial middle class, resentful at their lack of political voice, demanded a proper constitution. The Royal Court continued to enjoy an exceptionally pampered life. The arts flourished, and craftsmen catering to the aristocracy did well. All over Europe, Paris became a byword for luxury and the good life. At the same time, the state sank further into debt and ordinary people further into poverty. To offset the state's huge debts, repressive taxes were imposed. On 14 July 1789, spontaneous crowds (there had been rumblings of something afoot the previous day) converged on Les Invalides to grab the weapons stored there. From there, to the Bastille. The Revolution had started, and would lead France through many years of savage brutality and instability towards a new Republic.

**The Guillotine**

Dr. Joseph-Ignace Guillotin was a deputy of the National Assembly and in 1789 proposed the use of his machine as a democratic means of death. The machine was first set up in the place du Carrousel on 21 August 1792 for the execution of a Royalist general. As the Revolution progressed so did the executions and by 1794, during the *Grande Terreur*, 26 people a day were being guillotined. Those accused of crimes against the state were despatched on an industrial scale. This brought problems of disposal, with blood flowing in the city's gutters and bodies being thrown into mass graves.

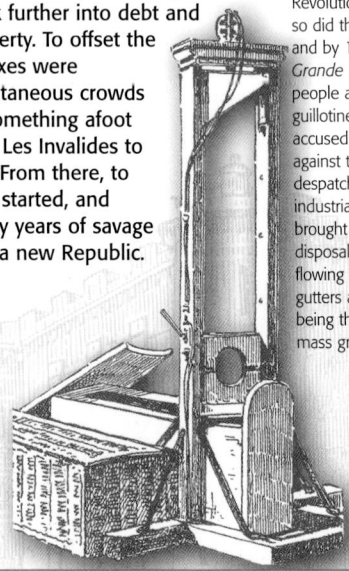

Dr. Joseph-Ignace Guillotin's 'philanthropic beheading machine'

## *1789*

## The Customs Wall

The attack on the Bastille on 14 July 1789 was preceded on 12 July by an attack on something less well known, the Customs Wall around Paris, built on the order of the Controller-General, Callone. In a desperate effort to raise money for the huge national debt (60 per cent of the budget went to pay the interest), Callone imposed a duty on goods entering and leaving the city. This was collected by private tax collectors who took a large cut for themselves, and were hated by the citizens of Paris for their brutal tactics. The wall was rather beautiful, the work of the chemist Antoine Lavoisier, who was also a tax collector. These well-fed gentlemen had, for once, miscalculated—after the wall came down, they were swiftly executed.

## 14 July 1789

The Revolution made a slow start. A bread shortage had caused months of angry revolt in Paris and on 12 and 13 July thousands of rioters surged through the city. On the morning of 14 July a group tricked its way into Les Invalides, seized its huge store of weapons and marched to the Bastille, the fortress-prison. The mob liberated the prisoners (all seven of them), decapitated the governor and paraded his head on a pole. This attack heralded a summer of violence and on 5 October thousands of women marched on Versailles to ask King Louis XVI for bread, which he gave them. Joined by their menfolk, they rampaged through the palace and took the King and Queen Marie-Antoinette to house arrest in Paris.

## The Marriage of Figaro

Beaumarchais' play *The Marriage of Figaro* was due to open in Paris in 1783, in a theatre owned by the Queen. She was looking forward to seeing it, but Louis XVI, realizing that its unprecendented attacks on the aristocracy were dangerous, stopped the performance and had the play banned, which led to riots in Paris. After some changes the play finally opened in another Paris venue the following year. When Figaro tells his master, 'You only took the trouble to be born… you're an ordinary person' the people of Paris roared with delight, as did the watching nobles, including Marie-Antoinette. An observer noted with amazement how the aristocracy slapped its own face while laughing at the same time.

## Festival of the Supreme Being

On 8 June 1794 (20 Prairial Year 2 by the Revolutionary calendar), the Revolution reached a pitch of insanity, and Paris witnessed the Festival of the Supreme Being, as artificial and ridiculous as any royal pageant. Deputies from the Convention marched along clutching wheat sheaves, girls in white distributed flowers, oxen pulled a printing press and a plough on a chariot and blind children sang inspiring songs. In the Champ de Mars, Maximilien Robespierre, one of the Revolution's leaders, set fire to a statue of Atheism, then descended from the top of a cardboard mountain to enthusiastic applause. 'Did the day of Creation…' he asked, 'shine with a light more agreeable?' Seven weeks later he was guillotined.

Being a leader of the Revolution did not protect Robespierre from the guillotine

Louis XVI (left) lost his life to the guillotine in 1793

The Dauphin Louis XVII (right) in prison

Place de la Concorde witnessed the bloody beheadings of more than 1,300 people

Place de la Bastille as it is today (far left) and during the violent Storming of the Bastille in July 1789 (left)

The absurd Festival of the Supreme Being

# *Napoleon's* Paris

Following the bloody days of The Terror, France was ruled by an intermediary government known as the *Directoire* (1795–1799). Problems arose at once–the war against surrounding countries threatened to turn against France and a violent royalism arose that sought to revive the *ancien régime*. An ambitious young Corsican army general emerged who felt able to deal with both issues–Napoleon Bonaparte (1769–1821). Given command of the army in Italy by the *Directoire* in 1796, he rapidly achieved victory. His next step, the invasion of Egypt, proved a mistake, but nevertheless his rise to power was now unstoppable. He became First Consul of the Republic after the 1799 *coup d'état* that overthrew the *Directoire*. To begin with, things looked good and the French border expanded. But in 1812 Napoleon made the mistake of invading Russia during winter. Ice and snow killed thousands of his soldiers. In 1814 the Russians invaded Paris and Napoleon was exiled to the island of Elba. He made a brief return in 1815, before meeting his final defeat at Waterloo a few months later. He was expelled to the island of St-Helena, where he died in 1821.

**A Republican Coronation**

Napoleon Bonaparte went through swift changes in under ten years–from extreme anti-royalist Jacobin supporter to army general serving the *Directoire*, to crowned head of state. His military successes, ability to restore order and sweeping vision of a modern France inspired the nation. Despite impeccable Republican credentials, in 1804 the military dictator decided he deserved to wear a crown. In an opulent ceremony fit for a king, Napoleon was crowned Emperor in Notre-Dame. The Pope, summoned to Paris for the purpose, gave his blessing. Since no one had authority to place the crown on Napoleon's head, in an act fraught with symbolism he did the job himself, after having first chivalrously crowned his wife Empress Josephine.

A young Napoleon Bonaparte

Empress Josephine's bedroom (left), in the Château de Malmaison

## *1799*

Napoleon departs for exile on the island of St-Helena

## Arc de Triomphe

Military triumph was the essence of Napoleon's right to wear a crown. The Emperor kept France in a constant state of belligerency against the rest of Europe, distributing conquered lands among friends and family. Only a year after his coronation, the greatest moment of glory came at Austerlitz, where French troops defeated the might of Austria. At the height of his power, Napoleon ordered a huge Roman-style triumphal arch to be built to commemorate his victories. The Arc de Triomphe was to stand in pride of place at the end of the Champs-Élysées. Construction had barely started when Napoleon's bubble burst. Work on the arch stopped until after his death.

## Napoleon's Elephant

To obliterate memories of the Revolution, Napoleon commissioned an enormous bronze elephant, 10m (33ft) high, for the site of the demolished Bastille prison. When it was finally built in 1814, the Empire could only afford a plaster elephant, which soon started to disintegrate into a bizarre, broken-down mess. No one seemed to know why it was there, or even why it was an elephant. A concierge was employed to look after the construction, but that didn't help. The elephant appears in the book *Les Misérables* as the home of the young Gavroche. Author Victor Hugo calls it a mysterious and mighty phantom. In 1846 the wretched beast was finally demolished, vanishing from the place de la Bastille as mysteriously as it had appeared.

## Bistro! Bistro!

When Russian soldiers occupied Paris in 1814 they liked to visit the small cafés in the city. Unsurprisingly, they got the cold-shoulder from their French waiters. *'Bystro! Bystro!'* (Quickly!) shouted the unhappy Cossacks and legend has it that this is the origin of this uniquely French type of restaurant. However, the word didn't enter the language until 1884 and there are other less attractive explanations for it. Bistro could originate from the word *bistre* (dull yellowy brown), meaning a smoky, gloomy place.

The Russians haven't made many notable contributions to French cuisine, so it's nicer to think they've sneaked in a term known for simple, but excellent, food.

## The Funeral of Napoleon

Napoleon's funeral at Les Invalides on 15 December 1840 was not a jolly affair. Inside, kings, princes and ancient heroes sat for hours in pious boredom. They were surrounded by black and purple drapes fringed with silver, hundreds of glowing candles glittering on marble, military decorations and the Imperial Crown itself. Outside, it was a different story. The day was bitterly cold and so the waiting crowd and the soldiers lining the route had to keep themselves warm somehow. A few people in the stands started to dance, which then spread to the crowds on the streets and then to the soldiers themselves, until a vast, happy round-dance snaked along the funeral route, only to stop when the coffin finally went by.

An older Napoleon, in uniform

Louis XVIII came to the throne in 1814, after Napoleon was exiled

# 1815

The Arc de Triomphe (left), intended as a celebration of Napoleon's victories

A Russian soldier in 1814 (left)

Napoleon's funeral cortège passes through place de la Concorde (below), in 1840

# 19th-Century Turmoil

The turbulence of the Napoleonic period, its war-making patriotism, far-reaching social changes and violent politics, continued through the rest of the 19th century. The people of Paris, marked out in the Revolution as more passionately radical than their provincial compatriots, continued to call for equality, democracy and workers' protection. The 1830 Uprising brought the 'citizen king' Louis-Philippe of Orléans to the throne. Yet Parisians seemed to hanker for grandiose, dictatorial leadership along the lines of a Sun King or a Bonaparte. Following the 1848 Revolution that finally did away with the French monarchy, a brief Second Republic gave way to yet another authoritarian, egotistical ruler, Napoleon's nephew, Napoleon III. He used his power to enhance Paris, especially during the transformation overseen by Baron Haussmann, when much of the city was rebuilt. Constant themes of Parisian life still remained, such as the poverty of workers, the lavish hedonism of the rich, and war. During the bloody episode of the Commune, in 1871, Paris even waged war against the rest of France. The century began with war against the Prussians, later saw the Prussians bombard Paris, and ended with another war looming. But for those with money, the mood was increasingly festive in *gay Paris*.

## Haussmann's Grand Design

Napoleon III adored luxury and prestige as much as his uncle had done. He and Empress Eugénie mixed with the crowned heads of Europe and came to exemplify the aristocratic style that Paris had suffered so much in trying to abolish. At the same time, the Emperor, like Bonaparte, had grand plans to improve the look of his capital city and so he commissioned Baron Haussmann to undertake massive urban improvement. Haussmann demolished large areas of the city, including almost everything on the historic Île de la Cité, sweeping away overcrowded and rebellious workers' districts. In their place he constructed wide, straight boulevards radiating from the riverside. The workers were rehoused in new suburbs away from the heart of the city.

Baron Haussmann redesigned much of Paris, including the area around the *Étoile* (left)

# 1815

The opening of the boulevard du Prince Eugene, by Napoleon III in 1862

The Eiffel Tower (right) was controversial when it opened in 1889

Louis Pasteur (below)

The Petit Palais (right), built for the 1900 Universal Exhibition

## The Siege of Paris

Thanks to the Emperor and Baron Haussmann, Paris had become the world's most beautiful and modern city. The Emperor had even agreed to improving workers' rights and an enjoyment of life permeated the city. But Napoleon III's pre-emptive declaration of war against Prussia in 1870 came as a blow to the city. Confronting the Prussians, the French suffered an immediate defeat and the country called for Napoleon III to abdicate. Later that year, Prussians surrounded the city and the siege of Paris began. For six winter weeks, nothing was allowed in or out and freezing Paris began to starve, resorting to eating rats, cats and even zoo animals. In January 1871, the bombardment began and France accepted defeat rather than see Paris destroyed.

## The Commune

The Prussian war infuriated Parisians, who felt that monarchist elements were to blame. To get away from the Paris mob, the government of the new, conservative National Assembly left the city for Versailles. In Paris, the people took the law into their own hands, establishing an anarchist-socialist Commune to run the city in March 1871, which planned to re-establish the gains of the Revolution. The Communards (*fédérés*) seized National Guard weapons and fought pitched battles in the streets against government troops. During the *Semaine Sanglante* (Bloody Week) of 21 to 28 May, the army ruthlessly regained control. Leading *fédérés* were executed in Père Lachaise cemetery. Around 10,000 Parisians were killed and 40,000 arrested.

## A saint in the rue du Bac

In 1830, while Revolution rocked Paris, Catherine Laboure, a nun in a convent on the rue du Bac, experienced three visions of the Virgin Mary. Standing on a globe with rays of light shining out, Mary commanded that a medal be struck that would give grace to anyone who wore it. Church authorities approved and the first medal was made in 1832. But illiterate Catherine, who had been a waitress before taking her vows, continued to live out her drab existence at the convent, where she looked after the poultry and was a gatekeeper. She was strangely uninterested in her visions, and her superiors branded her insignificant, cold and apathetic. She died in 1876.

## The Can-Can

Paris was the city of pleasure in the 1890s, with performers dancing the wildly daring Can-Can at the Moulin Rouge (immortalized in Henri Toulouse-Lautrec's lithographs). The dance may have started in Brittany in the 16th century, when women performed a similar dance by lifting their dresses and kicking their legs to the ceiling, although the version that came to Paris in the 1820s is probably a bawdy version of the quadrille. Two well-known dancers were Jane Avril and La Goulue. Avril was willowy and elegant, while La Goulue, big and earthy, was known as The Glutton due to her penchant for finishing off the customers' drinks. They both came to a melancholy end, drunk, poor and forgotten, with La Goulue selling matches in a Paris park.

Napoleon III, who ruled from 1848 to 1870

Jules Verne (1828–1905), author of *Around the World in 80 Days*

The writer Victor Hugo (1802–1885)

# 1900

An art nouveau Métro sign

Henri Toulouse-Lautrec's famous Moulin Rouge poster shows the dancer known as La Goulue

# The 20th Century

A savage century came to an end, but a worse one was to come, despite a fin-de-siècle atmosphere of frivolity and avant-garde art. The two world wars were the great disaster of the 20th century. In post-war years, the population of Paris grew rapidly, as did its prosperity, and the city itself expanded into new suburbs. Once more the preoccupations of Paris returned to luxury and fashion, sophisticated entertainment, good food and wine, avant-garde art, literature and now also film. A brief interlude of disorder in 1968 was a reminder that Paris had not lost its capacity for revolutionary politics. Nor had it lost its flair for architecture and development on a Napoleonic scale, with magnificent modern buildings and immense rebuilding schemes, like Mitterrand's *Grands Projets,* continuing to make Paris one of the world's greatest cities.

### *The Rite of Spring*

The premiere of the ballet *The Rite of Spring* in May 1913 was a genuine Parisian scandal. Stravinsky's wild music and Nijinsky's even wilder choreography were matched by a riot in the audience. The crowd made so much noise booing that Nijinsky had to stand in the wings shouting out the rhythms for his deafened dancers. The poor aesthetes in the stalls turned on the aristocrats in their boxes. The Comtesse de Pourtalès, tiara askew, shouted that no one had ever dared to make fun of her, when threatened by excitable young men who loved new art. The owner of the venue, Gabriel Astruc, leaned out of his box and screamed at the audience, 'First listen! Then boo!'

A drawing (left) from the front cover of *Art Goût Beauté*, in September 1922

Russian composer Igor Stravinsky (1882–1971), whose ballet *The Rite of Spring* caused uproar when it premiered in Paris in 1913

## 1900

Armistice talks at the Versailles Conference, 1919

German troops enter Paris in 1940 (above)

The costume worn by ballet dancer Vaslav Nijinsky in the 1912 production of Claude Debussy's *L'Apres Midi d'un Faune*, by the Ballets Russes

## City of Art and Literature

Le Consulat bar, on a street corner in Montmartre, together with À La Bonne Franquette across the road, were haunts of the large crowd of young artists gathering in the city. Such was Paris's reputation in the early years of the century that artists such as Pablo Picasso, Georges Braque and Marc Chagall came to stay or live in the city. Picasso, who moved to Paris in 1904, was one of few who did not derive his inspiration from the people, streets and bars of Montmartre, concentrating on more imaginative imagery and, with Braque, the development of Cubism. Between the Wars, many French and foreign writers came to immerse themselves in Paris, among them Gertrude Stein, Ernest Hemingway, Ezra Pound and Henry Miller.

## Occupation and Liberation

German troops and tanks marched proudly down the Champs-Élysées. Nazi Germany invaded France in May 1940, and a month later entered Paris. Many Parisians fled, and the government departed for Vichy. There was staunch resistance, but also collaboration.

In July 1942, 13,000 Jews were rounded up and deported to concentration camps. This was the turning point, and the silent majority began to form an underground resistance movement.

Paris's liberation in August 1944 saw thousands of people throng the Champs-Élysées in celebration. Resistance politician Charles de Gaulle swept to power.

## May 1968

Paris was caught up in the mood of anti-authoritarianism and liberty that swept the world in 1968. It started as a student sit-in against the regime at the out-of-town University of Nanterre, but a heavy-handed police response changed the mood to anger and confrontation. Action spread to the Sorbonne university, with demonstrators' demands expanding to include sweeping away all that was outdated and repressive in society. A heady air of revolution took hold as millions of discontented factory workers joined the fray. The army was called in but at first could not contain the situation. Yet by mid-June, less than a month later, order had been restored. Workers were unwilling to see the state toppled, but a far-reaching liberalization began to take place.

## Mitterrand's *Grands Projets*

On becoming the first Socialist President of the Fifth Republic, François Mitterrand indulged grandiose ambitions to enhance the capital. One of these is the gigantic Grande Arche, in the business district of La Défense, which marks the western end of an imaginery line across the city joining the Arc de Triomphe and the Louvre. The Louvre was enhanced by the glass pyramid, and the Opéra Bastille, a gigantic cultural venue, appeared in the working-class district of Bastille.

Other Mitterrand projects include the transformation of the former river port at Bercy and the building of the Institut du Monde Arabe and the new Bibliothèque Nationale.

General de Gaulle (1890–1970) ruled France briefly after World War II and again from 1958–69

François Mitterrand (1916–96), president from 1981–95

Jacques Chirac (*b.* 1932), who became president in 1995

2000

The prestigious Opéra Bastille (left)

La Grande Arche (below), finished in time for France's Bicentenary celebrations in 1989

# 21st-century Paris

**Paris is one of the world's most-loved cities, welcoming more than 28 million foreign visitors each year. The capital has a population of just over two million people, including students and temporary workers. In 1851, three per cent of French citizens were Parisian but by 2002 that figure had risen to four per cent. Around 11 million people live in the suburbs and satellite towns of the Île de France, and fast, inexpensive and relatively pleasant rail services bring these out-of-town Parisians into the city to work, shop, dine and be entertained.**

## Summer Heat

Summer 2003 took a tragic turn when hundreds of elderly Paris residents died of hyperthermia and dehydration, as temperatures soared to above 40°C.

In July, the heatwave was assumed to be nothing more than part of a national hot spell and television news reports advised people leaving town to take plenty of cold drinks and keep children cool. But by mid-August the crisis in Paris had grown, with nine-day waits for funerals, and the government added heatwaves to the list of national emergencies covered by the White Plan. This grants special powers to hospital chiefs and local authorities in the event of terrorist attacks and nuclear accidents.

High-speed TGV trains at the Gare de Lyon

## Paris Plage

Paris Plage, the beach by the Seine, is set to become a summer must-see in Paris. From mid-July to mid-August, when most Parisians desert the city, part of the Right Bank is transformed into a seaside. Palm trees (Parisian-style, in a chic row) sway over 100m of imported sand, along with 300 deckchairs, 150 parasols and striped changing tents.

Paris Plage was introduced in summer 2002 and Mayor Bertrand Delanoë has promised that it will be around for years to come.

## City of Protest

Parisians seem to feel it a matter of pride to pour into the streets to express their grievances by rallying, marching and putting up barricades. But while the Left demonstrates on the streets, when it is time to step into the polling booths it is the Right which has consistently won control of Paris.

The election of a Socialist mayor in 2001 meant that for the first time in almost a century the capital was to be ruled by the Left. The new mayor, Bertrand Delanoë, proudly declared 'For the first time since 1909, the forces for progress hold the majority. Paris is still the capital of the movement… a city that will neither conform nor submit'.

Paris mayor Bertrand Delanoë (above). Paris Plage (below)

# 2000…

Mayor Bertrand Delanoë launches Paris's bid for the 2012 Olympic Games

Enjoying the sun in an outdoor café in Les Halles

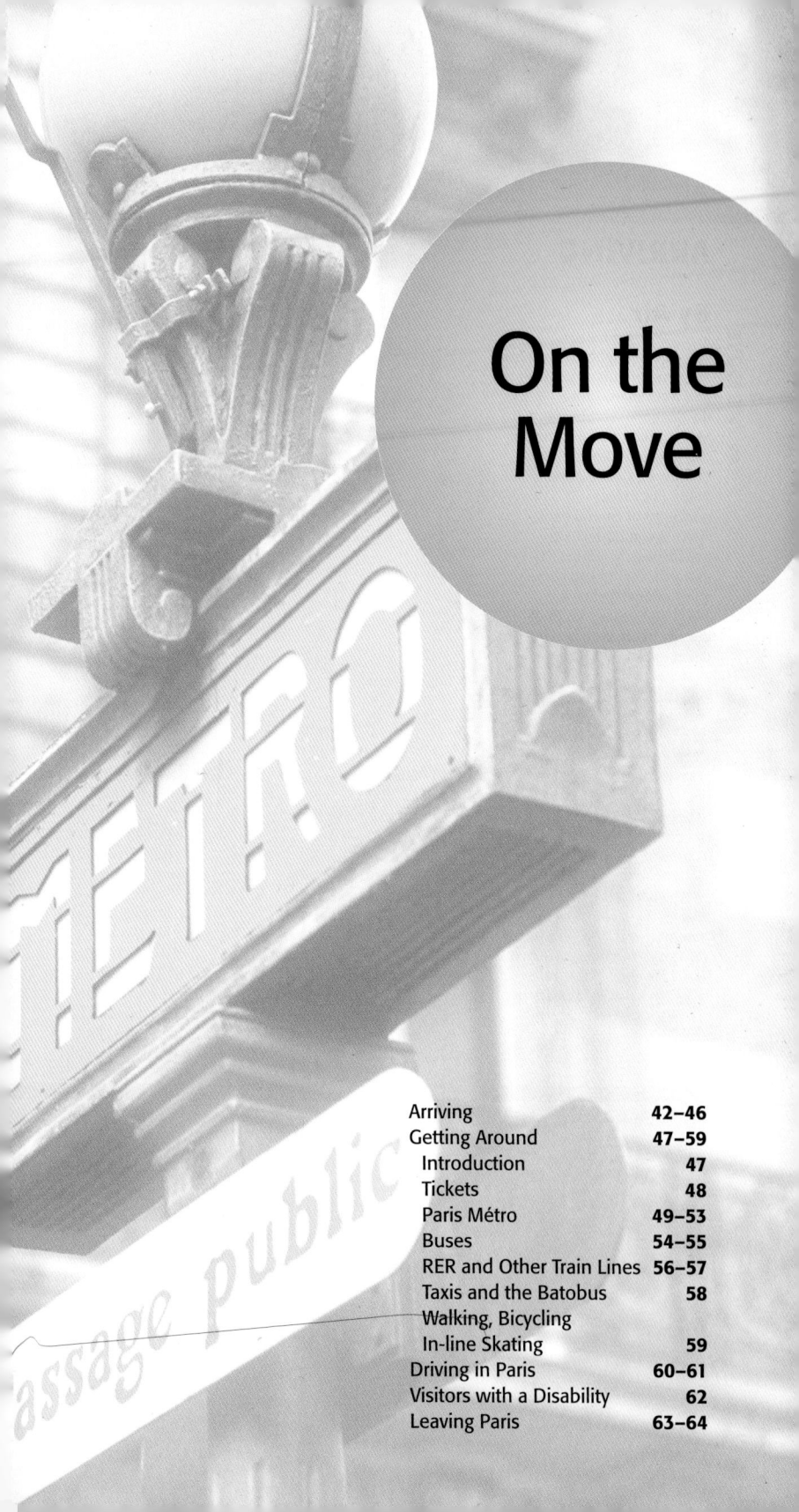


# On the Move


| | |
|---|---|
| Arriving | **42–46** |
| Getting Around | **47–59** |
| Introduction | **47** |
| Tickets | **48** |
| Paris Métro | **49–53** |
| Buses | **54–55** |
| RER and Other Train Lines | **56–57** |
| Taxis and the Batobus | **58** |
| Walking, Bicycling In-line Skating | **59** |
| Driving in Paris | **60–61** |
| Visitors with a Disability | **62** |
| Leaving Paris | **63–64** |

# ARRIVING



## By Air

You can get flights to Paris from most major European cities and from many other destinations worldwide. Major international carriers use the larger Roissy-Charles de Gaulle Airport, 23km (14 miles) northeast of central Paris. There are good rail and bus links. Orly Airport has domestic flights and some international flights. It is 14km (8.5 miles) south of the city heart, with bus but no direct rail links.

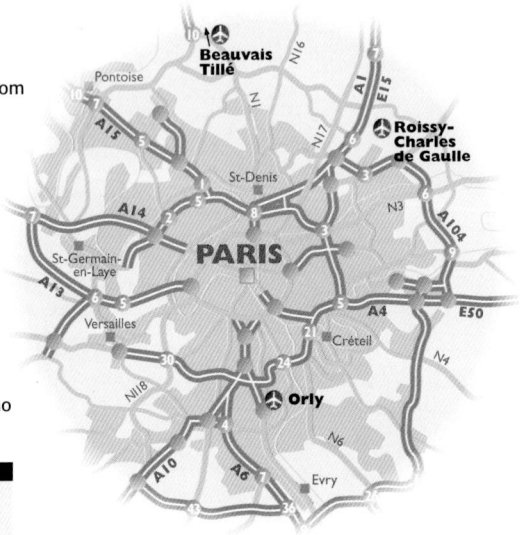


**TIPS**

- The tourist office in T1 of Roissy-Charles de Gaulle (arrivals level) is open from 7am to 10pm. The office on the arrivals level of Orly Ouest is open from 6am to 11.45pm.
- Smoking inside the airports is banned, except in designated smoking areas.
- When departing from Roissy-Charles de Gaulle make sure you know which terminal you are leaving from, as terminals 1 and 2 are a fair distance apart.
- When departing from any of the airports, allow plenty of time for extra security checks.

### ROISSY–CHARLES DE GAULLE

Paris's busiest airport has three terminals: T1, T2 and T3 (formerly T9). Terminal 2 is subdivided into 2A, 2B, 2C, 2D and 2F. Airlines operating out of T1 include Aer Lingus, British Midland, KLM, United Airlines and US Airways. T2 serves Air France, American Airlines, British Airways and others. Airlines using T3 include the low-cost EasyJet. Terminals do change so always check before setting off.

You'll find information desks, shops, restaurants, banks, bureaux de change, car rental firms and first aid facilities in T1 and T2. For security reasons there are no left luggage facilities. T3 has shops, cafés, a bureau de change and car rental outlets.

The airport has two RER stations—CDG1 for T1 and T3 and CDG2 for T2. Shuttle buses run from the terminals to both stations. You can then take RER line B into Paris. Buses also run to the city (see chart below).

**GETTING TO PARIS FROM THE AIRPORT**

| AIRPORT | TAXI | RER |
|---|---|---|
| **Roissy-Charles de Gaulle (CDG)** | Cost: €38–43.<br>Journey time: 30-60 min | RER line B takes you into the heart of Paris (Gare du Nord, Châtelet or St-Michel). Trains leave every 5–15 min, from 5am to 11.40pm.<br>Cost: €7.70.<br>Journey time: 35 min. |
| **Orly (ORY)** | Cost: around €25.<br>Journey time: 15–30 min. | The Orlyval train (Mon–Sat 6am–10.30pm, Sun 7am–11pm) takes you two stops to Antony, where you pick up RER line B.<br>Cost: €8.80. Journey time: 35 min. |
| **Beauvais Tillé (BVA)** | Cost: around €120.<br>Journey time: 1 hour 20 min. | None. |

*Checking the departures board at Roissy-Charles de Gaulle*

**ORLY**

Orly Airport has two terminals—Orly Sud and Orly Ouest. Shuttle buses or the Orlyval train link the two. The airport has shops, restaurants, bureaux de change, car rental firms and medical facilities. There are no direct rail links into Paris, but the Orlyval train takes you two stops to Antony, where you can change to RER line B. The Orlybus runs from the airport to Denfert-Rochereau Métro station; the Air France bus will take you farther into the city, to Les Invalides. Alternatively, take a shuttle bus to Pont de Rungis RER station then RER line C to Gare d'Austerlitz, St-Michel-Notre-Dame or Les Invalides.

**BEAUVAIS TILLÉ**

Beauvais Tillé is a small airport in Beauvais, north of Paris, in the Oise *département*. It is currently used by low-cost airlines. Facilities include a news vendor, restaurant and car rental desks. A bus connects with incoming flights and takes you to Porte Maillot, on the northwestern edge of Paris. It is also possible to take a taxi, although this is an expensive option.

## USEFUL TELEPHONE NUMBERS AND WEBSITES

### ROISSY-CHARLES DE GAULLE

**www.adp.fr** The official website of Roissy-Charles de Gaulle and Orly
**Information:** 01 48 62 22 80
**Lost Property, T1:** 01 48 62 13 34
**Lost Property, T2:** 01 48 16 63 83
**Police:** 01 48 62 31 22
**Air France:** 0802 802 802
**Air France bus to Paris:** 0892 350 820; www.cars-airfrance.com
**RATP (RER):** 0892 68 77 14; www.ratp.fr

### ORLY

**www.adp.fr** The official website of Orly and Roissy-Charles de Gaulle
**Information:** 01 49 75 15 15
**Lost Property, Orly Sud:** 01 49 75 34 10
**Lost Property, Orly Ouest:** 01 49 75 42 34
**Police:** 01 49 75 43 04
**Air France bus to Paris:** 0892 350 820; www.cars-airfrance.com
**Orlybus:** 01 40 02 32 94 (customer services); 0892 687 714 (information)
**RATP information (Orlyval train and RER):** 0892 687 714; www.ratp.fr

### BEAUVAIS TILLÉ

**Information:** 0892 682 066
**Website:** www.aeroportbeauvais.com

| MÉTRO | BUS | CAR |
|---|---|---|
| None. | The Air France bus runs from Terminals 1 and 2 to Montparnasse and Gare de Lyon every 30 min, 7am–9pm. Cost: €11.50. Journey time: 45 min–1 hour. Another Air France bus runs to the Arc de Triomphe every 15 min, 5.45am–11pm. Cost: €10. Journey time: 45 min–1 hour. The Roissybus runs every 15 min from Terminals 1, 2 and 3 to Opéra, 6am–11pm. Cost: €8.20. Journey time: 50 min. | Take the A1 south to Paris. Journey time: 30–60 min, depending on traffic. |
| None. | Air France runs from Orly Sud and Ouest to Les Invalides and Gare Montparnasse every 15 min, 6am–11pm. Cost: €7.50. Journey time: 30 min. The Orlybus runs from Orly Sud and Ouest to Denfert-Rochereau Métro station every 15–20 min, 6am–11.30pm. Cost: €5.70. Journey time: 30 min. | Take the A106, then A6A or A6B into Paris. Journey time: 15–40 min, depending on traffic. |
| None. | Bus to Porte Maillot. Cost: €10. Journey time: around 1 hour 15 min. | Take the N1, A16, N1 then A1. Journey time: 1 hour 20 min. |

## By Train

**The Channel Tunnel rail link has revolutionized travel between London and Paris, allowing you to reach France's capital from Britain's in less than three hours, without leaving the ground or boarding a boat. The Queen and François Mitterrand, France's president at the time, opened the tunnel in 1994, almost 200 years after the first designs were submitted for an undersea link between England and France. It is the longest undersea tunnel in the world, with 39km (24 miles) of its 50km (31 mile) length under the English Channel.**

*Paris is easily reached by train from all parts of Europe*

**BOARDING EUROSTAR**

- Up to 16 trains per day travel to Paris from London; some stop en route at Ashford International (UK) and Calais (France). There are also direct trains to Disneyland Resort Paris. The introduction of upgraded track has cut the journey time to Paris to 2 hours 35 minutes.
- Trains leave from Waterloo International Station, in central London, which is on the Northern, Bakerloo, Jubilee, and Waterloo-and-City underground lines. Various mainline train services also run to Waterloo.
- The Eurostar terminal is separated from the hubbub of the rest of the station. Automatic check-in facilities are available for passengers with suitable tickets, otherwise check in at the desks. You must do this at least 30 minutes before your train is due to leave.
- Before you reach the departure lounge you must go through airport-style security checks and passport control. French passport control is actually carried out at Waterloo.
- Once in the departure lounge there are newspaper and gift shops, cafés, lavatories, internet points and a post box.
- Boarding begins around 20 minutes before departure. Information screens in the lounge tell you where and when to board.
- Each train has 18 carriages (cars) so you could face a long walk along the platform. Trolleys (carts) are available, but you'll need a £1 coin as a deposit.
- Once on board, large cases must be stored on the luggage racks at the end of each carriage, although you can put smaller bags in the racks above your seat.

**THE JOURNEY**

- A buffet car serves drinks, snacks and light meals. There are lavatories and baby changing facilities on board. The journey through the tunnel takes around 20 minutes and an announcement is made just before you enter.

**ARRIVING**

- When you arrive in Paris's Gare du Nord station you don't need to go through passport control as this has been carried out at Waterloo. Watch for pickpockets at the station.
- The covered taxi stand is well signposted. Don't be too depressed by the long queue—it moves fairly quickly. A taxi into the heart of Paris usually costs €10 to €15. There are extra charges for luggage and for travel after 7pm and on Sundays.

**TIPS**

- You'll usually pay less for your ticket if you reserve it in advance. It is highly recommended that you do this, since non-reserved seats are limited.
- The train is split into Premium, First and Standard class. Premium and First class give you a meal, extra legroom, a reclining seat and free newspapers. Certain tickets also allow admission to the business lounges at Waterloo and Gare du Nord.
- Remember that you need your passport to travel between Britain and France (see Passports and Visas, page 297).
- The official luggage allowance is two suitcases and one piece of hand luggage. Luggage labels must be marked with your name and seat number.
- Luggage trolleys (carts) are available on the platforms at Waterloo and Gare du Nord, but you need a £1 or €1 coin (refundable). If you have a heavy case a trolley is a good idea as the walk along the platform can be long if your carriage (car) happens to be the last of 18.

*It is best to reserve tickets ahead*

- Gare du Nord is on Métro lines 4 (purple) and 5 (orange). Line 4 (direction Porte d'Orléans) will take you across the river to the Left Bank. If your hotel is on the Right Bank, you can change lines at Gare de l'Est, Strasbourg St-Denis, Réaumur Sébastopol or Châtelet. Line 5 (direction place d'Italie) is handy if you're heading to the Bastille area.
- Gare du Nord is also on two RER lines: D (green) and B (blue). Line B takes you to Châtelet, then on to the Left Bank (St-Michel-Notre-Dame and Luxembourg). The RER can be a confusing rail system to the uninitiated (see page 56) so if it's your first time in Paris it may be better to take the Métro or a taxi.

## LEAVING PARIS

- The Eurostar terminal is on the first floor of the Gare du Nord. There are a few gift shops and coffee bars, but facilities are not as comprehensive as at Waterloo. There is no mailbox, so rid yourself of any last-minute postcards before you get to the terminal.
- Electronic screens will tell you which of the two boarding points to use and when to board.
- When you arrive back at Waterloo, you'll need to show your passport to customs officials.

## FACTS AND FIGURES

- Construction work on the tunnel began in 1987 and was completed in 1991.
- At 50km (31 miles), it is the second-longest tunnel in the world, and the longest undersea tunnel.
- The tunnel is 40m (131ft) below the seabed.

**USEFUL NUMBERS**

**Eurostar:**
From within the UK:
08705 186 186
From outside the UK:
+ 44 1233 617 575
**www.eurostar.com**
**Lost luggage at Waterloo:**
020 7928 0660 (UK number)
**Lost luggage at Gare du Nord:**
01 55 31 58 40 (French number)

- Trains travel at up to 300 kph (186 mph).
- Each train is 400m (1,312ft) long.
- There are two main tunnels and a service tunnel. This doubles as a safety tunnel and is designed to stay smoke-free in the event of a fire.
- Trains have a driver's carriage at either end, so they can quickly change direction and exit the tunnel if an emergency arises ahead.
- French designer Philippe Starck is helping Eurostar with various refurbishments, which range from new staff uniforms to redesigned business lounges and train interiors.

*The busy Gare du Nord*

# By Car or Long-Distance Bus

**If you want to drive from the UK to France you can take either the Eurotunnel or a ferry, both of which run to Calais. From here it should take around 3 hours 15 minutes to drive to Paris. Driving to France from countries on mainland Europe is straightforward.**



**EUROTUNNEL**

If you are driving from the UK, you can load your car onto the Shuttle train at Folkestone for the 35-minute journey under the English Channel to Calais/Coquelles. There are up to four departures per hour, 24 hours a day. Book ahead.

To reach the Folkestone terminal take the M20 to junction 11A, then follow signs to the Channel Tunnel. French border controls take place in the UK.

You stay with your vehicle during the journey, although you can go to the lavatory or walk about within the air-conditioned carriage (car). There is an on-board radio station and staff are available if you need assistance.

To reach Paris from Calais you can take the A16 (E40) in the direction of Dunkerque, then join the A26 (E15). At the junction with the A1, head southbound on the A1 (E15), which takes you to Paris. You will have to pay *autoroute* tolls. See pages 60–61 for more driving information.

**Eurotunnel Contact Details**
08705 35 35 35 (UK number); **www.**eurotunnel.com

**TIPS**

- It is often less expensive to reserve Eurotunnel tickets online rather than by telephone.
- LPG vehicles cannot use the Eurotunnel.
- Look out for low-cost ferry deals in British newspapers.
- The phone numbers given on this page are UK-based. To call from the US, dial 011 44, then omit the initial zero from the number. To call from mainland Europe, dial 00 44, then omit the zero.

**BY SEA**

The cost of crossing to France from England by ferry varies widely according to the time, day and month of travel. Most companies require you to check in at least 30 minutes before departure, although you may need to arrive earlier.

**P&O Ferries and Seafrance** sail from Dover to Calais (journey time: 70 to 90 minutes). Facilities on board the ferries include shops, cafés, bureaux de change and lounges. From Calais, it takes around 3 hours 15 minutes to drive to Paris—for directions, see Eurotunnel.

The **Hoverspeed** catamaran cuts the journey between Dover and Calais to 50 minutes, although it can be more prone to cancellations in bad weather.

**Hoverspeed** operates a Newhaven to Dieppe service (journey time: 2 hours). From Dieppe, the drive to Paris takes around 2 hours 30 minutes.

**Brittany Ferries** sail from Portsmouth to Caen (journey time: 6 hours). The drive to Paris takes around 2 hours 40 minutes.

**P&O Ferries** sail from Portsmouth to Le Havre (journey time: 5 hours 30 minutes). The drive to Paris takes around 2 hours 25 minutes.

**Ferry Contact Details**
**Brittany Ferries:** 0870 366 5333 (UK); **www.**brittany-ferries.co.uk
**Hoverspeed:** 0870 240 8070 (UK); **www.**hoverspeed.co.uk
**P&O Ferries:** 0870 520 2020 (UK); **www.**poferries.com
**Seafrance:** 08705 711 711 (UK); **www.**seafrance.co.uk

**BY LONG-DISTANCE BUS**

Taking the bus from the UK can be a useful option if you're on a tight budget, although the journey from London takes almost eight hours. Eurolines runs from Victoria coach station to Paris up to five times a day, with pick-up points at Canterbury and Dover, in Kent. The Channel crossing is made either by Eurotunnel or ferry. You arrive at the bus terminal in avenue du General de Gaulle, in Bagnolet, on the eastern edge of Paris.

Reserve your ticket at least 30 days in advance to get the best prices.

**Eurolines Contact Details**
0870 514 3219 (UK); **www.**eurolines.co.uk

# GETTING AROUND

**Paris has a comprehensive, efficient and relatively inexpensive transportation network and you should have few problems finding your way around the city. The Métro (underground/subway) is the backbone of the network. Other useful options include buses, riverboats and the suburban RER trains. Finally, don't forget your own two feet—central Paris is compact and walking is a great way to get your bearings.**



The Métro is often the quickest way of getting from A to B, and with around 300 stations you're rarely more than five minutes' walk from a line. Trains vary from ultramodern to past-their-best, depending on the line, but services usually run with minimum delays (barring strike action). Once in the station, be prepared for long walks to reach the platform—especially at Châtelet—although you won't need to go down as deep as, say, the London Underground. During rush hour the trains can become uncomfortably crowded and you're unlikely to find a seat. Lines that connect key visitor attractions (such as Line 1) can be crowded all day.

Buses give you the chance to see the city as you travel and their routes are clearly marked at the stops and on the bus. But they are slower than the Métro and can become just as crowded in rush hour.

The Métro, some RER lines and most buses are operated by RATP.

Taxis are useful if you have lots of baggage or if you don't feel comfortable using the Métro at night.

**TRAVEL INFORMATION**

- You can pick up free Métro maps at every station.
- For 24-hour recorded information in English, Italian, Spanish and German, call 0892 684 114.
- To speak to an advisor (in French only) call 0892 687 714.
- The major stations have information desks, although communication can sometimes be limited if you don't speak French.
- The website **www.**ratp.fr has lots of helpful information, in French and English. Click on *Paris Visite* for advice for visitors.
- There are travel information points at the airports.

*Using the automatic ticket machines can save time*

**ON THE MOVE WITH CHILDREN**

- Children under the age of four travel free on the Métro, buses and RER.
- Children under the age of 10 receive a 50 per cent reduction on ticket prices.
- Some buses have ramps for pushchairs (and wheelchairs) at the central doors.
- Taking a pushchair on the Métro can be tricky, due to awkward ticket barriers and the many steps to and from platforms.

**TICKETS**

- The Métro and buses use the same tickets and travel cards (see page 48). These can also be used on the RER within central Paris.
- The city is divided into fare zones. Most of the key sights are in Zone 1, although the Grande Arche is in Zone 3, Roissy-Charles de Gaulle airport is in Zone 5 and Orly airport is in Zone 4.
- Buy tickets at Métro stations, on buses (single tickets only) and at some news-stands.
- To save time, use the ticket machines in station concourses. Instructions are given in a choice of languages.
- Most stations have ticket offices, generally open from 5.30am to midnight. If you don't speak French, take a copy of the RER or Métro map with you so you can point to where you want to go if necessary.
- Major credit and debit cards are accepted at stations, although cash is more convenient.
- A single ticket costs €1.30 and covers all Métro stations, RER stations within the heart of Paris and most buses (see page 48).
- If you are planning to make good use of the Métro and buses during your visit, a *carnet* (book) of ten tickets or a travelcard could be a better option.
- For more information on tickets and travelcards, see the chart on page 48.

**TIPS**

- Try to avoid using buses and the Métro during rush hour (roughly 7.30am–9.30am and 4.30pm–7pm).
- Smoking is banned on buses, the Métro and the RER.
- Buying a *carnet* of 10 tickets is better value than buying tickets separately for each bus or Métro journey, and also saves time waiting at the ticket office.
- If you are on your own, you may feel uncomfortable using the Métro late at night.

| TICKETS | | | |
|---|---|---|---|
| **TYPE** | **PRICE** | **VALID** | **EXTRA INFORMATION** |
| **Single ticket** | €1.30 | Tickets are valid on the Métro, the RER (within central Paris) and most buses. You don't have to use them on the day of purchase, but once you have stamped a ticket (by slotting it through the automatic barrier at Métro stations or in the machine on buses) it is valid for that journey only. | You can change Métro and RER lines within one journey on the same ticket, but you can't change from the Métro to a bus on the same ticket, or from one bus to another. |
| ***Carnet*** | €10 for 10 single tickets | As single tickets, see above. | This is cost-effective if you are planning eight journeys or more. |
| ***Mobilis*** | Zones 1–2: €5.20<br>Zones 1–3: €6.95<br>Zones 1–5: €12 | Valid for one day on the Métro, buses and RER, within the relevant zones. | A less expensive option than the one-day *Paris Visite* card (see below). |
| ***Paris Visite*, Zones 1–3** | 1 day : €8.35<br>2 days: €13.70<br>3 days: €18.25<br>5 days: €26.65<br>Children's passes (4–11 year-olds) are roughly half-price | Valid for an unlimited number of journeys on the Métro, bus, RER and Transilien services, within zones 1–3. The ticket is valid from the first occasion you use it. | If you need to travel for one day only or if you are staying within zone 1, the *Mobilis* pass (see above) is a less expensive option. But with the *Paris Visite* card you also receive special offers for various sights. Buy the ticket at Paris tourist offices or at stations. |
| ***Paris Visite*, Zones 1–5** | 1 day: €16.75<br>2 days: €26.65<br>3 days: €37.35<br>5 days: €45.70 | Valid for an unlimited number of journeys on the Métro, bus, RER and Transilien services within zones 1–5 (including Versailles, Disneyland Resort Paris and Orly and Roissy–Charles de Gaulle airports). | An expensive option. |
| ***La Carte Orange-Coupon Hebdomadaire*, Zones 1–2** | €14.50 | Valid for a week on the Métro, buses and RER within zones 1–2. | The card is officially intended for residents of the Île de France and runs from Monday to Sunday. So the earlier in the week you purchase it, the better the value. You'll need a passport-size photo. |
| ***La Carte Orange-Coupon Mensuel*, Zones 1–2** | €48.60 | Valid for a month on the Métro, buses and RER within zones 1–2. | See above. |

# Paris Métro

**Paris's Métro (Métropolitain) system is the lifeblood of the city, carrying around four million passengers each day. The first trains ran in 1900, during the Belle-Époque era. The network has since grown to 16 lines and 211km (131 miles) of track.**



The Métro system is efficient, inexpensive and relatively clean. It is the quickest way to travel for most journeys within the city.

Each line is colour-coded and numbered (1–14, 3b and 7b). Stations are identified either by a large M or by the famous art nouveau Métro signs. Steps, or occasionally escalators, lead down into a lobby, where you can buy tickets from either a manned booth or a machine. Larger stations have shops and cafés.

To reach the platforms, validate (*composter*) your ticket by slotting it into the machine at the automatic barrier, then collect it and keep it with you—inspectors make random checks. You'll often have a fairly long walk to the platform, so follow direction signs carefully. Signs will show the line number and colour. You also need to know the final destination of the train in the direction you wish to travel. Trains are frequent but get crowded during rush hour. An orange *Correspondance* sign on the platform gives directions to connecting lines. Blue signs marked *Sortie* indicate the exits.

## UNDERSTANDING THE MÉTRO MAP

The information below will help you understand the Métro map on pages 52–53 and on the inside back cover. Symbols used on the map in this book may differ slightly to the symbols found on the maps posted up at Métro stations.

**MÉTRO STATION**
A small triangle indicates a station with no interchanges.

**MAINLINE STATION**
This is shown by the SNCF symbol.

**LINES** Châtelet 11
Each line is colour-coded and is marked at each end with its number and final destination.

**STATION WITH INTERCHANGE**
Stations used by more than one line are marked with a white circle.

**END OF THE LINE** Châtelet 11
Terminus stations are placed in a white box.

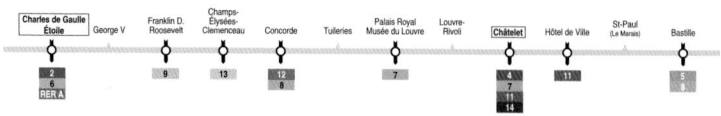


**ROUTE MAPS**
Route maps are posted up inside each train, allowing you to follow your journey.

**INTERCHANGING LINES**
On route maps, any connecting lines are marked underneath the station.

## HOW TO SURVIVE THE MÉTRO

- Trains run from 5.30am to around 12.30am.
- When waiting for the train, stand away from the edge of the platform.

- To open train doors press the button (on newer trains) or lift the handle (on older trains). Most trains on Line 1 have doors that open automatically.
- Let passengers leave the train before you enter.

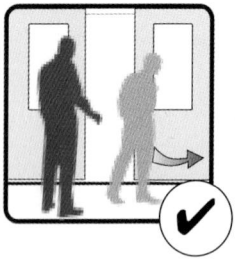

- A signal sounds when the automatic doors are about to close. Stand clear of the doors.

- Keep your bags close to you and watch out for pickpockets. Don't carry valuables in back pockets or rucksacks.

- Keep hold of your ticket, in case an inspector asks to see it.
- Watch for the gap between the train and the platform as you step onto and off the train.

- If you need to change lines, don't leave the interchange station or you will invalidate your ticket.
- If you find you're going in the wrong direction, come off at the next station and double-back. Follow directions to the correct platform, but stay within the automatic barriers or you'll invalidate your ticket.
- Once you have finished your journey, signs in the station indicate which exit leads to which road.
- As with many large cities, you'll probably come across people begging in Paris's Métro stations.

### DID YOU KNOW?

- Hector Guimard's famous art nouveau Métro entrances are at Abbesses and Porte Dauphine.
- Fittingly for a city known for its perfume, Paris's Métro stations are freshened up with a specially created musk and vanilla scent, known as *Madeleine*.
- Look out for Métro stations whose decoration reflects the location. Examples include Bastille, with murals depicting the uprising, and Louvre-Rivoli, with its museum-style displays.
- The newest line, number 14, has glass doors separating the platform and the tracks. On the trains, a PA system announces the station you are approaching.

### USEFUL LINES FOR REACHING THE SIGHTS

**Line 1 (yellow)** runs from east to west across the city, starting at Château de Vincennes and finishing at Grande Arche de la Défense. Key stops include Gare de Lyon, Bastille, Louvre-Rivoli and Concorde. It also runs up the Champs-Élysées—stopping at Champs-Élysées-Clemenceau, Franklin D. Roosevelt, George V and Charles de Gaulle-Étoile—allowing you to hop from one end of the avenue to the other.

**Line 4 (light purple)** connects the St-Germain-des-Prés district with the Right Bank. It also stops at Gare du Nord, location of the Eurostar terminal.

**Line 9 (light green)** takes you from the outskirts of the Bois de Boulogne, in the west of the city, up to the popular shopping areas of the Right Bank (Havre-Caumartin for Printemps and Chaussée d'Antin for Galeries Lafayette). It then continues east through République and Nation.

**Line 12 (dark green)** is useful if you're heading to Montmartre (use the Abbesses stop). It runs from the Left Bank. Useful stations en route include Solférino (for the Musée d'Orsay), Concorde and Madeleine.

**Line 14 (purple)** is handy if you are staying on the eastern side of the city, within walking distance

## HOW TO USE THE MÉTRO

Below is a typical Métro journey from Odéon to Charles de Gaulle–Étoile (the Arc de Triomphe).

**ODÉON**

- Find a map and note the colours and numbers of the lines you'll need.
- Purchase a single ticket or use one of your *carnet* tickets or a travel pass (see page 48).
- To reach the platforms, slot your ticket into the automatic barrier and pick it up when it re-emerges.
- Follow signs for Line 4 (light purple) in the direction of Porte de Clignancourt.
- Once at the platform, you shouldn't have too long to wait for a train.
- A route map on board the train allows you to follow your journey.

**CHÂTELET**

- Get off at Châtelet and follow the orange *Correspondance* signs for Line 1 (yellow), in the direction of La Défense.
- Bear in mind that Châtelet is one of the largest Métro stations, with a long walk between some platforms.
- Board the train, then get off at Charles de Gaulle–Étoile.
- Follow the blue *Sortie* (exit) signs and look for the street exit that you require.

**CHARLES DE GAULLE-ÉTOILE**

## TIPS

- When planning your route, don't confuse Métro lines with the suburban RER lines—both are usually shown on Métro maps. RER lines have letters rather than numbers and will usually flow off the map.
- The RATP website (www.ratp.fr) has a helpful route planner and also gives up-to-date traffic and travel information.
- To estimate your journey time, allow two minutes between each station. Remember that it could take five minutes to walk to the platform (especially in warrens such as Châtelet).
- For recorded travel information in various languages call 0892 684 114.
- To speak to a travel advisor (in French only) call 0892 687 714.
- Cash is more useful than credit cards when paying for tickets.
- Keep hold of your ticket until you have left the station, as you may come across an inspector.
- Street maps of the local areas are posted up in most station lobbies.



of the Gare de Lyon. This ultramodern line is the quickest way to reach the heart of the city, taking you straight to Châtelet with no stops, then on to Pyramides and Madeleine. In the other direction, it runs to Bercy then across the river to the Bibliothèque François Mitterrand.

*One of Paris's renowned art nouveau Métro entrances, at Abbesses, in Montmartre*

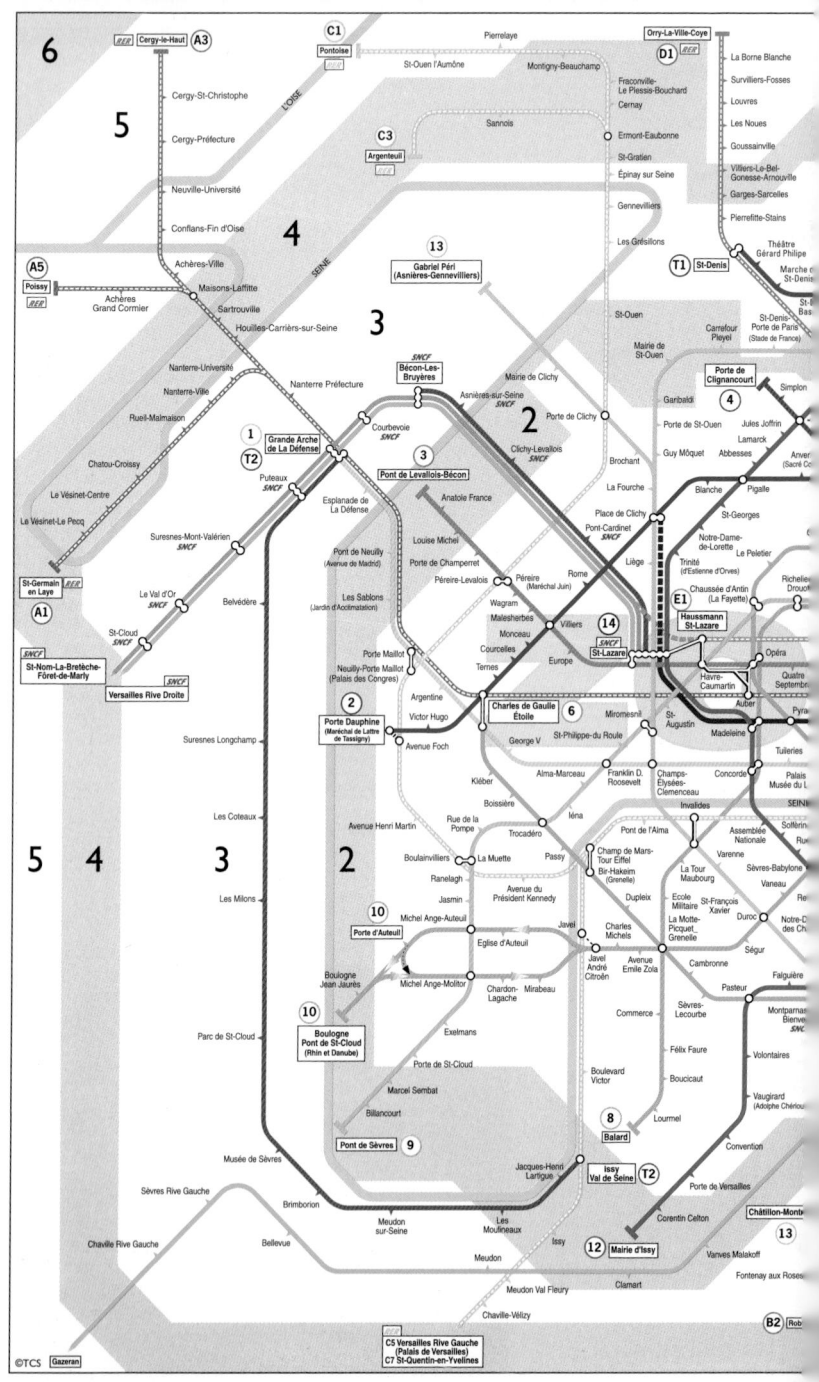
Cergy-le-Haut
A3
Cergy-St-Christophe
Cergy-Préfecture
Neuville-Université
Conflans-Fin d'Oise
Achères-Ville
A5
Poissy
Achères Grand Cormier
Maisons-Laffitte
Sartrouville
Houilles-Carrières-sur-Seine
LOISE
SEINE
C1
Pontoise
Pierrelaye
St-Ouen l'Aumône
Montigny-Beauchamp
C3
Argenteuil
Sannois
Orry-La-Ville-Coye
D1
La Borne Blanche
Survilliers-Fosses
Louvres
Les Noues
Goussainville
Villiers-Le-Bel-Gonesse-Arnouville
Garges-Sarcelles
Pierrefitte-Stains
Fraconville-Le Plessis-Bouchard
Cernay
Ermont-Eaubonne
St-Gratien
Épinay sur Seine
Gennevilliers
Les Grésillons
13
Gabriel Péri (Asnières-Gennevilliers)
T1
St-Denis
Théâtre Gérard Philipe
Marché de St-Denis
St-Denis-Porte de Paris (Stade de France)
St-Ouen
Carrefour Pleyel
Mairie de St-Ouen
Nanterre-Université
Nanterre-Ville
Rueil-Malmaison
Nanterre Préfecture
Bécon-Les-Bruyères
Mairie de Clichy
Asnières-sur-Seine
Porte de Clichy
Clichy-Levallois
Porte de Clignancourt
Garibaldi
Porte de St-Ouen
Jules Joffrin
Lamarck
Guy Môquet
Abbesses
Simplon
Brochant
La Fourche
Blanche
Pigalle
Place de Clichy
Pont-Cardinet
St-Georges
Notre-Dame-de-Lorette
Le Peletier
Liège
Trinité (d'Estienne d'Orves)
Chaussée d'Antin (La Fayette)
E1
Haussmann St-Lazare
Richelieu-Drouot
Opéra
Havre-Caumartin
Quatre Septembre
Auber
Madeleine
Tuileries
Palais du L
Concorde
Champs-Élysées-Clemenceau
Invalides
Solférino
Assemblée Nationale
Varenne
Sèvres-Babylone
Vaneau
Rue
Rer
Notre-D des Ch
Ségur
Cambronne
Falguière
Pasteur
Montparnas Bienve
Volontaires
Vaugirard (Adolphe Chériou
Convention
Porte de Versailles
Châtillon-Montr
13
Vanves Malakoff
Fontenay aux Roses
B2
Rob
St-Germain en Laye
A1
Chatou-Croissy
Le Vésinet-Centre
Le Vésinet-Le Pecq
Suresnes-Mont-Valérien
Le Val d'Or
Belvédère
St-Cloud
St-Nom-La-Bretèche-Forêt-de-Marly
Versailles Rive Droite
1
Grande Arche de La Défense
T2
Puteaux
Esplanade de La Défense
3
Pont de Levallois-Bécon
Courbevoie
Anatole France
Louise Michel
Pont de Neuilly (Avenue de Madrid)
Porte de Champerret
Péreire-Levalois
Péreire (Maréchal Juin)
Rome
Les Sablons (Jardin d'Acclimatation)
Wagram
Malesherbes
Villiers
Monceau
Courcelles
Ternes
Europe
14
St-Lazare
Porte Maillot
Neuilly-Porte Maillot (Palais des Congrès)
Argentine
Victor Hugo
2
Porte Dauphine (Maréchal de Lattre de Tassigny)
Avenue Foch
Charles de Gaulle Étoile
6
George V
St-Philippe-du Roule
Miromesnil
St-Augustin
Franklin D. Roosevelt
Alma-Marceau
Iéna
Kléber
Boissière
Rue de la Pompe
Trocadéro
Avenue Henri Martin
Pont de l'Alma
Champ de Mars-Tour Eiffel
Bir-Hakeim (Grenelle)
La Tour Maubourg
La Motte-Picquet-Grenelle
Ecole Militaire
St-François Xavier
Duroc
Suresnes Longchamp
Les Coteaux
Les Milons
Boulainvilliers
La Muette
Passy
Ranelagh
Jasmin
Avenue du Président Kennedy
Dupleix
10
Porte d'Auteuil
Michel Ange-Auteuil
Eglise d'Auteuil
Javel
Charles Michels
Javel André Citroën
Avenue Emile Zola
Boulogne Jean Jaurès
Michel Ange-Molitor
Chardon-Lagache
Mirabeau
Commerce
Sèvres-Lecourbe
Félix Faure
Boucicaut
Lourmel
Parc de St-Cloud
10
Boulogne Pont de St-Cloud (Rhin et Danube)
Exelmans
Porte de St-Cloud
Boulevard Victor
Marcel Sembat
Billancourt
8
Balard
Pont de Sèvres
9
Musée de Sèvres
Jacques-Henri Lartigue
Issy Val de Seine
T2
Sèvres Rive Gauche
Brimborion
Meudon sur-Seine
Les Moulineaux
Corentin Celton
Chaville Rive Gauche
Bellevue
Issy
12
Mairie d'Issy
Meudon
Meudon Val Fleury
Clamart
Chaville-Vélizy
C5 Versailles Rive Gauche (Palais de Versailles)
C7 St-Quentin-en-Yvelines
©TCS
Gazeran

Map Authorised User Ref: 9C02117/KG/PAR/GB V1.ZON - UDN.1

Aéroport-Charles de Gaulle 2 TGV (B3)
Aéroport-Charles de Gaulle 1
Parc des Expositions
Villepinte
Sevran-Beaudottes
Aulnay sous Bois
Sevran-Livry
Vert Galant
Mitry-Claye (B5)
Villeparisis
Blanc Mesnil
Drancy
Le Bourget
Aubervilliers-La Courneuve
Hôpital Delafontaine
La Courneuve 6 Routes
Stade Géo André
La Courneuve-8 Mai 1945 (7)
Drancy Avenir
Gaston Roulaud
Escadrille Normandie-Niéman
La Ferme
Libération
Hôtel de Ville de Bobigny
Bobigny-Pablo Picasso (T1) (5)
Cimetière de St-Denis
Cosmonautes
Hôtel de Ville de La Courneuve
Danton
Maurice Lachâtre
Hôpital Avicenne
Eglise de Pantin
Bobigny-Pantin Raymond Queneau
Basilique de Saint-Denis (Hôtel de Ville)
La Plaine-Stade de France (St-Denis-Aubervilliers)
Fort d'Aubervilliers
Hoche
Pantin
Noisy-le-Sec
E2: Chelles-Gournay
E4: Villiers-sur-Marne
(Le Plessis-Trévise)
Porte de la Chapelle (12)
Aubervilliers-Pantin Quatre-Chemins
Porte de la Villette
Corentin Cariou
Porte de Pantin (Parc de la Villette)
Télégraphe
Porte des Lilas (3b)
Mairie des Lilas (11)
Marx Dormoy
Crimée
Ourcq
(7b) Pré St-Gervais
Riquet
Laumière
Danube
Stalingrad
Jaurès
Bolivar
Botzaris
Place des Fêtes
St-Fargeau
Gallieni (Parc de Bagnolet) (3)
La Chapelle
Buttes Chaumont
Jourdain
Pelleport
Louis Blanc (7b)
Colonel Fabien
Pyrénées
(9) Mairie de Montreuil
Magenta
Château-Landon
Jacques Bonsergent
Belleville
Couronnes
Porte de Bagnolet
Gare de l'Est (Verdun)
Goncourt (Hôpital St-Louis)
Ménilmontant
Gambetta (3b)
Croix de Chavaux (Jaques Duclos)
Bonne Nouvelle
Château d'Eau
Parmentier
Père Lachaise
Strasbourg St-Denis
République
Temple
Rue St-Maur
Philippe Auguste
Robespierre
Réaumur Sébastopol
Arts et Métiers
Oberkampf
St-Ambroise
Alexandre Dumas
Porte de Montreuil
Sentier
Richard Lenoir
Voltaire (Léon Blum)
Filles du Calvaire
Étienne Marcel
Rambuteau
St-Sébastien-Froissart
Charonne
Avron
Maraîchers
Châtelet-Les Halles
Bréguet-Sabin
Rue des Boulets (Rue de Montreuil)
Nation (Place des Artilles)
Buzenval
Les Halles
Chemin Vert
Ledru Rollin
Faidherbe-Chaligny
Reuilly-Diderot
Châtelet (11)
St-Paul (Le Marais)
Bastille
Nation (2) (6)
Hôtel de Ville
Porte de Vincennes
Gare de Lyon
Châtelet (Pont au Change)
Pont Marie Cité des Arts
Sully Morland
Quai de la Rapée
Montgallet
Picpus (Courteline)
St-Mandé-Tourelle
Pont Neuf (La Monnaie)
Bel Air
St-Michel-Notre-Dame
Daumesnil (Félix Eboué)
Bérault
Maubert-Mutualité
Jussieu
(10) Gare d'Austerlitz
Dugommier
Michel Bizot
Vincennes
A2: Boissy St-Léger
A4: Marne-la-Vallée-Chessy
(Disneyland® Resort Paris)
Odéon
Cluny La Sorbonne
Cardinal Lemoine
Luxembourg
Place Monge
St-Marcel
Porte Dorée
Bercy
Cour St-Émilion
Porte de Charenton
Château de Vincennes (1)
Censier-Daubenton
Campo Formio
Chevaleret
Quai de la Gare
Liberté
Port Royal
Charenton-Écoles (Place Aristide Briand)
LA MARNE
Denfert-Rochereau
Les Gobelins
Nationale
Bibliothèque François Mitterrand (14)
Ecole Vétérinaire de Maisons-Alfort
Glacière
Corvisart
Place d'Italie (5)
Maisons-Alfort Stade
Raspail
St-Jacques
Tolbiac
Maisons-Alfort Les Juilliottes
Mouton-Duvernet
Olympiades
Ivry-sur-Seine
Cité Universitaire
Alésia
Maison Blanche
Porte de Choisy
Porte d'Ivry
Créteil-l'Echat (Hôpital Henri Mondor)
Maisons-Alfort Alfortville
Créteil Université
Gentilly
Porte d'Italie
Le Kremlin-Bicêtre
Pierre Curie
Le Vert-de Maisons
Créteil Préfecture (Hôtel de Ville) (8)
Porte d'Orléans (Général Leclerc) (4)
Villejuif-Léo Lagrange
Villeneuve Prairie
Villejuif-Paul Vaillant-Couturier
Mairie d'Ivry (7)
Villeneuve Triage
Villeneuve -St-Georges
Laplace
Ivry sur Seine
Montgeron-Crosne
Arcueil-Cachan
Vitry sur Seine
Yerres
Bagneux
Villejuif-Louis Aragon (7)
Les Ardoines
Brunoy
Boussy St-Antoine
Bourg la Reine
Rungis la Fraternelle
Orly Ville
Les Saules
Choisy le Roi
Parc de Sceaux
Pont de Rungis (Aéroport d'Orly)
Orlybus
Villeneuve le Roi
Vigneux-sur-Seine
Combs-la-Ville-Quincy
La Croix de Berny
Ablon
Athis-Mons
Lieusaint-Moissy
Orlyval
Antony
Juvisy-sur-Orge
Savigny-le-Temple Nandy
Orly Ouest
Orly Sud
B2: Robinson
B4: St-Rémy les Chevreuse
C2: Massy Palaiseau
C4: Dourdan-la-Forêt
C6: St-Martin d'Etampes
C8: Versailles-Chantiers
D4: Malesherbes
D2: Melun

# Buses

**Paris has a good network of buses, with more than 1,300 vehicles negotiating the city's traffic. Taking the bus is a good idea if you want to see the streets and sights rather than simply passing under them on the Métro, but don't expect to get anywhere quickly—the average speed is less than 13kph (8mph)!**

## GETTING AROUND BY BUS

- Most buses are painted easy-to-see turquoise and run from 7am to 8.30pm, although some continue until around 12.30am. You're unlikely to have to wait more than 5 or 10 minutes from Monday to Saturday, but services are reduced or, on some routes, non-existent on Sunday.
- The route number is displayed on the front of the bus, along with the final destination.
- Hold out your hand to stop the bus.
- If you need to buy a ticket, have the exact money ready as drivers do not carry much change. You can buy only single tickets on board. For information on travelcards see page 48.
- Enter at the front of the bus and show your travelcard or *carnet* ticket (see page 48) to the driver. *Carnet* tickets or single tickets must be stamped in the machine next to the driver.
- In rush hour you're unlikely to get a seat. Be prepared for a long and uncomfortable stand.
- If you are unsure of the route, you can track your journey on the route map in the bus.
- Just before your stop, press the red button to alert the driver that you want to get off. You'll see the *arrêt demandé* (stop requested) sign light up.
- Leave by the central doors.
- When planning your return journey, remember that buses do not necessarily follow the same route in both directions, so you may have to find a different bus to take you back.

### UNDERSTANDING BUS STOPS

**Bus Numbers**
Bus numbers are marked on the stop in the colour in which they appear on the route map. The number is also shown on the front of the bus.

**Routes**
The route is displayed on a large-scale map and every stop is marked. The stop you are standing at will be highlighted.

**Timetables**
Information is available about the hours and days each route operates.

**Bus Stop Types**
- Major bus stops are covered and have a small seat. Minor stops are marked by a pillar showing the bus numbers and routes.
- All bus stops are a distinctive turquoise.
- Major stops will also display a helpful map of the area, as well as the ubiquitous advertising posters.

### USEFUL ROUTES (OR SECTIONS OF ROUTES) FOR SIGHTSEEING

| ROUTE | KEY SIGHTS |
|---|---|
| 27 (southbound) | • Opéra Palais Garnier • Musée du Louvre • Pont Neuf • Pont St-Michel • Jardin du Luxembourg |
| 29 (eastbound) | • Opéra Palais Garnier • Bourse • Place des Victoires • Centre Georges Pompidou • Musée Carnavalet • Place des Vosges • Bastille |
| 42 (northbound) | • Tour Eiffel • Rond-Point des Champs-Élysées • Place de la Concorde • Place de la Madeleine |
| 69 (westbound) | • Bastille • Musée du Louvre • Musée d'Orsay • Les Invalides • Champ de Mars |
| 73 (eastbound) | • Arc de Triomphe • Champs-Élysées • Place de la Concorde • Assemblée Nationale • Musée d'Orsay |

## TICKET OPTIONS

- Buses use the same tickets as the Métro. A single ticket is valid for most central routes but you are not allowed to change buses on one ticket.
- You can buy single tickets on board, but not travelcards or *carnets* of 10 tickets. Have the exact change ready.
- Always stamp single tickets (including *carnet* tickets) in the machine near the driver, but not *Paris Visite, Mobilis* or *Carte Orange* passes. Keep your ticket until you have left the bus.

### FINDING INFORMATION

- The *Grand Plan Lignes et Rues,* available from Métro stations, has a useful bus map.
- www.ratp.fr has bus information in French and English, as well as a handy route planner.
- Call 0892 684 114 for a recorded message in various languages or 0892 687 714 to speak to an advisor (in French).

### OTHER SERVICES

**Airport buses:** See pages 42–43.
**Balabus:** The Balabus, aimed at visitors, runs from Gare de Lyon to La Grande Arche, taking in Bastille, Île de la Cité, place de la Concorde and the Champs-Élysées. It operates only on Sundays (afternoon to early evening), April to September, and costs between one and three single tickets.
**Montmartrobus and funicular:** See pages 108–109.
**Noctambus:** Night buses link Châtelet with the suburbs from 1am to 5.30am. Buses are identified by a letter and tickets cost €2.60. With waits of up to one hour, you may prefer to take a taxi.
**Tour buses:** See page 248.

*Buses are marked with their number and end destination*

## BUS BUSTER CHART

### CHANGE AT OR WALK TO/FROM:

- Place de la Concorde
- Châtelet
- Musée d'Orsay
- Opéra Palais Garnier
- Luxembourg
- Rond-Point des Champs-Élysées
- Trocadéro

**w = walk** *** = walk or take the Montmartrobus to/from Pigalle**

Use this chart to find out which buses will take you to your chosen destination. Follow the rows of squares horizontally and vertically from the name of the destinations until they meet. This square contains the number(s) of the bus(es) you'll need to catch. Bus numbers on white squares are direct. Numbers in shaded squares show that you have to change buses or take a bus some of the way and walk the rest. Start out on the first bus listed, then change to the second bus. Look at the key to find out where you must change buses or walk to/from. Note that the bus stop may be a few minutes' walk away from the destination.

**Routes are subject to change, and often differ on Sundays, so check an up-to-date timetable or bus map before setting out.**

| | ARC DE TRIOMPHE | BASTILLE | CENTRE GEORGES POMPIDOU | CIMETIÈRE DU PÈRE-LACHAISE | CONCIERGERIE | GRANDE ARCHE | GRAND PALAIS | INVALIDES | JARDIN DU LUXEMBOURG | JARDIN DES TUILERIES | MONTMARTRE | MUSÉE DU LOUVRE | MUSÉE MARMOTTAN | MUSÉE D'ORSAY | NOTRE-DAME | OPÉRA PALAIS GARNIER | PLACE DE LA CONCORDE | PLACE DES VOSGES | QUARTIER LATIN | SACRÉ-CŒUR | TOUR EIFFEL |
|---|---|---|---|---|---|---|---|---|---|---|---|---|---|---|---|---|---|---|---|---|---|
| ARC DE TRIOMPHE | | 22/20 | 22/29 | 73/69 | 22/21 | 73 | 73/w | 92 | 73/84 | 73 | 73/80 | 73/72 | 30/32 | 73 | 22/21 | 22 | 73 | 22/29 | 22/21 | 73/80 | 73/42 |
| BASTILLE | | | 76/w | 69 | 69/w | 69/73 | 69/w | 69 | 69/21 | 69 | 20/68 | 69 | 20/32 | 69 | 69/w | 20 | 69/72 | w/29 | 86/87 | 69/67* | 69 |
| CENTRE GEORGES POMPIDOU | | | | w/69 | 47 | 69/73 | w/72 | w/69 | w/21 | w/72 | w/67* | w/72 | 29/32 | w/69 | 47 | w/21 | w/72 | w | 47 | w/67* | w/69 |
| CIMETIÈRE DU PÈRE-LACHAISE | | | | | 69/w | 69/73 | 69/72 | 69/w | 69/21 | 69/w | 69/67* | 69 | | w/69 | 69/w | 69 | 69/72 | 69 | 69/21 | 69/67* | 69/w |
| CONCIERGERIE | | | | | | 72/73 | w/72 | 73/28 | 21 | 73/w | w/67* | 21 | 21/32 | 73 | w | w/69 | w/72 | w/69 | w/21 | w/67* | w/69 |
| GRANDE ARCHE | | | | | | | 73/w | 93 | 73/84/84 | 72 | 73/80 | 72 | 73/72 | 73 | 73/24 | 73/24 | 73 | 73/42 | 73/24 | 73/80 | 73/42 |
| GRAND PALAIS | | | | | | | | 83 | 93/42 | 93/80 | w/80 | 69 | w/32 | w/69 | 72/w | 72/w | w/72 | 72/21 | 72/21 | w/80 | w/42 |
| INVALIDES | | | | | | | | | 84 | 85 | 95 | 21 | 83/32 | 69 | 69/w | 69/w | 83/w | 82/w | 82 | 93 | 69/82 |
| JARDIN DU LUXEMBOURG | | | | | | | | | | w | *67 | w | 42/32 | 84 | w | 21 | 81/42 | w | 24 | 80 | 42 |
| JARDIN DES TUILERIES | | | | | | | | | | | 21 | 69 | 30/32 | w/73 | 80/73 | 72/69 | 72/42 | 84 | 85 | 42/80 | 80/42 |
| MONTMARTRE | | | | | | | | | | | | 72 | 21/32 | 69 | 69 | *67/69 | 81/42 | 72 | 21/24 | w | 69 |
| MUSÉE DU LOUVRE | | | | | | | | | | | | | 32/63 | 32/29 | 32/21 | 32/42 | 32/22 | 32/42 | 32/21 | 32/30* | 32/w |
| MUSÉE MARMOTTAN | | | | | | | | | | | | | | 69 | 69/w | 73 | 73/42 | 73 | 63 | 73/80 | 69 |
| MUSÉE D'ORSAY | | | | | | | | | | | | | | | w/21 | 21 | 21 | w/72 | w/21 | w/67* | w/69 |
| NOTRE-DAME | | | | | | | | | | | | | | | | 72/69 | 72/69 | 42 | 21/24 | 68* | 42 |
| OPÉRA PALAIS GARNIER | | | | | | | | | | | | | | | | | 69 | 69 | 96 | 42/80 | 69/67* |
| PLACE DE LA CONCORDE | | | | | | | | | | | | | | | | | | 21 | 85 | 85 | w/82 |
| PLACE DES VOSGES | | | | | | | | | | | | | | | | | | | 24 | 42 | 80/42 |
| QUARTIER LATIN | | | | | | | | | | | | | | | | | | | | 69 | 69 |
| SACRÉ-CŒUR | | | | | | | | | | | | | | | | | | | | | 42 |
| TOUR EIFFEL | | | | | | | | | | | | | | | | | | | | | |

# RER and Other Train Lines

**The RER train network travels through the city en route to the suburbs and can be a good time-saver if you are going from one side of town to the other. For trips farther afield, the Transilien network covers the Île de France region.**

## RER

The RER (Réseau Express Régional) dates from 1969 and is operated by RATP and SNCF. It serves Disneyland Resort Paris to the east, Roissy-Charles de Gaulle Airport to the north, Versailles to the west and the Orly Airport train link to the south. Trains run underground in central Paris and overground in the suburbs. Bear in mind that the RER can be confusing, so for a short trip you're usually better off using the Métro.

### Tickets

- A single Métro ticket is valid for RER journeys in central Paris and you can change lines (including Métro lines) on the same ticket. For journeys farther afield, you'll need to buy a separate ticket valid for the particular destination.
- Travelcards (see page 48) are valid if they cover all the zones you are going through.

- Keep hold of your ticket as you'll need to slot it through the automatic barrier to exit the station.

### Using the RER

- Trains run from around 5.30am to 12.30am.
- The RER has five lines, named A to E. Each line breaks into offshoots, which bear a number after the letter.
- Pick up a *Grand Plan Touristique* or another RER map from the station to identify the

**TIPS**

- The RATP website (www.ratp.fr) has a helpful route planner, as well as other travel information.
- To speak to an advisor (in French only), call 0892 687 714. To avoid confusion, remember that the French pronounce RER '*air-eu-air*'.
- Few visitors use the RER outside central Paris (unless they are going to Versailles, Disneyland or the airport) so you may feel conspicuous. Be aware that some of the suburbs the RER passes through are somewhat run-down, and the trains and platforms tend to have more graffiti than on the Métro. Outside peak periods, the trains may also be quite empty.
- Trains run fairly frequently in central Paris, but less so in the outlying areas.

**WHERE TO GO**

| DESTINATION | LINE | STOP | TIME | ZONE | NOTES |
|---|---|---|---|---|---|
| **Disneyland Resort Paris** | A4 | Marne-la-Vallée Chessy (Parc Disneyland) | 35 min | Zone 5 | You can buy passes for Disneyland Resort Paris from some RATP ticket offices, to save time later, although the passes do not include travel. |
| **Versailles** | C5 | Versailles-Rive Gauche | 35 min | Zone 4 | Versailles-Rive Gauche is the closest station to the chateau, but you can also travel to Versailles-Chantiers on C7 and C8. Tickets covering train travel and entrance are available (see page 244). |
| **Roissy-Charles de Gaulle Airport** | B3 | Aéroport Charles de Gaulle 1 or 2 | 35 min | Zone 5 | Use Charles de Gaulle 1 for Terminal 1 and Terminal 3. Use Charles de Gaulle 2 for Terminal 2. |
| **Orly Airport** | B4 | Antony | 30 min to Antony | Zone 3 (Antony) | From Antony, take the Orlyval train to the airport, which is in Zone 4. |
| **Chantilly** | SNCF (Gare du Nord) | Chantilly-Gouvieux | 30 min | Outside the zones | The chateau is a 30-min walk from the station. |

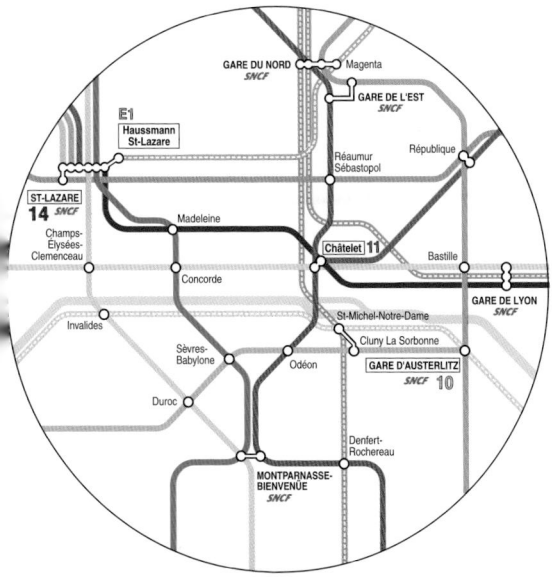


*Paris's mainline stations (left)*

**TIPS**

- SNCF's website (www.sncf.fr) has a useful route planner.
- For information over the phone, call 01 53 90 20 20.
- If you are leaving from a mainline station, give yourself plenty of time to buy a ticket and find the correct platform.
- Keep hold of your ticket in case an inspector joins the train.

*Signs show which RER lines stop at your station*

line and offshoot you need. The RER lines in central Paris are on the Métro map on pages 52–53.

- Information screens in the foyer should tell you which platform you need; or you could ask at the ticket desk.
- Slot your ticket into the automatic barrier and remember to retrieve it when it emerges.
- An increasing number of platforms have screens with information on arrival times for the next five trains.
- When leaving the train, follow blue *Sortie* signs if it is the end of your journey, or orange *Correspondance* signs if you need to change to another line.
- You'll need to slot your ticket into the automatic barrier to leave the station.

## TRANSILIEN TRAINS

The Transilien network, operated by SNCF, covers stations all over the Île de France. You are most likely to use these trains if you are taking an excursion to places such as Fontainebleau (see pages 242–243). Trains leave from mainline stations.

### Using Transilien Trains

- Buy tickets from the ticket desk or the machine. Prices vary according to destination. Travelcards are valid if they cover all the zones you travel through.
- Stamp your ticket before boarding, either in the automatic barrier if you pass through one or in the orange machine near the entrance to the platform.
- Timetables are available at the station. Platform numbers are shown on the information boards in the station concourse.
- Check there is a suitably timed train to bring you back into Paris.

*Waiting in line for tickets (right)*

# Taxis and the Batobus

Taxis are not exorbitantly expensive and can be a relatively stress-free way of getting around. Paris's 14,900 taxis are operated by a variety of companies, but all adhere to the same pricing structure.



### USING A TAXI

- The best way to find a taxi is to head to one of the city's 470 taxi stands, marked by a blue *Taxis* sign. You can phone for a taxi but this is more expensive as the meter starts running as soon as the taxi sets off to collect you.
- You can hail a taxi in the street, if you can find one that is free. A white light on the roof indicates the taxi is available. When the light is off, the taxi is busy.
- Smoking is allowed in some taxis. Look for the sign.
- Taxi drivers are permitted to refuse a journey if there are more than three people, if you have animals or if it involves taking you outside Paris.
- If you want a receipt, ask for *un reçu*.
- If you have any complaints, contact the Préfecture de Police, Service des Taxis, 36 rue des Morillons, 75015; tel 01 55 76 20 00. Quote the taxi's registration number.

### CHARGES

- Prices are regulated and tariffs should be displayed in each taxi. Always check the meter is reset when you enter the taxi. Daytime trips within central Paris should cost under €12.
- Some taxis accept bank cards but it is best to have cash available. It is usual to give a tip of around 10 per cent.
- The three tariffs (A, B and C) are set out in the prices chart (right), along with the surcharges.

### TAXI COMPANIES

Taxi companies include:
**Alpha Taxis:** tel 01 45 85 85 85
**Artaxi:** tel 01 42 06 67 10
**Taxis Bleus:** tel 0891 701 010; www.taxis-bleus.com
**Taxi G7:** tel 01 47 39 47 39; www.g7.fr

*Taxis can be a convenient way of getting around*

### THE BATOBUS

The Batobus is a relaxing way to get around, allowing you to hop on and off at eight stops along the Seine. It runs from April to October, from 10am to 7pm *(until 9pm June to end-September)*. Boats leave every 15–25 minutes, stopping at *quais* near the Eiffel Tower, Champs-Élysées, Musée d'Orsay, Louvre, St-Germain-des-Prés, Notre-Dame, Hôtel de Ville and Jardin des Plantes. A one-day pass costs €10, a two-day pass €12.50 and a month-long pass €20 (half price for children under 12). Single tickets are available. You can buy tickets at the stops or the tourist office. Tel 01 44 11 33 99; www.batobus.com.

| TAXI PRICES | | |
|---|---|---|
| **Pick up charge** | €2 (or €2.70 at mainline stations) | |
| ***Tarif A*** | €0.60 per km | Central Paris, 7am–7pm, Mon–Sat. |
| ***Tarif B*** | €1 per km | Suburbs 7am–7pm, Mon–Sat. Central Paris 7pm–7am and all day Sun and public hols. Daytime journeys to and from the airports. |
| ***Tarif C*** | €1.20 per km | Suburbs 7pm–7am and all day Sun and public hols. All day, every day outside the suburbs. Night journeys to and from the airports. |
| **Surcharges** | You will be charged €2.60 for a fourth passenger, €0.60 for an animal and €0.90 for each piece of luggage over 5kg. There is a minimum fare of €5. | |

# Walking, Bicycling, In-line Skating

**Paris is gradually accepting more eco-friendly ways of getting about. An increasing number of people travel by foot or bicycle—you may well find that some sights can be reached more quickly by either of these methods than by the Métro, with its labyrinthine corridors. Bicyclists need to keep their wits about them, but may find their journeys are quicker than by car or bus. In-line skating is also extremely popular, with up to 12,000 people turning out to the special rides on Friday nights.**



## WALKING

Métro stations are everywhere in Paris and this can make it tempting to hop on a train even for short journeys. But if the weather is good try going on foot instead—it's a great way to get to know the layout of the city. You can easily walk from one district to another and it is far more enjoyable than the Métro. One minute you can be on a main road teeming with people, the next you're in a quiet side street in a residential district with its well-used grassy square.

The down side is the amount of traffic on the busier streets, especially place de la Concorde, Pont Neuf and the roads running alongside the Seine.

**TIPS**

- Be aware that a green-man signal or a striped pedestrian crossing do not necessarily mean cars will stop.
- When crossing roads, British visitors need to remember that traffic drives on the right in France.
- Avoid walking in deserted areas at night.

## BICYCLING

With more than 200km (124 miles) of bicycle tracks and plenty of bicycle rental outlets, Paris is gradually opening up to bicyclists. Drivers, however, are taking a while to catch up and dodging the traffic on the city's roads remains a hair-raising experience. Even where there are designated bicycle lanes, you'll find parked cars blocking your route. Among the least stressful places to bicycle are the leafy Bois de Boulogne, in the west of the city (see page 236), the Bois de Vincennes in the east (see page 237) and certain *quais* along the Seine on Sundays, when cars are banned *(Sunday 9–5, March to November)*. The *Paris à Vélo* map, available from the tourist office, town hall or bicycle rental shops, gives details of bicycle routes.

Remember that if a bicycle lane is available, you must use it. You must also wear a helmet, have bicycle lights and a bell. Lock your bicycle well. Bicycles are not allowed on the Métro but are permitted on certain RER lines outside rush hour. A good option if you're keen to bicycle is to take a tour run by Paris à Vélo C'est Sympa or Roue Libre.

### Useful Contacts

**Roue Libre**
Bicycle rental and guided bicycle tours, run by the Métro operators RATP.
1 Passage Mondétour (Forum des Halles), 75001
Tel 0810 441 534

**Paris à Vélo C'est Sympa**
Bicycle tours during the day and night. Bicycle rental. Tours leave from 37 boulevard Bourdon, 75004, and reservation is compulsory.
Tel 01 48 87 60 01
www.parisvelosympa.com

## IN-LINE SKATING

In-line skating is popular in Paris, helped by the Pari-Roller rides on Friday evening, which can attract up to 12,000 participants. You need to be an experienced skater to take part in this three-hour ride and you must check your insurance cover. The skate departs from outside the Gare Montparnasse at 10pm (in good weather only).

*On your skates—it's environmentally friendly and fun*

An easier ride, run by Rollers et Coquillages, leaves from Nomades store, Bastille, on Sunday at 2.30pm.

If you want to skate on your own, remember that by law you must stay off the roads. You are not allowed to skate along the Champs-Élysées walkways or wear skates on the Métro, buses or RER.

### Useful Contacts

**Pari-Roller**
Friday-night ride leaves from Gare Montparnasse at 10pm, weather permitting.
www.pari-roller.com

**Nomades**
Skate rental.
37 boulevard Bourdon, 75004
Tel 01 44 54 07 44
www.nomadeshop.com

**Rollers et Coquillages**
Sunday afternoon skate.
Tel 01 44 54 94 42
www.rollers-coquillages.org

# DRIVING



## Driving in Paris

**The best advice for driving in Paris is to avoid it! You'll face heavy traffic, tricky and expensive parking and confusing one-way systems. In addition, fuel stations can be hard to find. It is far better to use the Métro or buses, or take a taxi. However, if you do decide to drive, here are some tips.**

**TIPS**

- The speed limit in central Paris is 50kph (31mph). On the ring road (*périphérique*) the limit is 80kph (49mph).
- Don't park or stop on any of the *axes rouges* (key routes through the city).
- In built up areas, give way to traffic approaching from the right (*priorité à droite*), unless signs advise you otherwise.
- Don't use the bus lanes.
- Try to avoid driving during rush hour, weekdays from around 7 to 9.30am and 4.30 to 7.30pm.
- The city's roads are least congested in August, when many Parisians escape to the coast. But August is also when most road repairs take place.

**FINDING YOUR WAY**

- Paris's complex network of frequently narrow streets can be very confusing. Always plan your route in advance.
- Useful maps include *Plan de Paris par Arrondissement*, published by Grafocarte, and *Paris par Arrondissement*, by Editions L'Indispensable.

**LOCAL DRIVING CUSTOMS**

- You may find the concept of lanes is not taken too seriously, nor are red traffic lights—but don't be tempted to follow suit as you can be fined €750 for ignoring a red light or stop sign.
- Parisian drivers can be aggressive.
- Cars move fast when they can.
- Watch for delivery vehicles that may block you in by double parking.

**PARKING**

**On-Street Parking**

- Charges usually apply from 9am to 7pm, Monday to Saturday. Sundays and holidays are generally free, but always check before parking your car on the street.
- You can park for up to two hours.
- Parking meters accept coins or special cards (buy these from tobacconists).
- Hourly rates vary from under €1 to over €2.

**Parking Areas**

- You'll usually find underground parking areas in shopping complexes, near large department stores, in business districts and in certain tourist areas. Look for the "P" sign.
- Prices vary, and charges can be by the hour, day, weekend, month or year.
- For more information on parking areas for cars or motorcycles, buy the 288-page guide *Parkings de Paris*, which lists more than 200 parking areas, above and below ground, and gives prices. It also contains street maps, and maps of the Métro, RER and bus routes. It costs €10 and can be bought at the Paris Tourist Office, bookshops or from Editions Com 3000, 21 rue Lamartine 75009 Paris (*tel 01 45 26 59 74; www.parkingsdeparis.com*).

**Parking on the Outskirts**

- To save parking charges, some people park in the suburbs and take the Métro, RER or bus into central Paris.
- Stick to one of the safer areas like Maison-Lafitte, Neuilly, St-Cloud or Levallois-Perret (see advice on visiting areas outside the *périphérique* in Finding Help, page 305).
- It is possible to park for free at some supermarkets—but don't stay overnight.

*You'll need to pay at the meter to park on many streets in Paris*

**Towing Away**

- If your car isn't where you left it, contact the local police station or the police headquarters (tel 01 53 71 53 71) for details of the car pound.

# General Driving Hints

**A car is useful if you want to take an excursion out of Paris, or move on to a second destination in France. A good system of *autoroutes* links Paris with the main cities: The A1 leads to the north, the A13 to Normandy and the northwest, the A4 to the east, the A10 to the west and southwest and the A6 to the Alps and the Riviera. The French drive on the right.**



### PLANNING

- You must have at least third-party motor insurance to drive in France. But fully comprehensive cover is strongly advised as third party in France covers less than in some countries.
- If driving your own car, display an international sticker near the rear registration plate.
- Adjust headlights of left-hand-drive vehicles for driving on the right in France.

### RENTING A CAR

- See page 299.

### ROADS

- The *autoroute* is the French counterpart of the British motorway or American expressway and is marked by an 'A' on maps and road signs. A few sections around key cities are free of charge, but tolls are charged on the rest (*autoroutes à péage*). Always have cash available as foreign credit cards may not be accepted.
- In France, a highway or trunk road is called a *Route Nationale* (N).
- The next level down is the *Route Départementale* (D), although these roads can still be wide and fast. There are also quieter country roads.

### THE LAW

- Always carry a passport or national ID card, a valid driving licence, the vehicle's registration document and a certificate of motor insurance.
- The minimum age to drive in France is 18.
- In built-up areas vehicles should give way to traffic coming from the right (*Priorité à droite*), unless signs advise otherwise. At roundabouts (traffic circles) with signs saying *Cédez le passage* or *Vous n'avez pas la priorité* traffic already on the roundabout has priority. On roundabouts without these signs, traffic entering has priority. A priority road can also be shown by a white diamond-shaped sign with a yellow diamond within it. A black line through the diamond indicates the end of priority.

A red-bordered triangle with a black cross on a white background, with the words *passage protégé*, also shows priority.
- You must wear a seatbelt. Children under 10 must travel in the back, with a booster seat, except for babies under nine months with a specially adapted rear-facing front seat (but not in cars with airbags).
- Do not overtake where there is a solid single central line.
- There are harsh penalties if the level of alcohol in the blood is 0.05 per cent or more. If you drink, don't drive.
- Always stop at stop signs.

### ROAD SIGNS

**Allumez vos Phares** Switch on your lights.
**Cédez le Passage** Give way.
**Chantier** Road works.
**Péage** Toll.
**Priorité à droite/gauche** Priority to the right/left.
**Rappel** Reminder (continue with the previous instruction).
**Route Barré** Road closed.
**Sens interdit** No entry.
**Sens unique** One way.
**Serrez à droite/gauche** Keep to the right/left.
**Stationnement interdit** No parking.
**Travaux** Roadworks.

### EQUIPMENT

- Carry a red warning triangle in case of breakdown.
- Have a spare-bulb kit to hand.

### FUEL

- Fuel (*essence*) comes as unleaded (*sans plomb*, 95 and 98 octane), lead replacement petrol (*LRP* or *supercarburant*), diesel (*gasoil* or *gazole*) and LPG.
- Many filling stations close on Sundays and at 6pm the rest of the week.
- Prices are high at filling stations on *autoroutes*.
- Filling stations can be far apart in rural areas, so never let your tank get too low.

### CAR BREAKDOWN

- Make sure you have adequate breakdown cover.
- If you break down on an *autoroute* or the Paris *périphérique*, you must call the police or the official breakdown service for that area. There are emergency telephones on the roadside.

| SPEED LIMITS | |
|---|---|
| Urban roads | 50kph (31mph) |
| Outside built-up areas | 90kph (56mph); 80kph (49mph) in wet weather |
| Dual carriageways (divided highways), and non-toll *autoroutes* | 110kph (68mph); 100kph (62mph) in wet weather |
| Toll *autoroutes* | 130kph (80mph); 110kph (68mph) in wet weather |

Visiting drivers who have held a licence for less than two years are not allowed to exceed the wet-weather limits, even in good weather.

# VISITORS WITH A DISABILITY



**Facilities are gradually improving for visitors with a disability. All renovated and newly constructed buildings are now well equipped and some buses and certain RER stations are accessible to wheelchair users. But if you have reduced mobility you're still likely to encounter challenges in getting around in Paris—kerbs can be high, ramps are few and elevators are sometimes too small.**

## ARRIVING

**By Air** Both Roissy-Charles de Gaulle and Orly airports are well equipped for people with disabilities. Shuttle buses between terminals have ramps for wheelchair users, as well as voice announcements for the visually impaired. The terminals have adapted lavatories, low-level telephones and reserved parking spaces. For more information, ask for the leaflet *Guide-Passager à Mobilité Réduite* (*Guide for Passengers with Reduced Mobility*; *fax requests to: 01 49 75 58 78 or email: DCCMP3@adp.fr*). Organizations that offer specialist transportation from the airports into Paris include Airhop (*01 41 29 01 29*), AMHAP (*01 56 61 91 00*) and GIHP (*01 55 33 56 56*). Reserve them in advance. Taxis are also an option. The Orlyval train (see page 42–43) is accessible to wheelchairs.

**By Train** The modern design of the Eurostar trains and terminals makes them wheelchair-friendly. Passengers using a wheelchair can also benefit from discounted tickets.

## GETTING AROUND

Paris's main way of getting around—the Métro—is virtually inaccessible to wheelchair users because of its countless steps, warren of passageways and inflexible automatic barriers. The exception is Line 14, which also has voice announcements as the train draws in, for passengers with visual impairments. Certain RER stations on lines A and B have elevators to the platforms, although some can be operated only by a member of staff (press the *Appel* button for assistance). RATP's Mission Accessibilité (*tel 01 49 28 18 84*) publishes a *Guide Pratique* listing the RER stations that are accessible to wheelchair users. Even when a station is listed as accessible, wheelchair users are still likely to need assistance to board the train. Most ticket offices have induction loops for people with hearing impairments.

Buses can be a useful way of getting around, as some have ramps, including routes 20, 21, 24, 26, 27, 30, 38, 39, 53, 60, 62, 80, 88, 91, 92, 94, 95 and 96. There are plans for 59 bus routes to be accessible to wheelchairs by 2006. Some buses, including routes 26, 63, 80, 84, 91, 92, 94 and 96, are fitted with voice announcements of the next stop for passengers with visual impairments. For information on accessible bus routes, look up the website of the operator RATP (*www.ratp.fr*) or pick up the map *Grand Plan Lignes et Rues—2* from stations.

RATP runs an accompaniment service (Les Compagnons du Voyage) to assist people with reduced mobility. You have to reserve in advance and a fee is charged (*tel 01 45 19 15 00*).

The UK-based Access Project publishes a helpful book giving detailed information on going to Paris, accommodation, sights and getting around (£10 donation; see below for contact details).

## USEFUL ORGANIZATIONS

**Access Project**
**www.accessproject-phsp.org/paris/about.htm**
39 Bradley Gardens, West Ealing, London, W13 8HE, UK
Detailed advice on getting around.

**Les Compagnons du Voyage**
Tel 01 45 19 15 00
An accompaniment service on the Métro, RER and buses.

**Holiday Care Service**
**www.holidaycare.org.uk**
Tel 0845 124 9971 (UK)
Travel and holiday information for people with disabilities. The organization produces an information pack on France (£5).

**RATP Mission Accessibilité**
**E mail: mission.accessibilite@ratp.fr**
19 place Lachambaudie, 75570, Paris Cedex 12
Tel 01 49 28 18 84
Set up by the bus and Métro operator RATP to work for improved access for people with disabilities.

**Infomobi**
**www.infomobi.com**
Information about buses, the Métro and RER trains in the Île de France for people with disabilities.

**Mobile en Ville**
**www.mobile-en-ville.asso.fr**
A website packed with information on disability access and related issues.

**Mobility International USA**
**www.miusa.org**
Promotes international travel and exchange schemes for people with disabilities.

**Paris Tourist Office**
**www.paris-touristoffice.com**
Useful information about wheelchair access in museums, on buses, the RER and at airports.

**Society for Accessible Travel and Hospitality (SATH)**
**www.sath.org**
A US-based organization offering advice for visitors with disabilities and promoting awareness of their travel requirements.

# LEAVING PARIS

France has a comprehensive rail network and moving between cities and other European countries is relatively simple. The network, run by SNCF, is made up of *Grands Lignes* (long-distance lines) and *Lignes Régionals* (regional lines). The *Grands Lignes* have the regular CORAIL trains and the faster TGV trains, which can travel at speeds of up to 300kph (186mph). The *Lignes Régionals* have TER trains (*Trains Express Régionaux*), called Transilien trains in Paris. Paris has six mainline stations, each serving different regions in France and the rest of Europe. There are good connections with the Métro and buses (and RER in some cases).

## TICKETS

- Most trains have first and second classes, both of which are perfectly acceptable.
- Fares are split into blue (normal) and red (peak). Reduced-rate fares are generally available for normal travel on mainline routes, excluding TGV and couchette services.
- Ticket prices vary according to the level of comfort (first or second class; called Comfort Level 1 and Comfort Level 2 on Thalys) and departure time. First class fares are roughly 50 per cent more expensive than second class.
- You can buy tickets in the stations, at SNCF offices around the city and through some travel agents. Tickets for TGV trains must be reserved. You can do this up to a few minutes before departure, although in peak season it is best to book well in advance. Couchettes must be booked at least 75 minutes before the train leaves its first station.
- Make sure you stamp your ticket in the orange machines on the platforms before you start your journey. You'll risk a fine if you forget to do this.
- If you are under 26, you can get a 25 per cent discount (called *Découverte 12–25*) on train travel. Seniors also receive discounts (called *Découverte Senior*).
- When you travel second class, there are lower rates for booking more than eight days in advance (ask for *Découverte J8*) and more than 30 days in advance (ask for *Découverte J30*).
- A variety of rail passes are available, which allow travel either within France only, or within France and certain other countries, or within the whole of Europe. You should buy these before you enter France, either through travel agents or Rail Europe (see page 64).

## CATERING SERVICE

- Catering facilities—ranging from sandwiches and salads to hot meals—are available on most TGV and Corail services, but at a price.
- A benefit of first-class travel is that you can have food served at your seat during meal times on most TGV trains. You'll need to reserve in advance, except on TGV *Méditerranée* trains.
- You can reserve meals when you purchase your train ticket. Ticket machines dispense meal vouchers.
- Hot and cold drinks, sandwiches and snacks are served on most trains.
- Overnight trains (and some day services) have vending machines dispensing hot and cold drinks and sweets.

**FASTEST JOURNEY TIMES FROM PARIS (APPROXIMATE)**

| | |
|---|---|
| **Amsterdam** | 4 hours 10 min |
| **Bordeaux** | 3 hours |
| **Brussels** | 1 hour 20 min |
| **Lille** | 1 hour |
| **Marseille** | 3 hours |

## OVERNIGHT TRAINS

- Most overnight trains offer either reclining seats, couchette berths or a sleeper car.
- Reclining seats are available only in second class. You can adjust the head and foot rests.
- In first class, couchettes are in four-berth compartments; in second class they are in six-berth compartments.
- Sleeper car compartments are for up to two people in first class and up to three people in second class.
- Trains travel to cities in France and to other European countries.

*TGV trains travel across France*

### STATION ASSISTANCE

- Larger stations have an information kiosk, which is usually easy to find.
- If you need assistance, look for a member of the station staff, identifiable by their red waistcoats.
- You'll need a €1 deposit to use the luggage trolleys (carts).
- Porters are on hand to help with your luggage in main stations. They wear red jackets and black or navy caps.

### LEFT LUGGAGE

- Some stations have a left-luggage office or coin-operated lockers. Electronic locks issue a printed ticket with a code number. You'll need to keep this ticket for when you return to collect your items.
- Don't store valuables in lockers.
- Security concerns mean that left-luggage facilities are not always available.

*A packed departures board (right).*
*The chart (below) indicates the key destinations served by mainline stations in Paris*

### UNDERSTANDING RAILWAY TIMETABLES

- You can pick up free timetables (*horaires*) at stations.
- SNCF timetables are usually published twice a year—the summer one lasts from late May to late September, and the winter one from late September to late May.
- There are two styles of timetable: one for the *Grandes Lignes*, covering high-speed TGV and other mainline services, and another for the regional TER trains.
- Be prepared to decipher French railway terminology. On *Grandes Lignes* timetables, two rows of boxed numbers at the top refer to the *numéro de train* (train number) and to the *notes à consulter* (footnotes). In TER timetables, the train number is not listed.
- Footnotes at the bottom explain when a particular train runs (*circule*). *Tous les jours* means it runs every day; *sauf dimanche et fêtes* means it doesn't run on Sundays and holidays. *Jusqu'au*, followed by a date, indicates the service runs only up until that date.

### USEFUL CONTACTS

**SNCF**
**www.sncf.com**
**www.voyages-sncf.com**
**www.tgv.com**
Tel 0892 353 535

**Thalys**
**www.thalys.com**
Trains to cities in northern Europe.
Tel 0892 353 536

**Rail Europe**
Sells a variety of European rail passes.
**www.raileurope.com**
(for US visitors)
**www.raileurope.co.uk**
(for UK visitors)

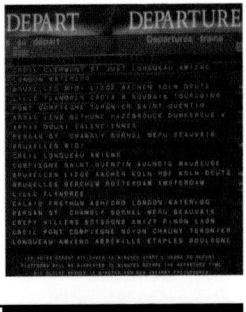


**MAINLINE STATION INFORMATION**

| STATION | MAJOR DESTINATIONS | MAJOR TRAIN OPERATOR | CONNECTIONS: MÉTRO | CONNECTIONS: RER | TOURIST DESTINATIONS INCLUDE |
|---|---|---|---|---|---|
| Gare d'Austerlitz | Central and southwest France, Spain, Portugal | CORAIL Trainhôtel Elipsos | Lines 5, 10 | Line C | Poitiers, Limoges, Madrid, Barcelona, the Alps |
| Gare de l'Est | Eastern France, Germany, Luxembourg, Switzerland, Austria, Eastern Europe | CORAIL | Lines 4, 5, 7 | None | Strasbourg |
| Gare de Lyon | Southeast France, Switzerland, Italy | TGV | Lines, 1, 14 | Lines A, D | Lyon, Nice, Grenoble, Milan, Florence, Geneva, Marseille |
| Gare Montparnasse | Western and southern France, Spain | TGV | Lines 4, 6, 12, 13 | None | Brest, Quimper, Nantes, Toulouse, Bordeaux |
| Gare du Nord | Northern France, UK, Germany, Holland, Belgium, Scandinavia | TGV, Thalys, Eurostar | Lines 4, 5 | Lines B, D, E | Brussels, London, Amsterdam, Lille |
| Gare St-Lazare | Northwest France | CORAIL | Lines 3, 12, 13 | Line E | Normandy |

TGV services also leave from Aéroport Charles-de-Gaulle TGV and Marne-La-Vallée Disneyland Resort Paris.

This section is divided into two parts: Sightseeing Areas guides you to the best things to see in six districts of Paris (shown on the map inside the front cover); the A–Z of Sights is an alphabetical listing of places to visit across the city, located on the maps on pages 66–69.

# The Sights


**Sights Locator Maps** **66–69**

**Sightseeing Areas** **70–75**
Le Marais **70**
Montmartre **71**
Champs-Élysées **72**
Around the Louvre **73**
The Islands and the Quartier Latin **74**
Around La Tour Eiffel **75**

**A–Z of Sights** **76–170**
For quick reference, the top sights are listed below, with the major ones highlighted in bold type.

**Arc de Triomphe and Champs-Élysées** **76–79**
**Centre Georges Pompidou** **82–86**
Cimetière du Père-Lachaise **88**
Conciergerie **89–91**
Grande Arche **94**
Île de la Cité **96–97**
Les Invalides **99–101**
Jardin du Luxembourg **102–103**
Jardin du Palais Royal **104**
Jardin des Tuileries **105**
Montmartre **108–109**
Musée Carnavalet **114–115**
**Musée du Louvre** **118–123**
Musée Marmottan Monet **124–125**
Muséum National d'Histoire Naturelle and Jardin des Plantes **127**
Musée National du Moyen Âge–Thermes de Cluny **128–129**
**Musée d'Orsay** **130–134**
Musée Picasso **135**
Musée Rodin **136**
**Notre-Dame** **137–141**
Opéra Palais Garnier **142**
Palais de Chaillot **143**
Panthéon **144**
Parc de la Villette **146–147**
Place de la Concorde **148**
Place des Vosges **150**
Quartier Latin **152–153**
**Sacré-Cœur** **154–157**
Sainte-Chapelle **158–160**
**Tour Eiffel** **164–169**
Tour Montparnasse **170**

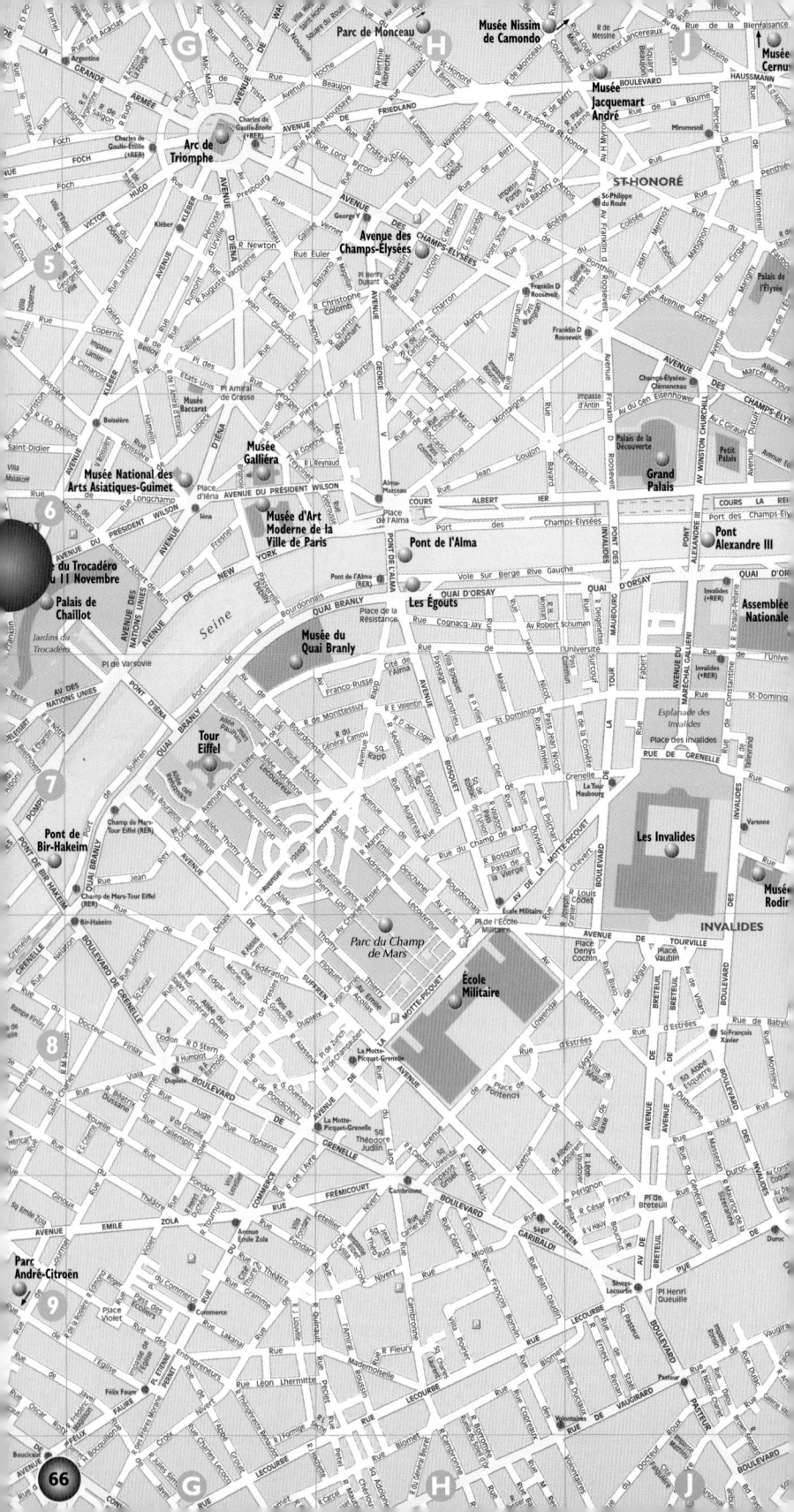
Parc de Monceau
Musée Nissim de Camondo
Musée Jacquemart André
Musée Cernu
Arc de Triomphe
Avenue des Champs-Elysées
ST-HONORÉ
Palais de l'Elysée
Musée Galliéra
Musée National des Arts Asiatiques-Guimet
Musée d'Art Moderne de la Ville de Paris
Pont de l'Alma
Grand Palais
Palais de la Découverte
Petit Palais
Pont Alexandre III
Palais de Chaillot
Les Égouts
Assemblée Nationale
Musée du Quai Branly
Tour Eiffel
Pont de Bir-Hakeim
Les Invalides
Musée Rodin
INVALIDES
Parc du Champ de Mars
École Militaire
Parc André-Citroën
Seine
66

Passage Verdeau
Drouot
Passage Jouffroy
Musée Grévin
Opéra Palais Garnier
Place de la Madeleine
Passage des Panoramas
Musée Fragonard
La Bourse
Place Vendôme
Bibliothèque Nationale de France
Galerie Colbert
Galerie Vivienne
Place des Victoires
Jeu de Paume
Place de la Concorde
Jardin du Palais Royal
Les H
Orangerie
Jardin des Tuileries
St-Eustache
Musée des Arts Décoratifs
Galerie Véro-Dodat
Fontaine des Innocents
Musée d'Orsay
Pont Royal
Musée du Louvre
St-Germain-l'Auxerrois
Seine
Pont des Arts
Institut de France
Musée de la Monnaie
Pont Neuf
Conciergerie
Sainte-Chapelle
Île de la Cité
ST-GERMAIN-DES-PRÉS
Musée National Eugène Delacroix
Maison de Verre
St-Germain-des-Prés
St-Julien-le-Pauvre
Notre-Dame
St-Séverin
St-Sulpice
Musée National du Moyen Age
La Sorbonne
QUARTIER LATIN
Palais du Luxembourg
Jardin du Luxembourg
Panthéon
St-Étienne-du-Mont
Tour Montparnasse
GARE ST-LAZARE
GARE DE MONTPARNASSE
67

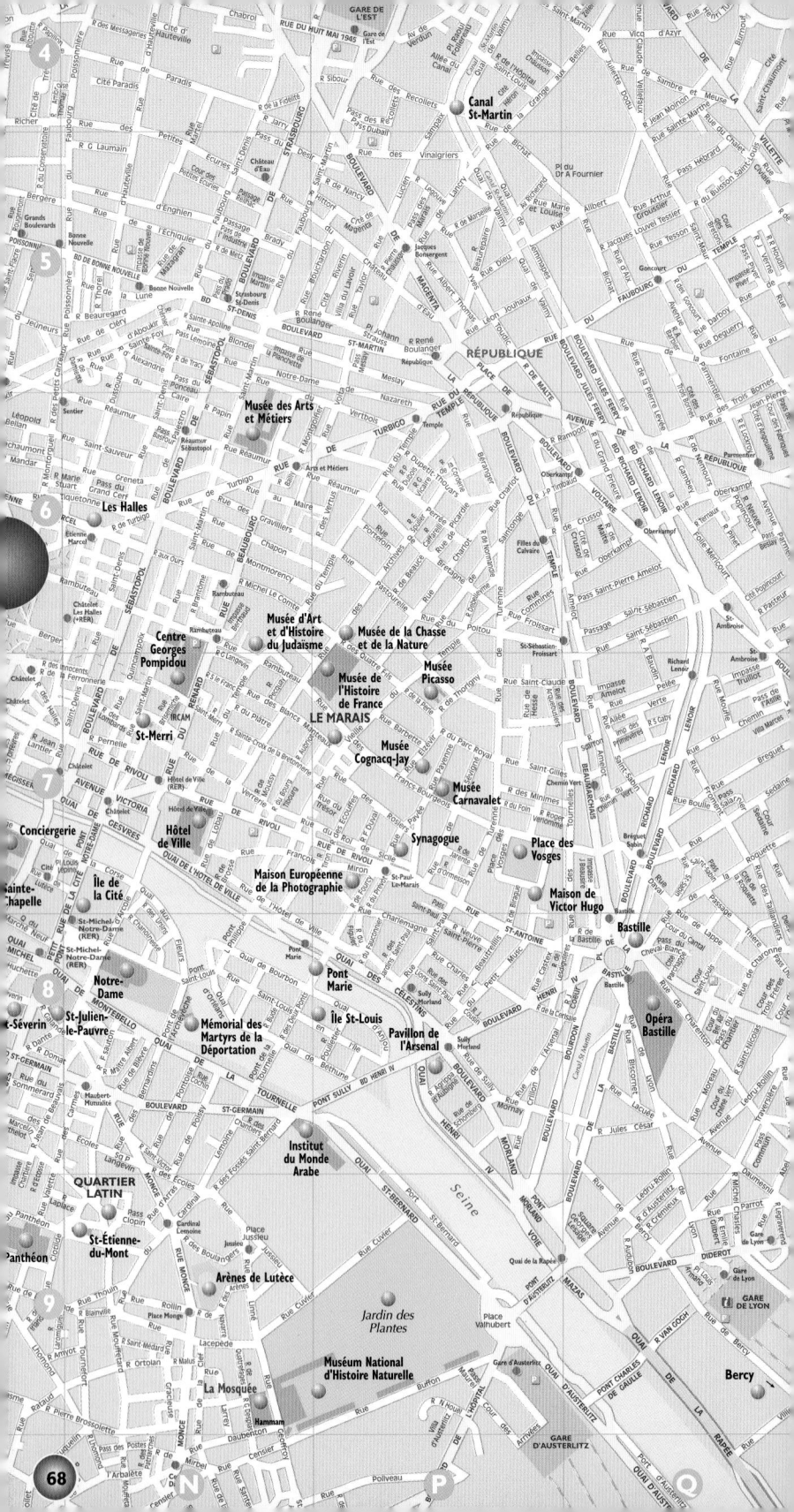
Canal St-Martin
Musée des Arts et Métiers
Les Halles
Musée d'Art et d'Histoire du Judaïsme
Musée de la Chasse et de la Nature
Centre Georges Pompidou
Musée de l'Histoire de France
Musée Picasso
LE MARAIS
Musée Cognacq-Jay
St-Merri
Musée Carnavalet
Conciergerie
Hôtel de Ville
Synagogue
Place des Vosges
Maison Européenne de la Photographie
Île de la Cité
Maison de Victor Hugo
Sainte-Chapelle
Bastille
Notre-Dame
Pont Marie
St-Julien-le-Pauvre
Île St-Louis
Opéra Bastille
Mémorial des Martyrs de la Déportation
Pavillon de l'Arsenal
Institut du Monde Arabe
QUARTIER LATIN
St-Étienne-du-Mont
Panthéon
Arènes de Lutèce
Jardin des Plantes
Muséum National d'Histoire Naturelle
La Mosquée
Bercy
RÉPUBLIQUE
Seine
GARE DE L'EST
GARE DE LYON
GARE D'AUSTERLITZ
68

Marché aux Puces de St-Ouen
Cimetière de Montmartre
Musée de Montmartre
MONTMARTHE
Espace Montmartre Salvador Dali
Sacré-Cœur
Moulin Rouge
Place des Abbesses
Pigalle
Musée Gustave Moreau
GARE ST-LAZARE
Passage Verdeau
Drouot
Passage Jouffroy
Musée Grévin
Opéra Palais Garnier
Passage des Panoramas
Place de la Madeleine
Musée Fragonard
La Bourse
Place Vendôme
Bibliothèque Nationale de France
Galerie Vivienne
Galerie Colbert
Place des Victoires
Jeu de Paume
Jardin du Palais Royal
Jardin des Tuileries
Les Halles
St-Eustache
Musée des Arts Décoratifs
Galerie Véro-Dodat
Fontaine des Innocents
Seine
Musée d'Orsay
Centre Georges
69

# Le Marais

**HOW TO GET THERE**

Place des Vosges
St-Paul, Bastille
29

Centre Georges Pompidou
Rambuteau, Hôtel de Ville
29, 38, 47, 75

**This district, on the Right Bank, is sandwiched between Les Halles and Bastille and is packed with museums, elegant mansions and quirky shops. The wacky Centre Georges Pompidou sits on its western border.**

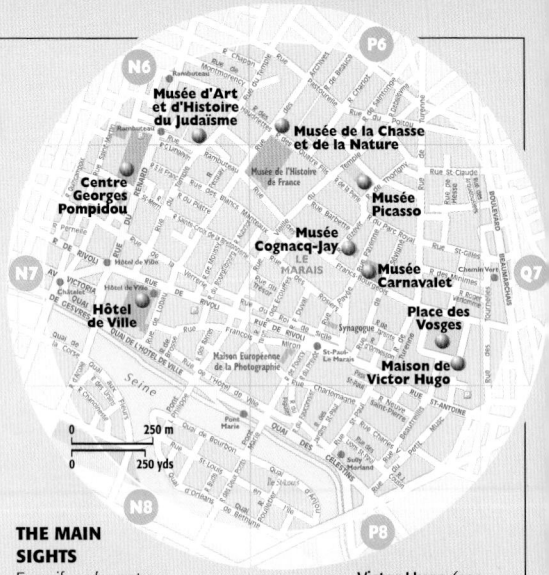


THE SIGHTS

The Marais gives you a taste of pre-Revolution Paris, when aristocrats vied to create the most elegant mansions and courtyards. Many of these ornate 17th- and 18th-century buildings remain and you can wander around those that have been converted into museums. The district is home to Paris's oldest square, place des Vosges, a leafy haven that takes you by surprise as you stumble upon it from the surrounding bustling streets. It is bordered by smart boutiques and cafés. You'll also find a lively Jewish quarter in the streets around the rue des Rosiers, in addition to stylish boutiques.

The Marais was originally marshland (*marais* means marsh). In the Middle Ages, the northern part was under the rule of the Knights Templar. By the 17th century, aristocrats were moving into the area and building their sumptuous mansions. For more information, see page 107.

*The elegant place des Vosges is Paris's oldest square*

**THE MAIN SIGHTS**

Even if you're not a particular fan of museums, try to visit one or two in the Marais, if only to see the interiors of these beautiful mansions. Save time to explore the fashionable shops and to relax in a café in the place des Vosges. To round off the day, a visit to the Centre Georges Pompidou will bring you sharply back to the 21st century.

**Centre Georges Pompidou**
One of the largest collections of modern art in the world, housed in a suitably spectacular 1970s building.
See pages 82–86.

**Musée Carnavalet**
Adjacent 16th- and 17th-century mansions contain a fascinating collection of memorabilia relating to the history of Paris.
See pages 114–115.

**Musée Picasso**
A must for Picasso fans, with more than 200 paintings, 160 sculptures and numerous drawings.
See page 135.

**Place des Vosges**
A calming, historic square, inaugurated in 1612 as the place Royale.
See page 150.

**OTHER PLACES TO VISIT**
Other museums include the **Musée Cognacq-Jay** (see page 113), the **Musée d'Art et d'Histoire du Judaïsme** (see page 112), the **Maison de Victor Hugo** (see page 106), and the **Musée de la Chasse et de la Nature** (see page 113). Paris's grand town hall, the **Hôtel de Ville**, stands on the southwestern border (see page 95).

*The eccentric Stravinsky Fountain, outside the Pompidou*

**WHERE TO EAT**

The Centre Georges Pompidou has a first-floor café as well as **Georges** restaurant (see page 268) on the sixth floor, where you can enjoy great city views. For a drink in a (relatively) tranquil, picturesque setting you can't beat the place des Vosges.

**Le Petit Gavroche**
Bistro with a good-value set menu and retro interior (see page 272).

**Piccolo Teatro**
Vegetarian cuisine with influences from across the world (see page 273).

# Montmartre

**HOW TO GET THERE**

Anvers, Abbesses, Blanche, Lamarck-Caulaincourt take you to the outskirts

Montmartrobus; buses 30, 31, 54, 68, 74, 80 have stops on the outskirts

**This hilltop village, to the north of the Right Bank, has two of Paris's most famous symbols, Sacré-Cœur and the Moulin Rouge. Parisians call it *La Butte* (the mound).**

Montmartre is a world apart from Paris, despite lying well within the city's boundary. It has managed to retain the atmosphere of its late-19th-century heyday, when artists such as Henri Toulouse-Lautrec were frequent visitors to its decadent dance halls. Away from the tourist honeypots of Sacré-Cœur and place du Tertre, quiet, cobbled streets take you back hundreds of years—Montmartre's oldest building dates from the mid-17th

*The entrance to the Espace Montmartre–Salvador Dalí*

century. Wander through these back streets and alleyways to see romantic tree-lined steps, squares, gardens and individually designed houses. There is even a small vineyard, tucked away on the rue des Saules.

Back on the tourist trail, there are wonderful views over Paris from the front steps of Sacré-Cœur. At nearby place du Tertre a bevy of street artists are waiting to paint your portrait or draw your caricature, should you wish.

For more information see pages 108–109. For a walk around Montmartre, see pages 226–227.

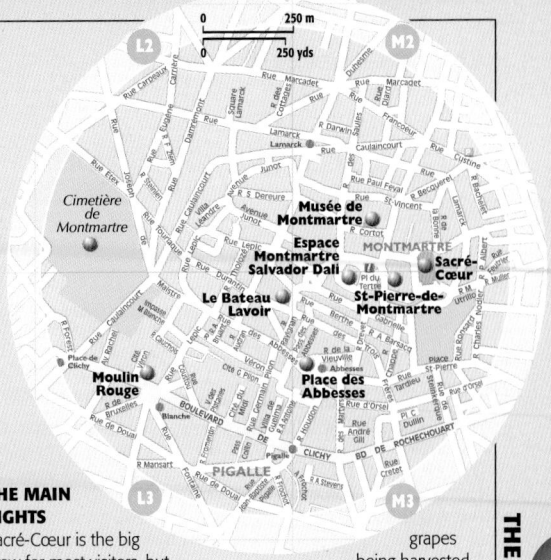


**THE MAIN SIGHTS**

Sacré-Cœur is the big draw for most visitors, but make sure you also explore Montmartre's quieter back streets. If you want to save your legs, the Petit Train de Montmartre (Promotrain) and the Montmartrain tour the area. The Musée de Montmartre will fill you in on the history.

**Cimetière de Montmartre**
Visit the graves of composer Hector Berlioz and artists Edgar Degas and Gustave Moreau.
See page 87.

**Espace Montmartre–Salvador Dalí**
The biggest Dalí collection in France.
See page 92.

**Moulin Rouge**
Paris's most famous cabaret venue still hosts glittering shows.
See page 111.

**Musée de Montmartre**
Montmartre's oldest building is a fitting venue for this museum.
See page 126.

**Sacré-Cœur**
A stunning basilica crowning Montmartre's hill.
See pages 154–157.

**OTHER PLACES TO VISIT**

At **place des Abbesses** (see page 145) you can admire one of Paris's few remaining art nouveau Métro entrances. Wander past the vineyard on rue des Saules on the first Saturday in October and you'll see the grapes being harvested.

The **Bateau-Lavoir studio,** where Pablo Picasso and Georges Braque conceived Cubism, once stood on place Émile-Goudeau, although it has been replaced with a concrete

*Sacré-Cœur looks at its best against a clear blue sky*

structure. Finally, if Sacré-Cœur is teeming with visitors, go to the quieter church of **St-Pierre-de-Montmartre**, nearby to the west.

**WHERE TO EAT**

Restaurants on place du Tertre can be rather pricey. For a light bite, there are cafés at place des Abbesses.

**Au Pied du Sacré-Cœur**
See page 261.

**La Galerie**
16 rue Tholozé, 75018
Tel 01 42 59 25 76
A good-value restaurant, open evenings only.

# Champs-Élysées

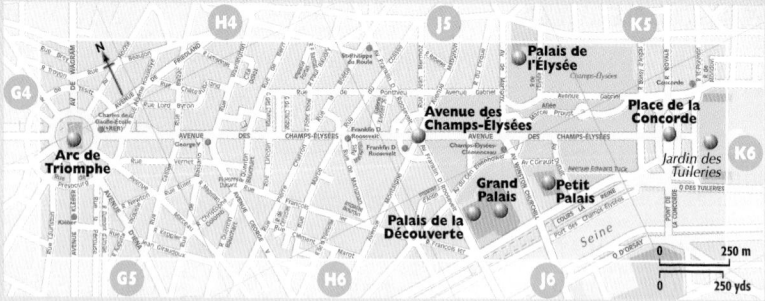


**HOW TO GET THERE**

Arc de Triomphe
Charles de Gaulle–Étoile
22, 30, 31, 52, 73, 92

Place de la Concorde
Concorde
24, 42, 72, 73, 84, 94

**Paris's most celebrated avenue sweeps majestically from the Arc de Triomphe to the historic place de la Concorde. It is over 2km**

*The Arc de Triomphe towers over the cars*

**(1.2 miles) long and 71m (232 feet) wide.**

This broad, tree-lined avenue bustles with activity. By day the wide walkways are packed with people visiting the shops, cafés and the *pièce de résistance*, the Arc de Triomphe. By night it is the turn of the clubs, cinemas and restaurants, either on the avenue itself or in the nearby streets. Many of Paris's luxury hotels and exclusive nightclubs cluster around the Champs-Élysées and nearby avenue Montaigne and Faubourg St-Honoré, and the temples of top chefs are generously sprinkled between the 8th and adjoining 17th *arrondissements*.

The Champs-Élysées dates from the early 17th century, when Marie de' Medici, wife of Henri IV, turned the area into a fashionable driveway. Landscape designer André Le Nôtre added his mark later that century, planting alleys of trees as an extension to the Tuileries gardens.

For more information, see pages 76–79.

**THE MAIN SIGHTS**

The Arc de Triomphe is the must-see sight, but the Grand Palais, southeast of the Rond-Point des Champs-Élysées, is also worth visiting. At the eastern end of the avenue, place de la Concorde is brimming with history (and cars).

**Arc de Triomphe**
Napoleon's grand arch.
See pages 76–79.

**Champs-Élysées**
Elegant, historic—and packed with people and traffic.
See pages 76–79.

**Grand Palais**
Prestigious art shows in an art nouveau palace.
See page 95.

**Jardin des Tuileries**
Gardens next to place de la Concorde.
See page 105.

**Palais de la Découverte**
A science museum with a planetarium. See page 95.

**Place de la Concorde**
The site of 1,300 grisly beheadings during the Revolution.
See page 148.

**OTHER PLACES TO VISIT**

The **Petit Palais** (see page 95) houses the Musée des Beaux-Arts de la Ville (Municipal Museum of Fine Arts), although it is closed for renovation until autumn 2005. It sits opposite the Grand Palais. Just north of the Champs-Élysées, on the rue Faubourg St-Honoré, the **Palais de l'Élysée** is the official home of the French President.

*The magnificent lobby of the Palais de la Découverte*

**WHERE TO EAT**

There are plenty of restaurants and cafés along the Champs-Élysées, mainly at the Arc de Triomphe end. Some charge a premium for the location so you may prefer to venture into the side streets. The Grand Palais and Palais de la Découverte both have cafés and the Jardin des Tuileries has open-air cafés.

**Asian**
A tea room and Asian restaurant (see page 260).

**Bistro Romain**
Italian cuisine at this chain restaurant (see page 262).

# Around the Louvre

**HOW TO GET THERE**

Musée du Louvre
Palais-Royal/Musée du Louvre
21, 27, 39, 48, 67, 69, 72, 74, 75, 76, 81, 85, 95
Forum des Halles
Les Halles
29, 38, 47
Châtelet–Les Halles

**Linked with royalty for centuries, the section of the Right Bank around the Louvre is known for its grandeur. The Louvre has a commanding position next to the Seine, with the Jardin des Tuileries to its west and the Palais Royal to its north.**

In its former life as a royal palace, the Louvre bestowed a certain amount of regal status on the surrounding area. Gradually other royal buildings sprang up around it, including the Tuileries Palace (destroyed by fire in 1871) and the Palais Royal. St-Germain-l'Auxerrois became the royal family's parish church. By contrast, nearby Les Halles was the market district, colonized by traders in the 12th century.

Now, art not royalty draws people to the Louvre, while the tranquil gardens of the Palais Royal offer the chance to escape the noise of the city. Farther north are the imposing Banque de France and Bibliothèque Nationale de France, as well as the circular, stately place des Victoires, with its smart shops. Les Halles lost some of its vitality when the covered market was dismantled in 1969. The jarringly modern shopping mall, the Forum des Halles, stands in its place, although nearby streets such as the cobbled rue Montorgueil give you a taste of the past.

*Relaxing by the pond in the Jardin des Tuileries*

**THE MAIN SIGHTS**

The Louvre is the main attraction by far, clocking up around 30,000 visitors each day. The Musée des Arts Décoratifs is also worth a visit. When you tire of art galleries, the Jardin des Tuileries and Jardin du Palais Royal are good places to relax. In Les Halles, the Forum des Halles may or may not be to your taste, and the area can be rather seedy at night. But don't miss the vast church of St-Eustache, based on Notre-Dame.

**Jardin du Palais Royal**
A peaceful garden surrounded by 18th-century arcades.
See page 104.

**Jardin des Tuileries**
Stately riverside gardens.
See page 105.

**Musée des Arts Décoratifs**
Decorative arts.
See page 111.

**Musée du Louvre**
Home to the *Mona Lisa*.
See pages 118–123.

**St-Eustache**
Paris's second-largest church.
See page 161.

**St-Germain-l'Auxerrois**
Parish church to royalty.
See page 162.

**OTHER PLACES TO VISIT**

**Pont des Arts** (see page 151) is Paris's most romantic bridge, while the **Pont Neuf** (see page 151) is the oldest. You can shop in the elegant **Place des Victoires** (see page 149) or the 19th-century malls of **Galerie Vivienne** and **Galerie Colbert** (see page 93). If the Louvre and the Musée des Arts Décoratifs have not satisfied your appetite for culture, visit the **Jeu de Paume** (see page 106) and the **Orangerie** (see page 142), in the Jardin des Tuileries.

*The vast church of St-Eustache*

**WHERE TO EAT**

**Le Bar à Soupes**
See page 262.

**Grand Colbert**
See page 268.

**Muscade**
See page 271.

# The Islands and the Quartier Latin

**HOW TO GET THERE**

Notre-Dame
- Cité, St-Michel, Châtelet
- 21, 24, 38, 47, 85, 96
- RER lines B, C St-Michel

Musée National du Moyen Âge–Thermes de Cluny
- Cluny–La Sorbonne
- 21, 27, 38, 63, 85, 86, 87, 96
- RER line B, C St-Michel

**Happily floating mid-stream in the Seine, the Île de la Cité and the Île St-Louis are as different in character as the two banks they separate. To their south, the Latin Quarter takes you back to medieval times.**

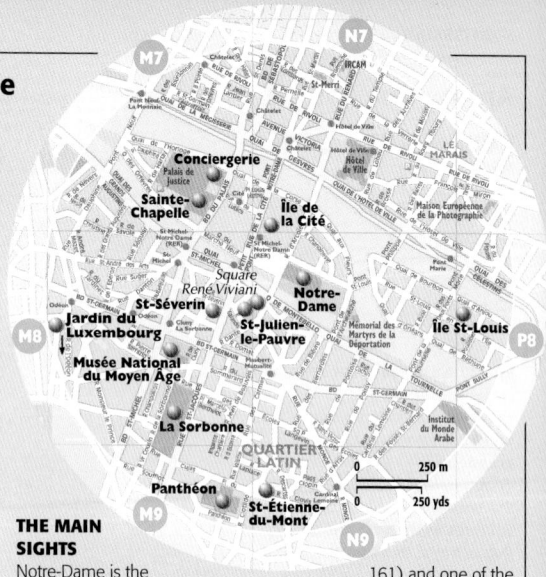


THE SIGHTS

The Île de la Cité is where Paris began, when a Celtic tribe known as the Parisii arrived in around 250BC. The Romans moved in 200 years later and set up the town of Lutetia. The island's prominence continued into the Middle Ages, with the building of a royal palace—now the Palais de Justice and Conciergerie—and Notre-Dame. Today the island is a hectic but attractive focal point for visitors (see pages 96–97). By contrast, the smaller Île St-Louis is refreshingly peaceful, with a far shorter history (see page 98).

Five bridges link the Île de la Cité with the Latin Quarter, Paris's intellectual heart (see pages 152–153). The Sorbonne university was founded here in the 13th century and the district takes its name from the language once spoken by the students.

*The Île St-Louis is more relaxed than the nearby Île de la Cité*

**THE MAIN SIGHTS**

Notre-Dame is the must-see sight on the Île de la Cité. The best way to appreciate the Latin Quarter is simply to wander through its medieval streets (see the walk, pages 228–229). Sights worth visiting en route include the Musée National du Moyen Âge, the mighty Panthéon and the Jardin du Luxembourg. Highlights on the Île St-Louis are the view of Notre-Dame and the legendary ice cream (see page 98).

**Conciergerie**
A notorious prison during the Revolution.
See pages 89–91.

**Jardin du Luxembourg**
Parkland in the heart of the city.
See pages 102–103.

**Musée National du Moyen Âge–Thermes de Cluny**
Objects from the Middle Ages, in one of the city's oldest mansions.
See pages 128–129.

**Notre-Dame**
A Paris landmark.
See pages 137–141.

**Panthéon**
A vast neoclassical mausoleum.
See page 144.

**Sainte-Chapelle**
Stunning stained glass.
See pages 158–160.

**OTHER PLACES TO VISIT**

Churches include **St-Séverin** (see pages 162–163), **St-Étienne-du-Mont** (see page 161) and one of the city's oldest, **St-Julien-le-Pauvre** (see page 162). You can admire the outside of **La Sorbonne** (see page 163), although the building is not open to the public. If you want to relax, try **square René Viviani** (see page 152).

*Work started on Notre-Dame in the 12th century*

**WHERE TO EAT**

There are plenty of cafés and restaurants, although you may find some rather touristy. The nearby St-Germain-des-Prés district is known for its cafés.

**Au Gourmet de l'Isle**
42 rue St-Louis-en-l'Île, Île St-Louis
Tel 01 43 26 79 27
Open: Wed–Sun 12–2, 7–10.30pm
A bistro with a good lunch menu.

**Le Bar à Huîtres**
33 rue St-Jacques
Tel 01 44 07 27 37
Open: daily noon–3am
Tasty seafood platters and shellfish.

# Around La Tour Eiffel

**HOW TO GET THERE**

Eiffel Tower
- Bir-Hakeim
- 42, 69, 82, 87
- RER line C, Champ de Mars/ Tour Eiffel

Palais de Chaillot
- Trocadéro
- 22, 30, 32, 63, 72, 82

**The Eiffel Tower stands on the banks of the Seine, at the edge of the stately 7th *arrondissement*. There are wonderful views of the monument from the terrace of the Palais de Chaillot, across the river in the wealthy 16th *arrondissement*.**

As well as boosting morale, Paris's Universal Exhibitions left several new landmarks on the horizon, including the Palais de Chaillot (1937) and the Eiffel Tower (1889). Although the tower attracted two million

*The Eiffel Tower is particularly impressive at night*

visitors in its first year, it was not without its critics, including the writers Guy de Maupassant and Émile Zola. But it soon became *the* symbol of Paris and visitors from across the world still come to admire its soaring structure and enjoy the vertigo-inducing views from the top. The tower is backed by the lawns of the Champ de Mars (Field of Mars), where the Romans fought the Celtic Parisii tribe in 52BC.
The area was landscaped in the mid-18th century, and the imposing École Militaire (Military Academy) was built at its southern end. Napoleon enrolled here, at the age of 15.

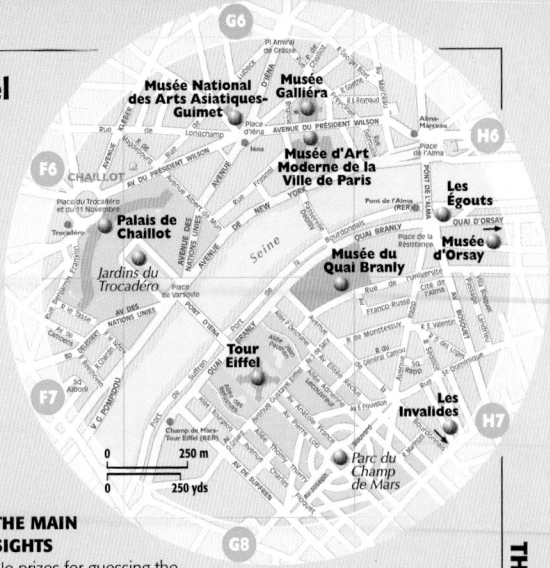


## THE MAIN SIGHTS

No prizes for guessing the key attraction—the Eiffel Tower pulls in around six million visitors each year. Across the Seine, the Palais de Chaillot contains a maritime museum and an anthropological museum. Three other museums cluster near the place d'Iéna, farther west.

**Musée d'Art Moderne de la Ville de Paris**
Modern art.
See page 112.

**Musée National des Arts Asiatiques-Guimet**
An intriguing collection of Oriental antiquities.
See page 126.

**Palais de Chaillot**
This curved, colonnaded palace has two museums, a theatre and great views of the Eiffel Tower.
See page 143.

**Tour Eiffel**
The ultimate symbol of Paris.
See pages 164–169.

## OTHER PLACES TO VISIT

The **Musée Galliéra** hosts temporary exhibitions of urban fashion (see page 116). On the Left Bank, the **Musée du Quai Branly** is due to open in 2005 (see page 126). For a museum with a (rather smelly) difference, visit Paris's sewers, **Les Égouts**, at place de la Résistance (see page 92). For a break, you can relax by the fountains of the **Jardins du Trocadéro** (see page 149), in front of the Palais de Chaillot.

## FARTHER AFIELD

**Les Invalides**, to the east of the Eiffel Tower, shelters the tomb of Napoleon in its golden-domed church (see pages 99–101). The **Musée d'Orsay** (see page 130–134) is farther east.

*Looking at the Palais de Chaillot from the Jardins du Trocadéro*

## WHERE TO EAT

The Eiffel Tower has a snack bar, as well as the **Altitude 95 restaurant** and the prestigious **Jules Verne restaurant** (book well in advance). **Le Totem** restaurant (see page 275) is at the Palais de Chaillot.

**Fakhr El Dine**
See page 267.

**Le Sept Quinze**
29 avenue de Lowendal
Tel 01 43 06 23 06
Open: Mon–Fri 12–2.30, 8–11, Sat 8pm–11pm. Closed three weeks in Aug
A welcoming bistro near the École Militaire.

LODI
MILLESIMO
DEGO
MONDOVI
ROVEREDO
BASSANO
S. GEORGES
MANTOUE
TAGLIAMENTO
SEDIMAN
MONT THABOR
CHEBREISSE
BASSIGNANO
SAN GIULIANO
DIETIKON
MUTTA THAL
GENES
LE VAR
MONTEBELLO
LE MINCIO
CALDIERO
CASTEL FRANCO
RAGUSE
GAETE

# Arc de Triomphe and Champs-Élysées

**Paris's most famous avenue, crowned by the mighty Arc de Triomphe.**

*The Champs-Élysées at night*

*Shields commemorating battles decorate the crown of the Arc; visitors on the viewing platform above appear tiny in comparison*

## SEEING THE ARC DE TRIOMPHE AND CHAMPS-ÉLYSÉES

The wide, leafy Champs-Élysées is a focal point for the French nation, witness to momentous events such as De Gaulle's triumphal liberation march in 1944 and the soccer World Cup celebrations in 1998. Despite the avenue's glamorous reputation, be prepared also for streams of traffic, swarms of busy people and rather brash cinemas, car showrooms and chainstores. If the Arc de Triomphe is your main goal, take the Métro to Charles-de-Gaulle-Étoile, which drops you just outside. However, if you don't mind a 20-minute stroll, a good place to begin is two-thirds of the way down, at Métro Champs-Élysées-Clemenceau. Leave the Métro station and take a look at the imposing Grand Palais on avenue Winston Churchill, (see page 95), then walk towards place Charles-de-Gaulle, with the Arc de Triomphe looming up majestically in front of you. You'll see greenery as far as the Rond-Point des Champs-Élysées, at which point the commercial side of the avenue takes over. At the top, use the underpass to cross to the Arc, where you can climb the 284 steps to the roof. The views are stunning. Once back down, you could get a bite to eat at one of the nearby cafés or hop on the Métro and travel the four stops to Concorde to see the start of the avenue. This is guarded by copies of the Marly Horses—the originals are in the Louvre.

| RATINGS | |
|---|---|
| Historic interest | ●●●● |
| Photo stops | ●●●● |
| Shopping | ●●● |
| Walkability | ●●● |

**TIPS**

- It takes at least 30 minutes to walk from one end of the Champs-Élysées to the other. You may prefer to take the Métro—Line 1 (yellow) runs the length of the avenue.
- Most cafés and restaurants are at the Arc de Triomphe end, although you may find better value in establishments in the side streets.
- The best time for photos from the top of the arch is just after it opens, when the light is clearer, or just before sunset.

## HIGHLIGHTS

### ARC DE TRIOMPHE

Napoleon conceived the Arc de Triomphe as a symbol of his military might—two centuries on the colossal monument is still an image of national pride. It plays a central role in many of France's key commemorations, including VE Day (8 May), Bastille Day (14 July) and Remembrance Day (11 November). Within its grounds are the

*The Arc de Triomphe (left) is a place of remembrance as well as a visitor attraction*

**BASICS**

**Arc de Triomphe**

66 G5•place Charles-de-Gaulle, 75008 ☎ 01 55 37 73 77

Daily 9.30am–11pm, Apr–end Sep; 10am–10.30pm rest of year. Closed 1 Jan, 1 May, 8 May, 14 July, 25 Dec

Free to wander around the base. Rooftop: adult €7, under 18 free

Charles de Gaulle–Étoile

22, 30, 31, 52, 73, 92

RER line A, Charles de Gaulle–Étoile

Giftshop €6

For information on guided tours call Monum on 01 44 54 19 30

Tomb of the Unknown Soldier, installed in 1920 after World War I, and a poignant Memorial Flame, added three years later.

There are wonderful views from the rooftop, 50m (164ft) above street level. From here you can admire Haussmann's web-like street design and look along the Grand Axis (see panel, page 79) towards place de la Concorde in one direction and the Grande Arche in the other. At night the city shimmers with lights. There is a small shop and museum on the way up. Back at ground level, save some time to admire the magnificent sculpted façade, the work of three different artists. Don't miss the fearsome winged figure of Liberty on François Rude's sculpture *La Marseillaise*, calling the French to defend their nation (northeastern pillar, facing the Champs-Élysées). On the southeast pillar Napoleon is depicted as a victorious Roman emperor. The 30 shields studding the crown of the arch each bear the name of a Revolutionary or Imperial victory.

*The tree-lined Champs-Élysées is always packed with people*

*There are stunning views from the top of the Arc—if you can face the climb*

*Flowers adorn the Tomb of the Unknown Soldier*

There is a ceremony at the Tomb of the Unknown Soldier daily at 6.30pm

www.monum.fr (in French and English. Click on *Visit the Monuments* to see the Arc de Triomphe)

**Avenue des Champs-Élysées**

66 H5•75008

Charles de Gaulle–Étoile, Georges V, Franklin D. Roosevelt, Champs-Élysées-Clemenceau

32, 42, 73 and others

Charles de Gaulle–Étoile

Wide selection (see page 258)

Wide selection (see page 258)

Plenty of shops

## AVENUE DES CHAMPS-ÉLYSÉES

This famous avenue is packed with cinemas, shops, cafés and car showrooms, and bustling with life. Although it is high on most visitors' itineraries, you are as likely to see Parisians going about their business as camera-snapping sightseers. The tree-lined avenue is over 2km (1.2 miles) long and 71m (232ft) wide, stretching between two of the city's most illustrious monuments—the Arc de Triomphe and the Egyptian obelisk in place de la Concorde. A short detour will lead you to other key buildings, including the Grand Palais (see page 95) and the Palais de l'Élysée, official residence of the French president.

The French come here to celebrate, whether it be winning the soccer World Cup or welcoming home participants in the Tour de France cycle race. The avenue has hosted some of France's most prestigious processions, including the funeral of writer Victor Hugo in 1885, General de Gaulle's liberation march in 1944 and the bicentenary celebrations of the French Revolution in 1989. Catch it on 14 July (Bastille Day) when most of the French army rolls past. Another good time to visit is during the Christmas illuminations.

## BACKGROUND

**The Champs-Élysées dates back to 1616, when Marie de Medici turned the area into a fashionable driveway. Then, landscape designer André Le Nôtre (of Versailles fame) added alleys of**

*Twelve streets radiate from the Arc de Triomphe*

### *GRAND AXIS*

The Arc de Triomphe is a key element of the *Grand Axis* that runs in an imaginary straight line across the city from the Louvre's Arc de Triomphe du Carrousel to the Grande Arche at La Défense (see page 92). To emphasize the progression along this route, the Grande Arche is twice as tall as the Arc de Triomphe, which in turn is twice as tall as the Arc de Triomphe du Carrousel.

*An eye-catching shop window*

### *ÉTOILE*

The Arc de Triomphe's traffic-ridden roundabout is still known as the *Étoile* (star), despite an official name-change to place Charles-de-Gaulle. The *Étoile* label comes from the 12 avenues that radiate from it like the tips of a star, a layout designed by Baron Haussmann in the 19th century. It may look impressive from the roof of the Arc de Triomphe but at ground level it seems to have resulted in all the cars in the capital converging on this one point!

*François Rude's striking sculpture* La Marseillaise *(above left), on the Arc de Triomphe's northeast pillar*

trees and gardens, prompting its current name, Elysian Fields. Walkways and fountains were installed in 1824 and the avenue became crowded with cafés, restaurants and a smart clientele. Napoleon Bonaparte commissioned the Arc de Triomphe in 1806, demanding an awesome memorial to the French army. In 1810 a wooden, life-size model was installed to celebrate the emperor's marriage to Marie-Louise, but the real thing was not ready until 1836, 15 years after his death. Various architects and sculptors worked on the monument, inspired by Rome's Arch of Titus and Arch of Septimius Severus. The arch's symbolic role was confirmed after World War I, when parades of victorious troops marched through.

**AVENUE DES CHAMPS-ÉLYSÉES MAP**

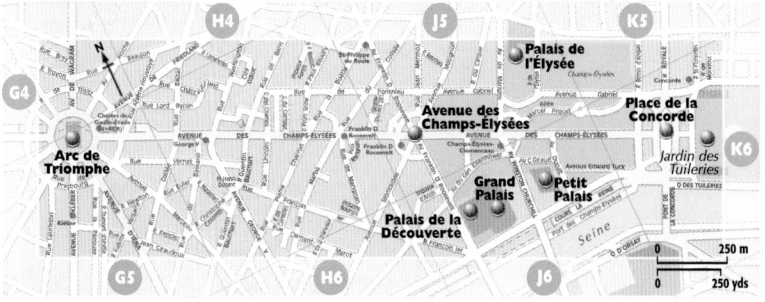

*Boules is a popular pastime at the Arènes de Lutèce*

## ARÈNES DE LUTÈCE

68 N9•Entrances at rue des Arènes, rue de Navarre and 47 rue Monge, 75005 Daily 9am–9.30pm in summer, 8–5.30 in winter Free Cardinal Lemoine, Jussieu 47, 67, 89 Best avoided after dark

This Gallo-Roman arena dates from the end of the second century AD and takes its name from the Roman name for Paris, Lutetia. It was destroyed in AD280, rediscovered in 1869, and restored in the early 20th century. Today, the arena ruins and the gardens are popular with students, boules-players, walkers and picnickers.

## ASSEMBLÉE NATIONALE (PALAIS BOURBON)

66 J6•Palais Bourbon, 33bis quai d'Orsay, 75007 01 40 63 99 99 One-hour guided tours every Sat at 10, 2, 3, unless the Assembly is sitting. Admission is limited to 30 people. Arrive at least 20 min before the start (no advance booking). Passports are required. Admission to public debates (Oct–end Jun) is limited to the first 10 people Assemblée Nationale 24, 63, 73, 83, 84, 94 RER line C, Invalides Free
www.assemblee-nationale.fr

The 18th-century Palais Bourbon sits on the banks of the Seine and is home to the French National Assembly, the lower house of the French Parliament. Its 577 members debate in the Chamber and have offices nearby. The palace, with its imposing neoclassical façade, was built for Louis XIV's daughter, Louise-Françoise de Bourbon. Its political role began in 1798, when the Council of the Five Hundred met there.
**Don't miss** The library ceiling (1838–1847), by Eugène Delacroix, depicts the history of civilization.

# BASTILLE

**See where the dramatic Storming of the Bastille took place—then enjoy a drink at one of the trendy cafés.**

68 Q8•Place de la Bastille and surrounding area, 75004/75011/75012 Bastille 20, 29, 65, 69, 76, 86, 87, 91 A good selection of cafés and restaurants (see page 258)

| RATINGS | |
|---|---|
| Historic interest | |
| Photo stops | |
| Shopping | |

Frenetic place de la Bastille, now bustling with street cafés and traffic, witnessed one of the pivotal events in France's history. Where in-line skaters and pedestrians now jostle for space, a Revolutionary mob stormed the Bastille prison in 1789 in a violent riot that signalled the start of the French Revolution.

The Bastille was built in 1380 as a fortress guarding the eastern entrance to Paris. It later became a jail for political prisoners, including the Marquis de Sade and Voltaire. Nothing remains of the building, although paving stones mark its outline. A visual reminder of Paris's turbulent past is the Colonne de Juillet (July Column), which stands 50m (164ft) tall on place de la Bastille's busy roundabout. It was constructed in 1840 to commemorate victims of another revolt, the 1830 uprising, and is topped by the winged *Spirit of Liberty*.

Bastille has been spruced up and is now a lively nightspot, with a wide choice of restaurants and bars. During the day you can shop in the hectic streets that radiate from the Colonne de Juillet. There is also a marina, art galleries and the ultramodern Opéra Bastille (see page 142). Walk down the rue de Lyon and you'll come to the Viaduc des Arts, an old railway viaduct converted into craft workshops and showrooms (9–129 avenue Daumesnil).

**Don't miss** To escape the noise and traffic of the Bastille, head down rue St-Antoine, then turn right into the peaceful rue de Birague. Here, browse in shops selling paintings, rugs and ceramics, then walk back in time through an archway to the tranquil place des Vosges (see page 150).

*The* Spirit of Liberty *watches over the busy place de la Bastille*

*The strikingly contemporary Palais Omnisports, at Bercy*

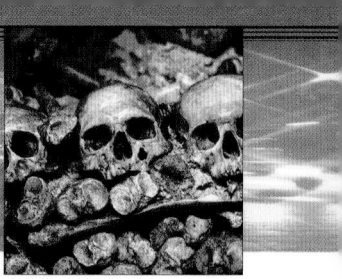

*Les Catacombes—not for the faint-hearted*

## BERCY

68 off Q9•Bercy, 75012 Bercy 24, 62, 87

Bercy spreads east from Gare de Lyon through a maze of new apartment and office blocks. Once known for its wine warehouses, it is undergoing intensive development. The most likely reason you'll come here is to see a rock concert or sporting event in the grass-walled Palais Omnisports (*www.bercy.fr*). Also of interest is the curvilinear former American Cultural Center, designed by Frank Gehry and due to be re-launched as a Museum of Cinema (see page 113). The freshly landscaped Parc de Bercy relieves the concrete jungle. At the far end, wine warehouses have been converted into the boutiques, bars and restaurants of Bercy Village (*www.bercyvillage.com*).

## BIBLIOTHÈQUE NATIONALE DE FRANCE–SITE FRANÇOIS MITTERRAND

332 Q11•quai François-Mauriac, 75013 01 53 79 59 59; guided visits 01 53 79 49 49 Upper Garden reading rooms: Tue–Sat 10–8, Sun 12–7 Adult one-day pass: €3, under 16 not admitted to reading room Bibliothèque François-Mitterrand 62, 89 Bibliothèque François-Mitterrand Bookshop/giftshop www.bnf.fr

Around 12 million books and numerous documents belong to the national library, so it's not surprising that it was forced to find additional premises towards the end of the 20th century. The new library, with its glass corner towers designed like four open books, stands on the eastern edge of the Left Bank. The public has access to books, the Internet and an excellent audiovisual section of videos, CDs and DVDs.

## BIBLIOTHÈQUE NATIONALE DE FRANCE–SITE RICHELIEU

67 M6•58 rue de Richelieu, 75002 01 53 79 59 59; guided visits 01 53 79 86 87 Library: daily 9–7 (from 12 Sun); Galerie Mansart, Galerie Mazarine and Crypte: Tue–Sat 10–7, Sun 12–7 (during exhibitions only) Bourse 20, 29, 39, 48, 67, 74, 85 Adult €4.50 for a two-day pass Guided visits first Tue of month www.bnf.fr

This former palace has been the prestigious base for France's national library since the early 18th century. It is close to the Louvre and Palais Royal and was once home to Cardinal Mazarin, Louis XIII's First Minister. In 1996 part of its collection moved to the new François-Mitterrand site (see this page), creating space to focus on manuscripts, maps, music, prints, photos and coins. Reading room access is reserved for those who prove a genuine research need, but you can see temporary exhibitions in the Galerie Mansart (devoted to photography), Galerie Mazarine and the Crypte.

**Don't miss** The Galerie Mazarine has a wonderful painted ceiling.

## LA BOURSE

67 M5•Palais de la Bourse, rue Vivienne, 75002 01 49 27 55 55 Guided tours between 9.30am and 4pm, Mon–Fri. Reserve ahead Adult €8.50, child €5.50 Bourse 20, 29, 39, 74, 85 www.euronext.com

Paris's money-spinning hub is in the Palais de la Bourse. Designed by architect Alexandre Brongniart, this neoclassical Napoleonic creation was built between 1808 and 1826. In1902 and 1907 two wings were added, giving the building the shape of a cross. Watch the action from the public gallery and learn about the importance of the stock exchange in France's economy with the help of audiovisual presentations.

## CANAL ST-MARTIN

68 P4•Canal St-Martin République, Jaurès, Jacques Bonsergent, Goncourt 26, 46, 75 Several companies offer boat trips including Canauxrama (see page 248)

The Canal St-Martin, in the eastern part of the city, makes a peaceful alternative to a boat trip along the Seine. You can also stroll along the tree-lined canal paths. The canal, which opened in 1825, is around 5km (3 miles) long and passes through nine locks and two swing bridges. It is spanned by many picturesque curved metal footbridges. The canal featured in the 2001 film *Le Fabuleux Destin d'Amélie Poulain* and in Marcel Carné's 1938 film *Hôtel du Nord*.

## LES CATACOMBES

330 L11•1 place Denfert-Rochereau, 75014 01 43 22 47 63 Tue–Sun 10–4 Adult €5, under 14 free Denfert-Rochereau 38, 68, 88 Not recommended for young children (or the faint-hearted!)

This labyrinth of tunnels—the world's largest repository of human bones—is the resting place of more than six million Parisians. The inscription above the entrance reads 'Stop! Here is the empire of death!'. Skulls and bones are arranged along the walls of these recesses, 20m (65ft) beneath the city. The tunnels were created in Roman times as quarries. Bones were transferred here from overcrowded cemeteries in 1785. During World War II the catacombs were used by the Resistance as a secret meeting place. Be prepared for lots of stairs and take a torch.

# Centre Georges Pompidou

**Paris's wackiest building, with one of the largest collections of modern art in the world.**
**Around six million visitors each year come to see works by Pablo Picasso, Andy Warhol, Jackson Pollock and many others.**

*You can see as far as Sacré-Cœur from the top floor*

*Learn more at the bookstore about the art you've just seen*

*Walkways are on the exterior, thanks to the inside-out design*

**RATINGS**

| | |
|---|---|
| Cultural interest | ●●●●● |
| Good for kids | ●●● |
| Photo stops (exterior and views) | ●●● |

**PANORAMA**

Don't miss the view over Paris from the top floor. Landmarks you can spot include Sacré-Cœur, the Eiffel Tower, Notre-Dame and the Panthéon.

## SEEING THE CENTRE GEORGES POMPIDOU

You'll either love or hate the brazen design of the Centre Georges Pompidou and you may well feel the same about the contemporary art it displays. The venue has sparked controversy since it opened in 1977, gracing the historic heart of Paris with an incongruously modern building that resembles a giant air-conditioning system. The main entrance, off the lively place Georges-Pompidou, takes you to level zero, where you can pick up a plan of the building and buy museum and exhibition tickets. If you want to visit both the Museum National d'Art Moderne and the temporary exhibitions, an all-gallery pass may be your best ticket option. To reach the museum, take the escalator to the entrance on level four, where you can rent an audioguide. Once inside the museum you may prefer to head straight to level five, which covers the first half of the 20th century, before returning to level four to tackle works from the 1960s to the present day. Temporary exhibitions are on levels one and six. If you need a break from the galleries, you can get a bite to eat in the café on level one or browse in the bookshop on level zero or the boutique on level one.

*One of the eccentric characters of the Stravinsky Fountain (right)*

Le Défenseur du Temps—*not your typical clock*

## HIGHLIGHTS

### MUSÉE NATIONAL D'ART MODERNE

Where the Musée d'Orsay (see pages 130–134) leaves off, the Museum of Modern Art takes over, featuring works from 1905 to the present day. Up to 2,000 pieces from the 50,000-strong collection are on display at any one time and range from Cubism by Georges Braque and Picasso to Pop Art by Andy Warhol and video art by Korean artist Nam June Paik. The approach to the museum is almost as unusual as the art it contains. You step onto an escalator inside a giant transparent tube that runs up the outside of the building. This takes you to the fourth floor, which covers 1960 to the present day, including works by the French New Realists, photographers, architects and video artists. There are also rooms dedicated to graphic art and new media. Pieces on display change annually, each autumn. For a chronological overview, start on the fifth floor, tame in comparison, which takes you

**SITE GUIDE**

**LEVEL -1**
Live events, Cinema 2

**LEVEL 0**
Lobby, including information, ticket office, post office, bookshop

**LEVEL 1**
Library, Cinema 1, exhibitions, café, design boutique

**LEVELS 2 AND 3**
Library

**LEVELS 4 AND 5**
Musée National d'Art Moderne

**LEVEL 6**
Exhibitions, restaurant, bookshop

back to the first half of the 20th century. The displays here change each spring and include works by Henri Matisse, Picasso, Braque, Juan Gris and Pollock. On both floors, glass walls flood the interior with natural light and give wonderful views.

**TEMPORARY EXHIBITIONS AND OTHER ATTRACTIONS**

Temporary exhibitions, on the first and sixth floors, are as much a draw as the Musée National d'Art Moderne. Recent themes have ranged from 'Hitchcock and Art' to the designer Philippe Starck. Other attractions on site include children's activities, two cinemas, dance and drama productions and a library. Nearby, at 1 place Igor Stravinsky, the experimental music venue IRCAM (Institute de Recherche et Coordination de l'Acoustique et de la Musique) stages concerts, workshops and lectures. On the other side of the Pompidou, on rue Rambuteau, the Atelier Brancusi is a reconstruction of Romanian sculptor Constantin Brancusi's workshop. Brancusi moved to Paris in 1904 and his studio has been re-created as he left it when he died in 1957.

**OUTDOORS**

On a sunny day, the square outside comes alive with jugglers, mime artists, fire-eaters and musicians. Try to see the surreal Stravinsky Fountain round the corner in place Igor Stravinsky. The zany

*The controversial exterior of the Centre Georges Pompidou*

characters, which squirt water at anyone who dares walk past, are each named after a work by the Russian composer. Finally, look out for Paris's newest public clock in rue Brantôme, the vicious looking brass and steel *Le Défenseur du Temps* (The Defender of Time). The defender fights beasts, representing earth, water and air, on the hour but can be seen at his most ferocious at noon, 6pm and 10pm.

## BACKGROUND

The Centre Georges Pompidou was the inspiration of Georges Pompidou, president of France from 1969 until his death in 1974. His vision was a venue where people could enjoy contemporary film, drama, dance, music and visual art. The outlandish complex took five years to build and was a controversial addition to Beaubourg, a run-down district of 18th- and 19th-century town houses. Designers Renzo Piano and Richard Rogers turned the building inside out by placing its 'guts' (all the piping) on the outside. This piping was coded with different shades of paint, with yellow for electrics, blue for air-conditioning, green for water and red for the elevators. Pompidou did not live to see the opening in 1977, but his vision for the arts venue proved sagacious—it was soon attracting 22,000 visitors a day, rivalling the Louvre in popularity. It closed for two years for renovation work in the autumn of 1997, reopening just in time for the new millennium.

## BASICS

**Centre Georges Pompidou**

68 N7•place Georges-Pompidou, 75004

01 44 78 12 33

Centre Georges Pompidou: Wed–Mon 11–10. Musée National d'Art Moderne and exhibitions: Wed–Mon 11–9 (last ticket 8). Thu, Fri until 11 for some exhibitions (last ticket 10). Closed Tue, 1 May. Library: Mon, Wed–Fri 12–9.40, Sat–Sun 11–9.40

Adult all-gallery pass €10. Musée National d'Art Moderne, Atelier Brancusi and Children's Gallery: adult €5.50, under 18 free; free first Sun of month. Exhibitions: prices vary (under 13 free)

Rambuteau, Hôtel de Ville

29, 38, 47, 75

Châtelet-Les-Halles

Georges restaurant on 6th floor, with good views

On first floor

Bookshops on levels 0, 4, 6; boutique on 1; post office on 0

€12 (French, English, German, Italian, Spanish, Japanese)

Audioguide €4.50

www.centrepompidou.fr (in French, with some information in English; includes photos of some of the works, details of events and exhibitions and practical information)

**IRCAM**

1 place Igor Stravinsky

01 44 78 48 43

Pick up a brochure or check the website for concert details

www.ircam.fr

**Atelier Brancusi**

55 rue Rambuteau

Wed–Mon 2–6

Joint ticket with Musée National d'Art Moderne and Children's Gallery: adult €5.50, under 18 free; free first Sun of month

*The spacious lobby buzzes with people throughout the day*

**TIPS**

- If you're a traditionalist when it comes to art, let yourself in (relatively) gently to the Museum of Modern Art by starting with the fifth floor (1905–1960) before tackling the more bemusing fourth floor (1960 to today).

- The museum's late opening hours allow you to enjoy a visit after an early evening meal (last ticket sold at 8pm; museum closes at 9pm).

- You may hear local people referring to the Centre Georges Pompidou as Beaubourg.

- The official guidebook has photos and information about 150 of the most important exhibits and is worth buying before you visit the Museum of Modern Art.

- If your mind is spinning from a day of modern art, you may enjoy a calming concert at the nearby church of St-Merri (see page 162), on Saturdays at 9pm and Sundays at 4pm.

**MODERN ART FOR THE UNINITIATED—AN EXPLANATION OF SOME OF THE MOVEMENTS OF MODERN ART**

**Abstract Expressionism:** This movement stemmed from the US and had two main subdivisions—Action Painting and Colour Field Painting. Action Painting focused on the act of painting, rather than the finished piece of art. The most famous artist of this genre was Jackson Pollock, who used sticks and syringes to drip paint onto the canvas, forming abstract shapes.
**Arte Povera:** Literally 'poor art', Arte Povera is an Italian-based genre that involves the use of cheap, everyday materials to create sculptures or art installations. Artists include Mario Merz and Giuseppe Penone.
**Cubism:** Created by Picasso, Braque, Fernand Léger and Gris in the early 20th century, Cubism was, in part, a backlash against Impressionism. People and objects are fragmented and portrayed using geometric shapes.
**Fauvism:** Uses bold blocks of pure colour, seen in the works of Matisse.
**Fluxus:** A movement launched in the 1960s. Rejected classic ideas of what a work of art is and focused on fluidity, chance and everyday objects and events. Artists include Ben and Joseph Beuys.
**Minimalism:** The emphasis is on simplicity and repetition, such as the works of Donald Judd and Brice Marden.
**New Realist:** New Realists used everyday objects in their works, which would sometimes be smashed or burned as a statement against society or fine art. Arman's collection of gas masks, entitled *Home, Sweet Home,* is an example of the genre.
**Pop Art:** An artistic take on popular culture and advertising. One of the most famous Pop Art pieces is Andy Warhol's *Marilyn Monroe* silkscreen. Other artists include Claes Oldenburg, Roy Lichtenstein and David Hockney.
**Surrealism:** A rejection of logic and realism for a surreal dream world. This movement was popular in the 1920s and 1930s, with artists such as René Magritte and Salvador Dalí.
**Video Art:** Experimenting with video footage as art, for example in the work of Nam June Paik.

*Napoleon trained to be an army officer at the imposing École Militaire*

*One of the many intriguing graves at Montparnasse Cemetery*

## CHAMP DE MARS AND ÉCOLE MILITAIRE

**Champ de Mars**
66 H8•Champ de Mars, 75007
0820 007 575 Always open
Free École Militaire 42, 69, 82, 87 RER line C, Champ de Mars-Tour Eiffel

**École Militaire**
66 H8•1 place Joffre, 75007
Visits by written application only
École Militaire 28, 80, 82, 87, 92

The green lawns of the Champ de Mars stretch out in a rectangular design between the Eiffel Tower and the imposing 18th-century École Militaire. It was on this site that Roman invaders battled it out with the Parisii in 52BC to win supremacy over the area, and the Parisians later beat off the Vikings.

The Champ de Mars was laid out in 1765 as an army parade ground. Its name, Field of Mars, refers to the Roman god of war. Over the years it has witnessed national celebrations, parades, international exhibitions, horse races and even ballooning experiments by the intrepid Montgolfier brothers. Today it is popular with families, joggers and visitors strolling in the shadow of the Eiffel Tower.

The colonnaded and domed École Militaire dominates the opposite end of the Champ de Mars. It was commissioned in 1751 by Louis XV and his mistress, Madame de Pompadour, who wanted somewhere to train impoverished young gentlemen. Architect Jacques-Ange Gabriel, who also worked on the place de la Concorde and Versailles's Petit Trianon, was responsible for the design. Work finished in 1773 and a new tax on playing cards and the lottery financed the grooming of France's military cadets, including none other than Napoleon Bonaparte. He entered the academy in 1784, aged 15.

## CIMETIÈRE DE MONTMARTRE

69 L2•20 avenue Rachel, 75018
01 43 87 64 24 Mon–Fri 8–6, Sat 8.30–6, Sun 9–6, Mar–end Nov; Mon–Fri 8–5.30, Sat 8.30–5.30, Sun 9–5.30, rest of year (last entry 15 min before closing) Free Place de Clichy/Blanche, then walk 30, 54, 74, 80, 95
www.paris.fr

Montmartre's cemetery is packed with graves of the famous, including composers Hector Berlioz and Jacques Offenbach and artists Edgar Degas and Gustave Moreau. The imposing tomb of Émile Zola is close to the flower-filled roundabout near the main entrance, although the writer's remains were moved to the Panthéon (see page 144) in 1906. The cemetery, created in 1798, also holds the grave of Louise Weber, the Moulin Rouge dancer known as La Goulue, who appeared in paintings by Toulouse-Lautrec. Jazz fans may want to find the tomb of the saxophone inventor, Adolphe Sax.

A notice board at the main entrance gives times and dates of guided visits.

## CIMETIÈRE DU MONTPARNASSE

330 K10•3 boulevard Edgar Quinet, 75014 01 44 10 86 50 Mon–Fri 8–6, Sat 8.30–6, Sun 9–6 (closes 5.30pm early Nov–mid-Mar) Free Edgar Quinet, Raspail, Montparnasse-Bienvenüe 28, 68

Montparnasse Cemetery opened in 1824 and is the final resting place of many notable former residents of the area. Here you can pay homage to an array of illustrious writers, composers, musicians, artists and sculptors, including Jean-Paul Sartre, Simone de Beauvoir, Charles Baudelaire, Guy de Maupassant, Constantin Brancusi, Camille Saint-Saëns, Ossip Zadkine and Samuel Beckett. Also buried here are car manufacturer André Citroën and Prime Minister Pierre Laval, who was executed for treason after World War II following his open collaboration with the Germans.

Adorning a tomb in the north-eastern corner of the cemetery is Brancusi's charmingly childlike sculpture *The Kiss*—supposedly a response to Rodin's famous work of the same name.

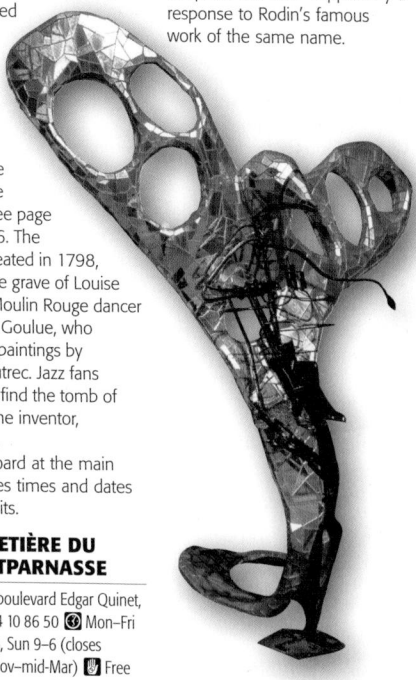

*This striking statue decorates a grave at Montparnasse Cemetery*

*The cobbled avenues of leafy Père-Lachaise Cemetery*

# CIMETIÈRE DU PÈRE-LACHAISE

**One of the most famous burial grounds in the world.**

You can visit the graves of luminaries such as Frédéric Chopin, Marcel Proust and Oscar Wilde at this vast cemetery, on the eastern edge of the city. Père-Lachaise covers 44 ha (108 acres) on the slopes of Ménilmontant and contains around 70,000 tombs. Tree-lined, cobbled paths are bordered by ornate tombstones and mausoleums. Far from gloomy, it is a great place for a peaceful walk on a sunny day.

### ENGLISH ORIGINS

The cemetery is named after Louis XIV's confessor, Père La Chaise, who once owned the land here. It was designed by Brongniart in 1803 to echo an English-style garden. At first, the cemetery was not popular, but once the graves of writers Molière and Jean de La Fontaine and the tragic lovers Abélard and Héloïse had been transferred here—precisely to encourage other Parisians to follow suit—it soon became the most fashionable place to be buried in Paris.

### RESTING PLACE OF THE FAMOUS

Père-Lachaise has become a place of pilgrimage—among the famous people buried here are composers Frédéric Chopin and Georges Bizet, Paris town planner Baron Haussmann, artists Amedeo Modigliani and Eugène Delacroix, singers Edith Piaf and Maria Callas, writers Marcel Proust, Honoré de Balzac and Oscar Wilde, actresses Simone Signoret and Sarah Bernhardt, actor Yves Montand and dancer Isadora Duncan. One of the most visited graves is that of Jim Morrison, lead singer of The Doors, who died in Paris in 1971. His once graffiti-covered tomb is now protected by a security guard. Fans still leave cigarette stubs, flowers and beads as a mark of respect. In August 2003, French actress Marie Trintignant was buried in the cemetery.

### MEMORIALS

The Mur des Fédérés, in the eastern corner of the cemetery, marks the site of the Communards' tragic last stand in 1871, when the 147 survivors of the Commune were lined up against the wall and executed by a government firing squad. They were buried where they fell, in a communal grave. There are also poignant memorials to the victims of Nazi concentration camps and to the Resistance fighters killed in World War II.

**RATINGS**

| | |
|---|---|
| Historic interest | ●●●● |
| Photo stops | ●● |
| Value for money | FREE |

**TIPS**

- Try to avoid visiting on very windy days as there is a danger of falling branches.
- The cemetery is huge and maps are dotted about, but if you are keen to visit particular graves it is best to obtain your own map beforehand (see below) to help you find your way.

**BASICS**

327 S6•boulevard de Ménilmontant, 75020 ☎ 01 55 25 82 10

Mon–Fri 8–6, Sat 8.30–6, Sun 9–6 (closes 5.30 early Nov to mid-Mar); last entry 15 min before closing

Free

Père Lachaise, Gambetta

61, 69

Guided tours in English Sat 3 (€6), Jul, Aug

You can buy a map from the news vendors or florists near the main entrances (avenue Père Lachaise and boulevard de Ménilmontant). You can also obtain a map from the cemetery office by the Père Lachaise entrance

*The tomb of 19th-century journalist Victor Noir (above)*

# Conciergerie

**The horrors of the French Revolution linger on in this dimly lit Gothic palace, where prisoners spent their final days before being led to the guillotine. The eerie complex also contains Europe's oldest surviving medieval hall, and the kitchens once used to cook food for royalty.**

*Dramatic lighting and Gothic turrets at the eerie Conciergerie*

| RATINGS | |
|---|---|
| Historic interest | ●●●● |
| Photo stops (from the Seine) | ●●● |

## SEEING THE CONCIERGERIE

Sailing past the Conciergerie's floodlit towers on an evening boat cruise, it is hard to imagine the fear that lurked within its walls during the five centuries it served as a prison. But step inside the gloomy main hall and the sense of oppression is palpable.

The entrance is on the boulevard du Palais, near the gateway to the Palais de Justice. If you also want to visit Sainte-Chapelle (see pages 158–160) you can buy a joint ticket. Pick up a plan at the entrance as signage inside isn't particularly clear. The first three rooms on your tour—the Salle des Gens d'Armes, the medieval kitchens and the Salle des Gardes—date from the Middle Ages, when the Conciergerie was a royal palace. To learn more about its gruesome role during the Revolution head for the Galerie des Prisonniers, off the southwestern corner of the main hall. Here you'll also find a reconstruction of Marie-Antoinette's cell.

## HIGHLIGHTS

### GOTHIC HALLS

On entry you are immediately plunged into semi-darkness in a vast Gothic chamber said to be Europe's oldest surviving medieval hall. Subtle uplighting adds to the eerie atmosphere of the Salle des Gens d'Armes, 63m (206ft) long and 8.5m (28ft) high. The hall dates from the 14th century, when it formed the lower floor of the Grand'Salle.

*Sculptures of Law and Justice flank the clock on the Tour de l'Horloge*

The king's staff ate here, up to 2,000 at a time, while royal banquets and marriage celebrations were held upstairs. Later, the hall was divided into separate storerooms, but was restored in the 19th century by Viollet-le-Duc. A spiral staircase leads up to the kitchens, where four walk-in fireplaces, each big enough to roast a couple of sheep, indicate the scale of medieval appetites. From the kitchens walk back into the Salles des Gens d'Armes and up to the Salle des Gardes, in the northwestern corner. This Gothic hall sat underneath the Grand'Chambre, where the Revolutionary court delivered death sentences like parking tickets to its unfortunate victims.

**RE-CREATIONS OF THE REVOLUTION**

The Galerie des Prisonniers was once the prison's most animated crossroads, where lawyers, visitors and inmates met. Here you'll find re-creations of the clerk's and concierge's offices, as well as the Salle de Toilette, where barbers cut off prisoners' hair before execution. There is also a poignant reconstruction of Marie-Antoinette's cell. The spartan furnishings (not original), torn wallpaper and stifling gaze of the prison guard paint a sorry picture of the queen's last days. Upstairs in the Room of the Sentenced, wall panels list the 2,780 people guillotined between March 1793 and May 1795. Farther along the eerie upstairs corridor, re-created cells give you a glimpse of the prisoners' harsh living conditions. The first cell, with no beds or lamp, was for the poorest prisoners, the *pailleux* (*paille* means straw). Prisoners with money shared a *chambre à la pistole*, with the relative luxury of beds and chairs. Finally, the famous or the very wealthy were granted their own cell, complete with a desk, bed, lamp and books.

### THE CHAPEL

At the end of the upper corridor, stairs take you down to the Chapelle des Girondins, named after the 21 condemned Girondins (left-wing members of the 1791 Legislative Assembly) who sat around a banqueting table here on the night before their execution. Leading off this room, the Chapelle Expiatoire stands on the site of Marie-Antoinette's actual cell. The chapel was commissioned by Louis XVIII to commemorate members of the royal family killed during the Revolution. The silver pattern on the walls represents tears.

## BACKGROUND

The Conciergerie is notorious for its role as a prison, but it began as a palace, part of a royal complex including Sainte-Chapelle and the Palais de Justice. The oldest parts of the Conciergerie date from the early 14th century, although a fortress probably stood on the western part of the Île de la Cité as far back as Roman times. In the late 14th century, Charles V chose to live elsewhere and its role changed to a law court and prison, with occasional use for royal functions. It was at this time that it gained its name, from the Concierge who oversaw the site. During the Revolution, the prison housed more than 4,000 inmates, up to 600 at a time. Conditions were crowded and disease was rife. Prisoners had nothing to do but wait in the dungeon-like interior for the often inevitable death sentence and the terrifying journey through the city to the guillotine. After the Revolution, the Conciergerie continued as a prison until 1914. It now offers visitors a chilling reminder of the darker side of Paris's history.

### BASICS

- 67 M7•2 boulevard du Palais, Île de la Cité, 75001
- 01 53 40 60 97; 01 53 73 78 52
- Daily 9.30–6. Closed 1 Jan, 1 May, 25 Dec
- Adult €5.50 (€8 for combined ticket with Sainte-Chapelle), free for under 18 (bring passport to prove age)
- Cité, Châtelet
- 21, 24, 27, 38, 58, 81, 85, 96
- RER line B, C St-Michel-Notre-Dame
- Bookshop
- Daily guided tours in French, English, Italian. No audioguides
- €6
- 

www.monum.fr (in French and English; easy to navigate, with lots of photos and historical information)

### TIPS

- If you intend to visit Sainte-Chapelle as well, go to the Conciergerie first and buy a joint ticket, to avoid the long queues at Sainte-Chapelle. However, try to get to Sainte-Chapelle before lunchtime, as it is generally more crowded in the afternoon.
- The Conciergerie's main halls are empty of furniture, making it harder to imagine the events that once took place here. Come prepared to work your imagination.
- On the Seine side of the building, take a look at the Tour de l'Horloge, site of Paris's first public clock, commissioned in 1370. The present clock dates from the 16th century and has sculptures of Law and Justice.

*The Salle des Gens d'Armes (above) is said to be Europe's oldest surviving medieval hall*

*The shape of things to come? Office blocks at La Défense*

*The entrance to Espace Montmartre–Salvador Dalí*

*Luxury treats at Ladurée, in the rue Royale, near Faubourg St-Honoré*

THE SIGHTS

## LA DÉFENSE

333 B2•92044 Grande Arche de La Défense 73 RER line A, La Défense A selection

You couldn't find a starker contrast with Paris's historic core than this high-rise business district on the city's western edge. In addition to office blocks, you'll find Les Quatre Temps shopping complex and the CNIT building (Centre of New Industries and Technologies), looking like an upturned shell. **Don't miss** The main draw for visitors is the imposing Grande Arche (see page 94), which rises 110m (360ft) above the enormous pedestrian-only square called Le Parvis. Stand on the white marble steps of this 300,000-tonne giant and the people wandering across the vast square seem utterly dwarfed by skyscrapers.

## DROUOT

69 M5•9 rue Drouot, 75009 01 48 00 20 20 Mon–Fri 11–6, Sat–Sun times vary. Closed Aug Free Richelieu-Drouot, Le Peletier 67, 74, 85
www.drouot.fr

Paris's leading auctioneers was founded in the 19th century and takes its name from the Comte de Drouot, Napoleon's aide-de-camp. There are 16 auction rooms and the auctions, in French, usually begin at 2pm. Viewing is from 11 to 6 the day before the sale and 11 to noon on the day of the sale. You'll find details on the website and in *La Gazette de l'Hôtel Drouot*, published weekly.

## LES ÉGOUTS

66 H6•place de la Résistance (Pont Alma). Entrance opposite 93 quai d'Orsay, 75007 01 53 68 27 81 Sat–Wed 11–5, May–end Sep; Sat–Wed 11–4, rest of year. Closed last three weeks in Jan Alma-Marceau 42, 63, 80, 92 RER line C, Pont-de-l'Alma Adult €3.80, child €3.05, under 5 free
www.paris.fr

Paris's sewers are a surprisingly popular visitor attraction. A worker guides you through part of the city's 2,100km (1,302 mile) subterranean network and shows you an audiovisual presentation. The sewers were built by Baron Haussmann in the latter part of the 19th century, and during World War II the Germans used some sections as offices. They have even made it onto the stage, featuring in the hit musicals *Les Misérables* and *Phantom of the Opera*.

## ESPACE MONTMARTRE–SALVADOR DALÍ

69 M3•11 rue Poulbot (off place du Tertre), 75018 01 42 64 40 10 Daily 10–6.30 (also 6.30–9.30pm, Jul–end Aug) Abbesses then walk 80, Montmartrobus Adult €7, child €6, under 8 free
www.dali-espacemontmartre.com

This surreal museum displays more than 300 weird and wonderful works by the Catalan artist Salvador Dalí (1904–1989), who came to live in Paris in the late 1920s. The disconcerting black-walled interior is a fitting backdrop for the sculptures and illustrations, which form the biggest Dalí collection in France.

## LES FAUBOURGS

### Faubourg St-Honoré

66 J5•Around rue du Faubourg St-Honoré St-Philippe du Roule, Miromesnil, Ternes 43, 52, 93

### Faubourg St-Antoine

68 off Q8•Around rue du Faubourg St-Antoine Bastille, Ledru Rollin, Faidherbe Chaligny, Nation 76, 86 RER line A, Nation

### Faubourg St-Germain

67 K8•West of St-Germain-des-Prés, including rue de Varenne Varenne 69, 87 RER line C, Invalides

### Faubourg Montmartre

69 M4–5•Around rue du Faubourg Montmartre Grands Boulevards, Le Peletier 48, 67, 74, 85

The *faubourgs* (fake boroughs) were Paris's first suburbs and for years the title had derogatory connotations. Now, far from being second-class, many have become highly sought-after areas. One of the oldest is the Right Bank's Faubourg St-Honoré, stretching along the road of the same name. Now a hub of Parisian wealth, it is packed with designer boutiques and is home to the Palais de l'Élysée, the French president's official residence.

Faubourg St-Antoine, which runs east from Bastille to the place de la Nation, was once an explosive district full of rebels. Now more peaceful in spirit, its identity remains linked with the crafts of its former artisans.

To find the real atmosphere of the faubourgs look in the area between Faubourg Montmartre and Faubourg Poissonière. From the grands boulevards, the Faubourg Montmartre winds uphill towards Pigalle and Montmartre, carrying in its wake a lively string of bars and inexpensive restaurants.

South of the river, Faubourg St-Germain was meadowland in medieval times, evolving into a bourgeois district in the 18th century. Many of the elegant mansions are now foreign embassies and government offices.

But even today *faubourg* can have a pejorative ring, with the comment 'he was born in the *faubourgs*' implying an unsophisticated background.

*The Fondation Cartier specializes in contemporary art exhibitions*

### FONDATION CARTIER

330 L10•261 boulevard Raspail, 75014 ☎ 01 42 18 56 51 ⏰ Tue–Sun 12–8 € Adult €5, child (11–24) €3.50, under 10 free Raspail 🚌 38, 68, 91 ? Nomadic Nights held on certain Thursdays at 8.30pm (advance booking necessary, tel 01 42 18 56 72) www.fondation.cartier.fr

The Fondation Cartier has been an avid promoter of contemporary art since it was founded in 1984. In 1994, it moved to central Paris, to the striking steel and glass building designed by architect Jean Nouvel. The light, spacious interior is the perfect setting for the permanent and temporary exhibitions of French and international art. Vast glass windows open onto a garden and small amphitheatre created by artist Lothar Baumgarten.

### FONTAINE DES INNOCENTS

67 M6•square des Innocents, near Forum des Halles, 75001 Châtelet, Les Halles 🚌 38, 47 (and all buses going along rue de Rivoli) Châtelet-Les-Halles Plenty in Les Halles ? Don't visit the fountain alone at night

Water has gushed from this superb Renaissance fountain since the mid-16th century, although the fountain has not always stood on this spot in Les Halles. It was originally on the corner of the rue St-Denis but was moved to its current position in the late-18th century to replace a cemetery that had run out of soil. The cemetery's two million skeletons were transferred to the Catacombes (see page 81). After the move, the fountain gained a fourth side, carved by Augustin Pajou. The original three-sided cascade was designed by Pierre Lescot and sculpted by Jean Goujon.

## LES GALERIES

**These elegant covered passageways, with glass skylights and decorative floors, were the stylish shopping malls of early 19th-century Paris.**

**Galerie Vivienne** 67 M6•4 rue des Petits-Champs/6 rue Vivienne/5 rue de la Banque, 75002 Bourse
**Galerie Colbert** 67 M6•6 rue des Petits-Champs, 75002 Bourse
**Passage des Panoramas** 69 M5•11 boulevard Montmartre/10 rue St-Marc, 75002 Grands Boulevards
**Galerie Véro-Dodat** 67 M6•19 rue Jean-Jacques Rousseau, 75001 Palais-Royale–Musée du Louvre
**Passage Jouffroy** 69 M5•10 boulevard Montmartre, 75009 Grands Boulevards
**Passage Verdeau** 69 M5•31 bis rue du Faubourg-Montmartre, 75009 Le Peletier
http://passagescouverts.free.fr (in French only)

| RATINGS | |
|---|---|
| Historic interest | ●●● |
| Specialist shopping | ●●●● |
| Value for money | FREE |

**TIPS**

- The *galeries* are an ideal place to visit on a rainy day. Browse in the boutiques, window shop or simply enjoy the ornate architecture, glass roofs and decorative floors.
- If your feet are aching, relax in a café under the skylights and let the surroundings waft you back to 19th-century Paris.

Between the late 18th and early 19th century a network of *galeries* were built on the Right Bank. Less than 30 of the original 140 passages survive. Many have been restored, others are dusty reminders of a bygone age. Elegant Galerie Vivienne, built in 1823, is perhaps the most fashionable, with its ornate cast-iron gates, high glass roofs, chandeliers and mosaic floors. It is home to Legrand, one of Paris's best wine-merchants, a toy shop, a bookshop established in 1826, stylish boutiques and a chic *salon de thé* with tables spilling out under the lofty skylights.

Parallel to it is the much-restored Galerie Colbert, dating from 1826 and now an annex of the Bibliothèque Nationale. It has interesting shops and a sophisticated brasserie, the Grand Colbert. Exhibitions are sometimes held in its galleries and auditorium. The Passage des Panoramas, built in 1800, is today a hive of specialist shops with eateries that include a tea room and an Italian trattoria.

The picturesque 1826 Galerie Véro-Dodat is named after two butchers and was one of first streets in Paris to be illuminated by gas. Today its black-and-white tiled floor, window-boxes and carved wooden mouldings make a shadowy, harmonious setting for an old-world restaurant, antiques shops and galleries. Passages Jouffroy and Verdeau are also worth visiting.

*Vivienne (top) is one of Paris's most fashionable galeries*

*The Grande Arche (above) towers 110m (360ft) over La Défense. One of the business district's contemporary art installations (left)*

**RATINGS**

Photo stops

**TIPS**

- The best view of the Arc de Triomphe is not from the roof of the Grande Arche but from the top of the 54 marble steps leading up to the elevators.
- To experience the bustle of business-focused La Défense, visit on a weekday.

**BASICS**

333 A2•1 parvis de la Défense, 92044, La Défense
01 49 07 27 57
Daily 10–7 (also Sat 7–8, Apr–end Sep); last entry 30 min before closing
Adult €7, child (6-17) €6
Grande Arche de la Défense
73
RER line A, La Défense
Restaurant on top floor, but no view
Small bookshop/giftshop on top floor
€6

www.grandearche.com (in French and English; information on exhibitions and photos of the views)

# GRANDE ARCHE

**Paris's most striking modern monument.**

The Grande Arche is best admired from below, looking up into the vast chasm that is greater than the height of Notre-Dame and the width of the Champs-Élysées. The futuristic monument-cum-office block was designed as a symbolic western gateway to Paris and focal point of the new business district, La Défense (see page 92). Work finished in 1989, in time for the Bicentenary of the French Revolution.

## TEST YOUR NERVES

Standing below the Grande Arche is an unnerving experience, as you look up at 300,000 tonnes of concrete, marble-cladding and glass rising 110m (360ft) above the ground. But if you think that's daunting, wait until you take the glass elevator that climbs up the cavity of the arch on what looks disconcertingly like a piece of scaffolding. When you reach the top, you might wonder if the hair-raising ride was worth it. The elevator deposits you in a closed-in area lacking the walls of windows you would expect from such a lofty position. To see the view you have to walk outside, up some steps onto a viewing platform. The panorama is partly obscured by wire fencing and the office blocks of La Défense. If you climb only one of Paris's tall buildings, the Grande Arche is probably not the one to choose. But if you have already seen the view from the Eiffel Tower and the Arc de Triomphe, the Grande Arche offers a new perspective on the city. On a clear day you can see along part of Paris's *Grand Axis* (see page 79), towards the Arc de Triomphe. Farther to the right is a quirky view of the Eiffel Tower, with the Tour Montparnasse lined up directly behind it—at first glance it looks as if the Eiffel Tower is surrounded by scaffolding. Back inside, there is a restaurant and temporary art exhibitions.

## LONG-AWAITED

The Grande Arche was the culmination of many unsuccessful attempts to find a nucleus for La Défense in the 1970s. The design, by Danish architect Johan Otto von Spreckelsen, was finally chosen in 1983 and the venture became one of President Mitterrand's *Grand Projets* (see page 39).

*Gleaming statues guard the roof of the Hôtel de Ville*

## LES HALLES

68 N6•75001 (the area bordered by rue Beaubourg, rue du Louvre, rue Réaumur and rue de Rivoli) Les Halles 29, 38, 47 Châtelet-Les-Halles Au Pied de Cochon, 6 rue Coquillère Les Halles can be seedy at night, especially along rue St-Denis
www.forum-des-halles.com

'The belly of Paris' (so said the writer Émile Zola) is a curious mixture of old and new, picturesque and seedy. It started life as a food market in the 12th century and continued this role until 1969, when the superb 1860s pavilions were demolished. A decade later they were replaced by the jarring Forum des Halles, a vast underground shopping mall. You can also visit the church of St-Eustache (see page 161) and the Fontaine des Innocents (see page 93).
**Don't miss** The atmosphere of Les Halles in years gone by remains in the surrounding streets, including the cobbled rue Montorgueil.

## HÔTEL DE VILLE

68 N7•place de l'Hôtel de Ville, 75004 01 42 76 40 40 Weekly guided tours in French, by appointment only; call 01 42 76 54 04 at least 7 days in advance Hôtel de Ville 38, 47, 58, 67, 70, 72, 74, 75, 96 Free guided tours
www.paris.fr

The imposing town hall, built in neo-Renaissance style in the late 19th century, is home to Paris's city council. Its predecessor was destroyed in the 1871 uprising.
**Don't miss** The place de l'Hôtel de Ville is a pedestrian-only haven in the middle of a mammoth traffic jam. Fountains at either end drown out some of the noise and it's a pleasant spot to admire the 136 statues of historical characters that decorate the town hall's façades.

# GRAND PALAIS

**An eye-catching exhibition hall hosting major art shows and a science museum.**

**Grand Palais**
66 J6•avenue Winston-Churchill, 75008 (entrance on avenue Général Eisenhower) 01 44 13 17 30; reservations 01 42 31 32 28 Wed–Mon 10–8 (also Wed 8–10pm) Depends on exhibition Champs-Élysées-Clemenceau 42, 73, 83, 93 Bookshop Depends on exhibition Audioguides available
www.rmn.fr/galeriesnationaldugrandpalais

**Palais de la Découverte**
66 J6•avenue Franklin D. Roosevelt, 75008 01 56 43 20 21 Tue–Sat 9.30–6, Sun 10–7 Adult €5.60, child €3.70, €3.10 extra for Planetarium Champs-Élysées-Clemenceau 28, 42, 52, 63, 72, 73, 80, 83, 93
www.palais-decouverte.fr

**RATINGS**

| | |
|---|---|
| Cultural interest | ●●●● |
| Historic interest | ●●● |
| Photo stops (exterior) | ●●● |

**TIPS**

- **It is best to book in advance for exhibitions at the Grand Palais, especially if you want to visit in the morning. Reserve tickets by telephone or via www.fnac.com**
- **The exhibits in the Palais de la Découverte may be of limited interest to children who do not speak French.**
- **Even if you don't want to visit the science museum, take a peek at its foyer, with mosaic floor and glass-domed ceiling.**

The Grand Palais, with its soaring glass and iron domes, occupies a commanding position between the Seine and the Champs-Élysées. It was built for the 1900 Universal Exhibition, along with the nearby Pont Alexandre III and Petit Palais. The aim was to form a prestigious axis running from the golden-domed Les Invalides to the Champs-Élysées. The colossal building is a striking mix of art nouveau and neoclassical and it is well worth walking around the outside before venturing inside to see the exhibitions.

The Palais hosts high-profile temporary art exhibitions, usually very popular, so be prepared for long waits for tickets (reservations are well worth the extra euros). On the western side, the Palais de la Découverte is a hands-on science museum aimed primarily at children, with a Planetarium. Topics range from climate change to the workings of the human heart.

Across the road is the Petit Palais, the focus of a €264 million restoration project due to finish in autumn 2005. The palace is closed during the renovations, but when it reopens it will resume its role as the Musée des Beaux-Arts de la Ville (Municipal Museum of Fine Arts), offering an eclectic collection of mainly 19th-century paintings. In the meantime, content yourself with the statue of a rather stern looking Winston Churchill in the grounds outside.
**Don't miss** There are wonderful friezes on the eastern and western façades of the Grand Palais.

# Île de la Cité

**The historical heart of Paris, packed with must-see sights and offering wonderful views of the Seine.**
**Key attractions include the Gothic Conciergerie, the glistening Sainte-Chapelle and the stately Notre-Dame cathedral.**

*The western tip of the Île de la Cité, joined to the Right and Left banks by the Pont Neuf (above). Inside the Mémorial des Martyrs de la Déportation (top)*

**RATINGS**

| | |
|---|---|
| Good for kids | ● ● ● |
| Historic interest | ● ● ● ● ● |
| Photo stops | ● ● ● ● ● |

**BASICS**

68 N7•Île de la Cité, 75001 and 75004
Cité (also Pont Neuf, St-Michel, Châtelet, Hôtel de Ville)
21, 24, 27, 38, 47, 58, 70, 85, 96
RER line B, C, St-Michel-Notre-Dame
On Île de la Cité, the nearby Île St-Louis and in the Latin Quarter
A selection

## SEEING THE ÎLE DE LA CITÉ

The Paris story began on the Île de la Cité more than 2,000 years ago. Today it is still a key part of the city, packed with visitors, traffic and fabulous architecture. The island sits in the middle of the Seine like a tug, towing the smaller Île St-Louis behind it. One of the best ways to appreciate its beautiful architecture is by boat, taking one of the trips that start from below the Pont Neuf, Paris's oldest bridge. From the water you'll see the elegant Notre-Dame rising high above the banks, and the stern façade of the Conciergerie, once Paris's most notorious prison. In the evening, lighting gives the island an almost magical glow. On foot, the Île de la Cité's charms may be harder to appreciate at first, thanks to the heavy traffic, frequent police sirens and seemingly impenetrable stream of tourists. But persevere and you'll be rewarded with some of Paris's key sights.

## HIGHLIGHTS

### KEY MONUMENTS

The Île de la Cité shelters three of Paris's most historic buildings—Notre-Dame (see pages 137–141), the Conciergerie (see pages 89–91) and Sainte-Chapelle (see page158–160). The most famous is Notre-Dame cathedral, but it is worth fitting all three into your visit. The eerie Gothic halls of the Conciergerie contrast wonderfully with the brightness of nearby Sainte-Chapelle, which in turn seems less intimate than Notre-Dame, despite its smaller size.

*The ornate gates of the Palais de Justice*

### THE QUIETER SIDE

When you have ticked off the key sights, there are quieter squares where you can relax and enjoy the views. The grassy square Jean XXIII is a good spot to sit and admire Notre-Dame, while square de l'Île de France, at the island's eastern tip, gives lovely views of the Seine and the Île St-Louis (see page 98). It is also home to the Mémorial des Martyrs de la Déportation (see page 107).

**Don't miss** The flower market in place Louis Lépine (see page 192) sells anything from delicate blooms to trees.

## BACKGROUND

A Celtic tribe called the Parisii settled here in around 250BC. The Romans arrived 200 years later, building the town of Lutetia, which expanded onto the Left Bank. They built a governor's palace and fortress on the western side of the Île de la Cité. In AD508 the king of the Franks made the island his capital, and in the Middle Ages it again became a seat of political power, gaining a royal palace (now the Palais de Justice and Conciergerie). Much of the island was cleared in the 19th century during Baron Haussmann's re-drawing of Paris. Today, it is no longer a political power base, but it retains the Palais de Justice (the Law Courts) and the Préfecture de Police. The island is also the official heart of the city—distances from Paris to the rest of France are measured from the bronze star in the square in front of Notre-Dame.

*A dazzling display at the flower market*

*Strolling past the Patrick Allain florist on the rue St-Louis-en-Île*

## ÎLE ST-LOUIS

68 P8•Île St-Louis, 75004 Pont Marie, Sully Morland 67, 86, 87 A selection

This leafy island sits discreetly behind the more conspicuous Île de la Cité. Visitors pack its main road, the narrow rue St-Louis-en-l'Île, to browse in the shops and sample the famous ice cream at Maison Berthillon (*closed Mon, Tue and Aug*). Architect Louis Le Vau designed many of the elegant town houses on the tiny island in the 17th century. He was so pleased with the result he decided to live there himself. **Don't miss** You'll get wonderful views of Notre-Dame from the western tip of the island.

## INSTITUT DE FRANCE

67 L7•23 quai de Conti, 75006 01 44 41 44 41 Entry by guided tour only: Sat, Sun, public hols, 10.30, 3; advance booking obligatory, tel: 01 44 41 44 35 Adult €3.10 Pont Neuf, Odéon, Louvre-Rivoli 24, 27, 58, 70 www.institut-de-france.fr

The Institut de France, with its striking cupola, has a prime position on the Left Bank. The building was designed in 1663 by Louis Le Vau and financed by Cardinal Mazarin, who wanted a college for provincial students. The college closed in 1790 and in 1805 Napoleon transferred the Institut de France to the building. The Institut, founded in 1795, aims to protect the arts, literature and the sciences and is made up of five Académies: Inscriptions et Belles-Lettres, Sciences, Beaux-Arts, Sciences Morales et Politiques and the prestigious Française. The Académie Française, founded in 1635, is limited to 40 members. Its rule over the standards of the French language is still very real and is embodied in the *Dictionnaire de la Langue Française.*

# INSTITUT DU MONDE ARABE

**A must for anyone interested in the history of the Arabic-Islamic world and for fans of contemporary architecture.**

| RATINGS | |
|---|---|
| Cultural interest | ●●●● |
| Historic interest | ●●● |
| Photo stops (exterior and views) | ●●● |

68 N8•1 rue des Fossés-St-Bernard, 75005 01 40 51 38 45 Tue–Sun 10–6 (last entry 5.15). Library: Tue–Sat 1–8 (closes at 6 Jul–Aug) Adult €4, child €3, under 12 free Jussieu, Cardinal-Lemoine, Sully-Morland 24, 63, 67, 86, 87, 89 Guided tours (in French): Tue–Fri 3pm, Sat–Sun 2pm and 4pm. Tours last 1 hour 30 minutes, €6.10

Le Ziryab panoramic restaurant (9th floor) Café Littéraire (ground floor) and Le Moucharabieh cafeteria (9th floor)

Shop (ground floor) selling books, CDs, ceramics and gifts

www.imarabe.org (in French, packed with information on the museum, library, exhibitions and events at the Institute; also information on Arab countries )

In 1974, France and 19 Arab countries decided to create the Institut du Monde Arabe (the Arab World Institute). The foundation document was signed in 1980 and the institute opened on the Left Bank in 1987. The stunning aluminium and glass building was dreamed up by a group of architects—Jean Nouvel, Pierre Soria, Gilbert Lezenes and Architecture Studio. Its design combines modern materials with the spirit of traditional Arab architecture. The southern façade consists of 240 identical metal light-sensitive screens, adjusted every hour, which electronically filter the sunlight as it enters the building. Their design is taken from carved wooden screens called *moucharabiehs,* used in buildings from Morocco to southeast Asia. The high-speed transparent lifts alone make a visit worthwhile, so let them take you to the ninth floor, where you can admire the river views from the terrace or eat in the elegant restaurant.

The entrance to the museum is on the seventh floor and the displays move chronologically to the sixth and fourth floors, with over 600 items on view. From Spain to India and from prehistoric times to the 19th century, the ceramics, bronzes, ivories, astrolabes, calligraphy, tapestries, textiles and carpets of this collection reflect the brilliance of the Arabic-Islamic civilization. There are also temporary exhibitions, including displays of photography and contemporary art.

The Institute is more than a museum. It houses a facility for Arab language and civilization, a cinema, an auditorium, a library of more than 50,000 books, research facilities and an audiovisual venue, and it publishes two magazines. Events include lectures, music, dance and drama performances, creative workshops and educational activities.

*Metal screens filter the sunlight at the Institut du Monde Arabe*

# Les Invalides

**Learn more about Napoleon Bonaparte and his military campaigns in the absorbing army museum.**
**Then see the emperor's tomb in the stunning, golden-domed Église du Dôme.**

*The imposing façade of Les Invalides, 195m (640ft) in length*

*The Church of the Dome, resting place of Napoleon*

## SEEING LES INVALIDES

On entering the stately grounds of Les Invalides you'll be following in the footsteps of many a military hero, including General de Gaulle and Winston Churchill. The august building started life as a hospital for wounded soldiers but now houses an army museum. The adjacent Église du Dôme shelters Napoleon's tomb. Unless you are a particular devotee of war history, you may be tempted to skip the Army Museum and head straight to Napoleon's tomb. Don't. The museum is one of the largest of its kind in the world and among the extensive collections of weapons, armour, flags, uniforms and paintings are some real gems. The museum is split into three wings—east, south and west—although renovation work means the west wing is likely to be closed until summer 2005. For the poignant World War II exhibition head to the south wing; to see the Musée des Plans-Reliefs, with its huge scale models of French towns, go to the fourth floor of the east wing. The entrance to the Église du Dôme is at the front of the church, on the south side of the complex.

## HIGHLIGHTS

### REMINDERS OF NAPOLEON

As you would expect, Napoleon Bonaparte features prominently in the Musée de l'Armée and you can see his frock coat, hat, coronation saddle and even his actual horse, Vizir (not for the squeamish). There is a re-creation of the room where he died in exile on the island of St-Helena and a variety of paintings, including Paul Delaroche's portrait of the emperor looking unusually undignified just before his abdication in Fontainebleau in 1814.

### WORLD WAR II EXHIBITION

Don't miss the World War II exhibition, which moves chronologically through the war years over three floors of the south wing. The evocative, sometimes chilling, displays use film footage, photos and day-to-day objects to convey the horrors of the war and the bravery of those who fought against Hitler. Exhibits include a BBC microphone, French Resistance equipment and a cheerful red, white and blue dress worn during the French Liberation celebrations.

**RATINGS**

| | |
|---|---|
| Good for kids | ● ● ● |
| Historic interest | ● ● ● ● |
| Photo stops (exterior) | ● ● ● |

**BASICS**

66 J7•Hôtel National des Invalides, 129 rue de Grenelle, 75007
01 44 42 37 72
Daily 10–6, Apr–end Sep (also 6–7pm, mid-Jun to mid-Sep, for the Église du Dôme); daily 10–5, rest of year. Closed 1 Jan, 1 May, 1 Nov, 25 Dec and 1st Mon of each month. (The west wing is closed for renovation until summer 2005)
Adult €7, under 18 free
La-Tour-Maubourg, Invalides, Varenne
28, 63, 69, 82, 83, 93
RER line C, Invalides
Selling salads, pizza and sandwiches
Giftshop/bookshop
€12
Guided tours available

www.invalides.org (in French and English; lots of practical and historical information)

**TIPS**

- The best way to appreciate the grandeur of Les Invalides is to approach the site from the Pont Alexandre III (see page 151).
- The Army Museum is busiest between 11am and 1pm.
- As an antidote to Les Invalides's war focus, unwind in the nearby gardens of the Musée Rodin (see page 136).

**THE COUR D'HONNEUR**

It is worth spending a few minutes admiring the architecture of this central courtyard. The arcades that surround it were thriving thoroughfares during Les Invalides's heyday in the late 17th and early 18th centuries. During this time the site was a mini-town, home to around 1,500 soldiers. At times demand for places was so high that only soldiers with 20 years' service were admitted. On arrival they were measured for their blue uniform and black hat, and issued with a comb, knife and wooden spoon. They were not allowed tobacco or to leave the site without permission, and punishments for wrongdoing included being placed on a water-only diet. There was a hospital on site, staffed by almost 40 nurses. From the courtyard, look up to the first floor and you'll see the small grey doors that led to the dormitories. The soldiers ate in dining halls surrounded by paintings of battle. Today Les Invalides is still home to around 100 war veterans.

## ÉGLISE DU DÔME

The golden dome of this church rises 107m (350ft) above the ground, a glistening monument to two of France's most influential and charismatic rulers, Louis XIV and Napoleon. The emperor's tomb sits in a grandiose crypt directly below the dome. He died in exile on the island of St-Helena in 1821 but his remains were brought back to France in 1840. It took another 21 years to create his mausoleum and the task was not without controversy as it involved excavating part of the church. Napoleon's remains are encased in six coffins, inside a red porphyry sarcophagus, set on an immense granite base. The twelve statues guarding the tomb represent his military campaigns. Behind the Église du Dôme stands the Soldier's Church, reached from the Cour d'Honneur. It was originally designed by Jules Hardouin-Mansart as part of a vast church with two separate entrances, one for the king (on the south side of what is now the Église du Dôme) and one for soldiers (on the north side of the Soldier's Church). In time, the two churches became separate entities, known respectively as the Église du Dôme and St-Louis-des-Invalides.

*Looking across the Cour d'Honneur to the golden dome of the Église du Dôme (far left)*

*Napoleon's tomb (left, inset), in the crypt of the Église du Dôme*

*Les Invalides looks no less commanding at night*

### BACKGROUND

Pompous, severe and authoritarian, Les Invalides was actually built to house wounded and elderly soldiers. Louis XIV was thinking of others for once when he commissioned Libéral Bruant to design the imposing building, with its 195m (640ft) façade. The first soldiers arrived in 1674 and were welcomed by the king himself. It took another 32 years before the gold-encrusted Église du Dôme was completed. Bruant's design for the church never got off the ground and in 1676 the king approved new plans by Versailles architect Jules Hardouin-Mansart. The church, dedicated to St. Louis, was finally completed in 1706. Its inauguration was a grand affair, attended by Louis XIV.

### ÉGLISE DU DÔME FLOORPLAN

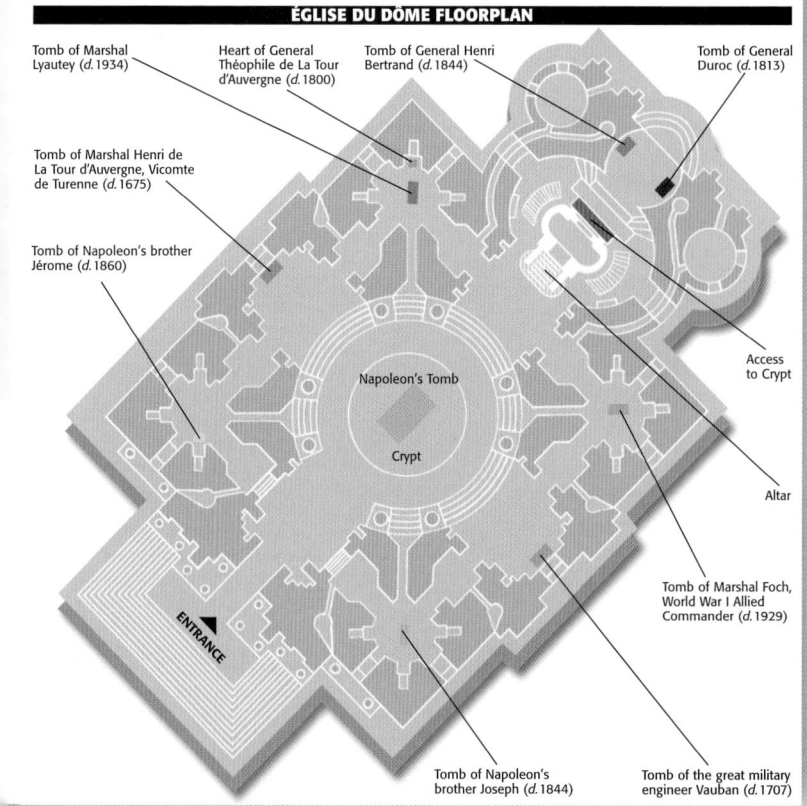

# Jardin du Luxembourg

**One of Paris's most popular parks, with a boating pond, children's activities, fabulous flower displays and an Italianate palace. A great place to escape the bustle of the nearby Latin Quarter and St-Germain-des-Prés.**

*A donkey ride is just one of the children's activities available…*

*…sailing model boats on the pond is another*

*The French Senate meets in the Palais du Luxembourg*

| RATINGS | |
|---|---|
| Good for kids | ●●●● |
| Photo stops | ●●● |
| Value for money | FREE |
| Walkability | ●●●● |

*Birds prefer the statues to the green metal chairs!*

## SEEING THE JARDIN DU LUXEMBOURG

The Jardin du Luxembourg, 24ha (60 acres), forms an attractive southern boundary to St-Germain-des-Prés and the Latin Quarter. Here, students come to relax after lectures and visitors find some breathing space between sightseeing. There are entrances all around the park and wide paths lead to the main attractions, including the octagonal pond and the Théâtre du Luxembourg. Plenty of seats and refreshments are available. The Palais du Luxembourg, home of the French Senate, is on the northern edge. Book ahead for guided tours.

## HIGHLIGHTS

### RELAXING IN SCENIC SURROUNDINGS

The park contains some of the most beautiful public flower displays in Paris and is landscaped in an appealing mixture of French, English and Italian styles. The focal point is a large octagonal pond, elegantly encircled by stone urns and statues of French queens and other notable women. In good weather the park is full of Parisians sunbathing, playing *boules* or chess, or jogging along the shady paths. Other attractions include tennis courts, a bandstand and even a bee-keeping school. The Musée du Luxembourg, in the former orangery, stages temporary exhibitions. Despite the crowds, the park is a welcome respite from the hectic Paris streets. But there is no forgetting you are in the heart of the city—the Eiffel Tower and Tour Montparnasse loom up on the horizon.

### PALAIS DU LUXEMBOURG

The Italianate Palais du Luxembourg is a reminder of the park's Florentine origins and is now home to the French Senate. It was commissioned for Marie de Medici in the 17th century and during the Revolution was commandeered as a prison.

*Feeding the birds*

## ACTIVITIES FOR CHILDREN

Children are well catered for, with donkey rides (during French school holidays only), puppet shows in the Théâtre du Luxembourg (Wednesday, Saturday and Sunday from 2pm) and the usual swings and slides. They can also try their hand at being skippers by renting remote-control model yachts to sail on the pond.

## STATUES

The Fontaine Médicis is a popular romantic spot to the east of the Palais du Luxembourg. The grotto was commissioned by Marie de Medici in the 17th century and sculptures include allegorical characters representing the rivers Seine and Rhône, as well as the queen's coats of arms. Later, a sculpture showing the angry Polyphemus preparing to throw a rock at the innocent lovers Acis and Galatea was added. At the western end of the park you can see a miniature Statue of Liberty.

## BACKGROUND

**Bored with the Louvre, Marie de Medici commissioned the gardens and palace in 1615, hoping for a reminder of her native Florence. She bought the land from Duke François of Luxembourg (hence the park's name) and asked architect Salomon de Brosse to use the Pitti Palace as inspiration. Work finished in the mid-1620s but Marie, widow of Henri IV, did not have long to enjoy her creation. She was exiled from France by the powerful Cardinal Richelieu and died penniless in Cologne. A petition of 12,000 signatures failed to save parts of the gardens from Baron Haussmann's development plans in the mid-19th century, but the remaining greenery continued to be a refuge for artists, writers and philosophers, including Ernest Hemingway, Victor Hugo and Jean-Paul Sartre.**

## BASICS

67 L9•rue de Vaugirard/rue de Médicis/boulevard St-Michel, 75006

Park: 01 42 34 23 89.
Senate: 01 42 34 20 00. Musée du Luxembourg 01 42 34 25 95

Times vary depending on season; generally dawn to dusk.

Free

Odéon

21, 27, 38, 58, 82, 83, 84, 85, 89

RER line B, Luxembourg

Open-air cafés, kiosk restaurant

Kiosk

Guided tours of the Palais du Luxembourg on the first Saturday of each month. To book a place call 01 44 54 19 49. To sit in on a Senate debate call 01 42 34 20 01

An oak tree dedicated to the victims of September 11, 2001, has been planted near the Statue of Liberty

www.senat.fr (in French, English, German and Spanish, with historical information and photos)

*The surprisingly contemporary fountain in the Cour d'Honneur (above). Strolling through the arcades (left)*

# JARDIN DU PALAIS ROYAL

**An oasis of calm only a few steps (and a million miles) from the bustle of the city.**

| RATINGS | |
|---|---|
| Good for kids | ●●● |
| Photo stops | ●●● |
| Specialist shopping | ●●● |
| Value for money | FREE |

**BASICS**

67 M6•place du Palais-Royal, 75001 (entrance to the gardens is through an arch to the left of the Palais Royal)

Daily 7am–11pm, Jun–end Aug; 7am–10.15pm, Apr–end May; 7am–9.30pm, Sep; 7.30am–8.30pm, Oct–Mar

Free

Palais-Royal/Musée du Louvre

21, 48, 67, 69, 72, 81

Restaurants and tea rooms around the outside, including Muscade tea room (see page 271).

Plenty of small shops in the arcades

This tranquil garden is the perfect place to recharge your batteries after a visit to the Louvre. The flower-filled enclave is separated from the 21st century by a cordon of handsome 18th-century arcades. These shelter traditional *salons de thé* and quirky shops selling anything from art, jewellery and clothes to pipes, silverware and model soldiers. In good weather the gardens are full of Parisians resting, reading and playing *boules*. The flower beds are vibrant, and a central statue and refreshing fountain add to the elegant calm. Children come to roller skate around the rather incongruous grey-and-white striped mini-columns in the Cour d'Honneur, a controversial 1986 addition by artist Daniel Buren. The courtyard's sleek water features blend more easily with the rest of the garden.

### THE PALACE

The Palais Royal was commissioned by Louis XIII's advisor, Cardinal Richelieu, in the 17th century and was originally called the Palais-Cardinal. Molière and his troupe of actors used to perform in the Théâtre du Petit Cardinal, which once stood at the southern corner of the palace. It was here in 1673 that the illustrious playwright fell ill, ironically during a production of *Le Malade Imaginaire* (The Hypochondriac). He died a few hours later. The nearby Comédie Française still stages his plays today. Louis XIV spent part of his childhood in the Palais Royal and authors Colette and Jean Cocteau lived within the grounds. Now the building houses the French Ministry of Culture and is not open to the public.

### UPRISING

The arcades and apartments surrounding the palace garden were constructed in the 18th century. Only a few years later, on 12 July 1789, Camille Desmoulins made a passionate speech in the garden that sparked the uprising in Bastille two days later (see page 33).

*There are plenty of seats by the pond if you feel like taking a break*



# JARDIN DES TUILERIES

**A chic park offering great views of Paris's most famous landmarks.**

Dominated at one end by the hectic place de la Concorde and at the other by the mighty Louvre, this isn't one of those parks that lets you forget you're in the heart of the city. But what the elegant, French-style grounds lack in seclusion they make up for in photo opportunities, with marvellous views of the Louvre, Eiffel Tower, Arc de Triomphe, Musée d'Orsay and Egyptian obelisk. The park, once considered the best-kept in Europe, runs alongside the Seine.

## ART AND NATURE

The grandest way to enter is through the gilded gates at the Concorde end. This brings you to the first of two large ponds, balanced at either end of the park—ideal for relaxing with a book. Two art galleries stand on terraces either side of this first pond, the Jeu de Paume (see page 106) and the Orangerie (see page 142). Look out for Henry Moore's *Reclining Figure* (1951), which sits on the steps leading up to the Orangerie. Follow the wide central avenue towards the Louvre and the gravel of the western half of the park gradually gives way to grass and well-tended flower beds. You'll pass allegorical statues, open-air cafés and children's playgrounds. All around people are relaxing. At the other end of the park, the neoclassical Arc du Carrousel acts as a symbolic gateway to the Louvre and is also the first arch in Paris's *Grand Axis*, the imaginary straight line linking the Louvre, the Arc de Triomphe and the Grande Arche.

## ITALIAN ORIGINS

The park was the inspiration of Catherine de Medici, who wanted an Italian-style garden to complement the Tuileries Palace, built in 1564. Lavish balls, concerts and fireworks ensured her garden became a key social venue. The park as we know it today dates from 1649, when Louis XIV asked his preferred landscape gardener, André Le Nôtre, to redesign it in the formal French style. He added the central avenue, as well as two raised walkways running along either side, and the garden soon became a fashionable promenading area. The palace went up in smoke at the hands of the Communards in 1871 but the garden survived. After years of neglect and pollution in the 20th century, it received a makeover in time for the start of the 21st century.

**RATINGS**

| | |
|---|---|
| Good for kids | ●●●● |
| Photo stops | ●●● |
| Value for money | FREE |
| Walkability | ●●●● |

**BASICS**

- 67 K6•Place de la Concorde, 75001
- 01 40 20 90 43
- Daily 7am–9pm, Apr–end Sep; 7.30am–7pm, rest of year
- Free
- Tuileries, Concorde
- 24, 68, 72, 73, 84, 94
- Open-air cafés
- Bookshop at Concorde end
- 
- No dogs allowed

**TIPS**

- Children can rent model yachts to sail on the pond at the Louvre end of the park.
- Free guided tours take place during the summer months. For more information see the notice boards or call 01 49 26 07 59.

*A sculpture of Balzac by Auguste Rodin*

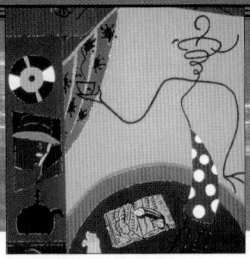

*You'll find both modern and traditional tapestries at Gobelins*

*The house where Victor Hugo once lived is now a museum*



## JEU DE PAUME

67 K6•Jeu de Paume, 1 place de la Concorde, 75008 ☎ 01 47 03 12 50 Tue 12–9.30; Wed–Fri 12–7; Sat–Sun 10–7. Concorde 24, 42, 52, 72, 73, 84, 94 Adult €6, child €4.50 ? Opening hours and prices are likely to change when the Centre National de la Photographie moves in

The illustrious Jeu de Paume started life as an indoor tennis court, metamorphosed into a world-famous art gallery, then lost its prize exhibits to the Musée d'Orsay. Since 1991 it has hosted contemporary art exhibitions, but there are plans to make it part of the Centre National de la Photographie in summer 2004.

The airy, neoclassical building, idyllically located in the Jardin des Tuileries (see page 105), was commissioned by Napoleon III as an indoor court for *réal* (royal) tennis, played with the *paume* (palm) of the hand. When lawn tennis took over in popularity the court was used for art exhibitions and after World War II it became one of the world's finest Impressionist museums. Its doors closed in 1986, after the exodus of its rich collection to the Musée d'Orsay.

## MAISON DE BALZAC

321 F7•47 rue Raynouard, 75016 ☎ 01 55 74 41 80 Tue–Sun 10–6. Closed public hols Free (except temporary exhibitions) Passy, La Muette 52, 70, 72 www.paris.fr

The writer Honoré de Balzac (1799–1850) lived in this pretty house on the Passy hillside from 1840 until 1847. Pursued by debtors, he lay low here using a false identity. It was also here, in a creative flow that often lasted all night, that Balzac penned some of his masterpieces, including *La Comédie Humaine*, *La Cousine Bette* and *Le Cousin Pons*. The house is now an intimate museum dedicated to his life and works. Many original editions, illustrations and manuscripts are on show and there is a library devoted to his works. You can also visit temporary exhibitions.

## MAISON EUROPÉENNE DE LA PHOTOGRAPHIE

68 P7•5–7 rue de Fourcy, 75004 ☎ 01 44 78 75 00 Wed–Sun 11–8 (last entry 7.30; closed during changeover of exhibitions) St-Paul 67, 69, 76, 96 In basement Adult €5, child €2.50, under 8 free; free to all Wed 5–8 www.mep-fr.org

The Maison Européenne de la Photographie is a stylish venue for dynamic exhibitions of contemporary photography. The galleries spread over five floors of the 18th-century Hôtel Hénault de Cantobre, as well as in a new wing built especially for the venue, which opened in 1996. A 100-seat auditorium screens films related to the exhibitions, and there is also a library and video-viewing facilities.

## MAISON DE VERRE

67 L8•31 rue St-Guillaume, 75007 Visits by written application only Rue du Bac 39, 63

The Maison de Verre, in St-Germain-des-Prés, is a temple to the purity of modernism. This extraordinary house was built between 1928 and 1932 by the art deco architect Pierre Chareau. Walls of glass bricks with steel frames and an airy geometric interior are the innovations that replaced a 17th-century town house. You need to apply in writing to tour inside the house.

## MAISON DE VICTOR HUGO

68 P7•6 place des Vosges, 75004 ☎ 01 42 72 10 16 Tue–Sun 10–6 Bastille, St-Paul 29 Permanent collections free. Temporary exhibitions: adult €5.50, child €2.50 www.paris.fr

Quirky Maison de Victor Hugo conjures up a vivid impression of literary life in 19th-century Paris. It is in the Hôtel de Rohan-Guéménée, where Victor Hugo lived from 1832 to 1848 with his wife and four children. He wrote part of his world-famous novel *Les Misérables* here, and met with fellow writers such as Alexandre Dumas and Alphonse de Lamartine.

As you climb the stone steps to the upper floors you'll see a series of old posters advertising theatrical productions of *Les Misérables*.

In the permanent exhibition on the second floor, the rooms are laid out to echo the interiors of Hugo's various homes, including one on the Channel Island of Guernsey, where he spent time in political exile. Memorabilia include a bust of Hugo by Auguste Rodin and furniture from actress Juliette Drouet's room in Guernsey, some of it carved and decorated by Hugo. There is also a reconstruction of the room where Hugo died in 1885.

Temporary exhibitions are staged on the first floor and there is a library on the third floor, although access to this is by appointment only.

**Don't miss** The luxurious wallpaper alone makes a visit to the permanent exhibitions on the second floor worthwhile. The *salon chinois* (Chinese room) is also striking.

*One of the many interesting shops in the Marais district*

*Browsing in the Marché aux Puces de St-Ouen*

## MANUFACTURE DES GOBELINS

✚ 331 N11•42 avenue des Gobelins, 75013 ☎ 01 44 54 19 33 ⏲ Visit by guided tour only (in French): Tue–Thu at 2 and 2.45. Arrive 10 minutes before the start of the tour. Closed public hols ₩ Adult €8, child €6, under 7 free Ⓜ Les Gobelins 🚌 27, 47, 83, 91

Originally a dyeworks set up by the Gobelin brothers in the 15th century, the Manufacture des Gobelins attracted the attention of Colbert, Louis XIV's astute minister, and by 1662 it had become the royal tapestry factory. It rapidly expanded to include furniture and carpet workshops. Much of the interior decoration of Versailles was woven, carved or inlaid here.

Today you see the centuries-old looms clicking away, worked by expert weavers. The 90-minute guided tour also takes in some of the workshops of the famous Beauvais tapestry and Savonnerie carpet factories.

## LE MARAIS

✚ 68 P7•Le Marais Ⓜ St-Paul, Rambuteau, Hôtel de Ville 🚌 29, 69, 75, 76, 96

Stretching west to east between Les Halles and the Bastille and north to south from the place de la République to the Seine, the Marais district has a beguiling combination of history, ornate architecture and trendy chic boutiques, bars, restaurants and galleries. The area was once an expanse of low-lying marshland, hence its name *marais* (marsh). Now it is home to cobblestone courtyards, medieval streets, beautiful mansions, a bustling Jewish quarter, and the oldest square in Paris—place des Vosges (see page 150).

During the 17th century aristocrats competed here to build the most elegant mansion. The area subsequently fell into neglect until, in 1962, Culture Minister-cum-writer André Malraux pointed out the historic value of numerous crumbling monuments, and a restoration scheme began.

Today it is impossible to wander through the Marais without stumbling across architectural masterpieces, even if you can only admire them from their courtyards. Many of these mansions (called *hôtels*) now house museums, including the Musée Picasso (see page 135), the Musée Carnavalet (see pages 114–115) and the Musée d'Art et d'Histoire du Judaïsme (see page 112). Other mansions to look out for include the Hôtel de Soubise (see pages 116–117), the Hôtel de Sully in rue St-Antoine and the Hôtel de Rohan in the rue Vieille-du-Temple.

**Don't miss** Enjoy a leisurely drink in the place des Vosges

## MARCHÉ AUX PUCES DE ST-OUEN

✚ 69 off M1•Porte de Clignancourt, 75018 (from the Métro station turn right onto avenue de la Porte de Clignancourt, past the tacky unofficial stands. Walk under the flyover and the market is on your left) ☎ 01 58 61 22 90 ⏲ Sat–Mon 9.30–6 (some stands open earlier) Ⓜ Porte de Clignancourt 🚌 56, 60, 85, 95, 137, 166, 255 🍴 Cafés and restaurants on rue des Rosiers ₩ Free ? Beware of pickpockets

www.parispuces.com

Pick up a piece of bygone Paris—or a cheap imitation—at what claims to be the world's largest antiques market, spread over 7ha (17 acres) north of Montmartre, just beyond the *périphérique*. Even if you have no intention of buying, you'll find an Aladdin's Cave of fascinating objects, ranging from Louis XV mirrors and luxurious 19th-century chandeliers to wacky 1970s furniture.

Don't be put off by the cluster of tacky stands along the approach to the market. Walk swiftly past them, under the flyover, then decide which of the 13 official markets you'll tackle first. There are around 2,000 shops and stalls to choose from. Watch out for pickpockets and remember that prices fluctuate according to the weather, so be prepared to haggle. Sunday afternoons are particularly busy. If you prefer breathing space, arrive early.

## MÉMORIAL DES MARTYRS DE LA DÉPORTATION

✚ 68 N8•Square de l'Île de France, Île de la Cité, 75004 ☎ 01 46 33 87 56 ⏲ Daily 10–12, 2–7 (2–5 in winter) Ⓜ Cité 🚌 24, 47 Ⓜ St-Michel-Notre-Dame 🍴 Plenty on Île de la Cité ₩ Free

This haunting monument commemorates the 200,000 French people who died in concentration camps during the Holocaust. The roof of the memorial sits in a peaceful grassy square on the eastern tip of the Île de la Cité, from where you can enjoy views of the river and the Île St-Louis.

By contrast, walk down the narrow staircase into the shadowy crypt and you are limited to mere glimpses of the Seine through iron bars, a chilling reminder of the incarceration experienced by the prisoners. A long, dark tunnel leading from the crypt is studded by 200,000 fragments of shining glass, one for each person who died. A light at the end symbolizes hope. This is no ordinary, lifeless monument—it gives an unsettling reminder of the horrors of World War II.

# Montmartre

**A village within a city, with cobbled streets, quirky museums, stunning views and the mighty Sacré-Cœur basilica.**
**Follow in the footsteps of artists Toulouse-Lautrec, Pierre-Auguste Renoir and Pablo Picasso… and a headless saint.**

*For the price of a Métro ticket, the funicular (above) will save you a lengthy climb up to Sacré-Cœur*

*A traditional merry-go-round (right inset)*

| RATINGS | |
|---|---|
| Good for kids | ● ● ● |
| Historic interest | ● ● ● ● |
| Photo stops | ● ● ● ● ● |

**TIPS**

- Le Petit Train de Montmartre (Promotrain) offers a 40-minute tour of Montmartre's main sights, starting from place Blanche and including a stop at place du Tertre (10–7; until midnight at weekends and in summer; adult €5, child €3). The Montmartrain runs a similar circuit.

- Montmartre's cemetery (see page 87) is well worth a visit to search out the graves of Hector Berlioz, Jacques Offenbach, Émile Zola and other composers and writers.

## SEEING MONTMARTRE

The hilltop village of Montmartre, to the north of the city core, has a split personality. There are teeming tourist traps, including place du Tertre and the front steps of Sacré-Cœur, but venture a few minutes off the beaten track and you'll find quiet cobbled streets, white-washed cottages and all the atmosphere of a small village. The Métro will take you to the outskirts of the district, but to reach the key sights you'll have to either walk or take the Montmartrobus, which runs a circular route from place Pigalle, past Sacré-Cœur, and north to the Métro station Jules Joffrin. You can avoid the daunting walk up the steps to Sacré-Cœur by taking the funicular from square Willette (costing one Métro ticket each way).

## HIGHLIGHTS

### TOURIST MONTMARTRE

Montmartre is crowned by the Basilique du Sacré-Cœur (see pages 154–157), a dazzling white neo-Byzantine creation whose domes and turrets look stunning against a blue sky. There are sweeping views over Paris from its front steps. The nearby place du Tertre (literally 'Hillock Square') is Paris's highest point and swarms with visitors and street artists. The restaurant La Mère Catherine, at number 6, was founded in 1793 and was said to have given rise to the name *bistro*. Legend has it that in 1814 Russian troops, who had become regulars at the restaurant, would shout *bystro* (quickly) to hurry along their food (see page 35). You can sometimes try Montmartre's own wine here, made from grapes grown in the area's only remaining vineyard, on rue des Saules.

### VILLAGE MONTMARTRE

Place du Tertre is tourist Montmartre at its peak, but only a few minutes' walk away are quieter streets, including rue de l'Abreuvoir, rue des Saules and rue Girardon. Make sure you save some time to wander through this less showy side of Montmartre (see walk, pages 226–227), where you'll find cobblestones, romantic tree-lined steps and even two windmills. It's hard to remember you're still in France's capital. At 22 rue des Saules is the tiny but legendary cabaret venue Au Lapin Agile, once frequented by Picasso and still providing entertainment. Nearby, at 12 rue Cortot, is the Musée de Montmartre (see page 126), where you can learn more about the history of the area. A short walk away, off rue Lepic, is one of Montmartre's two remaining windmills, the Moulin de la Galette, built in 1622 and formerly known as Le Moulin du Blute-fin. Legend claims that one of its millers, Pierre-Charles Debray, was strung up on its sails in 1814 for trying to stop the invading Cossacks, although it is more likely he was killed by a stray bullet. Later in the 19th century the Debray family converted the mill into a popular open-air dance hall, providing inspiration for many artists, including Renoir and Vincent Van Gogh. Nearby is the Moulin Radet, now part of a restaurant called Moulin de la Galette.

*A decorative shopfront (above)*

*A street artist (left) in place du Tertre*

## ARTISTS' MONTMARTRE

Montmartre earned an almost mythical status at the end of the 19th century, thanks to its community of artists and its raunchy nightlife. Toulouse-Lautrec immortalized scenes of dancing girls at the world-famous cabaret venue Moulin Rouge (see page 111), while Renoir captured the exuberance of a ball at the Moulin de la Galette. Twentieth-century artists who converged on Montmartre included Picasso and Georges Braque, who gave birth to Cubism in the Bateau-Lavoir studios, on place Emile-Goudeau. The original timber building burned down in 1970 and was replaced by a concrete studio, now closed to the public. To view some 20th-century art head for the surreal Espace Montmartre—Salvador Dalí (see page 92).

## BACKGROUND

**Montmartre started life as a place of worship, a far cry from its later hedonistic reputation. The Romans built a temple to Mercury here, naming the hill Mons Mercurii. It was later called Mont des Martyrs, following the murder of Paris's first bishop, St. Denis, in the 3rd century AD. He was said to have picked up his head and taken it to a nearby fountain to wash away the blood, before collapsing (see his statue in square Suzanne-Buisson). Montmartre's religious connection was renewed in the 12th century, when Louis VI founded a Benedictine Abbey there. With monks around, the area was soon filled with vineyards. By the end of the 17th century around 30 windmills stood on the hill and Montmartre prospered with the production of wine, flour and gypsum (plaster of Paris) for the city below. Gypsum quarrying stopped in the early 19th century because the hill was in danger of collapsing. Montmartre became known for its decadent cabarets at the end of the 19th century. Nowadays the district is no longer the hub of Paris's nightlife, but visitors still come to La Butte (the mound) for a taste of its Bohemian past.**

### BASICS

69 M2•75018

Anvers, Abbesses, Blanche, Lamarck Caulaincourt

Montmartrobus; 30, 54, 68, 74, 80 have stops around the edge of Montmartre

La Maison Rose, rue de l'Abreuvoir, 01 42 57 66 75 (open 12–3 and 7–11; closed Wed lunch and Tue and Thu dinner). There are plenty of restaurants and cafés in the area, many of them very touristy

A selection

www.montmartrenet.com (in French and English; packed with history, practical information and photos)

*Café-culture still reigns in Montparnasse*

## MONTPARNASSE

329 K10•Montparnasse
Montparnasse-Bienvenüe, Vavin, Edgar Quinet 28, 58, 82, 88, 89, 91, 92, 94, 95, 96

Montparnasse was a popular district with artists and writers in the early 20th century, attracting the likes of Amedeo Modigliani, Marc Chagall and Ernest Hemingway. Legendary meeting places (including La Coupole, see page 266) still exist, haunted by shadows of literary and artistic giants from the 1920s and 1930s.

Although Montparnasse's main boulevards have lost some of their charm, sacrificed to the whims of consumerism, the area's many theatres, cafés, cinemas and cabarets remain lively.

Tour Montparnasse (see page 170) looms over the district and you get wonderful views from the public gallery on the 56th floor. The tower, 209m (685ft) high, was built in the early 1970s as part of a huge urban development project. Across a windy esplanade is the Gare Montparnasse, one of the most confusing stations in Paris.

Years of hectic redevelopment in Montparnasse have replaced atmospheric narrow streets with uninspiring apartment blocks. Some corners are worth seeking out, however, such as 16 rue Antoine Bourdelle, where you can visit the Musée Bourdelle (*Tue–Sun 10–5.40*). The museum focuses on the sculptor Émile-Antoine Bourdelle (1861–1929), a former pupil of Auguste Rodin, who once lived and worked in this picturesque house.

Also worth a visit is the Cimetière du Montparnasse (see page 87) where many notable former residents are buried, including Jean-Paul Sartre and Guy de Maupassant.

THE SIGHTS

# LA MOSQUÉE

**A gem of 20th-century European Islamic architecture, with exquisitely carved arcades and a magnificent minaret, 33m (108ft) high.**

| RATINGS | |
|---|---|
| Cultural interest | ●●●● |
| Historic interest | ●●● |
| Specialist shopping (souk) | ●●● |

68 N9•La Mosquée: place du Puits-de-l'Ermite, 75005; Hammam: 39 rue Geoffroy St-Hilaire La Mosquée: 01 45 35 97 33; Hammam: 01 43 31 18 14 La Mosquée: guided tours in French: Sat–Thu 9–12, 2–6. Hammam: Men: Tue 2–9, Sun 10–9. Women: Mon, Wed, Thu, Sat 10–9, Fri 2–9 La Mosquée: adult €3, child €2, under 7 free. Hammam: prices vary for different treatments Jussieu, Place Monge, Censier-Daubenton 47, 67, 89 Restaurant: 39 rue Geoffroy St-Hilaire *Salon de Thé*: 39 rue Geoffroy St-Hilaire Small bookshop at La Mosquée. A souk at 39 rue Geoffroy St-Hilaire sells ceramics, jewellery, bags, postcards, lampshades and other items In the Hammam www.la-mosquee.com (in French and English, includes practical information about the Hammam)

The splendid Paris Mosque is one of the Left Bank's most pleasant surprises, with its impressive square minaret and ornate decoration. It was built between 1922 and 1926, with French funds, to commemorate North African military support during World War I.

Faithful to ornate Hispano-Moorish architecture, its roofs are green tiled, its fountains are pink marbled and its doors are exquisitely carved. The grand patio was inspired by the Alhambra in Granada, Spain, and has decorative mosaics and fine cedar and eucalyptus woodwork. The finely carved arcades are also decorated with intricate mosaics. A spiritual base for Paris's Muslim community, the prayer room is exceptional for its ornamentation and fine carpets. The courtyard garden is a symbol of Muslim paradise. The Mosque is also home to a library and an Islamic teaching facility.

The rest of the Mosque complex is accessible from rue Geoffroy St-Hilaire and includes a restaurant, a *salon de thé* and the Hammam (Turkish baths). The Hammam is the perfect escape from the bustle of city life. Seated around a marble fountain, let your mind drift to exotic shores. Later, you can sit at an outdoor table in the pretty courtyard of the *salon de thé*, sipping mint tea and eating couscous. There is also a shop, reminiscent of a small souk, crammed with an array of distinctive items.

*Mosaics decorate the arcades at La Mosquée*

*A windmill in name only—the world-famous Moulin Rouge*

### MOULIN ROUGE

69 L3•82 boulevard de Clichy, 75018 ☎ 01 53 09 82 82 Shows nightly at 9pm and 11pm. Dinner at 7pm Dinner and show €130–€160. Show only €82–€92 Blanche 30, 54, 68, 74
www.moulin-rouge.com

The Moulin Rouge is the famous symbol of Montmartre. Its decadent, pleasure-seeking reputation was initially fuelled by Toulouse-Lautrec's posters and more recently by the 2001 film *Moulin Rouge*, starring Nicole Kidman and Ewan McGregor. The 'Red Windmill' was never actually a windmill but was launched as a cabaret venue in 1889. It soon became known for its saucy shows, featuring scantily-clad cancan girls who entertained an audience from all walks of life. Over the years many stars have made guest appearances, including Edith Piaf, Frank Sinatra, Liza Minnelli and Elton John. You can still see lively shows here (at a price), complete with the famous *cancaneuses* dancers.

### MUSÉE DES ARTS ET MÉTIERS

68 N6•60 rue Réaumur, 75003 ☎ 01 53 01 82 00 Tue–Sun 10–6 (also Thu 6–9.30pm). Closed public hols Arts et Métiers, Réaumur-Sébastopol 20, 38, 39, 47 Adult €6.50, under 18 free
www.arts-et-metiers.net/

Art meets science at this quirky museum, with a fascinating collection of early scientific machinery, vintage cars and mechanical toys. You can see a primitive calculating machine invented by Blaise Pascal, one of Thomas Edison's phonographs and a mechanical toy created for Marie-Antoinette. A Formula 1 racing car sits incongruously in the former chapel.

## MUSÉE DES ARTS DÉCORATIFS

**A remarkable collection of decorative arts from the Middle Ages to the present day.**

67 L6•107 rue de Rivoli, 75001 ☎ 01 44 55 57 50 Tue–Fri 11–6 (also Wed 6–9pm), Sat–Sun 10–6; last entry 30 min before closing. Closed public hols Adult €5.40, under 18 free Palais-Royal/Musée du Louvre, Tuileries 21, 27, 39, 48, 69, 72, 81, 95 Phone in advance for details of guided tours: 01 44 55 59 26 Bookshop and gift shop
www.ucad.fr

| RATINGS | |
|---|---|
| Cultural interest | ●●●● |
| Historic interest | ●●● |

The Union Centrale des Arts Décoratifs (UCAD) was founded at the end of the 19th century by a group of industrialists whose aim was to display beauty in function. Today UCAD is composed of a decorative arts library, three schools and four museums. Three of the museums, including the Musée des Arts Décoratifs, are housed in the Pavillon de Marsan and Rohan wing of the Louvre.

The Musée des Arts Décoratifs has more than 150,000 items covering almost every aspect of the decorative arts, from ceramics, glass and embroidery to wood and metalwork. Collections include the Middle Ages and Renaissance, art nouveau, art deco, modern and contemporary and a further five specialist departments: glass, toys, drawings, wallpaper and jewellery.

Owing to extensive renovations, only the Middle Ages and Renaissance galleries have been open to the public for the last few years. Temporary exhibitions are organized while work is in progress and the specialist departments can be viewed by appointment. The 17th–20th century collections are due to reopen at the end of 2004. The nine rooms of the Middle Ages and Renaissance department contain a rich collection reflecting religious art and domestic life from the 13th–16th centuries. Paintings, sculptures and furniture from churches and monasteries alternate with exquisite objects from daily life. The Galerie des Retables contains a fine collection of European altarpieces carved in wood and stone. Tapestries are on display in the Salle de la Vie Rurale dans la Tapisserie. The Salle du Maître de la Madeleine contains medieval sculptures and paintings and the Cabinet de Travail, a delightful period room, is decorated with refined marquetry panelling. The Salle des Vitraux contains French and Italian furniture, Flemish tapestries, 16th-century stained-glass and objets d'art.

*A tapestry from the museum's medieval collection (above)*

*Explore modern art and design*

## MUSÉE D'ART MODERNE DE LA VILLE DE PARIS

66 G6•11 avenue du Président Wilson, 75016 01 53 67 40 00 Closed for renovation until late 2004; then Tue–Fri 10–6, Sat–Sun 10–7 Free. Temporary exhibitions: adult €4.50, under 13 free Iéna, Alma-Marceau 32, 63, 72, 92
www.paris.fr

Temporary exhibitions of outstanding quality help keep this modern art museum within an international sphere. The collection covers Fauvism, Cubism, Surrealism, Abstraction and Nouveau Réalisme. *La Danse* (1932), a mural by Henri Matisse, hangs in a room entirely devoted to the artist.

Next door to the museum, the Palais de Tokyo houses the Centre d'Art Contemporain (see page 198).

**Don't miss** Raoul Dufy's 1937 mural *La Fée Electricité*, is a staggering 60m (197ft) by 10m (33ft).

## MUSÉE BACCARAT

66 G5•11 place des États-Unis, 75016 01 40 22 11 00 Mon–Sat 10–6. Closed public hols Boissière, Kléber 22, 30, 32, 82 Adult €3, under 18 free Giftshop Guided tours available in French, English, German and Japanese
www.baccarat.fr

Baccarat began making window-panes, mirrors and goblets in the village of Baccarat, in Lorraine, in 1764. The company fired up its first crystal kiln in 1816, and since then prestigious clients have included Louis XVIII, Tsar Nicholas II of Russia and Napoleon III. The operation moved to Paris in 1831. The museum displays around 5,000 examples of Baccarat's work.

**Don't miss** Look out for items made for the many World Fairs attended by Baccarat.

# MUSÉE D'ART ET D'HISTOIRE DU JUDAÏSME

**Discover the rich cultural heritage of the Jewish community in France and beyond**

68 N6•Hôtel de St-Aignan, 71 rue du Temple, 75003 01 53 01 86 60 Mon–Fri 11–6, Sun 10–6. Closed Saturday Rambuteau, Hôtel de Ville 29, 38, 47, 75 Café Adult €6.10, under 18 free Audioguide included in the entry price Substantial bookshop
www.mahj.org (in French only; see photos of the collections and find out about temporary exhibitions)

| RATINGS | |
|---|---|
| Cultural interest | ●●●● |
| Historic interest | ●●● |
| Specialist shopping (books) | ●●● |

This museum vividly illustrates the development of Jewish culture from the Middle Ages to the present day, in France and further afield. It also highlights the contribution members of the Jewish community have made to European life and art. The main focus is on French Jews, although you can also see items from the rest of Europe, as well as North Africa.

An audioguide, included in the entry price, directs you chronologically through the museum. Themes include the Middle Ages, the Emancipation of the Jews after the French Revolution, intellectual and artistic achievements in the 19th century and the tragedies and triumphs of the modern era. Medieval exhibits include a rare Hanukkah lamp, dating from before the expulsion of the Jews in the 14th century. Later items include a vivid Jewish marriage contract from 1752 and a 19th-century Algerian wedding outfit. Artists represented include Marc Chagall and Amedeo Modigliani. The archives of the Dreyfus Affair contain around three thousand letters, photographs, books and official documents relating to the case of French Jewish army captain, Alfred Dreyfus, who was falsely convicted of passing secrets to the Germans in 1894.

The museum opened in 1998 in the Hôtel de St-Aignan, a restored 17th-century mansion named after an early owner, the Duc de St-Aignan. The mansion became home to Jewish immigrants from Eastern Europe in the 19th century and during World War II its residents were arrested by the Germans and sent to concentration camps. Their memory is kept alive by an art installation by Christian Boltanski, called *Les habitants de l'Hôtel de Saint-Aignan en 1939* (1998).

*An ironwork detail at the 17th-century Hôtel de St-Aignan*

*The Cernuschi Museum*

*Canaletto's* View of the Canal of Santa Chiara

## MUSÉE CERNUSCHI

68 off J4•7 avenue Vélasquez, 75008 01 45 63 50 75 Closed for renovation but due to reopen in late 2004 (Tue–Sun 10–5.40. Closed public hols) Monceau, Villiers 30, 94 Free (except temporary exhibitions) www.paris.fr

Banker Henri Cernuschi went on an 18-month world tour in the 1870s and came back with an enchanting assortment of ancient art from China and Japan. On his death in 1896 he left the collection to the City of Paris, along with his neoclassical mansion next to the idyllic Parc de Monceau (see page 145). Since then, further items of oriental art have been added, including the prized 8th-century painting *Chevaux et Palefrenier (Horses and Groom)*. Ancient statuettes, jade objects and pottery are all on display, as well as contemporary Chinese paintings. The approach to the museum is attractive, whether through the picturesque Parc de Monceau or the beautiful gilded gates that lead into avenue Vélasquez from the boulevard Malesherbes.

## MUSÉE DE LA CHASSE ET DE LA NATURE

68 P6•Hôtel de Guénégaud, 60, rue des Archives, 75003 01 53 01 92 40 Tue–Sun 11–6. Closed public hols Rambuteau 29, 75 Adult €4.60, child €2.30

The Museum of Hunting and Nature is packed with stuffed animals, hunting weapons, paintings and decorative arts. It may not be to everyone's taste, but it gives an insight into an activity pursued since time immemorial. The collection of hunting weapons spans prehistory to the 19th century and includes knives, crossbows, swords, airguns and rifles. Some displays are dedicated to big-game hunting, with souvenirs of the museum's founder, François Sommer. There are also hunting-related paintings, including works by François Desportes (court artist at Versailles), Jean-Baptiste-Siméon Chardin and Carle Vernet. The museum is housed in the Hôtel de Guénégaud, a Marais mansion built in 1650 by François Mansart, great-uncle to Versailles architect Jules Hardouin-Mansart. The 20th-century writer and politician André Malraux once lived here.

## MUSÉE DU CINÉMA

68 off Q9•51 rue de Bercy, 75012 01 44 34 06 60 Bercy 24, 62, 87 www.51ruedebercy.com

This cinema museum is due to open in 2005, in the former American Cultural Center, a striking curved building created by architect Frank Gehry. The site will include the Henri Langlois Cinema Museum, four cinemas, the Cinémathèque Française, a film library, an exhibition room, a bookshop and a restaurant.

## MUSÉE COGNACQ-JAY

68 P7•Hôtel Donon, 8 rue Elzévir, 75003 01 40 27 07 21 Tue–Sun 10–6. Garden open 10–12.15, 4–5.35, mid-May to mid-Sep (in good weather) St-Paul 29, 96 Free www.paris.fr

The Musée Cognacq-Jay is a discreet, unassuming museum whose charm far exceeds its small size. Part of its appeal is the setting, in an elegant mansion furnished in 18th-century style. Narrow corridors and stairways lead to intimate chandeliered rooms, packed with paintings, porcelain, sculpture and objets d'art. The collection was put together in the early 20th century by Ernest Cognacq and his wife Louise Jay, founders of La Samaritaine department store. Their busts are displayed near the reception.

In 1990 the collection was transferred to the 16th-century Hôtel Donon, in the Marais district. Works by Rembrandt, Jean Honoré Fragonard and Giovanni Battista Tiepolo are among the pieces on display. There is also a garden (summer only) and a small bookshop.

If you can read French, information cards placed at key points around the museum will fill you in on the collection. If not, just enjoy the refined atmosphere—a taste of the life led by wealthy Parisians in the 18th century.

**Don't miss** The Venetian scenes by Canaletto are impressive.

## MUSÉE EDITH PIAF

327 R6•5 rue Crespin du Gast, 75011 01 43 55 52 72 Visit by appointment only: Mon–Wed 1–6, Thu 10–12. Closed Jun and Sep Free (donations appreciated) Ménilmontant 96

Edith Piaf, known by her nickname the Little Sparrow, was born Edith Giovanna Gassion in 1915. Brought up in the working-class east end of Paris, she began her career as a singer in local bars and cafés. Although she achieved international acclaim in the 1930s, appearing in many plays and films, she is best remembered for songs such as *La vie en rose* and *Non, je ne regrette rien*.

This small museum is crammed with Piaf memorabilia, including posters, letters, photographs, dresses and shoes. A visit is worthwhile if only to hear her original records playing in the background as you look around. Nearby is the Cimetière du Père-Lachaise (see page 88) where you can visit her grave—thousands of people attended her funeral here in 1963.

# Musée Carnavalet

**Immerse yourself in the turbulent history of Paris. See prison keys from the Revolution, Napoleon Bonaparte's picnic case and lavish furniture from the reign of Louis XV.**

*Ivy-clad arcades (above)*

*The museum is housed in two elegant mansions (far right)*

| RATINGS | |
|---|---|
| Cultural interest | ●●● |
| Historic interest | ●●●●● |
| Value for money | FREE |

**TIPS**

- Staff shortages mean some rooms are closed at times.
- Explanation panels are in French only, so you may like to buy the guidebook before you begin your tour.

**GALLERY GUIDE**

**HÔTEL CARNAVALET**
**Ground floor:** Middle Ages to 16th century. Also Grand Salon de l'Hôtel d'Uzès.
**1st floor:** 17th and 18th centuries (to end of Louis XVI's reign).

**HÔTEL LE PELETIER DE ST-FARGEAU**
**Ground floor:** 19th century, from Napoleon I to 1848.
**1st floor:** 19th and 20th centuries (from Napoleon III).
**2nd floor:** the Revolution.

**ORANGERIE**
Paris's beginnings, from pre-history to Roman times.

## SEEING THE MUSÉE CARNAVALET

Step into these adjoining mansions and you'll be setting off on an intriguing journey through Paris-past. Paintings, memorabilia and sumptuous re-creations of period rooms evoke the spirit of the city in previous eras, including the French Revolution and the reign of Napoleon I. The emphasis is on conveying an atmosphere rather than listing historical facts, so if you're expecting a detailed account of each era you may be disappointed. But if you want a taste of the high life during Louis XV's rule or a glimpse of the terrors of the Revolution, this is the place to come. The museum is housed in two mansions—the Hôtel Carnavalet and the adjoining Hôtel Le Peletier de St-Fargeau. Use the main entrance on rue de Sévigné, rather than the entrance on rue des Francs-Bourgeois. This takes you into the Hôtel Carnavalet. There is an information desk here where you can ask for a plan of the museum (in English). Be sure to do this—you'll have little hope of making sense of the layout of the site without it. To reach the Hôtel Le Peletier de St-Fargeau, walk across the *galerie* on the first floor.

## HIGHLIGHTS

### THE REVOLUTION

The museum has a poignant collection of memorabilia from the French Revolution on the second floor of the Hôtel Le Peletier de St-Fargeau. You can see a set of keys from the Bastille prison, comic strips by Le Sueur and furniture used by the royal family while they were in prison. Paintings include works by Hubert Robert, who was imprisoned during the Revolution, and a portrait of the Revolutionary leader Robespierre, who later fell victim to the guillotine himself. A collection of fans, plates, clocks and furniture show that Revolutionary slogans infiltrated even household goods.

### HOW THE OTHER HALF LIVED

A world away from the horrors of the Revolution, the lavish tastes of Paris's richer residents through the years are brought to life by vivid re-creations of their rooms. On the ground floor of the Hôtel Carnavalet, the Grand Salon de l'Hôtel d'Uzès evokes the opulence of pre-Revolution days, with a profusion of gold, mirrors and chandeliers. Architect Claude-Nicolas Ledoux designed the original room in 1767. On the first floor, rooms 21 and 22 are dedicated to the mansion's most famous resident, Madame Sévigné, and include two portraits of her. Rooms 27 to 48 depict Paris during the reign of Louis XV (1715–1774). Literary and theatrical life is illustrated in room 47, with brightly painted wooden statuettes from the Théâtre Séraphin. The reign of Louis XVI (1774–93) is covered in rooms 49 to 64. Don't miss the charming Boudoir Circulaire in room 51 and the stunning wallpaper throughout the first floor, made at the Gobelins workshops (see page 107) and based on 18th-century designs.

### 19TH AND 20TH CENTURY DISPLAYS

Highlights from the Napoleonic era include the Emperor's 110-piece picnic case and his death mask (on the ground floor of the Hôtel Le Peletier de St-Fargeau). Reconstructions on the first floor of the Hôtel Le Peletier de St-Fargeau include the elegant art nouveau interior of the famous jewellers, Fouquet (1900), and Madame Wendel's 1920s Queen-of-Sheba ballroom. Also worth seeing is the re-creation of Marcel Proust's room, soundproofed with cork to protect the reclusive writer from unwanted noise.

## BACKGROUND

The building is a piece of history in itself—an ornate mansion built in the 1540s for the president of the Paris *parlement*, Jacques des Ligneris. Architect François Mansart put his stamp on the site in 1660, when he added a new wing. Shortly after, the celebrated lady of letters, Madame de Sévigné, moved in. The idea for a museum of Parisian history originally came from Baron Haussmann, the man responsible for reshaping the city in the 19th century (see page 36). The Hôtel Carnavalet was chosen and the museum opened in 1880. More than a century later, in 1989, the collections were able to expand into the adjoining Hôtel Le Peletier de St-Fargeau.

### BASICS

68 P7•23 rue de Sévigné, 75003 (also an entrance on rue des Francs-Bourgeois)
01 44 59 58 58
Tue–Sun 10–6
Free (except temporary exhibitions)
St-Paul
29, 96
Bookshop with a comprehensive selection of history-related titles
€9
In French Tue, Wed, Sun 3pm; in English on first Sun in month at 3pm

www.paris.fr/musees/musee_carnavalet (in French but photos of the collections and a museum plan are easily accessible)

*The bedroom at the Musée Gustave Moreau*

*Come face to face with fashion designer Jean-Paul Gaultier and the opera singer Maria Callas at the Musée Grévin*



## MUSÉE FRAGONARD

67 L5•Musée Parfum: 9 rue Scribe, 75009. Théâtre-Musée des Capucines: 39 boulevard des Capucines, 75002 ☎ Musée Parfum: 01 47 42 04 56. Théâtre-Musée des Capucines: 01 42 60 37 14 ⏰ Mon–Sat 9–5.30 (rue Scribe: open until 6 and Sun, Apr–end Oct) Free Opéra 21, 27, 42, 68 www.fragonard.com

This museum tells the story of perfume-making over 3,000 years, from Ancient Egyptian times to the present day. It is split into two parts, in two buildings near the Opéra Palais Garnier. The Musée Parfum is in a 19th-century town house in rue Scribe and the Théâtre-Musée des Capucines is in an attractive theatre dating from 1900. Both are home to fascinating collections of perfumery paraphernalia, from bottles and burners to paintings and photographs. There are displays explaining how perfume is made, including an overview of the raw materials. At the Musée des Capucines a miniature factory with 19th-century copper distilling equipment demonstrates extraction methods.

Fragonard has been creating perfumes since 1926 and uses a mixture of traditional and modern techniques. Products are on sale at factory prices in the gift shops.

## MUSÉE GALLIÉRA–MUSÉE DE LA MODE DE LA VILLE DE PARIS

66 G6•Palais Galliéra, 10 avenue Pierre Ier de Serbie, 75016 ☎ 01 56 52 86 20 ⏰ Tue–Sun 10–6 (during exhibitions only). Closed public hols Iéna 32, 63, 72, 92 RER line C, Pont de l'Alma Adult €7, under 14 free (prices may vary according to exhibition) Audioguide is included in entry ticket www.paris.fr

Urban fashion from the 18th century to the present day is the theme of the temporary exhibitions held here, which draw from a collection of 80,000 objects. Dresses by Jean-Paul Gaultier, outfits worn by Marlene Dietrich and ball gowns from the 19th-century are among the items that have appeared here.

## MUSÉE GRÉVIN

69 M5•10 boulevard Montmartre, 75009 ☎ 01 47 70 85 05 ⏰ Mon–Fri 10–6.30, Sat, Sun 10–7 (last entry 1 hour before closing) Grands Boulevards 20, 39, 48, 74, 85 Adult €16, child (6–14) €9, under 6 free ? You can buy tickets in advance at FNAC, Carrefour, Auchan, Virgin Megastore and the tourist office www.grevin.com

If you are hoping to spot a celebrity or two while in Paris, why not cheat a little and visit this waxwork museum? Here you can mingle with Sean Connery, Julia Roberts and Bruce Willis at a cocktail party, join George W. Bush, Queen Elizabeth II and Vladimir Putin in the Élysée Palace and watch Auguste Rodin and Salvador Dalí at work in their studios. You'll find the ubiquitous Elvis Presley and Marilyn Monroe among the 500 waxwork models, and even Lara Croft.

When you've had enough of 21st-century glitz, step back in time to Paris's turbulent past. The French Revolution is re-created with plenty of blood and gore, and you can also witness the assassination of Henri IV and meet Napoleon and Louis XIV.

The Musée Grévin (also known simply as Grévin) is the Parisian answer to Madame Tussaud's and was launched in 1882 by cartoonist and sculptor Alfred Grévin and journalist Arthur Meyer. Since 2001, a group of journalists known as the Académie Grévin has met twice a year to decide which famous faces should be immortalized in wax. Recent additions include the French philosopher Bernard-Henri Lévy, US senator Hillary Clinton and singer Céline Dion.

## MUSÉE GUSTAVE MOREAU

69 L4•14 rue de la Rochefoucauld, 75009 ☎ 01 48 74 38 50 ⏰ Wed–Mon 10–12.45, 2–5.15 Trinité Adult €4, under 18 free, free to all on 1st Sun of month Bookshop

This studio-museum, on the edge of Pigalle, offers an intriguing view of how a late-19th-century artist lived. On the lower floors you'll find the studios of the Symbolist painter Gustave Moreau (1826–1898), teacher to Henri Matisse. Upstairs is a reconstruction of his private apartment, where you can see the kind of paintings, objects and furniture he chose to surround himself with. Paintings gracing his walls included works by Edgar Degas and Théodore Chassériau.

It was Moreau himself who wanted his house to be preserved for posterity as a museum. His wish has been accomplished and the museum now displays around 800 of his own evocative paintings and drawings, many of them with biblical or mythological themes.

## MUSÉE DE L'HISTOIRE DE FRANCE (HÔTEL DE SOUBISE)

68 P7•Hôtel de Soubise, 60 rue des Francs-Bourgeois, 75003 ☎ 01 40 27 60 96 ⏰ Mon and Wed–Fri 10–12.30, 2–5.30, Sat–Sun 2–5.30. Closed public hols Rambuteau, Hôtel de Ville 29, 75, 96 Adult €3.50, under 18 free Giftshop/bookshop www.archivesnationales.culture.gouv.fr

*Musée Jacquemart André, in a splendid 19th-century mansion*

*The 18th-century Hôtel de Soubise, fit for a princess*

The star attraction of the Museum of French History is its sumptuous setting. The Hôtel de Soubise, in the Marais district (see page 107), was built by Delamair in the early 18th century for the Princesse de Soubise.

Delamair incorporated into his design the 14th-century double-towered entrance on the rue des Archives, a remnant of a medieval manor originally on the site.

The Prince's Apartment (*Appartement du Prince*), on the ground floor, is lavishly decorated by painters including Carle Van Loo and François Boucher. The artistry continues upstairs in the Princess's Apartment (*Appartement de la Princesse*).

The history museum itself is document-based and so probably not of great interest to non-French speakers. It draws on the National Archives for its exhibitions, a rich store that includes letters written by Charlemagne and Joan of Arc, the wills of Louis XIV and Napoleon I, and Marie-Antoinette's last correspondence before her execution.

There are plans to broaden the museum's scope in future to explore the way historical events are interpreted.

Classical music concerts are held in the Chambre du Prince on Saturdays at 5.30. Call 01 40 20 09 34 for details.

## MUSÉE JACQUEMART ANDRÉ

66 J4•158 boulevard Haussmann, 75008 ☎ 01 45 62 11 59 Daily 10–6 Daily 11.30–5.30 St-Philippe-du-Roule, Miromesnil 22, 28, 43, 52, 80, 83, 84, 93 RER line A, Charles-de-Gaulle-Étoile Adult €8, child €6, under 7 free, family €25

**www.**musee-jacquemart-andre.com

Banker Edouard Jacquemart and his painter wife Nélie André were keen collectors of European art and amassed an impressive private collection of European masterpieces. In 1875 they built a stately mansion to display their acquisitions, complete with a ballroom, picture gallery and ornate swirling staircase. Nélie outlived her husband, but when she died she respected his wish to donate the mansion and its contents to the Institut de France. It opened as a museum in 1913.

More than 90 years on you can wander through the elegant picture gallery, music room, grand salon and other parts of the mansion where paintings, sculptures and tapestries are displayed. The collection includes paintings and sculptures by Italian artists (including Canaletto, Botticelli and Della Robbia), Flemish and Dutch masters (Van Dyck, Rembrandt and Hals) and French artists (Boucher, David and Fragonard). As well as the permanent collection, the museum hosts popular temporary exhibitions.

An audioguide, in a choice of six languages, is included in the entry price.

**Don't miss** The former dining room (now the café) has a ceiling painted by Giovanni Battista Tiepolo. The walls are decorated with 17th-century tapestries from Brussels.

## MUSÉE DE LA MONNAIE

67 M7•Hôtel de la Monnaie, 11 quai de Conti, 75006 ☎ 01 40 46 55 35 Tue–Fri 11–5.30, Sat–Sun 12–5.30 Adult €8, under 16 free, free to all on 1st Sun of month Pont Neuf, Odéon 27, 58, 70 Audioguide included in entry price. Guided tour of the workshops (advance booking): Wed and Fri 2.15pm, €3 (free for under 16) The shop sells coin collections, books, historical medals, posters. The Paris Mint shop, at 2 rue Guénégaud (Mon–Sat 10–6.15), sells items produced in its workshops

**www.**monnaiedeparis.fr

Elegant Hôtel de la Monnaie, on the Left Bank alongside the Seine, housed the workshops of the Paris Mint from the 18th century until 1973. Today the workshops produce commemorative coins and medals. The *hôtel* is also home to a coin and medal museum, dating back to the 19th century. Here you can learn about the development of minting techniques.

# Musée du Louvre

**One of the world's largest museums. Legendary works of art include the *Mona Lisa, Venus de Milo* and a 4,000-year-old Egyptian sphinx.**

*The museum entrance*

*Illustrated papyrus from the Egyptian collection*

*A ticket allows same-day re-entry to the museum*

## SEEING THE MUSÉE DU LOUVRE

The Louvre is one of the most famous art galleries in the world and it covers a vast period, from around 7,000BC to 1848. There is no way you'll be able to see all 35,000 works on display in one visit, so you need to be selective. If you don't know where to begin, consider taking one of the *Visite-Découverte* guided tours. The free museum plan, available from the information desk, also highlights the key works.

The main entrance is through I.M. Pei's striking glass pyramid in the middle of the large Napoleon Courtyard. From here escalators take you down to the gleaming marble underground foyer, with its cloakroom, information desk and entrances to the museum's three wings, Richelieu, Sully and Denon. If you already have a ticket or a museum pass, you can enter through the passage Richelieu, off the rue de Rivoli, where queues are usually shorter. Other access points are through the Carrousel du Louvre shopping area and the Porte des Lions (closed on Fridays). When it's time for a break, the museum has a choice of cafés and restaurants. Alternatively, you can leave the site and find a café nearby, as your ticket allows re-entry on the same day.

| RATINGS | |
|---|---|
| Cultural interest | ●●●●● |
| Historic interest | ●●●●● |
| Shopping (art books) | ●●●●● |

## HIGHLIGHTS

### *MONA LISA*

When Leonardo da Vinci set up his easel in Florence in the early 16th century to paint the *Mona Lisa*, little did he know he was creating what was to become one of the world's most famous works of art. The diminutive painting, only 77cm (30in) tall and 53cm (20in) wide, is on the first floor of the Denon wing, surrounded by bullet-proof glass and a constant crowd of admirers. The identity of the woman is not known for certain, although she is believed to be the wife of Francesco del Giocondo, hence the portrait's other name, *La Gioconda*. Da Vinci painted the work between 1503 and 1506. François I obtained the painting soon after its completion. It has since spent time in Versailles and in the former Tuileries Palace and has even hung in Napoleon I's bedroom. In 1911 an Italian stole the portrait, wanting to return it to its native Florence. It was recovered two years later, after a police hunt that won it worldwide fame.

*I.M. Pei's pyramid theme continues inside (left)*

**BASICS**

67 M7•99 rue de Rivoli, 75001
01 40 20 50 50. Recorded information in 5 languages: 01 40 20 51 51. Auditorium: 01 40 20 51 86
Wed–Mon 9–6 (last entry 45 min before closing); late opening until 9.45pm Mon (Richelieu wing only) and Wed (whole museum). Closed Tue, 1 Jan, Easter Sun, 1 May, Pentecost Sunday, 1 Nov, 25 Dec
Palais-Royal/Musée du Louvre
21, 27, 39, 48, 67, 68, 69, 72, 74, 75, 76, 81, 85, 95
Châtalet-les-Halles
Adult €7.50 (€5 after 3pm and on Sundays), under 18 free. Temporary exhibitions in the Hall Napoléon €7. Tickets are valid all day, so re-entry is allowed. Tickets combining entrance and rail travel are available at railway stations. The museum is free on the 1st Sun of each month and 14 July (except for exhibitions in the Hall Napoléon)
Range of guidebooks. Free leaflet available at information
Various guided tours are available in English and French, including the *Visite-Découverte* (Discovery Visit) in English at 11, 2 and 3.45 (11.30 only on Sun; not first Sun of month) and in French at 11.30. Audioguides are available in French, English, German, Spanish, Italian and Japanese. Pick them up from the entrances to the three wings of the museum (€5). Special tours are available for those with reduced mobility. There is also a sculpture gallery for those with visual impairments. Ask at the information desk for a leaflet about disability access
Cafés and restaurants
Large bookshop
www.louvre.fr (in French, English, Spanish and Japanese; see the works and take a virtual tour)

*The Puget Courtyard (right)*

*You can see part of the Louvre's medieval base on the lower level (below)*



### *VENUS DE MILO* AND *THE WINGED VICTORY OF SAMOTHRACE*

The eternally serene *Venus de Milo* (ground floor, Sully) is the most famous of the Louvre's Greek antiquities. She was discovered on the island of Melos in 1820. As Aphrodite, the goddess of love, she portrays the Greek image of perfect beauty. The marble statue was created around 100BC, during Greece's Hellenistic period, although its simple style harks back to Classical Greek sculpture.

Among the other Greek antiquities, don't miss the *Winged Victory of Samothrace* (first-floor landing, Denon), soaring 3m (9.8ft) high. The statue was sculpted in 190BC to celebrate a maritime victory and shows the goddess Victory, as if on the prow of a boat. The fluid style of the carving gives the impression the sea wind is blowing through her dress and wings. The sculpture had to be painstakingly reassembled from 300 pieces found on the island of Samothrace in 1863.

### ETRUSCAN AND ROMAN ART

While Ancient Greek civilization was thriving, the Etruscans were carving out their own civilization in northern Italy. Highlights of their art include a charming terracotta sarcophagus (*c* 530BC) showing a husband and wife reclining on wineskins (ground floor, Denon). Both wear the contented smiles that are a common feature of Etruscan sculpture. The Louvre's collection of Roman art (ground floor, Denon) includes mosaics, sculpture, plates, vases and sarcophagi.

### THE EGYPTIAN COLLECTION

You get a captivating glimpse of life at the time of the pharaohs, as much as 5,000 years ago, in the Egyptian rooms. The collection is the largest of its kind outside Egypt, containing 55,000 items, around 5,000 of which are on show. There are commanding sphinxes and statues of the all-powerful pharaohs, but just as fascinating are the smaller, everyday items, including mirrors, combs, necklaces and intricately carved spoons for applying cosmetics. Don't miss the pink granite Grand Sphinx, part pharaoh, part lion, that once protected the corridors of a holy shrine (ground floor, Sully). Its exact age is unknown, but stylistic details suggest it could be more than 4,600 years old.

The collections are presented thematically on the ground floor of the Sully wing, where topics include fishing, funerals and writing. On the first floor the displays are chronological, starting with prehistory, tracing the rule of the pharaohs and ending just before the arrival of the Romans in 333BC. To see how Egyptian culture developed under Roman rule you can continue your tour in the lower floor of the Denon wing.

### FRENCH HISTORICAL/ALLEGORICAL PAINTINGS

These vast paintings, on the first floor of the Denon wing, draw you into the action not simply through their immense size but also in the vivid detail. Some of the subjects would have seemed uncomfortably contemporary when the paintings were first unveiled. Théodore Géricault's *The Raft of the Medusa* (1819) portrays a controversial French shipwreck that took place near Senegal three years earlier. Only 15 of the 150-strong crew survived, clinging to a hastily constructed raft, and there were rumours of cannibalism and treachery. Early viewers of the paintings were shocked by the realism of the corpses.

Dead bodies also appear in Eugène Delacroix's *Liberty Leading the People* (1830), although the presence of the allegorical figure Liberty brings a sense of triumph to the destruction and chaos. The painting depicts the uprising of 1830.

Jacques-Louis David's neoclassical painting *The Coronation of Napoleon I* seems rather cold when set against the passion of Delacroix and Géricault's works. Almost 10m (33ft) wide, it was commissioned by the Emperor himself, and completed in 1807.

**TIPS**

- The museum is least crowded first thing in the morning and during late-opening on Monday and Wednesday. Sunday is the busiest day.

- Remember that the museum is closed on Tuesday.

- The entrance fee is reduced to €5 after 3pm and on Sundays.

- To avoid long waits for tickets, use a *Carte Musées-Monuments* (see page 307) or pre-book your ticket by phone, Internet, FNAC (01 42 31 32 28; small commission charged) or at certain department stores. This allows you to use the passage Richelieu entrance.

- You can view many of the Louvre's paintings and other exhibits on the website, allowing you to decide before your visit where to focus your attention.

- Staff shortages mean that not all the rooms are open every day. If there are particular things you want to see, check the website for the schedule of closures.

- If you visit on Monday evening, ask the information desk for the *Nocturnes du Lundi* leaflet which takes you on a quick tour of 26 key exhibits.

*Old meets new in the architecture of the Napoleon Courtyard (above right)*

*In this cross section of the Louvre, (below), Sully wing is behind you*

**OTHER HIGHLIGHTS**

- *The Lacemaker* by Jan Vermeer (1670–71; Richelieu, 2nd floor)
- *Dying Slave* by Michelangelo (1513–15; Denon, ground floor)
- *The Marly Horses* by Coustou (1743–45; Richelieu, Cour Marly)
- Cour Khorsabad, (Richelieu, ground floor)
- *The Wedding Feast at Cana* by Veronese (1562–63; Denon, first floor)
- Medieval fortifications (lower ground floor)

## BACKGROUND

The building dates back to the 14th century, when Charles V transformed Philippe-Auguste's 12th-century fortress into a medieval castle. Nearly two centuries later, the wily Renaissance king François I instigated considerable rebuilding, and also

**MUSÉE DU LOUVRE CROSS-SECTION**

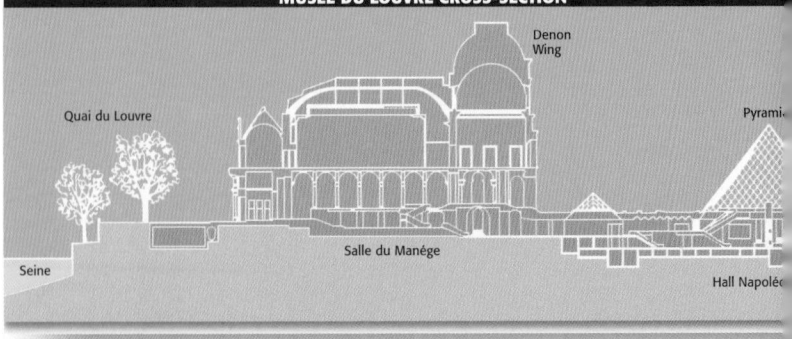

launched the Louvre's art collection, bringing the *Mona Lisa* and its creator, Leonardo da Vinci, to France. Various kings carried out improvements to the building, until Louis XIV moved the court to Versailles in the 17th century. During the Revolution, an art museum opened to the public in the Grand Galerie.

Napoleon I celebrated his marriage to Marie-Louise in the Louvre in 1810, and lived in the nearby Tuileries Palace, which has since burned down. He immediately set about creating a central courtyard dominated by the Arc du Carrousel, building a new wing and adding floors. His numerous victories overseas, and the subsequent looting, added significantly to the Louvre's stock.

The latest improvements, in the 1980s and 1990s, saw the creation of I.M. Pei's stunning glass pyramid, as well as extensive renovations to the museum's galleries.

**GALLERY GUIDE**

The Louvre operates a useful system of colour-coding on its maps, which should help you find what you are looking for. The departments are:

**Egyptian Antiquities (green):** The main collection is on the ground and first floor of Sully. Roman and Coptic Egypt on the lower floor of Denon.

**Greek, Etruscan and Roman Antiquities (blue):** First and ground floor of Sully, ground floor of Denon. Pre-Classical Greece is on Denon's lower floor.

**Oriental Antiquities and Arts of Islam (yellow):** Arts of Islam are on the lower ground floor of Richelieu. The Cour Khorsabad is on the ground floor of Richelieu and Antique Iran and Levant are on the ground floor of Sully.

**Paintings (red):** Paintings from France, Flanders, Holland and Germany are on the second floor of Richelieu and Sully, except for historical/allegorical French paintings, on the first floor of Denon. Italian and Spanish paintings are on the first floor of Denon; English on the first floor of Sully.

**Drawings and Prints (pink):** French drawings are on the second floor of Sully. Other drawings and prints are on the first floor of Denon.

**Objets d'Art (mauve):** First floor of Richelieu and Sully.

**Sculptures (beige):** French sculptures are on the ground and lower ground floors of Richelieu. Italian sculptures are on the ground and lower-ground floors of Denon.

**History of the Louvre (brown):** Remains of the medieval fortress are on Sully's lower ground floor.

**Arts of Africa, Asia, Oceania and the Americas (white):** In the Pavillon des Sessions (on loan from the Musée du Quai Branly, see page 126).



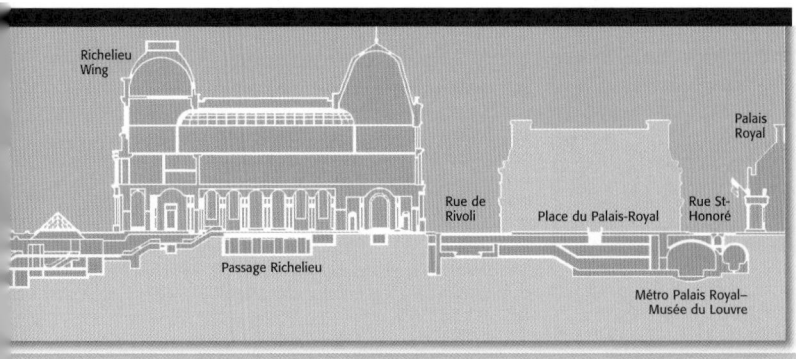

# Musée Marmottan Monet

**The world's largest collection of paintings by Claude Monet, in an intimate town house.**
**You can also see medieval manuscripts, Napoleonic furniture and paintings by Monet's contemporaries.**

*Monet's* Impression–soleil levant *(above), which gave Impressionism its name*

| RATINGS | |
|---|---|
| Cultural interest | ●●●● |
| Historic interest | ●●● |

## SEEING THE MUSÉE MARMOTTAN MONET

It's a bit of a trek out to this museum in the leafy 16th *arrondissement* but you'll be rewarded with a feast of famous paintings by Monet and his contemporaries. The intimate setting in a discreetly elegant 19th-century town house makes a pleasant change from Paris's larger, more impersonal museums. And if the Impressionist works fail to satisfy your appetite, there are also paintings and furniture from the Napoleonic period, as well as more than 300 illustrated pages from medieval and Renaissance manuscripts. It's a curious but compelling combination.

The walk to the museum from La Muette Métro station is well signed and takes you through the pleasant Jardins du Ranelagh. There is no café at the museum, so you may wish to bring your own refreshments to have in the park on the way back.

*This 'illuminated' letter R depicts St. Catherine of Alexandria*

## HIGHLIGHTS

### MONET

Without a doubt, the main draw for visitors is the Monet collection, built up over the last 50 years through donations from the artist's son, Michel, and various other collectors. Many of the 60 paintings on display are in the purpose-built basement gallery–remarkably light and airy considering its underground location. Clouds of irises, wisteria and water lilies fill many of the frames, inspired by the artist's 43 years at Giverny. Various views of the Thames are also on display, including *Londres: Le Parlement, Reflets sur la Tamise* (1899–1901). Monet worked on almost 100 paintings of the river during a visit to London at the turn of the 20th century. The gallery has a selection of works from the *Rouen Cathedral* series, created during two visits to Rouen in 1892 and 1893. Don't miss the influential *Impression–soleil levant* (*c*1873), which gave the Impressionist movement its name. The masterpiece depicts the port at Le Havre and focuses on one of Monet's preferred themes–the play of light on water. It is the only painting behind glass, after it was stolen in 1985 and recovered five years later in Corsica.

### OTHER IMPRESSIONISTS

The Impressionist collection, on the upper floor, includes works by Edgar Degas, Gustave Caillebotte, Camille Pissarro, Berthe Morisot and Pierre-Auguste Renoir. Look for Renoir's beguiling *Claude Monet lisant* (Claude Monet reading; 1872). Monet was particularly fond of this portrait, painted by his friend, and kept it until his death.

### THE EMPIRE COLLECTION

Highlights from the Empire period include the Geographical Clock (1813) on the ground floor, originally made for Napoleon and later altered by Louis XVIII.

### THE ILLUMINATIONS

The museum has around 300 medieval and Renaissance illustrated pages, collectively known as the Illuminations, on the ground floor. These were amassed by art dealer Georges Wildenstein and were donated to the museum by his son in 1980. Many of the pages come from French and Italian religious manuscripts and are vividly illustrated with saints and biblical characters. Others are from Books of Hours, compilations of prayers and religious sayings. Some show scenes from feudal life in the 15th century.

## BACKGROUND

The Marmottan Museum did not start life as a showcase for Monet's work. It takes its name from art historian Paul Marmottan, who left his house and collection of Empire paintings and furniture to the nation in 1932. The collection, built up by both Paul and his father Jules, also includes paintings from the Flemish, Italian and German primitives. It wasn't until later that various donors added the Impressionist works that have now become the museum's main attraction.

Monet was born in Paris in 1840 and died in Giverny 86 years later. During his life he drew inspiration from his travels around France, as well as those to London, Norway, Holland and Italy. But it was in the gardens of Giverny, his home from 1883 until his death, that he produced some of his most famous works. You can see family portraits near the steps to the basement gallery.

*The museum has a collection of elegant furniture*

### TIPS

- Look out for the amusing *Le Havre* caricatures (c1858), on the first floor, markedly different in style to Monet's later, more famous paintings.
- The museum lets you see some of Monet's most famous works in a refreshingly tranquil setting. But if you are in Paris for only a few days you may find it easier to see the Impressionist collection in the more central Musée d'Orsay (see pages 130–134).
- If you have time, you may like to combine a trip to the Musée Marmottan Monet with a visit to the Musée National des Arts Asiatiques-Guimet (see page 126) or the Musée Galliéra (see page 116), a few stops back on Métro line 9, at Iéna.

### BASICS

321 off E7•2 rue Louis-Boilly, 75016
01 44 96 50 33
Tue–Sun 10–6 (last entry 5.30). Closed Mon, 1 Jan, 1 May, 25 Dec
Adult €6.50, child €4, under 8 free
La Muette (then a 10-minute walk; follow signs from the station)
22, 32, 52
RER line C, Boulainvilliers
Giftshop/bookshop
€8.50

www.marmottan.com (French and English; a comprehensive website showing the major works and giving news and practical information about the museum)

### GALLERY GUIDE

**LOWER FLOOR**
Monet collection.

**GROUND FLOOR**
The Illuminations, the Primitives, the Empire Collection and the bookshop.

**UPPER FLOOR**
Other Impressionist works and temporary exhibitions.

Two Cranes on the Edge of a Pond, *from the Musée Guimet*

*Paintings in the Musée National Eugène Delacroix, in the former home of the artist*



## MUSÉE DE MONTMARTRE

69 M2•12 rue Cortot, 75018 ☎ 01 46 06 61 11 Tue–Sun 10–12.30, 1.30–6 Lamarck-Caulaincourt, then walk Montmartrobus, 80 Adult €4.50, child €3, under 10 free

Montmartre's history is arguably the most enchanting of all Paris's districts, with its walking beheaded saint, prosperous windmills and infamous nightlife. You can find out more at the unassuming Musée de Montmartre, in a delightful 17th-century mansion that once belonged to Rose de Rosimond, a member of Molière's stage troupe. The house, behind Montmartre's one remaining vineyard, later welcomed the painter Pierre-Auguste Renoir.

## MUSÉE NATIONAL DES ARTS ASIATIQUES-GUIMET

66 G6•6 place d'Iéna, 75016 ☎ 01 56 52 53 00 Wed–Mon 10–6 Museum and temporary exhibitions: adult €7, under 18 free. Temporary exhibitions only: adult €5.50, under 18 free, free to all on 1st Sun of month Iéna, Boissière 22, 30, 32, 63, 82 Free audioguides (lasting around 90 min) are available in several languages. For information on guided tours, see the schedule at the entrance
www.museeguimet.fr

This museum, which opened in 1889, has a remarkable display of Oriental antiquities, built up by industrialist Émile Guimet (1836–1918). Around 45,000 items are on display, including sculptures, carvings, paintings and artefacts from Korea, China, Japan, Tibet, Afghanistan, Thailand, Pakistan and India.

The stunning collection of Khmer art (6th–19th centuries) includes serene stone buddhas and Hindu gods. The museum also has richly painted Tibetan and Nepalese *tankas* (portable paintings). The Indian department includes bronze deities from southern India and Moghul and Rajput miniatures. The rich Chinese department has a vast ceramics collection.

Japanese religious art is represented in the museum annexe, the Buddhist Pantheon at 19 avenue d'Iéna (*Wed–Mon 9.45–5.45*).

## MUSÉE NATIONAL EUGÈNE DELACROIX

67 L7•6 rue de Furstemberg, 75006 ☎ 01 44 41 86 50 Wed–Mon 9.30–5 (last entry 4.30) Adult €4, free for under 18, free to all 1st Sun of month St-Germain-des-Prés, Mabillon 39, 63, 95
www.musee-delacroix.fr

Romantic painter Eugène Delacroix (1798–1863) spent the last six years of his life in this apartment. His living quarters and studio are now a small museum. On display are his paintings, drawings, pastels, sketches, furniture and personal documents. You can see many of his major works in the Louvre (see pages 118–123) and the Musée d'Orsay (see pages 130–134).

## MUSÉE NISSIM DE CAMONDO

66 off H4•63 rue de Monceau, 75008 ☎ 01 53 89 06 50 Wed–Sun 10–5. Closed public hols Villiers, Monceau 30, 84, 94 Adult €4.60, under 18 free
www.ucad.fr

The elegance of the furniture and ornaments on display in this stylish town house hides a tragic family story. Moïse de Camondo left his house and collection to the State on his death in 1935, stipulating that it should be named in memory of his son, Nissim, who was killed in action during World War I. Less than 10 years after Moïse's death, his daughter and her family were killed at Auschwitz.

The mansion is laid out as an 18th-century home and contains Moïse's tasteful collection of decorative arts, mainly from the second half of the 18th century. Vases once owned by Marie-Antoinette, a graceful roll-top desk by Jean François Oeben and furniture embellished with Sèvres porcelain are among the items on display. You can also see a silver dinner service made for Empress Catherine II of Russia.

Despite its 18th-century furnishings, the mansion was built in the early 20th century to designs inspired by Versailles's Petit Trianon. The kitchens and servants quarters have been restored as they would have been for the brief period when the mansion was a working home.

## MUSÉE DU QUAI BRANLY

66 G7•29–55 quai Branly, 75007 (east of the junction with avenue de la Bourdonnais) ☎ During the construction period: 01 56 61 70 00 Due to open mid-2005 Pont de l'Alma 42 Champ de Mars Tour Eiffel
www.quaibranly.fr

The cultural heritage of Africa, Asia, Oceania and the Americas is the focus of this new museum, due to open in mid-2005, near the Eiffel Tower. Themes will range from African musical instruments to the relationship between man and the natural world.

Some exhibits will come from the former Musée des Arts d'Afrique et d'Océanie and from the Musée de l'Homme, in the Palais de Chaillot (see page 143).

*Tree-lined avenue in the Jardin des Plantes (above). A greenhouse shimmers in the sunlight (right)*

# MUSÉUM NATIONAL D'HISTOIRE NATURELLE AND JARDIN DES PLANTES

**These beautifully laid out gardens contain several natural history museums, tropical greenhouses and one of the oldest zoos in the world.**

The Jardin des Plantes is one of the city's prettiest parks and an ideal place for a stroll. Its wide tree-lined avenue, flanked by museums on one side and gardens on the other, is especially picturesque in autumn when the leaves are changing hue. Paths lead off to the gardens with flowers, statues and a great view of the striking Grande Galerie de l'Évolution (see below). The Jardin des Plantes was founded in 1626 by two of Louis XIII's physicians as the royal garden of medicinal plants. It opened to the public in 1640 and was extended by the naturalist Buffon in the 18th century.

## MUSÉUM NATIONAL D'HISTOIRE NATURELLE

The Natural History Museum is made up of several separate galleries within the Jardin des Plantes. The highlight is the Grande Galerie de l'Évolution, in a mammoth glass-roofed structure built in 1889 and renovated in the early 1990s. Contemporary displays cover themes ranging from evolution and the diversity of the living world to endangered and extinct species. The Galerie de Paléontologie, which opened in 1898, has fossils dating back millions of years. The Galerie d'Anatomie Comparée focuses on the classification of more than 1,000 vertebrates, while the Galerie de Minéralogie and Géologie displays gems, precious minerals and giant crystals.

## PLANTS AND ANIMALS

Tropical greenhouses, including a winter garden and a Mexican greenhouse, shelter thousands of plant species. The Alpine garden is home to more than 2,000 species originating from mountainous regions including the Alps, Corsica and the Himalayas. The Ménagerie opened in 1794 and houses around 1,100 mammals, birds and reptiles, in addition to a Microzoo for insects and spiders.

**RATINGS**

| | |
|---|---|
| Good for kids | ●●●●● |
| Historic interest | ●●● |
| Photo stops | ●●● |

**BASICS**

68 P9 ☎ 01 40 79 30 00
Gare d'Austerlitz, Jussieu, Place Monge 24, 57, 61, 63, 67, 89, 91
Gift and bookshops

**Jardin des Plantes**
57 rue Cuvier, 75005 Daily 7.30am–8pm in summer; 7.30–5.30 in winter Free

**Grande Galerie de l'Évolution**
36 rue Geoffroy St-Hilaire, 75005 Wed–Mon 10–6 (also Thu 6–10). Closed 1 May Adult €7, under 18 free €4.60

**Galeries de Paléontologie et d'Anatomie Comparée**
57 rue Cuvier, 75005 Wed–Mon 10–5 (also Sat–Sun 5–6, Apr–end Sep). Closed 1 May Adult €5, under 18 free

**Galerie de Minéralogie & Géologie**
36 rue Geoffroy St-Hilaire, 75005 Wed–Mon 10–5 (also Sat–Sun 5–6, Apr–end Sep). Closed 1 May Adult €5, child €3, under 4 free

**Les Serres (Greenhouses)**
57 rue Cuvier, 75005 Wed–Mon 1–5 (also Sat–Sun 5–6, Apr–end Sep). Closed 1 May Adult €2.50, child €1.50, under 4 free

**Ménagerie (Zoo)**
57 rue Cuvier, 75005 Daily 9–6 in summer; 9–5 in winter Adult €6, child €3.50, under 4 free
www.mnhn.fr (mainly in French)

# Musée National du Moyen Âge–Thermes de Cluny

**A collection of medieval tapestries, altarpieces and statues that takes you back to the days of courtly love and feudal living.**

Sight, *from the 15th-century* Lady and the Unicorn *series*

*Take a close-up look at some vivid stained glass*

*Carvings on the exterior of the 15th-century mansion*

**RATINGS**

| | |
|---|---|
| Cultural interest | ●●●● |
| Historic interest | ●●●● |
| Photo stops (exterior) | ●●● |

**TIPS**

- You don't have to pay to enter the Gothic courtyard off place Paul-Painlevé. It's a pleasant spot to sit for a few minutes and the turrets and gargoyles are worth a look.

- This is a good museum for English speakers, as the explanation notices are written in English as well as French.

## SEEING THE MUSÉE NATIONAL DU MOYEN ÂGE–THERMES DE CLUNY

The Cluny Museum offers an intriguing glimpse into medieval life. Animated tapestries, dazzling necklaces, headless statues and religious paraphernalia are among the 23,000 exhibits, displayed in an intimate Gothic mansion in the Latin Quarter. What makes the collection so compelling is that you get a close-up view of objects that you usually admire only from a distance. Vivid stained-glass windows you would normally crane your neck to see are suddenly down at eye level, while altarpieces created to sit imposingly at the far end of a church are right in front of you. The detail is exceptional.

Entrance to the museum is through a splendid Gothic courtyard, whose gargoyles and turrets put you in the mood for the exhibits inside. Pick up a free plan at the ticket desk, then start your tour by walking through the bookshop to room 2. From here it is easy to find your way around as you simply follow the numerical order of the rooms, 2 to 12 on the lower floor and 13 to 23 on the upper floor. After your visit, you can take a break in the medieval gardens, whose entrance is on the corner of boulevards St-Michel and St-Germain.

## HIGHLIGHTS

### TAPESTRIES

Vivid tapestries paint an enchanting, if idealized, picture of medieval life. Walking, bathing and reading are among the everyday activities portrayed in the 16th-century series *La Vie Seigneuriale* (Manorial Life; room 4). The floral background, known as *mille fleurs,* was a popular artistic device at the time. Don't miss the 16th-century *Les Vendanges* (room 12), created in the southern Netherlands and portraying a busy grape harvest. The six allegorical tapestries of *La Dame à la Licorne* (The Lady and the Unicorn; room 13) were woven in silk and wool in the 15th century in the Netherlands. Each of the first five tapestries shows a lady acting out one of the five senses. In the enigmatic sixth piece, *À mon seul désir* (*To my only desire*), she returns the necklace she has been wearing to its box, symbolizing, it is thought, a refusal to give in to worldly passions.

### THE HEADS OF NOTRE-DAME

The concert hall (room 8) displays a surreal collection of heads that were knocked off statues on the west front of Notre-Dame by zealous Revolutionaries who thought they represented French kings. In fact, the statues, dating from the 13th century, were of biblical characters. Historians assumed the heads had been destroyed, until they were unearthed in a bank vault in 1977.

### GALLO-ROMAN BATHS

The museum is on the site of Paris's most ancient Gallo-Roman baths, the ruins of which can still be seen. In the second century AD bathers would progress through three stone chambers offering different water temperatures—warm in the *tepidarium*, hot in the *caldarium* and cold in the *frigidarium*. Much of the vast *frigidarium* still remains and has been incorporated into the lower floor of the museum (room 9). It is an imposing chamber, with walls 2m (6ft) thick, rising 15m (49ft) high. In one corner stands Paris's oldest sculpture, the recently renovated *Pilier des Nautes* (AD30). A network of Roman vaults leads off from the *frigidarium*. Outside, you can see the ruins of the Roman gymnasium from the boulevard St-Germain.

## BACKGROUND

**The turreted Hôtel de Cluny, one of Paris's oldest mansions, was built at the end of the 15th century as a pied-à-terre for a wealthy order of Benedictine monks from Cluny, in Burgundy. Illustrious residents included Mary Tudor, sister of Henry VIII, who was widowed at age 16 after a three-month marriage to Louis XII, and James V of Scotland. In the early 19th century the art collector Alexandre du Sommerard bought the property—it is his rich finds that form the basis of the museum today.**

### BASICS

67 M8•6 place Paul-Painlevé, rue du Sommerard, 75005
01 53 73 78 16; 01 53 73 78 00
Wed–Mon 9.15–5.45. Closed public hols
Adult €5.50, under 18 free, free to all on 1st Sun of month
Cluny-La-Sorbonne
21, 27, 38, 63, 85, 86, 87, 96
RER line B, C St-Michel
Bookshop/giftshop
€13.90
Guided tours available in English

**www.**musee-moyenage.fr (main website in French only; boutique in French and English. See photos, read background information, browse the boutique, or find out about concerts, guided tours and family activities)

*The museum is housed in one of the city's oldest mansions (above)*

# Musée d'Orsay

**A vast collection of world-famous Impressionist paintings joins other art from the mid-19th century to early 20th century. Housed in a magnificent Industrial Age train terminus, with a soaring glass and iron roof and wonderful station clock.**

*The soaring roof allows plenty of light into the museum*

End of an Arabesque, *by Edgar Degas (1877)*

*The elegant exterior of the former train station*

**TIPS**

- A *Carte Musées–Monuments* (see page 307) gives you free entrance and allows you to skip the queues.
- Tuesday, Saturday and Sunday are the museum's busiest days. Thursday evening is the quietest time to visit.
- To see Monet's paintings in a more tranquil setting, visit the Musée Marmottan Monet (see pages 124–125).
- The Musée d'Orsay is closed on Monday, unlike the Louvre and Centre Georges Pompidou, which close on Tuesday.
- Entrance is free to teachers, art students and professional artists.
- The café on the upper floor gives you a stunning (and slightly surreal) view of Paris through the glass of the huge station clock. If the wait for a table is daunting, try the self-service cafeteria just above it. There is also a lavish restaurant on the middle level.

*Children learning about Carpeaux's* La Danse *(right)*

## SEEING THE MUSÉE D'ORSAY

The Musée d'Orsay's collection spans 1848 to 1914, a crucial period in Western art that witnessed such giants as Claude Monet, Pierre-Auguste Renoir and Paul Cézanne. Chronologically, the museum fits neatly between the Louvre and the Centre Georges Pompidou. Most people come to see the breathtaking Impressionist collection, which includes Monet's *Houses of Parliament,* Vincent Van Gogh's *The Church at Auvers-sur-Oise* and Renoir's *Ball at the Moulin de la Galette.* But Impressionism forms less than a third of the vast display, which also includes sculpture, Symbolist and historical paintings, photography and art nouveau furniture. The building is an attraction in itself, with its vast main hall, lavish ballroom and wonderful station clocks.

In recent years, queues for the museum have stretched far along the Seine, although alterations to the entrance are likely to improve the situation. Plans for automatic ticket machines may also speed things up. To see the works chronologically, start with the lower level, then take the escalators to the upper level, before finishing on the middle level.

## HIGHLIGHTS

### MONET

The Impressionist and post-Impressionist collections (upper level) are a real treat, with airy galleries filled with row upon row of legendary works by Renoir, Edgar Degas, Monet, Edouard Manet, Van Gogh and others. Monet, one of the father figures of Impressionism, is well represented, with works such as *Régate à Argenteuil* (c1872), *Nymphéas Bleus* (c1916–19) and *La Gare St-Lazare* (1877). There are five paintings from the 28-strong *Cathédrales de Rouen* series, painted between 1892 and 1894. Monet rented a studio opposite the cathedral to allow him to paint the building in different lights and weather conditions. More from the series can be seen at the Musée Marmottan Monet (see pages 124–125).

### RENOIR

Renoir's cheerful *Le Bal du Moulin de la Galette* (1876; upper level) portrays Montmartre when it was the hub of Paris's nightlife. Renoir

*Marking time—the surreal station clock*

painted it while actually at the open-air dance hall, on the site of the Galette windmill (see page 108). Notice the play of light and shade on the dancers, a key Impressionist theme, and the way the dancers seem almost to merge with their surroundings. Like many artists of the time, Renoir had studios in Montmartre and was a regular at the Moulin de la Galette.

**VAN GOGH**

Van Gogh is among the most prominently displayed post-Impressionists (upper floor), with masterpieces including the vivid *La Chambre à Arles* (1889), the sinisterly swirling *L'Église d'Auvers-sur-Oise* (1890) and the relaxed *La Sieste* (1889–90). His turquoise self-portrait of 1889 was painted in the same year he admitted himself to a psychiatric hospital in St-Rémy-de-Provence. It is one of the last of the artist's 40 self-portraits and shows him as pale and gaunt. Van Gogh suffered from severe depression and hallucinations and a year after painting this portrait he killed himself.

*Van Gogh's* L'Église d'Auvers-sur-Oise *(1890)*

**SCULPTURE ON THE LOWER LEVEL**

Even if your sole reason for visiting the museum is the Impressionist collection on the upper level, don't leave without wandering through the central aisle on the lower floor. This is the best place to catch the atmosphere of the building—part museum, part Belle-Époque train station—with its ornate clock, magnificent glass roof and contrastingly solid stone-clad floor and walls. In addition to allowing you to admire the building, the central aisle is also a gallery for 19th-century neoclassical sculpture. Near the east end, look out for Jean-Baptiste Carpeaux's *La Danse* (1869), formerly part of the façade of the Opéra Palais Garnier (see page 142) and controversial when it was first unveiled because of the detail in the nude figures. Also worth spotting, in the entrance hall, is François Rude's ferocious bust *Génie de la Patrie* (1836), moulded from a larger bas relief on the Arc de Triomphe.

**HIGHLIGHTS ON THE MIDDLE LEVEL**

The middle level brings you up to just before World War I. Here you can see examples of Naturalism (Jules Dalou, Fernand Cormon), Symbolism (Edward Burne-Jones and Arnold Böcklin) and the Nabis

school. Most striking here are Auguste Rodin's sculptures (including the powerful *Balzac*) and those of his followers Camille Claudel, Medardo Rosso, Émile-Antoine Bourdelle and the rounded forms of Aristide Maillol. This floor also displays some superb applied arts, concentrating on art nouveau furniture and objects, including creations by Charles Rennie Mackintosh (room 27, between floors, at the east end of museum).

**THE BALLROOM**

Don't miss the lavish Salles des Fêtes (room 51), tucked away at the end of the middle level. The extravagantly chandeliered and mirrored room was originally part of the station's hotel and served both as a reception room and venue for special events. In 1958 General de Gaulle declared his return to government here to a gathering of reporters.

**RATINGS**

| | |
|---|---|
| Cultural interest | ●●●●● |
| Historic interest | ●●● |
| Shopping (art books) | ●●●● |

*Part of the museum's extensive sculpture collection (below, left)*

*An art nouveau dining room designed by Alexandre Charpentier (below, middle)*

*Learning from the masters, in the Impressionist gallery (below)*

## BACKGROUND

The imposing Orsay station and its accompanying hotel were constructed along the banks of the Seine in just two years, in time for the Exposition Universelle in 1900. Victor Laloux designed the soaring glass and iron roof, together with the wildly ornate Belle-Époque restaurant and ballroom; all still intact. The station boasted all modern facilities, including elevators and underground tracks. But in 1939 the advent of longer electric trains forced it to close for long-distance travel (it was still used for suburban trains). During the war it became a mail depot, then a reception venue for freed prisoners of war. Later, various films were shot here, including Orson Welles' *The Trial*. Public protest saved the station from demolition, and final approval was given to turn it into a museum in 1977. Italian architect Gae Aulenti masterminded the conversion of the interior, encasing both the walls and floors with stone, and President François Mitterrand opened the museum in December 1986.

**BASICS**

67 K7•62 rue de Lille, 75007. Entrance (when improvement works have finished) on place de la Légion d'Honneur.

01 40 49 48 14; 01 40 49 48 48

Tue–Wed and Fri–Sat 10–6, Sun 9–6, Thu 10–9.45 (the museum opens at 9 from late Jun to late Sep); last ticket 45 min before closing. Closed 1 Jan, 1 May, 25 Dec

Adult €7, under 18 free, free to all on 1st Sun of month. Temporary exhibitions cost extra.

Solférino

24, 63, 68, 73, 83, 84, 94

RER line C, Musée d'Orsay

On the middle level (11.30–2.30, 3.30–5.30; dinner 7–9.15 on Thu)

Café des Hauteurs on upper level, with wonderful view of the old station clock; self-service café just above it

Giftshop and bookshop

A wide selection of books, including *Pocket Guide* (€5.50) and *Guide to the Musée d'Orsay* (€15)

Guided tours in English Tue–Sat 11.30; in French Tue–Sat 11 (€6). Audioguides (€5) in English, French, Italian, Spanish, Japanese, German

Close at 5.15

www.musee-orsay.fr (English, French and Spanish. Practical and historical information about the site, as well as photos of some of the paintings)

*The central sculpture aisle, with its ornate station clock*

## GALLERY GUIDE

There may be changes to the layout of the museum when renovation work is completed. During the building work, the main entrance has been on quai Anatole France.

**KEY**

- **Architecture**
- **Decorative Arts**
- **Painting**
- **Photography**
- **Sculpture**
- **Temporary Exhibitions**

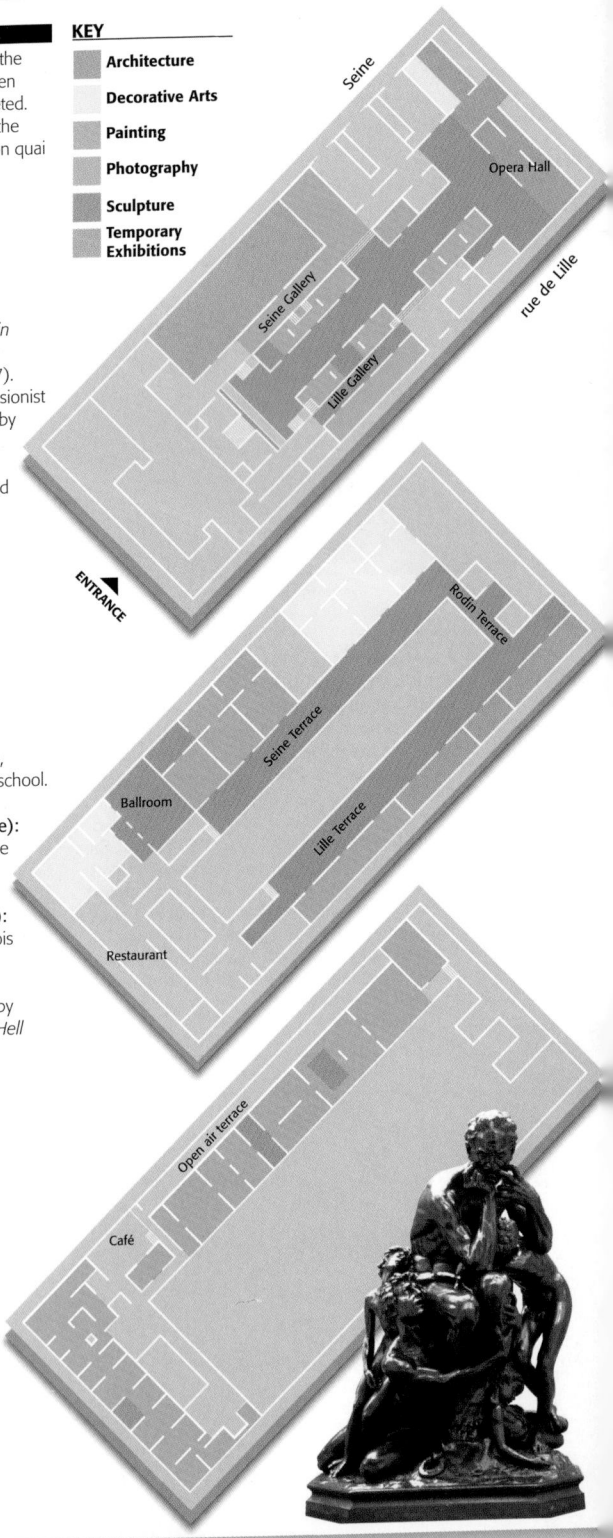


### LOWER LEVEL

**Central Aisle:** Sculpture, including Carpeaux's *Ugolin* (1860) and Louis-Antoine Barye's *Seated Lion* (1847).
**Side galleries:** Pre-Impressionist paintings, including works by Eugène Delacroix and Gustave Courbet.
Also historical paintings and early works by Monet, Renoir and Manet.

### MIDDLE LEVEL

**Ballroom.**
**Side galleries:** Symbolism, Naturalism and the Nabis school. Also decorative arts.
**Seine Terrace (mezzanine):** Sculpture, including Camille Claudel's *Middle Age* (1899–1903).
**Lille Terrace (mezzanine):** Sculpture, including François Pompon's *Polar Bear* (1922–23).
**Rodin Terrace:** Sculpture by Rodin, including *Gates of Hell* (1880–1917) and *Balzac* (1897).
**Restaurant.**

### UPPER LEVEL

**Galleries:** Impressionist and post-Impressionist paintings, sculpture by Degas, Renoir and Paul Gauguin.
**Café des Hauteurs.**

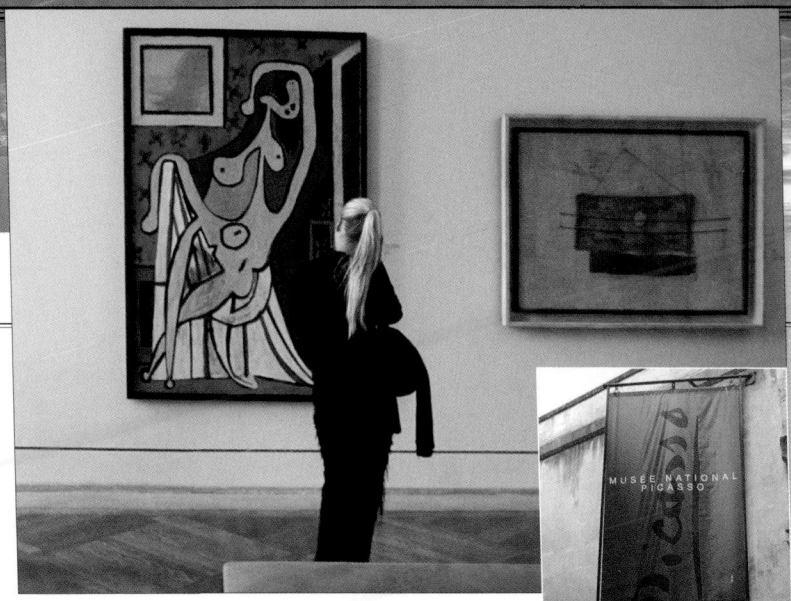

*The Picasso Museum has more than 200 paintings by the artist*

# MUSÉE PICASSO

**An outstanding collection of works by Pablo Picasso—a must for anyone interested in 20th-century art.**

The grand opening of this museum in 1985 put an end to 11 years of wrangling over the death duties of Pablo Picasso (1881–1973). Thanks to a law allowing payment of these duties in the form of works of art, the French State received one quarter of Picasso's collection from his heirs. The collection, including 203 paintings, 158 sculptures, 16 collages and more than 1,500 drawings and prints, was extended further after the death of Picasso's wife in 1990. Also on display is Picasso's personal collection of works by his mentors and contemporaries, including Paul Cézanne, Pierre-Auguste Renoir, Joan Miró, Georges Braque and Henri Matisse.

## THE WORKS

The art is arranged chronologically, from Picasso's early 1900s Blue and Pink periods, through his years of Cubist experimentation with Georges Braque, to the 1930s and beyond. Look out for the *Trois Femmes à la Fontaine* (1921) at the top of the staircase to the left, and the sculpture of *La Guenon et Son Petit* (*the Baboon with Young;* 1951) in room 18, whose head is made from two toy cars.

Other highlights are his *Self-Portrait* (1901) in room 1, *The Goat* (1950) in room 16, *The Bathers* (1918) and *Two Women Running on the Beach* (1922) in room 6 and the tragic yet moving *Seated Old Man* (1970–71) in room 20. The collection captures the freshness and inventiveness that ran through the core of Picasso's long and creative life.

## MANSION SETTING

The museum is in the Hôtel Salé, a beautiful 17th-century mansion in the Marais district. After changing hands several times the mansion was acquired by the Ville de Paris in 1962 and in 1976 architect Roland Simounet began work to convert the interior to the Musée Picasso. The chandeliers and furniture were designed by Diego Giacometti and extensive, and expensive, renovation work was needed before the museum opened to the public. A small room dedicated to the history of the Hôtel Salé displays black-and-white photographs and information on the building and its occupants over the years.

**RATINGS**

| | |
|---|---|
| Cultural interest | ●●●● |
| Historic interest | ●●● |

**TIPS**

- Even for those who are not ardent Picasso fans, the museum is still worth a visit to admire the interior of the magnificent Hôtel Salé.
- Wall plaques in each of the rooms give detailed information (in English) about the works on display.

**BASICS**

68 P7•Hôtel Salé, 5 rue de Thorigny, 75003
01 42 71 25 21
Wed–Mon 9.30–6, Apr–end Sep; 9.30–5.30 rest of year; last entry 45 min before closing. Closed 1 Jan, 25 Dec
Adult €5.50, under 18 free
St-Paul, Chemin Vert, St-Sébastien Froissart
29, 69, 75, 96
Guided tours Mon and Fri 2.30 (€6)
€3
Garden café, mid-Apr to mid-Oct
Bookshop and giftshop
www.musee-picasso.fr (in French)

*Strolling past* The Walking Man *(1900–1907)*

| RATINGS | |
|---|---|
| Cultural interest | ●●●● |
| Good for kids (garden) | ●●● |
| Photo stops (garden) | ●●● |
| Value for money (garden) | ●●●● |

**TIPS**

- The garden-only ticket lets you view some of Rodin's most important works for only €1; children should enjoy the play area.
- If the Rodin Museum whets your appetite for open-air sculpture, try the Musée de la Sculpture en Plein Air, on quai St-Bernard, which has around 40 avant-garde works. (Visit during the day only.)
- There are few information boards in the garden, so rent an audioguide or pick up a free leaflet from the Hôtel Biron.

**BASICS**

66 J7•77 rue de Varenne, 75007
01 44 18 61 10
Tue–Sun 9.30–5.45, Apr–end Sep (gardens stay open until 6.45); Tue–Sun 9.30–4.45, rest of year
Adult €5, under 18 free, free to all on 1st Sun of month. Garden only: €1
Varenne
69, 82, 87, 92
RER line C, Invalides
Garden café Bookshop/giftshop
€9.50 Audioguides €4. Guided tours once a week In the gardens

www.musee-rodin.fr (French, English; with photos of Rodin and his works)

# MUSÉE RODIN

**In this museum's soothing gardens, hidden in the heart of the city, you can wander past Auguste Rodin's world-famous sculptures or relax among the roses.**

The Musée Rodin's open-air gallery, spread over 3ha (7 acres) of beautiful garden, makes a great escape from more strenuous sightseeing. After a stroll through the grounds, you can see more of Rodin's works in the Hôtel Biron, the airy 18th-century mansion where he once lived.

### THE GARDEN

Don't miss the brooding bronze *Le Penseur* (*The Thinker*; 1880–1904), thought to represent the Italian poet Dante and originally placed outside the Panthéon, or the gruesome doorway *La Porte de l'Enfer* (*The Gates of Hell*; 1880–1917), inspired by Dante's *Divine Comedy*. *Les Bourgeois de Calais* (*The Burghers of Calais*; 1884–89) depicts six burghers who gave up their lives to save their townsfolk during a siege by the English in the 14th century, while *Balzac* (1891–98) is a rather unflattering portrayal of the writer in his dressing gown.

### THE HÔTEL BIRON

Inside the elegant mansion, you can follow Rodin's artistic evolution chronologically, from his early academic sketches and paintings to his vigorous watercolours. The highlight is the passionate white marble *Le Baiser* (*The Kiss*; 1882–98), one of Rodin's best-known pieces. There are also works by the artist's contemporaries, including Camille Claudel, Pierre-Auguste Renoir, Vincent Van Gogh and Claude Monet.

### THE ARTIST

Rodin was born in Paris in 1840 and showed an early aptitude for drawing. In 1857 he applied to study sculpture at the École des Beaux-Arts but was rejected because tutors felt his style was old fashioned. Most of his famous pieces date from the latter half of his life. In 1908 Rodin moved into the ground floor of the rococo Hôtel Biron (1730), where other residents included Jean Cocteau, Henri Matisse and Isadora Duncan. In 1916 he welcomed a decision to turn the mansion into a museum of his work, but he died in 1917, two years before the plans became reality.

# Notre-Dame

**This beautiful Gothic cathedral is one of France's most visited religious sites. Climb the towers for wonderful views over the city or take a boat trip to admire the famous flying buttresses.**

*Take a closer look at the gargoyles—if you can face the climb*

*A postcard stand in the bustling square in front of the cathedral*

*Sunset over Notre-Dame*

## SEEING NOTRE-DAME

Notre-Dame anchors the Île de la Cité with its powerful presence and more than 850 years of history. The cathedral is as famous a symbol of Paris as the Eiffel Tower and around 10 million people enter its doors each year. Despite this, it retains an inspiring sense of calm.

Entry is through the huge doorways of the west façade, in the touristy place du Parvis Notre-Dame. You can buy a guidebook at the bookstand just inside the cathedral, before wandering around the dimly lit interior. There are fewer crowds in the early morning, when the cathedral is also at its brightest. If you're not in a hurry, you may like to visit the Treasury, reached from the south side of the choir. The entrance to the crypt is outside, on the place du Parvis du Notre-Dame.

Keep some time for strolling around the outside of Notre-Dame to admire the architecture, including the buttresses. One of the best views of the exterior is from the Seine, on a boat trip that circles the Île de la Cité. Finally, if your legs will agree to it, there are wonderful views from the top of the towers. Queues are shortest in the morning, Tuesday to Friday.

## HIGHLIGHTS

### WEST FAÇADE

The symmetrical west façade, dominated by Notre-Dame's towers, appears rather heavy and angular compared with the elegant curves and spires you see from the eastern side. But it is packed with sculptures, originally painted and intended as a Bible for the illiterate. The 28 large statues lined up between the doors and the windows form the Gallery of the Kings. Although the figures represent biblical characters, revolutionary zealots mistook them for French kings and beheaded them. The statues you see today are 19th-century replicas, but you can see some of the original heads at the Musée National du Moyen Âge (see pages 128–129). Below the Gallery of the Kings, the left portal is dedicated to the Virgin Mary, the central portal shows the Last Judgement and the right portal, dedicated to St. Anne, shows Mary holding the infant Jesus, while Louis VII and Bishop Sully kneel in worship.

**RATINGS**

| | |
|---|---|
| Historic interest | ●●●● |
| Photo stops (views) | ●●●●● |

**TIPS**

- Try to visit just before a service, to experience the palpable sense of anticipation as lights are gradually turned on and people gather to worship.
- Instead of paying tourist prices in the nearby cafés and restaurants, enjoy a picnic in the grassy square Jean XXIII, on the southern side of the cathedral.

## TOWERS

It's a tough climb, but it is worth tackling the towers, 69m (226ft) high, for the views over Paris and a closer look at the gargoyles. You'll be following the fictional footsteps of Notre-Dame's bell ringer, Quasimodo. Two-thirds of the way up (and a mere 285 steps) is the gargoyle parapet known as the Galerie des Chimères, where you can enjoy views across the Latin Quarter to the Tour Montparnasse, as well as along the Seine and across the Île de la Cité to Sainte-Chapelle. This is a great place to photograph the quirky gargoyles, added in the 19th century by Viollet-le-Duc (see background, page 140). A wooden staircase in the South Tower leads to the 13-tonne Emmanuel bell, recast in 1686 and evoking memories of a tormented Quasimodo. A separate spiral staircase leads up to the top of the South Tower (another 115 steps), where the panoramic views take in Sacré-Cœur to the north, the Arc de Triomphe to the west, the modern Bibliothèque Nationale to the east and the Panthéon to the south. At the top, take a moment to consider how the view must have changed since the towers were completed in 1245.

## THE WINDOWS

Notre-Dame has stunning stained glass and it is hard to imagine how the cathedral must have looked in the 18th century, when officials replaced many of the medieval windows with clear glass to let in more light. Much of the current stained glass dates from the 19th and 20th centuries. The south rose window, 13m (42ft) in diameter, is especially glorious when the sun shines through, adding extra vibrancy to the purple hues. Christ stands in the heart of the window, encircled by angels, apostles, martyrs and scenes from the New Testament. Opposite, the middle of the north rose window shows Mary holding a young Jesus. Old Testament prophets, priests and kings fill the rest of the window, one of the cathedral's few originals.

## CHOIR SCREEN, ALTAR AND NOTRE-DAME DE PARIS

Don't miss the cathedral's intricately carved and painted 14th-century choir screen, restored in the 1960s. Its enchanting depictions of gospel scenes include the Wise Men bringing their gifts to baby Jesus, Jesus riding into Jerusalem on a donkey, and the Last Supper.

The modern bronze high altar in the middle of the cathedral was consecrated in 1989. It depicts gospel writers Matthew, Mark, Luke and John and Old Testament prophets Isaiah, Ezekiel, Daniel and Jeremiah.

Nearby you can see the most famous of Notre-Dame's 37 statues of the Virgin Mary. Known as Notre-Dame de Paris, it dates from the 14th century and was installed in the cathedral in the 19th century.

## CHAPELS

The cathedral is lined with small chapels, added during the 13th and 14th centuries and dedicated to saints. Guilds used to meet in these chapels and each May Day they would donate a painting to the cathedral. Some of these works of art remain on display today, including pieces by 17th-century artists Charles Le Brun and Eustache Le Sueur.

## BASICS

**Cathedral**

68 N8•place du Parvis Notre-Dame, 75004
01 42 34 56 10
Daily 8–6.45. Closed on some religious feast days
Free
Cité, St-Michel, Châtelet
21, 24, 38, 47, 85, 96
RER lines B, C St-Michel
Plenty on Île de la Cité and in the nearby Latin Quarter
Small bookshop in the cathedral. Larger bookshop/giftshop halfway up the tower
A wide choice in many languages
Guided tours: in French, daily at noon and Mon and Sat at 2pm; in English, Wed–Thu at noon, Sat at 2.30. Extra tours in English in August.
Organ recitals at 4.30 on Sun

**Towers**

6 place du Parvis Notre-Dame (entrance is on the northwestern corner of the cathedral)
Daily 9–7.30 Jul–end Aug (until 11pm Sat–Sun); 9.30–7.30 Apr–end Jun and Sep; 10–5.30 rest of year; last entry 45 min before closing
Adult €5.50, under 18 free

**Treasury**

Entrance is within the cathedral, on the southern side near the choir
Mon–Sat 9.30–6, Sun 1.30–5.30
Adult €2.50, child €1

**Crypt**

1 place du Parvis Notre-Dame
01 55 42 50 10
Tue–Sun 10–6
Adult €3.30, child €2.20

www.monum.fr (in French and English)

*Notre-Dame—a symbol of Paris*

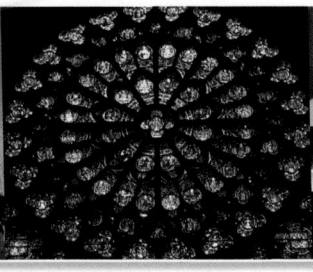

*The vibrant south rose window*

*Prayer candles*

*The portal of the Last Judgement (left), on the west façade*

**FACTS AND FIGURES**

- The cathedral is 128m (420ft) long and its transept is 48m (157ft) wide.
- The spire is 90m (295ft) high. The towers are 69m (226ft) high.
- More than 1,300 oak trees were felled to make the cathedral's wooden frame.
- The organ dates from the early 18th century and has 7,800 pipes.

### TREASURY AND CRYPT

Notre-Dame's Trésor holds medieval manuscripts, religious paraphernalia and relics, including the Crown of Thorns, bought for an exorbitant amount by Louis IX (see page 160). It's not a vital part of the Notre-Dame experience, but the gold and jewel-encrusted items give an insight into the wealth and power wielded by the Church over the years. The cathedral's Crypt is often overlooked by visitors, perhaps because the entrance is outside, on the opposite side of the place du Parvis Notre-Dame. Down here you'll see Roman foundations and archaeological finds.

## BACKGROUND

In the 12th century, Bishop Maurice de Sully decided that Paris needed its own cathedral. Pope Alexander III laid the foundation stone in 1163 and the choir was constructed in just under 20 years. Guilds of carpenters, stone-carvers, iron forgers and glass craftsmen worked on the grand project but it took almost 200 years to complete, finishing in 1345. For years Notre-Dame doubled as a meeting place for trade unions and a dormitory for the homeless. Its cathedral school was renowned throughout Europe. But by the time Napoleon was crowned in the cathedral in 1804 it was in a state of disrepair. Victor Hugo, author of *The Hunchback of Notre-Dame*, campaigned for its restoration, concerned at the absence of countless statues (toppled during the Revolution), the lack of stained glass and the amputation of the spire in 1787. His ranting met with some success. The statues in the Gallery of Kings were eventually reproduced and a 90m (295ft) spire was erected. Viollet-le-Duc oversaw the restoration in the mid-19th century. His work included replacing some of the clear-glass windows with stained glass and modestly adding a statue of himself among the Apostles. It wasn't until after World War II that the rest of the windows were replaced. Today, Notre-Dame remains an important place of worship, as well as one of Paris's top visitor attractions.

*The striking silhouette of Notre-Dame at sunset (above)*

*The vast interior (left)*

**NOTRE-DAME FLOORPLAN**

Porte Rouge
High altar
Louis XIV
Pietà
Portail du Cloître
North rose window
Louis XIII
Choir stalls
Entrance to tower
Notre-Dame de Paris
Portail de St-Étienne
ENTRANCE
Portail de la Vierge
Portail de Jugement Dernier
Portail de Sainte-Anne
South rose window

*The strikingly modern Opéra Bastille*

## OPÉRA BASTILLE

68 Q8•place de la Bastille (box office: 120 rue de Lyon), 75012 ☎ 01 40 01 19 70 (information); 0892 899 090 (reservations) Box office: Mon–Sat 11–6.30 Guided tours: adult €10, child (under 17) €5 Guided visits last 1 hour 15 minutes–check on the notice board in the box office for details www.opera-de-paris.fr

The geometric marble façade of this modern opera house dominates place de la Bastille (see page 80). The 2,700-seat auditorium hosts prestigious productions (see page 202). The imposing building made its presence felt even before it was constructed. The project, championed by President Mitterrand in the early 1980s, ran into controversy when a design by a relatively unknown architect, Carlos Ott, was selected from more than 700 entries. The opera house attracted further criticism for its ungainly volume and its cost, but it was ready to open for the bicentenary of the French Revolution in 1989.

## ORANGERIE

67 K6•Jardin des Tuileries, 75001 Closed until autumn 2004, then Wed–Mon 10–6 Concorde 24, 42, 52, 72, 73, 84, 94

The stately Orangerie started life as a greenhouse but is now an art gallery housing eight of Monet's world-famous *Water Lily* paintings. It was constructed in 1852, in Second Empire style, to overwinter orange trees from the Jardin des Tuileries (see page 105). It became an art gallery in the early 20th century, and now shelters the Walter-Guillaume collection of around 140 Impressionist and 20th-century paintings. Artists represented include Pierre-Auguste Renoir, Paul Cézanne and Pablo Picasso.

# OPÉRA PALAIS GARNIER

**This architectural masterpiece, designed by Charles Garnier, was the largest theatre in the world when it opened in 1875.**

| RATING | |
|---|---|
| Cultural interest | ●●●● |
| Historic interest | ●●● |
| Photo stops (exterior) | ●●● |

67 L5•place de l'Opéra, 75009 ☎ 01 40 01 22 63. Box office: 08 92 89 90 90. Museum: 01 47 42 07 02 Daily 10–5 (open until 6pm, mid-Jul to mid-Sep). Closed 1 Jan, 1 May and when there is a matinée performance/special event. The auditorium is closed during rehearsals and shows Adult €6, child €3, under 10 free Opéra 20, 21, 22, 27, 29, 42, 52, 53, 66, 68, 81, 95 Guided tours last 1 hour 30 minutes and cost €10; in French, daily at noon; in English, Sat at 12.30pm (except when there is a matinée performance). Telephone in advance: 01 40 01 25 17 €6 Gift shop www.opera-de-paris.fr (an informative site, in French, with some English pages, including practical information, history, events calendar and photo gallery)

The sumptuous Opéra Palais Garnier was commissioned by Napoleon III and inaugurated in 1875. Charles Garnier beat more than 170 hopefuls in a competition to design the prestigious building. Work finished 15 years after the official acceptance of his riotous design.

The opera house was for a time the largest theatre in the world (11,000sq m/118,404sq ft), a fittingly lavish epitaph to the architecture of the Second Empire. The stage can accommodate up to 450 performers and the opulent auditorium holds around 2,200 spectators under a domed ceiling painted by Marc Chagall in 1964. The Italianate, horseshoe-shape auditorium has red and gold décor and a huge crystal chandelier.

The decorative façade has been likened to a huge ornamental wedding cake. Look out for Carrier-Belleuse's provocative lamp-bearing statues and the copy of Jean-Baptiste Carpeaux's sculpted group *La Danse* to the right of the front arcade (the 1869 original is now in the Musée d'Orsay). A small library-museum presents the history of the Opéra and includes paintings, photographs and operatic memorabilia. Temporary exhibitions are held throughout the year. Many operatic performances are today staged at the Opéra Bastille (see left). The Opéra Palais Garnier is almost exclusively devoted to ballet (see page 202).

**Don't miss** The splendid marble and gilt Grand Staircase and the baroque Grand Foyer are highlights inside.

*Charles Garnier's lavish opera house, crowned by a statue of Apollo*

*A model ship on display at the Musée National de la Marine*

# PALAIS DE CHAILLOT

**From the terrace of the elegant Palais de Chaillot there is a breathtaking view across the Seine to the Eiffel Tower.**

The colonnaded Palais de Chaillot was built for the *Exposition Universelle* of 1937 and offers stunning views of the Eiffel Tower, and the Champ de Mars beyond. Its curved wings are dotted with gleaming bronze statues and the wide terraces, overlooking the fountains of the Jardins du Trocadéro, bustle with street artists, souvenir sellers, food kiosks and visitors admiring the Eiffel Tower. The palace currently houses two museums and the Théâtre National de Chaillot (*tel 01 53 65 30 00; www.theatre-chaillot.fr*), which sits beneath the terrace, between the two wings.

## MUSEUMS

The Musée National de la Marine and the Musée de l'Homme are in the palace's west wing. The Musée National de la Marine is one of the largest maritime museums in the world and was founded by Charles X in 1827. It focuses on French naval history from the 18th century to the present day and displays paintings, naval instruments and a vast array of model ships. There is also a workshop where you can watch the models being restored. The Musée de l'Homme has anthropological and ethnographical collections, including items from Asia, Africa and South America. Its Salon de la Musique displays around 500 musical instruments from around the world. Part of the collection is due to move to the Musée du Quai Branly in 2005 (see page 126).

## THE FUTURE

The eastern wing of the palace was badly damaged by a fire in 1997 and as a result its two museums are now closed. One of them, the Musée des Monuments Français, created in 1882 by the architect Viollet-le-Duc, is under restoration and is due to reopen in 2005, under a new name—the Cité de l'Architecture et du Patrimoine. The museum will focus on French architecture, from the Middle Ages to the 20th century. The other museum, the Musée du Cinéma Henri-Langlois and the Cinémathèque Française, will become part of the new Maison du Cinéma complex, also due to open in 2005, in the former American Cultural Center, in Bercy, on the other side of the city (see page 113).

**RATINGS**

| | |
|---|---|
| Good for kids | ●●● |
| Historic interest | ●●● |
| Photo stops (views) | ●●●● |

**BASICS**

66 F6•17 place du Trocadéro et du 11 Novembre, 75016

**Musée National de la Marine**

01 53 65 69 69
Wed–Mon 10–6 (last entry 5.15). Closed 1 Jan, 1 May and 25 Dec
Adult €7, child (6–18) €3.85, under 6 free
Trocadéro
22, 30, 32, 63, 72, 82
Audioguides (French, English; €4) available for temporary exhibitions
Bookshop/gift shop
www.culture.fr/marine and www.musee-marine.fr

**Musée de l'Homme**

01 44 05 72 72
Wed–Mon 9.45–5.15; last entry 30 min before closing. Closed public hols
Adult €5, child €3
Trocadéro
22, 30, 32, 63, 72, 82
*Le Totem* restaurant
Bookshop/gift shop
www.mnhn.fr

*The monumental columns of the Panthéon (above). Writer Voltaire (right) is one of the French greats buried here*

# PANTHÉON

**Originally a basilica, this striking monument is now the final resting place of some of France's greatest citizens.**

The neoclassical grandeur of the Panthéon is an arresting sight after you have wandered through the warren-like streets of the Latin Quarter to reach it. This colossal mausoleum contains the tombs of many illustrious citizens, including writers Victor Hugo, Émile Zola and Voltaire, scientists Marie and Pierre Curie, Braille inventor Louis Braille, and World War II Resistance martyr Jean Moulin. To be 'pantheonized' is one of the greatest accolades in France and arguments still ignite periodically about who merits a re-burial here.

### GIVING THANKS

The monument was commissioned by Louis XV as a basilica dedicated to St. Geneviève, patron saint of Paris, in thanks for his recovery from gout. The king laid the foundation stone in 1764 and work finished in 1790, by which time the original architect, Jacques Germain Soufflot, had died. Only a year later, in 1791, the Revolutionaries seized the building, bricking up the windows and changing its function to a secular Temple of Fame.

### VISITING THE PANTHÉON

You enter the building through an imposing peristyle, based on the grandiose frontage of Rome's Pantheon. The sculpted pediment portrays France's heroes receiving their rewards. Inside the vast, cross-shaped chamber the atmosphere feels austere. Religious heroes are prominent in many of the paintings in the naves, including St. Geneviève (western nave and choir), the beheaded St. Denis (western nave), Joan of Arc (northern nave) and St. Louis (northern nave). The Revolution also features in paintings and sculptures. Look up into the dome—the scientist Foucault hung a pendulum here in 1851 to prove the earth rotates. To climb to the colonnade beneath the dome, 35m (115ft) high, you must take a guided tour—and tackle 206 steps. Downstairs in the huge, shadowy crypt you can see the tombs of Voltaire, Victor Hugo, Émile Zola, Marie Curie and others.

**RATINGS**

| | |
|---|---|
| Historic interest | ●●● |
| Photo stops (exterior and views) | ●●● |

**TIPS**

- **See the notice board outside the Panthéon for times for the guided tours up to the dome's circular colonnade.**
- **If you don't feel like climbing to the colonnade, you can still enjoy views of the Eiffel Tower from the top of the Panthéon's steps.**

**BASICS**

- 67 M9•place du Panthéon, 75005
- 01 44 32 18 00
- 10–6.30, Apr–end Sep; 10–6 rest of year; last entrance 45 min before closing. Closed public hols
- Adult €7, under 18 free
- Cardinal-Lemoine
- 21, 27, 84, 85, 89
- RER B, Luxembourg
- Small bookshop/giftshop
- €6
- Guided tours in French. Ring ahead for other languages
- Near crypt

www.monum.fr (in French and English; click on the Panthéon symbol for historical information or to add your comments to the virtual visitors' book)

*The Parc de Monceau, a few Métro stops from the Arc de Triomphe*

*The magnificent art nouveau Métro entrance at place des Abbesses*

## PARC ANDRÉ-CITROËN

66 off F9•rue Balard, rue Leblanc, quai André-Citroën, 75015 0820 007 575 Mon–Fri 8.30–dusk, Sat–Sun 9–dusk Balard, Javel 42, 88 RER line C, Boulevard Victor Free
www.paris.fr

As the name suggests, this futuristic park replaced a vast Citroën car factory in the south-west of Paris. Nearly 14 hectares (35 acres) of ultramodern landscaping lead down to the Seine, burying embankment traffic in their wake. Specialist gardens are colour-coded and you'll find zany experimentation with metal and water. Even the customary Orangery has had the postmodern treatment, evolving into two gigantic high-tech glasshouses. The park opened in 1992, following Citroën's decision to move its factory out of Paris in the 1970s.

## PARC DE MONCEAU

66 off H4•boulevard de Courcelles, 75008 0820 007 575 7am–10pm, Apr–end Sep; 7am–8pm, rest of year Monceau 30, 84, 94 Free
www.paris.fr

It's worth taking a trip out to this timeless park, northeast of the Arc de Triomphe, with its fake ruins, tree-shaded pond and magnificent wrought-iron gates. The weekend is best, when the park buzzes with joggers, families and residents of the classy surrounding area. From the Métro station, with its art nouveau entrance, you enter the park through tall, gilded wrought-iron gates. Inside, there's a pond bordered with fake Roman columns, a pyramid, a rotunda, various statues and plenty of trees and flowers. For children there are donkey rides, swings and a merry-go-round. The park was landscaped in the English style by Thomas Blaikie in 1783 and became a public park in 1861. Nearby attractions include the Musée Cernuschi (see page 113) and the Musée Nissim de Camondo (see page 126).

## PARC MONTSOURIS

330 off L11•boulevard Jourdan/avenue Reille, 75014 0820 007 575 Daily 7am–8pm, Nov–end Mar; daily 7am–9pm rest of year Free Porte d'Orléans 21, 88 RER line B, Cité Universitaire

Parc Montsouris, in the south of the city, is a vast English-style park, laid out in 1878. The site was originally a granite quarry and was once dotted with windmills. Now paths twist up gentle slopes among a large variety of trees and plants. There are also play areas and a lake with a waterfall. The park is home to a meteorological observatory.

This pocket of green was a popular hideaway with artists and literati when the nearby artists' studios were inhabited by luminaries such as Georges Braque, Salvador Dalí and Henry Miller.

## PAVILLON DE L'ARSENAL

68 P8•21 boulevard Morland, 75004 01 42 76 33 97 Tue–Sat 10.30–6.30, Sun 11–7 Sully-Morland 67, 86, 87 Free
www.pavillon-arsenal.com

If you want to learn more about how Paris has evolved as a city, this architectural and town-planning information site is worth a visit. At ground level, a permanent exhibition uses drawings, models, documents and photographs to explain the development projects that have shaped the city. There is also a huge scale model, a bookshop and a seating area where you can read newspapers, including foreign titles. The upper floors of the skylit venue host temporary exhibitions.

The iron and glass building was constructed in 1879, near an area where gunpowder was made, hence the name.

## PIGALLE

69 L3•south of Montmartre 75009/75018 Pigalle 30, 54, 67, Montmartrobus

The name Pigalle is synonymous with the blatant sex trade that has flourished there for decades. There are sleazy bars, sex shops and peep shows in the boulevard Rochechouart and surrounding streets. In the 19th century, the painters Pierre-Auguste Renoir and Henri Toulouse-Lautrec were frequent visitors, scouting around place Pigalle looking for models among the dancers.

## PLACE DES ABBESSES

69 M3•place des Abbesses, Montmartre, 75018 Abbesses Montmartrobus A selection

Place des Abbesses is less touristy than place du Tertre, farther up the Montmartre hill, so makes a quieter coffee stop.

The square has a magnificent art nouveau Métro entrance, which leads into Paris's deepest station, 40m (131ft) below ground. The church of St-Jean-l'Évangéliste (1904) picks up on the art nouveau theme, with decorative windows that enliven the rather ugly red-brick cladding. This conspicuous brickwork earned it the nickname St-Jean-des-Briques. The square takes its name from the abbey which once stood on the site. A mischievous legend claims that Henri de Navarre, who later became King Henri IV, had a fling with the abbess in 1590.

**Don't miss** Seek out the Mur des Je t'Aime (see page 22).

# Parc de la Villette

**One of the world's largest scientific and cultural sites. This urban park combines arts and sciences with nature.**

THE SIGHTS

**BASICS**

**Cité des Sciences et de l'Industrie**
320 S1•30 avenue Corentin-Cariou, 75019 ☎ 01 40 05 80 00
Explora exhibitions: Tue–Sat 10–6, Sun 10–7. Planetarium: Tue–Sun, shows every hour from 11–5 (except 1pm). Aquarium: Tue–Sat 10–6, Sun 10–7. Géode: Tue–Sat 10.30–9.30, Sun 10.30–7.30 (times vary Mon and public hols). *Argonaute*: Tue–Fri 10.30–5.30, Sat–Sun 11–6. Cinaxe: Tue–Sun, shows every 15 min from 11–1 and 2–5 (times vary on public hols)
Explora exhibitions: adult €7.50, child €5.50, under 7 free. Planetarium: adult €2.50 (plus admission to Explora), under 7 free. Cité des Enfants: €5 per person for a 90-minute session. Aquarium: free. Géode: €8.75, child €6.75. Argonaute: €3. Cinaxe: €5.20, child €4.50.
Porte de la Villette
75, 139, 150, 152, PC2, PC3
Canauxrama organizes canal trips to the Parc de la Villette, see page 248.
Explora exhibitions: Audioguides (€3.80) available in several languages, including English. Géode: Headsets, in English, available free from the information point
Mini-guide to the exhibitions: €3. Guide to the Cité des enfants: €3
*Le Hublot*, level -2
Several Gift shop/bookshop
Children under 3 are not admitted to the Géode, *L'Argonaute*, Cinaxe, Planetarium and Cité des Enfants.
www.cite-sciences.fr
www.lageode.fr

**Cité de la Musique**
320 S2•221 avenue Jean-Jaurès, 75019
☎ 01 44 84 45 45 (information); 01 44 84 44 84 (reservations)
Tue–Sat 12–6, Sun 10–6 (until 8 for concerts)
Museum: adult €6.10, under 18 free
Porte de Pantin
75, 151, PC2, PC3
Café de la Musique
Bookshop and gift shop
www.cite-musique.fr

## SEEING THE PARC DE LA VILLETTE

The ultramodern Parc de la Villette catapults you into a futuristic world. Its innovatively landscaped 55ha (135 acres) have a range of cultural and leisure activities, including a science museum, music complex, hemispheric cinema, exhibition venue and concert hall.

The park is northeast of the city's heart and is easily reached by Métro. For the Cité de Sciences et de l'Industrie take line seven to Porte de la Villette. For the Cité de la Musique take line five to Porte de Pantin. A covered walkway runs the length of the park, linking the two attractions. The walk takes around 15 minutes. The reception desks in the Cité des Sciences et de l'Industrie have information in several languages. You can also pick up a schedule (*Le Programme)* of the shows, films and presentations here. Reserve shows, films and activities as soon as you arrive at the Cité des Sciences et de l'Industrie because they are very popular.

## HIGHLIGHTS

### CITÉ DES SCIENCES ET DE L'INDUSTRIE

This giant, futuristic science and technology venue is packed with high-tech, hands-on displays, in addition to shows, audiovisual presentations, optical illusions and interactive experiments.
The Explora exhibitions, on levels 1 and 2, cover five main themes: The Universe; Water and the Earth; Challenges of the Living World; Industry; and Communication. There is a planetarium on level 2 and the excellent Cité des Enfants on level 0. Here games and fun experiments encourage children to learn. The Louis-Lumière cinema, on level 0, shows 3D films and the Aquarium, on level -2, has more than 200 species of marine life from Mediterranean waters. The Cité des Sciences et de l'Industrie also has a Médiathèque (a multimedia library), a health village (offering information), a cyber-base and the Cité des Métiers (providing careers guidance).

### LA GÉODE, *L'ARGONAUTE* AND LE CINAXE

Just south of the Cité des Sciences, across the moat, stands the space-age Géode cinema. This gigantic sphere measures 36m (118ft) in diameter. The exterior is covered with curved triangles of polished steel creating a spectacular distorted mirrored effect. Inside, you can see films on a 1,000sq-m (10,764sq-ft) hemispheric screen—the images are 10 times larger than in a normal cinema. Next to the Géode you can explore the *Argonaute*, a military submarine that was launched in 1957 and served in the Toulon submarine squadron for 24 years. On the western side of the Cité des Sciences stands the 56-seater Cinaxe—one of the biggest simulator cinemas in the world. The high-tech simulator moves in synchronization with the film. 3-D glasses add to the excitement of this bumpy ride.

### CITÉ DE LA MUSIQUE

The highlight here is the Musée de la Musique, a fascinating music museum displaying around 900 musical instruments, dating from the Renaissance to the present day. As you walk around, an infrared audioguide plays the music of the instruments in front of you.

Paintings, sculptures and beautiful models of concert halls are also displayed. Concerts are staged in the amphitheatre, with its baroque organ. The Cité also contains research facilities, a media library, music and dance information rooms and the Conservatoire National Supérieur de Musique de Paris.

| RATINGS | |
|---|---|
| Cultural interest | ●●● |
| Good for kids | ●●●●● |
| Photo stops | ●●● |

## BACKGROUND

Parc de la Villette was created in the 1980s, designed by architect Bernard Tschumi. He transformed the former abattoir into landscaped grounds containing water features, themed gardens, children's playgrounds, cultural sites, cafés and events venues. The site straddles the Canal de l'Ourcq and is decorated with red metal follies. The city abattoirs stood here from 1867 until 1974 and their cattle hall was transformed into La Grande Halle, now used for trade fairs and concerts. The Cité des Sciences et de l'Industrie opened in 1986, on the same day that Halley's Comet passed near the earth. Its concrete, steel and glass building, surrounded by a moat, was designed by Adrien Fainsilber. The Cité de la Musique, designed by Christian de Portzamparc, is one of the newer arrivals at the park. It opened in 1995.

## CONCERTS

On the eastern edge of the park, a 6,000-seat venue called Zénith stages pop and rock concerts. Music events are also held in the 15,000-seat Grande Halle.

*The Cité des Sciences et de l'Industrie (above, left). Enjoying a drink in the Café de la Musique (above, middle). You never know what you might find at Parc de la Villette (above)*

**PARC DE LA VILLETTE**

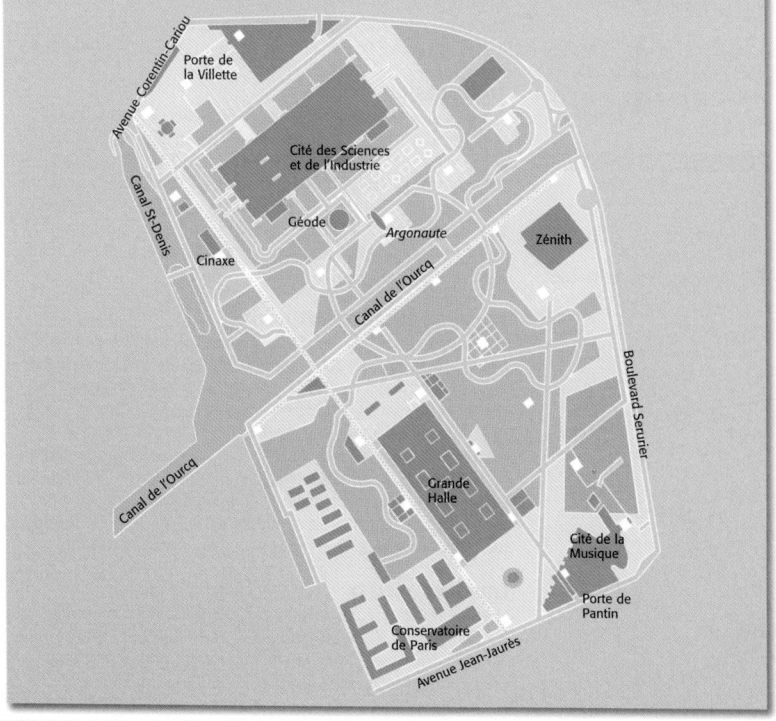

*One of the fountains in the place de la Concorde (above). Hieroglyphics on the obelisk, Paris's oldest monument (left)*

**RATINGS**

| | |
|---|---|
| Historic interest | ●●●● |
| Photo stops | ●●●● |

**TIPS**

- Use the pedestrian crossing when walking to the middle of the square—but be careful, as the traffic does not always stop when it should.
- Take time to appreciate the wonderful views from the heart of the square, especially up the Champs-Élysées.

**BASICS**

67 K6•place de la Concorde, 75008
Free
Concorde
24, 42, 72, 73, 84, 94
In the nearby Jardin des Tuileries

# PLACE DE LA CONCORDE

**Paris's largest square is home to the city's oldest monument. It also played a gruesome role during the Revolution.**

Hectic place de la Concorde was once an area of swampland but now buzzes with people and traffic. It sits on the intersection of two principal axes and standing in the middle you get four dramatic views. To the west is the Champs-Élysées, leading to the Arc de Triomphe, and to the east you can look past the ornate gates of the Jardin des Tuileries down towards the Louvre. North along the rue Royale is La Madeleine church and to the south, across the Pont de la Concorde, is the colonnaded Palais Bourbon, home to the Assemblée Nationale.

## ROYAL DESIGN

The square was designed by Jacques-Ange Gabriel and laid out between 1755 and 1775 to accommodate an equestrian statue of the reigning king, Louis XV. Gabriel designed the two properties flanking the rue Royale—the Hôtel Crillon and the Hôtel de la Marine—in addition to the stone pavilions in each corner of the octagonal square. These are topped with female statues each representing a major French city—Lille, Strasbourg, Lyon, Marseille, Bordeaux, Nantes, Brest and Rouen.

## HORRORS OF THE REVOLUTION

The square was originally called place Louis XV but was renamed place de la Révolution during the Revolution. The statue of Louis XV was removed and the guillotine erected in its stead. Between 1793 and 1795 more than 1,300 people were beheaded here, including Louis XVI and his queen, Marie-Antoinette. With the cooling of revolutionary passions in 1795, the square was renamed the place de la Concorde, in the hope of a less troubled future. Soon after, Guillaume I Coustou's magnificent *Chevaux de Marly* (1743–45) were added to the entrance of the Champs-Élysées. The ones you see today are replicas—the orginals are now in the Louvre.

## EGYPTIAN OBELISK

In 1833 Mohammed Ali, Viceroy of Egypt, presented King Louis-Philippe with a 230-tonne, pink granite obelisk, 23m (75ft) high. It is around 3,300-years-old, engraved with hieroglyphics, and was once used to measure the sun's shadow at the Temple of Thebes.

*Place de la Madeleine is the place to go for luxury food*

*Gold statues adorn the Palais de Chaillot, on place du Trocadéro*

*Shopping in place Vendôme*

## PLACE DE LA MADELEINE

67 K5•place de la Madeleine, 75008
Madeleine
24, 42, 52, 84, 94

The colossal church of La Madeleine (*Mon–Sat 8.30–7, Sun 7.30–7*) dominates this square. It is supported by 52 enormous Corinthian pillars and resembles a Greek temple. The triangular pediment bears a sculpted frieze of the Last Judgement. Construction began in 1764, but did not finish until 1842. The church has had a varied career, narrowly avoiding being transformed into a railway station, stock exchange, bank and yet another temple to Napoleon. It is now a popular venue for society weddings and funerals and has seen the coffins of notables such as Frédéric Chopin and Marlene Dietrich.

After you have climbed the steps to the main entrance, turn around to admire the view down the rue Royale to the obelisk in the place de la Concorde (see page 148), across the river to the Palais Bourbon (see page 80) and beyond to the golden cupola of Les Invalides (see pages 99–101).

**Don't miss** Food connoisseurs should visit Fauchon, the exclusive foodstore synonymous with the best of French food. There are plenty of other food shops and restaurants on the square, as well as a small flower market.

## PLACE DU TROCADÉRO ET DU 11 NOVEMBRE

321 F6•place du Trocadéro et du 11 Novembre, 75016 Trocadéro
22, 30, 32, 63

Semi-circular place du Trocadéro et du 11 Novembre faces the monumental wings of the Palais de Chaillot (see page 143), the fountains of the Jardins du Trocadéro and, across the Seine, the Eiffel Tower. Six avenues radiate from it and an equestrian statue of World War I Allied Commander Marshal Foch stands at its heart.

The square was named after an Andalusian fort occupied by the French in 1823 and was given its present shape in 1858, when a first palace was built. This palace was replaced with the Palais de Chaillot, built for the 1937 Universal Exhibition. There are plenty of cafés and restaurants in the area.

## PLACE VENDÔME

67 L5•place Vendôme, 75001
Opéra, Tuileries 21, 27, 29, 68, 72, 81, 95
www.paris.fr

Stately place Vendôme is the supreme symbol of Parisian chic. You'll need a hefty bank balance to venture into its exclusive jewellery stores, and its hotel, the Ritz, is among the most prestigious in the world. Noted residents of the square have included Frédéric Chopin, who died at number 12, and Anton Mesmer, founder of the theory of mesmerism, who held experiments at number 16. Marcel Proust, Ernest Hemingway and Coco Chanel were guests at the Ritz, and Diana, Princess of Wales, dined there before her fateful car journey across Paris in August 1997.

Louis XIV commissioned the classical square in 1685, choosing Versailles architect Jules Hardouin-Mansart, who had impressed him with his design for place des Victoires (see below). The focal point was an equestrian statue of the king, but this fell victim to the mob during the Revolution. In 1810 it was replaced by a 44m (144ft) bronze column, based on Trajan's column in Rome, but this was pulled to the ground during another revolution, the Paris Commune of 1871.

It was rebuilt and now supports a Caesar-like statue of Napoleon I. The square's turbulent past has caused its name to be changed frequently over the years, with titles including place des Conquêtes, place Louis le Grand, place des Piques and place Internationale.

Keep an eye out for traffic while admiring the square—despite the cobbles, it is not pedestrian-only.

## PLACE DES VICTOIRES

67 M6•place des Victoires, 75002
Bourse, Sentier 29
www.paris.fr

Elegant, circular place des Victoires is tucked quietly at the end of the busy shopping street, rue Étienne Marcel. Its curved mansions house the chic boutiques of Kenzo, Cacharel and other leading fashion names. The square was laid out in 1685 by the architect Jules Hardouin-Mansart, who also worked on Versailles. It was commissioned by the Maréchal de la Feuillade to celebrate the victories of the Sun King, Louis XIV. A statue of the king was destroyed during the Revolution and later replaced by an equestrian sculpture by Bosio.

**Don't miss** Look down rue Catinat to see the imposing Banque de France.

*Napoleon tops the column in place Vendôme (left)*

*Tranquil place des Vosges (above).*
*A carving on one of the elegant buildings lining the square*

**RATINGS**

| | |
|---|---|
| Historic interest | ●●●● |
| Photo stops | ●●● |

**TIPS**

- Sunday afternoon is a good time to catch the square, as this is when Parisians come for a stroll, to the accompaniment of outdoor musicians

- To find out more about Paris life during the place des Vosges's heyday, visit the nearby Musée Carnavalet (see pages 114–115).

**BASICS**

68 P7•place des Vosges, 75004
Bastille, St-Paul, Chemin Vert
29, 96

# PLACE DES VOSGES

**Paris's oldest square is the perfect place to while away a few hours, relaxing in an outdoor café or enjoying the fountains.**

Picturesque place des Vosges is steeped in history and only minutes away from the busy, modern Bastille district. It is a great example of the Paris phenomenon where you can be on a traffic-filled road teeming with people one minute, and in a quiet grassy square the next, seemingly miles from 21st-century bustle. Here you can browse in the boutiques, antiques shops and art galleries in the arcades surrounding the square or sip hot chocolate in one of the cafés.

## PLACE ROYALE

A royal palace originally stood on this site but was demolished in the 16th century by Catherine de Medici when her husband, Henri II, was killed in a tournament here. Later, Henri IV commissioned the symmetrical place Royale, one of the first examples of town planning in Paris. The square was inaugurated in 1612, amid spectacular celebrations. In 1800, it was renamed place des Vosges in tribute to the first French *département* to pay its new taxes.

## SYMMETRY

The square's harmonious form is created by 36 red brick- and stone-faced houses, nine on each side, with arcaded ground floors and steep pitched roofs. These striking buildings surround a formal garden containing fountains, trees, gravel paths, a children's play area, ornate lampposts and a statue of Louis XIII. The north and south façades of the square retain a royal touch, as each has a larger, central house, respectively the Pavillon de la Reine (Queen's pavilion), and the Pavillon du Roi (King's pavilion). The Pavillon de la Reine is now a four-star hotel (see page 292).

## FAMOUS RESIDENTS

Many famous characters have inhabited the square's mansions and apartments. Princesses, duchesses, official mistresses, Cardinal Richelieu, the Duc de Sully, writer Alphonse Daudet and, more recently, the painter Francis Bacon and the architect Richard Rogers have all gazed out at its perfect symmetry. Another French author, Victor Hugo, penned many a manuscript at number six, his home from 1832 to 1848, and now a museum (see page 106).

*A winged Pegasus shimmers on top of the Pont Alexandre III*

*The Pont des Arts, linking the Louvre with the Institut de France*

*The Pont Neuf, Paris's oldest bridge*

## PONT ALEXANDRE III

66 J6•cours La Reine/quai d'Orsay Invalides, Champs-Élysées-Clémenceau 63, 83, 93 RER line C, Invalides

Four gilded bronze Pegasus figures watch over this wildly ornate bridge, which sparkles in the setting sun. The bridge forms a link between Les Invalides (see pages 99–101) on the Left Bank and the Grand Palais and Petit Palais (see page 95) on the Right, its glory marred only by the stream of traffic.

Symbolic of the optimism of the Belle Époque, it was built for the 1900 *Exposition Universelle* and dedicated to a new alliance between Russia and France. The foundation stone was laid by Tsar Nicholas II, son of Alexandre III, and the façade bears the coats of arms of both Paris and Russia. The bridge is crammed with elaborate decoration by more than 15 artists.

## PONT DE L'ALMA

66 H6•place de l'Alma/place de la Résistance Alma-Marceau 42, 63, 72, 80, 92 RER line C, Pont de l'Alma

The first Pont de l'Alma was built in 1856 to commemorate a victory over the Russians by the Franco-British alliance in the Crimean War. The bridge developed subsidence and was replaced in 1974. The underpass running along the Seine here is where the fatal car crash involving Diana, Princess of Wales happened in August 1997. The Liberty Flame, placed near the entrance in 1987 by the *International Herald Tribune* as a symbol of American and French friendship, has become a memorial to the People's Princess.

**Don't miss** A statue of a Zouave soldier from the original bridge is now a high-water marker.

## PONT DES ARTS

67 L7•quai du Louvre/quai de Conti Louvre-Rivoli 24, 27, 39, 69, 72

This is one of Paris's most romantic bridges and is also a popular place for street performances and impromptu parties. Also known as the Passerelle (footbridge) des Arts, it links the Louvre (hence its name) with the Institut de France, and was rebuilt in 1984 with seven steel arches. Napoleon commissioned the original cast-iron bridge, Paris's first. It had nine arches and was completed in 1804.

## PONT DE BIR-HAKEIM

321 F7•quai Branly, 75015 Bir-Hakeim, Passy 72

The Pont de Bir-Hakeim was built between 1903 and 1905, replacing a 19th-century footbridge. The two-tiered art nouveau bridge has a walkway, roadway and a viaduct for the Métro. It is made up of two unequal metal structures on either side of the allée des Cygnes. Trains rattle across the top level, which is supported by cast-iron pillars. Originally called the Passy Viaduct, the bridge was renamed the Pont de Bir-Hakeim in 1949, in memory of the victory of General Koenig in Libya in 1942.

## PONT MARIE

68 P8•voie Georges Pompidou/Île St-Louis Pont Marie 67

This stone bridge, linking the Île St-Louis with the Right Bank, had a controversial beginning. Île St-Louis property developer Christophe Marie first suggested the bridge in 1605, but objections from officials at Notre-Dame delayed completion until 1635. Disaster struck in the spring thaw of 1658. The bridge was top-heavy with tall houses (all the more *écus* for the developer) and a powerful flood caused two arches, along with the homes, shops and occupants they supported, to topple into the Seine. The bridge was subsequently rebuilt—without any new houses.

## PONT NEUF

67 M7•Île de la Cité Pont Neuf 24, 27, 58, 70

Ironically, the New Bridge is actually Paris's oldest surviving bridge, dating from 1604. It was Henri II's idea, in 1556, in order to ease his journey between the Louvre Palace and the abbey of St-Germain-des-Prés. The bridge opened almost half a century later, when the flamboyant Henri IV inaugurated it by galloping across on his charger. His equestrian statue still stands there, although it is a replacement of the original, which was melted down during the Revolution. For years this was the site of a permanent funfair. In 1985, the land-artist Christo ceremoniously wrapped the entire bridge.

## PONT ROYAL

67 L7•quai des Tuileries, rue du Bac Palais-Royal 24, 68, 69, 72 RER line C, Musée d'Orsay

The Pont Royal was a gift from Louis XIV, replacing a wooden bridge that had been destroyed by fire. The king chose one of his most prized architects, Jules Hardouin-Mansart, to design the graceful stone structure, and the bridge was in place by 1689. Nobles used it to travel from the exclusive Faubourg St-Germain district to the Tuileries Palace. In the 18th century, the bridge became the site of major Parisian festivities and fireworks. The hydrographic scales on each end pillar show high-water levels.

# Quartier Latin

**Mingle with students in this historic district, with its Roman ruins, medieval alleyways and abundance of cafés. Other attractions include a medieval museum, a 12th-century church and the soothing Luxembourg Garden.**

*St. Michael slays a dragon in the bustling square bearing his name*

*Browsing through the street stalls on the boulevard St-Michel*

*Enjoying a café-break—a popular pastime in the Latin Quarter*

**RATINGS**

| | |
|---|---|
| Historic interest | ●●●● |
| Photo stops | ●●●● |
| Shopping | ●●● |
| Walkability | ●●● |

**TIPS**

- For a stroll through the Latin Quarter see pages 228–229.

- You could while away an hour or so browsing in the English-language bookshop Shakespeare and Company (see page 182). Or head for the Gothic courtyard of the Musée National du Moyen Âge to admire the turrets and gargoyles.

**BASICS**

68 N9•Left Bank between Carrefour de l'Odéon and Jardin des Plantes, 75005

St-Michel, Cluny La Sorbonne, Odéon

21, 24, 27, 38, 63, 84, 85, 86, 87, 89

RER line B, C, St-Michel-Notre-Dame

Selection of restaurants and cafés (see page 258)

Clothes stores and bookshops

*The renowned bookstore Shakespeare and Company (top, far right)*

## SEEING THE LATIN QUARTER

The Latin Quarter is an essential part of the Paris experience. Its picturesque narrow side streets take you back to the Middle Ages, while the presence of many students gives the area a refreshing vibrancy. No other district of Paris claims so many bookshops or colleges, and there is also a host of historic churches, cinemas, jazz clubs and restaurants. You'll find a relaxed and youthful atmosphere compared to the frenetic, business-focused Right Bank. Here, the cliché of students and artists lingering for hours in cafés is actually true.

Your first taste of the Latin Quarter is likely to be the chaotic place St-Michel, with its imposing fountain symbolizing St. Michael slaying the dragon. From here there are views of Notre-Dame (see pages 137–141) on the nearby Île de la Cité. The busy boulevard St-Michel (or *Boul Mich* to students) runs from place St-Michel along the length of the district and teems with students, visitors and magazine kiosks. Unless you want to browse in its clothes stores and bookshops, it is best to venture onto the picturesque side streets.

## HIGHLIGHTS

### WANDERING IN MEDIEVAL STREETS

The area to the east of place St-Michel is a warren of winding, historic alleyways, redolent of the Middle Ages. You'll find small specialist shops in the streets off the *quais* and Greek restaurants in rue de la Huchette and rue de la Harpe. It is worth seeking out the small 12th-century church of St-Julien-le-Pauvre (see page 162) and the beautiful stained-glass windows of St-Séverin (see pages 162–163). The tranquil square René Viviani, off the quai de Montebello, is home to what is said to be Paris's oldest tree, planted in the early 17th century.

### LITERARY LIFE

Farther south, in the area around the Sorbonne, you can plunge into the heart of academia and probably find a café once frequented by Latin Quarter intelligentsia such as Paul Verlaine or Jean-Paul Sartre. This is also where you'll find the Panthéon (see page 144), final resting place of France's scientific, literary and political heroes.

*Crossing the Pont des Arts*

### GALLO-ROMAN BATHS

On the corner of boulevards St-Michel and St-Germain are the remains of the Gallo-Roman baths. The vast stone chamber that housed the Frigidarium (cold bath) is now part of the Musée National du Moyen Âge (see pages 128–129).

### GREEN LUNG

On the Latin Quarter's southern boundary, the flower-filled Jardin du Luxembourg (see pages 102–103) is the perfect place to rest your aching feet after a day exploring the streets.

## BACKGROUND

The Latin Quarter owes its scholarly, literary and artistic reputation to the founding of the Sorbonne university in the 13th century (see page 163) in an area known as the Montagne Ste-Geneviève. An animated crowd of European students soon flocked here, turning the university into a Catholic city-within-a-city. Other colleges grew up around it and the area gained the name Latin Quarter, after the language used by the students for everyday conversation. In the 15th century the introduction of printing presses made the rue St-Jacques France's publishing headquarters. Later, the district acquired a reputation for undisciplined and bohemian inhabitants, making it fertile soil for the Revolution. In May 1968, its rebellious streak re-emerged when students took to the streets (see page 39).

## RIVE DROITE

✚ •North of the Seine

The Right Bank (*Rive Droite*) is by far the larger of Paris's two parts and so is harder to define than the southern Left Bank (*Rive Gauche*). Kings built their palaces here, Baron Haussmann created his wide arteries and every ruler left at least one monument. The area boasts the Musée du Louvre, the outlandish Centre Georges Pompidou and two prestigious opera houses. Cushioning the grandeur are newer, burgeoning districts, including Bercy and La Villette, and spruced up older ones, such as the Marais. The Right Bank also contains the city's banking and business heart. In the far north is the former hilltop village of Montmartre.

## RIVE GAUCHE

✚ •South of the Seine

The Seine curves gently round the southern part of the city, known as the Left Bank, which is significantly smaller than the Right Bank. Despite this, many Left Bank residents claim they hardly ever cross the Seine; they have their Roman ruins, galleries, literary cafés and colleges in the Latin Quarter and St-Germain. France's rulers sit in the Palais Bourbon and Palais du Luxembourg and the 7th *arrondissement* is packed with stately residential avenues. Many of the landmarks that make up Paris's skyline are here: the Eiffel Tower, Les Invalides and the tall shadow of Tour Montparnasse. The four glass towers of the new national library, the Bibliothèque François Mitterrand, crown a huge redevelopment project in the 13th *arrondissement*, which is also the starting point for Paris's newest Métro line (14).

# Sacré-Cœur

**A gleaming white neo-Byzantine basilica, where you'll get wonderful views over Paris. Its stunning golden mosaic, inside, is one of the largest of its kind and its bell is one of the heaviest in the world.**

*Panoramic views over Paris (above). Sacré-Cœur during a service (left)*

*You never know who may be peering down at you*

*Cardinal Guibert, who sanctioned plans for the basilica in 1872*

## SEEING SACRÉ-CŒUR

The mighty Sacré-Cœur basilica is one of Paris's most prominent landmarks, shimmering at the top of Montmartre's hill. Its eastern-inspired dome is the second-highest point in Paris and the views from the top stretch up to 50km (31 miles). This sweeping panorama is the main attraction for its many visitors, who gather in hordes on the front steps. But walk inside the hushed interior, especially during Mass, and it is an altogether more spiritual experience.

The basilica is not the most accessible place, sitting north of central Paris, without an adjoining Métro station. Take the Métro to Anvers or Abbesses, then walk to square Willette, where a funicular (or flight of steep steps for the energetic) takes you the final way up the hill. Enter the basilica from the front doors on place du Parvis du Sacré-Cœur. If Mass is in progress, you may find your movements restricted, but otherwise you are free to roam. To climb to the dome or visit the crypt, leave the basilica and turn right, to a side door on the west of the building. Tickets for the Dome are issued from a machine here.

## HIGHLIGHTS

### PANORAMA

The views from Sacré-Cœur make the trip out here worthwhile even if you don't want to visit the basilica itself. Try to choose a clear day, when you'll see farther across the city and when the contrast between the glistening white domes of the basilica and the blue sky behind is at its most dramatic. If you are short of time, the view from the front terrace should keep your camera satisfied. Among the landmarks you can see are Notre-Dame, the gold dome of Les Invalides, and Tour Montparnasse. For striking views of the Eiffel Tower, head round the corner into rue Azaïs.

If you have the time (and energy), it is worth climbing the dome. The entrance, shared with the crypt, is on the western side of the basilica, in rue du Cardinal Guibert. A steep spiral staircase leads to the colonnade, where you'll have a vertigo-inducing view down into

**RATINGS**

| | |
|---|---|
| Historic interest | ●●●● |
| Photo stops (views) | ●●●●● |

**TIPS**

- Sacré-Cœur is a 10-minute walk from Abbesses or Anvers Métro stations. Or you could take the Montmartrobus to the base of the funicular.
- The funicular costs one Métro ticket each way—you'll probably consider it worthwhile when you see how many steps lead up to the basilica!
- Try to visit just before a service takes place (times are posted on the website). The basilica can seem rather sombre otherwise.

*If you don't use the funicular, it's a long climb up to the basilica (right)*

**FACTS AND FIGURES**

- Sacré-Cœur's hilltop location makes its bell tower and dome the second-highest points in Paris, after the Eiffel Tower. The bell tower is 84m (275.5ft) tall, 67cm (26in) higher than the dome.

- The basilica was originally designed by Paul Abadie, a pupil of Viollet-le-Duc, although six more architects were called in over the 39-year building project.

- The unstable ground under the basilica meant that pillars had to be sunk 33m (108ft) into the ground.

- The Savoyarde bell plays a C, while the four smaller bells, Félicité, Louise, Elisabeth and Nicole, play C, D, G and E.

the basilica, as well as out across Paris. The bronze statue you see just in front of the colonnade shows St. Michael killing a demon. Behind the dome stands the main bell tower, which houses one of the world's largest bells, the 19-tonne La Savoyarde.

The basilica itself is best viewed from below, in place St-Pierre, where the turrets and towers rise up majestically into the sky, seeming to bridge the gap between earth and heaven. For more unusual views, wander around the back of the basilica (see walk, pages 226–227).

### MOSAIC

Inside the basilica, the vast golden mosaic that hovers over the choir is a striking focal point. It is one of the largest of its kind, covering 475sq m (5,145sq ft), and was created by Olivier Merson between 1900 and 1922. Christ stands in the middle, with outstretched arms and a golden heart. Immediately surrounding him, the Virgin Mary, Joan of Arc, St. Michael, the Pope and a figure representing France look up in reverence. Farther to the left, the characters in the lower row represent the earthly church, while above you can see members of the heavenly church, including St. Peter and St. Paul. To the right, the lower row portrays the builders of Sacré-Cœur, while above them are French saints, including St. Louis and St. Geneviève. God the Father and the Holy Spirit are represented on the ceiling and the Latin inscription below the mosaic reads 'To the most holy Heart of Jesus, France, fervent, penitent and grateful'.

## SCULPTURES

Joan of Arc and St. Louis guard the entrance to the basilica, on horseback in sculpted bronze. A stone statue of Christ stands high above them, in an arched recess. Gospel stories are portrayed on the bronze doors. Inside, look for the statue of *Our Lady of Peace*, in the Virgin Chapel, by Georges Serraz. Other sculptures include a silver statue of Christ, *Le Sacré-Coeur*, by Eugène Benet, and a silver *Virgin and Child* by Paul Brunet. Further statues can be seen in the crypt, including archbishop Cardinal Guibert, who approved the building of the basilica in 1872, and a *Pietà* by Jules Coutan.

## BACKGROUND

**Sacré-Cœur was commissioned as atonement for the deaths of 58,000 people during the Franco-Prussian war of 1870–71 and the bloody events of the Commune (see page 36). Money was donated from across France and the first stone was laid in 1875. Various problems hampered the building work, including unstable ground on a hill full of gypsum quarries, and the basilica was not ready until 1914. Then World War I intervened, and Parisians had to wait until 1919 for the consecration. The stained-glass windows were destroyed by bombs in 1944. Despite its setbacks—and the constant stream of visitors—the basilica has not lost its focus as a place of worship. More than 130 years after the vow to build Sacré-Cœur, priests still work in relays to maintain constant prayer for forgiveness for the horrors of war.**

### BASICS

69 M2•place du Parvis du Sacré-Cœur
01 53 41 89 00
Basilica: daily 6am–11pm. Dome and crypt: daily 9.15–5.30 (also 5.30–7 in summer)
Basilica: free. Dome: adult/child €5
Anvers/Abbesses, then walk to funicular
Montmartrobus
Cafés and restaurants in Montmartre (see page 258)
Small bookshop/giftshop
€5 (in French, English, German, Spanish and Italian)
There is a lift at 35 rue du Chevalier de la Barre to help people with disabilities gain access to the basilica

www.sacre-coeur-montmartre.com (in French, with some pages in English; find out more about the history and life of the basilica)

*The basilica looks most striking when viewed from below*

# Sainte-Chapelle

**Stunning stained-glass windows turn this 13th-century royal chapel into a shimmering jewel, hidden within the Palais de Justice complex. It was here that St. Louis brought his holy relics in the 13th century.**

*Intricate carvings in the upper chapel*

*This window depicts Judith's prayer*

*The golden arches of the lower chapel*

## SEEING SAINTE-CHAPELLE

It's not quite heaven, but the celestial rays of blue, red and golden light streaming through the windows of Sainte-Chapelle certainly seem out of this world. The only downside is the crowds, which, as with Rome's Sistine Chapel, can detract from what should be an awe-inspiring experience.

You reach the chapel through a shared entrance with the Palais de Justice, on the boulevard du Palais, where your bags will be screened. From here, walk round to the main entrance of the chapel. The wait for tickets can be long, but you can avoid this if you have a *Carte Musées-Monuments* (see page 307) or a joint ticket with the Conciergerie (see pages 89–91). The entrance leads you first into the lower chapel, where there is a small gift-shop. A steep spiral staircase takes you to the upper chapel.

## HIGHLIGHTS

### THE WINDOWS

When you step into the upper chapel you are immediately hit by colour coming at you from all directions, not only from the glorious windows but also from the patterned floor, the golden columns and the painted lower walls. Fifteen windows, up to 15m (49ft) tall, and a glorious rose window depict more than 1,100 biblical scenes, from the Creation to the Apocalypse. Two-thirds of the windows are 13th-century originals, the oldest stained glass in Paris. The panels tell key biblical stories, starting with Genesis in the window on the left as you enter and working clockwise round the chapel to the Apocalypse in the rose window. The only non-biblical theme is in the final window, which tells how the holy relics came to Paris.

### CARVINGS

Although the windows are undoubtedly the highlight of the upper chapel, take time to notice other features, such as the incredible detail of the sculpted golden foliage on the capitals (including oak leaves, holly, thistle and hops) and the statues of the apostles, which appear to be supporting the pillars (an allusion to their role as pillars of the Christian faith). Some are 19th-century copies—the originals are in the Musée National du Moyen Âge (see pages 128–129).

**RATINGS**

| | |
|---|---|
| Cultural interest | ●●● |
| Historic interest | ●●●● |

**BASICS**

- 67 M7•4 boulevard du Palais, Île de la Cité, 75001
- 01 53 73 78 52
- 9.30–6 (last entry 5.30). Closed 1 Jan, 1 May, 25 Dec
- Adult €5.50, under 18 free. Joint ticket with Conciergerie €8
- Cité, Châtelet
- 21, 24, 27, 38, 85, 96
- RER line B, C St-Michel-Notre-Dame
- Small gift shop in lower chapel
- €6
- Daily 11, 3
- Off the Cour de la Sainte-Chapelle, in the Palais de Justice complex

www.monum.fr (in French and English)

*Louis IX demanded a grand setting to display his holy relics—he certainly got that with the glorious Sainte-Chapelle (left)*

**TIPS**

- The upper chapel can become extremely crowded. The quietest times to visit are Tuesday to Friday morning.

- You can buy a joint ticket for the Conciergerie (see pages 89–91) and Sainte-Chapelle. Buy this at the Conciergerie, where the queues are often shorter.

- To help decipher the windows in the upper chapel, pick up an information card from the stand by the exit.

- Try to visit when the sun is shining, to experience the windows at their iridescent best. Sunset is the best time to see the Rose Window, although the chapel is likely to be crowded then.

- If you have binoculars, bring them with you, to help you see the higher windows.

- For details of the candlelit concerts held in the chapel ask the ticket office or tourist information office.

### THE LOWER CHAPEL

Before reaching the brilliance of the upper chapel, you walk through the dark lower chapel, originally used by palace staff and dedicated to the Virgin Mary. Its blue, red and gold ceiling is decorated with fleurs-de-lys, symbol of the French monarchy, while some of the pillars bear Castilian towers, from the coat of arms of Louis IX's mother. The paintwork dates from the mid-19th century, when attempts were made to reproduce the medieval style. This followed damage caused during the Revolution, when the chapel was used as a flour warehouse.

## BACKGROUND

Sainte-Chapelle was commissioned by Louis IX (St. Louis) in the 13th century to house holy relics, and to promote the king's authority as a divinely appointed leader. It was constructed in the royal palace complex (now the Palais de Justice) in less than six years. The architect is not known for certain, although it was possibly Pierre de Montreuil, who also worked on Notre-Dame. He made clever use of discreet pillars to support the 670sq m (7,169sq ft) of stained glass without the need for walls. The relics were displayed on a wooden-canopied platform that you can still see today in front of the altar. They included what was reputed to be the Crown of Thorns, pieces of the Cross and drops of Christ's blood. Louis IX was so eager to take possession of these objects that he paid the Emperor of Constantinople 135,000 *livres* for the Crown of Thorns alone—more than three times the building costs of the chapel. The Crown of Thorns is now kept in Notre-Dame's Treasury. The other relics, along with the silver- and copper-plated reliquary in which they sat, were melted down during the Revolution.

After the Revolution the chapel was used as an archive for court documents. It was restored in the mid 19th-century, when its fifth (and current) spire was constructed, rising 75m (245ft) above the ground.

**UPPER CHAPEL FLOORPLAN**

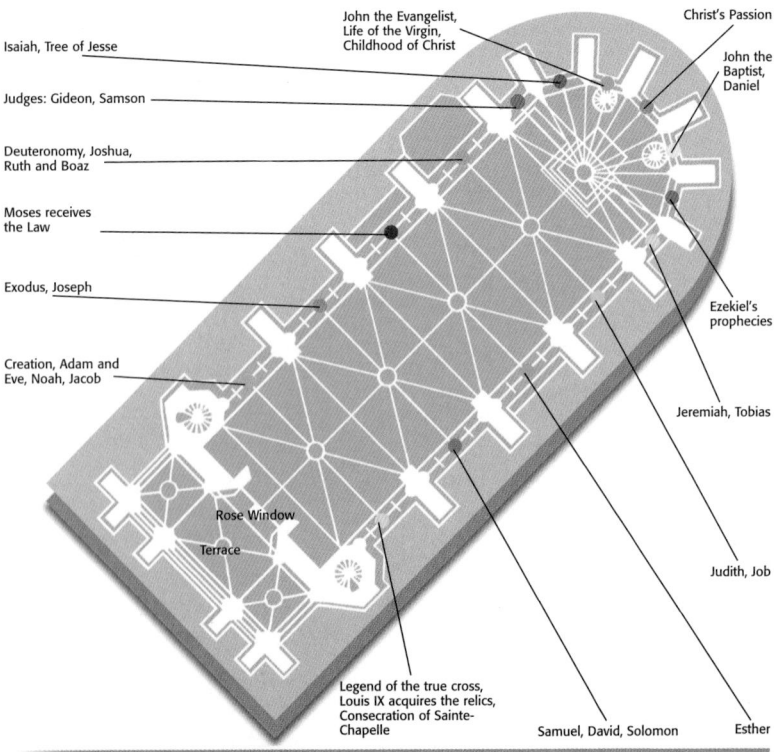

*Henri de Miller's curious sculpture* L'Écoute, *outside St-Eustache*

### ST-ÉTIENNE-DU-MONT

68 N9•place Ste-Geneviève ☎ 01 43 54 11 79 Mon 2–7.30, Tue–Sun 8–7.30 Cardinal Lemoine 84, 89 Free

As you approach St-Étienne-du-Mont from the place du Panthéon the church seems utterly dwarfed by its mighty companion. But the closer you get, the more it steals your attention with its intricately carved façade and delicate bell tower.

Work started in 1492, replacing a smaller chapel that was part of the abbey of Ste-Geneviève. It continued until 1626, which explains the bizarre architectural mix of Gothic, Renaissance and Classical. Paris's archbishop was assassinated in the church in 1857.

**Don't miss** The delicately fretted rood-screen is a highlight.

### ST-EUSTACHE

67 M6•2 impasse St-Eustache, 75001 ☎ 01 42 36 31 05 Daily 9–7.30 (until 8 in summer) Les Halles 29, 67, 74, 85 RER lines A, B, D, Châtelet-les-Halles Free www.st-eustache.org

Paris's second-largest church stands in the busy Les Halles district (see page 95), next to the incongruously modern Forum des Halles. The Gothic structure is second in size only to Notre-Dame, on which it is based. Building work started in 1532 and continued for more than 100 years. Since then, the church has played a prominent role, hosting Louis XIV's first communion, Cardinal Richelieu's baptism and the premières of Liszt's *Grand Mass* and Berlioz's *Te Deum*.

The church's musical reputation continues today, with regular concerts, including organ recitals on Sundays from 5.30 to 6pm.

## ST-GERMAIN-DES-PRÉS

**A charming district with narrow lanes, chic boutiques, the oldest church in Paris and an abundance of cafés, restaurants, antiques shops and art galleries.**

67 L7•75006 St-Germain-des-Prés, Odéon, St-Sulpice, Mabillon 39, 63, 70, 86, 87, 95, 96

| RATINGS | |
|---|---|
| Historic interest | ●●●● |
| Shopping | ●●● |

St-Germain-des-Prés, in the heart of the Left Bank, is eternally magnetic to visitors and residents alike, with a more leisurely pace than on the other side of the river. At its core is the Église St-Germain-des-Prés (see page 162), the oldest church in Paris, dating from the 11th century. Its picturesque bell tower is symbolic of the area. Nearby, in the tranquil rue de Furstemberg, is the Musée National Eugène Delacroix (see page 126).

The pulse of the district is along the boulevard St-Germain, running west from the Latin Quarter to join the government buildings and bourgeois mansions of the 7th *arrondissement*. Lively cafés on this boulevard—the rendezvous of the literary élite—include the illustrious Café de Flore, once frequented by Jean-Paul Sartre, Brasserie Lipp and Café Les Deux Magots, a former haunt of Ernest Hemingway.

South of the boulevard, the streets widen and the atmosphere changes. From the church of St-Sulpice (see page 163) to the pretty Jardin du Luxembourg (see pages 102–103), through the shopping streets of rue Bonaparte, rue de Sèvres and rue de Grenelle, this is the St-Germain of fashion boutiques and publishing houses. Trendy bars replace crowded cafés and furniture shops line the boulevard Raspail leading to the crossroads of Sèvres-Babylone, home of Paris's first department store, Le Bon Marché. North of the boulevard, towards the Seine, remains an arty area, packed with small cinemas, art galleries, antiques shops, the École Nationale Supérieure des Beaux-Arts and the Hôtel de la Monnaie (see page 117).

**Don't miss** The green stalls of *Les bouquinistes* (the booksellers) line the banks of the Seine.

*Enjoying a drink at Les Deux Magots, in front of the church of St-Germain-des-Prés*

*The church of St-Germain-l'Auxerrois, near the Louvre*

*St-Julien-le-Pauvre is one of the oldest churches in Paris…*

*…but not quite as old as St-Germain-des-Prés*



## ST-GERMAIN-L'AUXERROIS

67 M7•place du Louvre ☎ 01 42 60 13 96 Daily 8.20–7. No visits during services (Mass: Mon–Sat 8.20, 12.15, 6.30, Sun 10, 11.15, 5.30, 9.15) Louvre-Rivoli, Pont Neuf 21, 67, 69, 74, 85 Free

Kings from the nearby Louvre palace used St-Germain-l'Auxerrois as their parish church until the Revolution and you can still see the royal pew, near the pulpit. Other highlights include the beautiful stained-glass windows, the carved choir screen and the 18th-century organ, moved from Sainte-Chapelle in 1791. The site's religious connections date back to AD500, when an oratory was built here. In later years it was used to hastily baptize children whose lives were in danger from floods. The current church was built between the 13th and 16th centuries but lost its religious role during the Revolution and became, for a time, a police station, town hall, barn and printers' workshop. Viollet-le-Duc restored the building in the 19th century.

The church's bell (1529) notoriously signalled the onset of the bloody St. Bartholomew's Day Massacre in 1572 (see page 29).

**Don't miss** The church makes a pleasant stop after a visit to the Louvre. You can sit on benches on the grassy area outside and admire the Louvre's façade.

## ST-GERMAIN-DES-PRÉS (ÉGLISE)

67 L8•3 place St-Germain-des-Prés, 75006 ☎ 01 55 42 81 33 Mon–Sat 8–7.40, Sun 9–8 Free St-Germain-des-Prés 39, 63, 86, 95 www.eglise-sgp.org

The Église St-Germain-des-Prés is the oldest church in Paris and lies at the heart of the district that bears its name (see page 161). The Merovingian king, Childebert I, founded an abbey here in the 6th century. The current church was consecrated by Pope Alexander III in 1163, although its bell tower dates from the previous century. The mix of Romanesque and Gothic styles is the result of many additions over the years. The structure was badly damaged during the Revolution and only one of the three original towers remains. The massive 12th-century flying buttresses are still intact. During the 19th century, the church underwent various restorations, and the murals in the nave and choir, by Flandrin, date from this period.

**Don't miss** The tomb of the philosopher René Descartes (1596–1650) lies in the St-Benoît side chapel.

## ST-JULIEN-LE-PAUVRE

67 M8•1 rue St-Julien-le-Pauvre, 75005 ☎ 01 43 54 52 16 (for concert information call 01 42 26 00 00) 9.30–1, 3–6.30 St-Michel 24, 47 RER lines B, C St-Michel-Notre-Dame Free

This small church, one of the oldest in Paris, is tucked away in a quiet corner of the Latin Quarter, near the tranquil square René Viviani (see page 152). It dates from the 12th century and is said to stand on the site of a Merovingian burial ground. In the late Middle Ages the church had strong ties with the nearby university and elections for the rectors took place within its walls. During the Revolution it became a salt store, then in 1889 it was given to the Melkite Church (Greek-Catholic).

Inside the low-ceilinged building are various religious paintings and sculptures, although subdued lighting makes it hard to appreciate them fully. There is also an iconostasis (an Orthodox rood-screen where icons hang) dating from around 1900. The church hosts classical music concerts.

## ST-MERRI

68 N7•78 rue St-Martin, 75003 ☎ For concert information: 01 42 71 40 75 Daily 3–7 Hôtel de Ville 38, 47 RER lines A, B, D, Châtelet-Les-Halles Free

St-Merri, a short walk from the Centre Georges Pompidou, is named after the Right Bank's patron saint. The 16th-century church is a superb example of Flamboyant Gothic. It contains Paris's oldest bell, made in 1331 and a remnant from the medieval chapel that once stood on the site. Inside, the stained-glass windows feature Joseph in Egypt, St. Nicholas of Myre, St. Agnès and the Paris merchant Étienne Marcel.

The *Carnaval des Animaux* composer Camille Saint-Saëns was organist here in the 1850s. Today, you can enjoy free concerts on Saturdays at 9pm and Sundays at 4pm.

**Don't miss** The ornate pulpit was carved in 1753 by the sculptor P. A. Slodtz, one of two brothers who worked on the church in the 18th century.

## ST-SÉVERIN

67 M8•1 rue des Prêtres St-Séverin, 75005 ☎ 01 42 34 93 50 Mon–Sat 11–7.30, Sun 9–8.30 St-Michel 21, 24, 27, 38, 47, 85 RER lines B, C, St-Michel-Notre-Dame Free ? There is a ramp for wheelchair users at the back of the church, off rue St-Jacques www.saint-severin.com

This beautiful church, in the Latin Quarter, would probably attract more visitors were it not for the grander Notre-Dame a few

*Gargoyles decorate the church of St-Séverin*

*The fountain in place St-Sulpice*

*S for Sorbonne*

minutes walk across the river. As it is, the Gothic St-Séverin remains a well-kept secret, but its beautiful stained glass makes it worth seeking out.

The church dates from the 13th century, although a fire led to much of it being rebuilt in the 15th century. Highlights include the Chapelle du Saint-Esprit, the double ambulatory and the palm-tree vaulting. The church originally took its name from a 6th-century hermit called Séverin the Solitary, although its allegiance later changed to a 5th-century Swiss abbot of the same name, whose statue now stands outside.

Ask at the church office for the information leaflet (in English), which gives a plan of the building and details about its key features.

**Don't miss** Among the historic panes of stained glass it is refreshing to see some contemporary designs, installed in 1970, at the top end of the church. The vibrant windows, designed by Jean Bazaine, represent the Seven Sacraments.

## ST-SULPICE

67 L8•place St-Sulpice, 75006
☎ 01 46 33 21 78 Mon–Sat 7.30am–7.30pm, Sun 7am–7.30pm Free St-Sulpice 63, 70, 86, 87, 96

St-Sulpice is a masterpiece of classical architecture. It took six architects and 134 years to build the enormous church, 119m (390ft) long and 57m (187ft) wide. Work finished in 1780. The imposing façade is flanked by two asymmetrical towers; the south tower, still unfinished, is 5m (16ft) shorter than the north. One of the architects who worked on the towers was Jean-François Chalgrin.

St-Sulpice is home to one of the world's largest church organs, but has many other treasures, including 17th-century stained-glass windows, paintings by Carle Van Loo and carvings and statues by sculptors Edme Bouchardon, Jean-Baptiste Pigalle, the Slodtz brothers and Louis-Simon Boizot.

The opulently carved and gilded pulpit was designed in 1788 by Charles de Wailly. Paintings by 17 renowned artists were commissioned to hang in the transept and the chapels in the 19th century.

Look out for the astronomical gnomon (sundial) in the form of a bronze meridian line stretching from the south to the north transept. At noon on the winter solstice the image of the sun is reflected onto a white marble obelisk while at noon on the summer solstice the light falls onto a marble plaque in the south transept.

**Don't miss** Murals by Eugène Delacroix are in the Chapelle des Anges, the first chapel on the right.

## LA SORBONNE

67 M8•1 rue Victor Cousin, 75005
☎ 01 40 46 22 11 Closed to the public (guided tours are available for groups but you must write in advance for a reservation)
Cluny–La Sorbonne 21, 27, 38, 63, 85, 86, 87 RER B, C, Cluny–La Sorbonne
www.Sorbonne.fr

La Sorbonne is the symbol of France's great spirit of learning. The university dates from the 13th century, when Robert de Sorbon, chaplain to St. Louis, set up a college to house poorer theology students. For centuries the university maintained an independent attitude to the state, recognizing the English Henry V as King of France, condemning Joan of Arc and fiercely opposing the 18th-century philosophers. This continued into the 20th century, with the student revolt of 1968 (see page 39).

Cardinal Richelieu was responsible for rebuilding the dilapidated college in the 17th century, although Lemercier's domed chapel, where the Cardinal now lies, is all that remains. Today's amphitheatres and endless corridors date from the 19th century.

The premises are now used by four separate universities—Paris Sorbonne, Sorbonne Nouvelle, Panthéon-Sorbonne and René Descartes.

Occasional exhibitions are held in the Chapelle de la Sorbonne and you can catch something of the college atmosphere in the student-filled place de la Sorbonne.

**Don't miss** Although the university is closed to the general public, you can sneak a glimpse of the imposing courtyard off the rue de la Sorbonne.

## SYNAGOGUE

68 P7•10 rue Pavée, 75004
☎ 01 48 87 21 54/01 42 44 81 51
Visits by request only. Telephone between 10 and 4, Sun–Thu Free St-Paul
69, 76, 96

The synagogue lies in the heart of the Marais district's Jewish quarter (see page 107). It was built in 1913 to designs by architect Hector Guimard, best remembered for his fanlighted Métro entrances. Guimard was one of the leading lights in the French art nouveau movement and was prolific between 1895 and 1910. He continued to work until 1930 but, distressed by the rise of Fascism, he emigrated with his Jewish wife to the United States, where he died in 1942.

# Tour Eiffel

**The Eiffel Tower is the symbol of Paris and one of the world's most famous monuments. From the top, there are breathtaking views across the city and beyond.**

*Across the Champ de Mars to the Tour Montparnasse*

*The Eiffel Tower looks stunning at night*

*It's a long way up!*

**RATINGS**

| | |
|---|---|
| Good for kids | ● ● ● |
| Historic interest | ● ● ● |
| Photo stops | ● ● ● ● ● |

**TIPS**

- To skip the wait for the lifts, walk up the stairs to level one, then catch the lift to level two. The climb isn't too daunting.
- The wait for the lift is generally shorter at night.
- Pushchairs are allowed up the tower only if they are collapsible.
- If you want to dine at the elegant Jules Verne restaurant book well ahead.

## SEEING LA TOUR EIFFEL

Whether you see it as a 'hollow candlestick' or an elegant emblem of Paris, you can't ignore the Eiffel Tower. Its sleek iron silhouette, rising up 324m (1,063ft), finds its way into many of the city's best views.

Around six million people visit the Iron Lady each year, so be prepared for a long wait (and the indefatigable attentions of trinket salesmen). Before you buy a ticket, you'll need to decide whether you want to go as far as level one (57m/187ft), level two (120m/394ft) or level three (280m/918ft), and whether you'll take the elevator or brave the stairs (to levels one and two only). The price will vary accordingly. The stairs are at the south pillar. The two-level elevators, with room for 80 people, are in the north, west and east pillars, although only one or two are operational at any one time. These take you as far as levels one and two, then you face another wait for a second, smaller elevator that takes you on the three-minute journey to level three. The plush Jules Verne restaurant, on level two, has a separate elevator at the south pillar.

## HIGHLIGHTS

### THE VIEW

The view is the reason you climb the Eiffel Tower, whether it's for the magnificent sweep across the city or to test your nerves peering down 120m (394ft) through the glass window on the floor of level two. The tower was the world's tallest building for 40 years, and from the gallery on level three you can see up to 75km (46 miles) on a clear day. If you can't face the vertigo-inducing top level, the views are just as impressive on level two, where you can see the city in more detail. There is also a viewing gallery on level one, with information boards. Sights to look out for include the Arc de Triomphe (north), the elegantly colonnaded wings of the Palais de Chaillot (northwest), the gardens of the Champ de Mars (southeast), with the Tour Montparnasse farther back, and the golden dome of Les Invalides (east). The views are often at their best in the run up to sunset, when the light is kinder to cameras. At night a totally different picture unfolds, as hundreds of thousands of lights sketch out the city.

*A few of the 18,000 metal sections and 2.5 million rivets holding together the tower (right)*

*There are great views of the Eiffel Tower from the Palais de Chaillot and the place du Trocadéro, across the Seine*

**THE LIGHTS**

Make sure you catch a glimpse of the tower at night, even if you want to reserve your actual visit for daylight. A staggering 10,000 light bulbs contribute to the glittering spectacle. More than 350 spotlights illuminate the latticework, topped by a rotating beacon that can be seen up to 80km (50 miles) away. One of the best ways to appreciate the shimmering display is on a boat trip (see pages 234–235), when the tower takes you by surprise as you turn the corner at the Pont de l'Alma. On foot, the views from the Palais de Chaillot (see page 143) are memorable.

The tower was originally lit by gas, before electricity was introduced in time for the Universal Exhibition in 1900. In 1925, car manufacturer André Citroën bankrolled a dramatic display of lights advertising his company. The current 350,000-watt system was inaugurated on New Year's Eve 1985. It replaced an unpopular system that beamed light onto the tower from more than 1,000 spotlights on the Champ de Mars, dazzling visitors inside. The rotating beacon was added in 1999. Special displays were staged for the centenary of the tower in 1989 and for the countdown to the new millennium. During the year 2000, 20,000 extra bulbs shimmered on the hour.

**THE ANTICS**

The Eiffel Tower has inspired more than its fair share of eccentric behaviour. In 1912 a would-be Icarus plunged to his death when his cape failed to act as wings, as he had hoped. In 1928 a watchmaker tried out an innovative new design for a parachute but, once again, it failed to open and he rapidly met his maker. A bicyclist who pedalled down the steps to win a bet in 1923 was more successful, although he was arrested when he reached the bottom. Mountaineers have scaled the tower, pilots have tried to fly through its pillars and in 1909

the Comte de Lambert circled 100m (328ft) above it in a flying machine. More recently, in 1984, a British couple survived an unofficial parachute jump from level three and in 1989 Philippe Petit walked a tightrope strung up between the tower and the Palais de Chaillot.

Humans are not the only ones involved in antics at the tower. While animals are usually banned, in 1948 a circus elephant was allowed to walk up the stairs!

### OTHER ATTRACTIONS

On level three, a panoramic photo helps you to identify monuments on the skyline. You can also discover the distance from the tower of various capital cities (none of them within sight!). Once you have soaked up the view, you can learn more about the history of the tower from the short film shown at Cineiffel (level one). Other attractions on the first floor include the Observatory, where you can monitor the tower's sway, and the Feroscope, focusing on all things iron. You can also see the original hydraulic elevator pump and a piece of the original spiral staircase, as used by Monsieur Eiffel himself. If you want to boast of your whereabouts to your friends back home, you can have your postcards franked with *Tour Eiffel* at the post office (*open 10–7*).

## BACKGROUND

### CONTROVERSIAL BEGINNINGS

**Slammed as a 'hollow chandelier' and 'tower of Babel' when it was built in 1889, the Eiffel Tower went on to become the emblem of Paris. Gustave Eiffel took only two years to complete the unconventional monument, finishing just in time for the 1889 Universal Exhibition. At the peak of the construction work, the tower grew 30m (98ft) a month. Despite this breakneck**

### FACTS AND FIGURES

- During the storms of 1999, the sway at the top of the tower measured 9cm (3.5in).
- The tower weighs 10,100 tonnes. It has 18,000 metal sections and 2.5 million rivets.
- In hot weather it expands by up to 15cm (5.8in).
- 370 people committed suicide by jumping from the tower, until protective shields were installed in 1971.
- Around 200 million people have visited the tower.
- There are 1,665 steps to the top.
- It takes 60 tonnes of paint to spruce up the tower.
- The elevators cover the equivalent of 100,000km (62,000 miles) each year.

**BASICS**

66 G7•quai Branly, Champ de Mars, 75007

01 44 11 23 23

Daily 9am–midnight, mid-Jun to end Aug; 9.30am–11pm rest of year (stairs close at 6.30); last entry 30 min before closing

Bir-Hakeim

42, 69, 82, 87

RER line C, Champ de Mars–Tour Eiffel

**By elevator**: adult €3.70 (level one), €7 (level two), €10.20 (level three), child €2.30 (level one), €3.90 (level two), €5.50 (level three). **By stairs**: adult/child €3.30. Under 3 free

In a variety of languages

Altitude 95 on level one, Jules Verne on level two

Snack bars on ground floor, level one and level two

Monum leads occasional guided tours. Call 01 44 54 19 30

Gift shops on levels one and two. Post office on level one

Wheelchair access to first and second levels only

www.eiffel-tower.com (in English) or www.tour-eiffel.fr (in French)

**FLOOR GUIDE**

**LEVEL ONE**

Cineiffel, Observatory, Feroscope, gift shop, post office, viewing gallery, Altitude 95 restaurant, snack bar, hydraulic elevator pump, part of the original spiral staircase.

**LEVEL TWO**

Jules Verne restaurant, glass-floor viewing window, gift shops, viewing gallery, snack bar.

**LEVEL THREE**

Viewing gallery, panoramic photo, reconstruction of Gustave Eiffel's office.

operation, when the opening day came, Gustave Eiffel and a gaggle of officials still had to walk up the 1,665 steps to the top because the elevators weren't working. The tower is a feat of engineering, weighing more than 10,000 tonnes and made up of 18,000 iron parts. No one knew then that it would become the symbol of Paris—it was due to be demolished after 20 years. By the time its allotted two decades were up it had as many fans as opponents. It was eventually saved simply for its broadcasting antennae. Its growing popularity vindicated the opinions of literary and artistic allies such as Guillaume Apollinaire, Raoul Dufy, Maurice Utrillo and Camille Pissarro. The objections of Paul Verlaine, Émile Zola and Guy de Maupassant were relegated to history. For 40 years the tower basked in the glory of being the highest structure in the world until New York's Chrysler Building usurped the title. It gained another 20m (66ft) in 1957 when television antennae were added. Famous visitors have included Thomas Edison, King George VI and his wife Queen Elizabeth (later to become the Queen Mother) and the Shah of Persia.

**TOWERING FIGURE**

Gustave Eiffel beat more than 100 other entrants in the competition to design a focal point, 300m (984ft) high, for the 1889 Universal Exhibition. The resulting tower is the ultimate symbol of his skill and imagination, but the 'magician of iron' has left hundreds of other constructions all over the world. Born in 1832 in Burgundy, he was already working on Bordeaux bridge at the age of 26. Bridges soon became his area of expertise: Iron and the hydraulic methods he used for installing their supports helped to build his reputation. Factories, churches, a synagogue (rue des Tournelles), shops (Le Bon Marché), banks and, over a period of 18 years, 31 railway viaducts and 17 major bridges all came within his creative sphere. Egypt, Peru, Portugal, Hungary and Bolivia all have their Eiffel monuments. He even designed the frame for New York's Statue of Liberty. Eiffel kept an office in his most famous tower until his death. You can see a reconstruction of the room, complete with waxwork figures, on level 3. A bust of the engineer, by Bourdelle, stands near the north pillar. He died in 1923, at the age of 91.

*The north pillar of the tower (above right)*

*Looking across the fountain-filled Jardins du Trocadéro to the Eiffel Tower (left)*

*Viewing the Eiffel Tower from the 59th-floor terrace (above). The Tour Montparnasse from below (left)*

# TOUR MONTPARNASSE

**An enormous tower with panoramic views across Paris and beyond.**

The Tour Montparnasse dominates the Paris skyline, rising 209m (685ft) over the Montparnasse district. For awe-inspiring views of the city let the ear-popping lift whizz you up to the enclosed, air-conditioned viewing gallery on the 56th floor, in just 38 seconds. From here you can spot many of Paris's major attractions, including the Eiffel Tower, Les Invalides, the Arc de Triomphe, Sacré-Cœur, the Louvre, Musée d'Orsay, Centre Georges Pompidou, St-Germain-des-Prés, Église St-Sulpice, Notre-Dame and the Panthéon. A mini-cinema projects a 20-minute film by Albert Lamorisse showing aerial views of Paris. There are also temporary exhibitions and displays. Farther up, the 59th floor is the highest open-air terrace in Paris—and not for the faint-hearted. You can see up to 40km (25 miles) on a clear day.

## OFFICE BLOCK

The tower has 58 floors, each covering an area of almost 2,000sq m (21,528sq ft). There is also a 59th-floor terrace. Offices occupy 52 floors, with a workforce of around 5,000 people. Only two floors are open to the public, the 56th floor and the 59th floor terrace. The tower is 62m (203ft) long, 32m (105ft) wide and weighs 120,000 tonnes. Its foundations reach a depth of 70m (230ft). It has a concrete core with a steel structure. The façades are predominantly glass, aluminium and bronze.

## AN EYESORE?

The Tour Montparnasse was built between 1969 and 1973, as part of a huge urban development project to modernize Montparnasse. It was designed by architects Beaudouin, Cassan, De Marien and Saubot and stands on the site of the old railway station—the Métro runs directly underneath it. The tower has always been highly controversial. President Georges Pompidou, who authorized its construction, took a helicopter tour to observe the completed job and is reported to have said to his urban planners 'That's enough, we stop right there'. It is still considered an eyesore by many Parisians, and remains one of the capital's least liked buildings, despite the spectacular views it offers.

**RATINGS**

Photo stops

**TIPS**

- **The 59th-floor open-air terrace is closed on very windy days.**
- **If you're short on time, don't stop to watch the film—enjoy the amazing views instead.**
- **The guidebook has photographs of different viewpoints. Major landmarks are identified, with a short accompanying description.**

**BASICS**

67 K9•33 avenue du Maine, 75015
01 45 38 52 56
Daily 9.30am–11.30pm Apr–end Sep, 9.30am–10.30pm (11 Fri, Sat) rest of year; last elevator up 30 min before closing
Adult €8, child (under 14) €5.50. 56th floor only: adult €7, child €5
Montparnasse-Bienvenüe
28, 48, 82, 89
Gare Montparnasse
€2.50
Le Ciel de Paris

www.tourmontparnasse56.com (in English, French and German, with practical and historical information)

# What to Do

This chapter gives information on things to do in Paris other than sightseeing.
Shops and performance venues are located on the maps at the beginning of each section.


**Shopping** **172–192**
Locator Maps **172–175**
Introduction **176**
Paris Shopping Areas:
Faubourg St-Honoré **177**
Le Marais **178**
Around Opéra **179**
Palais Royal/Les Halles **180**
St-Germain-des-Prés **181**
Shopping Directory **182–192**

**Performance** **193–208**
Introduction **193**
Locator Maps **194–197**
Arts Venues **198**
Cabaret **198–199**
Cinemas **199–201**
Circus **201**
Classical Music, Dance and Opera **201–203**
Comedy **203**
Contemporary Live Music **203–205**
Theatre **205–208**

**Nightlife** **209–215**
Bars **209–213**
Cafés **213–214**
Clubs **214–215**
Gay and Lesbian **215**

**Sports and Activities** **216–220**
**Children's Paris** **221**
**Festivals and Events** **222**

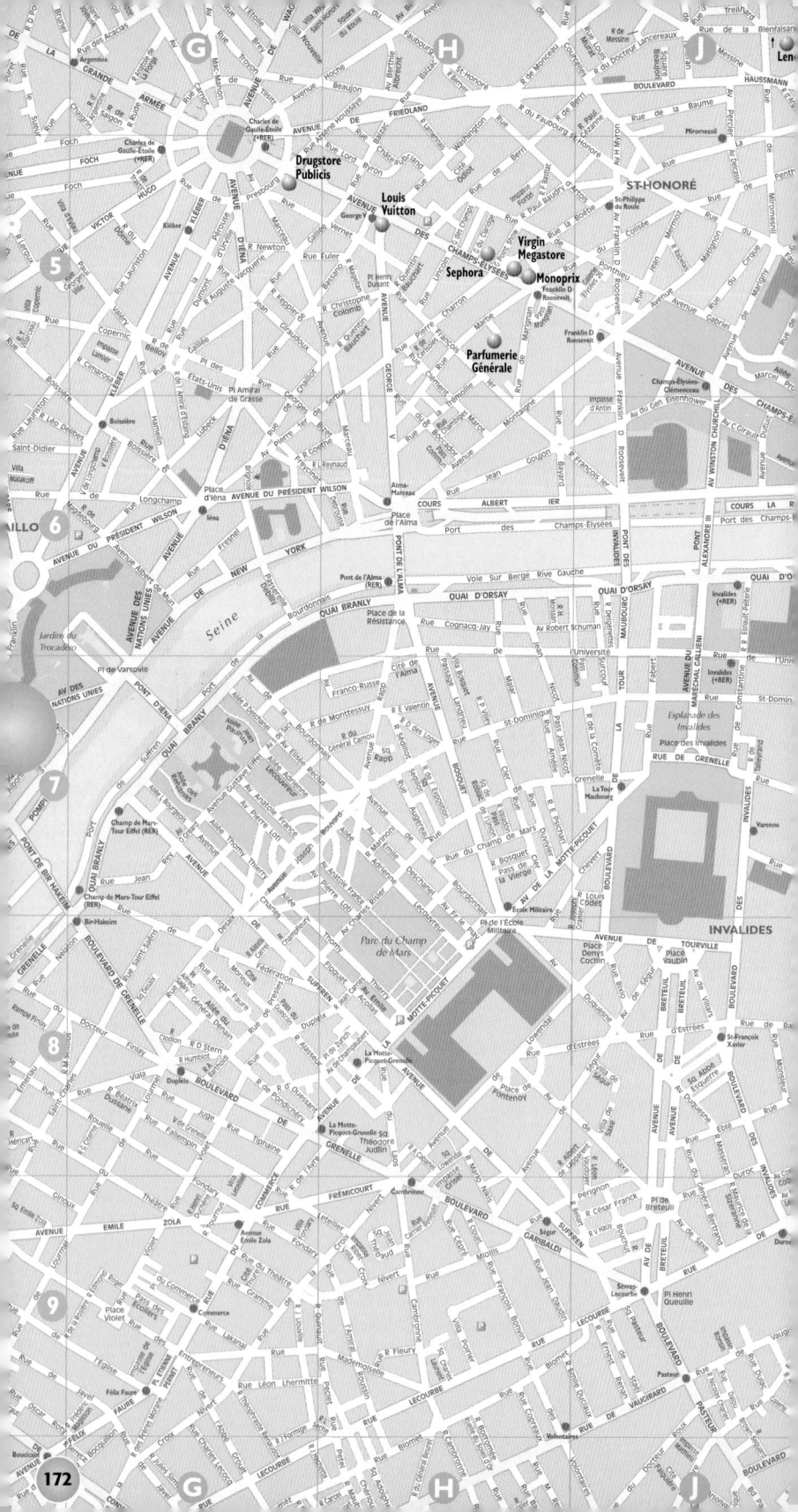
Drugstore Publicis
Louis Vuitton
Virgin Megastore
Sephora
Monoprix
Parfumerie Générale
ST-HONORÉ
INVALIDES
Seine
Jardins du Trocadéro
Esplanade des Invalides
Parc du Champ de Mars
Champ de Mars-Tour Eiffel (RER)
Pl de Varsovie
Place de la Résistance
Place d'Iéna
Place de l'Alma
Place Denys Cochin
Place Vauban
Pl Henri Queuille
Pl de l'Etoile
Pl de l'Alma
Pl de l'Ecole Militaire
Pl de Breteuil
Pl de Fontenoy
Pl Amiral de Grasse
Pl de la Motte-Picquet-Grenelle
Pl Théodore Judlin
Pl Henry Dunant
Pl de Varsovie
Pl Jean Rostand
Pl Jean Rostand
Pl Jean Rostand

Judith Lacroix
Le Printemps
Galeries Lafayette
Comme des Garçons
Fauchon
Lavinia
Chanel
Maria Luis
Vanessa Bruno
WHSmith
Colette
Le Shop
Bill Tornade
Salons du Palais Royal Shiseido
Kiliwatch
Agnès B
Barbara Bui
La Droguerie
Why?
Agatha
La Samaritaine
Zara
Cité de la Femme - Etam
Galerie Captier
L'Occitane
Barthélémy
La Hune
Taschen
Marché aux Fleurs
Galerie Antoinette Jean
Shakespeare and Company
Lollipops
The Conran Shop
Poilâne
Maritté & François Girbaud
Pierre Hermé
Christian Tortu
Le Bon Marché
Au Nom de la Rose
Gibert Joseph
Au Vieux Campeur
Marché du Boulevard Raspail
Anne Maisonneuve
Salle Raspail
Jardin des Tuileries
Jardin du Luxembourg
Seine
ST-GERMAIN-DES-PRÉS
QUARTIER LATIN
HALL
GARE ST-LAZARE
Place de la Concorde
Place Vendôme
Place du Carrousel
Musée d'Orsay (RER)
Musée du Louvre
Pont Neuf
Pont des Arts
Pont Royal
Pont de Sèvres
Pont de Bercy
Pont Neuf
Pont Marie
Pont Saint-Louis
Pont Saint-Michel
Pont Notre-Dame
Pont Saint-Louis
Pont Marie
Pont Neuf
Pont Royal
Pont des Arts
Pont Neuf

4
5
6
7
8
9
Jamin Puech
Antoine & Lilli
Artazart
Jacques Boissergent
RÉPUBLIQUE
Goncourt
Bonne Nouvelle
Strasbourg St-Denis
Réaumur Sébastopol
Arts et Métiers
Temple
Oberkampf
Filles du Calvaire
LES HALLES
Barbara Bui
Etienne Marcel
Kiliwatch
Why?
Châtelet Les Halles (+RER)
Rambuteau
Patyka
St-Sébastien-Froissart
Richard Lenoir
St-Ambroise
Dom Christian Koban
Xuly Bet
Olivers and Co
Biche de Bère
LE MARAIS
Mariage Frères
Hôtel de Ville
Chemin Vert
Jean-Claude Monderer
BHV
Nim
Un Dimanche à Venise par Kalliste
Ventilo
Antik Batik
Place des Vosges
Bréguet Sabin
Marché aux Fleurs
St-Michel-Notre-Dame (RER)
St-Paul-le-Marais
Marché Réuni
BASTILLE
Pont Marie
Shakespeare and Company
Sully Morland
Isabel Marant
Librairie Ulysse
Dépôt Vente de Paris Les Fées d'Herbe XX
Au Vieux Campeur
Maubert-Mutualité
Marché d'Aligre
QUARTIER LATIN
Cardinal Lemoine
Place Jussieu
Seine
Quai de la Rapée
Place Monge
Jardin des Plantes
Place Valhubert
Gare d'Austerlitz
Natures et Decouvertes, Nicolas, Résonances
GARE D'AUSTERLITZ
174

Alan Archéologie du XXe Siècle
St-Ouen (RER)
Cimetière de Montmartre
MONTMARTRE
PIGALLE
Loorica
Judith Lacroix
Jamin Puech
Le Printemps
Galeries Lafayette
Fauchon
Lavinia
Chanel
Maria Luis
Vanessa Bruno
WHSmith
Colette
Le Shop
Bill Tornade
Kiliwatch
Salons du Palais Royal Shiseido
LES HALLES
Barbara Bul
Agnès B
La Droguerie
Agatha
Cité de la Femme - Etam
Whyt
Jardin des Tuileries
Seine
175

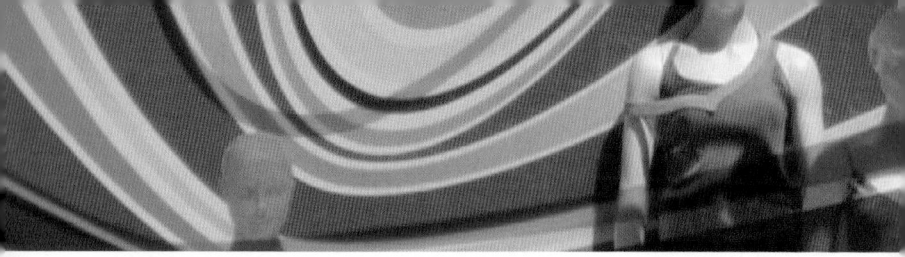

# SHOPPING

When it comes to shopping, Paris has it all: fine department stores, quirky and super-chic boutiques, inexpensive chain stores, big and small flea markets, and everything in-between.

**FASHION**

Clothing, of course, is the thing to buy in Paris, still the world's fashion capital in spite of

serious competition from London, New York and Milan. All the top-name designers have boutiques in the city, concentrated on Faubourg St-Honoré and avenue Montaigne and in St-Germain-des-Prés. For those on a tighter budget, *dépôt-vente* (second-hand) shops sell Madame's (and occasionally Monsieur's) designer cast-offs from last year's collections, often at very reasonable prices. The rue d'Alésia is lined with stock shops selling labels at discounts of up to 70 per cent. La Vallée Outlet Shopping Village, outside Paris, sells designer clothing at discounts of up to 60 per cent (*take the RER line A4 to Val d'Europe, 45 minutes from Paris*). Designer corners can be found in the three top department stores: the exclusive Left Bank Le Bon Marché and the huge Right Bank stores Galeries Lafayette and Printemps. The BHV and La Samaritaine department stores are less expensive and not as chic. The former is famous for its fully stocked DIY basement. High-street chain stores are concentrated in Forum des Halles and on the Champs-Élysées, rue de Rivoli and boulevard St-Michel, while one-off boutiques are clustered in Le Marais and St-Germain-des-Prés, with a scattering of more youthful, offbeat shops along the Canal St-Martin, in Montmartre near Métro Abbesses and on and around rue Oberkampf.

If shoes are your thing, head directly for rue du Cherche-Midi and rue de Grenelle, in the 6th and 7th *arrondissements* respectively, for the top names in shoe designs.

**PERFUME**

Paris is also perfume capital of the world. All the department stores sell the major names in fragrances and every district has a perfumery.

**FOOD**

There is plenty of choice for food lovers, from foie gras to fine wine and champagne, in shops such as Hédiard and Fauchon in place de la Madeleine, the Grande Épicerie de Paris next to Le Bon Marché department store, and Lafayette Gourmet in Galeries Lafayette. Many *boulangeries* make their own chocolate (look for the word *chocolatier*) and special chocolate shops abound, but you can also get bars of high-quality chocolate (70 per cent or higher cocoa content) in any supermarket.

**ANTIQUES AND BOOKS**

For antiques and second-hand bargain hunters, the Marché aux Puces de St-Ouen (see page 107) is a virtual city of antiques and bric-a-brac, while smaller markets at Porte de Montreuil and Porte de Vanves may also offer bargains. Roving flea markets (*brocantes*), often set up in the streets on weekends, are always fun to browse through. Fine antiques shops are clustered around quai Voltaire and rue de Beaune in the 7th *arrondissement* and in the Louvre des Antiquaires, where some 250 vendors sell their wares, across rue de Rivoli from the museum.

For rare books, wander through the 5th and 6th *arrondissements* and along the *quais* of the Seine, lined with booksellers' stalls.

**PRACTICALITIES**

Stores are generally open from 9 or 10am to 7 or 7.30pm. Most stores close on Sunday, although many of the boutiques in the Marais are open on Sunday afternoon. Small boutiques may close on Monday morning and every lunchtime. Most stores accept major credit cards. Always say *bonjour* and *au revoir* to sales staff. If they offer unwanted assistance, say *Je regarde* ('just looking').

**SHOPPING AREAS**

Pages 177–181 highlight five areas in Paris that are particularly good for shopping.

# Faubourg St-Honoré

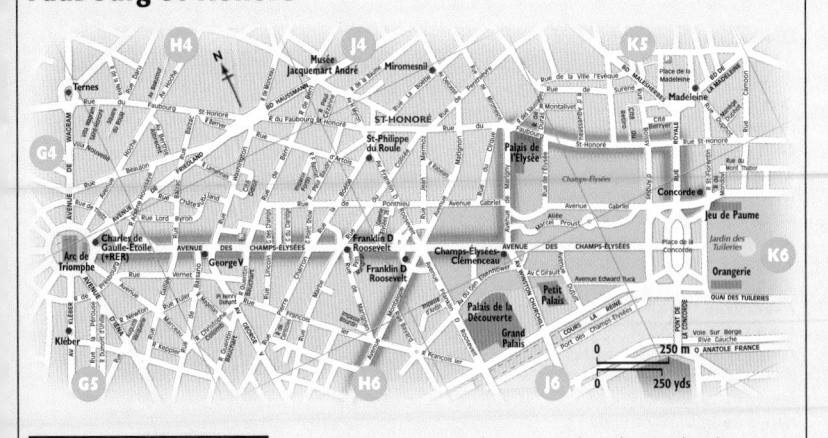
H4
J4
K5
G4
K6
G5
H6
J6
Ternes
Musée Jacquemart André
Miromesnil
ST-HONORÉ
St-Philippe du Roule
Palais de l'Élysée
Madeleine
Place de la Madeleine
Concorde
Jeu de Paume
Jardin des Tuileries
Orangerie
Charles de Gaulle-Étoile (RER)
Arc de Triomphe
George V
Franklin D. Roosevelt
Champs-Élysées-Clemenceau
Petit Palais
Palais de la Découverte
Grand Palais
Kléber
AVENUE DES CHAMPS-ÉLYSÉES
Champs-Élysées
Avenue Gabriel
Avenue Edward Tuck
QUAI DES TUILERIES
Place de la Concorde
Rue Royale
Rue Lord Byron
Rue Marbeuf
Rue Vernet
Rue Boissy d'Anglas
Rue Cambacérès
Rue Caumartin
Rue Tronchet
Rue Duphot
Rue Saint-Honoré
Rue Rivoli
Rue de la Paix
Rue Scribe
Rue Auber
Rue Daunou
Rue Pasquier
Rue Tronchet
Rue Vignon
Rue Boissy d'Anglas
Rue Cambacérès
Rue Caumartin
Rue Tronchet
Rue Duphot
Rue Saint-Honoré
Rue Rivoli
Rue de la Paix
Rue Scribe
Rue Auber
Rue Daunou
Rue Pasquier

# Le Marais

**HOW TO GET THERE**

St-Paul

**This historic quarter, with its narrow streets and 17th- and 18th-century town houses, is a haven for small, one-off boutiques and one of the few areas where you can be sure to find many shops open on a Sunday afternoon. It is also the city's gay quarter and a hub for the Jewish community, which is concentrated on the rue des Rosiers, where Jewish bakeries, restaurants and shops mingle with trendy clothing boutiques such as L'Eclaireur (No. 3 ter), purveyor of avant-garde designer labels.**

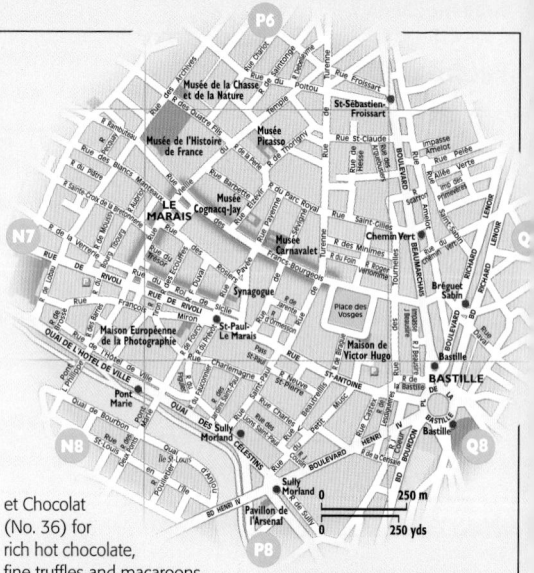


**RUE DU ROI DE SICILE**

From St-Paul Métro station, take rue Pavée to rue du Roi de Sicile and turn left. First stop is

*Chocoholics should head for the rue Vieille-du-Temple*

Mizoram (No. 10), selling haute couture from India, with a wonderful selection of hand-made accessories. Alternatives (No. 18) is one of the few *dépôt-vente* (second-hand) shops that caters for both men and women—it offers names such as Helmut Lang and Comme des Garçons. The trendier-than-thou Noir Kennedy boutique sells the latest fashions from Delphine Murat and Fake London Genius, among others.

**RUE VIEILLE-DU-TEMPLE**

Take a right onto rue Vieille-du-Temple. If you need chocolate to keep you going, stop in at Cacao et Chocolat (No. 36) for rich hot chocolate, fine truffles and macaroons made in France with South American chocolate. Next door is Nil Darende, selling bright, attractive accessories and clothing for women by a selection of international designers at reasonable prices. Catherine Martineau (No. 42) makes all the jewellery and accessories she sells in her tiny shop. The Fiesta Galerie (No. 43), always fun to browse in, specializes in American design furnishings from the 1950s to 80s, plus some European pieces.

**RUE DES FRANCS-BOURGEOIS**

Take another right onto the boutique-packed rue des Francs-Bourgeois. On the corner is Issey Miyake's minimalist A.POC shop (No. 47), featuring his simple, wearable designs in original fabrics. Next to it is Art du Bureau, selling handsome designer office accessories, watches and handbags, followed by Muji (No. 47), with its inexpensive clothing for men and women, as well as homewares and office supplies in the shop next door. La Chaise Longue (No. 20) is a great place to pick up gifts for yourself or others, with many of its homewares and accessories based on 1950s designs. For wearable women's clothing with an exotic touch, go to Abou d'Abi Bazar (No. 10). Autour du Monde Home offers stylish furnishings and accessories for the home, as well as bright women's clothing.

**WHERE TO EAT**

**L'ÉTOILE MANQUANTE**

34 rue Vieille-du-Temple, 75004
Tel 01 42 72 48 34; www.cafeine.com
Open daily 9am–2am
**An attractive modern café**

*Window-shopping in the the rue des Francs-Bourgeois*

**serving light meals such as salads, soups, sandwiches and charcuterie or cheese platters between noon and 1.30am. Hot dishes are also offered at lunchtime. For dessert, try Christian Constant's delicious ice cream. Check out the starlit, stainless-steel lavatories.**

**COUDE FOU**

12 rue du Bourg-Tibourg, 75004
Tel 01 42 77 15 16
Open Mon–Sat 11–10.30, Sun 7pm–10.30pm
**A busy little restaurant decorated with rustic murals of farm life. The traditional French food is hearty and tasty.**

# Around Opéra

**HOW TO GET THERE**

Chaussée-d'Antin-Lafayette
Auber

**The main shopping attractions near Paris's beautifully restored 19th-century Opéra Palais Garnier are the two major department stores, Galeries Lafayette and Printemps. In one or the other, you'll find everything imaginable in terms of clothing, accessories, shoes, perfumes and cosmetics, home furnishings and household linen. A short walk away is place de la Madeleine, with all you need to satisfy your cravings for luxury foods.**

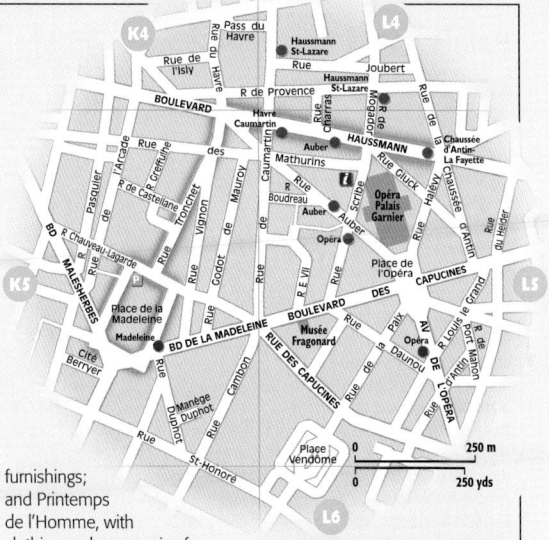


**BOULEVARD HAUSSMANN**

When you step out of the Chaussée-d'Antin-Lafayette Métro station, you'll be right in front of Galeries Lafayette (No. 40). The

*The impressive glass dome and balconies at Galeries Lafayette*

Magasin Coupole (named for its enormous stained-glass dome) sells everything but menswear, which is next door in Lafayette Homme—also the home of the first-floor Lafayette Gourmet food hall. Walkways on the first and second floors of the Magasin Coupole lead to the second and third floors of Lafayette Homme.

Down the street at No. 64 is Galerie Lafayette's main competitor, Printemps, which has three buildings: Printemps de la Mode, with eight floors of women's and children's fashions; Printemps de la Maison, selling everything for the home, from pots and pans to ethnic furnishings; and Printemps de l'Homme, with clothing and accessories for men. For a panoramic view of Paris and a close look at the art nouveau cupola, take the elevator to the ninth floor of Printemps de la Maison. Both department stores have cafés and restaurants, personal shopper services and regular fashion shows.

The streets around the two stores are inhabited mostly by chain stores such as Gap France, H&M and C&A.

**RUE TRONCHET AND PLACE DE LA MADELEINE**

The shop-lined rue Tronchet has outlets such as Jacadi (No. 17; appealing but expensive childrenswear) and La Bagagerie (No. 12; luggage and handbags). It takes you to place de la Madeleine, where a number of stores offer gourmet foods. The famous Fauchon (No. 26) has a pastry shop, a gourmet grocery store with foods from around the world and a tea room. On the other side of the square is Hédiard (No. 21), with similar offerings of exotic foods and its own restaurant. The flagship store of the Nicolas wine chain (No. 31) has a huge cellar stocked with everything from the priciest to most inexpensive bottles. Other gourmet goodies can be found at the Caviar Kaspa boutique and restaurant (No. 17) and Maison de la Truffe (No. 19), which specializes in truffles and foie gras. For something crystal to serve them in, go to Baccarat (No. 11).

**WHERE TO EAT**

**LAFAYETTE GOURMET**
40 boulevard Haussmann, 75009
Tel 01 42 82 34 56
Open Mon–Sat 9–8, Thu 9–9
**What could be more chic than**

*Shopping in place de la Madeleine, southwest of Opéra*

**eating lunch in the middle of a gourmet supermarket? Choose the food stand that appeals to you and find a chair. The fruit and vegetable stand has salads, quiches, vegetable soup and freshly squeezed juices. Other counters offer Italian food, cheese dishes, grilled meats and fresh fish.**

**L'ECLUSE**
15 place de la Madeleine, 75008
Tel 01 42 65 34 69
www.leclusebaravin.com
Open daily 11.30am–1am
**This chain of six wine bars is reliable for its tasty meals, fine wines and friendly service.**

# Palais Royal/Les Halles

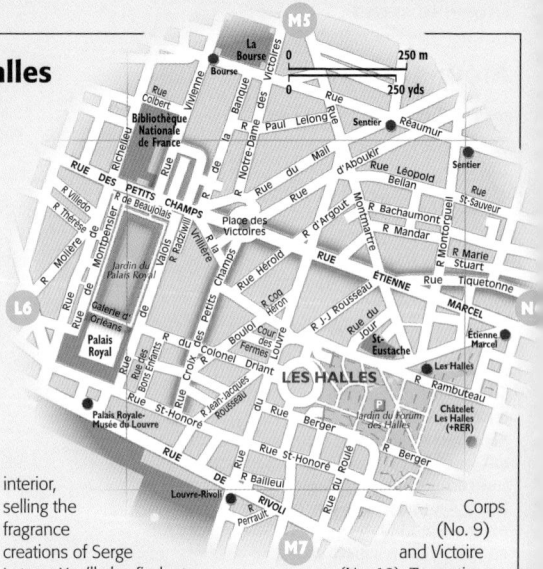


**HOW TO GET THERE**

Palais-Royal/Musée du Louvre

**The Forum des Halles is an underground shopping mall marked by a mirrored, above-ground architectural eyesore. It's a good option if you're looking for chain stores, but it's not particularly Parisian. The Carrousel du Louvre is a classier underground mall with museum boutiques, a nature-themed store and a branch of Virgin Megastore. If you want to see Paris while you shop, go to the beautiful Jardin du Palais Royal, Galerie Vivienne and place des Victoires, all of which are worth visiting in their own right, as well as for shopping.**

**JARDIN DU PALAIS ROYAL**

Enter the Palais Royal from the rue St-Honoré side, have a look

*A wacky window display at Jean-Paul Gaultier*

at Daniel Buren's interestingly incongruous striped columns, then continue into the main courtyard, where you can rest in the garden or shop in the surrounding arcades. Among the more interesting shops are Didier Ludot's three boutiques selling vintage haute couture by such fashion legends as Chanel, Dior and Balenciaga (No. 20 galerie de Montpensier), accessories (No. 24) and, on the eastern side, nothing but little black dresses—all vintage—and fur coats (No. 125 galerie de Valois). Nearby, is the Salons du Palais Royal Shiseido boutique (No. 142), with its dimly lit mauve interior, selling the fragrance creations of Serge Lutens. You'll also find art galleries and unusual shops such as Drapeaux de France (1 place Colette), with a huge collection of toy soldiers.

**GALERIE VIVIENNE**

Leave the Palais Royal from the galerie de Beaujolais side and walk up rue Vivienne. Start a visit to the Galerie Vivienne at Jean-Paul Gaultier (No. 6) for a look at the designer's ready-to-wear and couture clothes in a chic, spacious boutique. From here wander into the elegant passageways of the early 19th-century gallery (which connects with the parallel Galerie Colbert) to browse in a series of interesting shops. Décor de Cuisine (No. 32) sells antique kitchen utensils and furnishings. La Marelle (No. 21) is an excellent *dépôt-vente* (second-hand clothing shop) with designer labels for women and children. Legrand Filles et Fils (1 rue de la Banque), a purveyor of fine wine, wine-related books and utensils, and gourmet foods, also has a wine bar and holds regular tastings.

**PLACE DES VICTOIRES**

Exit the Galerie Vivienne onto rue des Petits Champs (which becomes rue de la Feuillade), turn left and walk the short distance to the stately 17th-century place des Victoires, a circular 'square' created by Louis XIV. Here you'll find the boutiques of Kenzo (No. 3), Thierry Mugler (No. 8), Esprit de Corps (No. 9) and Victoire (No. 10). To continue your shopping, walk down either the rue Croix des Petits Champs back towards rue de Rivoli or down rue Étienne Marcel to the newly trendy rue Tiquetonne.

*Take a break in the beautiful 19th-century Galerie Vivienne*

**WHERE TO EAT**

**A PRIORI THÉ**

35–37 galerie Vivienne, 75002
Tel 01 42 97 48 75
Open Mon-Fri 9–6, Sat 9–6.30, Sun 12.30–6.30

**Tea room serving hot dishes and salads at lunchtime and delicious desserts at teatime. Brunch on Sunday.**

**RESTAURANT DU PALAIS ROYAL**

43 rue de Valois, 75001
Tel 01 40 20 00 27
Open Mon–Sat 12.30–2.30, 7–10

**A handsome restaurant, with outdoor tables in the Palais Royal garden in warm weather.**

# St-Germain-des-Prés

**HOW TO GET THERE**

St-Germain-des-Prés

**Once the domain of small boutiques, art galleries and antiques shops, St-Germain-des-Prés has been transformed over the past decade by the arrival of designer boutiques. Smart as it is, the area hasn't yet replaced the Faubourg St-Honoré as the city's couture hub and retains much of its historical and some of its bohemian charm.**

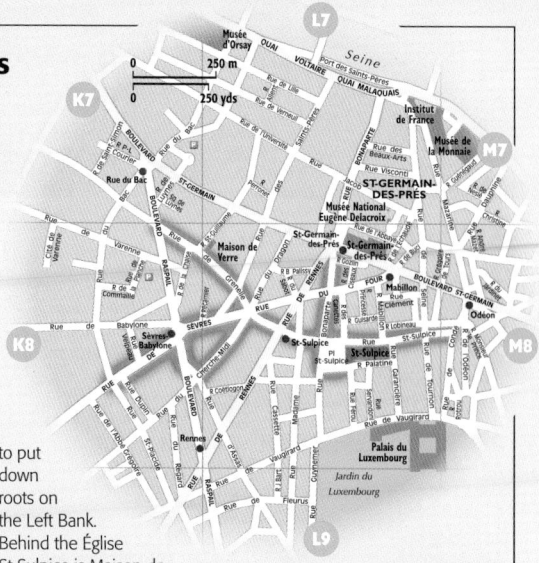


**RUE BONAPARTE**

Admire the gracious tower of the Église St-Germain-des-Prés as you come out of the St-Germain-des-Prés Métro station. Across the street is the Louis Vuitton store (6 place St-Germain-des-Prés), with its famous trunks and more modern travel wares. Head south down rue Bonaparte. You

*Designer labels, such as Prada, are abundant in Paris*

can't miss the Emporio Armani store, complete with an Italian restaurant, on the corner of boulevard St-Germain. Back on rue Bonaparte, you'll pass the boutiques of Hugo Boss (No. 47), Georges Rech (No. 54), Max Mara (corner of rue du Four), Ventilo (No. 59) and Cacharel (No. 64). Stop in at Pierre Hermé (No. 72), the smartest patisserie in town, for exquisite pastries, macaroons or chocolates, but be prepared to wait, especially on weekends. Move on to Yves Saint-Laurent Rive Gauche (6 place St-Sulpice) across the street, the first big-name designer boutique to put down roots on the Left Bank. Behind the Église St-Sulpice is Maison de Famille (29 rue St-Sulpice), with original household goods and linen, and chic yet sober clothing for men and women. An option here is to continue down the shop-lined rue St-Sulpice and venture off into the side streets to discover a variety of boutiques.

**RUE DU CHERCHE-MIDI**

From place St-Sulpice, take rue du Vieux-Colombier (passing more shops, including Agnès B at No. 6) to rue du Cherche-Midi, where one stylish shoe shop follows another, among them Robert Clergerie (No. 5), with everything from strappy high-heeled sandals to fur-covered slip-ons with toes as sharp as daggers. Take a right at place Alphonse Deville and a left down rue de Sèvres to browse in Le Bon Marché (No. 24), Paris's oldest and most elegant department store. Alternatively, go right along rue de Sèvres and then left down rue de Grenelle.

**RUE DE GRENELLE**

Here you'll find even smarter shoe shops, including Stephane Kélian (No. 13 bis) and Patrick Cox (No. 21), as well as designer labels Sonia Rykiel (Nos. 4 and 6), Prada (No. 5) Miu Miu (No. 16) and Martine Sitbon (No. 13). For something a little different, check out the 'barbaric' furniture designs at En Attendant les Barbares (No. 35) and the designer perfumes at Editions de Parfums Frédéric Malle (No. 37).

**WHERE TO EAT**

**CAFÉ DE FLORE**

172 boulevard St-Germain, 75006
Tel 01 45 48 55 26
www.cafe-de-flore.com
Open daily 7.30am–1.30am

*Relax at an outdoor table at the Café de Flore*

**You can't get more Parisian than the Flore, still popular with French and international celebrities despite the tourist invasion. Prices are steep for café food (club sandwiches, omelettes and salads), but the art deco interior, professional service from white-aproned waiters, and bustling Left Bank ambience make it worth it.**

**LE PETIT ST-BENOÎT**

4 rue St-Benoît, 75006
Tel 01 42 60 27 92
Open Mon–Sat noon–2.30, 7–10.30
**Simple, hearty French dishes at this Left Bank institution.**

# Shopping Directory

This selection of shops, arranged by theme, includes some of Paris's countless fashion boutiques, specialist food shops, markets, department stores, antiques shops and bookstores.


- See pages 172–175 for shopping locator maps
- See pages 190–191 for chain stores
- See page 298 for clothing sizes


## BOOKS

### ARTAZART

Map 174 P5
83 quai de Valmy, 75010
Tel 01 40 40 24 00
www.artazart.com

This bookshop on the banks of the Canal St-Martin specializes in visual arts, including design, architecture, photography and fashion. A small gallery welcomes work by up-and-coming artists. The friendly and well-informed staff may even offer you coffee.

Mon–Wed, Fri 11–8, Thu 11–10, Sat, Sun 2–8
Jacques Bonsergent

### GIBERT JOSEPH

Map 173 M8
26 boulevard St-Michel, 75006
Tel 01 44 41 88 88

You'll find an impressive range of books here, covering nearly every subject, from travel to maths via religion! Look out for used books, which are usually in pristine condition but come at a discounted price. This shop is very popular with students from the nearby Sorbonne university.

Mon–Sat 10–7.30 St-Michel

### LA HUNE

Map 173 L8
170 boulevard St-Germain, 75006
Tel 01 45 48 35 85

This is the haunt of the literary crowd, as is prestigious Café Flore, nearby. There is little in the fields of poetry and art that you won't find here. Book signings and literary evenings in the presence of eminent writers are organized regularly.

Mon–Sat 10am–midnight, Sun 11–8
St-Germain-des-Prés

### LIBRAIRIE ULYSSE

Map 174 P8
26 rue St-Louis en l'Ile, 75004
Tel 01 43 25 17 35
www.ulysse.fr

The books (both new and used), maps and magazines here span almost every country in the world. The shop is also a congenial venue for people exchanging stories, souvenirs and tips, and planning further adventures.

Tue–Sat 2–8 Sully Morland

### TASCHEN

Map 173 M8
2 rue de Buci, 75006
Tel 01 40 51 79 22
www.taschen.com

This art bookshop is itself a work of art: Its interior was designed by Philippe Starck (there are tawny tones and a large screen at the back shows silent films). Publications by this German house include books on photography, painting, eroticism and architecture.

Sun–Thu 11–8, Fri–Sat 11am–midnight Odéon

### SPECIAL

### SHAKESPEARE AND COMPANY

Map 173 M8
37 rue de la Bûcherie, 75005
Tel 01 43 26 96 50
www.shakespeareco.org

An American bookstore, Shakespeare and Company (see page 20) is named after the famous bookshop started by Sylvia Beach in the 1920s. This place is special, with its old floor tiles, little well full of coins and floor-to-ceiling shelves. The stock includes both new and used books. There is a small library upstairs, where books can be browsed.

Daily noon–midnight
St-Michel

### W.H.SMITH

Map 173 K6
248 rue de Rivoli, 75001
Tel 01 44 77 88 99
www.whsmith.fr

A piece of England in the heart of Paris. France's biggest English bookseller stocks just as many English books and newspapers as its sister stores across the Channel. British daily papers are available on the day of publication.

Mon–Sat 9–7.30, Sun 1–7.30
Tuileries

## MUSIC

### VIRGIN MEGASTORE

Map 172 H5
52–60 avenue des Champs-Elysées, 75008
Tel 01 49 53 50 00
www.virginmega.fr

This megastore, surrounded by bars and cinemas, stays open late, so you can pop in and

sample the latest CDs, DVDs and books before a film or after a drink. There is also a café-restaurant upstairs.

Daily 10am–midnight
Franklin D. Roosevelt

## ANTIQUES

### ALAN ARCHÉOLOGIE DU XXE SIÈCLE

Map 175 off L1
45 rue Anselme, 93400, St-Ouen
Tel 01 40 10 93 08

Alan has turned his home into a giant second-hand shop. Everything is for sale, from the soap he is using to his furniture—some beautiful 1950s, 60s and 70s vintage pieces—via his clothes. A warm welcome is guaranteed.

Sat–Sun 11.30–7; by appointment rest of the week Mairie de St-Ouen

### DÉPÔT VENTE DE PARIS

Map 174 off Q8
81 rue Lagny, 75020
Tel 01 43 72 13 91
www.depotventedeparis.com

This is France's biggest second-hand shop, where everything is on sale or return: more than 1,000 pieces of furniture and nearly 100,000 items. There are some direct imports from Asia (eight arrivals per year). Many of its rentals are to the movie industry.

Mon–Sat 10–7 Nation

### GALERIE CAPTIER

Map 173 L7
33 rue de Beaune, 75007
Tel 01 42 61 00 57

The antique Chinese furniture (17th to 19th century) and old Japanese screens here have been chosen by owners Bernard and Sylvie Captier, who regularly travel to Asia to

search out exotic and refined works of art.

Mon 2.30–7, Tue–Sat 10.30–7
Rue du Bac

### SALLE RASPAIL

Map 173 L10
224 boulevard Raspail, 75014
Tel 01 56 54 11 90

This second-hand shop stocks antiques from the 18th, 19th and 20th centuries. The selection is wide enough to have some funky 1970s pieces sitting next to a chest of drawers from the 19th century. It's likely that everyone will be tempted by something, all the more because only quality pieces are displayed here.

Tue–Fri 11–8, Sat 11–7 Raspail

### XXO

Map 174 off Q8
78 rue de la Fraternité, 93200 Romainville
Tel 01 48 18 08 88
www.xxo.com

XXO stands for Extra Extra Original, and the furniture purchased, sold and rented out is indeed quite original. Exclusively distributing 1950s to 80s furniture, this shop has classics such as Colombo chairs and lip-shaped sofas.

Mon–Fri 9.30–6.30, Sat 2–6.30
Not close to a Métro stop
A few minutes' drive from Porte de Bagnolet

## GIFTS

### ANNE MAISONNEUVE

Map 173 L9
112 boulevard Raspail, 75006
Tel 01 42 22 42 70
www.annemaisonneuve.com

This shop will make you want to travel. Every visit is relaxing—you are soothed by the sound of Zen fountains and intoxicated by the smell of fragrant wood. Anne Maisonneuve has brought back beautiful wooden bowls, sea-grass mats and jewellery from Indonesia and the Philippines. She also designs her own pieces, including original greetings cards.

Mon–Sat 11–8.30 Notre-Dame des-Champs, Vavin, St-Placide

### DOM CHRISTIAN KOBAN

Map 174 N7
21 rue Ste-Croix de la Bretonnerie, 75004
Tel 01 42 71 08 00
www.dom-shop.com

Designer Christian Koban caters to the urban home, at more than affordable prices.

Trendy objects and pieces of furniture offer sleek lines, but with a funky twist. The shop also has some truly kitsch but amusing trinkets.

Mon–Sat 11–8, Sun 2–8
Hôtel de Ville

### LES FÉES D'HERBE

Map 174 off Q8
23 rue Faidherbe, 75011
Tel 01 43 70 14 76

Les Fées d'Herbe sounds like *l'effet d'herbe* ('the grass effect') but is, in fact, a play on the streetname, Faidherbe. The shop stocks paper dragonflies, exotic artificial flowers and distinctive china, as well as real plants, including herbs for the kitchen and beautiful rare orchids.

Tue–Fri 10–1, 1.30–7.30, Sat 10.30–7.30
Faidherbe Chaligny

### WHY?

Map 175 N6
93 rue Rambuteau, 75001
Tel 01 40 26 39 56
www.why.fr

This is a shop where pigs really do fly. Expect the most unusual, the funniest and definitely the kitschest items (including zebra-print fur wallets and pink inflatable ottomans). Here, you'll find things you'd never thought of buying and may never need, but they are sure to make you laugh.

Daily 11–8 Les Halles

## FOOD AND DRINK

### BARTHÉLÉMY (STÉ)

Map 173 K7
51 rue de Grenelle, 75007
Tel 01 42 22 82 24

Established in 1904, this is a cheese-lover's paradise, selling Brie, Mont d'Or (from Jura), Roquefort and much more. The old-fashioned shop supplies both the Élysée Palace and Matignon, home to France's president and prime minister respectively.

Tue–Sat 8–1, 4–7.30
Rue du Bac

## SPECIAL

### FAUCHON

Map 173 K5
26 place de la Madeleine, 75008
Tel 01 47 42 60 11

This is the tastiest (and possibly most expensive) delicatessen in Paris. Foie gras, fine condiments, great wines: The very best of French cuisine has been

available here since 1886. And not only French: Beluga caviar, the best vintages of the finest spirits from all over the world, and many more exotic delicacies can also be found. There is also a tea room.

Mon–Sat 9.30–7 Madeleine

### DRUGSTORE PUBLICIS

Map172 G5
133 avenue des Champs-Élysées, 75008
Tel 01 44 43 79 00

This is a night owls' paradise. When other shops have closed, you can come here for newspapers, tobacco and alcohol, cosmetics, pharmaceutical products and much more—but you'll pay quite a premium. There is also a restaurant for light meals, including salads and *croques*.

Mon–Sat 9am–2am, Sun 10am–2am Charles de Gaulle-Étoile

### LAVINIA

Map 173 K5
3–5 boulevard de la Madeleine, 75001
Tel 01 42 97 20 20
www.lavinia.es (in Spanish)

You'll find more than 5,000 wines and 1,000 spirits spread over three floors here. There is also wine paraphernalia, books, a bar and a restaurant.

Mon–Fri 10–8, Sat 9–8
Madeleine

### LENÔTRE

Map 172 off J4
15 boulevard de Coucelles, 75008
Tel 01 45 63 87 63
www.lenotre.fr

Lenôtre has long been famous for its fine foods and pastries, but the launch of the *macarré*, a bright and surprisingly square-shaped macaroon, has made it even more fashionable. Unusual varieties include chocolate-cherry and aniseed-blackcurrant.

Daily 9am–9pm Villiers

### MARIAGE FRÈRES

Map 174 N7
30 rue du Bourg-Tibourg, 75004
Tel 01 42 72 28 11
www.mariagefreres.com

Founded in 1854, this tea house is a Parisian institution.

It stocks hundreds of teas from all over the world, including some exclusive house blends. If you are passionate about tea, sample some here or take a new discovery home. China and tea-based delicacies are also for sale: The *matcha* tea-scented salt is a must.

Daily 10.30–7.30 Hôtel de Ville

**NICOLAS**
Map 174 off Q9
24 cour St-Émilion, 75012
Tel 01 44 74 62 65
www.nicolas.com
This chain of wine shops offers a good selection of vintages, ranging from its small vineyards' collection through to more prestigious names. This particular shop also has an adjoining wine bar—perfect for sampling before buying.
Shop: daily 10am–9pm; Wine bar: daily noon–11pm Cour St-Émilion

**OLIVIERS & CO**
Map 174 P7
47 rue Vieille-du-Temple, 75004
Tel 01 42 74 38 40
www.oliviers-co.com
Dedicated to olive oil, Oliviers & Co stocks vintages from all over the Mediterranean, plus many products in which it is a core ingredient (tapenade, olive oil biscuits). Also spices, olive-wood bowls and utensils.
Daily 11–8 Hôtel de Ville

**PIERRE HERMÉ**
Map 173 L8
72 rue Bonaparte, 75006
Tel 01 43 54 47 77
Couture pastries? Chef Pierre Hermé works in association with a designer so his creations are as visually exciting as they are tasty. His gold-leaf ornamented chocolate cake is legendary. Be prepared for a wait at his small boutique, more like a jeweller's shop than a patisserie, but remember, satisfaction is at the other end of the line.
Tue–Sun 9–7 St-Sulpice, Mabillon

**POILÂNE**
Map 173 L8
8 rue du Cherche-Midi, 75006
Tel 01 45 48 42 59
www.poilane.fr
What is often regarded as the best French bread is still baked here from secret family recipes. The country nut-and-raisin bread is a must, but

other delicacies include the traditional baguette, croissant and rye loaf.
Mon–Sat 7.15am–8.15pm
Sèvres-Babylone, St-Sulpice

## FASHION

**ANTIK BATIK**
See page 186.

**ANTOINE ET LILI**
Map 174 P4
95 quai de Valmy, 75010
Tel 01 40 37 41 55
www.antoineetlili.com
Knick-knacks from all over the world, oriental beauty products and vivid outfits in luxurious fabrics: This is hippie-chic kingdom. There are two shops here—one for clothes, another for gifts—and also a small restaurant.
Mon 11–7, Tue–Fri 11–8, Sat 10–8, Sun 9–2, 3–6 Jacques Bonsergent, Gare de l'Est

**BARBARA BUI**
Map 175 N6
23 rue Étienne Marcel, 75001
Tel 01 40 26 43 65
www.barbarabui.com
The lines are sleek, original and often have a sexy twist, but are never provocative. You'll find tailored jackets, fitted tops, tight trousers and an impressive range of high-heeled shoes. The collection is aimed at the urban woman and is classy, modern and feminine.
Daily 10.30–7.30
Étienne Marcel

## SPECIAL

**AGNÈS B**
Map 175 M6
6 rue du Jour, 75001
Tel 01 45 08 56 56
www.agnesb.fr

Sober yet trendy, Agnès B's fashion is the epitome of young Parisian chic. Sharply cut clothes with original details are her signature, and her little waistcoat with press studs is a classic.
The designer is also worth celebrating for her artistic engagement—she sponsors many budding creators.
Mon–Sat 10–7, Sun 9–2, 3–6
Les Halles

**BILL TORNADE**
Map 175 M6
44 rue Étienne-Marcel, 75002
Tel 01 42 33 66 47
www.billtornade.com
Bill Tornade sells beautiful fabrics, 1960s-style jackets, pinstripe suits and fine Italian leather shoes.
Some outfits are part of a limited edition, for a rather exclusive touch.
Mon–Sat 11–7.30
Étienne Marcel

SPECIAL

**ANTIK BATIK**
Map 174 P7
18 rue de Turenne, 75004
Tel 01 44 78 02 00
Come here for the finest of ethnic chic: Embroidered blouses made of cotton or silk, long batik-printed stoles, a collection of bags that look as if they were bought at a souk, and which offer the perfect finishing touch. There is even some sexy lingerie, with sheer fabrics and little sequins.
Tue–Sat 11–7, Sun–Mon 2–7
Hôtel de Ville

**CHANEL**
Map 173 K5

31 rue Cambon, 75001
Tel 01 42 86 28 00
www.chanel.com
The tweed suit and the little black dress, Coco Chanel's signature outfits, keep on being re-invented by Karl Lagerfeld, head of this fashion house since 1984. Classy, sexy and feminine, Chanel's designs embody Parisian elegance.
Mon–Sat 10–7 Madeleine

**COLETTE**
Map 173 L6
213 rue St-Honoré, 75001
Tel 01 55 35 33 90
www.colette.fr
Exclusive shopping par excellence! Come here for cutting-edge design from one of the industry's rising names, or for imported beauty products that are difficult to find elsewhere. A glance at the press box will ensure you keep abreast of the trends. The water bar downstairs offers more than a hundred different brands of bottled water.
Mon–Sat 10.30–7.30 Tuileries, Pyramides

**COMME DES GARÇONS**
Map 173 K5
54 rue du Faubourg St-Honoré, 75008
Tel 01 53 30 27 27
Japanese designer Rei Kawakubo's approach to fashion is almost architectural. Her asymmetrical cuts produce sleek lines and one of her outfits can remodel a body. The collection caters to those looking for something unique, modern and with a couture accent. Comme des Garçons's perfume is also sold here.
Mon–Sat 11–7 Madeleine, Concorde

**ISABEL MARANT**
Map 174 Q8
16 rue de Charonne, 75011
Tel 01 49 29 71 55
Now a regular on the catwalk, Isabel Marant has updated Parisian elegance by giving it a bit of a bohemian bourgeois twist. Silk paisley shirts, big woollen wrap-over tops: This is casual chic at its best.
Mon–Sat 10.30–7.30 Bastille

**JUDITH LACROIX**
Map 175 M4
15 rue Hippolyte-Lebas, 75009
Tel 01 42 82 12 50
www.judithlacroix.com
This young designer originally made a name for herself with her successful children's range—notably using a fabric which resembled a page from a child's homework book. After her work was distributed at leading outlets such as Barneys in New York, she opened her own boutique in 2002 and extended her range to include womenswear.
Mon–Sat 10–7
Notre-Dame-de-Lorette

**KILIWATCH**
Map 175 M6
64 rue Tiquetone, 75002
Tel 01 42 21 17 37
Kiliwatch offers the very best in retro gear. Every garment has been carefully chosen, so the vintage Hawaiian shirts and bright 1970s skirts often come at a price. A line of new denim outfits completes the collection. Be sure to check the press box which displays the sharpest fashion and design reviews.
Mon 2–7, Tue–Fri 11–7, Sat 11–7.30
Étienne Marcel

**MARIA LUISA**
Map 173 K6
40 rue du Mont-Thabor, 75001
Tel 01 47 03 48 08
Maria Luisa Poumaillou is one of Paris's leading trendsetters. The best of fashion's avant-garde can be found at her boutique: Philip Treacy hats, Manolo Blahnik shoes. Fashionistas will appreciate the shop's modern interior design, signature of architect Laurent Buttazzoni.
Mon–Sat 10.30–7 Concorde

**MARITHÉ + FRANÇOIS GIRBAUD**
Map 173 L8
7 rue du Cherche-Midi, 75006
Tel 01 53 63 53 63
www.girbaud.com
Come here for designer streetwear in innovative fabrics and lines. The jeans collection is particularly futuristic. This branch showcases one of botanist Patrick Blanc's suspended gardens—more than 200 plants hang from a wall.
Mon 11–9, Tue–Sat 10–7
Sèvres-Babylone, St-Sulpice

**SPECIAL**

**VANESSA BRUNO**
Map 173 L6
12 rue Castiglione, 75001
Tel 01 42 61 44 60
This French designer's feminine creations spice up classicism with a modern twist; check out the sequined canvas shopping bag or satin knickerbockers. Old also meets new in the shop's interior, with wooden floorboards, lofty pillars and a succession of bare and lacquered walls.
Mon–Sat 10.30–7.30 Tuileries

**NIM**
Map 174 N7
16 rue du Bourg-Tibourg, 75004
Tel 01 42 77 19 79
Half gallery, half shop, Nim explores the world of denim. You'll find Levi's innovative Red label range here or you can choose a piece customized by a young designer.

Tue–Sat 1–8, Sun 3–7
Hôtel de Ville

**LE SHOP**
Map 175 M6
3 rue d'Argout, 75002
Tel 01 40 28 95 94
www.leshop-paris.com
This massive industrial space has the most fashionable brands of streetwear: Carhartt, Loona, Lady Soul, Tim Bargeot. Shop to the sounds of techno mixed by great DJs. There is also a bar.
Mon 1–7, Tue–Sat 11–7
Étienne Marcel

**XULY BËT**
Map 174 P7
1 rue Pierre-Lescot, 75001
Tel 01 42 33 50 40
Malian designer Lamine Kouyate adds an ethnic twist to glamour. His creations show the influence of his native Africa (distinctive, patterned fabrics), but the sexy cuts are more reminiscent of a daring couture designer such as Versace. There are some beautiful tight-fitting dresses, often with red stitching. Alongside the clothes is a collection of objects for the home, handmade in Africa.
Daily 11–2, 3–7 Chemin Vert

**ZARA**
Map 173 M7
128 rue de Rivoli, 75001
Tel 01 44 82 64 00
www.zara.com
The Emporio Armani-inspired collection (neutral tones and sleek lines for a casual chic look) offers unbeatable value for money. Alongside this main range there are funkier clothes for teenagers and children and a smaller collection for men.

Mon–Sat 10–8 Châtelet

**SHOES AND ACCESSORIES**

**GALERIE ANTOINETTE JEAN**
Map 173 M8
65 rue St-André des Arts, 75006
Tel 01 43 26 23 29
www.galerie-antoinettejean.com
This gallery promotes young designers and artists. The walls display a collection of Haitian paintings. On the shelves there are bags, scarves and jewellery; each of the

carefully crafted pieces is an original design.
Daily noon–7 Odéon, St-Michel

**JAMIN PUECH**
Map 175 N4
61 rue d'Hauteville, 75010
Tel 01 40 22 08 32
Beaded or embroidered, ornamented with little leather flowers or golden chains: Each bag offers precious and unique details, and is quite simply a work of art. Jamin Puech has brought jewellery to leather craft and is now one of Paris's fashion-scene darlings.
Mon, Sat 11–7, Tue–Fri 10–7
Poissonnière, Bonne Nouvelle

**JEAN-CLAUDE MONDERER**
Map 174 P7
22 rue des Francs-Bourgeois, 75004
Tel 01 48 04 51 41
On the picturesque rue des Francs-Bourgeois, this shop is for men and women who love

elegant, original footwear. Fine materials, remarkable finishing and interesting designs are Monderer's trademarks.
Mon 10.30–7, Tue–Sat 10.30–7.30, Sun 2–7 St-Paul

**LOLLIPOPS**
Map 173 L8
40 rue du Dragon, 75006
Tel 01 42 22 09 29
www.lollipops.fr
Bags, scarves, hats and some jewellery form this chic but playful collection, with its interesting use of materials such as wool, suede and velvet. Products are displayed by colour, so it is easy to find matching pieces.
Mon noon–7, Tue 11–7, Wed–Fri 10.30–7, Sat 10.30–7.30 St-Sulpice

**LOORICA**
Map 175 N3
8bis rue des Gardes, 75018
Tel 01 44 92 01 26
www.loorica.com
Ever thought that a red shell of polypropylene could hold your wallet? Loorica designs bags that look so futuristic you could take them aboard a spacecraft. This shop is on the so-called *rue de la Mode* (Fashion Street). Young and promising designers have been offered workspace here at a discounted rate to attract them to this formerly run-down but now up-and-coming district. Credit cards are not accepted.
Mon–Sat 10–7
Barbès Rochechouart

**LOUIS VUITTON**
Map 172 H5
101 avenue des Champs-Élysées, 75008
Tel 01 53 57 24 00
www.vuitton.com
The beige and brown chequered pattern and the

interlaced LV initials are the house's signature and a symbol of chic par excellence. You'll find coordinated leather goods, from suitcases to key rings via wallets, but also some high quality clothes with classy finishing touches.
Mon–Sat 10–8 George V

**UN DIMANCHE À VENISE PAR KALLISTÉ**
Map 174 P7
7 rue des Francs-Bourgeois, 75004
Tel 01 42 76 02 65
www.dimancheavenise.com
Here, the shoes are constantly re-invented. In winter, high-heeled boots appear in interesting materials such as fake crocodile leather, while in summer, stilettos may be adorned with pearl butterflies. The workmanship and finish are always impeccable.
Tue–Sat 10.30–7, Sun–Mon 2.30–7
St-Paul

**VENTILO**
Map 174 P7
11 rue de Sévigné, 75004
Tel 01 44 54 09 82
The ethnic chic attitude promoted by this fashion label has been extended to accessories. In this former Hungarian grocery store, with a Chinese-inspired interior, you'll find shoes, embroidered scarves and hand-painted bags, as well as candles and incense.
Tue–Sat 10.30–2, 3–7, Sun 1–7
St-Paul

## JEWELLERY

**AGATHA**
Map 173 L6
99 rue de Rivoli 75001
Tel 01 42 96 03 09
www.agatha.fr
Agatha offers classic jewellery at very fair prices. Semi-precious stones and silver and gold-plated materials are the keys. Why not treat yourself to a (fake) diamond *pavé* ring? The regularly changing collection of watches, pendants, rings and bracelets often features the brand's mascot, a fox terrier.

Mon–Sat 10–7 Châtelet

**BICHE DE BÈRE**
Map 174 N7
15 rue des Innocents, 75001
Tel 01 40 28 94 47
Nelly Biche de Bère, who trained as an industrial designer, creates original, easy-to-wear jewellery. Gold or silver-plated materials often have a hammered appearance and simple geometrical shapes.
Mon–Sat 11–7.30 Châtelet

## HEALTH AND BEAUTY

**L'OCCITANE**
Map 173 K7
90 rue du Bac, 75007
Tel 01 42 22 55 28
www.loccitane.fr
The essence of Provence is captured here in perfumed soaps, olive-oil based creams and fragrances. There are per-

fumes for the home and herbal incenses such as fig tree and sandalwood.
Mon–Sat 10.30–7 (closed Wed–Thu 2.30–3.30, Mon, Tue, Fri 2.30–3)
Rue du Bac, Sèvres-Babylone

**PARFUMERIE GÉNÉRALE**
Map 172 H5
6 rue Robert Estienne, 75008
Tel 01 43 59 10 62
www.parfumeriegenerale.com
You would be forgiven for thinking you had stepped into a contemporary art gallery here. It's all fitted carpet made up of large, bright stripes (very Pop Art), immaculate walls punctuated with bright, flashy shelves, and a huge counter where most of the products are window-displayed. This futuristic perfumery sells the most exclusive brands.
Mon–Sat 11–7
Franklin D. Roosevelt

**PATYKA**
Map 174 N7
14 rue Rambuteau, 75003
Tel 01 40 29 49 49
In this *patyka* ('chemist's shop' in Hungarian), you'll find natural beauty products devised according to ancient French and Hungarian recipes. Their *huile absolue* (absolute oil) is a must: This concentrate of essential oils is almost a panacea. The products come in pretty glass bottles.
Daily noon–8 Rambuteau

**SALONS DU PALAIS ROYAL SHISEIDO**
Map 173 M6
142 Galerie de Valois, 75001
Tel 01 49 27 09 09
www.salons-shiseido.com
Everything here is special: The nearby Palais Royal, the prune and lilac theme that imitates a *Directoire*-period boudoir, and perfume bottles designed by Serge Lutens—a world exclusive. You'll also find the full range of Shiseido beauty products.
Mon–Sat 10–7 Louvre-Rivoli, Palais Royal-Musée du Louvre

**SEPHORA**
Map 172 H5
70 avenue des Champs-Élysées, 75008
Tel 01 53 93 22 50
www.sephora.com
This well-stocked perfumery has a slightly futuristic interior, with sleek lines and shiny black and red surfaces. Fragrances, displayed in alphabetical order, come with a description of their core

ingredients and the moods they evoke. A full range of cosmetics is available, including some brands hard to find elsewhere in France.
Mon–Sat 10am–midnight, Sun 11am–midnight Franklin D. Roosevelt

**SPORTING GOODS**

**AU VIEUX CAMPEUR**
Map 173 M8
48 rue des Écoles, 75005
Tel 01 53 10 48 48
www.auvieuxcampeur.fr
No less than 22 adjoining boutiques cover a range of sports goods, including winter sports, mountain climbing and scuba diving. The professional staff offer advice, and you can try out some of the equipment, for example on their indoor rock-climbing wall.
Mon, Tue, Thu 11–7.30, Wed 11–9, Sat 10–7.30 Maubert Mutualité

**HOME AND GARDEN**

**THE CONRAN SHOP**
Map 173 K8
117 rue du Bac, 75007
Tel 01 42 84 10 01
www.conran.com
Celebrated English designer Sir Terence Conran is a hit with the Parisian crowd. Fine materials, a post-1970s influence, and sometimes an ethnic twist give Conran's furniture a modern elegance. Bathroom, kitchen and garden accessories complete the range. Fine foods from all over the world are also sold in this impressive building, designed by Gustave Eiffel.
Mon–Fri 10–7, Sat 10–7.30
Sèvres-Babylone

**LA DROGUERIE**
Map 175 M6
9 rue du Jour, 75001
Tel 01 45 08 93 27
www.ladroguerie.com
Beads, buttons, ribbons and wool are invitations to let your imagination fly. This shop sells everything you'll need to make your own jewellery, knit, or customize your home.
Mon 2–6.45, Tue–Sat 10.30–6.45
Les Halles

## CHAIN STORES

| NAME | Menswear | Womenswear | For children | Shoes | Cosmetics and toiletries | Sports equipment and clothing | Accessories | Household items | Books, music and DVDs | Perfume | CONTACT NUMBER |
|---|---|---|---|---|---|---|---|---|---|---|---|
| Alain Manoukian | ✔ | ✔ | | ✔ | | | ✔ | | | | 04 75 07 50 50 |
| André | | | ✔ | ✔ | | | ✔ | | | | 01 53 26 28 28 |
| Bata | | | ✔ | ✔ | | | ✔ | | | | 01 47 76 40 04 |
| The Body Shop | | | | | ✔ | | ✔ | | | ✔ | 01 53 05 51 51 |
| Caroll | | ✔ | | ✔ | | | ✔ | | | | 04 75 07 50 50 |
| Celio | ✔ | | | | | | ✔ | | | | 01 49 48 13 00 |
| Courir | | | ✔ | ✔ | | | ✔ | | | | 01 46 15 55 00 |
| Du Pareil au Même | | | ✔ | ✔ | | | ✔ | | | | 01 69 81 46 46 |
| Etam | | ✔ | | ✔ | | | ✔ | | | | 01 44 76 73 73 |
| FNAC | | | | | | | | | ✔ | | 01 53 53 64 64 |
| Foot Locker | | | ✔ | ✔ | | ✔ | ✔ | | | | 01 70 20 00 57 |
| Gap | ✔ | ✔ | ✔ | ✔ | | | ✔ | | | ✔ | 01 44 88 28 28 |
| Go Sport | ✔ | ✔ | ✔ | ✔ | | ✔ | ✔ | | | | 04 76 28 20 20 |
| H&M | ✔ | ✔ | ✔ | | | | ✔ | | | | 01 53 20 71 11 |
| Kookaï | | ✔ | | | | | ✔ | | | | 01 43 52 52 52 |
| Mango | | ✔ | | ✔ | | | ✔ | | | | +34 93 860 24 24 |
| Marionnaud | | | | | | | | | | ✔ | 01 48 08 69 69 |
| Minelli | | | | ✔ | | | ✔ | | | | 01 53 35 86 10 |
| Monoprix | ✔ | ✔ | ✔ | ✔ | ✔ | | ✔ | ✔ | | ✔ | 01 55 20 74 42 |
| Morgan | | ✔ | | | | | ✔ | | | | 01 49 34 06 95 |
| Naf Naf | ✔ | ✔ | ✔ | ✔ | | | ✔ | | | | 01 48 13 88 88 |
| Pimkie | | ✔ | ✔ | ✔ | | | ✔ | | | | 03 20 81 48 48 |
| Promod | | ✔ | | ✔ | | | ✔ | | | | 03 20 01 10 00 |
| Virgin Megastore | | | | | | | | | ✔ | | 01 49 53 50 00 |
| Zara | ✔ | ✔ | | ✔ | | | ✔ | | | | +34 981 185 400 |



### NATURES ET DECOUVERTES

Map 174 off Q9
9 cour St-Émilion, 75012
Tel 01 53 33 82 40
www.natureetdecouvertes.com

This chain celebrates the richness of nature. Garden furniture and accessories are available alongside natural products (gems, incense) and instruments to better appreciate nature (telescopes, microscopes, barometers). There are also educational games, CDs, candles and some inspiring books.

Daily 11–9 Cour St-Émilion

### RÉSONANCES

Map 174 off Q9
13 cour St-Émilion, 75012
Tel 01 44 73 82 82

Every object here is evocative of a particular atmosphere: Pure wax and old ceramics may remind you of your granny's home, while the bright vases should suit any modern interior. The shop is part of Bercy Village, a pedestrianized street where outlets offer the latest trends.

Daily 11–9 Cour St-Émilion

## FLORISTS

### AU NOM DE LA ROSE

Map 173 L8
4 rue de Tournon, 75006
Tel 01 46 34 10 64
www.aunomdelarose.fr

Only one kind of flower is sold here—the rose. There are numerous varieties and hues, for some truly original bouquets. This was the first Au Nom de la Rose shop, established in 1991. There are now around 20 in France.

Daily 9am–9pm (Closed Sun in summer) Odéon

### CHRISTIAN TORTU

Map 173 M8
6 carrefour de l'Odéon, 75006
Tel 01 43 26 02 56

Named after its owner, this was one of the first florists to include elements other than flowers in the bouquets—

Paris, like any other Western European capital, has its fair share of chain stores as well as its individual boutiques. Branches of the stores in the chart below can be found across the city. There are also individual listings for Etam (see below), Monoprix (see page 192), Virgin Megastore (see page 183) and Zara (see page 187).

| NUMBER OF SHOPS | DESCRIPTION | WEBSITE |
|---|---|---|
| 10 | Stylish clothes and accessories for women and men. | www.alain-manoukian.com |
| 70 | Footwear for men, women and children. | www.vivarte.fr |
| 51 | Smart and sporty shoes and boots for men, women and children. | www.bata.com |
| 9 | Make-up and skin and body products for men and women. | www.thebodyshop.com |
| 20 | Elegant clothes and accessories for women. | www.caroll.com |
| 24 | Popular clothing and accessories store for men. | www.celio.com |
| 14 | Sports footwear and accessories (watches and bags) for the whole family. | www.courir.com |
| 30 | Clothes, toys, pushchairs (strollers) and equipment for babies/children. | www.dpam.com |
| 35 | Inexpensive fashion, lingerie and accessories for women. | www.etam.com |
| 7 | Books, music, DVDs, computer equipment and concert tickets. | www.fnac.com |
| 10 | Sports shoes and sporty accessories such as sunglasses, watches and bags. | www.footlocker.com |
| 6 | Everyday clothes and accessories for the whole family. | www.gap.com |
| 10 | Sports clothing, shoes, equipment and accessories for all. | www.gosport.fr |
| 6 | A must for fashion lovers on a budget. High fashion at rock-bottom prices. | www.hm.com |
| 13 | Fashion and accessories for women. | www.kookai.com |
| 6 | Fashion and accessories for women. | www.mango.es |
| 89 | Perfume store with branches all over the city. | www.marionnaud.com |
| 12 | Funky shoes and boots. | www.vivarte.fr |
| 47 | Department store selling food, household items, clothes and cosmetics. | www.monoprix.fr |
| 14 | Fashions for women. | www.morgandetoi.com |
| 11 | Clothes for women and children (Naf Naf) and men (Chevignon). | www.nafnaf.com |
| 8 | Clothes and accessories at rock-bottom prices for women and girls. | www.pimkie.fr |
| 15 | Reasonably-priced clothes for women. | www.promod.com |
| 5 | DVDs, videos, books, CDs, posters, computer games and concert tickets. | www.virgin.com |
| 21 | Stylish clothes and accessories for men and women. | www.zara.com |



some fruits and branches for example. Tortu's original creations also include vases (some made of wax) and scented candles.
Mon–Sat 10–8 Odéon

## DEPARTMENT STORES

### BHV (BAZAR DE L'HÔTEL DE VILLE)

Map 174 N7
52 rue de Rivoli, 75001
Tel 01 42 74 90 00
www.bhv.fr

The City Hall Bazaar has been operating since 1856 and is incredibly well stocked. Clothes, furniture, home goods—just about everything you could possibly need or think of has been gathered under one roof.
Mon–Tue, Thu–Sat 9.30–7.30, Wed 9.30–9 Hôtel de Ville

### LE BON MARCHÉ

Map 173 K8
24 rue de Sèvres, 75007
Tel 01 44 39 80 00
www.lebonmarche.fr

You'll find the classiest brands and goods here. The modernist interior adds to the elegant atmosphere. Don't miss the beauty centre on the ground floor and the food hall in an adjoining building, stocking delicacies from all over the world.
Mon–Wed, Fri 9.30–7, Thu 10–9, Sat 9.30–8 Sèvres-Babylone, Vaneau

### CITÉ DE LA FEMME—ETAM

Map 173 M7
67–73 rue de Rivoli, 75001
Tel 01 44 76 73 73

No less than seven floors house this store, where you'll find the full range of Etam clothing (including lingerie, Tammy collection for teenagers and Maternité collection for pregnant women). There are also some home goods, a restaurant with a beautiful view of the bustling rue de Rivoli and even a crèche (*open Wed, Sat and public holidays*).
Mon–Wed, Fri–Sat 10–8, Thu 10–9
Châtelet

**GALERIES LAFAYETTE**
Map 175 L5
40 boulevard Haussmann, 75009
Tel 01 42 82 34 56
www.galerieslafayette.com
Inaugurated in 1912, the main building of this grand old department store has an impressive stained-glass dome, balconies and gilded balustrades. It is a luxurious setting for the hundreds of brands stocked here, including

fashion and beauty items, accessories, home goods and fine foods.
Mon–Wed, Fri–Sat 9.30–7.30, Thu 9.30–9 Chaussée d'Antin

**MONOPRIX**
Map 172 H5
52 avenue des Champs-Élysées, 75008
Tel 01 53 77 65 65
www.monoprix.fr
Monoprix offers all the conveniences the urban crowd is looking for. There is food, cosmetics and fashion, as well as facilities such as photocopying and a photo booth. This branch of Monoprix stays open late.
Mon–Sat 9am–midnight
Franklin D. Roosevelt

**PRINTEMPS**
Map 175 L4
64 boulevard Haussmann, 75009
Tel 01 42 82 50 00
www.printemps.com
Since 1865 it has been this store's ambition to be the most modern of its time. Under its main building's impressive stained-glass cupola, there are six floors of women's fashion and Europe's largest perfume department. There is also a men's store, and a department dedicated to home decoration.
Mon–Wed, Fri–Sat 9.15–7, Thu 9.15am–10pm Havre-Caumartin

**LA SAMARITAINE**
Map 173 M7
19 rue de la Monnaie, 75001
Tel 01 40 41 20 20
www.lasamaritaine.com
Brands and goods galore on the banks of the Seine. You name it, this place probably has it: home goods, furniture,

clothes and a great deal more. Don't miss the view from the rooftop on the 10th floor of this art deco building—it is one of the best in Paris (*open Apr–end Oct*). There's also a café and a restaurant.
Mon–Wed, Fri 9.30–7, Thu 9.30–9, Sat 9.30–8 Pont Neuf

## MARKETS

**MARCHÉ D'ALIGRE**
Map 174 off Q8
Place d'Aligre, 75012
This is one of Paris's liveliest markets. Many restaurants send staff here to shop for fresh fruit and vegetables, fish and meat. Some merchants sell by auction, and everyone joyfully jostles everybody else—a truly Parisian experience.
Tue–Sun 6.30–1 Ledru-Rollin, Faidherbe Chaligny

**MARCHÉ DU BOULEVARD RASPAIL**
Map 173 K8
Boulevard Raspail, 75006
Organically grown fruit and vegetables are sold here, as well as organic honey, bread and wine. Another organic market is held on boulevard des Batignolles on Saturday mornings.
Tue, Fri and Sun 9–1 Rennes

**MARCHÉ AUX FLEURS**
Map 174 N7
Place Louis Lépine, Île de la Cité, 75004
This market has a lovely setting on the Île de la Cité, close to Notre-Dame. You'll find a wide selection of plants and flowers displayed near the

banks of the river or in greenhouses, with a couple of specialist stands (such as orchids or herb gardens).
Mon–Sat 8–7 Cité

**MARCHÉ AUX PUCES DE ST-OUEN**
See page 107.

**MARCHÉ RÉUNION**
Map 174 Q8
Place de la Réunion, 75020
Fruit and vegetables are available here at rock-bottom prices. Come near to closing time for the best deals: After noon, everything is sold by auction, in French and in Arabic, and the market starts to resemble a souk. Fish, flowers and bread are also on offer.
Thu and Sun 8–2 Alexandre Dumas

# PERFORMANCE

Paris has a rich heritage in the performing arts, ranging from the classics through to avant-garde, at venues from small clubs to huge auditoriums. To find out what's on, see the listings in magazines such as *Pariscope* and *L'Officiel des Spectacles*.

**THEATRE**
The founding of the Comédie Française (*www.comedie-francaise.fr*) in 1680 kick-started a national love of the theatre. Paris now stands at the forefront of stage performances, with a wealth of classical, avant-garde and foreign-language plays. French theatre tends to be rather intellectual—the Comédie Française (see page 206) still concentrates on the classics. Many theatres are closed from mid-July to September.

**DANCE**
Modern and contemporary dance is an active force within French arts. Leading the way is the Centre Georges Pompidou (see pages 82–86), with performances by French and international companies.

**CLASSICAL MUSIC**
Paris has no world-renowned orchestra and live classical music has less of a high profile here than in some European capitals. However, several ensembles, such as the Orchestre de Paris (*www.orchestredeparis.com*), have an annual schedule. Versailles' *Grandes Eaux Musicales* (see page 246) are also popular. Churches often host reasonably priced classical music concerts—look for posters on the notice-boards for details.

**JAZZ**
Paris is one of Europe's leading jazz venues, with a plethora of small clubs, including New Morning (see page 205), catering to an army of aficionados. Jazz festivals include the Autumn Festival du Jazz and Paris Jazz (see page 222).

**BALLET AND OPERA**
The ornate Opéra Palais Garnier (see page 202) and Opéra Bastille (see page 202) lead the field. The Opéra Bastille opened in 1989 and is a striking example of modern architecture. Reserve well ahead for performances.

**CINEMAS**
The French are renewing their interest in home-grown films and around half the tickets sold in cinemas in France are for French productions. But you should always be able to find an English-language movie if you want to—your best bet is one of the multiplex cinemas. Look for the symbol 'VO' (*version originale*) on their listings, which shows that a non-French film is being shown in its original language. For something more Parisian in character, try one of the many art house cinemas.

**CABARET**
Paris's glittering cabaret venues are world famous and tend to attract tourists rather than locals. Many offer a joint dinner-and-show ticket and you can unload a small fortune on the sometimes exorbitantly priced drinks.

**BOOKING TICKETS**
Most theatre box offices sell tickets to their own performances and will accept phone bookings with payment by credit card. If you are calling from abroad, be aware that box offices often have '089' premium-rate numbers. It may be less expensive to use the venue's general administration number, then ask to be put through to the box office (*bureau de location*). FNAC stores (*www.fnac.com*) are ticket agents. For rock/pop/jazz concerts try Virgin Megastore (*www.virginmega.fr*), or for multi-venue arts festivals try the tourist office. The Kiosque Théâtre sells cut-price tickets for the day of the performance for most Paris theatres. There are outlets at 15 place de la Madeleine and at Gare Montparnasse.

Matinée performances are often less expensive than evening shows and tickets for that day's performances (if available) are also sold at a price reduction.

**DRESS CODES**
Evening theatre, operatic and orchestral performances require smart but not necessarily formal clothing, although you can dress to the hilt if you want to. For other types of performance, casual clothing is perfectly acceptable.

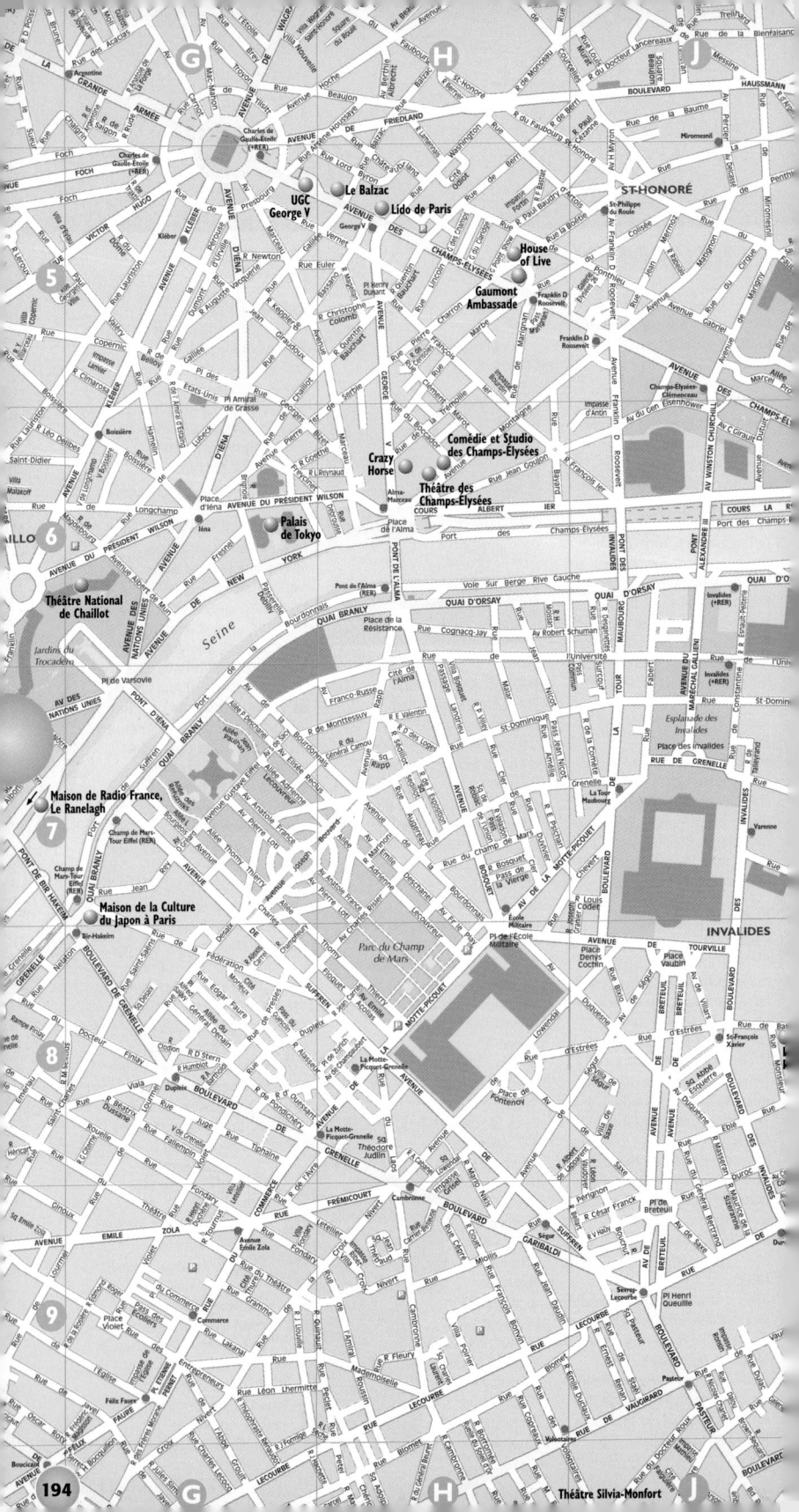
UGC George V
Le Balzac
Lido de Paris
House of Live
Gaumont Ambassade
Comédie et Studio des Champs-Élysées
Crazy Horse
Théâtre des Champs-Élysées
Palais de Tokyo
Théâtre National de Chaillot
Maison de Radio France, Le Ranelagh
Maison de la Culture du Japon à Paris
Théâtre Silvia-Monfort
Seine
Jardins du Trocadéro
Parc du Champ de Mars
Esplanade des Invalides
ST-HONORÉ
INVALIDES
GRANDE ARMÉE
FRIEDLAND
HAUSSMANN
CHAMPS-ÉLYSÉES
AVENUE DU PRÉSIDENT WILSON
PONT DE L'ALMA
QUAI D'ORSAY
QUAI BRANLY
AVENUE DES NATIONS UNIES
PONT D'IÉNA
PONT DE BIR-HAKEIM
BOULEVARD DE GRENELLE
AVENUE DE LA MOTTE-PICQUET
AVENUE DE TOURVILLE
BOULEVARD GARIBALDI
AVENUE EMILE ZOLA
AVENUE DE VAUGIRARD
5
6
7
8
9
G
H
J

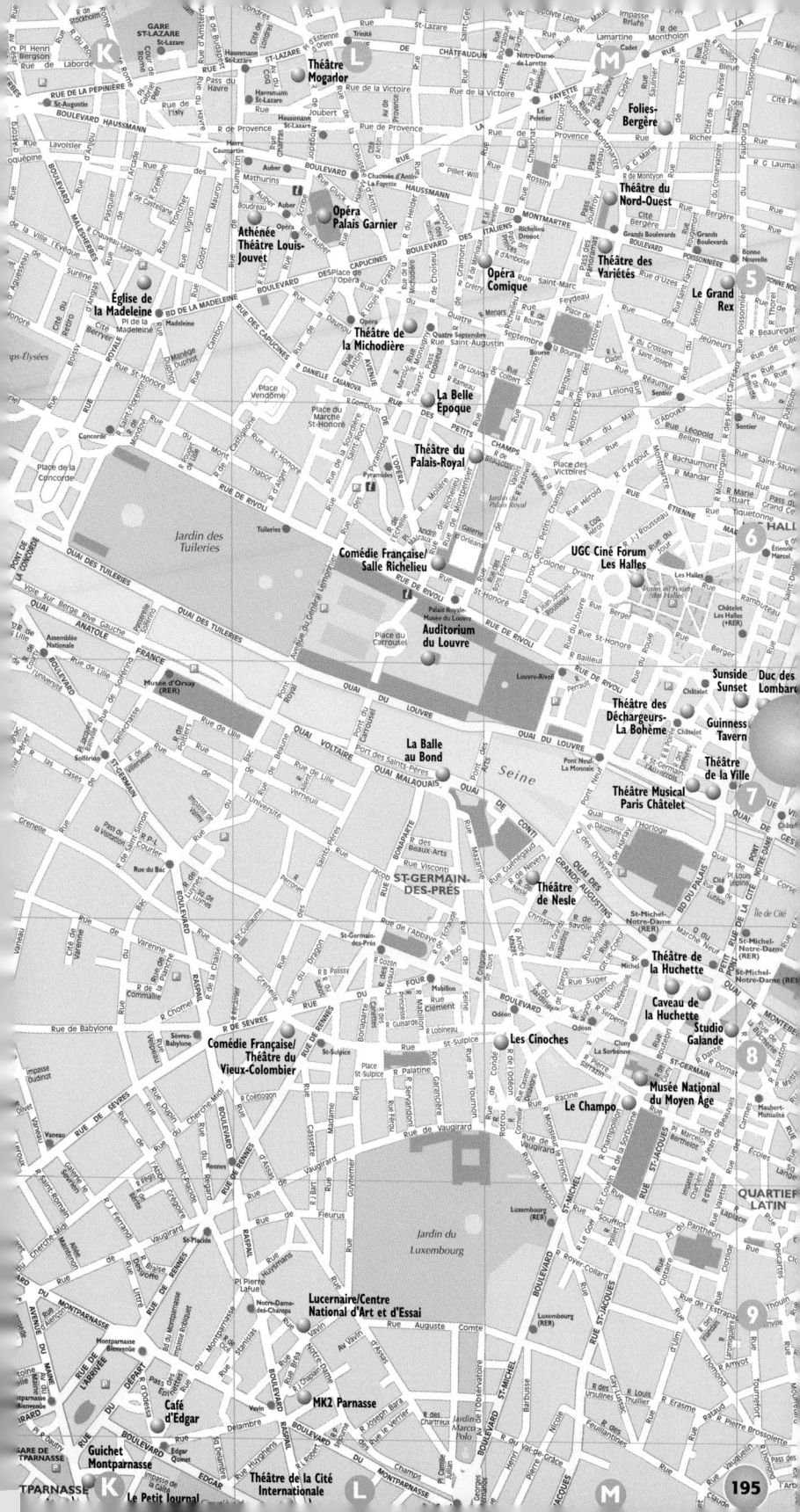
Théâtre Mogador
Folies-Bergère
Théâtre du Nord-Ouest
Opéra Palais Garnier
Athénée Théâtre Louis-Jouvet
Église de la Madeleine
Théâtre des Variétés
Opéra Comique
Le Grand Rex
Théâtre de la Michodière
La Belle Époque
Théâtre du Palais-Royal
Jardin des Tuileries
Comédie Française/ Salle Richelieu
UGC Ciné Forum Les Halles
Auditorium du Louvre
Sunside Sunset
Duc des Lombards
Théâtre des Déchargeurs-La Bohème
Guinness Tavern
La Balle au Bond
Théâtre de la Ville
Théâtre Musical Paris Châtelet
Seine
ST-GERMAIN-DES-PRÉS
Théâtre de Nesle
Théâtre de la Huchette
Caveau de la Huchette
Studio Galande
Comédie Française/ Théâtre du Vieux-Colombier
Les Cinoches
Musée National du Moyen Âge
Le Champo
Jardin du Luxembourg
Lucernaire/Centre National d'Art et d'Essai
MK2 Parnasse
Café d'Edgar
Guichet Montparnasse
Théâtre de la Cité Internationale
Le Petit Journal
QUARTIER LATIN
K
L
M
5
6
7
8
9

New Morning
Le Brady
Théâtre de la Mainate
Java
Tambour Royal
Le Grand Rex
Palais des Glaces
LA RÉPUBLIQUE
LES HALLES
Théâtre Moilière
Cirque d'Hiver Bouglione
Satellit Café
Ménagerie de Verre
Sunside Sunset
Duc des Lombards
Essaion
Café de la Gare
Guinness Tavern
IRCAM
Les Blancs Manteaux
LE MARAIS
Point-Virgule
Théâtre de la Bastille
Café de la Danse
BASTILLE
Caveau de la Huchette
Flèche d'
La Scè
Studio Galande
Opéra Bastille
QUARTIER LATIN
Seine
Jardin des Plantes
La Cartoucherie, Opéra du Château de Versailles, Parc Floral de Paris
Gaumont Grand Écran Italie,
GARE D'AUSTERLITZ
GARE DE LYON
GARE DE L'EST
196

Au Lapin Agile
MONTMARTRE
Cimetière de Montmartre
Théâtre des Deux Anes
Cinéma des Cinéastes
Moulin Rouge
Théâtre de la Ville-Salle des Abbesses
Théâtre de l'Atelier
Élysée Montmartre
Chez Madame Arthur
Bouffes du Nord, Cabaret Sauvage, Cité de la Musique, La Géode, Glaz'Art
Hébertot
Carrousel de Paris
Le Divan du Monde
La Cigale
Théâtre Fontaine
PIGALLE
Casino de Paris
GARE ST-LAZARE
Théâtre Mogador
Folies-Bergère
New Morning
Athénée Théâtre Louis-Jouvet
Théâtre du Nord-Ouest
Opéra Palais Garnier
Théâtre des Variétés
Opéra Comique
Le Grand Rex
Théâtre de la Madeleine
La Belle Époque
Théâtre du Palais-Royal
LES HALLES
Jardin des Tuileries
Comédie Française/ Salle Richelieu
UGC Ciné Forum Les Halles
Théâtre Molière
Auditorium du Louvre
Seine
Sunside Sunset
Duc des Lombards
Café de
197

## Arts venues

**CITHÉA**
See page 204.

**FLÈCHE D'OR**
Map 196 off Q8
102bis rue de Bagnolet, 75020
Tel 01 43 72 04 23
www.flechedor.com
This former railway station is home to a remarkable avant-garde venue. The varied schedule reflects its dynamism: concerts, balls, poetry readings and exhibitions. There is a bar.
Tue–Fri 6pm–2am, Sat–Sun 10am–2am €2–6
Gambetta

**GLAZ'ART**
Map 197 off N3
7–15 avenue de la Porte de la Villette, 75019
Tel 01 40 36 55 65
www.glazart.com
Named after a group of pro-art activists and located in a refurbished bus station, this experimental café has avant-garde performances (including concerts, exhibitions, video projections) in a decadent, arty atmosphere.
Sun–Fri 8.30pm–2am, Sat 10pm–5am Around €10
Porte de la Villette

**LES LUCIOLES**
Map 196 off Q6
102 boulevard de Ménilmontant, 75011
Tel 01 40 33 10 24
This unpretentious little café is the kingdom of slam, a new genre that mixes poetry and rap, where poems are chanted rather than read. Everyone is welcome to try; a drink is offered per poem.
Performance: Sun 3pm Free
Ménilmontant

**LA MAROQUINERIE**
Map 196 off Q6
23 rue Boyer, 75020
Tel 01 40 33 30 60
Once a fine leather shop (as its name in French indicates), La Maroquinerie is a springboard for new talent. Eclectic, audacious and ever-changing schedule, with literary conversations, techno music concerts, drama and more.
Mon–Sat 11am–1am €15–17
Gambetta

**PALAIS DE TOKYO**
Map 194 G6
13 avenue du Président Wilson, 75016
Tel 01 47 23 38 86
www.palaisdetokyo.com
Dedicated to contemporary art, this venue is attempting to revive the spirit of Andy Warhol's factory. Contrasting

with its chic surroundings, this large space, with its exposed concrete, hosts temporary exhibitions, concerts, film projections and debates.
Varies Gallery: €5 Iéna, Trocadéro

**LA SCÈNE**
Map 196 off Q8
2bis rue des Taillandiers, 75011
Tel 01 48 06 50 70
This concert venue and its adjoining restaurant are in an old warehouse. There is a lounge bar upstairs, where the concerts can be seen (but not heard). Electro and acoustic music features, sometimes accompanied by video projections.
Varies €10 Ledru-Rollin

**THÉÂTRE MOLIÈRE—MAISON DE LA POÉSIE**
Map 196 N6
157 rue St-Martin, 75003
Tel 01 44 54 53 00
www.maisondelapoesie-moliere.com
The Molière theatre, dating from 1791, is home to the 'House of Poetry', where activities include readings, sometimes with music or dance. Festivals explore the literature of other countries.
Varies €14–22 Auditorium
Rambuteau

## Cabaret

**AU LAPIN AGILE**
Map 197 M2
22 rue des Saules, 75018
01 46 06 85 87
This Montmartre cabaret has been a meeting place for

artists for nearly 150 years. On the walls, many souvenirs tell of this glorious past. French singers and poets perform here nightly in a cordial but intimate atmosphere.
Show: Tue–Sun 9pm–2am
Show and drink: €24 Lamarck-Caulaincourt

**LA BELLE ÉPOQUE**
Map 195 L5
36 rue des Petits-Champs, 75002
Tel 01 42 96 33 33
www.belleepoqueparis.com
The truly sparkling show *La Vie est Belle* (Life is Beautiful) includes the cancan, which the audience is then invited to dance. Fine French cuisine is served during the show.
Show: daily 9pm Show and dinner: €70–100 Pyramides

**CARROUSEL DE PARIS**
Map 197 L3
40 rue Fontaine, 75009
Tel 01 42 82 09 16
www.carrouseldeparis.fr
After a diverse show—French cancan, comedians, magic tricks and much more—it is your turn to come onto the dance floor. One of the few cabarets/clubs.
Show: Sat–Thu 8.30pm, Fri 9.30pm
Show and dinner: €49 Blanche

**CHEZ MADAME ARTHUR**
Map 197 M3
75bis rue des Martyrs, 75018
Tel 01 42 54 40 21
Impersonators of both sexes play famous French singers, including Sheila and Sylvie Vartan. A bit of cancan spices up your dinner, with dancing until the early hours after the show.
Show: daily 9pm €47 (weekends and holidays €63) Pigalle

**CRAZY HORSE**
Map 194 H6
12 avenue George V, 75008
Tel 01 47 23 32 32
www.crazy-horse.fr
This Parisian institution was established in 1951. Its 'Teasing' show presents dancers who, because of savvy lighting effects, appear to be almost nude. Dinner is served during the show.
Shows: Tue–Sun 8.30pm, 11pm
Show and dinner: €125
Alma-Marceau, George V

**FOLIES-BERGÈRE**
Map 197 M4
32 rue Richer, 75009
Tel 01 44 79 98 70

The legendary Folies-Bergère opened in 1869 and became famous for its risqué shows. It now hosts Broadway-style musicals. Dinner is served by uniformed waiters before or after the show.
Show: Tue–Sun 7pm Show and dinner: €127–132 Cadet, Grands Boulevards

**LIDO DE PARIS**
Map 194 H5
116bis avenue des Champs-Élysées, 75008
Tel 01 40 76 56 10
www.lido.fr
A prestigious address for this cabaret, which offers a titillating show, with scantily-dressed dancers and magic tricks, and some fine French cuisine, under the direction of chef Paul Bocuse.

Show: daily 7.30pm Show: €90. Show and dinner: €130–160
George V

**MOULIN ROUGE**
Map 197 L3
82 boulevard de Clichy, 75018
Tel 01 53 09 82 82
www.moulin-rouge.fr
The 'Red Windmill' opened in 1889 and became even more

of a Parisian institution after the eponymous Hollywood movie in 2001 (see page 111). Fine food is served in the magnificent building while you watch the titillating *Féerie* show.
Shows: daily 9pm, 11pm
Show: €82–92. Show and dinner: €130–160 Blanche

**OPÉRA COMIQUE**
See page 202.

## Cinemas

**LE BALZAC**
Map 194 H5
1 rue Balzac, 75008
Tel 01 45 61 10 60
www.cinemabalzac.com
Le Balzac is famous for its screenings of American independent films (shown in the original language) and for the debates that often follow. The biggest of the three screens often has photography exhibitions. Bar on site.
Daily 2–10 Adult €7, child €5.50
George V, Charles de Gaulle–Étoile

**LE BRADY**
Map 196 N5
39 boulevard de Strasbourg, 75010
Tel 01 47 70 08 86
Here you can see a mix of action movies, cult classics and some B-movies.
Daily 1.30–10 Adult €5.70, child €5.40 Château d'Eau

**LE CHAMPO**
Map 195 M8
51 rue des Écoles, 75005
Tel 01 43 54 51 60
Come here for cult classics. Numerous retrospectives explore the work of directors such as the Marx Brothers and Jacques Tati. Films are shown in their original language.
Daily noon–10 Adult €7, child €4.50–5.50 St-Michel, Odéon, Cluny-La Sorbonne

### CINÉMA DES CINÉASTES

Map 197 K3
7 avenue de Clichy, 75017
Tel 01 53 42 40 20

In a former cabaret venue designed by Gustave Eiffel, this three-screen complex shows avant-garde films, usually in their original language. Bar-restaurant on site.

Daily 1.30–10.30 Adult €6.60, child €5.40 Place de Clichy

### LES CINOCHES

Map 195 M8
1 rue de Condé, 75006
Tel 01 46 33 10 82

Les Cinoches screens relatively recent movies, but ones that one day may be considered classics. Most are shown in their original language. On Wednesday, Saturday and Sunday there are plenty of children's movies too.

Daily 2–9.30 Adult €6.10, child €4.50 Odéon

### L'ENTREPÔT

Map 195 off K10
7–9 rue Francis de Pressencé, 75014
Tel 01 45 40 07 50

A cinema that film buffs dream of: Cult movies and art films, from all periods and parts of the world, are screened in their original language. There are many themed retrospectives. Bar-restaurant on site.

Daily 2–midnight Adult €6.90, child €5.60 Pernety

### GAUMONT AMBASSADE

Map 194 H5
50 avenue des Champs-Élysées, 75008
Tel 01 40 30 30 31
www.gaumont.com

This prestigiously sited seven-screen cinema has a varied schedule: from mass-market productions to art films via some premières. All are shown in their original language.

Daily 2–10 Adult €9, child €6.50 Franklin D. Roosevelt

### GAUMONT GRAND ÉCRAN ITALIE

Map 196 off P10
30 place d'Italie, 75013
Tel 0892 696 696
www.gaumont.com

Hollywood blockbusters can be fully experienced here in digital stereo sound and on Paris's largest screen. The two smaller screens have a more diverse schedule. Foreign films are usually shown in their original language.

Daily 1–10 Adult €8–9, child €5.50–7 Place d'Italie

### LA GÉODE

Map 197 off N3
26 avenue Corentin-Cariou, 75019
Tel 0892 684 540
www.cite-sciences.fr

La Géode is at the Parc de la Villette (see pages 146–147). A gigantic hemispheric screen and an auditorium with digital stereo sound really take you

into the movie. No recent releases are screened as only films specially adapted to this technology can be shown.

Daily 10.30–8.30 Adult €8.75, child €6.75 Porte de la Villette

### LE GRAND REX

Map197 N5
1 boulevard Poissonnière, 75002
Tel 0892 680 596

Paris's last grand old cinema, founded in 1936, has a lavish auditorium and one of Europe's largest screens. Mass-market productions dominate the bill. Some films are shown in their original language.

Wed–Sun 10–7 (and public hols) Adult €7.50, child €6.50 Bonne Nouvelle

### MK2 PARNASSE

Map 195 L9
11 rue Jules-Chaplain, 75006
Tel 0836 681 407
www.mk2.com

Minutes from Tour Montparnasse, this small cinema is an eminent member of the MK2 chain, which puts the emphasis on independent films. There are many themed weeks and retrospectives and all films are in their original language.

Daily 1.30–10 Adult €9, child €4.50 Vavin

### LA PAGODE

Map 194 J8
57 rue de Babylone, 75007
Tel 01 45 55 48 48

Housed in a Chinese pagoda, this cinema has two screens and the larger one has lavish surroundings. Cult classics and recent arty releases fill the schedule. Films are shown in their original language. There is a small tea room on site.

Daily 2–10 Adult €7.30, child €5.80 St-François-Xavier

**STUDIO GALANDE**
Map 195 M8
42 rue Galande, 75005
Tel 01 43 54 72 71
www.studiogalande.com
Cult movie *The Rocky Horror Picture Show* is on here every Friday and Saturday—come dressed up if you like. The rest of the week screenings vary from art films to cartoons.
Daily 2–10.30 Adult €7, child €5.35 St-Michel, Maubert Mutualité

**UGC CINÉ FORUM LES HALLES**
Map 195 M6
7 place de la Rotonde, 75001
0892 700 000
www.ugc.fr
Films are shown in their original language at this 19-screen complex. Look out for the jumbo-sized pictures of film stars in the hall.
Daily 9am–10.30pm Adult €8.90, child €5.50 Châtelet-Les Halles

**UGC GEORGE V**
Map 194 G5
146 avenue des Champs-Élysées, 75008
0892 700 000
www.ugc.fr
Of all the cinemas on the Champs-Élysées, this probably offers the largest choice. Foreign films are shown in their original language.
Daily 10.30–10 Adult €8.70, child €5.50 Charles de Gaulle-Étoile

## Circus

**CIRQUE D'HIVER BOUGLIONE**
Map 196 Q6
110 rue Amelot, 75011
Tel 01 49 29 09 78
www.cirquedhiver.com
This lavishly decorated 19th-century arena has been home to the Bouglione family circus since 1934. Alongside traditional performances by trapeze artists, clowns and wild animals, concerts are sometimes held here.
Varies €21–78
Oberkampf, Filles du Calvaire

## Classical Music, Dance and Opera

**AUDITORIUM DU LOUVRE**
Map 195 L6
Le Louvre, 75001 (entrance by the Pyramid)
Tel 01 40 20 55 00
www.louvre.fr
This 420-seat auditorium has an impressive setting, beneath I. M. Pei's Louvre Pyramid. The excellent and varied schedule includes sacred music, film themes and recitals.
Concerts: Wed 8pm, Thu 12.30pm €23 (Wed), €10 (Thu)
Auditorium Louvre-Rivoli

**CENTRE NATIONAL DE LA DANSE**
Map 196 N7
9 rue Geoffroy l'Asnier, 75004
Tel 01 42 74 06 44
www.cnd.fr
The National Dance Centre puts on shows here and at other venues. There are also debates, lectures and films on many aspects of dance, as well as professional workshops.
Varies Varies St-Paul, Pont Marie

**CITÉ DE LA MUSIQUE**
Map 197 off N3
221 avenue Jean-Jaurès, 75019
Tel 01 44 84 44 84
www.cite-musique.fr
This postmodern building at the Parc de la Villette (see pages 146–147) hosts opera,

jazz, classical and world music concerts.
Varies Varies Porte de Pantin

**ÉGLISE DE LA MADELEINE**
Map 195 K5
Place de la Madeleine, 75008
Tel 01 44 51 69 00
www.eglise-lamadeleine.com
This neoclassical church, dating from 1842, hosts free organ recitals at least two Sundays a month. Chamber music, symphony orchestras and vocal performances complete its schedule.
Free organ recitals: some Sun 4pm. Times of other performances vary
Varies Madeleine

**MAISON DE LA CULTURE DU JAPON À PARIS**
Map 194 G7
101bis quai Branly, 75015
Tel 01 44 37 95 00
www.mcjp.asso.fr
This modern, open-plan, glass and steel building showcases Japanese culture. Some dance performances, both modern and traditional, are staged. The modular auditorium can hold up to 300 people.
Varies €12 Bir-Hakeim

**MAISON DE RADIO FRANCE**
Map 194 off F7
116 avenue du Président-Kennedy, 75016
Tel 01 56 40 15 16
www.radio-france.fr
Top-notch symphony orchestras, jazz concerts and operas are all presented here, either as live broadcasts or pre-recorded for subsequent broadcasts.
Varies Free (or small charge)
Kennedy Radio France

**MÉNAGERIE DE VERRE**
Map 196 off Q6
12 rue Léchevin, 75011
Tel 01 43 38 33 44
A glass roof and concrete walls distinguish this venue, formerly a printing house. You can see modern dance performances and some multi-disciplinary festivals: video, dance and visual arts. Credit cards are not accepted.
Performance: daily 8.30pm
Varies Parmentier

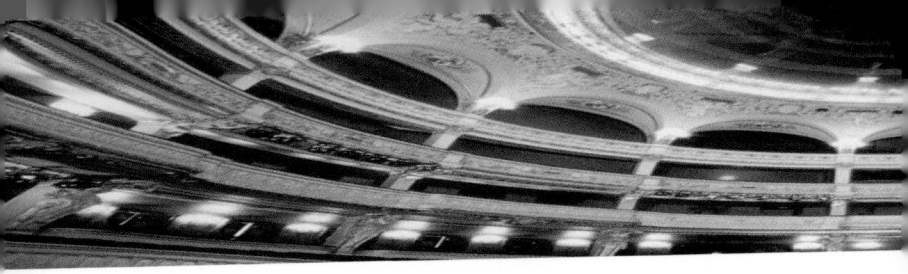

### MUSÉE NATIONAL DU MOYEN ÂGE–THERMES DE CLUNY

Map 195 M8
6 place Paul-Painlevé, 75005
Tel 01 53 73 78 16
www.musee-moyenage.fr

This medieval mansion is home to a museum dedicated to the Middle Ages (see pages 128–129), but it also hosts classical and chamber music concerts. It's a unique setting.
Performances: Fri 12.30pm, Sat 4pm Free with admission to museum (€5.50) Cluny–La Sorbonne

### OPÉRA BASTILLE

Map 196 Q8
120 rue de Lyon, 75012
Tel 0892 899 090
www.opera-de-paris.fr

This massive modern auditorium, with its 2,700 seats, opened in 1989, amid much controversy (see page 142). Operas and symphony

orchestras benefit from its exceptional acoustics and there is also some ballet.
Varies €10–110 Auditorium Bastille

### OPÉRA DU CHÂTEAU DE VERSAILLES–OPÉRA ROYAL

Map 196 off Q9
Château de Versailles, RP 834, 78008
Tel 01 30 83 78 98
www.chateauversailles.fr

The auditorium at the Château de Versailles was originally built for Louis XVI's wedding, and opened in 1770. Ballet, opera and drama are all performed here, in an impressive setting, surrounded by statues, trompe l'oeil marble and a painted ceiling.
Varies Varies Auditorium Versailles Rive Droite, Versailles Rive Gauche, Versailles Chantier

### OPÉRA COMIQUE

Map 197 M5
5 rue Favart, 75002
Tel 0825 000 058
www.opera-comique.com

The lavish interior here has frescoes on the ceiling and gilded mouldings. Music afi-

cionados will appreciate the eclectic mix of events, from symphony orchestras to variety shows, via operettas.
Varies Varies Auditorium Richelieu-Drouot

### OPÉRA PALAIS GARNIER

Map 197 L5
Place de l'Opéra, 75009
Tel 0892 899 090
www.opera-de-paris.fr

This architectural masterpiece was built during the 19th century by Charles Garnier (see page 142). It provides a lavish, prestigious setting for visiting ballet and opera companies, as well as symphony orchestras.
Varies €10–110 Auditorium Opéra

### PARC FLORAL DE PARIS

See page 205.

### TAMBOUR ROYAL

Map 196 Q5
Passage Piver, rue du Faubourg du Temple, 75011
Tel 01 48 06 72 34

This small theatre (100 seats) should satisfy music lovers of all kinds: Opera, operetta and musicals, as well as occasional plays that make use of music, are all to be found here.
Varies €12–16 Auditorium Goncourt, Belleville

### THÉÂTRE DE LA BASTILLE

Map 196 off Q7
76 rue de la Roquette, 75011
Tel 01 43 57 42 14
www.theatre-bastille.com

Formerly a cinema, this venue shows avant-garde plays and dance performances. Keen on hosting new talent, it also welcomes big names such as German choreographer Pina Bausch.
Performances: Tue–Sat 7.30pm, 9pm, Sun 3.30pm, 5pm €19 Auditorium Bastille

### THÉÂTRE DES CHAMPS-ÉLYSÉES

Map 194 H6
15 avenue Montaigne, 75008
Tel 01 49 52 50 50
www.theatrechampselysees.fr

This grand auditorium, with red velvet seats and balconies, hosts performances of opera, ballet, classical and chamber music, as well as some jazz and solo variety singers, including Jane Birkin in 2003.
Performances: almost daily at around 8–8.30pm Varies Auditorium Franklin D. Roosevelt, Alma-Marceau

**THÉÂTRE DE LA CITÉ INTERNATIONALE**
Map 195 off L10
21 boulevard Jourdan, 75014
Tel 01 43 13 50 50
Paris's International Halls of Residence are home to this imposing complex of three auditoriums (with 500, 280 and 150 seats), created in 1968. Dance performances and contemporary plays form most of the schedule.
Performances: Mon–Tue and Thu–Sat evening, Sun afternoon €15–18 Auditorium Porte d'Orléans Cité Universitaire

**THÉÂTRE MUSICAL PARIS CHÂTELET**
Map 195 M7
2 rue Edouard Colonne, 75001
Tel 01 40 28 28 40
www.chatelet-theatre.com
Built in 1862, this venue is famed for its grandeur, with candelabra and gilded mouldings. It attracts an audience of classical music lovers who like to dress up for the orchestra, concerts, ballet and opera staged here.
Performance: daily (concerts 8pm/opera 7.30pm) Varies Auditorium Châtelet

**THÉÂTRE LE RANELAGH**
See page 208.

**THÉÂTRE SILVIA–MONFORT**
See page 208.

**THÉÂTRE DE LA VILLE**
See page 208.

**THÉÂTRE DE LA VILLE–SALLE DES ABBESSES**
See page 208.

## Comedy

**LES BLANCS-MANTEAUX**
Map 196 P7
15 rue des Blancs-Manteaux, 75004
Tel 01 48 87 15 84
This café-theatre, in a 17th-century mansion, stages one-man comedy shows and sketches. *Plateaux d'Humour* (Humour Platters), which present budding talent, are on Wednesdays.
Show: daily 8pm €14 Hôtel de Ville

**CAFÉ D'EDGAR–THÉÂTRE D'EDGAR**
Map 195 K9
58 boulevard Edgar Quinet, 75014
Tel 01 42 79 97 97
This is a pioneer of the café-theatre style launched in the 1970s. Today, it still offers small-production comedy acts that appeal to a wide audience and is a springboard for new talent.
Performance: Mon–Sat 8pm or 8.15pm €14 and €17 Edgar Quinet

**CAFÉ DE LA GARE**
Map 196 N7
41 rue du Temple, 75004
Tel 01 42 78 52 51
Well hidden in a listed courtyard, this venue perpetuates the tradition of the café-theatre. The actor Gerard Depardieu made his debut here.
Every evening, times vary Around €20 Hôtel de Ville

**GUICHET MONTPARNASSE**
Map 195 K10
15 rue du Maine, 75014
Tel 01 43 27 88 61
This small auditorium (50 seats) stages lively comedy shows, often involving promising young actors.
Shows: Wed–Sat 7pm, 8.30pm or 10pm €17 Auditorium Montparnasse-Bienvenüe

**PALAIS DES GLACES**
Map 196 Q5
37 rue du Faubourg-du-Temple, 75010
Tel 01 42 02 27 17
This theatre, with its two auditoriums, occupies an old cinema. There are comedy acts of all kinds, but one-man shows dominate the bill.
Show: Tue–Sat evening €18–28 Auditorium République

**POINT-VIRGULE**
Map 196 N7
7 rue Ste-Croix de la Bretonnerie, 75004
Tel 01 42 78 67 03
See all sorts of comedy acts at this venue, renowned for its Humour Festival in September. Credit cards are not accepted.
Shows: daily 8pm, 9.15pm, 10.15pm €15 Hôtel de Ville

**THÉÂTRE DES DÉCHARGEURS –LA BOHÈME**
See page 207.

**THÉÂTRE DES DEUX ANES**
See page 207.

**THÉÂTRE DE LA MICHODIÈRE**
See page 207.

**THÉÂTRE DES VARIÉTÉS**
See page 208.

## Contemporary Live Music

**LA BALLE AU BOND**
Map 195 L7
Facing 3 quai Malaquais, 75006 (Apr–end Sep); facing 55 quai de la Tournelle, 75005 (Oct–end Mar)
Latin Quarter and St-Germain-des-Prés
Tel 01 40 51 87 06
www.laballeaubond.fr
Moored on the banks of the Seine, this barge hosts all

kinds of concerts, including rock, blues and French song. The views are beautiful and the acoustics good.
Concert: daily around 9pm €7 Pont Neuf (location 1), Maubert Mutualité (location 2)

**BATOFAR**
Map 196 off Q10
Port de la Gare, 75013
Tel 01 56 29 10 33
www.batofar.org
This lightship is moored between Bercy and Tolbiac bridge, on the banks of quai de la Gare, and hosts some of the best techno and house music DJs. Its mixed schedule also includes experimental video nights. There is a restaurant on board and a bar on the deck.
Sun–Thu 8pm–3am, Fri–Sat 8pm–dawn €10 Quai de la Gare, Bibliothèque François Mitterrand

**CABARET SAUVAGE**
Map 197 off N3
Parc de la Villette, 75019
Tel 01 42 09 01 09
Modern architecture (glass, red and silver steel) is the setting for this 'cabaret', where you can listen to world music, electronica, R & B and more. There is a jovial ball on Sundays.
Show: daily around 8.30pm (but very flexible). Sunday ball: 6pm €8–20 Porte de la Villette

**CAFÉ DE LA DANSE**
Map 196 Q8
5 passage Louis-Philippe, 75011
Tel 01 47 00 57 59
www.chez.com/cafedeladanse
There's an intimate feel to this 500-seat auditorium, with its small platform and exposed brick walls. Pop, rock and world music dominate the bill, with some drama and dance. There is a small bar on site. Credit cards are not accepted.
Performance: daily around 8.30pm Around €20 Bastille

**CAVEAU DE LA HUCHETTE**
Map 195 M8
5 rue de la Huchette, 75005
Tel 01 43 26 65 05
Minutes from the Sorbonne university, this popular, two-floor club has hosted famous jazz musicians.
Performance: daily 9.30pm €9–13
St-Michel, Cluny–La Sorbonne

**LA CIGALE**
Map 197 M3
120 boulevard de Rochechouart, 75018
Tel 01 49 25 89 99
This former grand old theatre, dating from 1887, has been modernized with a striking black and red theme. The venue now hosts musicals, rock and pop, and music festivals.
Varies Varies Anvers, Pigalle

**CITÉ DE LA MUSIQUE**
See page 201.

**CITHÉA**
Map 196 off Q8
114 rue Oberkampf, 75011
Tel 01 40 21 70 95
www.cithea.com
The eclectic yet arty schedule here includes live music (world, jazz, rock, techno) and video projections. Late opening makes Cithéa the perfect venue once the numerous nearby bars have closed.
Daily 5pm–5.30am Entry: Fri–Sat €4, rest of the week free. Concerts: €6 Parmentier

**LE DIVAN DU MONDE**
Map 197 M3
75 rue des Martyrs, 75018
Tel 01 44 92 77 66
This small, inviting concert hall runs theme nights, with an emphasis on world music. It also welcomes new talent. Ze Party on Fridays has live performances in a circus atmosphere.
Performance: varies. Ze Party: Fri 11pm–6am Ze Party: €15 Pigalle

**DUC DES LOMBARDS**
Map 196 N7
42 rue des Lombards, 75001
Tel 01 42 33 22 88
A Parisian institution, the most prestigious jazz musicians have regularly performed at this intimate club. Their performances have culminated in memorable jam sessions.
Performance: Mon–Sat 9.15pm €19 Châtelet

**ÉLYSÉE MONTMARTRE**
Map 197 M3
72 boulevard Rochechouart, 75018
Tel 01 44 92 45 36
www.elysee-montmartre.com
Over a century old, this establishment has retained its original interior and is now host to some of the best pop-

rock concerts. It is also famous for its ball and techno nights.
Varies About €23 (depending on performance) Anvers

**GUINNESS TAVERN**
Map 196 N7
31bis rue des Lombards, 75001
Tel 01 42 33 26 45
www.rocktavern.com
Live rock music is played here every day of the year, from the great classics of the 1970s to contemporary tunes, in a convivial wooden interior. The draught Guinness helps to warm the atmosphere.
Concert: daily 10pm Free
Châtelet

**HOUSE OF LIVE**
Map 194 H5
124 rue de la Boétie, 75008
Tel 01 42 25 18 06
You can enjoy free rock and blues concerts at this café/bar, close to the Champs-Élysées.
Concert: Tue–Thu 11.30pm, Fri–Sat midnight Free George V

**IRCAM**
Map 196 N7
1 place Igor-Stravinsky, 75004
Tel 01 44 78 48 16
www.ircam.fr
Founded in 1975 by composer Pierre Boulez, this institute brings together musicians and research scientists for a

thorough exploration of the subject of music. It is affiliated to the Centre Georges Pompidou (pictured), where some performances are held.
Varies Varies
Rambuteau, Hôtel de Ville, Châtelet

**JAVA**
Map 196 Q5
105 rue du Faubourg-du-Temple, 75010
Tel 01 45 32 57 63
Latino bands often play at this concert hall. Salsa and other Latino strains, orchestrated by talented DJs, keep you dancing until the early hours. Formerly a cabaret, the venue has been swinging since 1920 and saw famous French singer Edith Piaf make her debut.
Thu–Sat 11pm–5am, Sun 2–7pm
Varies Goncourt

**MAISON DE RADIO FRANCE**
See page 201.

**NEW MORNING**
Map 196 N5
7–9 rue des Petites-Écuries, 75010
Tel 01 45 23 51 41
This famous club has welcomed the world's most prestigious jazz musicians over the years. Bossa nova and salsa are also played here.
Concert: 9pm (days vary) Varies
Château d'Eau

**PARC FLORAL DE PARIS**
Map 196 off Q9
Esplanade du Château de Vincennes, 75012
Tel 01 73 04 75 75
www.parcfloraldeparis.com
This beautiful park, with its hundreds of plant species, hosts an annual jazz festival from June to July and a classical music festival during August and September. See top-class performances in this exceptional open-air setting. Credit cards are not accepted.
Concerts: Sat, Sun afternoon, May–end Sep Concerts: free. Entry to the park: €1.50 (Mon–Tue, Thu–Fri), €3 (Wed, Sat–Sun) Château de Vincennes

**LE PETIT JOURNAL MONTPARNASSE**
Map 195 K10
13 rue du Commandant-Mouchotte, 75014
Tel 01 43 21 56 70
This club, offering quality jazz and cuisine, has hosted some of France's best-loved jazz musicians. It is sister venue to the Petit Journal on the Latin Quarter's boulevard St-Michel.
Concert: Tue–Sat 10pm €16
Montparnasse-Bienvenüe

**SATELLIT CAFÉ**
Map 196 Q10
44 rue de la Folie-Méricourt, 75011
Tel 01 47 00 48 87
www.satellit-cafe.com
This self-proclaimed Parisian ambassador of world music, which can hold up to 250 people, has a varied schedule including Latino, blues, African, Balkan,

Mediterranean strains and much more.
Concert: daily 8.30pm Around €10 Oberkampf

**SUNSIDE SUNSET**
Map 196 N7
60 rue des Lombards, 75001
Tel 01 40 26 46 60
Young European talent frequently heats up this little cellar during frenzied, memorable jam sessions. For jazz-lovers who like to wander off the beaten track.
Concerts: daily 9pm, 10pm (sometimes closed Mon) €18 Châtelet

**THÉÂTRE DES CHAMPS-ELYSÉES**
See page 202.

## Theatre

**ATHÉNÉE–THÉÂTRE LOUIS JOUVET**
Map 195 L5
24 rue Caumartin, 75009
Tel 01 53 05 19 19
Built in 1896 and now a listed building, this magnificent venue has a 700-seat auditorium. It stages the classics of drama, opera and chamber music.
Performances: Tue–Sat evening, Sun matinée (closed Jul–end Aug)
€16–22 Auditorium
Havre- Caumartin

**BOUFFES DU NORD**
Map 197 off N3
37bis boulevard de la Chapelle, 75010
Tel 01 46 07 34 50
www.bouffesdunord.com
World-famous producer Peter Brook has been managing this venue since 1974 and he continues to direct some of the drama productions here. There are also occasional classical music concerts.
Performances: Tue–Sat 8.30pm, Sat–Sun matinée (times vary)
€14–25 Auditorium
La Chapelle

### LA CARTOUCHERIE

Map 196 off Q9
Route du Champ-de-Manoeuvre, 75012
Tel 01 43 74 72 74 (Aquarium)
01 43 74 24 08 (Soleil)
01 43 28 36 36 (Tempête)
01 43 28 97 04 (Chaudron)
01 48 08 39 74 (Épée de Bois)
www.theatre-du-soleil.fr

**At the heart of the Bois de Vincennes, in a former cartridge depot (*cartoucherie*), you'll find several playhouses: Aquarium, Soleil (Sun), Tempête (Tempest), Chaudron (Cauldron) and Épée de Bois (Wooden Sword). They all host contemporary, avant-garde plays.**

Performances: Tue–Sat evening, Sun afternoon €17 Auditorium Château de Vincennes (then free shuttle, bus number 112 or walk)

### CASINO DE PARIS

Map 197 L4
16 rue de Clichy, 75009
Tel 01 49 95 22 22
www.casinodeparis.fr

**You won't find any slot machines here. Concerts, musicals and plays are on the bill at this legendary venue, which played host to Joséphine Baker in the 1920s.**

Performances: Mon–Sat 8pm or 8.30pm, Sun 4pm or 5pm €21–51 Auditorium Trinité d'Estienne d'Orves

### COMÉDIE FRANÇAISE/ SALLE RICHELIEU

Map 195 L6
2 rue de Richelieu, 75001
Tel 01 44 58 15 15
www.comedie-francaise.fr

**The Comédie Française is France's most prestigious**

**troupe of actors, established by Molière in 1680. Today, the repertoire is made up of the classics, including works by Shakespeare and Molière.**

Performance: daily 8.30pm €11–30 Auditorium Palais Royal-Musée du Louvre

### COMÉDIE FRANÇAISE/ THÉÂTRE DU VIEUX-COLOMBIER

Map 195 L8
21 rue du Vieux-Colombier, 75006
Tel 01 44 39 87 00
www.comedie-francaise.fr

**This 330-seat venue, with a modern design, was established in 1913. It is associated with the Comédie Française (see above), who interpret contemporary plays here.**

Performances: Tue–Sat evening, Sun afternoon €26 Auditorium St-Sulpice

### COMÉDIE ET STUDIO DES CHAMPS-ÉLYSÉES

Map 194 H6
15 avenue Montaigne, 75008
Tel 01 53 23 99 19

**Set amid luxury shops, this elegant art nouveau venue, with 631 seats, hosts various**

**theatrical productions, including comedy and drama. There are also occasional variety shows. (Not to be mistaken with the Théâtre des Champs-Élysées, at the same address.)**

Varies Varies Auditorium Alma-Marceau, Franklin D. Roosevelt

### ESSAÏON

Map 196 N7
6 rue Pierre-au-Lard, 75004
Tel 01 42 78 46 42

**This former 12th-century cellar is home to two auditoriums: Genet (100 seats) and Beckett (70 seats). It stages small productions by living, French-speaking writers.**

Performances: Tue–Fri 8.30pm, Sat 5pm, 8.30pm €20 Auditorium Rambuteau, Hôtel de Ville

### HÉBERTOT

Map 197 off K3
78bis boulevard des Batignolles, 75017
Tel 01 43 87 23 23

**Built in 1830, this venue takes it name from Jacques Hébertot, who was manager here from 1940–1973. Quality classics and contemporary plays are on the schedule.**

Performances: Tue–Fri 9pm, Sat 6pm, 9pm €15–40 Auditorium Villiers, Rome

### LUCERNAIRE/CENTRE NATIONAL D'ART ET D'ESSAI

Map 195 L9
53 rue Notre-Dame-des-Champs, 75006
Tel 01 45 44 57 34
www.lucernaire.fr

**This complex has three cinemas, a drama school, art gallery, bar, restaurant and two theatres. The 'Black' and 'Red' auditoriums, with 130 seats each, stage performances of the classics and quality contemporary plays.**

Performances: Tue–Sat evening €22 Auditorium Vavin, Notre-Dame des-Champs

### THÉÂTRE DE L'ATELIER

Map 197 M3
Place Charles Dullin, 75018
Tel 01 46 06 49 24

**The descendant of the Théâtre de Montmartre, which was established here in 1822, this venue subsequently became a cinema before reopening as the present theatre in 1922. It focuses on well known works.**

Performances: Tue–Fri 8.30pm, Sat 5pm, 8.30pm, Sun 3.30pm €7–39 Auditorium Anvers

**THÉÂTRE DE LA CITÉ INTERNATIONALE**
See page 203.

**THÉÂTRE DES DÉCHARGEURS –LA BOHÈME**
Map 195 M7
3 rue des Déchargeurs, 75001
Tel 01 42 36 00 02 (theatre);
01 42 36 00 50 (La Bohême)
This elegant 17th-century building houses a small theatre (100 seats) with a varied repertoire and, in the basement, a café-theatre, La Bohème, where one-man shows and other comedy acts take place.
Performances: Tue–Sat around 8.30pm €15 Auditorium
Châtelet-Les Halles

**THÉÂTRE DES DEUX ANES**
Map 197 L3
100 boulevard de Clichy, 75018
Tel 01 46 06 10 26
www.2anes.com
Since 1922, the Théâtre des Deux Anes (Theatre of the Two Donkeys) has remained true to its motto: 'to bray and let laugh'. Its satirical comedies, frequently mocking the French political scene, are sure to entertain.
Performances: Tue–Fri 8.30pm, Sat 4.30pm, 8.30pm, Sun 3.30pm €33–37 Auditorium Blanche

**THÉÂTRE DUNOIS**
Map 196 off P10
108 rue du Chevaleret, 75013
Tel 01 45 84 72 00
This theatre, established in 1987, caters specifically to a young audience. There are puppet shows, adaptations of children's books and some choreography—magical and poetic.
Performances: Wed, Sat, Sun afternoon €16, children under 15 €7 Auditorium Chevaleret

**THÉÂTRE FONTAINE**
Map 197 L3
10 rue Fontaine, 75009
Tel 01 48 74 74 40
A former dance hall turned theatre in 1951, this 650-seat venue stages high-quality acts. Contemporary plays and enduring classics are interpreted by well-known actors.
Performances: Tue–Fri 9pm, Sat 6pm, 9pm €16–30 Auditorium
Blanche, St-Georges, Pigalle

**THÉÂTRE DE LA HUCHETTE**
Map 195 M8
23 rue de la Huchette, 75005
Tel 01 43 26 38 99
Two of Ionesco's masterpieces, *La Cantatrice Chauve* (The Bald Soprano) and *La Leçon* (The Lesson), have been performed here six days a week for over 50 years. This small venue, in the Latin Quarter, is a Parisian institution.
Varies €16–24 Auditorium
St-Michel

**THÉÂTRE DE LA MAINATE**
Map 196 Q5
36 rue Bichat, 75010
Tel 01 42 08 83 33
www.lamainate.com
This venue caters specifically to very young children, from two to eight years old. There are puppet shows, fairytale readings and kids cabaret with a clown and magic tricks on Sundays. Children's birthday parties can also be held here. Credit cards are not accepted.
Performances: Wed (and during French school holidays) 10.30am, 2.30pm, 4pm, Sat 4pm, Sun 3.30pm, Sep–end May €9 Auditorium
République, Goncourt

**THÉÂTRE DE LA MICHODIÈRE**
Map 197 L5
4bis rue de la Michodière, 75002
Tel 01 47 42 95 22
Since its opening in 1925, this theatre has been true to the formula that secured its success: top-quality comedies interpreted by the best actors—Arletty in the 1930s, Roland Giraud nowadays.
Performances: Tue–Fri 8.30pm, Sat 5pm, 9pm €8–36 Auditorium
Quatre Septembre

**THÉÂTRE MOGADOR**
Map 197 L4
25 rue de Mogador, 75009
Tel 01 53 32 32 00
Musicals and operettas make up the majority of the shows at this 1,700-seat auditorium. Comedy and dance are also on the bill.
Performances: Tue, Fri, Sat evening, Wed, Sat, Sun afternoon €17–42 Auditorium Trinité d'Estienne d'Orves

**THÉÂTRE MOLIÈRE–MAISON DE LA POÉSIE**
See page 198.

**THÉÂTRE NATIONAL DE CHAILLOT**
Map 194 G6
1 place du Trocadéro, 75016
Tel 01 53 65 30 00
www.theatre-chaillot.fr
This theatre, in the imposing Palais de Chaillot, stages pro-

ductions of all kinds, from top-quality contemporary works to classics.
Performances: Tue–Sat 8.30pm, Sun 3pm €18–30 Auditorium
Trocadéro

### THÉÂTRE NATIONAL DE LA COLLINE

Map 196 off Q6
15 rue Malte-Brun, 75020
Tel 01 44 62 52 52
www.colline.fr

Housed in a modern building, this is the first national theatre exclusively dedicated to performing the work of contemporary playwrights. There are two auditoriums: the Grand Théâtre (760 seats) and the Petit Théâtre (200 seats).
Performances: Tue–Sat evening, Sun afternoon €25 Auditorium Gambetta

### THÉÂTRE DE NESLE

Map 195 M7
8 rue de Nesle, 75006
Tel 01 46 34 61 04

This vaulted basement, in a 17th-century mansion, hosts American plays produced in English, as well as top-notch French plays and performances for children (puppet shows, shadow theatre and more).
Performances: Tue–Sat evening, Wed and Sat afternoon €6–15 Auditorium Odéon, Pont Neuf

### THÉÂTRE DU NORD-OUEST

Map 197 M5
13 rue du Faubourg-Montmartre, 75009
Tel 01 47 70 32 75

Edith Piaf performed here in the 1930s, when this venue was a cabaret. It has been a theatre, with two auditoriums, since 1997, and the classics on the bill are re-interpreted by young companies.
Varies €20 Auditorium Grands Boulevards

### THÉÂTRE DU PALAIS ROYAL

Map 195 L6
38 rue Montpensier, 75001
Tel 01 42 97 59 81
www.theatrepalaisroyal.com

This elegant theatre, with its red velvet seats and gilded panels, is within the gardens of the Palais Royal and was built in 1783. Plays and comedy acts dominate the schedule but some classical music can also be enjoyed here.
Performances: Mon–Sat 9pm, Sun 4.30pm Varies Auditorium Bourse, Palais Royal-Musée du Louvre

### THÉÂTRE LE RANELAGH

Map 194 off F7
5 rue des Vignes, 75016
Tel 01 42 88 64 44

This 340-seat venue, built in 1890, has a somewhat rococo interior with carved wood panels and a lacunar ceiling. The high-quality, varied schedule includes classics, contemporary plays and opera.
Performances: Tue–Sat evening, Sun afternoon €23 and €30 Auditorium La Muette

### THÉÂTRE SILVIA-MONFORT

Map 194 off J10
106 rue Brancion, 75015
Tel 01 56 08 33 88

The comedienne Silvia Monfort was given this theatre by the city of Paris and she went on to produce excellent plays, dance shows and concerts. Today, the schedule is as eclectic as ever.
Performances: Tue–Sat 8.30pm, Sun 4pm €22 Auditorium Porte de Vanves

### THÉÂTRE DES VARIÉTÉS

Map 197 M5
7 boulevard Montmartre, 75002
Tel 01 42 33 09 92
www.theatre-des-varietes.fr

Established in 1807, this 900-seat venue, with a listed façade, hosts top-quality drama and comedy. It has been managed by actor Jean-Paul Belmondo since 1991.
Performances: Tue–Fri 8.30pm, Sat 9pm, Sun 3.30pm €12–46 Auditorium Bourse, Grands Boulevards

### THÉÂTRE DE LA VILLE

Map 195 M7
2 place du Châtelet, 75004
Tel 01 42 74 22 77
www.theatredelaville-paris.com

Forever associated with Sarah Bernhardt, who used to play here at the beginning of the 20th century, this grand theatre (1,000 seats) hosts plays and modern dance.
Performances: Tue–Fri 8.30pm, Sat 3pm, 8.30pm €15-22 Auditorium Châtelet

### THÉÂTRE DE LA VILLE–SALLE DES ABBESSES

Map 197 L3
31 rue des Abbesses, 75018
Tel 01 42 74 22 77
www.theatredelaville-paris.com

This auditorium offers the same type of productions as its sister venue, the Théâtre de la Ville (see above): contemporary plays and dance performances.
Performances: Tue–Sat 8.30pm, Sun 3pm €15-22 Auditorium Abbesses

### VINGTIÈME THÉÂTRE

Map 196 off Q6
7 rue des Platrières, 75020
Tel 01 43 66 01 13

This unpretentious venue stages dance, comedy, French song and more. Conferences and debates on pertinent themes are sometimes held alongside the performances.
Performances: Tue–Fri evening, Sat matinée and evening €19 Auditorium Ménilmontant

# NIGHTLIFE

Loyalties change rapidly in Paris but the listings in magazines such as *Pariscope* and *L'Officiel des Spectacles* should help keep you up-to-date with the places to be seen at. The action doesn't start until after midnight at most clubs, and usually continues until dawn on Fridays and Saturdays. You'll often have to pay an entrance fee, and dress smartly to get past the bouncers. If clubbing isn't your scene, there are thousands of bars across the city, ranging from small and friendly to fiery Latino or trendy-chic.

## Bars

**15 PISTON PÉLICAN**
Rue de Bagnolet, 75020
Tel 01 43 70 35 00
This unpretentious yet trendy bar has an exceptionally convivial atmosphere. It is Bistro-style, with a large bar, old prints, lots of wood and a tiny terrace that looks out onto an interesting street.
Mon–Fri 8am–2am, Sat–Sun 10am–2am Alexandre Dumas

**L'ATELIER RENAULT**
53 avenue des Champs-Élysées, 75008
Tel 01 49 53 70 00
www.atelier-renault.com
The Renault car showroom also has a bar, restaurant and trend laboratory, with exhibitions, events and fashion shows. The place has been transformed into a massive loft, worlds away from a regular car dealer.
Daily 10am–1am
Franklin D. Roosevelt

**BAR HEMINGWAY**
Hôtel Ritz, 15 place Vendôme, 75001
Tel 01 43 16 30 30
www.ritzparis.com
Within the Ritz hotel, this bar pays tribute to the celebrated writer. Papa himself used to enjoy the elegant atmosphere, where old malts, champagne and cigars are de rigueur.
Tue–Sat 6.30pm–2am
Opéra, Madeleine

**BARFLY**
49–51 avenue George-V, 75008
Tel 01 53 67 84 60
This bright bar used to be a newspaper depot. It is popular with the show business crowd, who come here for a drink or for the innovative fusion food.
Daily noon–2am George V

**BAR DU MARCHÉ**
75 rue de Seine, 75006
Tel 01 43 26 55 15
This venue has a retro-style interior and a terrace looking out onto a lively market street. Waiters, dressed like Parisian urchins, bustle around. It's so Parisian that it's even popular with locals.
Daily 8am–2am Mabillon

**BARRAMUNDI**
3 rue Taitbout, 75009
Tel 01 47 70 21 21
India meets Africa for the style, and chill-out world music spices up the atmosphere. This place is a hit with the fashion crowd, who come here for a drink in the bar or fusion food in the restaurant.
Mon–Fri noon–2.30, 7pm–2am, Sat 7pm–5am Richelieu-Drouot

**BA-TA-CLAN CAFÉ**
50 boulevard Voltaire, 75011
Tel 01 49 23 96 33
Named after the eponymous adjoining concert hall, this bar welcomes the same trendy clientele. The interior has ochre walls and rattan furniture, and the large terrace is heated when necessary.
Daily 7am–2am Oberkampf

**BELLE HORTENSE**
31 rue Vieille-du-Temple, 75004
Tel 01 48 04 71 60
www.cafeine.com
Wine and literature, two of life's pleasures, are combined here. If the first should be consumed with moderation, no restrictions apply when it comes to the second. The shelves, full of books, invite you to discover new authors.
Daily 5pm–2am Hôtel de Ville

**BOCA CHICA**
58 rue de Charonne, 75011
Tel 01 43 57 93 13
www.labocachica.com
A fiesta mood reigns at this fully spiced-up tapas bar with its bright stools, long steel bar and funky lighting. Come here for a drink or a bite to eat, and enjoy the lively Latino rhythms.
Sun–Thu 10am–2am, Fri–Sat 10am–5am Ledru-Rollin

**BOTTLE SHOP**
5 rue Trousseau, 75011
Tel 01 43 14 28 04
This unpretentious but trendy café-bar in the lively Bastille area has a small terrace outside, a wooden interior and a convivial atmosphere. Brunch is served on Sundays.
Daily 11.30am–2am
Ledru-Rollin

SPECIAL

**CAFÉ DE L'INDUSTRIE**
16 rue St-Sabin, 75011
Tel 01 47 00 13 53
www.cafedelindustrie.com
A wooden interior, punctuated by exotic curios and pictures of actors, marks this modern bistro. It's very popular with the lively Bastille area's trendy crowd.
Sun–Fri 10am–2am
Bréguet Sabin, Bastille

**BUBBLES**
6 rue Edouard VII, 75009
Tel 01 47 42 77 95
www.bubbles-paris.com
This modern and bright bar is entirely dedicated to champagne. More than one hundred vintages are on offer; some can be bought here and taken out. There is also a restaurant upstairs.
Tue–Sat noon–2am Madeleine, Opéra

**CAFÉ DES ANGES**
66 rue de la Roquette, 75011
Tel 01 47 00 00 63
The small terrace here consists of just one row of bistro tables, but it's perfect for people-watching. The retro interior has wooden tables, a mosaic-tiled floor, a long bar and a lively atmosphere.
Daily 8am–2am Bastille

**CAFÉ CHARBON**
109 rue Oberkampf, 75011
Tel 01 43 57 55 13
A former coal merchant's, dating from 1890, this café-bar is full of character, with large mirrors and frescoes on the walls. One of the trendiest of rue Oberkampf's many bars, it is absolutely packed in the evenings.
Daily 8am–2am Rue St-Maur

**CAFÉ MARTINI**
11 rue du Pas-de-la-Mule, 75004
Tel 01 42 77 05 04
The beamed ceiling, deep carpets, ochre walls and jazz music create a warm and welcoming atmosphere in this café, close to the place des Vosges.
Daily 8.30am–2am Chemin Vert

**CAFÉ RUC**
159 rue St-Honoré, 75001
Tel 01 42 60 97 54
A smart interior—red velvet, columns and indirect lighting—coupled with a prestigious address on a street famous for its couture shops, make this place a hit with the fashion crowd.
Daily 8am–2.30am Palais Royal-Musée du Louvre

**CANNIBALE CAFÉ**
93 rue Jean-Pierre Timbaud, 75011
Tel 01 49 29 95 59
The retro interior here includes a long bar, moleskin wall-seats and large mirrors. Cannibale Café is a convivial venue, which has its crowd of regulars but also warmly welcomes anyone passing through.
Daily 8am–2am Couronnes

**CHAO BA CAFÉ**
22 boulevard de Clichy, 75018
Tel 01 46 06 72 90
This is an island of exoticism in the middle of Paris's red light district. Rattan furniture, bamboo, indirect lighting and chill-out music take you on a visual and aural journey. A DJ takes to the decks at weekends.
Sun–Thu 8.30am–2am, Fri–Sat 8.30am–5am Pigalle

**CHINA CLUB**
50 rue de Charenton, 75012
Tel 01 43 43 82 02
www.chinaclub.cc
A mixture of art deco and colonial influences make this a thoroughly chic venue. There is a large bar and some comfortable Chesterfield sofas—the perfect place to sip cocktails. The restaurant serves fine Chinese cuisine and there is a smoking room upstairs.
Sun–Thu 7pm–2am, Fri–Sat 7pm–3am Bastille, Ledru-Rollin

**CORCORAN'S**
110 boulevard de Clichy, 75018
Tel 01 42 23 00 30
This venue takes you to Dublin: Guinness on tap, old Irish adverts on the walls and a big screen for watching sport. Good pub food, including fish and chips and stews, is served at lunchtime.
Sun–Wed 11am–3.30am, Thu 11am–4.30am, Fri–Sat 11am–5.30am Place de Clichy

**CUBANA CAFÉ**
45 rue Vavin, 75006
Tel 01 40 46 80 81
www.cubanacafe.com
Revolutionary Cuba at the heart of chic Paris—this evocation of La Havana comes complete with posters, pictures and slogans on the walls, and cigars and rum-based cocktails on the menu.
Sun–Thu 11am–3am, Fri–Sat 11am–5am Vavin

**DE LA VILLE CAFÉ**
36 boulevard Bonne-Nouvelle, 75010
Tel 01 48 24 48 09
The monumental staircase, stained glass and wrought-iron work give this café a theatrical touch. Lounge music is provided by good DJs.
Daily 11am–2am
Bonne Nouvelle

**LES EDITEURS**
4 carrefour de l'Odéon, 75006
Tel 01 43 26 67 76
www.leseditiers.fr
Les Editeurs is frequented by the literary crowd. The warm, wooden interior, comfortable red velvet armchairs and subdued lighting make the perfect setting for reading—you're invited to pick up a book from its library.
Daily 8am–2am Odéon

**SPECIAL**

**LES DEUX-MAGOTS**
170 boulevard St-Germain, 75006
Tel 01 45 48 55 25
A hub for philosophers and artists in the 1950s, and popular with Hemingway, this establishment has kept some

of its literary feel thanks to the proximity of La Hune bookshop. A Parisian institution.
Daily 7.30am–1am
St-Germain des-Prés

**L'ENDROIT**
67 place du Docteur-Félix-Lobligeois, 75017
Tel 01 42 29 50 00
The stylish modern interior has long, black leather wall-seats, indirect lighting and a massive semi-circular bar. The good vibes, with ambient techno and trip hop, suit its trendy clientele.
Daily noon–2am Rome

**LES ÉTAGES**
35 rue Vieille-du-Temple, 75004
Tel 01 42 78 72 00
This building has a budget-chic style, with used armchairs and sofas that must have had a glorious past. Imaginative cocktails are served in the lively downstairs bar; you'll find a more intimate mood in the rooms upstairs.
Daily 3.30pm–2am
Hôtel de Ville

**L'ÉTOILE MANQUANTE**
34 rue Vieille-du-Temple, 75004
Tel 01 42 72 48 34
www.cafeine.com
This café, full of interesting artwork, is an invitation to daydream. Look up at the pop art sky-like ceiling and don't forget to check out the lavatories, with their abundance of steel and video screens.
Daily 9am–2am Hôtel de Ville

**FAVELA CHIC**
18 rue du Faubourg-du-Temple, 75011
Tel 01 40 03 02 66
www.favelachic.com

Sexy-sounding cocktails (the *caipirinha* is a must) and world music spun by DJs are on the bill at this hot Brazilian bar. Some South American food is also available.
Tue–Sat 7.30pm–2am Free entry (most of the time) République

**FOOTSIE**
10–12 rue Daunou, 75002
Tel 01 42 60 07 20
Close to Paris's stock market, this bar, named after London's stock index, operates according to the same principle: The drinks prices fluctuate according to supply and demand.
Mon–Thu noon–3, 6pm–2am, Fri–Sat noon–3, 6pm–4am Opéra

**FUMOIR**
6 rue de l'Amiral-de-Coligny, 75001
Tel 01 42 92 00 24
Relax in voluptuous calm—sink into one of the deep armchairs and browse the international newspapers. You can also indulge in a cigar if you wish.
Daily 11am–2am Louvre-Rivoli

**SPECIAL**

**FOURMI**
71 rue des Martyrs, 75018
Tel 01 42 64 74 28
Named 'La Fourmi' (the Ant) in reference to La Fontaine's fable, this convivial venue—popular with the arty crowd—has a beautiful retro style with a large bar, small wooden tables and ochre walls. The concert hall La Cigale (see page 204) is nearby.
Mon–Thu 8am–2am, Fri–Sat 8am–4am, Sun 10am–2am
Pigalle

**HARRY'S NEW YORK BAR**
5 rue Daunou, 75002
Tel 01 42 61 71 14
www.harrys-bar.fr
Hundreds of cocktails are on offer here, perfectly mastered

by highly professional barmen. The chic interior combines wood with red moleskin.
Daily 11am–4am Opéra

**HAVANITA**
11 rue de Lappe, 75011
Tel 01 43 55 96 42
Club armchairs, palm trees and fans make up the interior; rum-based cocktails and cigars the menu. This little piece of Cuba is on a pedestrianized street where bars are legion.
Daily 4pm–2am Bastille

**KLEIN HOLLAND**
36 rue du Roi de Sicile, 75004
Tel 01 42 71 43 13
www.dutchbars.com
This is the haunt of the Dutch in Paris, who gather here when their national soccer team is

playing. The beer is inexpensive and there is a pub atmosphere.
Daily 5pm–2am Hôtel de Ville

**LIZARD LOUNGE**
18 rue du Bourg-Tibourg, 75004
Tel 01 42 72 81 34
www.hip-bars.com
This lively pub has a wooden interior and beer on tap. Concerts take place in the

basement. Not surprisingly, it is a hit with the Brits.
Daily noon–2am Hôtel de Ville

**LA MERCERIE**
98 rue Oberkampf, 75011
Tel 01 43 38 81 30
Once a haberdasher's shop, this is now an arty, comfortable venue with used, but soft, sofas, and paintings by young artists on the walls.
Mon–Fri 5pm–2am, Sat–Sun 3pm–2am Ménilmontant

**OPA**
9 rue Biscornet, 75012
Tel 01 49 28 97 16
www.opabastille.com
Good sounds, with electronica but also 1980s classics, and late opening, make this two-level loft the perfect stop before a night out clubbing.
Tue–Thu 7pm–2am, Fri–Sat 7pm–6am Free entry most weekdays, Fri–Sat around €10 Bastille

**PAPOU LOUNGE**
74 rue Jean-Jacques Rousseau, 75001
Tel 01 44 76 00 03
Come here for a total change of scene: Asian and African curios, exotic cocktails, inventive cuisine and music with a global theme.
Mon–Fri 10am–2am, Sat 11am–2am, Sun 5pm–midnight
Étienne Marcel, Les Halles

**LE PETIT FER À CHEVAL**
30 rue Vieille-du-Temple, 75004
Tel 01 42 72 47 47
www.cafeine.com
Named after its horseshoe-shaped bar, where you can order a coffee or a glass of wine, this venue has a small terrace and retro dining room serving bistro food.
Daily 9am–2am Hôtel de Ville

**LES PHILOSOPHES**
28 rue Vieille-du-Temple, 75004
Tel 01 48 87 49 64
www.cafeine.com
This café has a smart bistro interior and lots of artwork on the walls. The main attraction, however, is its lovely outside terrace overlooking a quiet, picturesque cul-de-sac.
Daily 9am–2am Hôtel de Ville

**PIANO VACHE**
8 rue Laplace, 75005
Tel 01 46 33 75 03
This temple of rock has been swinging for over 30 years and is still a good place to listen to acoustic music while enjoying draught beer.
Mon–Fri noon–2am, Sat–Sun 9pm–2am; school holidays daily 6pm–2am Maubert Mutualité

**THE POLO ROOM**
3 rue Lord Byron, 75008
Tel 01 40 74 07 78
www.poloroom.com
The atmosphere is reminiscent of an old polo club, and the class and comfort this implies: little salons, wood and bottle-green interior. Choose from the menu of cocktails including perfectly mastered martinis.
Mon–Thu 5pm–1am, Fri 5pm–2am, Sat 6pm–2am, Sun 6pm–1am
Charles de Gaulle-Étoile

**RÉSERVOIR**
16 rue de la Forge-Royale, 75011
Tel 01 43 56 39 60
www.reservoirclub.com
The luxurious yet funky style mixes leopard print, red velvet, wrought iron and interesting light fixtures. Besides the place's *je ne sais quoi*, it's the lively atmosphere and occasional concerts which draw the trendy crowd.
Mon–Thu 8pm–2am, Fri–Sat 8pm–4am, Sun noon–5am
Ledru-Rollin

**RHUMERIE**
166 boulevard St-Germain, 75006
Tel 01 43 54 28 94
www.larhumerie.com
The perennial colonial interior of this venue is the key to its attraction. Punch, palm trees and rattan furniture let you forget that the sun isn't always there. And when it is, a cocktail on the terrace is a must.
Daily 9am–2am Mabillon

**SANCERRE**
35 rue des Abbesses, 75018
Tel 01 42 58 08 20
www.sancerre.com
The theme here is reminiscent of the film *Le Fabuleux Destin d'Amélie Poulain*: a retro interior and a small terrace facing one of Montmartre's picturesque streets. The bar is popular with an arty crowd of regulars and visitors.
Daily 7am–2am Abbesses

**SANZ SANS**
49 rue du Faubourg St-Antoine, 75011
Tel 01 44 75 78 78
Gold and red velvet give a classy touch to this trendy bar, where good DJs, playing techno and R & B, regularly spice up the atmosphere. Restaurant upstairs.
Mon 9am–2am, Tue–Sat 9am–5am, Sun 6pm–2am Bastille

**SCHERKHAN**
144 rue Oberkampf, 75011
Tel 01 43 57 29 34
Deep sofas, chill-out music and an imposing stuffed tiger set the atmosphere. A warm welcome awaits you at this address in rue Oberkampf (nicknamed 'Thirst Street' as it is packed with bars).
Daily 5pm–2am Ménilmontant

**WEB BAR**
32 rue de Picardie, 75003
Tel 01 42 72 66 55
www.webbar.fr
This lofty establishment, with its mezzanine and glass roof, used to be a silversmith's workshop. It is now an Internet café, and more: Video projections, concerts and exhibitions also take place.
Mon–Fri 8.30am–2am, Sat 11am–2am, Sun 11am–midnight
Temple

**XO**
307 rue du Faubourg St-Antoine, 75011
Tel 01 43 71 73 45
You'll find loads of retro character at this 'Old Express Café', which is what XO stands for: a large bar, beautiful steel light fixtures and a window-display of old toys. Good, simple food is served, including salads and tarts.
Mon–Sat 7am–2am, Sun 8am–6pm
Faidherbe Chaligny, Nation

## Cafés

**APPAREMMENT CAFÉ**
18 rue des Coutures-St-Gervais, 75003
Tel 01 48 87 12 22
A café that feels like home. Comfortable armchairs surround coffee tables and there is a library, plus board games—it's also possible to have something to eat here.
Mon–Fri noon–2am, Sat 4pm–2am, Sun 12.30–midnight St-Paul, Fille du Calvaire

**BAZOOKA CAFÉ**
9 rue Nicolas Flamel, 75004
Tel 01 42 74 45 82
Formerly named Onix café, this chic and trendy spot is near the Centre Georges Pompidou and close to Paris's gay district. You'll find good music and vibes in the evening.
Daily 3pm–2am
Châtelet

**SPECIAL**

**CAFÉ BEAUBOURG**
43 rue St-Merri, 75004
Tel 01 48 87 63 96
This modern, stylish café-restaurant has a terrace

spilling out onto the piazza Beaubourg. It is one of the best spots in Paris for people-watching and is a good place to stop after visiting the nearby Centre Georges Pompidou.
The simple recipes are perfectly mastered.
Sun–Thu 8am–1am, Fri–Sat 8am–2am Rambuteau

**SPECIAL**

**CAFÉ DE FLORE**
172 boulevard St-Germain, 75006
Tel 01 45 48 55 26
Once the haunt of celebrated writers and philosophers (Jean-Paul Sartre used to be a regular), this café still welcomes customers all day long, for a snack or a drink, in elegant surroundings.
Daily 7.30am–1.30am
St-Germain-des-Prés

**CAFÉ DE L'ATELIER**
95 boulevard du Montparnasse, 75014
Tel 01 45 44 98 81
This café welcomes you round the clock for a drink or a snack, inside or on its terrace (heated when necessary). It is a young and trendy spot in a district otherwise home to timeless venues such as the brasserie La Coupole.
Daily 24 hours Vavin

**CAFÉ DE LA MAIRIE**
8 place St-Sulpice, 75006
Tel 01 43 26 67 82
Spilling onto a picturesque square, the terrace of this café is the perfect spot to appreciate the French way of life. Snacks are available. Credit cards are not accepted.
Mon–Fri 7am–2am, Sat 8am–2am
St-Sulpice, Mabillon

**CHAISE AU PLAFOND**
10 rue du Trésor, 75004
Tel 01 42 76 03 22
www.cafeine.com/chaise2.htm
Nestled in a quiet cul-de-sac, this café has a very pleasant terrace that is heated when necessary. The beautiful wooden interior has amusing details (have a look into the bathroom peepholes). Good standard bistro food is served.
Daily 9am–2am St-Paul, Hôtel de Ville

**LOU PASCALOU**
14 rue des Panoyaux, 75020
Ménilmontant
Tel 01 46 36 78 10
You're guaranteed to receive a warm welcome at this unpretentious yet arty little café. Sit on the delightful terrace and sample one of the best mint teas in Paris.
Daily 9am–2am Ménilmontant

**LE MABILLON**
164 boulevard St-Germain, 75006
Tel 01 43 26 62 93
Near the Sorbonne university, Le Mabillon is popular with students and trendy twenty-somethings who appreciate the café's red velvet interior and electric atmosphere.
Daily 7.30am–6am Mabillon, St-Germain-des-Prés

**PAUSE CAFÉ BASTILLE**
41 rue de Charonne, 75011
Tel 01 48 06 80 33
High ceilings, ancient tiled floors and a welcoming U-shaped bar create a beautiful interior for this hip café-restaurant. The terrace is pleasant on spring and summer days.
Mon–Sat 7.45am–2am, Sun 9am–8pm Bastille, Ledru-Rollin

## Clubs

**DUPLEX**
2bis avenue Foch, 75016
Tel 01 45 00 45 00
www.leduplex.fr
Near the Champs-Élysées, this is a club for well-to-do twenty-somethings. Smart gear is de rigueur. A bowling alley and some dance, house and techno beats spice up the action.
Tue–Sun 11.30pm–6am €19 Fri–Sat, €15 Sun, Tue–Thu (includes one drink) Charles de Gaulle-Étoile

**SPECIAL**

**LES BAINS**
7 rue du Bourg-l'Abbé, 75003
Tel 01 48 87 01 80
Once a favourite with celebrities, this club lost some of its attraction with the departure of the Guettas, its former owners and true king and queen of Paris nightlife. It's still a good place to groove to the sound of disco though.
Daily 11.30pm–6am
€ 20 Étienne Marcel

**L'ÉTOILE**
12 rue de Presbourg, 75016
Tel 01 45 00 78 70
www.letoileparis.com
Dressing smartly should grant you the right to enter this temple of chic and trendy Parisian nightlife. Disco, dance and techno are played, the setting is beautiful and the terrace has a superb view of the Arc de Triomphe.
Wed–Sun 11pm–5am Free
Charles de Gaulle-Étoile

**LA FABRIQUE**
53 rue du Faubourg St-Antoine, 75011
Tel 01 43 07 67 07
www.fabrique.fr
In a district packed with bars, you can enjoy a beer—brewed on the premises—and dance to techno music. There is also a restaurant.
Mon–Tue noon–2am, Wed–Fri noon–5am, Sat–Sun 5pm–5am
Free until midnight, €10 thereafter (includes one drink) Bastille

**FOLIE'S PIGALLE**
11 place Pigalle, 75009
Tel 01 48 78 55 25
www.folies-pigalle.com
A nightclub emblematic of Paris's red light district. A young crowd moves to the sound of house in a highly-charged atmosphere. On Sundays the rhythms are more varied.
Tue–Fri midnight–6am, Sat–Sun midnight–noon €20 Pigalle

**LE GIBUS**
18 rue du Faubourg-du-Temple, 75011
Tel 01 47 00 78 88
www.gibus.fr
Once a temple of underground culture, this club has become a true ravers' heaven. Hard beats keep the mid-20s crowd dancing until the early hours. Trance on Wednesdays and Fridays, house on Saturdays.
Wed, Fri–Sat midnight–7am
Free on Wed, €13 Fri, €18 Sat
République

**LATINA CAFÉ**
114 avenue des Champs-Élysées, 75008
Tel 01 42 89 98 89
www.radiolatina.com
The complete Latino experience is spread over three floors and includes a bar, a restaurant and a club. There are live bands, DJs and even some salsa classes (Sundays).
Daily 10pm–5am €16 Fri, Sat (includes 2 drinks); €7 Sun, Mon (but free for women); free Tue, Wed; €10 Thu (but free for women) George V

**LA LOCO**
90 boulevard de Clichy, 75018
Tel 01 53 41 88 88
www.laloco.com
Three dance floors, with a beautiful steel design, offer pop and electronica, house club and gay club. On Fridays and Saturdays, the 'Wake Up' parties keep you dancing till 10am.
Tue–Wed and Sun 11pm–5am, Thu–Sat till 6am €10 Sun–Thu, €20 Fri–Sat Blanche

**LOUNGE BAR DU ZEBRA SQUARE**
3 place Clément-Ader, 75016
Tel 01 44 14 91 91
The intimate surroundings suit the somewhat older clientele (35-plus), comfortably seated on Chesterfield sofas, listening to the music. This is part of a complex that includes the Hôtel Square and the Zebra Square restaurant.
Mon–Sat 8pm–4am
Free Passy, Ranelagh

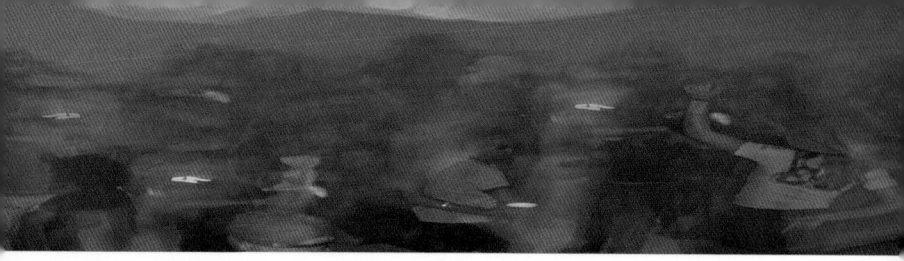

**SPECIAL**

**NEW RÉGINE'S CLUB**
48 rue de Ponthieu, 75008
Tel 01 43 59 21 60
The club may claim to be new, but Regine has been at the heart of the city's social scene forever. The restaurant-club draws a clientele of elegant forty-somethings, but it's the younger crowd who usually occupy the dance floor.
Tue–Sun 11pm–5am
Free Franklin D. Roosevelt

**SPECIAL**

**V I P ROOM**
76 avenue des Champs-Élysées, 75008
Tel 01 56 69 16 66
A clientele of VIPs do indeed enjoy this club, which has a superb baroque interior (red velvet, leopard print, candelabra). Be ready for selective entry: the beautiful or the seriously rich.
Tue–Sun 11.30pm–5am
Free Franklin D. Roosevelt

**MOLOKO**
26 rue Fontaine, 75009
Tel 01 48 74 50 26
www.lemoloko.com
In Paris's red light district, this club has an eclectic range of music, including R & B and salsa. There is a dance floor on the ground floor and a lounge bar upstairs.
Daily 11pm–7am Free
Blanche

**NIRVANA**
3 avenue Matignon, 75008
Tel 01 53 89 18 91
This restaurant and club has a luxurious, contemporary style, with Indian influences. It is on one of Paris's smartest avenues. Valet parking.
Daily 8pm–4am Free
Franklin D. Roosevelt

**LE NOUVEAU CASINO**
109 rue Oberkampf, 75011
Tel 01 43 57 57 40
www.nouveaucasino.net

It didn't take long for this club to develop a regular clientele after opening in 2001. Excellent DJs, a beautiful interior (lots of steel and vivid hues) and an excellent location in a busy district are the keys to its success.
11pm–5am (days vary) Around €10 Parmentier, Ménilmontant, Rue St-Maur

**REX CLUB**
5 boulevard Poissonnière, 75002
Tel 01 42 36 10 96
The best international DJs have come here to spin—including Carl Cox and Daft Punk. For an attentive crowd of house/techno connoisseurs, this is the place to go.
Wed–Sat 11.30pm–5am €10–14
Bonne Nouvelle

**WAGG**
62 rue Mazarine, 75006
Tel 01 55 42 22 00
A smaller dance floor (up to 350 people) gives this venue its welcoming atmosphere. The house and dance music draws a trendy mid-20s to mid-30s crowd here, in the heart of St-Germain-des-Prés.
Wed–Sun 11.30pm–5am
€12 Fri–Sat, €10 Thu and Sun, free on Wed St-Germain-des-Prés, Odéon

## Gay and Lesbian

**BANANA CAFÉ**
13–15 rue de la Ferronnerie, 75001
Tel 01 42 33 35 31
www.bananacafeparis.com
A strictly gay clientele enjoys the house and techno rhythms at this club. The themed interior changes every week (oriental, Latino, etc). There is also a piano-bar downstairs.
Daily 6pm–6am €9 Fri, Sat; free rest of the week Châtelet

**PULP**
25 boulevard Poissonnière, 75002
Tel 01 40 26 01 93
This is the only lesbian club in Paris. House and techno are spun by talented DJs, mainly female. Some parties are open to gay men and everyone is welcome on Wednesdays and Thursdays.
Wed–Sat midnight–6am
Around €10 Grands Boulevards

**QUEEN**
102 avenue des Champs-Élysées, 75008
Tel 01 53 89 08 90
www.queen.fr
This trendy club has a prestigious address on the Champs-Élysées and attracts a straight as well as gay crowd. House and garage music is mixed by international DJs. Themes and atmospheres vary each day of the week.
Daily midnight–7am €12 Mon, €10 Tue–Thu and Sun, €20 Fri–Sat
George V

# SPORTS AND ACTIVITIES

Highlights of the Parisian sporting calendar include the Roland Garros International Tennis Grand Slam tournament (late May to early June), the final leg of the Tour de France bicycle race in July (see page 222) and the Prix de l'Arc de Triomphe horse race in October. There are also many rugby and soccer internationals. The Paris St-Germain soccer team play at the Parc des Princes, although France's international soccer and rugby matches are held at the Stade de France (*tel 01 55 93 00 00; ticketline 0892 700 900; www.stadefrance.fr*).

Participatory sports are not high on most people's agenda during a visit to Paris, but if you want to sweat off some calories head to the Bois de Boulogne (see page 236) and Bois de Vincennes (see page 237) for bicycling, jogging or boating. There are also gyms and swimming pools dotted around the city. For golf, contact the Fédération Française de Golf (*tel 01 41 49 77 00*). Boules, or pétanque, is a less strenuous option and is popular in parks and grassy squares.



## Spectator Sports

### SOCCER

**PARC DES PRINCES**
24 rue du Commandant-Guilbaud, 75016
Tel 0825 075 078 (closed Fri and public hols)
www.psg.fr
Inaugurated in 1972, the park has been home to Paris-St-Germain (PSG) soccer club since 1990. Within its boundaries you'll also find the Musée National du Sport (National Sport Museum), a shop with PSG merchandise and a restaurant, the 70.
Varies Porte d'Auteuil, Porte de St-Cloud

### STADIUMS

**STADE PIERRE DE COUBERTIN**
82 avenue Georges-Lafont, 75016
Tel 01 45 27 79 12
Built for the 1937 International Exhibition, destroyed during World War II and rebuilt in 1946, this 4,500-seat stadium now hosts all sorts of competitions, ranging from fencing and French boxing to handball and dance.
Varies Porte de St-Cloud

**STADE ROLAND-GARROS**
2 avenue Gordon-Bennett, 75016
Tel 01 47 43 48 00
www.rolandgarros.org
This stadium is home to the eponymous tennis tournament (see page 222). It has 24 tennis courts and can hold up to 39,000 spectators.
Varies Porte d'Auteuil

### SWIMMING

**PISCINE GEORGES-VALLEREY**
148 avenue Gambetta, 75020
Tel 01 40 31 15 20
Built in 1924 for the Olympic Games and renovated in 1989, this vast swimming pool has a translucent sunroof (open when weather permits) and a 1,500-seat terrace. You can see

competitions here or come for a swim yourself. Credit cards are not accepted.
Mon, Fri 11.30–5, Tue, Thu 11.30–10, Wed 10–5, Sat, Sun 9–7
€4 entrance Porte des Lilas

## Activities

### AQUA PARK

**AQUABOULEVARD**
4–6 rue Louis Armand, 75015
Tel 01 40 60 10 00
www.aquaboulevard.com
Alongside the aquapark, with toboggans and whirlpools, there are six squash courts, six tennis courts, a putting range, and several restaurants and shops. Fitness and dance classes are also on offer.
Mon–Thu 9am–11pm, Fri 9am–midnight, Sat 8am–midnight, Sun 8am–11pm Entry to aquapark: €20
Balard, Porte de Versailles

### BILLIARDS

**ACADÉMIE DE BILLARDS**
84 rue de Clichy, 75009
Tel 01 48 78 32 85
www.academie-billard.com
Occupying a former brasserie built in 1880, this billiard hall has a lot of character. Play American and French billiards, snooker and pool. You'll find both professionals and amateurs here.
Daily 10–6 Around €10 per hour
Place de Clichy

### BOWLING

**BOWLING DE MONTPARNASSE**
25 rue du Commandant-Mouchotte, 75014
Tel 01 43 21 61 32
This venue has 16 bowling lanes, pool billiards and some video games. Every Friday and Saturday night you can bowl in the dark, with the lanes illuminated by fluorescent lighting.
Sun–Thu 10am–2am, Fri 10am–4am, Sat 10am–5am
€4.30–5.80 per game, per person
Montparnasse-Bienvenüe

## BICYCLING

### PARIS À VÉLO C'EST SYMPA

37 boulevard Bourbon, 75011
Tel 01 48 87 60 01
www.parisvelosympa.com

A bicycle ride is one of the best ways to discover Paris. Various guided tours are available in French and English: Heart of Paris, Paris at Dawn and Unusual Paris. Unaccompanied bicycle and tandem rental is also available.

Tour at noon and 2pm, days vary according to number of bookings €30 for a 3-hour ride Bastille

## DANCE

### CENTRE DE DANSE DU MARAIS

41 rue du Temple, 75004
Tel 01 42 72 15 42
www.parisdanse.com

A picturesque courtyard is home to this music school, restaurant (The Studio), café-theatre (Café de la Gare) and dance school, where you can take all sorts of classes: ballet, rock, flamenco, salsa, tango, African, tap-dancing and more.

Varies according to classes €15 per 90-min class Rambuteau, Hôtel de Ville

### CENTRE DE DANSE MOMBOYE

25 rue Boyer, 75020
Tel 01 43 58 85 01
www.ladanse.com/momboye

Here you'll find dances from all over the world, including salsa, tango and belly dancing, and especially African, from Senegal, Congo and the Ivory Coast. Percussion and gospel classes also on offer.

Classes: Mon–Fri 5.45pm, 7.15pm, 8.45pm, Sat–Sun 10, 11.30, 1pm €14 per 90-minute class Gambetta

### ROCK 'N' ROLL DANCE CENTER

6 impasse Lévis, 75017
Tel 01 43 80 90 23
www.cours-de-danse.com

All partner dances are taught here: Rock, salsa, boogie-woogie, bebop, West Coast swing, Latino, samba, and much more. Enjoy the rock party on Fridays and salsa on Saturdays.

Mon–Thu 3–10.30, Fri 3–8, Sat 1–6, closed Sun Varies according to class Villiers

## FLYING

### TSAR AVIATION

Aérodrome, 95000, Pontoise
Tel 01 46 56 69 80

During a 30-minute flight lesson with a trained pilot you can experience aerobatics, including looping and somersaults. Certificates are awarded after the session.

Depends on booking and weather €400 per flight A15, exit Cormeilles, then take the 915 and follow the signs

## GOLF

### GOLF DU BOIS DE BOULOGNE

Hippodome d'Auteuil, 75016
Tel 01 44 30 70 00
www.golfduboisdeboulogne.com

Paris's largest golf course, within a race track, includes an area where you can practise your swing, a putting green and a crazy-golf area with small greens interspersed with bunkers and watercourses.

Daily 8–8 (closed on race days) No membership required. €4 per bucket of balls, €4 per half hour of crazy golf Porte d'Auteuil

## HELICOPTER TOURS

### PARIS HÉLICOPTÈRES

Zone Aviation Affaires, Aéroport, 93350 Le Bourget
Tel 01 48 35 90 44
www.paris-helicoptere.com

Want to see all Paris's main sights in less than 30 minutes? Take a monument-spotting tour over Paris. Longer tours are also available, for a bird's-eye view of the Château de Versailles and farther afield.

Every Sunday afternoon (book ahead) €122 for a 25-min tour Le Bourget 152 (Musée de l'Air stop)

## HORSE-RIDING

### HARAS DES HAUTES FONTAINES

Rue Maria-Valla, 77171, Solers
Tel 01 64 06 74 21
www.haras-de-solers.com

This equestrian centre, in the leafy outskirts of Paris, organizes classes, competitions and rides in the nearby forest on a regular basis. A pony club welcomes children over three.

Vary widely Around €20 per hour Gare de Gretz Take the D 318 direction Provins

## HOT-AIR BALLOON TOURS

### FRANCE MONTGOLFIÈRES

63 boulevard de Ménilmontant, 75011
Tel 01 47 00 66 44
www.franceballoons.com

A hot-air balloon tour enables you to see Paris's surroundings as you soar above villages, chateaux, rivers and forests. You can also go to Burgundy and the Loire's chateaux. Some

trips include a hotel stay.

Tours from mid-Mar to end Nov; book ahead From €165 for 3.5-hour tour Père Lachaise

### MONTGOLFIÈRES AVENTURES

8 villa Hallé, 75014
Tel 01 40 47 61 04
www.montgolfieres-aventures.fr

Enjoy breathtaking views of the Loire's chateaux, the Périgord or Paris's surroundings. Champagne and a first-flight certificate are awarded upon landing.

All year long; book ahead €210 per person Mouton Duvernet

## IN-LINE SKATING

### RANDONNÉE EN ROLLERS

Meet in front of Nomades: 37 boulevard Bourdon, 75004
Tel 01 44 54 07 44

In partnership with Nomades sports store, the Rollers and Coquillages Society organizes mass in-line skating through Paris every Sunday afternoon. The 3-hour circuit changes regularly.

Sun 2.30pm Free Bastille

## KARTING

### KART'IN

23 rue du Puits Dixme, 94320, Thiais
Tel 01 49 79 79 79
www.kart-in.fr

The racing circuit here is regularly modified, so it never becomes routine. Times are displayed on a big screen to

maximize the thrill. You can watch the races from the restaurant alongside the track.

Tue–Thu 6pm–midnight, Fri 6pm–2am, Sat 3pm–2am, Sun 3–9pm €20 for 10 min

## MARTIAL ARTS

### ÉCOLE D'ARTS MARTIAUX ERIC PARISET

207 rue de Charenton, 75012
Tel 01 43 42 40 42
www.jujitsuericpariset.com

Ju-jitsu is the main focus here, but judo and *atemi-waza* are also taught. The school is famous for its numerous books and videos on the subject and Eric Pariset himself takes most of the classes.

Varies Private lesson with Eric Pariset €46 (no membership required) Dugommier

### ENJOY BY FKC

36 rue de Nantes, 75019
Tel 01 40 35 05 05
www.enjoy-fkc.com

Founded by a full contact expert, this fitness venue offers a wide range of martial arts lessons including kick boxing, kung fu and tae kwondo. Fitness classes are also available and there is a sauna on the premises.

Mon–Fri 9am–10pm, Sat 9–7, Sun 9–1 €20 per day, around €40–60 per month on an annual basis Corentin Cariou

### FALUN GONG

Jardin du Luxembourg, 75006

Similar to t'ai chi, falun gong consists of a series of exercises aimed at combatting anxiety and increasing vitality. The charming surroundings of the Luxembourg Garden are an added bonus. Meet next to Marie de Medici statue.

Sat–Sun 9.30am–11am Free Luxembourg

### LE TEMPLE DES ARTS MARTIAUX

21 rue de l'Amiral Roussin, 75015
Tel 01 43 06 38 87
www.temple-arts-martiaux.fr

Close to the Eiffel Tower, one of Europe's largest martial arts facilities offers a dazzling range of activities: capoeira, tae kwondo, French boxing, nin jutsu and more. There is also a gym and sauna.

Mon–Sat 8am–10pm €15 for a 75-minute lesson regardless of level and discipline. No membership required Cambronne, Avenue Émile Zola

## PAINTBALL

### 100% LOISIRS

6 place Léon Deubel, 75016
Tel 01 45 27 87 04
www.paintballidf.com

This shop stocks paintball equipment and arranges paintball parties. These take place in the outskirts of Paris, near the Velizy II shopping mall, in woods with many unoccupied buildings.

Full day 11–5; half day 9–1 or 1–5 €31 per day, €23 per half-day Porte de St-Cloud

### ATOMIK PAINTBALL

16–18 rue de la Cour-des-Noues, 75020
Tel 01 43 66 02 58
www.atomik.fr

All the required equipment is available here; the paintball battles take place in a forest near Cergy Pontoise. Wooden walls and little cabins have been erected to spice up the game.

Shop: Mon–Sat 10–7 €10 field entrance, €34 field entrance plus rental of equipment for a battle of 6 hours max Gambetta

## PELOTA

### LE TRINQUET

8 quai St-Éxupéry, 75016
Tel 01 40 50 09 25

A convivial pelota school, where it's possible to play indoor and out. The indoor court boasts terraces and, surprisingly, a glass wall onto which the ball is thrown. There is a bar on the premises.

Daily 7am–midnight €28 per hour Porte de St-Cloud

## SPORTS CLUBS

### CLUB MONTMARTROIS

50 rue Duhesme, 75018
Tel 01 42 54 49 88
www.club-montmartrois.fr

Among the 30 activities on offer are fitness, cardio-training, yoga, stretching and dance. There is a steam room (women only) and sauna (one for men, one for women).
Mon–Fri 8am–9.30pm, Sat 8.30–7, Sun 9–5 Day membership €15
Lamarck-Caulaincourt

### CLUB QUARTIER LATIN

19 rue Pontoise, 75005
Tel 01 55 42 77 88
www.clubquartierlatin.com

No membership is required and late opening and a whole array of classes and equipment (aquagym, cardio-training, squash and sauna) are on offer. This club is popular both with visitors and local students.
Mon–Fri 9am–midnight, Sat–Sun 9.30–7 €15 per day
Cardinal Lemoine

## SPORTS COMPLEX

### CENTRE T.E.P. DAVOUT

134 boulevard Davout, 75020
Tel 01 43 61 39 26

This complex contains two tennis courts, a track with a hockey pitch in the middle, two concrete courts where you can play handball or volleyball, and a running track.
Mon–Fri 8am–10pm, Sat 8am–8.30pm, Sun 8–6:30
Free use of equipment (except tennis courts: €5.75 per hour)
Porte de Montreuil, Porte de Bagnolet 57, 76

## SPORTS PARK

### PARC DE BELLEVILLE

Rue des Couronnes, 75020

Created in 1998, this park has a terraced layout and offers wonderful views of Paris. A walkers' and joggers' paradise, it also has basketball courts and soccer pitches.
Daily 6am–dusk Free
Couronnes, Belleville

## SQUASH

### SQUASH FRONT DE SEINE

21 rue Gaston-de-Caillavet, 75015
Tel 01 45 75 35 37

Here you'll find eight courts, a sauna and a bar where you can reconcile yourself with your opponent after a fierce game. Free initiation is on Mondays by appointment. Classes also available.
Mon–Fri 9am–11pm, Sat–Sun 9–8
€12 per person per half-hour
Charles Michels

### SQUASH MONTMARTRE

14 rue Achille Martinet, 75018
Tel 01 42 55 38 30
www.slot-montmartre.com

Facilities at this friendly squash club include four courts, a gym, sauna, solarium, clubhouse and restaurant.
Mon–Fri 10am–10.30pm, Sat–Sun 10–7 €10 for 30 min, €14 for 45 min Lamarck-Caulaincourt

## SWIMMING

### PISCINE DE LA BUTTE AUX CAILLES

5 place Paul Verlaine, 75013
Tel 01 45 89 60 05

This swimming pool, built in the 1920s, has lots of character, with Italian tiles and a vaulted roof. The indoor pool is open all year; the outdoor pool during summer.
Tue 7–8, 11.30–1, 4.30–6.30, Wed 7–6.30, Thu–Fri 7–8, 11.30–6, Sat 7–8, 10–6, Sun 8–5.30 €3
Place d'Italie

### PISCINE JEAN TARIS

16 rue Thuin, 75005
Tel 01 55 42 81 90

This swimming pool's main attractions are its location, in the Latin Quarter near the Panthéon, and the view: The large windows face a leafy garden. There is one big pool and a smaller one for children. Credit cards are not accepted.
Tue and Thu 7–8, 11.30–1, Wed 7–8, 11.30–5.30, Fri 7–8, 11.30–1, 5–8, Sat 7–5.30, Sun 8–5.30
€3 Cardinal Lemoine

### PISCINE MUNICIPALE DE REUILLY

13 rue Hénard, 75012
Tel 01 40 02 08 08

With its large windows, this modern pool is bright and airy. A solarium, two main pools and a smaller one for children are on site. Credit cards are not accepted.
Mon 12–1, Tue and Fri 7–8, 12–1, Wed 7am–8am, 12–5, Thu 12–1, 4–9.30, Sat 10.30–5, Sun 8–5 €3
Montgallet

## TENNIS

### TENNIS DU LUXEMBOURG

Jardin du Luxembourg, 75006
Tel 01 43 25 79 18

The Luxembourg Garden is a prestigious and pleasant setting for these six tennis courts. No membership and competitive rates mean it can be difficult to get a booking.
Daily 8:30am–4:30pm, till 9:30pm in summer €3 for 30 min, €6 per hour Luxembourg

### TENNIS MONTPARNASSE

25 allée du Capitaine-Dronne, 75015
Tel 01 43 20 89 00

Above Montparnasse railway station, in the middle of a garden, these five outdoor tennis courts are in a pleasant and practical location.
Mon–Sat 9am–10pm, Sun 9–5.30
Mon–Fri €10 per hour, Sat–Sun €19
Montparnasse-Bienvenüe

## YOGA

### CENTRE SIVANANDA DE YOGA VEDANTA

123 boulevard de Sébastopol, 75002
Tel 01 40 26 77 49
www.sivananda.org/paris

Run by Vedanta monks, true to ancestral Indian tradition, this venue offers an holistic approach to yoga with relaxation classes, but also an introduction to the philosophy of yoga and positive thinking.
Daily 11–8 €99 for eight 90-min lessons, or €13 per lesson
Réaumur Sébastopol

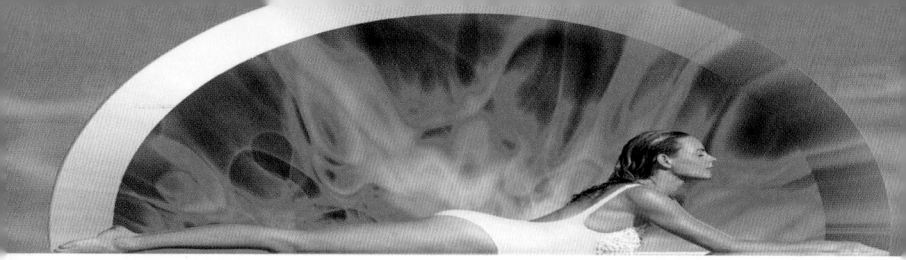

# Health and Beauty

## AQUATHERAPY

### AQUAMASSAGE AT PRINTEMPS

64 boulevard Haussmann, 75009
Tel 01 42 82 50 00
www.aquamassage.co.uk

Department store Printemps was the first in Paris to offer this revolutionary technique: An aquamassage that doesn't get you wet. A machine which looks like a sunbed surrounds your body with a completely waterproof envelope while 36 high-powered water jets

give you a heavenly massage. Seven different massages are available.

Mon–Sat 9.30–7 (Thu till 10pm) €15 for 10 min Havre-Caumartin

## BEAUTY SALONS

### INSTITUT LANCÔME

29 rue du Faubourg St-Honoré, 75008
Tel 01 42 65 30 74
www.lancome.com

Here you can have fully personalized treatments, including facials, masks and massages, for 60, 90 or 120 minutes.

Mon–Sat 10–7 Face treatments €70, body treatments €77 Concorde, Madeleine

### MICHEL MASTEY

93 avenue Kléber, 75016
Tel 01 45 53 30 85

This institute offers manicures using Nailtiques products, barely known in France, though some Hollywood stars swear by them: therapeutic oil (the whole hand is massaged), Formula 2 treatment for broken nails, Formula 1 to keep them healthy.

Mon–Sat 9.30–6 Manicure €30 Trocadéro

### VENUS ET MARS

26–28 avenue Marceau, 75008
Tel 01 56 89 10 01

Treat yourself to a facial or a massage after getting your hair cut here. Indulge yourself further in the small boutique selling clothes and accessories before relaxing with a cup of tea or an organic fruit juice in the tea room. Inspired by New York concept stores, this bright and airy salon, with its lofty mezzanine, offers just about everything a pampering addict could dream of.

Mon–Sat 9–7 Haircut €75; Tibetan, Chinese or Moroccan massage €37–€110 Alma-Marceau

## BEAUTY TREATMENTS

### LE AMAK

45 avenue George V, 75008
Tel 01 40 73 40 73

This is one of the few institutes in Paris to use Botox (in powder form only). Amak also offers anti-stress treatments such as massages and fitness classes in its smart venue next to the Champs-Élysées. Men are also welcome.

Daily 10–8 (Thu and Sun till 9) Botomax €160, 90-min Indian massage €100 George V

### INDRAJIT GARAI

10 place de Clichy, 75009
Tel 01 48 78 21 39

Indrajit Garai offers state-of-the-art Ayurvedic Indian massages. Having worked in Spain and London, he has set up this practice at his Parisian home. He collaborates with physiotherapists for a therapeutic approach. Credit cards are not accepted.

Varies. Advance booking essential €90 for 90 min Place de Clichy

### SENSO PIU

71 avenue Raymond-Poincaré, 75016
Tel 01 45 53 29 23

Peace and harmony may be on the horizon, thanks to a variety of treatments of oriental inspiration: Ayurvedic Indian massages with warm oils, biokinergy (reaching mind and body balance by working on certain muscles) and the tchong-mo massage (a stimulation of energy meridians). This latter was created here and remains exclusive to the institute. Men and women are welcome.

Mon–Fri 10.30–7, Sat 10.30–1 60-min tchong-mo massage €61 Victor Hugo, Trocadéro

## THALASSOTHERAPY

### VILLA THALGO

218–220 rue du Faubourg St-Honoré, 75008
Tel 01 45 62 00 20
www.thalgo.fr

This high-class institute brings thalassotherapy to the heart of Paris. The seven-hour session includes bodyscrub, seaweed wrap, balneotherapy, jet shower, aquagym and massages. One-hour and half-day treatments are also available. Both women and men are welcome.

Mon, Tue, Thu 8.30–8.30, Wed and Fri 8.30–7, Sat 9–7 60-min treatment €60 Ternes, Charles de Gaulle-Étoile

## TURKISH BATHS

### HAMMAM DE LA MOSQUÉE DE PARIS

See page 110.

# CHILDREN'S PARIS

Many of the city's museums and galleries arrange children's activities (often on Wednesday or Saturday) and provide worksheets. Entry is often free to under 18s. Parks such as the Jardin du Luxembourg have amusements for youngsters, including puppet shows, model yachts and playgrounds. Outside the city limits, there are the popular theme parks of Disneyland Resort Paris (see pages 240–241) and Parc Astérix.

## Farms and Wildlife Parks

**FERME OUVERTE DE GALLY**
Route de l'aérodrome, 78000
St-Cyr-l'École
Tel 01 30 14 60 60
www.gally.com
During a visit to this working farm, children can get close to cows, chickens, rabbits and other animals. They can also take part in farm activities such as apple pressing and honey collection.
Farm: Mon, Tue, Thu, Fri 4–5.30, Wed 10–12.30, 2–6, Sat, Sun 10–6.30. Garden: daily 9.30–7 Farm: adult €3.30, child (3–12) €2.50. €2 per child for each activity St-Cyr
A13 exit 6 take direction Bailly Noisy le Roi exit St-Cyr-l'École

**PARC ZOOLOGIQUE DE PARIS**
See page 237.

**PARC ZOOLOGIQUE DE THOIRY**
Château de Thoiry, 78770, Thoiry
Tel 01 34 87 52 25
www.thoiry.tm.fr
A 35-minute drive from Paris, this park takes you on safari. You can drive through the animals' territory and spot zebras, tigers, monkeys, flamingoes and more. Part of the zoo can be toured on foot. The castle is also worth a visit.
Daily 10–6 (until 5 in winter)
Zoo: adult €17.80, child (3–12) €13
A13 direction Versailles, exit Bois d'Arcy direction Dreux. Take N12 exit Pontchartrain then D11 to Thoiry

## Museums

**CITÉ DES SCIENCES ET DE L'INDUSTRIE**
See pages 146–147.

**MUSÉE GRÉVIN**
See page 116.

**MUSÉUM NATIONAL D'HISTOIRE NATURELLE**
See page 127.

## Parks and Gardens

**JARDIN D'ACCLIMATATION**
Main entry: boulevard des Sablons, Bois de Boulogne, 75016
Tel 01 40 67 90 82
With its ponds and tree-lined alleys, this 'garden within a wood' is a walker's paradise. There are many activities for children including minigolf, playgrounds, bowling, wildlife discovery, theatre and sports. A trip on the little train is a good way to discover the wood.
Daily 10–7 (until 6 in winter)
Adult €2.50, children under 3 free
Les Sablons

**MAISON DU JARDINAGE**
41 rue Paul-Belmondo, 75012
Tel 01 53 46 19 19
This 'House of Gardening', with ponds and an orange grove, is in Bercy Park. It hosts exhibitions on the environment and has a vegetable plot maintained by Parisian children. Gardening classes, with varying themes according to the season, are held here.
Tue–Sun 1–5.30, Oct–end Mar; Tue–Fri 1–6, Sat, Sun 1–5.30 rest of year
Park: Free. 90-min gardening classes around €5.30 Bercy

**PARC FLORAL DE PARIS**
See page 237.

**PARC DE LA VILLETTE**
See pages 146–147.

## Theatre

**THÉÂTRE DE LA MAINATE**
See page 207.

## Theme Parks

**AQUABOULEVARD**
See page 216.

**CLUB MED WORLD**
39 Cour St-Émilion, 75012
Tel 0810 810 410 or 01 44 68 70 09
www.clubmedworld.fr
Club Med World offers activities organized around three main themes: Travel (with a travel agency on site), tastes (with food from all over the world) and talents (circus, dance and rock-climbing lessons).
Tue, Wed 11am–2am, Thu–Sat 11am–6am, Sun 11am–7pm
Prices vary for each activity Cour St-Émilion

**DISNEYLAND RESORT PARIS**
See pages 240–241.

**PARC ASTÉRIX**
A1 Paris–Lille Highway, 60128, Plailly
Tel 03 44 62 30 30
www.parcasterix.fr
Characters from the famous cartoon books starring Astérix and Obélix await you here. There are plenty of shows and attractions and at the Gauls'

village a scale model depicts Paris through the centuries.
Generally Mon–Fri 10–6, Sat, Sun 9.30–7, Apr to mid-Oct; but some additional closures, so phone ahead
Adult €31, child (3–11) €23, children under 3 free Roissy-Pôle

# FESTIVALS AND EVENTS

See page 307 for France's national holidays.

**FÊTE DES ROIS**
6 January
Epiphany (or the Festival of the Kings) is celebrated with a special almond cake called a *galette des rois*.

**CHINESE NEW YEAR**
Late January/early February
Chinatown erupts into celebration, between the avenue d'Ivry and avenue de Choisy.
Tolbiac

**MARATHON INTERNATIONAL DE PARIS**
First Sunday in April
Tel 01 41 33 15 68
www.parismarathon.com
Paris's marathon attracts more than 30,000 runners. It starts at the Champs-Élysées and finishes in avenue Foch, just behind the Arc de Triomphe.
Charles de Gaulle–Étoile

**FOIRE DE PARIS**
April/May
Paris Expo, Porte de Versailles, 75015
Tel 01 49 09 60 60
or 0892 692 694
www.foiredeparis.fr
Garden, home and leisure are the themes of the International Paris Fair.
Porte de Versailles

**LABOUR DAY**
1 May
Trade unions arrange processions through the streets and people buy symbolic bouquets of lily-of-the-valley.

**PRINTEMPS DES RUES**
May
Tel 01 47 97 36 06
www.leprintempsdesrues.com
A weekend of outdoor events, held at various locations. There is a different theme each year.

**ROLAND-GARROS**
May–June
Stade Roland Garros, 2 avenue Gordon-Bennett, 75016
Tel 01 47 43 48 00
www.rolandgarros.com
The prestigious French Tennis Open, lasting two weeks.
Porte d'Auteuil

**FOIRE ST-GERMAIN**
June
In and around place St-Sulpice
Tel 01 43 29 61 04
www.foiresaintgermain.org
This village fair dates back to the 12th century.
St-Sulpice

**FÊTE DE LA MUSIQUE**
21 June
Tel 01 40 03 94 70
www.fetedelamusique.culture.fr
Free concerts are held all over the city, with everything from jazz and classical to techno.

**PARIS JAZZ**
June–July
Parc Floral, Route de la Pyramide, Bois de Vincennes, 75012
Tel 01 73 04 75 75
www.parcfloraldeparis.com
The sound of jazz fills the Parc Floral, courtesy of musicians from Europe and America.
Château de Vincennes

**BASTILLE DAY**
14 July
Fireworks and fire station balls on 13 July, followed by a military parade down the Champs-Élysées on 14 July.

**TOUR DE FRANCE**
July
Tel 01 41 33 15 00
www.letour.fr
The participants of this popular bicycle race cross the finish line on the Champs-Élysées.

**PARIS QUARTIER D'ÉTÉ**
July–August
Tel 01 44 94 98 00
www.quartierdete.com
Drama, music and dance in Paris's parks, gardens, streets and squares.

**FESTIVAL DE CINÉMA EN PLEIN AIR**
July–August
Parc de la Villette, 75019
Tel 01 40 03 75 75
www.villette.com
Open-air film festival.
Porte de la Villette, Porte de Pantin

**FESTIVAL D'AUTOMNE**
Mid-September to December
Tel 01 53 45 17 17
www.festival-automne.com
Avant-garde cultural festival, featuring dance, performance and music at various venues.

**FIAC (FOIRE INTERNATIONAL D'ART CONTEMPORAIN)**
5 days in October
Pavillon du Parc, Paris Expo, Porte de Versailles
Tel 01 43 95 37 00 (Paris Expo); information 0892 692 694
www.fiac-online.com
This vast modern art fair is a key social event.
Porte de Versailles

**NUIT BLANCHE**
October
Tel 0820 007 575
www.nuitblanche.paris.fr
Concerts and other events take place in unusual venues across the city, through the night.

**BEAUJOLAIS NOUVEAU**
Third Thursday in November
Bars spill out into the street as the first bottles of the year's Beaujolais reach Paris.

Paris is best explored on foot and this section describes five walks that take in key parts of the city. The locations of the walks are marked on the map on the inside front cover of the book.
This section also gives suggestions for excursions farther afield and details of a river trip.

**Walks**


| | |
|---|---|
| Le Marais | **224–225** |
| Montmartre | **226–227** |
| Quartier Latin | **228–229** |
| Rive Droite | **230–231** |
| St-Germain-des-Prés | **232–233** |


**River Trip**


| | |
|---|---|
| Along the Seine | **234–235** |


# Out and About

**Excursions**


| | |
|---|---|
| Bois de Boulogne | **236** |
| Bois de Vincennes | **237** |
| Chantilly | **238–239** |
| Disneyland Resort Paris | **240–241** |
| Fontainebleau | **242–243** |
| Versailles | **244–247** |

**City Tours** **248**

# LE MARAIS WALK

**The Marais is one of the prettiest districts in central Paris, home to elaborate mansions (known as *hôtels*), medieval streets, huge doorways with ornate handles, pretty gardens and squares, a bustling Jewish quarter and the oldest square in Paris, the place des Vosges.**

## THE WALK

**Length:** 3km (2 miles)
**Allow:** 2 hours
**Start/end:** St-Paul Métro station
**How to get there:** St-Paul
69, 76, 96

Leave St-Paul Métro station and head east along rue St-Antoine, passing the impressive façade of the church of St-Paul-St-Louis (1627–1641) on the right. At number 62, on your left, is the ❶ Hôtel de Sully.

**This magnificent 17th-century mansion was once home to Henri IV's chief minister, the Duc de Sully. Today it houses the headquarters of Monum, the Centre des Monuments Nationaux.**

Turn left into the peaceful rue de Birague which leads to the ❷ place des Vosges (see page 150).

**This picturesque square was commissioned by Henri IV and completed in 1612. During the 17th century it was home to significant figures such as Cardinal Richelieu, Louis XIII's hypochondriac minister, and the playwright Molière. In the 19th century writer Victor Hugo moved in. His house, number 6, is now a museum (see page 106).**

Continue around the square, walking under the arcades, past restaurants, galleries and shops. Look into the garden entrance of number 28, the Pavillon de la Reine, now a hotel (see page 292). If you feel like a drink, stop at one of the cafés with its tables spread out under the arcades.

Leave the square by rue des Francs-Bourgeois. On your right is the ❸ Musée Carnavalet (see pages 114–115), built in 1548 and later home to the writer Madame de Sévigné. As you walk past you can see the beautiful courtyard and gardens.

**The Musée Carnavalet, in two adjoining mansions, focuses on the story of Paris, from prehistory to the 20th century. The Revolution, Napoleon Bonaparte and art nouveau interiors are among its themes.**

Turn right into rue Payenne. The gardens on the right and courtyards on the left are in typical 17th-century Marais style. Notice the elaborate wooden gates of the Hôtel de Châtillon, on your left, at number 13.

Follow rue du Parc Royal to the left, walk around place de Thorigny and then turn right into rue de Thorigny, to reach the Hôtel Salé, built in 1656, and now home to the ❹ Musée Picasso (see page 135).

**Here you can see a vast collection of Picasso's works—more than 250 paintings, 160 sculptures and 1,500 drawings. There are also pieces by his contemporaries, notably Paul Cézanne, Joan Miró, Georges Braque and Henri Matisse.**

Turn left along rue Debelleyme, passing some contemporary art galleries, and then left again down rue Vieille-du-Temple. On the left you will see the lovely gardens of the Musée Picasso.

Halfway down on your right at number 87, you pass the carved gates of the Hôtel de Rohan and, on the corner of rue des Francs-Bourgeois, the picturesque turret (1510) of the Maison de Jean Hérouët.

Turn right here, past more elegant mansions and the Crédit Municipal (municipal pawnshop) at number 55 on your left. On the right is the courtyard of the ❺ Hôtel de Soubise.

**This mansion was constructed between 1705 and 1708 and is now home to the National Archives and the Musée de l'Histoire de France (see pages 116–117).**

Turn left into rue des Archives and take the next left into rue des Blancs-Manteaux. This brings you back to rue Vieille-du-Temple. Turn right and after a short walk turn left to follow ❻ rue des Rosiers.

**This bustling street is the hub of the Jewish district, full of specialist shops as far as rue Pavée. Chic boutiques and trendy furniture stores trade alongside traditional Jewish fast-food stalls, cafés and bookshops.**

Turn right into rue Pavée. On the left you'll pass the synagogue, designed by Hector Guimard (see page 163). Continue south to return to St-Paul Métro station.

**WHEN TO GO**

During the day, when the shops and museums are open.

**WHERE TO EAT**

The place des Vosges has plenty of cafés. Ma Bourgogne, at number 19, and Nectarine, at number 16, both have outdoor tables under the arcades.

*The cloisters of the Église des Billettes, in rue des Archives*

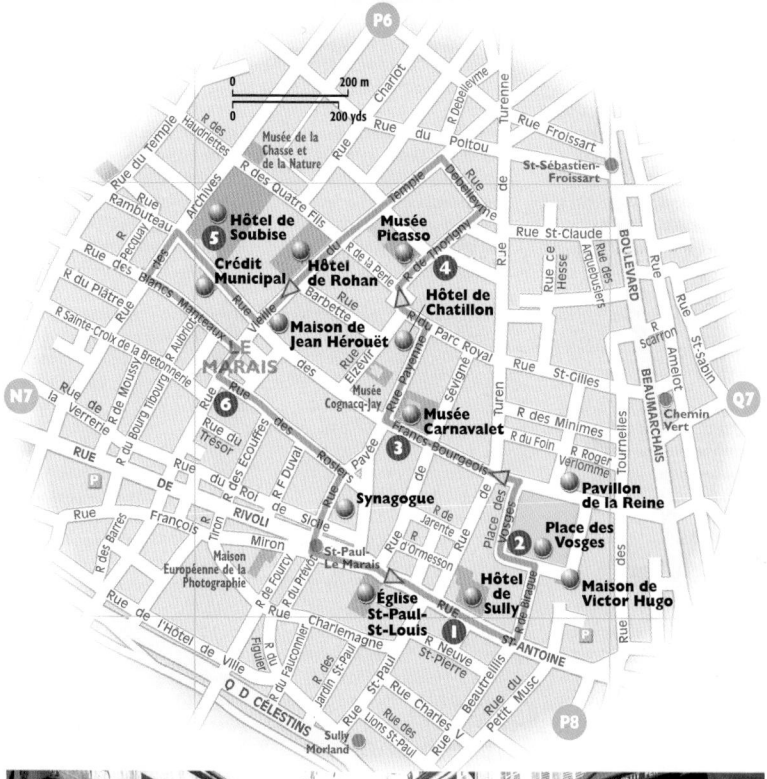

*A bustling street scene in Le Marais (above)*
*The brightly painted L'Oiseau Bariole bar (left)*
*Classic elegance at the Hôtel de Soubise (far left)*

# MONTMARTRE WALK

**There is so much more to Montmartre than the towering Sacré-Cœur basilica, impressive though this is. This walk shows you the lesser-known side of Paris's hilltop village, with its picturesque cottages, cobbled streets and panoramic views.**

**THE WALK**

**Length:** 3km (2 miles)
**Allow:** 2 hours
**Start:** place Blanche
**End:** place des Abbesses
**How to get there:** Blanche 30, 54, 68, 74

Starting from place Blanche, walk west along boulevard de Clichy, past the ❶ Moulin Rouge on your right.

**When the Moulin Rouge (see page 111) first opened its doors in 1889, its vivacious cancan dancers were an immediate hit. The venue still stages cabaret shows, now aimed at visitors.**

Turn right into avenue Rachel and carry on to the entrance of the ❷ Cimetière de Montmartre (see page 87).

**Here you can seek out the tombs of the writer Stendhal, composer Hector Berlioz and saxophone inventor Adolphe Sax.**

Leave the cemetery at avenue Rachel and walk up the steps on the right to rue Caulaincourt (a flyover). Turn right onto this road and walk to the junction with rue Joseph de Maistre. Turn right along rue Joseph de Maistre. After a few minutes, turn very sharp left up rue Lepic. Van Gogh lived at number 54 of this winding road from 1886 to 1888.

Follow the curve until you come to the junction with rue Tholozé. Look up to the left, past the green arch, to the ❸ Moulin de la Galette. Farther along the road, on the corner with rue Girardon, is the Moulin Radet.

**The Moulin de la Galette (literally the 'biscuit windmill') became a dance hall in the 19th century and was the inspiration behind Pierre-Auguste Renoir's painting *Le Bal du Moulin de la Galette* (1876). The windmill is now privately owned. The Moulin Radet now forms part of a restaurant, confusingly called the Moulin de la Galette.**

Turn left into rue Girardon, cross avenue Junot and enter the pleasant ❹ square Suzanne-Buisson, on the left.

**The square is named after a World War II resistance heroine. The macabre statue here is of the 3rd-century bishop St. Denis, who was beheaded by the Romans. Legend has it that he picked up his head and washed off the blood in a fountain on this spot.**

Facing the statue, turn right and leave the square into place Casadesus, in rue Simon Dereure. Turn right into the allée des Brouillards. Renoir lived in one of the houses on the left in the 1890s. The 18th-century mansion on the right was once a dance hall and a shelter for homeless artists.

Continue to place Dalida, named after the singer and actress who died in 1987, then walk up the cobbled rue de l'Abreuvoir. Formerly a country lane, the road takes its name from the watering trough *(l'abreuvoir)* that once stood at number 15. Number 14 attracted many of Montmartre's artists when it was the Café de l'Abreuvoir, while number 12 was home to Camille Pissarro from 1888 to 1892. If you're feeling hungry, stop for lunch at La Maison Rose (The Pink House).

Turn left after La Maison Rose and walk down the steep cobbled rue des Saules to the legendary cabaret spot, Au Lapin Agile. Turn right (east) along rue St-Vincent, past Montmartre's vineyard on your right. Cross rue du Mont Cenis, once home to Hector Berlioz (number 22), and walk uphill to rue de la Bonne. This leads into the hidden-away ❺ Parc de la Turlure.

**This tranquil park, well off the tourist trail, gives you magnificent views over Paris, as well as an unusual perspective on Sacré-Cœur.**

Wander up through the park, then exit onto rue du Chevalier de la Barre. Continue along rue du Cardinal Guibert to the entrance to ❻ Sacré-Cœur, on place du Parvis du Sacré-Cœur.

**The neo-Byzantine basilica of Sacré-Cœur (see pages 154–157) was commissioned as atonement after the Franco-Prussian war (1870–1871). Building work took nearly 45 years.**

Leave Sacré-Cœur and turn right along rue Azaïs, with its stunning views over the city. Turn right up rue St-Eleuthère to ❼ St-Pierre-de-Montmartre.

**Humbler than its grand companion, this peaceful church was originally part of the 12th-century Benedictine abbey of Montmartre.**

Enter the touristy place du Tertre (see page 108) and leave by the gift-shop strewn rue Norvins. Turn second left, through place Jean-Baptiste Clément. Turn right into rue Ravignan, and continue round to the left into the tree-shaded ❽ place Émile Goudeau.

**On the right of this square, look for the Bateau-Lavoir, where Pablo Picasso, Juan Gris and Georges Braque had studios and where Cubism was born. The original ramshackle wooden building burned down in 1970, but has since been rebuilt.**

To leave the square, walk down a small flight of steps and continue down rue Ravignan until you reach rue des Abbesses. Turn left here to ❾ place des Abbesses (see page 145).

Before stopping for a drink at place des Abbesses, take a look at the art nouveau Métro entrance and the unusual façade of the church of St-Jean-l'Évangéliste (1904), nicknamed St-Jean-des-Briques for its profusion of red bricks.

*The Moulin de la Galette restaurant, crowned by the Moulin Radet*

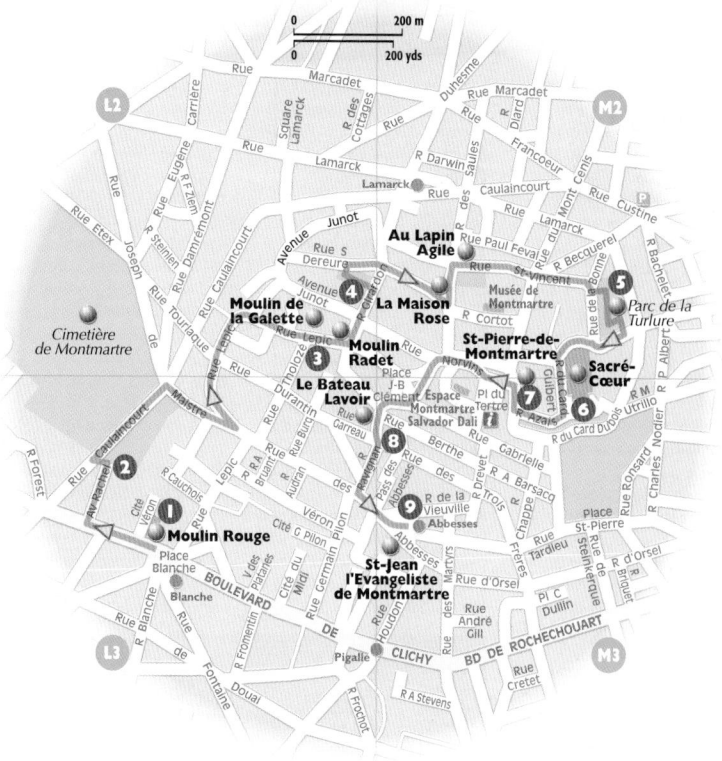
0 200 m
0 200 yds
L2
M2
L3
M3
Cimetière de Montmartre
Moulin de la Galette
Au Lapin Agile
La Maison Rose
Moulin Radet
Le Bateau Lavoir
St-Pierre-de-Montmartre
Sacré-Cœur
Parc de la Turlure
Moulin Rouge
St-Jean l'Evangeliste de Montmartre
Place des Abbesses
Abbesses
Place Blanche
Pigalle
Place St-Pierre
Place Clémenceau Espace Salvador Dali
Lamarck
Caulaincourt
Marcadet
Junot
Rue Lepic
Rue Caulaincourt
Rue Etex
Rue Tourlaque
Rue Damrémont
Rue Eugène Sue
Rue Steinlen
Rue Forest
Rue Cauchois
Rue Véron
Rue Durantin
Rue Garreau
Rue Berthe
Rue Gabrielle
Rue Tardieu
Rue d'Orsel
Rue André Gill
Rue Houdon
Rue Frémentin
Rue Blanche
Rue de Douai
Rue Fontaine
Rue Frochot
Rue Cretet
Rue Custine
Rue Ronsard
Rue Charles Nodier
Rue Albert
Rue Bachelet
Rue Becquerel
Rue Paul Féval
Rue Cortot
Rue Utrillo
Rue Norvins
Rue Chappe
Rue de Steinkerque
Rue Duhesme
Rue Caulaincourt
Rue Lamarck
Rue Darwin
Rue Francœur
Rue Saules
Rue Caulaincourt
Rue Maistre
Av. Rachel
Av. Junot
Av. Rachel
Av. Junot
Av. Steinlen
Av. Damrémont
Av. Eugène Sue
Av. Forest
Av. Rachel
Av. Junot

# QUARTIER LATIN WALK

**This walk takes you beyond the swarming boulevard St-Michel to the quiet cobbled alleyways, peaceful gardens, historic churches and laid-back cafés of the Latin Quarter.**

**THE WALK**

**Length:** 2.5km (1.5 miles)
**Allow:** 1 hour
**Start/end:** place St-Michel
**How to get there:** St-Michel 21, 24, 27, 38, 85, 96 RER line C, St-Michel-Notre-Dame

Start at place St-Michel and walk across to the ❶ Fontaine St-Michel.

**The sculpture symbolizes St. Michael slaying a dragon. Place St-Michel is the main gateway to the Latin Quarter from the Île de la Cité. Numerous visitors, students and Parisians pass through here every day.**

Cross boulevard St-Michel and walk down the medieval rue de la Huchette. Cross over rue de Petit Pont. Turn left, then immediately right into rue de la Bûcherie, with its views of Notre-Dame. Continue to ❷ square René Viviani.

**This is a pleasant place to sit for a few moments, admiring the flowers and enjoying the gurgle of running water from the fountain. The acacia here is said to be one of the oldest trees in Paris, dating from the early 17th century.**

Leave the square near the partly Gothic church of ❸ St-Julien-le-Pauvre (see page 162).

**This small, low-ceilinged church is one of the oldest in Paris, dating from the 12th century. You may find its sculptures and paintings hard to make out in the subdued lighting.**

From the church, follow the road round to rue St-Jacques. Cross rue St-Jacques and walk down rue St-Séverin, alongside the church of ❹ St-Séverin (see pages 162–163).

**The church dates from the 13th century, although much of it had to be rebuilt in the 15th century after a fire. To visit, turn left into rue des Prêtres St-Séverin. Don't miss the vivid stained-glass windows at the far end, installed in 1970 and representing the Seven Sacraments.**

Continue along rue St-Séverin to medieval rue de la Harpe, which, to the left, leads to boulevard St-Germain. Cross the boulevard to the medieval garden of the Musée National du Moyen Âge—Thermes de Cluny. Turn right up the boulevard, then left onto ❺ boulevard St-Michel.

**This traffic-thundering road, with its clothes stores, bookshops and newsstands, is the Latin Quarter's main artery.**

Walk up boulevard St-Michel, then turn right onto rue de l'École de Médecine. Turn left onto rue André Dubois, then up the steps to reach ❻ rue Monsieur le Prince. Turn left onto this road.

**Rue Monsieur le Prince closely follows the line of Paris's old city wall, built by King Philippe-Auguste, who reigned in the late 12th and early 13th centuries. Today it has shops and inexpensive restaurants, including the bistro Polidor at number 41, which was launched in 1845.**

Just before Polidor, turn right into rue Racine, then walk along to place de l'Odéon, dominated by the 18th-century Odéon Théâtre de l'Europe. Wander down the rue de l'Odéon, with its unusual shops, to reach ❼ Carrefour de l'Odéon.

**If you feel like a rest, you could stop for a coffee in one of the cafés here.**

Continue to boulevard St-Germain. Cross the boulevard and walk down ❽ rue de l'Ancienne Comédie.

**On your right you'll pass Paris's oldest café, Le Procope, founded in 1686 and now a restaurant (see page 273).**

At the Buci crossroads turn sharp right onto rue St-André-des-Arts. This leads back to place St-Michel. You could have a drink in one of the nearby cafés or cross the Pont St-Michel to explore the Île de la Cité.

## WHEN TO GO

Daytime is best for this walk, when the shops and churches are open.

## WHERE TO EAT

There is a choice of cafés on Carrefour de l'Odéon, or Pizza Milano at place St-Michel.

## NEARBY ATTRACTIONS

The Latin Quarter has plenty to occupy you, including the Musée National du Moyen Âge–Thermes de Cluny (see pages 128–129), the stately Panthéon (see page 144) and the refreshing Jardin du Luxembourg (see pages 102–103). You can while away a few hours in some of the many cafés or shop for clothes along boulevard St-Michel (pictured right).

*Avid readers will find plenty of bookstands (left) in the Latin Quarter; bookshops include Shakespeare and Company (right)*

# RIVE DROITE WALK

**A relaxing walk that combines restful gardens with chic shops.**

**THE WALK**

**Length:** 3.5km (2 miles)
**Allow:** 1 hour 30 minutes
**Start/end:** place de la Concorde
**How to get there:** Concorde
24, 42, 72, 73, 84, 94

Carefully cross the stream of traffic flowing through ❶ place de la Concorde to take a look at the obelisk in the heart of this historic square (see page 148).

**Place de la Concorde was designed in the mid-18th century as a regal setting for an equestrian statue of Louis XV. The square, originally named after the king, was promptly re-titled place de la Révolution when the guillotine arrived. Louis XVI and Marie-Antoinette were among the 1,300 people executed here. The pink granite obelisk came to Paris from Luxor, Egypt, in the 1830s and is around 3,300 years old.**

Cross to the ornate gates of the ❷ Jardin des Tuileries and stroll through this vibrant public garden (see page 105).

**The Tuileries is one of the oldest public gardens in Paris and offers fabulous views of the Louvre, the Eiffel Tower, place de la Concorde and the Arc de Triomphe. Parisians come here to relax by the two large ponds when the sun comes out, or stroll along the terraces on either side of the park.**

At the end of the park, turn left to reach rue de Rivoli. Turn right onto rue de Rivoli and walk alongside the ❸ Louvre.

**Many of France's rulers have left their mark on the Louvre, including Charles V, François I and Napoleon. The original medieval fortress was transformed into a castle in the 14th century, then became a royal palace, before assuming its present role as one of the most prestigious museums in the world.**

Cross rue de Rivoli into place du Palais Royal. From here, cross rue St-Honoré and bear left, towards the Comédie Française. Enter the ❹ Jardin du Palais Royal through a discreet arch on the left of the palace.

**This garden (see page 104) is only moments from the traffic and crowds of rue de Rivoli but a million miles away in atmosphere. You enter through a courtyard decorated with curious grey-and-white striped mini-columns, designed by the artist Daniel Buren in 1986. The garden, with its vivid flowerbeds, is surrounded by elegant 18th-century arcades with individual shops.**

Walk to the end of the garden and leave on the left side, past the historic restaurant Le Grand Véfour—look through the window at the lovely painted ceiling. This brings you to rue de Beaujolais. Turn right onto here, left up rue Vivienne, followed by a left turn onto rue des Petits Champs. You'll pass the ❺ Bibliothèque Nationale de France (see page 81) as you walk along this road.

**This building was once the palace of 17th-century prime minister Cardinal Mazarin, but has housed France's national library since the 18th century. By the 1990s the mammoth collection had outgrown the site and in 1996 an additional library (see page 81) opened in the 13th *arrondissement*, named after former president François Mitterrand.**

Continue until you reach avenue de l'Opéra. Cross the avenue and walk up towards the ❻ opera house (see page 142).

**The sumptuous Opéra Palais Garnier was designed by Charles Garnier and opened in 1875. It is an extravagance of marble, gold and sculpture and was once the largest opera house in the world.**

Just before place de l'Opéra, turn left down rue de la Paix, brimming with elegant jewellery shops. This leads to the even more exclusive ❼ place Vendôme (see page 149).

**You'll need a hefty bank balance to go shopping in this supreme symbol of Parisian chic, with its jewellery shops and world-famous Ritz Hotel. Be careful of the traffic—the cobbles give the false impression that the square is pedestrian-only.**

Cross the square and walk down rue de Castiglione, with its elegant shopping arcades. Turn right onto rue de Rivoli, which returns you to place de la Concorde. Back in the square, don't miss the view down the Champs-Élysées to the Arc de Triomphe.

*The Palais Royal courtyard*

*The obelisk in place de la Concorde (above) once stood at the Temple of Luxor.*
*Reading in the Jardin des Tuileries (below)*

**WHEN TO GO**

The best time to do this walk is during the day, when the shops are open and the Jardin des Tuileries is at its best. If you decide to take an evening stroll, avoid the Jardin des Tuileries and walk up rue de Rivoli instead.

**WHERE TO EAT**

For a meal try the chic but traditional brasserie Le Grand Colbert, at 4 rue Vivienne, near the Jardin du Palais Royal (*daily, noon–1am*). For tea and cake visit the chic Muscade tea room, within the *jardin* grounds, at 36 rue Montpensier/67 galerie Montpensier (*Tue–Sun 10–11.30, 3–6; until 8pm Sep–end Apr*).

*The imposing entrance to the Bibliothèque National de France (above).*
*Elegant place Vendôme (below)*

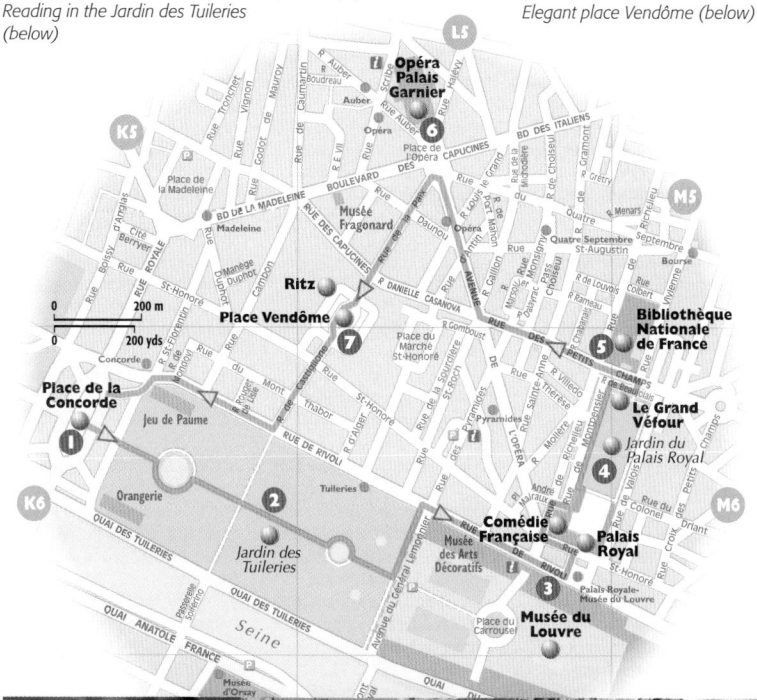

# ST-GERMAIN-DES-PRÉS WALK

**This walk takes you through the picturesque lanes of St-Germain-des-Prés, along the Left Bank of the Seine and around the beautiful Jardin du Luxembourg.**

**THE WALK**

**Length:** 3km (2 miles)
**Allow:** 2 hours 30 minutes
**Start:** St-Sulpice Métro station
**End:** St-Germain-des-Prés Métro station
**How to get there:** St-Sulpice
63, 70, 84, 86, 87, 96.

Leave St-Sulpice Métro station and walk east along rue du Vieux Colombier to place St-Sulpice. Straight ahead, across the square, is the immense ❶ Église St-Sulpice (see page 163).

**St-Sulpice church displays a mixture of architectural styles and dominates the square and its elaborate fountain. It took 134 years and six architects to build the church and even now the south tower remains unfinished. Treasures inside include murals by Eugène Delacroix, an extravagant pulpit and one of the world's largest organs.**

From the main entrance of the church, head south down rue Férou. At the end, cross over rue de Vaugirard and turn right. Almost immediately on your left is an entrance to the ❷ Jardin du Luxembourg (see pages 102–103).

**The landscaped Jardin du Luxembourg, commissioned by Marie de Medici in the early 17th century, is one of the most popular parks in Paris. The Palais du Luxembourg, within its grounds, is now home to the French Senate.**

Leave the gardens by the northern exit, to the right of the Palais du Luxembourg. Cross the road and head north along rue Rotrou. Pass the neoclassical Odéon Théâtre de l'Europe on the right. When you reach place de l'Odéon turn around to admire the theatre's colonnaded façade.

Walk across the square and carry on up rue de l'Odéon to the crossroads, carrefour de l'Odéon. Continue north a short distance until you reach boulevard St-Germain. Cross over, turn right and then almost immediately left into the ❸ cour du Commerce St-André.

**This narrow cobblestone passage was built in 1776 on the site of a tennis court. It became a hive of revolutionary activity, with Jean-Paul Marat printing his pamphlet at number 8, the anatomy professor Dr. Guillotin perfecting his 'philanthropic beheading machine' at number 9 and Revolutionary leader Georges Danton living at number 20.**

Turn left into rue St-André-des-Arts and almost immediately right at the carrefour de Buci into rue Dauphine. Walk to the end of this bustling street and you arrive at the Pont Neuf, the oldest bridge in Paris. Turn left, before the bridge, onto quai de Conti. On your left is the neoclassic façade of the ❹ Hôtel de la Monnaie.

**The workshops of the Paris Mint were here from the 18th century. The *hôtel* now houses the Musée de la Monnaie (see page 117), a coin and medal museum. Around 2,000 coins and hundreds of medals and tokens are on display, as well as prints, documents and engravings. The museum also shows the development of minting techniques.**

Cross over the road to walk along the edge of the Seine. Next to the Hôtel de la Monnaie, on the left, you'll see the splendid dome of the Institut de France (see page 98), home of the Académie Française. Notice the beautiful Pont des Arts footbridge, composed of seven steel arches, spanning the river to the Louvre. As you walk along you'll see ❺ *les bouquinistes* (booksellers) lining the banks of the Seine.

**Their green bookstalls, selling second-hand books, postcards and prints, have a history dating back 300 years. In the early days, the booksellers used to transport their goods in wheelbarrows across the river to sell them on the banks of the Seine.**

Head south down rue Bonaparte. On your right you'll pass the most celebrated fine art school in Paris, the École Nationale Supérieure des Beaux-Arts. Turn left into rue Jacob and then right into rue de Furstemberg. At number 6, in the corner of a charming little square, you'll find the ❻ Musée National Eugène Delacroix (see page 126).

**The artist Eugène Delacroix lived in St-Germain-des-Prés for the last six years of his life, from 1857 to 1863. His apartment has been converted into a museum, where you can see some of his paintings and sketches, in addition to his personal possessions.**

Head left down rue de l'Abbaye. Continue to head east on rue de Bourbon le Chateau. When you reach rue de Buci, home to one of Paris's most popular markets (*closed Mondays*), turn right. Turn right again and walk along boulevard St-Germain, passing the southern side of the ❼ Église St-Germain-des-Prés (see page 162) on your right. Continue until you come to place St-Germain-des-Prés; turn right into the square, where you'll find the entrance to the church.

**The Église St-Germain-des-Prés dates from the 11th century and is the oldest church in Paris. Damaged during the Revolution, the church was restored in the 19th century. The huge 12th-century flying buttresses of the choir are still intact.**

The walk ends at St-Germain-des-Prés Métro station, on boulevard St-Germain, on the southern side of the church.

*Browsing in the rue de Buci (right)*
*Elegant Le Bon Marché department store (below)*

Seine
Pont des Arts
École Nationale Supérieure des Beaux-Arts
Institut de France
Pont Neuf
Musée de la Monnaie
Palais de Justice
Sainte-Chapelle
Île de la Cité
Musée National Eugène Delacroix
ST-GERMAIN-DES-PRÉS
Maison de Verre
St-Germain-des-Prés
Odéon
St-Sulpice
Musée National du Moyen Âge
Odéon Théâtre de l'Europe
Palais du Luxembourg
La Sorbonne
Jardin du Luxembourg
0 200 m
0 200 yds
L7
M7
K8
N8
L9
M9

*Jean-Paul Sartre was once a regular at the Café de Flore*

**WHEN TO GO**

It is best to do this walk during the day, when the museums, gardens and churches are open. The market in the rue de Buci is closed on Mondays.

**WHERE TO EAT**

Two of the city's most famous cafés are on the boulevard St-Germain, at the end of the walk. Les Deux Magots is at number 170 and Café de Flore is at number 172. There are also plenty of other cafés and restaurants along the route.

# ALONG THE SEINE

**A river cruise along the Seine is a great way to view some of Paris's key sights from a different perspective. It is also ideal if you are short on time—in just over an hour you can see many of the famous landmarks.**

## THE RIVER TRIP

**Length:** 11km (7 miles)
**Allow:** Just over 1 hour
**Start/end:** square du Vert-Galant, Pont Neuf
**How to get there:** Pont Neuf
24, 27, 58, 67, 70, 72, 74, 75
From the Métro station walk over the Pont Neuf bridge. Just over halfway across, on the right, is a sign for the Vedettes du Pont Neuf. Go down the steps to the square du Vert-Galant, on the Île de la Cité, and turn right. The boarding platform is straight ahead.

The boat leaves from the pretty square du Vert-Galant and heads west, passing one of Paris's largest department stores, La Samaritaine, on the right (see page 192). The first bridge you pass under is the pedestrian-only Pont des Arts. This was originally built in 1804 but replaced in 1984. It is one of the most romantic bridges in Paris and is also a popular meeting place for artists. On the Right Bank you can see the ❶ Museé du Louvre (see pages 118–123).

**The Louvre, one of the largest museums in the world, was once the residence of the kings and queens of France. It now houses an outstanding collection of art, from ancient times to the 19th century.**

After passing under the Pont du Carrousel and the Pont Royal you'll see the façade of the ❷ Musée d'Orsay (see pages 130–134) on the Left Bank.

**The museum, in the former Orsay railway station, displays fine and applied arts from 1848–1914. It has one of the best Impressionist collections in the world.**

The next two bridges are the Passerelle de Solférino, spanning the river between the Jardin des Tuileries and the Musée d'Orsay, and the Pont de la Concorde, built with stones from the Bastille prison, which was destroyed during the French Revolution. On the Left Bank is the home of the Assemblée Nationale, the 18th-century Palais Bourbon (see page 80), and on the Right Bank is ❸ place de la Concorde (see page 148).

**Place de la Concorde, laid out between 1755 and 1775, is the largest square in Paris. At its heart stands the city's oldest monument, an Egyptian obelisk 23m (75ft) high and around 3,300 years old.**

The boat passes under the ornate Pont Alexandre III, built for the 1900 Exposition Universelle and dedicated to the Franco-Russian alliance. On the Right Bank you can see the Grand Palais and Petit Palais (see page 95) and on the Left Bank, in the distance, is ❹ Les Invalides (see pages 99–101).

**Here you'll find the Musée de l'Armée, with fascinating displays of military art and equipment. Napoleon's tomb is in the Église du Dôme.**

After passing under the Pont des Invalides, the Pont de l'Alma and the Passerelle Debilly, the boat rounds a bend and you are greeted by a spectacular view of the ❺ Eiffel Tower (see pages 164–169) on the Left Bank.

**The tower, symbol of Paris, was constructed between 1887 and 1889, is 324m (1,063ft) high and has more than six million visitors each year. The views from the top are breathtaking.**

The Pont d'Iéna spans the river between the Eiffel Tower on the Left Bank and the Jardins du Trocadéro on the Right Bank. The boat passes under this bridge before turning and heading back in the opposite direction to the

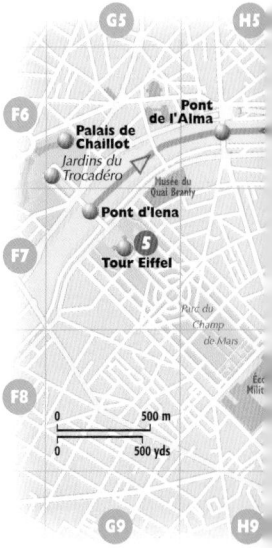


*Relaxing on steps leading down to the river (right).*
*Ornate Pont Alexandre III (below)*

Île de la Cité. As you sail along look out for the houseboats and brightly painted restaurant-barges moored along the banks of the Seine. You'll see the grand cupola of the Institut de France on the right before you pass under the southern side of the ❻ Pont Neuf.

**The 'new bridge' is actually the oldest in Paris, dating from the 17th century. It was the first bridge across the Seine to be built without houses on it.**

The next two bridges are the Pont St-Michel, leading to the Latin Quarter and the Sorbonne university (see page 163), and the Petit Pont, the smallest bridge in Paris. On the Île de la Cité you can see the beautiful ❼ Cathedral of Notre-Dame (see pages 137–141).

**Notre-Dame was constructed between the 12th and 14th centuries and is a masterpiece of Gothic architecture. Notice its impressive flying buttresses and its spire, 96m (315ft) high.**

Several bridges farther along the river, to your right, lies the Institut du Monde Arabe (see page 98) and the outdoor sculptures of the Musée de la Sculpture en Plein Air. The boat now turns to circle around the picturesque Île St-Louis (see page 98). After three more bridges, including the romantic Pont Marie, you can see Paris's town hall, the Hôtel de Ville (see page 95), on the Right Bank.

As the boat sails back along the other side of the Île de la Cité (and under another three bridges), you'll pass the city's oldest hospital, the Hôtel-Dieu, and the Conciergerie (see pages 89–91). Look out for the 16th-century clock, the Tour de l'Horloge, on the façade of the ❽ Conciergerie.

**Originally part of a royal palace, the Conciergerie later became a prison. More than 2,600 people held here during the Revolution were sent to the guillotine, including Queen Marie-Antoinette.**

The boat passes back under the Pont Neuf and the cruise ends where it began.

**BASICS**

☎ 01 46 33 98 38

🕒 10.30, 11.15, noon, and every half-hour from 1.30 to 6.30, then 8, 9, 9.30, 10 and 10.30, daily Mar–end Oct and Sat–Sun all year (except 1.30, 10.30pm Nov–Feb); Mon–Fri 10.30, 11.15, noon, 2, 2.45, 3.30, 4.15, 5, 5.45, 6.30, 8, 9 and 10 rest of year. Times may vary

€ Adult €9, child (4–12) €4.50, under 4 free

Pick up a free route map from the boarding platform

www.pontneuf.net

*Several companies offer boat trips along the Seine, including Bateaux Parisiens (above)*

**WHEN TO GO**

Evening is a great time to go on this trip, when the monuments are lit up. Day or night, try to go when the weather is good so you can sit on deck and get the best views.

**WHERE TO EAT**

There is a small bar on the boarding platform and vending machines on the boat.



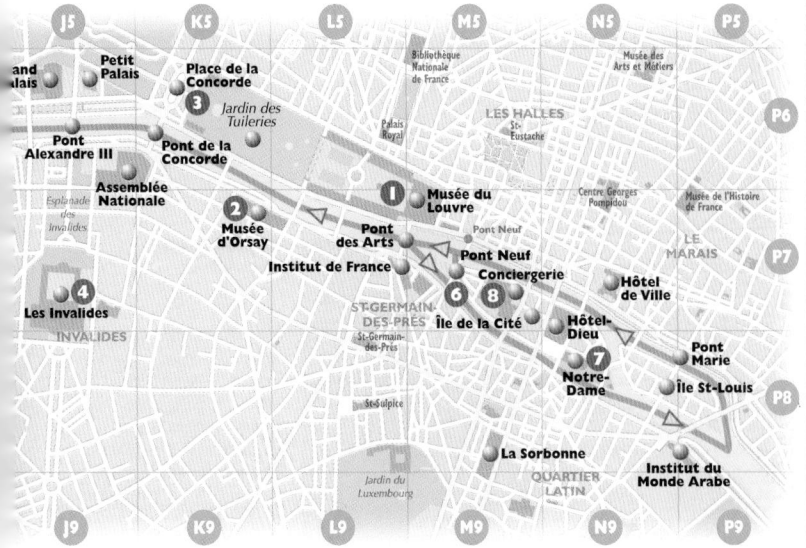

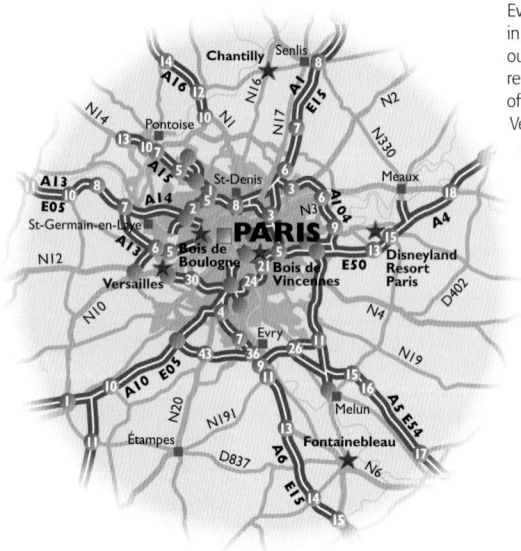


Even if you have only a few days in Paris, it can be worth venturing out of the city to see what the rest of the Île-de-France has to offer. The opulent palaces of Versailles and Fontainebleau, the art galleries of the Château de Chantilly or the woods of the Bois de Boulogne and Bois de Vincennes all make a pleasant day trip. If you have children in tow, you could take them to Disneyland Resort Paris, only a short train ride away.

EXCURSION ONE

# BOIS DE BOULOGNE

**The Bois de Boulogne is Paris's western lung, with 845 hectares (2,090 acres) of parkland, lakes, flower gardens, waterfalls and follies.**

OUT AND ABOUT

### Parc de Bagatelle

✉ Route de Sèvres à Neuilly
☎ 01 40 67 97 00
🕐 Daily, hours vary according to time of year
🚌 Porte de Neuilly, then bus 43 or 93; Porte Maillot, then bus 244
€ Adult €3, child (7–25) €1.50, under 7 free

### Jardin d'Acclimatation

✉ Boulevard des Sablons
☎ 01 40 67 90 82
🕐 Daily 10–7, Jun–end Sep; 10–6, rest of year
🚌 Les Sablons
€ Adult and child over 3 €2.50, under 3 free
www.jardindacclimatation.fr

### Jardin Shakespeare

✉ Pré-Catelan
🕐 Daily, hours vary
🚌 Porte Maillot, then bus 244

### Jardin des Serres d'Auteuil

✉ 3 avenue de la Porte d'Auteuil
☎ 01 40 71 74 00
🕐 Daily 10–5 (until 6 in summer)
🚌 Porte d'Auteuil
€ Adult €1, child 50c

### GREEN SPACE

The Bois de Boulogne lies just outside the *périphérique* and draws joggers, bicyclists and people who want to escape the city for an hour or two. There are cafés and restaurants, two lakes linked by waterfalls, follies, winding paths, an open-air theatre, two racecourses and more than 140,000 trees.

A highlight is the Parc de Bagatelle, on the northwestern edge. Its small chateau, built in 1775, looks out over a romantic park laid out by landscape gardener Thomas Blaike. There are more than 700 types of roses.

Farther north, the Jardin d'Acclimatation is good for children, with playgrounds, mini-golf, puppet shows, a toy train and the 'Explor@dome'.

Moving south, the Jardin Shakespeare has an open-air theatre staging productions in French and English, as well as a garden laid out with flowers, herbs and trees mentioned in Shakespeare's plays and sonnets.

In the Jardin des Serres d'Auteuil, in the south, 19th-century greenhouses shelter tropical plants. A short walk away is Roland-Garros, home of the French Tennis Open.

### BACKGROUND

Like the Bois de Vincennes on the eastern side of the city (see page 237), the Bois de Boulogne was used for hunting in medieval times, before becoming an aristocratic leisure ground in the 18th century. Napoleon III and his town planner Baron Haussmann were responsible for the park's current layout.

*The Bois de Boulogne is great for bicycling*

# BOIS DE VINCENNES

**The Bois de Vincennes forms the perfect antidote to hectic city life. Only a Métro ride from central Paris, it has three lakes, a historic castle, a beautiful floral park and one of France's largest zoos. On a sunny day, you may find it hard to drag yourself back to the city.**

## BASICS

**Château de Vincennes**

✉ avenue de Paris, 94300 Vincennes
☎ 01 48 08 31 20
🕒 Daily 10–noon, 1–6 May–end Aug; 10–noon, 1–5 rest of year. You are free to wander around the grounds, but admission to the chapel is by guided tour only. Tours, booked at the reception, are in French only. Ask for the English notes before you start
€ Grounds: free. 45-minute tour: €4.60 (under 18 free); 75-minute tour €6.10 (under 18 free)
www.monum.fr (French and English)

**Parc Zoologique de Paris**

✉ 53 avenue de St-Maurice, 75012
☎ 01 44 75 20 10
🕒 9–6 in summer (until 6.30 Sun); 9–5.30 in winter
🍴 ☕
€ Adult €8, child €5
www.mnhn.fr (click on *à visiter* then *parcs zoologique* to reach the zoo)

**Parc Floral**

✉ Off Esplanade du Château
☎ 01 73 04 75 75
🕒 9.30–8 in summer; 9.30–5 in winter
€ Adult €1.50, child €0.75; more expensive Wed pm, Sat, Sun
☕ Two cafés, open daily in summer, Wed and Sat–Sun in winter
www.parcfloraldeparis.com

## HOW TO GET THERE

The **Bois de Vincennes** is 6km (4 miles) east of central Paris

**Métro:** Château de Vincennes for the chateau and the Parc Floral; Porte Dorée for the Parc Zoologique de Paris

**Bus:** 46, 56, 115, 118, 124, 318, 325 for the chateau; 46, 112 for the Parc Floral; 46, 86, 325 for the Parc Zoologique

## CHÂTEAU DE VINCENNES

The Château de Vincennes has led a far from quiet life, despite its peaceful surroundings. Louis XIV spent his honeymoon within these walls, Winston Churchill attended a war conference in the underground chambers and the Germans executed prisoners in the courtyards during the Occupation of Paris.

Today, you can wander around the grounds and try to piece together the range of architectural styles, from the 14th-century medieval keep to the 17th-century classical Pavillon du Roi and Pavillon de la Reine and the 19th-century Pavillon des Armes. The keep is closed for restoration until around 2005, but you can take a guided tour around the chapel, based on Paris's Sainte-Chapelle. Inside you can see Paris's second oldest bell, the 700kg (1,540 lb) Vincennes bell, commissioned for the keep by Charles V in 1369. Whole sections of the chapel's windows were destroyed during the storms of 1999, although the stunning Rose Window survived unharmed.

## PARC ZOOLOGIQUE DE PARIS

Giraffes, penguins and pandas are not usually on the visitor's itinerary in Paris, but if you feel like a change from museums and monuments this could fit the bill. The zoo, part of the Muséum National d'Histoire Naturelle (see page 127), is home to around 1,200 animals. A highlight is the *Grand Rocher* (literally 'big rock'), a man-made mini-mountain, 65m (213ft) high, with goats careering up and down its slopes. You can take a lift to the top of the rock to enjoy an unusual view of Paris.

## PARC FLORAL

The floral gardens are a lovely place to wander after a visit to the nearby Château de Vincennes. The flower displays are exceptional and attractions for children include mini-golf, quad-biking and the Théatre pour Enfants (certain days only). The park has a striking dahlia garden, an iris garden, medicinal plants, a Valley of Flowers and forests of rhododendrons and azaleas. It also houses France's national collection of camellias and geraniums. A Jazz Festival gets the park jiving from mid-May to the end of July and a classical music festival is held in August and September.

## BACKGROUND

The Bois de Vincennes was a rich royal hunting ground in the 12th century, sectioned off by one of Philippe-Auguste's walls. By Louis XV's reign it had become a popular promenading area and in the 19th century Baron Haussmann landscaped it for the working-class population of eastern Paris. The woods suffered serious damage in the storms of 1999.

## TIPS

- **If your French is not very strong, think twice before embarking on the Château de Vincennes tour. Much of the route covers grounds in which you can wander freely anyway.**
- **The zoo is most crowded on Wednesday afternoons and at weekends.**

*A leafy street near the Château de Vincennes*

# CHANTILLY

**This fairytale Renaissance chateau, surrounded by a moat, sits in beautiful parkland and is home to an outstanding art collection.**

## BASICS

### Château de Chantilly—Musée Condé

✉ BP 70243, 60631, Chantilly
☎ 03 44 62 62 62
🕐 Museum and park: Wed–Mon 10–6, Mar–end Oct (park daily until 7, Jul–end Aug); Wed–Mon 10.30–12.45 and 2–5 (park open 10.30–5) rest of year
€ Museum and park: adult €7, child (4–12) €2.80, (13–17) €6. Park: adult €3.50, child (4–12) €2
Guided tours need to be booked in advance
Several to choose from, prices vary
? The Small Apartments can be visited by guided tour only. Buy tickets from the Gift shop.
Gift shop
www.chateaudechantilly.com (French, English; includes historical information and details of activities, events and temporary exhibitions)

### Musée Vivant du Cheval

✉ Grandes Écuries, BP 60242, 60631 Chantilly
☎ 03 44 57 40 40; information: 03 44 57 13 13; reservations: 03 44 57 91 79
🕐 Mon, Wed–Fri 10.30–6.30 (last admission 5.30); Sat, Sun and public hols 10.30–7 (last admission 6), Apr–end Oct (also open Tue 10.30–5.30 May–end Jun and 2–5.30 Jul–end Aug). Mon, Wed–Fri 2–6 (last admission 5); Sat, Sun and public hols 10.30–6.30 (last admission 5.30), rest of year.
€ Adult €8, child (4–12) €5.50, (13–17) €6.50
? Equestrian demonstrations (lasting 30 min) take place at 11.30, 3.30 and 5.30 (3.30 only, weekdays in winter)
www.musee-vivant-du-cheval.fr (plenty of information in English, including details of shows, events and demonstrations)

## HOW TO GET THERE

**Chantilly** is 40km (25 miles) north of Paris

**By train:** Gare du Nord to Chantilly-Gouvieux (30 min). It takes around 30 min to walk from the train station to the chateau. There are occasional buses or you can get a taxi from outside the station.

**By car:** Take the autoroute du Nord (A1) and leave on the Survilliers-St-Witz exit. Alternatively take the N16 or N17.

## OVERVIEW

The Château de Chantilly is one of the most picturesque castles in the region. It is surrounded by attractive parkland, with the forest of Chantilly beyond, and contains a magnificent art collection.

The town of Chantilly is one of the leading training venues in Europe for race horses and is home to a world-famous racecourse and the Musée Vivant du Cheval horse museum.

Chantilly has two culinary claims to fame—the delicious whipped and sweetened cream known as *crème chantilly* and the 17th-century master chef Vatel. He met a tragic end in 1671, when he committed suicide because he didn't have enough fish to feed the visiting Louis XIV and his courtiers.

## CHÂTEAU DE CHANTILLY

Chantilly was founded by a Roman named Cantilius but it was the famous head of the French army, High Constable Anne de Montmorency, who played a key role in developing the site in the 16th century. He decided to transform the medieval castle into a Renaissance chateau, and added the Petit Château, which still survives today.

Chantilly passed into the hands of the powerful Condé family in the mid-17th century and the prince, known as the Grand Condé, called in Versailles landscape architect André Le Nôtre to create the Grand Canal, lakes, waterfalls, ornamental ponds and a maze. The chateau became a popular venue for festivals and other gatherings, and literati who attended included Jean de La Fontaine and Molière.

During the Revolution much of the Grand Château was pillaged and destroyed and the building was used as a prison. In around1830 Henri d'Orléans, Duke of Aumale, inherited the property, then commissioned Honoré Daumet to carry out a major restoration in 1875. In 1886 the duke gave Chantilly to

*A winged statue on the Island of Love, in the English Garden*

*The Château de Chantilly dates from the 14th to 19th centuries*

the Institut de France, stipulating that his art collections should be preserved and the chateau must open to the public. The Musée Condé opened in April 1898, less than a year after his death.

**MUSÉE CONDÉ**

The art and furnishings on display here date from the Renaissance to the 19th century. The picture galleries have works by French, Italian, Dutch, English, Flemish and Spanish painters, in addition to 18th-century Chantilly porcelain and 19th-century Chantilly lace. Look out for works by Raphael, Jean Fouquet, Fra Angelico, Eugène Delacroix and Camille Corot. In a skylit room called The Tribune there are masterpieces by Antoine Watteau, Eugène Delacroix and Jean Auguste Dominique Ingres. The Psyche Gallery has 42 stunning 16th-century stained-glass windows and The Sanctuary exhibits Raphael's *Trois Grâces* (1500–1505) and 40 miniatures by Jean Fouquet (1445). The library has a vast collection of rare and important books—don't miss a reproduction of the illuminated medieval manuscript *Très Riches Heures du Duc de Berry* (15th century). The Chapel has beautiful stained-glass windows from Ecouen and the word *L'Espérance* (Hope) decorates the ceiling.

Tours of the Large Apartments take in the Prince's bedchamber, the Music Room and the Great Condé Victory Gallery. The sumptuously furnished Small Apartments of the Duke and Duchess of Aumale (guided tours only) were decorated in the 19th century with wood panels, marquetry furniture, brocade drapes and family portraits. The Small Monkey Gallery, painted in the 18th century, is covered in decorative panels with monkey motifs.

**THE PARK**

The grounds cover around 115ha (276 acres) and are ideal for strolling. Attractions include the Grand Canal, the waterfall, the 18th-century Anglo-Chinese garden, Le Nôtre's 17th-century French gardens, the Maison de Sylvie and the romantic English Garden with its Island of Love, Swan Lake, Temple of Venus and Beauvais waterfall. There is also the Enghien Castle, a children's play area, a kangaroo enclosure and Le Hameau (the Hamlet), built in 1774 for the Prince of Condé.

In the spring and summer you can sail along the moats and canals in an electric boat, take a nostalgic trip in a horse-drawn carriage or go for a ride on a little train.

**MUSÉE VIVANT DU CHEVAL**

The stables (Grandes Écuries), with their striking façade, were built for Louis-Henri, Duke of Bourbon, in the 18th century. According to legend, he believed he would be reincarnated as a horse after his death. The stables, 186m (610ft) long, were intended to accommodate 240 horses and more than 400 hounds for stag and boar hunts. Today they are devoted to the Living Horse Museum. Created in 1982 by Yves Bienaimé, this internationally renowned museum is considered the biggest and most beautiful of its kind. You can see horses of different breeds, equestrian exhibits, works of art and riding demonstrations.

**TIPS**

- **There are information cards in several languages in each room of the Musée Condé.**
- **Holders of a *Carte Musées-Monuments* (see page 307) receive free entry to the Musée Condé.**

**WHERE TO EAT**

**Château de Chantilly:** La Capitainerie restaurant and tea room (*open all year; closed Tue and evenings; tel 03 44 67 40 00*).

**The Hamlet:** Les Goûters Champêtres restaurant, serving regional dishes (*mid-Mar to mid-Nov; tel 03 44 57 46 21*).

**Park:** La Courtille, offering snacks, drinks and ice creams (*Mar to mid-Nov; tel 03 44 57 46 21*).

**Musée Vivant du Cheval:** Le Carrousel restaurant (*Sat, Sun and public hols, mid-Oct to early Mar; Wed–Mon, rest of year; tel 03 44 57 19 77*).

# DISNEYLAND RESORT PARIS

**Experience the magic of Disneyland—a must for kids of all ages.**

## BASICS

BP 100, Marne-la-Vallée, 77777 Cedex 4

01 60 30 60 30

**Disneyland Park:** Mon–Fri 10–8, Sat, Sun 9–8, Jan–end Mar; daily 9–8 Apr–early Jul; 9am–11pm, early Jul–end Aug; Mon–Fri 10–8, Sat–Sun 9–8, Sep–late Oct; daily 9–8, late Oct–early Nov; Mon–Fri 10–8, Sat–Sun 9–8, early Nov to mid-Dec; daily 9–8, mid-Dec to end Dec (9am–1am 31 Dec)

**Walt Disney Studios Park:** Mon–Fri 10–6, Sat, Sun 9–6, Jan–end Mar; daily 9–6, early Apr–end Aug; Mon–Fri 10–6, Sat–Sun 9–6, Sep–late Oct; daily 9–6, late Oct–early Nov; Mon–Fri 10–6, Sat–Sun 9–6, early Nov to mid-Dec; daily 9–6, mid-Dec to end Dec

1-day Theme Park ticket (valid for either Disneyland Park or Walt Disney Studios Park): adult €39, child (3–11) €29, under 3 free.

3-day Theme Parks Hopper Ticket (valid for both theme parks): adult €107, child (3–11) €80, under 3 free. Prices may vary according to season

P €8 per day; free if you are staying at a Disneyland Paris hotel

Shops and boutiques sell a huge range of items, including clothes, toys, books, ornaments and postcards

? Height and age restrictions apply to some of the rides

www.disneylandparis.com (packed with information in several languages, with entertainment schedules and details about hotels and restaurants. You can also book tickets)

## HOW TO GET THERE

**Disneyland Resort Paris** is 32km (20 miles) east of Paris

**By train:** RER line A runs from Châtelet-les-Halles and Gare de Lyon to Marne-la-Vallée/Chessy (around 40 min). The station is 100m (320 ft) from the entrances to both theme parks

**By car:** take the A4 motorway (Autoroute de l'Est), in the direction of Metz/Nancy. Leave at exit 14, to Parcs Disneyland

## OVERVIEW

Disneyland Resort Paris attracts millions of visitors to its two theme parks—Disneyland Park and Walt Disney Studios Park. The resort, in the Marne-la-Vallée countryside east of Paris, opened in 1992 to a blaze of publicity. It was Disney's fourth theme park, following in the footsteps of California, Florida and Tokyo. The Walt Disney Studios Park opened in 2002. Other attractions include the Disney Village entertainment complex, seven hotels and a 27-hole golf course.

## DISNEYLAND PARK

You can visit five different 'lands' at the 56ha (140-acre) Disneyland Park, each with its own themed rides, restaurants and shops.

Main Street USA takes you back in time with its nostalgic scenes from an American town at the turn of the 19th century. Seasonal parades bring scenes from Disney's animated films to life, with jugglers, clowns, dancers and, of course, the famous Disney characters (see the website for dates and times).

Fantasyland, especially popular with younger children, includes Sleeping Beauty's Fairytale Castle, the It's a Small World ride and the enchanting Pays de Contes de Fées canal cruise.

Adventureland boasts the swashbuckling Pirates of the Caribbean, Adventure Isle and the high-speed Indiana Jones and the Temple of Peril ride.

Frontierland, with its canyons, gold mines and rivers, offers two thrill-seeker attractions—the Big Thunder Mountain runaway train and the ghostly Phantom Manor.

Discoveryland was inspired by Jules Verne's visions of the future and the Mystery of the Nautilus

*You never know who you may bump into (inset, top right). It wouldn't be Disney without those famous ears (inset, right). Sleeping Beauty's fairytale castle (right)*

*Swashbuckling activities at Adventureland*

ride is based on the film *20,000 Leagues Under the Sea*. Reaching top speeds of 68kph (43mph), the Space Mountain–from the Earth to the Moon roller coaster is not for the faint-hearted. The spectacular Star Tours flight simulator whisks visitors onto an interplanetary journey.

**WALT DISNEY STUDIOS PARK**

The Walt Disney Studios Park is based on the concept of the popular Disney–MGM Studios in Florida. It is divided into four zones, each aiming to create the atmosphere of a real film studio. The 33m (105ft) water tower, crowned with Mickey's instantly recognizable black ears, dominates the Front Lot. Studio 1 in this zone gives an insight into what goes on behind the scenes in the world of cinema. In Animation Courtyard you can watch the Animagique 3D animated show in a 1,100-seat venue. Or, let yourself be whirled away on the Flying Carpets over Agrabah ride. The Production Courtyard offers the thrilling Catastrophe Canyon ride, while in the Backlot you can experience the excitement of the Rock 'n' Roller Coaster Starring Aerosmith and the fantastic Stunt Show Spectacular featuring cars, motorbikes and jet skis.

**DISNEY VILLAGE**

The entertainment complex Disney Village sits between the Theme Parks and the Disney hotels. The Village, open until the early hours, is bustling with themed restaurants, bars, shops, street artists and multi-screen cinemas. You could end the day with the popular dinner-spectacular Buffalo Bill's Wild West Show or dance the night away at Hurricanes nightclub.

**TIPS**

- **Disneyland Resort is easily accessible from Paris and makes a terrific day trip.**
- **Look for the information areas (City Hall in Disneyland Park and Studio Services in Walt Disney Studios Park), which provide entertainment schedules, maps and general information.**
- **The free FASTPASS system is available on some of the more popular rides, reducing waiting time.**

**WHERE TO EAT**

There are dozens of restaurants to choose from and the cuisine ranges from French, Italian and English to Bavarian, Mexican and, of course, American. There are waiter-service and self-service restaurants as well as an array of snack bars. Booking in advance is recommended for the popular sit-down restaurants.

All photography © Disney

# FONTAINEBLEAU

**The Château de Fontainebleau rivals Versailles in grandeur and historic interest but has the bonus of fewer crowds. It is steeped in regal and imperial resplendence, with 1,900 opulent rooms and exquisite landscaped gardens.**

## BASICS

✉ Château de Fontainebleau, Fontainebleau, 77300
☎ 01 60 71 50 70/60
🕒 Renaissance Rooms, Sovereign's State Apartments and Napoleon I's Imperial Apartment: Wed–Mon 9.30–6, Jun–end Sep; Wed–Mon 9.30–5 rest of year. Last admission 45 min before closing.
Small Apartments and Napoleon I Museum: guided tour only.
Chinese Museum: times vary.
Gardens: daily 9–7, May–end Sep; 9–6 Mar–end Apr, Oct; 9–5 Nov–end Feb
€ Adult €5.50, under 18 free, free to wander in the grounds.
Small apartments and Napoleon I museum adult €3
☛ See the notice board at the ticket desk for times. Audioguides are in French, English, Italian and Japanese, and cost €2.20 (€3.60 if you have received free admission to the palace)
ℹ 4 rue Royale (next to the Château de Fontainebleau bus stop); tel 01 60 74 99 99
**www.**musee-chateau-fontainebleau.fr (in French only, but easy to navigate if you have a basic knowledge of the language. If not, click on *Visite virtuelle* for photos of the highlights)

## HOW TO GET THERE

**By train:** Gare de Lyon to Fontainebleau-Avon, roughly every hour, on the Transilien line (around 45 min). From Fontainebleau-Avon station the A/B bus takes you to the chateau in around 15 min

**By car:** take the A6 motorway from the Porte d'Orléans and leave at the Fontainebleau exit

## OVERVIEW

Fontainebleau has witnessed some momentous events in French history, including the birth of Louis XIII in 1601 and Napoleon signing his deed of abdication in 1814. The site was popular with royalty as far back as the 12th century, when kings went hunting in the 17,000ha (40,800 acres) of forest. The keep in the Oval courtyard is the only remnant of a medieval castle dating from these times.

The pivotal period for Fontainebleau was the 16th century, when François I commissioned a sumptuous royal residence, enticed by the hunting opportunities. He employed the cream of Italy's artists and craftsmen to decorate the palace's interior and laid out the garden with lakes and canals.

A century later, the gardens were re-landscaped by André Le Nôtre, the man responsible for Versailles's stately parterres. Subsequent rulers put their stamp on the palace with numerous modifications, including Napoleon, who chose it as a suitably majestic base and had it completely refurnished in 1804.

## RENAISSANCE ROOMS

François I wanted Fontainebleau to be packed with prestigious art and this is reflected in the lavish decoration of Les Salles Renaissance.

The highlight is the Salle de Bal, the ceremonial ballroom, which hosted many a glittering occasion. The dazzling 30m (98ft) hall is decorated with wood panels and frescoes illustrating mythological and hunting themes. Vast windows bathe the room in light and give lovely views over the Oval Courtyard on one side and the Grand Parterre on the other. An imposing fireplace by Philibert Delorme stands at the far end. Pre-recorded Renaissance music helps you imagine the festivities once enjoyed here. In the Galerie François I you can see frescoes painted by the Florentine artist Rosso, a disciple of Michelangelo. For years they lay hidden behind other paintings and were rediscovered only in the 19th century.

## SOVEREIGN'S STATE APARTMENTS

Les Grands Appartements des Souverains are even more opulent than the Renaissance Rooms. Hardly an inch of space on the walls or ceilings has escaped intricate decoration. Don't miss the huge tapestries in the Salon François I and in the next-door Tapestry Room, created at the Gobelins factory. The ornate bed in the Empress's Bedchamber was made for Marie-Antoinette, although she never actually slept in it.

Napoleon Bonaparte converted the former king's bedchamber into a Salle du Trône (throne room) in 1808. The preposterously extravagant room is a decorative mixture of Louis XIII, XIV and XV styles.

## NAPOLEON I'S IMPERIAL APARTMENT

These rooms offer a fascinating insight into some of the more personal aspects of Napoleon's life, although they are not his private apartments (Small Apartments)—they can be seen

*The exuberant Galerie François I dates from the 16th century*

*You can go rowing on the Carp Pond in summer*

by guided tour only. His ceremonial bedchamber is suitably lavish, while the Petite Chambre à Coucher de l'Empereur is more humble, with a camp bed. This room doubled as Napoleon's study, as you can see from the large desk. The Salon Particulier de l'Empereur witnessed a key moment in France's history on 6 April 1814, when Napoleon signed his abdication papers at its round table.

**THE GROUNDS**

Fontainebleau's grounds are stunning and in good weather you should allow at least an hour to wander through them. For a self-guided walk (8km/5 miles), pick up the *circuit découverte* leaflet at the information desk.

A good place to start is the stately Cour du Cheval Blanc (Courtyard of the White Horse), at the entrance to the chateau. Napoleon bid farewell to his Imperial Guard at the horseshoe staircase here in 1814, before his exile on the island of Elba. The courtyard is also known as the Cour des Adieux in his memory.

To the right of the courtyard (as you face the chateau) is the Jardin Anglais (English Garden), dating from the early 19th century. To the left is the Jardin de Diane. From here, a pleasant stroll around the chateau leads to the elegant Grand Parterre, with its square central pond. Beyond is the 1.2km (0.75 mile) canal, created in 1606 by Henri IV. Be sure to continue round to the vast Carp Pond, separating the Jardin Anglais from the Grand Parterre and formerly used for water tournaments. In calm weather the reflections on the water are wonderful.

**TIPS**

- Gare de Lyon is a large station and finding the correct platform for Fontainebleau can be confusing. It helps to know that the lettered platforms are in the main concourse area, while the numbered platforms are at the far end of platform A. For a timetable of trains to Fontainebleau-Avon, ask at the ticket desk that deals with RER and Métro trains.

- Combined rail and entrance tickets are available.

- Holders of a *Carte Musées-Monuments* (see page 307) receive free entry to the castle.

**WHERE TO EAT**

There is no café, so bring your own refreshments. Picnics are allowed in the park, but not the gardens. There are cafés and restaurants in the town.

*The chateau, beautifully mirrored in the Carp Pond*

# VERSAILLES

**Versailles is France's ultimate royal palace, an opulent monument to the super-ego of the Sun King, Louis XIV. More like a town than a chateau, it was the seat of French power for more than 100 years and kept members of the royal family safely cushioned from their subjects in Paris—until the invasion of the bloodthirsty Revolutionary mob. Now the invaders are visitors, who come to see the lavish State Apartments and majestic, fountain-filled formal gardens.**

## BASICS

Versailles, 78000

01 30 83 78 00

Grands Appartements: Tue–Sun 9–6.30, May–end Sep; Tue–Sun 9–5.30 rest of year. Grand and Petit Trianon: daily 12–6.30, Apr–Oct; 12–5.30 rest of year. Gardens: daily 9–6. Fountains play: Sun 11–12, 3.30–5 Apr–end Sep (also Sat Jul–end Sep and other occasional days). Park: daily dawn–dusk. On public hols phone ahead to check opening times

See Getting Your Bearings, below

La Flottille (01 39 51 41 58) and La Petite Venise (01 30 97 19 44)

Café in the Cour de la Chapelle. Two snack bars in the grounds

Guided tours are available. Book at 9am. Audioguides for the State Apartments (€3.50) come in 8 languages. You need to leave a passport, credit card or driving licence as a deposit.

Entrance H is for visitors with disabilities. There is a lift to the State Apartments

Keep some coins available for the lavatories

www.chateauversailles.fr (in French, English and Spanish; practical information, historical background and photos. You can also check when the fountains are playing)

## HOW TO GET THERE

**By train:** RER line C takes 30 min to Versailles Rive-Gauche, followed by a 10-min walk to the palace. A mainline train from Gare Montparnasse takes 15 min to Versailles Chantiers, followed by a 20 min walk. The mainline train from Gare St-Lazare takes 25 min to Versailles Rive-Droite, followed by a 15-min walk

**By car:** take autoroute A13 to the Château Versailles exit, then follow signs

## GETTING YOUR BEARINGS

- Many people expect to be immediately overawed by the grandeur of Versailles, but instead, your first impression could well be confusion. The palace has a bewildering number of entrances and ticket options, and when you finally start the tour you'll find very few of the rooms have information boards. It's a good idea to rent an audioguide before you start.
- It's ambitious to try to see everything in one visit, but if that's your aim consider buying a *passeport* at the station in Paris (€20.80 Apr–end Oct, €14.50 rest of year). This covers train travel to Versailles Rive-Gauche or Versailles Chantiers and entry to the Grands Appartements (State Apartments), the Chambre du Roi (King's Chamber), the gardens, the Grand and Petit trianons, the fountain display and the Coach Museum; the Petits Appartements are excluded.
- For a less hectic day, limit yourself to the Grands Appartements (State Apartments; €7.50; entrance A), which include the King's State Apartment, the Hall of Mirrors and the Queen's Apartment. Then enjoy the gardens (€3 Mar—end Oct; free rest of year; €6 when fountain show is on; under 10 free).
- Optional extras include the Chambre du Roi (€4, including audioguide; entrance C, or C2 if you have a *passeport*); the Petits Appartements (reservations at entrance D; €7.50, plus €4–€6 for a compulsory tour). The

Grand Trianon and Petit Trianon (€5) are a 25-minute stroll away, or you can save your legs by taking the mini-train (adult €5; child (3–12) €3.20.

- A *Carte Musées-Monuments* (see page 307) gives free access to the Grands Appartements, the Grand Trianon and Petit Trianon.
- Entrance to Versailles is free for under 18s, and for everyone on the first Sunday of the month (October to end March).

**KING'S STATE APARTMENT**

The Appartement du Roi, part of the Grands Appartements, is a sumptuous shrine to the power and grandeur of Louis XIV. The ceilings are painted with scenes of thunderous gods and the walls

*The Latona Fountain (right), with the Grand Canal in the distance. The Treaty of Versailles, ending World War I, was ratified in the lavish Hall of Mirrors (below)*

*The Marble Courtyard*

are richly clad with marble and gilded bronze. Each room is dedicated to an Olympian deity symbolizing a royal virtue or duty. The sun god Apollo, closely linked to the cult of the Sun King (Louis XIV), gives his name to the throne room. The ceiling painting in the Hercules Drawing Room depicts 142 characters.

**HALL OF MIRRORS**

The Galerie des Glaces, also part of the Grands Appartements, bathes you in a sea of chandeliers, natural light and opulence. More than 350 mirrors catch the light pouring in through the huge arched windows, which in turn give spectacular views of the gardens and canal. The hall, 73m (240ft) long, was designed by Jules Hardouin-Mansart and completed in 1686. Since then it has served as a venue for royal wedding celebrations, a place for greeting foreign dignitaries and even a corridor. The Treaty of Versailles was ratified here in 1919. The omnipresent Louis XIV is depicted in the ceiling paintings by Charles Le Brun, showing episodes from the king's reign.

**QUEEN'S APARTMENT**

The Appartement de la Reine runs parallel to the King's State Apartment, with the Hall of Mirrors forming a lavish corridor between the two. In the Queen's Bedchamber the Queen suffered the ordeal of giving birth in public, to prove royal heirs were genuine. Marie-Antoinette was the last queen to occupy the room and portraits of her family decorate the walls. The exuberant feather-canopied bed is a copy. A poignant portrait of the queen with three of her children hangs in the Antechamber of the Grand Couvert. The empty crib refers to her youngest daughter, Sophie, who died before the portrait was painted.

**FOUNTAINS**

Versailles's fountains are famous and it is a pity that on most days they remain still. To catch them in full flow, visit during one of the *Grandes Eaux Musicales*. It comes as no surprise that Louis XIV's most-loved deity, the sun god Apollo, plays a prominent role. The Apollo Fountain, guarding the entrance to the Grand Canal, shows the sun god rising out of the water on a chariot, symbolizing the rise of the Sun King's reign. Closer to the chateau, the Latona Fountain depicts Apollo's mother asking Jupiter to turn the Lycian peasants into frogs. Don't miss the Neptune Fountain, past the North Parterre.

**THE GROUNDS**

Versailles has the largest palace grounds in Europe (100 ha/247 acres), tamed by André Le Nôtre into a geometry so perfect that even nature seemed to obey the Sun King's commands. Louis XIV sailed a flotilla of ships on the 1.6km (1 mile) Grand Canal—today, you can rent rowing boats.

**BACKGROUND**

Versailles had relatively humble beginnings, as a hunting lodge for Louis XIII. In 1661, Louis XIV

*Part of Le Hameau, a rustic hamlet built for Marie-Antoinette*

**TIPS**

- The busiest days are Tuesday and Sunday, as well as holiday weekends. The palace is closed on Mondays.
- A pre-purchased ticket (a *Carte Musées-Monuments* or a combined rail/palace *passeport*) allows you to avoid some of the queues.
- Be prepared for lots of waiting in line—for a ticket, for an audioguide and for the lavatories.

**WHERE TO EAT**

There is plenty of choice on site, with two restaurants, a café and two snack bars. On a summer Sunday it is best to book ahead for the restaurants. Alternatively, you can bring a picnic to eat in the park.

decided to move his court to the deserted swamp, 20km (12.5 miles) southwest of Paris, an astute way of isolating the nobility and his ministers while keeping an eye on his not too-distant capital. He brought in the greatest architects of the day, Louis Le Vau and Jules Hardouin-Mansart, and building work continued right up to his death in 1715. A town soon sprang up to accommodate the court and the smaller palaces of the Grand Trianon and the Petit Trianon were later created as a royal love nest. The building project put a severe strain on France's finances but the palace remained the seat of power until 1789, when a revolutionary mob seized Louis XVI and forced him back to Paris.

**VERSAILLES**

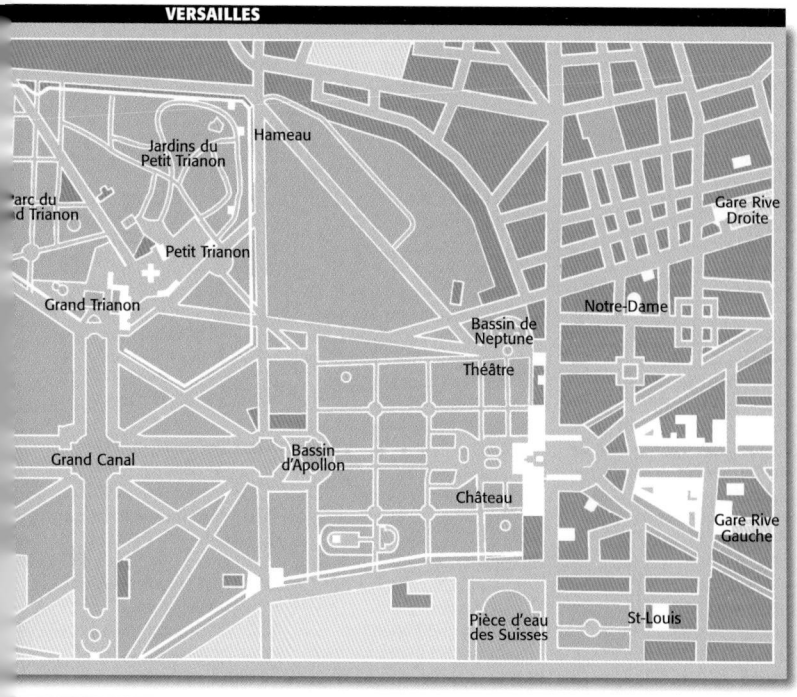

**No visit to Paris is complete without a boat trip down the Seine (see pages 234–235). Bus tours can also be worthwhile if you want a quick and comfortable introduction to the city. Alternatively, to really get under the skin of a *quartier*, try a walking tour.**

## BICYCLE TOURS

See page 59.

## BOAT TRIPS

### BATEAUX MOUCHES

Tel 01 40 76 99 99 (recorded information in English); 01 42 25 96 10 (reservations)
www.bateaux-mouches.fr
Board at the Pont de l'Alma for a boat trip down the Seine in a glass-roofed boat. The tour lasts one hour 10 minutes. Dinner cruises are available.
Daily every 20–30 min, 10am–11pm, summer. Daily 11, 2.30, 4, 6, 9, winter
Adult €7, child (4–12) €4, under 4 free

### BATEAUX PARISIENS

Tel 01 44 11 33 44
www.bateaux-parisiens.com
Take a one-hour cruise along the Seine in a glass-topped boat. Audioguides are available in 12 languages. You can also opt for a dinner cruise. Board near the Eiffel Tower.
Daily every 30 min, 10am–11pm, Apr–end Oct; every hour, 10–10, Nov–end Mar
Adult €9, child €4.10, under 3 free

### CANAUXRAMA

Tel 01 42 39 15 00
www.canauxrama.com
Take a trip along the picturesque Canal St-Martin, the waterway that featured in the 2001 film *Le Fabuleux Destin d'Amélie Poulain*. The trip, lasting two hours 30 minutes, starts at Port de l'Arsenal, at Bastille, and takes you up to Parc de la Villette. Book ahead.
Daily 9.45, 2.30 (in summer boats also leave from La Villette at 9.45, 2.45)
Mon–Fri: adult €13, child (6–12) €8, under 6 free; Sat, Sun €13 to all

### VEDETTES DU PONT NEUF

Tel 01 46 33 98 38
www.pontneuf.net
Cruises along the Seine, starting from the Pont Neuf. The trip lasts one hour and takes you up to the Eiffel Tower, and back down round the Île de la Cité.
See page 235
Adult €9, child (4–12) €4.50, under 4 free

## BUS TOURS

### LES CARS ROUGES

Tel 01 53 95 39 53
www.carsrouges.com
See the major sights from an open-top, double-decker bus, hopping on and off when you like at any of the nine stops. Commentary is available in French and English. The circuit lasts two hours 15 minutes.
Daily every 10–20 min, 9.30am–early evening
Two-day pass: adult €12, child (4–12) €7, under 4 free

### CITYRAMA TOUR

4 place des Pyramides
Tel 01 44 55 61 00
www.cityrama.com
Cityrama offers a two-hour city tour on a double-decker bus, with recorded commentary in 13 languages. Other excursions include Paris by Night, Versailles and Giverny.
City tour: daily 9.30, 10.30, 11.30, 1.30, 2.30, 3.30, summer; daily 9.30, 10.30, 1.30, 2.30, winter
City tour: adult €30, under 12 free

### L'OPEN TOUR

Tel 01 42 66 56 56
www.paris-opentour.com
Hop-on, hop-off open-top double-decker buses run four circuits—the Paris Grand Tour, Montmartre, Montparnasse and Bastille/Bercy. There is recorded commentary in French and English.
Daily every 10–15 min, first bus 10am, last round trip 6pm, Apr–Oct; daily every 25–30 min, first bus 9.30, last round trip 4, Nov–Mar
One-day pass: adult €24, child (4–11) €12, under 4 free; two-day pass: adult €27, child €12, under 4 free

### PARIS VISION

214 rue de Rivoli, 75001
Tel 01 42 60 30 01
www.parisvision.com
Paris Vision offer tours by bus and minibus. These range from the two-hour Discovery Tour around the city, with recorded commentary, to trips out to Versailles, Giverny and Chartres.
Discovery Tour: daily 10.30, 3.30
Discovery tour: adult €24, child (4–11) free

## WALKING TOURS

### MONUM

7 boulevard Morland, 75004
Tel 01 44 54 19 30
Walking tours (in French) across the city. The walks last 90 minutes and tickets are allocated on a first-come, first-served basis. Pick up a schedule from the tourist office or Monum museums.
Adult €8, child €6

### PARIS WALKING TOURS

Tel 01 48 09 21 40
www.pariswalkingtours.com
Take a two-hour walking tour through the city, with English commentary. Themes range from Hemingway's Paris to The French Revolution.
Call ahead for times and places, or look up the website
Adult €10, child €5

# Eating


| | |
|---|---|
| Locator Maps | **250–253** |
| Eating Out in Paris | **254** |
| Cuisine Guide | **255** |
| Menu Reader | **256–257** |
| Restaurants by Area | **258** |
| Restaurants by Cuisine | **259** |
| A–Z of Restaurants | **260–277** |
| Chain Restaurants | **278** |

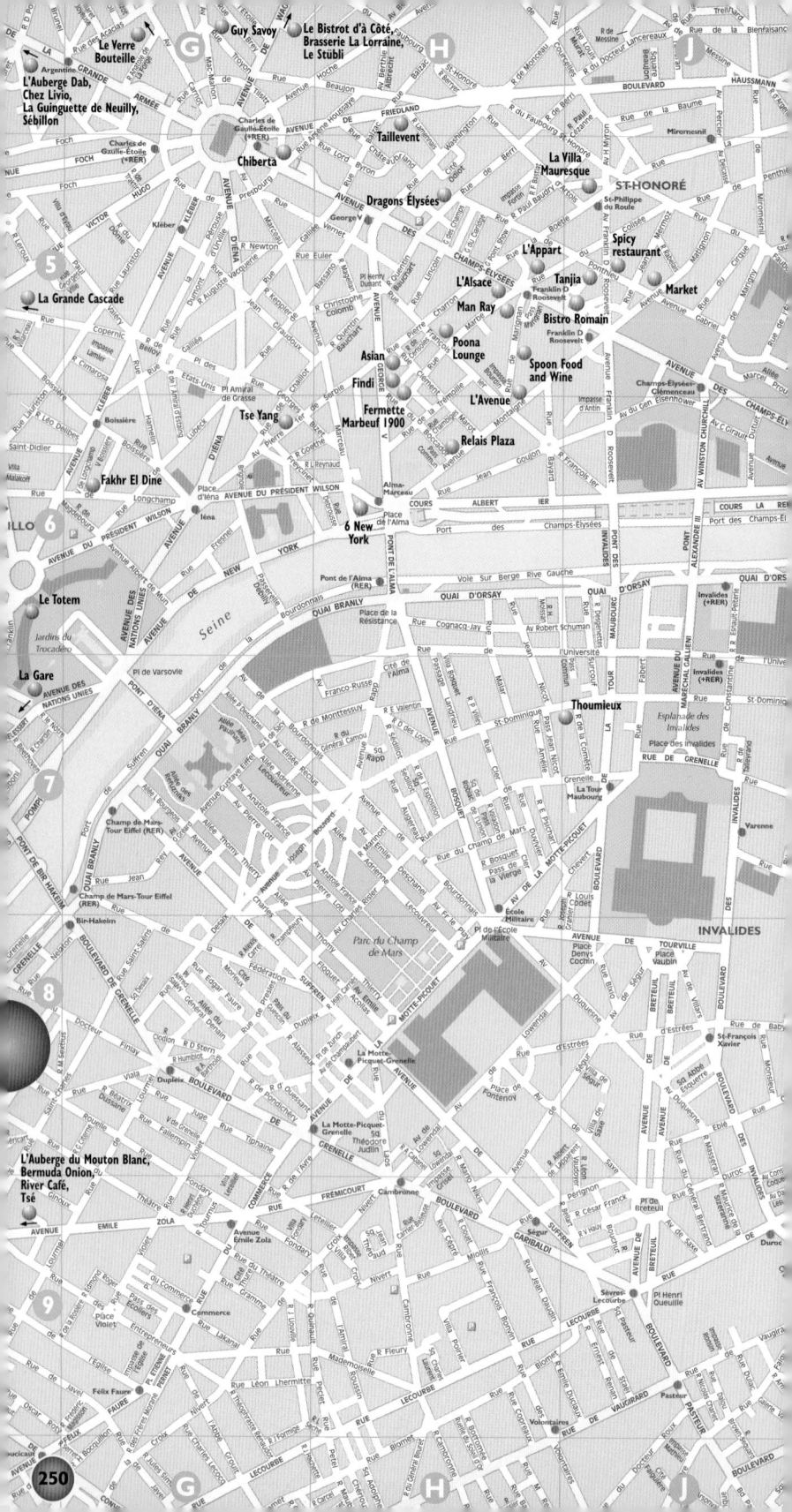
Le Verre Bouteille
Argentine
L'Auberge Dab, Chez Livio, La Guinguette de Neuilly, Sébillon
Guy Savoy
Le Bistrot d'à Côté, Brasserie La Lorraine, Le Stübli
Taillevent
Chiberta
Dragons Élysées
La Villa Mauresque
ST-HONORÉ
Spicy restaurant
L'Appart
Tanjia
Market
L'Alsace
Man Ray
Bistro Romain
La Grande Cascade
Poona Lounge
Asian
Spoon Food and Wine
Findi
L'Avenue
Fermette Marbeuf 1900
Tse Yang
Relais Plaza
Boissière
Fakhr El Dine
6 New York
Le Totem
Seine
La Gare
Thoumieux
Champ de Mars-Tour Eiffel (RER)
Bin-Hakeim
Parc du Champ de Mars
INVALIDES
L'Auberge du Mouton Blanc, Bermuda Onion, River Café, Tsé
Avenue Émile Zola
Commerce
Ségur
Pasteur
Volontaires
Sèvres-Lecourbe
Félix Faure
Duroc
Varenne
Dupleix
Cambronne
Place de Fontenoy
Place Denys Cochin
Place Vaubin
Esplanade des Invalides
Place des Invalides
Champs-Élysées Clémenceau
Invalides (RER)
Pont de l'Alma (RER)
Alma-Marceau
Place de l'Alma
Place de la Résistance
Place de l'Iéna
Place de Varsovie
Jardins du Trocadéro
Pl Henri Queuille
St-François Xavier
Pl du Brésil
Pl de l'École Militaire
École Militaire
La Tour Maubourg
Champ de Mars-Tour Eiffel (RER)
Iéna
Boissière
Ségur
Duroc
Varenne
Invalides
Pont de l'Alma (RER)
Alma-Marceau
Pl Henri Queuille
Sèvres-Lecourbe
Pasteur
Volontaires
Cambronne
Dupleix
Bin-Hakeim
Champ de Mars-Tour Eiffel (RER)
Thoumieux
Invalides (RER)
Pont de l'Alma (RER)
Iéna
Boissière
Ségur
Duroc
Varenne
Invalides
Pont de l'Alma (RER)
Alma-Marceau
Pl Henri Queuille
Sèvres-Lecourbe
Pasteur
Volontaires
Cambronne
Dupleix
Bin-Hakeim
Champ de Mars-Tour Eiffel (RER)
Thoumieux
Invalides

K
L
M
5
6
7
8
9
GARE ST-LAZARE
St-Lazare
Trinité
Notre-Dame de Lorette
Cadet
Le Peletier
Hausmann St-Lazare
Auber
Opéra
Chaussée d'Antin La Fayette
Richelieu Drouot
Grands Boulevards
Bonne Nouvelle
Hard Rock Café
La Taverne
Le Grand Café
Place de Capucines
L'Envue
Le Céladon
Madeleine
Ladurée
Il Cortile
Buddha Bar
Toraya
Maxim's
Concorde
Place Vendôme
Place du Marché St-Honoré
Jean-Paul Hévin
Grand Colbert
Muscade
Place des Victoires
Bourse
Sentier
Le bar à soupes
Au Pied de Cochon
Les Halles
Joe Allen
Pharamond
Chez Vong
Jardin des Tuileries
Tuileries
Il Palazzo
Palais Royal-Musée du Louvre
Place du Carrousel
Louvre-Rivoli
Châtelet
Châtelet Les Halles (+RER)
Au Pie de Chamea
Assemblée Nationale
Musée d'Orsay (RER)
Seine
Pont Neuf
La Monnaie
Solférino
Le Ferme St-Simon
Pont des Arts
Yugaraj
Relais Louis XIII
Le Paradis du Fruit
ST-GERMAIN-DES-PRÉS
Le Petit St-Benoit
Barroco
Jacques Cagna
Alcazar
La Rôtisserie d'en Face
Boulangerie Paul
Le Procope
St-Germain-des-Prés
Odéon
Coffee Parisien
St-Sulpice
Les Bouchons de François Clerc
Cité
Ile de la Cité
St-Michel Notre-Dame (RER)
Sèvres-Babylone
Café Cassette
Bouillon Racine
Villa Medici Chez Napoli
Vaneau
Rennes
St-Placide
Luxembourg (RER)
Jardin du Luxembourg
QUARTIER LATIN
Notre-Dame-des-Champs
Montparnasse Bienvenüe
Le Ciel de Paris
La Coupole
Vavin
Edgar Quinet
GARE DE MONTPARNASSE
Cimetière du
251

Brasserie Flo
Rital et Courts
Chez Prune
Chez Jenny
La Boulangerie La Mère Lachaise
Joe Allen
Pharamond
Chez Vong
404
Georges
Au Pied de Chameau
Le P'tit Gavroche
Trésor
Piccolo Teatro
Vins des Pyrénées
Hippopotamus
Bofinger
Blue Elephant
Le Bistrot du Peintre
Chez Paul
Barrio Latino
Les Grandes Marches
Nos Ancêtres les Gaulois
Les Bouchons de François Clerc
La Rôtisserie du Beaujolais
Tour d'Argent
Khun Akorn
Chai numéro 33
RÉPUBLIQUE
LES HALLES
LE MARAIS
BASTILLE
QUARTIER LATIN
Seine
Jardin des Plantes
GARE DE L'EST
GARE DE LYON
GARE D'AUSTERLITZ
252

1
2
3
4
5
6
Au Pied du Sacré Coeur
Cimetière de Montmartre
MONTMARTRE
L'Oriental
PIGALLE
Hard Rock Café
Brasserie Flo
La Taverne
Le Grand Café
Le Céladon
Ladurée
Il Cortile
Toraya
Jean-Paul Hévin
Grand Colbert
Muscade
le bar à soupes
LES HALLES
Joe Allen
Chez Vong
Pharamond
Au Pied de Cochon
Il Palazzo
Jardin des Tuileries
Seine
253

# EATING OUT IN PARIS

**Paris is often described as the capital of gastronomy so a meal out has to live up to a big reputation. France claims to have invented haute cuisine and the standard it sets for its best restaurants—the Michelin rosette—is famed throughout the world as the epitome of gastronomic excellence.**

Top chefs such as Alain Senderens and Guy Savoy dictate the food fads of tomorrow. Alain Ducasse even has an out-of-town cookery school where you can learn his fusion-food techniques, while the Cordon Bleu school in central Paris teaches the rules of classic cuisine. If your budget isn't up to the crème-de-la-crème of Paris's restaurants, there are hundreds of less expensive choices, from regional French cuisine to North African, Lebanese or Japanese. Be prepared to take time over your meal—good food is a way of life for many Parisians and meals are something to be enjoyed, rather than rushed.

### RESTAURANTS

Restaurants have higher prices than brasseries or bistros but will often provide a refined setting, elegant cuisine and a good wine list. For a special treat, look for multi-starred Michelin chefs such as Alain Ducasse and Guy Savoy. Dress smartly and book in advance. The *menu dégustation*, only found in the finest restaurants, is a prix-fixe menu offering a sample of the finest dishes accompanied by a selection of appropriate wines.

### BRASSERIES AND BISTROS

Brasseries are lively but informal restaurants that open long hours. Some have wonderful 19th-century settings. Popular dishes include *steak-frites* and *choucroute* (sauerkraut). Bistros are often small, family-run restaurants serving traditional cooking, with a limited choice of wines. A new breed of bistros is now springing up, launched by some of Paris's top chefs as satellite venues to their flagship restaurants.

### CAFÉS, BARS AND SALONS DE THÉ

Cafés and bars serve coffee, tea (not particularly recommended in Paris), soft drinks, alcohol and snacks. Most open from around 9am (some earlier) until well into the evening and many have outdoor seating, perfect for people-watching. *Salons de thé* (tea rooms) open from noon until late-evening and some are in grand settings (such as Ladurée, see page 270).

### CUTTING COSTS

If you are on a budget, have your main meal at lunchtime, when most restaurants serve a *menu du jour,* or daily menu, of two or three courses with a glass of wine for around 50 per cent of the cost in the evening. Most restaurants will offer prix-fixe meals in the evening with three, four or more courses, the best of which is the *menu gastronomique*.

### OPENING TIMES

Most restaurants and bistros keep strict serving times. Restaurants open at 12, close at 2.30, then reopen at 7.30. Most Parisians take an hour for lunch and either eat in the staff canteen or in a local bistro. The evening meal is the most important meal of the day and is usually taken *en famille* at around 9pm. Restaurants stop taking orders between 10pm and 11pm. If you want to eat later, try a brasserie or some of the venues in Les Halles area. Some restaurants close at weekends and during July and August.

### ETIQUETTE

Most restaurants include service in the price of dishes. This is indicated by *service compris* or *s.c.* If the service is exceptional you can leave a tip. Elegant dressing is part of French life and you should dress up to enjoy the experience that is a top class French restaurant. While few restaurants have a strict dress code, most Parisians dress smartly when they dine out. Address staff as *Monsieur* and *Mademoiselle*. By law, restaurants and cafés must provide a no-smoking section.

## REGIONAL FRENCH

The advantage of dining in Paris is that you can eat the great regional dishes without leaving town. Below is a quick guide to French regional cuisine. For the names of individual dishes, see the Menu Reader, pages 256–257. For restaurants serving regional French cuisine, see Restaurants by Cuisine, page 259.

Petit Chèvre Chaud, *made with goats' cheese*

### The Mediterranean

The sultry climate of Languedoc-Roussillon and Provence encourages wonderful fresh produce. The staples of dishes *à la Provençale* include wild herbs, virgin olive oil and garlic. *Ratatouille*—tomatoes, courgettes (zucchini) and aubergines (eggplants) cooked slowly in olive oil—epitomizes the cuisine of the region. In days gone by meat was tough (raised on the poor sun-shrivelled grasslands of the upper hills) and cooked slowly in casseroles such as *daubes* or *estouffades* to bring out the taste. The most famous is *cassoulet*, a slow-cooked dish of sausages and duck or goose with beans.

### The Pyrenees and the southwest

The cuisine of the southwest offers some of the quintessential French luxury foods—truffles (a fungus), cèpes (a form of mushroom) and foie gras (goose or duck liver). Unlike in the south-east, goose fat is the base of most dishes, the most famed of which is *confit d'oie* (preserved goose cooked in its own fat). Seasonal crops of walnuts and prunes are particularly prized, as is air-dried ham from Bayonne. Some of France's finest wines come from this region, including the *grand crus* of Bordeaux. Cognac produces the most exquisite French brandies.

### Brittany and Normandy

Brittany still looks to the sea for its culinary inspiration with excellent oysters, shellfish and fresh fish. The dish lobster *à l'Armoricaine* was invented in the Côtes-d'Armor. Lambs raised on the salt flats of the coastal plains around the Baie du Mont-St-Michel and the Cotentin Peninsula are said to have a hint of salt in their meat. Normandy's cuisine concentrates on two main products—pork and apples. Every morsel of the pig is used—even the intestines are transformed into delicious *andouilles* (sausages). Apples don't form the accompaniment to pork but are turned into excellent cider and calvados (apple brandy). Pancakes are the predominant desserts of the region and Normandy produces one of the country's finest cheeses, Camembert.

*Camembert cheese, from Normandy*

### Alsace-Lorraine

Alsace-Lorraine, in the northeast, has bounced between France and Germany for centuries and dishes like *choucroute* (pickled cabbage with sausage, smoked ham and pork) or *cervelas* (sausage) salad are popular, accompanied by wines such as riesling and gewürztraminer. Quiche Lorraine was invented here. Munster is a soft fermented cheese from the Vosges mountains, often with added cumin.

### Jura and the Alps

Until recently these mountain areas had to be self-sufficient in winter and prepared foods accordingly. They still have an excellent reputation for *charcuterie* (dried and prepared meats) and jams. Gratin and fondues are traditional winter dishes.

### Burgundy and the northern Rhône

Praised by the French as the birthplace of cuisine during the Middle Ages, Burgundy matches its top-notch wines with sublime dishes such as *boeuf bourguignon* (beef in red wine), *coq au vin* (male chicken in red wine sauce) and surprisingly delicious *escargots* (snails).

## VEGETARIAN

Traditional French dishes are usually meat or fish based, but some restaurants specialize in non-meat dishes (see page 259).

## WORLD

Paris has a vast selection of restaurants serving non-French cuisine, ranging from Italian and Belgian to Japanese, Chinese and Thai. North African dishes are popular and couscous restaurants can be found in every *quartier*. Couscous is wheat grain (coarse semolina) steamed over broth then heaped in a moist, buttery pile and topped with fresh vegetable stew. This comes with your choice of meat—the best bet is usually *brochettes d'agneau* (lamb kebabs) or *méchoui* (roast lamb). The other mainstay of Moroccan, Algerian and Tunisian cuisine is the *tajine*. Baked in a clay dish, *tajine* is a meat stew (lamb or chicken) with added olives, almonds, prunes and conserved lemons. You can find Chinese restaurants all over the city, especially in Chinatown in the 13th *arrondissement*. For kosher restaurants try Le Marais's Jewish Quarter.

## HAUTE CUISINE

Haute cuisine is top-quality cooking practised by chefs such as Guy Savoy and Alain Ducasse. In recent years it has been influenced by nouvelle cuisine, leading to lighter dishes.

### THE MEDITERRANEAN

...**à la languedocienne:** with tomatoes, aubergines, *cèpes* (a type of mushroom) and garlic.

... **à la niçoise:** with olive oil, garlic, tomatoes, onion and herbs, plus olives, capers, anchovies and tarragon.

... **à la provençale:** with olive oil, garlic, tomatoes, onion and herbs.

**Bouillabaisse:** fish stew served with *aïoli* (garlic mayonnaise) or *rouille* (chilli and garlic mayonnaise).

### BRITTANY, NORMANDY AND THE LOIRE

**Agneau de prés-salés:** lamb from animals raised on the salt marshes.

**Beurre blanc:** butter whipped with white wine vinegar and shallots.

**Châteaubriand:** a thick cut of tenderloin steak for two people with shallot, herb and white wine sauce.

**Coquille St-Jacques:** scallop served hot in its shell in a cream sauce topped with melted cheese or toasted breadcrumbs.

**Cotriade:** fish stew.

**Brandade de morue:** paste of salt cod mixed with milk, garlic and olive oil.

**Cargolade:** stew of snails in wine.

**Cassoulet:** a thick stew of haricot beans and garlic with goose and pork sausage.

**Daube:** meat stewed in wine.

**Foie gras à la toulousaine:** goose liver in pastry.

**Pistou:** sauce comprising ground garlic, basil and cheese bound with olive oil.

**Ratatouille:** tomatoes, onions, courgettes (zucchini) and aubergines (eggplants) slow-cooked in garlic and olive oil.

**Salade niçoise:** tomatoes, French beans, anchovies, olives, peppers and boiled eggs.

**Soupe de poisson:** a soup of puréed mixed fish.

### THE PYRENEES AND THE SOUTHWEST

...**à la basquaise:** meat served with Bayonne ham, cèpes and potatoes.

...**à la bordelaise:** with red wine sauce accompanied by mixed vegetables.

...**à la landaise:** dishes cooked in goose fat with garlic.

...**à la périgourdine:** accompanied by a truffle or foie gras sauce, or stuffed with truffles or foie gras.

**Confit de canard:** pieces of duck that are salted, cooked and then preserved in their own fat.

**Foie gras:** the enlarged liver of maize-fed geese or ducks, cooked and served in slices hot or cold.

**Lièvre à la royale:** hare boned and stuffed with bacon cooked in wine and served with a truffle sauce.

**Magret de canard:** boned duck breast, grilled or fried.

**Crêpes and galettes:** pancakes with either sweet or non-sweet fillings.

**Far:** a thick, sweet tart with prunes, similar to a flan.

**Homard à l'armoricaine:** lobster served flambéed in a cream and wine sauce.

**Moules marinières:** mussels in a white wine, shallot and parsley sauce.

**Noisette de porc aux pruneau:** loin of pork with prunes.

**Plat (assiette or plateau) de fruits de mer:** seafood platter consisting of mixed crayfish (*langouste*), oysters (*huîtres*), prawns/shrimps (*crevettes*), mussels (*moules*), crab (*crabes*) and whelks (*boulots*), served on ice.

**Sauce normande:** made with cider and cream.

**Tarte tatin:** upside-down apple tart.

### THE NORTH AND ALSACE-LORRAINE

**Bäeckeoffe:** mixed meat cooked in wine with potatoes and onions.

**Carbonnade flamande:** beef slow cooked in beer and spices.

**Choucroute garnie:** pickled cabbage cooked in wine with pork, sausage and smoked ham, served with boiled potatoes.

**Chou rouge à flamande:** red cabbage cooked with apples in vinegar and sugar.

**Jambon en croûte:** ham in a pastry case.

**Quiche Lorraine:** egg custard tart with bacon, onion and herbs.

**Salade de cervelas:** cold sausage in vinaigrette sauce.

**Waterzooi:** a soup originating from Belgium, made of a vegetable and cream stew, with either chicken or freshwater fish.

## BURGUNDY AND THE NORTHERN RHÔNE

**Andouille:** tripe and pork sausage served cold.
**Andouillette:** tripe and pork sausage served hot.
**Boeuf bourguignon:** beef slow cooked with onions and mushrooms in red wine.
**Boudin:** blood pudding/sausage.
**Coq au vin:** male chicken with mushrooms and onions stewed in red wine (traditionally Chambertin).
**Escargots à la bourguignonne:** snails in garlic and parsley butter.
**Jambon persillé:** ham and parsley in jelly served cold in slices.

## SAUCES

**Béchamel:** a classic sauce of flour, butter and milk. Often a base of other sauces such as Mornay, with cheese.
**Béarnaise:** egg-yolk, vinegar, butter, white wine, shallots and tarragon.
**Diane:** cream and pepper sauce.
**Chasseur:** hunter's style, with wine, mushrooms, shallots and herbs.
**Demi-glace:** brown sauce of stock with sherry or Madeira wine.
**...à la meunière:** a method of serving fish, fried in butter then served with butter, lemon juice and parsley.

**Pommes à la lyonnaise:** fried sliced potatoes and onions.
**Poulet de Bresse:** chicken from Bourg en Bresse (considered the best in France).
**Poulet (or jau) au sang:** chicken in a blood-thickened sauce.
**Quenelles de brochet:** individual fish mousses with cream sauce.
**Saladier à la lyonnaise:** cooked sheep's feet and pig's trotters, ox tongue and calf's head served with vinaigrette dressing.

## JURA AND THE ALPS

**Diots:** pork sausages.
**Fondue:** two different types: *au fromage*, cubes of bread dipped into molten cheese mixed with wine (and sometimes kirsch); or *bourguignonne*: cubes of meat cooked in oil, then dipped into sauces.
**Gratin dauphinois:** sliced potatoes baked in milk with nutmeg.
**Gratin savoyard:** sliced potatoes with cheese cooked in stock.

## CORSICA

**Aziminu:** a type of *bouillabaisse* (see The Mediterranean).
**Brocciu:** a sheep's cheese found only on Corsica.
**Fiadone:** cheesecake with lemon.
**Fritelles de brocciu:** fried doughnuts of cheese and chestnut flour.
**Oursins:** sea urchins, a local delicacy.
**Piverunta:** lamb stew with bell peppers.
**Raffia:** a skewer of roasted lamb offal.
**Sanglier:** wild or semi-wild pig.
**Tianu di fave:** pork stew with haricot beans.

## HOW TO ORDER STEAK

The French taste is for meat to be lightly cooked. Lamb will automatically come rare (unless you demand otherwise). If you order steak, you will be asked how you would like it cooked. The options are as follows:

**Bleu:** blue, the rarest steak, served warm on the outside but uncooked and cool in the middle.
**Saignant:** bloody, or rare, the steak is cooked until it starts to bleed and is warm in the middle.
**À point:** literally 'at the point'. The meat is cooked until it just stops bleeding. Many restaurants serve steak *à point* with some blood in the middle. Those who want a warm pink middle but no visible blood could try asking for steak *plus à point*. It's not an official French term, but good restaurants should oblige.
**Bien cuit:** 'well cooked', served with only a narrow pink middle. If you want no pink to remain, ask for it *bien bien cuit*, although your waiter may not be able to hide his disdain!

## RESTAURANTS BY AREA

These restaurants are listed alphabetically on pages 260–277.

**Auteuil**
L'Auberge du Mouton Blanc
La Gare
La Grande Cascade
Tsé

**Bastille**
Barrio Latino
Bistrot du Peintre
Blue Elephant
Bofinger
Chez Paul
Les Grandes Marches
Hippopotamus

**Belleville/Père Lachaise**
La Boulangerie
La Mère Lachaise
Rital et Courts

**Bercy**
Chai Numéro 33

**Champs-Élysées**
6 New York
L'Alsace
L'Appart
Asian
L'Avenue
Bistro Romain
Chiberta
Dragons Élysées
Fermette Marbeuf 1900
Findi
Guy Savoy
Man Ray
Market
Poona Lounge
Relais Plaza
Spicy Restaurant
Spoon Food and Wine
Taillevent
Tanjia
La Villa Mauresque

**Concorde**
Buddha Bar
L'Envue
Farnesina
Il Cortile
Ladurée
Maxim's
Toraya

**Grands Boulevards**
Brasserie Flo
Le Céladon
Le Grand Café
Hard Rock Café
La Taverne

**Grenelle**
Benkay
Bermuda Onion

**Les Halles**
Au Pied de Chameau
Au Pied de Cochon
Chez Vong
Georges
Joe Allen
Pharamond

**Île St-Louis**
Nos Ancêtres Les Gaulois

**Invalides**
La Ferme St-Simon
Thoumieux

**Latin Quarter**
Les Bouchons de François Clerc
Mavrommatis
La Rôtisserie du Beaujolais
La Tour d'Argent

**Louvre/Palais Royal**
Le Bar à Soupes
Café Marly
Grand Colbert
Jean-Paul Hévin
Muscade
Il Palazzo

**Le Marais**
404
Le Petit Gavroche
Piccolo Teatro
Le Trésor
Vin des Pyrénées

**Montmartre**
Au Pied du Sacré-Cœur
L'Oriental
Le Virage Lepic

**Montparnasse**
Le Ciel de Paris
La Coupole

**Mouffetard**
Marty

**Nation**
Khun Akorn

**République**
Chez Jenny
Chez Prune

**St-Germain-des-Prés**
Alcazar
Au Relais Louis XIII
Barroco
Bouillon Racine
Boulangerie Paul
Café Cassette
Coffee Parisien
Jacques Cagna
Le Paradis du Fruit
Le Petit St-Benoît
Le Procope
La Rôtisserie d'en Face
Villa Medici Chez Napoli
Yugaraj

**Ternes**
L'Auberge Dab
Le Bistrot d'à Coté
Brasserie La Lorraine
Le Stübli
Le Verre Bouteille

**Trocadéro**
Fakhr El Dine
Le Totem
Tse Yang

**Outside the Périphérique**
Chez Livio (Neuilly)
La Guinguette de Neuilly (Neuilly)
River Café (Issy-les-Moulineux)
Sébillon (Neuilly)

## RESTAURANTS BY CUISINE

**American**
Coffee Parisien
Hard Rock Café
Joe Allen

**Belgian**
Bouillon Racine

**Chinese**
Tse Yang

Guy Savoy
Jacques Cagna
Maxim's
Muscade
Le Procope
Relais Plaza
Taillevent
Le Totem
La Tour d'Argent

**French—Regional**
L'Alsace

**Japanese**
Benkay

**Latin American**
Barrio Latino
Barroco

**Lebanese**
Fakhr El Dine

**North African**
404

**French—Bistro**
Au Pied du Sacré-Cœur
Le Bistro d'à Côté
Bistrot du Peintre
Les Bouchons de François Clerc
La Boulangerie
Café Cassette
Chez Paul
Chez Prune
La Guingette de Neuilly
La Mère Lachaise
Le Petit St-Benoît
Le Petit Gavroche
La Rôtisserie du Beaujolais
Le Verre Bouteille
Le Virage Lepic

**French—Brasserie**
L'Auberge Dab
Bofinger
Brasserie Flo
Brasserie La Lorraine
Café Marly
La Coupole
Fermette Marbeuf 1900
Le Grand Café
Grand Colbert
Marty
Nos Ancêtres Les Gaulois
La Rôtisserie d'en Face
Sébillon

**French—Elegant**
Au Relais Louis XIII
Le Céladon
Chiberta
Le Ciel de Paris
L'Envue
La Grande Cascade
Les Grandes Marches

L'Appart
L'Auberge du Mouton Blanc
Au Pied de Cochon
Chez Jenny
La Ferme St-Simon
Pharamond
La Taverne
Thoumieux
Vin des Pyrénées

**Fusion**
6 New York
Bermuda Onion
Buddha Bar
Man Ray
Market
Spoon Food and Wine

**Greek**
Mavrommatis

**Grill/Rotisserie**
La Gare
Hippopotamus

**Indian**
Poona Lounge
Yugaraj

**Italian**
Bistro Romain
Chez Livio
Il Cortile
Farnesina
Findi
Il Palazzo
Rital et Courts
Le Trésor
Villa Medici Chez Napoli

Au Pied de Chameau
L'Oriental
Tanjia
La Villa Mauresque

**Pan-Asian**
Asian
Chez Vong
Dragons Élysées
Spicy Restaurant
Tsé

**Tea Room**
Asian
Boulangerie Paul
Jean-Paul Hévin
Ladurée
Muscade
Le Stübli
Toraya

**Thai**
Blue Elephant
Khun Akorn

**Trendy**
Alcazar
L'Appart
L'Avenue
Chai Numéro 33
Georges
Man Ray
Market
Poona Lounge
Spoon Food and Wine
Tanjia

**Vegetarian**
Le Paradis du Fruit
Piccolo Teatro

# Restaurants

The prices given are for a two-course lunch (L) for two people and a three-course dinner (D) for two people, without drinks. The wine price is the starting price for a bottle of wine.

**404**
Map 252 N6
69 rue des Gravilliers, 75003
Le Marais
Tel 01 42 74 57 81
This fashionable Moroccan restaurant is under the same ownership as Momo, off London's Regent Street. It serves excellent North African cuisine, including *tagines* and couscous, in chic Berber surroundings.
Daily 12–2.30, 8–midnight
L €35, D €68, Wine €20
Arts et Métiers

**6 NEW YORK**
Map 250 H6
6 avenue de New York, 75016
Champs-Élysées
Tel 01 40 70 03 30
This restaurant, named after its address, opened in 2002 and is reminiscent of an elegant Manhattan dining room.

The striking contemporary interior, with its sleek lines and light wood, is both stylish and peaceful, with subdued lighting from candle-shaped lamps. On the menu you'll find fusion dishes such as lobster and sun-dried tomato risotto, pork and bean casserole and black and white chocolate millefeuilles. The menu changes every three months.
Mon–Fri 12.30–2, 7.30–10.30, Sat 7.30–11
L €70, D €90, Wine €23
Alma Marceau

**ALCAZAR**
Map 251 M7
62 rue Mazarine, 75006
St-Germain-des-Prés
Tel 01 53 10 19 99
www.alcazar.fr
English designer Terence Conran's bar-restaurant is popular with a fashionable Parisian crowd. The key to its success? Some of the best fish

in the capital, a vast and elegant dining room and impeccable service. The menu also includes sophisticated non-fish dishes such as grilled lamb. Upstairs there's a lounge-bar where international DJs take to the decks. Perfect for a pre-dinner drink, Alcazar is also worth a visit for its excellent Sunday brunch, which comes with the option of a head massage.
Daily noon–3pm, 7pm–2am
L €44, D €90, Wine €16
Odéon

**L'ALSACE**
Map 250 H5
39 avenue des Champs-Élysées, 75008
Champs-Élysées
Tel 01 53 93 97 00
www.restaurantalsace.com
This little piece of eastern France is an integral part of the Parisian landscape and is open round the clock. Brasserie-style cuisine forms the menu, with a choice of seafood platters, sauerkraut, apple strudel and iced *gugelhupf* (cake). The interior is equally regional, with comfortable wall seats, inlaid wood and large mirrors. There is a pleasant terrace for spring and summer days.
Daily 24 hours
L €60, D €80, Wine €15
Franklin D. Roosevelt

**L'APPART**
Map 250 H5
9–11 rue du Colisée, 75008
Champs-Élysées
Tel 01 53 75 16 34
The unusual dining room in this two-floor house is like a comfortable library, lined with bookshelves and with beautiful Persian rugs covering the wooden floors. Expect inventive cuisine with a Mediterranean accent, such as pan-roasted veal in a creamy mustard and mushroom sauce. Before Sunday brunch, there's a children's brunch with a pastry workshop, the results of which you can take home.
Tue–Sat 12.30–2.30, 7.30–11.45, Sun–Mon 12.30–2.30, 7.30–11
L €40, D €60, Wine €20
Franklin D. Roosevelt

**ASIAN**
Map 250 H5
30 avenue George V, 75008
Champs-Élysées
Tel 01 56 89 11 00
www.asian.fr
This is a tea room by day and a bar-restaurant at lunch and dinner. The delightful interior uses pale wood columns, Chinese wall lamps and a forest of bamboo. The oriental cuisine includes dishes such as the Dragons' Duel (finely cut and marinated raw salmon and tuna with lemon) or *Chao Chao* (pork spare-ribs

marinated for three days and glazed with honey).
Tea room: daily 3–7. Restaurant: Sun–Fri noon–3, 7.30pm–1am, Sat 7.30pm–1am
L €50, D €120, Wine €25
George V

**L'AUBERGE DAB**
Map 250, off F4
161 avenue Malakoff, 75016
Ternes/Porte Maillot
Tel 01 45 00 32 22
This stylish brasserie is popular with the business crowd from the nearby Palais des Congrés, where trade shows are held. The menu focuses on traditional dishes, using seafood, fish and grilled meat. Wooden booths are perfect for those who want some privacy, and there's a lovely terrace for dining al fresco in spring and summer.
Daily noon–2am
L €80, D €100, Wine €15
Porte Maillot

**L'AUBERGE DU MOUTON BLANC**
Map 250 off F9
40 rue d'Auteuil, 75016
Auteuil
Tel 01 42 88 02 21
Molière, Jean Racine and Jean de La Fontaine were some of the famous writers who came here for discussions over a glass of wine. More than three centuries later, the place still has plenty of charm. Inside there are wooden panels, exposed bricks and elegantly laid tables. The menu has traditional, regional cuisine, including leg of lamb, calf's head and steak tartare.
Daily noon–3, 7–midnight
L €58, D €58, Wine €12
Michel-Ange Auteuil

**AU PIED DE CHAMEAU**
Map 252 N7
20 rue Quincampoix, 75004
Les Halles
Tel 01 42 78 35 00
www.aupieddechameau.fr
The Thousand-and-One-Nights décor takes you to a Moroccan souk. A spectrum of wool

hanging above your head, curios and handicrafts neatly displayed on carved wooden shelves and the entrancing smell of incense set the scene, but the show has just begun. It continues with performances by belly dancers, and could end in Casablanca, the nightclub in the basement, if you fancy a dance. The food reflects the North African theme, with traditional *tagine* (meat and vegetable stew) and couscous.
Daily noon–2, 8pm–1am
L €60, D €80, Wine €17
Châtelet

**AU PIED DE COCHON**
Map 251 M6
6 rue Coquillère, 75001
Les Halles
Tel 01 40 13 77 00
www.pieddecochon.com
This Parisian institution is a blessing for hungry night owls. It has been open around the clock, every day of the week, since 1946. Take your place in the elegant dining room, feast your eyes on the fresco-covered walls and the beautiful lighting, then your palate with one of France's

regional special dishes. Vegetarians will want to avoid the pig's trotters, the house signature dish. Seafood is plentiful and the French onion soup a must.
Daily 24 hours
L €46, D €100, Wine €17
Les Halles

**AU PIED DU SACRÉ-CŒUR**
Map 253 L2
square Caulaincourt, 75018
Montmartre
Tel 01 46 06 15 26
www.aupieddusacrecoeur.free.fr
As the name states, this restaurant is at the foot of Sacré-Cœur. Warm tones enhanced by indirect lighting and wooden furniture define the stylish, inviting interior. In fair weather you can eat out on the terrace. The cuisine ranges from traditional dishes such as pan-fried foie gras or grilled steak in pepper sauce to more innovative creations such as poultry stuffed with prawns. The finest French ingredients are always used.
Tue–Sun noon–3, 7.30–midnight
L €40, D €60, Wine €15
Lamarck-Caulaincourt

**AU RELAIS LOUIS XIII**
Map 251 M7
8 rue des Grands-Augustins, 75006
St-Germain-des-Prés
Tel 01 43 26 75 96
Manuel Martinez—previously chef at La Tour d'Argent (see

page 276)—set up his own restaurant in this 16th-century town house in 1996. There are exposed bricks in the vaulted cellar and beamed ceilings in the main dining room and in the upstairs salon. The rich menu includes lobster, foie gras, cep ravioli and vanilla and whisky millefeuilles.
Tue–Sat noon–2.30, 7.30–10.30
L €90, D €150, Wine €30
Odéon

**L'AVENUE**
Map 250 H6
41 avenue Montaigne, 75008
Champs-Élysées
Tel 01 40 70 14 91
This restaurant is the haunt of film stars and models, and the *cantina* for designers from the nearby couture house, Dior. It is one of the hippest places in town and its stylish interior is both contemporary and elegant, with burgundy velvet armchairs and wall seats and handsome white candelabra. Although people-watching is the main activity here, the food is also worth your attention. Seafood fans should enjoy the crab mille-feuille and tuna steak with balsamic vinegar sauce. The chocolate cake is delectable.
Daily noon–12.30am
L €70, D €100, Wine €19
Alma-Marceau

**LE BAR À SOUPES**
Map 251 M6
5 rue Hérold, 75001
Louvre/Palais Royal
Tel 01 45 08 49 84
At this venue, a few steps from the Palais Royal and the Louvre, you can choose from six varieties of fresh soup each day, with options including curried tomato and red bean, and coconut milk and carrot. Inside it's like a simple but charming *cantina*, with wooden tables and chairs, large paintings of vegetables and exposed brick walls. The restaurant is completely non-smoking. There is also a Bar à Soupes at Bastille.
Mon–Fri noon–3.30
Bowl of soup €5
Sentier, Palais Royal Musée du Louvre

**BARRIO LATINO**
Map 252 Q8
46 rue du Faubourg St-Antoine, 75012
Bastille
Tel 01 55 78 84 75
A hit with the fashionable crowd, this bar-restaurant would like to take you to Cuba, or rather, to a funky, kitsch version of the real thing. Look out for the Che Guevara mosaic on the fourth floor. Try a Tequila Special or a Mojito at one of the cocktail bars, then sample some Mexican-style food, including guacamole, chicken *quesadillas* (folded tortillas filled with meat or vegetables) and more.
Daily 11.30am–2am
L €37, D €74, Wine €15
Bastille

**BARROCO**
Map 251 M7
23 rue Mazarine, 75006
St-Germain-des-Prés
Tel 01 43 26 40 24
This is chic Brasilia, in perfect harmony with its stylish district, and in contrast to some other Parisian venues with a South American theme, where kitsch and fun are de rigueur. The welcoming interior has comfortable striped velvet armchairs, wooden tables, elegant tableware and a library. The cuisine is equally good, combining Brazilian zest with French delicacy. The menu includes fish and seafood cooked in coconut milk, lamb ribs and sweet potatoes. There is live South American music on Tuesdays and Fridays.
Tue–Sat 7pm–2am, Sun–Mon 5pm–12.30am
No lunch, D €76, Wine €16
Odéon

**BENKAY**
Map 250 off F8
61 quai de Grenelle, 75015
Grenelle
Tel 01 40 58 21 26
You can enjoy good *teppan-yaki* and panoramic views from this modern Japanese restaurant, on the 4th floor of the Novotel Paris Tour Eiffel. The set lunch menus are reasonably priced.
Daily 12–2, 7–10
L €60, D €120, Wine €23
Bir Hakeim

**BERMUDA ONION**
Map 250 off F9
16 rue Linois, 75015
Grenelle
Tel 01 45 75 11 11
This restaurant is close to one of Paris's miniature Statues of Liberty, copies of the original statue given to America. It has a bright and airy veranda with modern, elegant furniture and a stunning view of the Seine. The cuisine reinterprets French classics. Try duck in vanilla sauce with fresh fruit, or pineapple carpaccio with a pina colada sorbet. It's one of the places to be seen in, especially for Sunday brunch, and there's a DJ every night.
Mon–Sat 8pm–2am, Sun noon–4, 8pm–2am
L €60, D €80, Wine €16
Charles-Michels

**BISTRO ROMAIN**
Map 250 J5
26 avenue des Champs-Élysées, 75008
Champs-Élysées
Tel 01 53 75 17 84
Drapes, classical-style paintings and subdued lighting set the baroque tone here, reminiscent of an Italian opera house. The menu is not quite so refined, not venturing far from bowls of pasta, but those with big appetites will be delighted to learn that the carpaccio and chocolate mousse come on an all-you-can-eat basis. There are 12 Bistro Romains in Paris.
Daily 11.30am–1am
L €30, D €40, Wine €14
Franklin D. Roosevelt

**LE BISTROT D'À CÔTÉ**
Map 250 off G4
10 rue Gustave Flaubert, 75017
Ternes
Tel 01 42 67 05 81
www.michelrostang.com
This is part of a small chain of bistros created by chef Michel Rostang, offering high-quality regional cooking. A large blackboard in the dining room displays the specials, which vary according to what's available in the market. Hearty dishes include pig's trotters or chicken with mashed potatoes. The interior is typical bistro-style and there is an interesting collection of curios.
Daily noon–2.30, 7–11
L €60, D €80, Wine €15
Courcelles

**BISTROT DU PEINTRE**
Map 252 off Q8
116 avenue Ledru-Rollin, 75011
Bastille
Tel 01 47 00 34 39
This beautiful art nouveau bistro, established in 1903, has wood panels, soft lighting and large mirrors. Not surprisingly, the 'painter's bistro' displays numerous paintings, including a beautiful oil of La Goulue, the celebrated cancan dancer. You can eat in the welcoming bar, which has a couple of tables in the first room, in the other dining room upstairs or on the small terrace in spring and summer. The high-quality traditional French cuisine includes chicory, diced bacon and poached egg salad, duck à l'orange and steak tartare.
Daily noon–midnight
L €50, D €60, Wine €11
Ledru Rollin

**BLUE ELEPHANT**
Map 252 Q7
43 rue de la Roquette, 75011
Bastille
Tel 01 47 00 42 00
www.blueelephant.com
This venue, in the fashionable Bastille district, is part of a small international chain of Blue Elephant restaurants. Here, the beautifully laid wooden tables are set in the middle of a small jungle, surrounded by luxurious plants and cascading water. The menu offers the very best of Thai cuisine, prepared by a team of more than a dozen chefs. Typical dishes include chicken soufflé in banana leaves and *chiang rai* (minced pork with green peppers).
Mon–Fri noon–2.30, 7–midnight, Sat 7–midnight, Sun noon–2.30, 7–11
L €60, D €100, Wine €15
Bastille

**BOFINGER**
Map 252 Q8
5–7 rue de la Bastille, 75004
Bastille
Tel 01 42 72 87 82
This elegant brasserie, which claims to be the oldest in Paris, has a lavish art nouveau interior with an impressive stained-glass ceiling, mirrors, plenty of carved wood and lots of plants. The beautifully prepared French classic dishes

include lobster, oysters, duck, steak tartare and *choucroute* (sauerkraut).
Mon–Fri noon–3, 6.30pm–1am, Sat–Sun noon–1am
L €40, D €60, Wine €22
Bastille

**LES BOUCHONS DE FRANÇOIS CLERC**
Map 252 N8
12 rue de l'Hôtel Colbert, 75005
Latin Quarter
Tel 01 43 54 15 34
www.lesbouchonsdefrancoisclerc.com
Masterminded by chef François Clerc, this small chain of restaurants (there are five in Paris) boasts France's least expensive fine wine list, and probably also one of the most comprehensive, with about 400 vintages. Fine French cuisine is also on the menu: beef carpaccio, foie gras, veal kidneys with garlic and parsley and crème brûlée. Each branch of the chain has its own character. At this address, the dining room is in an elegant 18th-century mansion, with beamed ceilings, exposed brick and a vaulted cellar.
Mon–Fri noon–2.30, 7–10.30, Sat 7-10.30
L €56, D €82, Wine €12
St-Michel, Maubert Mutualité

**BOUILLON RACINE**
Map 251 M8
3 rue Racine, 75006
St-Germain-des-Prés
Tel 01 44 32 15 60

The bright and airy dining room here is in a listed historic building, with a dazzling art nouveau interior. There are wrought-iron chairs and candelabra, emerald green wall tiles and plenty of mirrors. The excellent Belgian food includes *waterzooi* (traditional Belgian soup) and shrimp croquettes. As you would expect in a Belgian restaurant, there is a comprehensive range of beers.
Daily noon–2.15, 7.30–11
L €30, D €80, Wine €25
Cluny La Sorbonne, Odéon

**LA BOULANGERIE**
Map 252 off Q6
15 rue des Panoyaux, 75020
Belleville/Père Lachaise
Tel 01 43 58 45 45
www.restaulaboulangerie.com
This is an unpretentious little bistro with good food and a convivial atmosphere. It's housed in a former bakery and retains many of its original features, such as the bright floor tiling. Various curios add to the character of the place. The menu is traditional French and changes every two months. Popular dishes include duck à l'orange, the ubiquitous grilled steak and chocolate cake.
Mon–Fri noon–3, 7.30–10.30, Sat 7.30–10.30
L €40, D €60, Wine €14
Père Lachaise

**BOULANGERIE PAUL**
Map 251 L8
77 rue de Seine, 75006
St-Germain-des-Prés
Tel 01 55 42 02 23
This bakery, on the same street as a lively fruit and vegetable market, sells a range of breads, including multi-grains, onion and even bacon bread. The pastries are just as appetizing and you can eat or have a tea, coffee or hot chocolate sitting on leather chairs at rustic wooden tables, enjoying the smell of freshly baked bread.
Daily 7.30am–8pm
Tea €3, slice of cake €4
Odéon

**BRASSERIE FLO**
Map 252 N5
7 cour des Petites Écuries, 75010
Grands Boulevards
Tel 01 47 70 13 59
Brasserie Flo is a Parisian institution, established in 1886. It is housed in a listed building with a wonderful turn-of-the-century interior, with stained-glass panels, green leather booths and wooden panels on the ceiling. The actress Sarah Bernhardt was a regular here when she performed at the nearby Théâtre de la Renaissance. The menu includes steak, fresh seafood and Alsatian special dishes such as sauerkraut. For dessert, try the profiteroles or *vacherin* (ice cream and meringue).

Daily noon–3, 7pm–1.30am
L €50, D €80, Wine €25
Château-d'Eau

**BRASSERIE LA LORRAINE**
Map 250 G4
2 place des Ternes, 75008
Ternes
Tel 01 56 21 22 00
www.brasserielalorraine.com
This brasserie, at the foot of the Arc de Triomphe, explores regional French cuisine, with

the menu including *choucroute* (sauerkraut) and Burgundy snails. The restaurant has been around for 70 years and its main attraction is seafood, with sea urchin and oysters on the menu. There's even a take-out service at the seafood bar. The elegant dining room is bright and has a retro feel, with red padded seats and 1950s-style lighting fixtures. There are also plenty of tables outside for spring and summer dining.
Daily 11.30am–12.30am
L €60, D €100, Wine €20
Place des Ternes

**BUDDHA BAR**
Map 251 K5
8 rue Boissy d'Anglas, 75008
Concorde
Tel 01 53 05 90 00
Buddha Bar is just off the place de la Concorde. It is popular with the business and fashion crowd and the strict door policy reflects this. Once inside, expect the exotic and the kitsch, but be aware that this is not a place for

meditation. There is a bar upstairs and a restaurant downstairs, run by a Japanese-Californian chef who creates high-quality imaginative fusion food. The menu changes every four months and includes Peking-style duck, seared tuna in a sesame crust, and desserts such as chocolate cake and lemon pie.
Mon–Fri noon–3, 6pm–2am, Sat–Sun 6pm–2am
L €64, D €120, Wine €14
Concorde

**CAFÉ CASSETTE**
Map 251 L8
73 rue de Rennes, 75006
St-Germain-des-Prés
Tel 01 45 48 53 78
This modern venue is not far from the place St-Sulpice and is good for a meal in all weathers. It has a large terrace with bistro tables and chairs, a veranda with conical orange lighting fixtures, a bar and a comfortable salon. There are three menus, one for the restaurant, with salmon tartare and grilled steak, one for the café, with lighter dishes such as salads and club sandwiches,

and one for those who just want a drink or desserts.
Daily 7am–1am
L €26, D €40, Wine €15
St-Sulpice, Rennes

**CAFÉ MARLY**
Map 251 L6
93 rue de Rivoli, 75001
Louvre/Palais Royal
Tel 01 49 26 06 60

There are wonderful views of the Louvre pyramid from this elegant brasserie, whose interior covers contemporary minimalism and Napoleon III style. There are sleek armchairs whose backs are adorned with gold rings and gilt-edged black wood panels. The menu has typical brasserie food with the occasional more modern offering such as rare tuna in a sesame crust or steak tartare.
Daily 8am–1.15am
L €70, D €100, Wine €20
Palais-Royal/Musée du Louvre

**LE CÉLADON**
Map 251 L5
15 rue Daunou, 75002
Grands Boulevards
Tel 01 47 03 40 42
www.leceladon.com
Celadon (willow-green) lends tone to every aspect of this stylish restaurant. You'll find this pale green on the Chinese porcelain curios that decorate the dining room, and on the fabric which covers the Regency-style armchairs. This refinement is matched by chef Christophe Moisand's cuisine, an interesting variation on

some French classics. Green asparagus is served in a nutty sauce, roasted veal is accompanied by capers and dried tomatoes and, for dessert, you'll need an open mind to try the unusual upside-down tomato and candied olive tart with olive oil ice cream.
Mon–Fri noon–2, 7.30–10
L €90, D €118, Wine €17
Opéra

**CHAI NUMÉRO 33**
Map 252 off Q9
33 cour St-Emilion, 75012
Bercy
Tel 01 53 44 01 01
www.chai33.com
This former wine and spirit storehouse is in the middle of Bercy, a district once home to Paris's warehouses. It has been refurbished in contemporary style, with soft brown armchairs and water lily-shaped wooden tables. Some original features have been retained, such as the exposed brick walls and the wine cellar. You'll be invited by the wine waiter to visit the cellar to choose the best accompaniment to your meal. The menu includes steamed fish served with potatoes, and steak tartare.
Daily 11.45–3, 7–midnight
L €40, D €70, Wine €15
Cour St-Emilion

**CHEZ JENNY**
Map 252 P6
39 boulevard du Temple, 75003
République
Tel 01 44 54 39 00
www.chez-jenny.com

Chez Jenny is named after the Alsatian Robert Jenny, who established the restaurant in 1930, not far from place de la République. Several types of sauerkraut are on offer—including one with champagne—and you can also choose seafood and special dishes such as saveloy sausage salad. Desserts include iced *gugelhupf* (cake) with egg custard. The decoration also pays tribute to the northeastern region of France, with frescos depicting its landscapes and marquetry by regional artist Charles Spindler.
Daily noon–1am
L €50, D €70, Wine €14
République

**CHEZ LIVIO**
Map 250 off F4
6 rue de Longchamp, 92200
Neuilly-sur-Seine
Neuilly
01 46 24 81 32
This little piece of Italy reflects the warmth and conviviality of its nation. The tables are on a terrace which is uncovered as soon as weather permits. It is a beautiful setting, with green, trellis-covered walls, black-and-white floor tiling, red woven osier chairs and matching tablecloths.
The traditional Italian cuisine includes mushroom risotto, fresh pasta and breaded veal escalope. Chez Livio is definitely one of the liveliest venues in this chic, residential district.
Daily midday–2.30, 7–10.45pm
L €30, D €50, Wine €11
Pont-de-Neuilly

**CHEZ PAUL**
Map 252 Q8
13 rue de Charonne, 75011
Bastille
Tel 01 47 00 34 57
This charming little bistro, not to be confused with the restaurant of the same name on rue de la Butte-aux-Cailles, was formerly an artisans' haunt, at the time when the Bastille area was famous for its furniture industry. It still looks authentic, although the clientele today is far more fashion-conscious. The menu includes good, French staples such as *gratin dauphinois* (sliced potatoes baked with cream) and grilled steak.
Daily noon–12.30am
L €40, D €70, Wine €13
Bastille

**CHEZ PRUNE**
Map 252 P5
36 rue Beaurepaire, 75010
République
Tel 01 42 41 30 47
The terrace at this bistro gives lovely views of the Canal St-Martin. The interior reflects the owner's enthusiasm for salvaging items from second-hand shops. The bistro is perfect for a drink or a light bite (try a cheese and cold meat platter) or for brunch, a feast of croissant, scrambled eggs, ham, salmon, orange juice and tea or coffee.

Daily 8am–2am
Cold meat or cheese plate €7, brunch €15
Jacques Bonsergent, République

**CHEZ VONG**
Map 253 N6
10 rue de la Grande Truanderie, 75001
Les Halles
Tel 01 40 26 09 36
This exotic, elegant Chinese restaurant is on a pedestrian-only street in the bustling Les Halles district. Inside there are lanterns and candles, dark wood, exposed brick walls and a profusion of tropical plants. Chef-proprietor Vai-Kuan Vong has created a menu that

includes both Cantonese and Vietnamese cuisine. The lobster with ginger and the pigeon are surprisingly good.
Mon–Sat noon–2.30, 7pm–12.30am
L €50, D €90, Wine €15
Châtelet-Les-Halles

**CHIBERTA**
Map 250 G5
3 rue Arsène-Houssaye, 75008
Champs-Élysées
Tel 01 53 53 42 00
www.lechiberta.com
Chef Eric Coisel's cuisine follows the seasons, but you can expect the same high quality (and prices) all year round. Indulgent dishes include black truffle cooked in champagne and served on toast with a Madeira butter. The discreetly elegant interior has tawny hues, neatly dressed tables and abstract paintings on the walls.

Mon–Fri noon–2, 7–10.30, Sat 7–10.30
L €100, D €200, Wine €15
Charles de Gaulle–Étoile

**LE CIEL DE PARIS**
Map 251 K9
Tour Montparnasse, 33 avenue du Maine, 75015
Montparnasse
Tel 01 40 64 77 64
www.cieldeparis.com
This restaurant, on the 56th floor of the Tour Montparnasse, claims to be the highest restaurant in Europe and gives stunning views over the city. The sleek, contemporary dining room has dark tones and Tulip Knoll armchairs, and chef Jean-François Oyon's creations are rich and impressive. The menu changes with the season and examples include pan-sautéed fillet of beef with a truffle sauce, lobster risotto, crab with poached quails eggs and fried scallops with a parsley purée.
Daily noon–2.30, 7–10.45
L €64, D €104, Wine €30
Montparnasse Bienvenüe

**COFFEE PARISIEN**
Map 251 L8
4 rue Princesse, 75006
St-Germain-des-Prés
Tel 01 43 54 18 18
As the name suggests, this is a hybrid of a place—a Parisian bistro serving American diner-style food. It's at the heart of St-Germain-des-Prés, in a picturesque pedestrian-only street. Inside you'll find square wooden tables and wall seats, and the occasional picture of John F. Kennedy. It's an excellent place for a lazy Sunday brunch, with American classics such as eggs

Benedict, chicken wings and one of the best cheeseburgers in Paris on the menu.
Daily noon–midnight
Cheeseburger €12, eggs Benedict €12, coffee €3
Mabillon, St-Germain-des-Prés

**IL CORTILE**
Map 251 K5
37 rue Cambon, 75001
Concorde
Tel 01 44 58 45 67
Chef Tjaco Van Eyken, who was trained by a disciple of cooking maestro Alain Ducasse, perfectly masters Italian cuisine here. Each dish, such as crab and lobster-stuffed cannelloni and *pancetta* (cured pork belly) and chanterelle mushroom risotto, contains the best ingredients. The interior design is equally refined, with a Florentine-style fresco on one of the walls and neatly dressed tables. In the summer months, you can dine al fresco on the terrace, where an Italianate fountain makes you forget you're in Paris.
Mon–Fri noon–2.30, 7.30–10.30
L €84, D €130, Wine €25
Concorde

**SPECIAL**

**LA COUPOLE**
Map 251 L9
102 boulevard du Montparnasse, 75014
Montparnasse
Tel 01 43 20 14 20
www.coupoleparis.com
Dine in this Parisian institution, established in 1927, and you'll be following in the footsteps of Pablo Picasso, Ernest Hemingway and Man Ray. The elegant art deco brasserie is a symbol of Montparnasse's artistic heyday. The bright and airy dining room has fresco-adorned pillars, an imposing sculpture and Cubist floor tiles. You'll find all the brasserie classics on the menu, including seafood platters, sauerkraut and steak tartare.
Daily 8.30am–1am (Sat until 1.30am)
L €44, D €60, Wine €20
Vavin

**DRAGONS ÉLYSÉES**
Map 250 H5
11 rue de Berri, 75008
Champs-Élysées
Tel 01 42 89 85 10
The high standard of service and smart address, close to the Champs-Élysées, make this restaurant perfect for a

business or more formal lunch. The menu includes Chinese and Thai dishes such as stuffed crab, spring rolls and Peking-style pork. The unique selling point is the gigantic, underfoot aquarium, with more than 1,000 fish.
Daily noon–2.30, 7–11.30
L €50, D €60, Wine €14
George V

**L'ENVUE**
Map 251 K5
39 rue Boissy d'Anglas, 75008
Concorde
Tel 01 42 65 10 49
This restaurant, just off the Champs-Élysées, has an interior of grey tones peppered

with splashes of pink and blue. The matching tableware, enhanced by fresh flowers, was designed by co-owner Valérie Balard. Chef Patrice Kelsen's innovative French cuisine includes pear and strawberry duck, and chicken with coriander semolina.
Mon–Sat 8am–2am
L €50, D €80, Wine €15
Concorde, Madeleine

**FAKHR EL DINE**
Map 250 G6
30 rue de Longchamp, 75016
Trocadéro
Tel 01 47 27 90 00
www.fakhreldine.com
This restaurant has been popular with both Parisian and Lebanese diners for more than

15 years. The menu includes *warak enab* (stuffed vine-leaves with rice and parsley) and *kharouf mehchi* (stuffed lamb with rice). Try the traditional *meze,* a selection of up to twenty hot and cold hors d'oeuvres. The extra-sweet desserts are just as tempting, and the *baklava* (puff pastry with pistachio nuts and honey) is a must.
Daily noon–3, 7.30–11.30
L €40, D €46, Wine €15
Trocadéro

**FARNESINA**
Map 251 K5
9 rue Boissy d'Anglas, 75008
Concorde
Tel 01 42 66 65 57
Farnesina, in the pedestrian-only section of the rue Boissy d'Anglas, is close to the luxury Hôtel Crillon. Inside, there are pale wooden tables and designer beige armchairs. A collection of teapots gives the place a welcoming feel. The menu is classic Italian, with dishes such as ravioli and beef *carpaccio* with rocket (arugula) and

parmesan. Save room for the superb tiramisu.
Mon–Fri 12.30–2, 7.30–10
L €80, D €100, Wine €20
Concorde

**LA FERME ST-SIMON**
Map 251 K7
6 rue de St-Simon, 75007
Invalides
Tel 01 45 48 35 74
www.fermestsimon.com
Decorated like an elegant country house, with exposed beams, candelabra and flowery curtains, this 'farm' is in reality surrounded by embassies and government ministries. Chef Francis Vendehende's cuisine is refined-rustic, with dishes such as smoked salmon and calf's kidney pasta with foie gras, and roasted sea bass with wild mushrooms and polenta. The menu changes weekly and there's an excellent wine list.
Mon–Fri noon–4, 7.30–10, Sat 7.30–10
L €56, D €90, Wine €18
Rue-du-Bac

**FERMETTE MARBEUF 1900**
Map 250 H6
5 rue Marbeuf, 75008
Champs-Élysées
Tel 01 53 23 08 00
www.fermettemarbeuf.com
There is a profusion of stained glass, decorative wall tiles and beautiful lighting inside this restaurant. In such a splendid setting you could almost forget about the food, but chef Gilbert Isaac's wonderful creations ensure you don't. These include grilled seabass fillet with artichoke, braised

veal sweetbreads, cold tomato soup with avocado mousse, sole fillets with basil and fresh pasta and Grand Marnier soufflé.
Daily noon–3, 7–11.30
L €50, D €60, Wine €15
Franklin D. Roosevelt

**FINDI**
Map 250 H5
24 avenue George V, 75008
Champs-Élysées
Tel 01 47 20 14 78
www.findi.net
Among the elegant clientele, you may recognize some celebrities staying at the nearby Four Seasons George V hotel. Rich red carpets, plush armchairs, subdued lighting and a library create an intimate

atmosphere, although the interior is surprisingly modern. The food is Italian, with dishes such as lasagne with truffle butter and vegetables, tagliatelle with prawns and veal escalopes stuffed with scamorza cheese, sage and polenta. There is also a delicatessen selling salami, wine and cheese.
Daily noon–3, 7–midnight
L €58, D €80, Wine €25
George V

**LA GARE**
Map 250 off F7
19 chaussée de la Muette, 75016
Auteuil
Tel 01 42 15 15 31
La Gare is popular with residents of this chic district and, as its name suggests, occupies an old railway station. The tables are set up on the railway platforms and diners are seated on old carriage benches. The menu includes grilled chicken, lamb and beef, and the rapid service is perfect for those who have another train to catch.
Daily noon–3, 7–midnight
L €46, D €58, Wine €17
La Muette

**LE GRAND CAFÉ**
Map 253 L5
4 boulevard des Capucines, 75009
Grands Boulevards
Tel 01 43 12 19 00
www.legrandcafe.com
Theatregoers, seafood-lovers and an eclectic flock of night owls make up the clientele of this restaurant, which is open day and night, every day of the year. The interior is beautiful ,

art nouveau, with an impressive stained-glass ceiling and fanciful furniture. Fish is king here and is served grilled, poached or *meunière* (in lemon and butter). The menu also includes some French meat dishes, such as fillet of Charolais beef with peppercorns or grilled with a Béarnaise sauce.
Daily, 24 hours
L €40, D €70, Wine €18
Opéra

**SPECIAL**

**GEORGES**
Map 252 N7
Centre Georges Pompidou
Place Georges-Pompidou, 75004
Les Halles
Tel 01 44 78 47 99
www.centrepompidou.fr
You are on the top floor of the Centre Georges Pompidou, with a stunning view over Paris. The dining room could be a work of modern art itself, with its sleek lines and shells of metal and bright rubber. Nouvelle cuisine is served, including mushroom cappuccino (a light and foamy soup) and crab millefeuille (in puff pastry). Save room for dessert, as the melt-in-the-mouth chocolate cake is one of the restaurant's signature dishes.
Wed–Mon noon–2am
L €80, D €100, Wine €20
Rambuteau

**GRAND COLBERT**
Map 251 M6
2 rue Vivienne, 75002
Louvre/Palais Royal
Tel 01 42 86 87 88
There's something quintessentially Parisian about this chic brasserie, which dates from 1830. The listed building has high ceilings, black-and-white floor tiles, Café-de-Paris-style lamps and an army of highly professional waiters wearing the traditional black-and-white

*garçon* uniform. The menu includes seafood platters, sauerkraut and steaks.
Daily noon–1am
L €35, D €50, Wine €14
Bourse

**LA GRANDE CASCADE**
Map 250 off F5
Allée de Longchamp, 75016
Auteuil (Bois de Boulogne)
Tel 01 45 27 33 51
www.lagrandecascade.fr
Napoleon III built this pavilion at the foot of La Grande Cascade (the Great Waterfall) for his visits to the Bois de Boulogne. It was converted into a restaurant in 1900 and its Belle-Epoque interior has a profusion of candelabra and red velvet drapes. The vast windows in the circular dining room give magical views of the woods. Chef Richard Mebkhout creates fine French cuisine, including black truffle macaroni glazed with port.

Daily 12.30–2.30, 7.30–9.30
L €120, D €300, Wine €25
Porte d'Auteuil

**LES GRANDES MARCHES**
Map 252 Q8
6 place de la Bastille, 75012
Bastille
Tel 01 43 42 90 32
www.lesgrandesmarches.com
*Les grandes marches* (the big steps) refer to those of the

Opéra Bastille, although this open two-floor house also has its own stylish staircase. Go to the upper floor for wonderful views of place de la Bastille. The modern decoration includes plenty of steel surfaces and subtle lighting. Chef Christian Constant oversees the creation of innovative French dishes such as Loué chicken with pistachio

and mustard juice, and caramel-coated monkfish with butter orange juices. The restaurant is also renowned for its superb seafood platters.
Daily noon–midnight
L €66, D €82, Wine €15
Bastille

**LA GUINGUETTE DE NEUILLY**
Map 250 off F4
12 boulevard Georges-Seurat, 92200
Neuilly-sur-Seine
Neuilly
01 46 24 25 04
www.laguinguette.net
Dine on the banks of the Seine at this restaurant, on the Île de la Grande Jatte. In the best French tradition, the tables have red-and-white tablecloths; on the walls, oars and pictures of fishing scenes evoke life by the river. The cuisine is equally traditional, simple but tasty, with choices such as grilled steak with fried potatoes and roasted sea bass with mixed vegetables.
Daily midday–2, 7.30–11
L €56, D €70, Wine €17
Pont de Levallois

**HARD ROCK CAFÉ**
Map 253 M5
14 boulevard Montmartre, 75009
Grands Boulevards
Tel 01 53 24 60 00
www.hardrockcafe.com
You'll find rock music, beers on tap and American food (their hamburgers, grilled fajitas and Texas T-Bone steaks aren't at all bad) at this chain restaurant. Rock memorabilia

include Eric Clapton's guitar and some of the Beatles' original scores. This is not the place for a romantic dinner, but a good spot to hang out with friends.
Daily noon–2am
L €18, D €40, Wine €5
Grands-Boulevards

**SPECIAL**

**GUY SAVOY**
Map 250 G4
18 rue Troyon, 75017
Champs-Élysées
Tel 01 43 80 40 61
www.guysavoy.com
Guy Savoy's motto is that cooking is the art of taking foodstuffs and transforming them into pure happiness. Art is indeed on the menu

with delicacies such as poached-grilled pigeon and giblets in a beetroot and mushroom millefeuille, or the split langoustines with citrus fruit and peas.

Art is also on the walls, with many modern paintings. There are fine white linen tablecloths and black wooden chairs. This is a true culinary experience, just minutes away from the Champs-Élysées.
Mon–Fri noon–2, 7–10.30, Sat 7–10.30
L €300, D €300, Wine €90
Charles de Gaulle–Étoile

**HIPPOPOTAMUS**
Map 252 Q8
1 boulevard Beaumarchais, 75004
Bastille
Tel 01 44 61 90 40
www.hippopotamus.fr
This restaurant is part of a chain (there are about 20 in Paris) known for its grilled meat. Salads, steak tartare and carpaccio are also on the menu, and your dinner could start with some goat's cheese on toast or a terrine. It's worth a visit if you're looking for reasonable prices and a convivial, child-friendly atmosphere.
Daily 8am–12.30am
L €30, D €40, Wine €15
Bastille

**JACQUES CAGNA**
Map 251 M7
14 rue des Grands-Augustins, 75006
St-Germain-des-Prés
Tel 01 43 26 49 39
www.jacques-cagna.com
For over 30 years, two-star chef Jacques Cagna has been reinventing gourmet cuisine. Here you can expect true delicacies, such as veal rib in a ginger and lime sauce and

grilled langoustines. The restaurant is in a 17th-century town house, overseen by the chef's sister Annie. The beautiful interior has beamed ceilings, wood panels and Flemish paintings.
Tue–Fri noon–2, 7.30–10.30, Mon and Sat 7.30–10.30
L €100, D €200, Wine €30
St-Michel, Odéon

**JOE ALLEN**
Map 253 N6
30 rue Pierre Lescot, 75001
Les Halles
Tel 01 42 36 70 13
www.joeallen.com
This relaxed American bar and restaurant is in a small street in the bustling Les Halles district.

The brick walls are covered with pictures and you dine by candlelight in the evenings. The venue has been a hit with the show-business crowd since 1972, partly due to the professional barmen, but also because of the high quality of the all-American food.
Daily noon–1am
L €40, D €50, Wine €14.50
Etienne-Marcel

SPECIAL

**JEAN-PAUL HÉVIN**
Map 251 L6
231 rue St-Honoré, 75001
Right Bank
Tel 01 55 35 35 96
www.jphevin.com
Jean-Paul Hévin, winner of the international prize for chocolate-making and a member of the French chocolate and confectionery

academy, is behind this tea and chocolate house. The hot chocolate is delicious and provides the perfect excuse to sample other dishes, such as the orange or raspberry chocolate cake or the almond and chocolate macaroon. The design is equally evocative of the celebrated ingredient, with chocolate tones, wood panels and co-ordinating rattan furniture.
Mon–Sat noon–6.30
Hot chocolate €6, slice of chocolate cake €5
Tuileries

**KHUN AKORN**
Map 252 off Q8
8 avenue de Taillebourg, 75011
Nation
Tel 01 43 56 20 03
The Thai menu here offers a wide range of dishes, including *larb neua* (beef cooked in lemon and spices), duck in red curry sauce and crispy noodles. Each dish can be spiced according to how hot you want it to be. The interior design avoids kitsch although you'll still find some statues of dragons, carved wooden panels and chairbacks. There's also a pleasant terrace for spring and summer days.
Tue–Sun noon–2, 7.30–11
L €48, D €80, Wine €15
Nation

**LADURÉE**
Map 251 K5
16 rue Royale, 75008
Concorde
Tel 01 42 60 21 79
www.laduree.fr
This was the first tea room in Paris, established in 1862. It started life as a bakery but became a tea room as demand grew for its delicious pastries. The fin-de-siècle

painter commissioned to decorate it used techniques employed in world-famous masterpieces such as the ceiling of the Sistine Chapel and the Opéra Palais Garnier. You can sample the very best teas and pastries in an elegant setting. Among the delicacies, the macaroon is an absolute must. It comes in its original varieties—rose, Yunnan tea, apricot and ginger—but also some which change with the seasons. All are a treat.
Daily 8.30–7
Tea €7, 4 mini macaroons €5
Concorde, Madeleine

**MAN RAY**
Map 250 H5
34 rue Marbeuf, 75008
Champs-Élysées
Tel 01 56 88 36 36
www.manray.fr
Lavish Asian-influenced interior design, dreamed up by Cancio Martins, marks this restaurant. The bright and airy space has giant statues of Buddha, a glass mosaic ceiling and a little waterfall, with the bar on the mezzanine floor. The menu brings French, Japanese and Thai tastes together, with sushi, grilled meat and sautéed fish. It's been a hit with the Parisian jet set since its launch in 1999.
Mon–Fri noon–2.30, 7.30–midnight, Sat–Sun 7.30–midnight
L €40, D €80, Wine €25
Franklin D. Roosevelt

SPECIAL

**MARKET**
Map 250 J5
15 avenue Matignon, 75008
Champs-Élysées
Tel 01 56 43 40 90
www.jean-georges.com
Interior designer Christian Liaigre has created a bare yet polished interior, with soft tones, pale wood furniture and panels punctuated by pieces of primitive art. There is the same pared-down approach to the menu, which offers the produce of a raw bar, notably a large choice of oysters, and fusion food by chef Jean-Georges Vongerichten. Try the black truffle pizza or the 'black plate', an hors d'oeuvre selection including shrimps on a skewer, ginger lobster roll, raw tuna and spiced quail. At the weekend you also have the option of brunch.
Daily noon–3, 7.30pm–12.30am (Sun–Mon closes at 11.30pm)
L €64, D €120, Wine €24
Franklin D. Roosevelt

**MARTY**
Map 252 off N10
20 avenue des Gobelins, 75005
Mouffetard
Tel 01 43 31 39 51
This 1930s-style brasserie, on the first floor, offers delicious fresh shellfish, fish and meat dishes. There is a restaurant on the ground floor, although it is slightly more expensive. The venue is well placed for a meal after a visit to the Gobelins factory (see page 107).
Daily 12–12
L €60, D €70, Wine €13
Les Gobelins

**MAVROMMATIS**
Map 252 N10
42 rue Daubenton, 75005
Latin Quarter
Tel 01 43 31 17 17
www.mavrommatis.fr
This restaurant is round the corner from the lively rue Mouffetard, where cafés and restaurants are legion. It is run by two brothers, Andreas and Evagoras Mavrommatis, with Andreas in the kitchen. The interior is elegant but unpretentious, with pale wood

and weaved osier chairbacks set off by fresh flowers. All the classics of Greek cuisine are here: preserved lamb and yoghurt with honey, vine leaves, moussaka and, of course, the syrup-soaked *baklava* (pastry with honey and pistachios) for dessert.

Tue–Sun noon–2.30, 7–11
L €60, D €90, Wine €20
Censier Daubenton

**MAXIM'S**
Map 251 K6
3 rue Royale, 75008
Concorde
Tel 01 42 65 27 94
www.maxims-de-paris.com
This Belle-Époque restaurant was established in 1893 by café waiter Maxime Gaillard and acquired in 1981 by designer Pierre Cardin. It is now a hub of Parisian social life and has proved so

successful that other Maxims have opened across the world, in New York, Beijing and Geneva. But it has managed to remain light years away from the atmosphere of some chain restaurants. Attentive service, refined French cuisine and a prestigious location all contribute to its touch of class.
Mon–Sat noon–2.30, 7.30–10
L €250, D €300, Wine €40
Concorde

**SPECIAL**

**MUSCADE**
Map 251 L6
36 rue Montpensier, 75001
Louvre/Palais Royal
Tel 01 42 97 51 36
www.muscade-palais-royal.com
This high-class venue has an exceptional setting in the Palais Royal gardens and an elegant interior, with black-and-white floor tiles and Regency chairs. The lunch menu and one of the dinner menus have a Mediterranean accent and change every six months. At Muscade they are passionate about cakes, which you can enjoy as a dessert or as part of a traditional afternoon tea. This includes chocolate macaroons, fig and saffron caramel *pastilla* (Middle Eastern filo pastry) and ginger and lemon cake. Other

delicacies include muffins, chocolate gateaux and tarts.
Tea room: Tue–Sun 10–11.30, 3–6 (also 6–8pm Sep–Apr)
Tea €4, slice of cake €6
Pyramides, Palais-Royal/Musée du Louvre

**LA MÈRE LACHAISE**
Map 252 off Q6
78 boulevard de Ménilmontant, 75020
Belleville/Père Lachaise
Tel 01 47 97 61 60
This convivial bistro is as fashionable as it is authentic. It has a great terrace in summer, and two dining rooms, one with a retro feel (tiled floor, wrought iron and wooden tables) and the other, with silver fabric-covered walls. The menu has unpretentious high-quality food such as big salads, tartares and tarts, and a good brunch on Sundays. The name echoes the nearby Père Lachaise cemetery, where many celebrities, including Jim Morrison, are buried (see page 88).
Daily 8am–2am
L €30, D €40, Wine €12
Père Lachaise

**NOS ANCÊTRES LES GAULOIS**
Map 252 N8
39 rue St-Louis-en-l'Ile, 75004
Ile St-Louis
Tel 01 46 33 66 07
www.nosancetreslesgaulois.com
This fun Gallic-themed restaurant has been going strong since it opened in 1969. There's a rustic feel to the place, with exposed stone walls, beamed ceilings and decorative agricultural tools. The idea is simple–one fixed-price menu, including unlimited wine from the barrel, an all-you-can-eat buffet of starters (cold meats and salads) and a choice of freshly grilled kebabs, lamb chops, steaks and other meats from the open fireplace. Vegetarians be warned.
Daily 7pm–1.30am
D €35 (including wine)
Pont-Marie

**L'ORIENTAL**
Map 253 M3
76 rue Martyrs, 75018
Montmartre
Tel 01 42 64 39 80
www.loriental-restaurant.com
Although this restaurant is barely a stone's throw from Sacré-Cœur in touristy Montmartre, you could be in another world. Lanterns, mosaics, curtains and mirrors create a luxurious Moroccan palace feel. The cuisine is North African, with *pastillas* (a kind of filo pastry), sophisticated *tajines* (meat cooked in a cone-shaped terracotta dish) such as king's lamb with figs, almonds and dates, the essential couscous and a mint tea to conclude.
Tue–Sat noon–2.30, 7.30–10
L €40, D €58, Wine €14
Abbesses, Pigalle

**IL PALAZZO**
Map 251 L6
7 rue de l'Échelle, 75001
Louvre/Palais Royal
Tel 01 42 60 30 21
www.leshotelsdeparis.com
This stylish corner of Italy is close to the Louvre, within the prestigious Hôtel Normandy. Inside, there's a mix of baroque and contemporary styles, with the fresco-adorned ceiling and drapes contrasting with the muted tones of the

furniture. The cuisine is a modern interpretation of Italian classic, with black truffle, mushroom and cheese *schiacciata* (similar to pizza), or the surprising Chianti and eel risotto.
Tue–Sat noon–2.30, 7.30–11
L €62, D €140, Wine €28
Palais-Royal

**LE PARADIS DU FRUIT**
Map 251 M7
29 quai des Grands-Augustins, 75006
St-Germain-des-Prés
Tel 01 43 54 51 42
The concept of this chain restaurant will delight vegetarians and health food fans alike, as you get to compose your own meal and drink from a large selection of fresh fruit and vegetables. The massive salads come with taramasalata, guacamole, cheese and other side dishes. Carnivores needn't despair as there are also some meat side orders, such as spiced chicken on a skewer. There are nine Paradis du Fruit in

Paris, and at this branch there is a small terrace where you can enjoy views of the Seine on spring and summer days.
Tue–Sat noon–2am, Sun–Mon noon–midnight
L €30, D €50, Wine €12
St-Michel

**LE PETIT GAVROCHE**
Map 252 N7
15 rue Ste-Croix de la Bretonnerie, 75004
Le Marais
Tel 01 48 87 74 26
Le Petit Gavroche ('the Parisian urchin', from a character in Victor Hugo's *Les Misérables*) is the place for French food enthusiasts on a budget. The set menu is a bargain, and invariably offers three choices of starter, main course and dessert. There's nothing

particularly fancy here, with plates of crudités, filling pies and the house tart on the menu, but you won't leave hungry. The retro interior, with old French posters and some curios, is an added bonus.
Mon–Sat 8am–11.30pm
L €30, D €40, Wine €7
Hôtel de Ville

**LE PETIT ST-BENOIT**
Map 251 L7
4 rue St-Benoît, 75006
St-Germain-des-Prés
Tel 01 42 60 27 92
This popular bistro is a St-Germain classic and the look has barely changed since the 1930s. Photos on the walls show some of the writers and intellectuals who have visited. The menu includes traditional soups, terrines and dishes such as rabbit with mustard. You can sit outside in summer. Credit cards are not accepted.
Mon–Sat 12–2.30, 7–10.30. Closed Aug
L €22, D €32, Wine €15
St-Germain-des-Prés

**PHARAMOND**
Map 253 N6
24 rue de la Grande-Truanderie, 75001
Les Halles
Tel 01 40 28 45 18
www.le-pharamond.com
This restaurant, established in 1832, is in a listed historic building. It has an extravagant art nouveau interior with ceramic murals, floor tiles, huge mirrors, mosaics and a dramatic spiral staircase. There are two dining rooms and a

private salon on the third floor. They serve traditional food from the Normandy region such as Caen-style tripe with cider, calvados (apple brandy) and potatoes and melt-in-the-mouth chocolate cake.

This is a Parisian institution, in keeping with the best tradition of Les Halles, which is the former home of Paris's food market.
Mon–Sat noon–2.30, 7.30–10.30
L €50, D €80, Wine €15
Les Halles

**PICCOLO TEATRO**
Map 252 P7
6 rue des Ecouffes, 75004
Le Marais
Tel 01 42 72 17 79
This restaurant was a pioneer of vegetarian cuisine at the time of its launch in 1976 and is now firmly established at the heart of the picturesque Marais district. The menu includes dishes from all over the world, using exotic ingredients such as Indonesian *tempeh* (fermented soya). A wide

range of *gratins* (cheese-topped dishes), soups and salads are on the menu, some with evocative names—*Calling the Sun* is aubergine (eggplant), mozzarella and basil gratin.

Daily noon–3, 7–11.30
L €30, D €40, Wine €12
St-Paul

**POONA LOUNGE**
Map 250 H5
25 rue Marbeuf, 75008
Champs-Élysées
Tel 01 40 70 09 99
Poona Lounge combines Indian-influenced dining with Parisian clubbing. The cuisine includes dishes such as lemon

pepper duck, cheese naan and chicken sandwich.

The ethnically inspired interior is smart and the resident DJ keeps the place lively until the early hours.

Daily 9am–5am
L €38, D €40, Wine €19
Franklin D. Roosevelt

**LE PROCOPE**
Map 251 M8
13 rue de l'Ancienne-Comédie, 75006
St-Germain-des-Prés
Tel 01 40 46 79 00
www.procope.com
This former Parisian café, now an elegant dining room, was once frequented by the philosophers Voltaire and

Rousseau. Benjamin Franklin is said to have drafted part of the American constitution here. The menu includes grilled beef fillet, coq au vin and basil sorbet. Fish fans can choose from mackerel terrine with potatoes, fish soup or one of the rich seafood platters.

Sun-Wed noon–midnight, Thu–Sat noon–1am
L €60, D €100, Wine €15
Odéon

**RELAIS PLAZA**
Map 250 H6
15 avenue Montaigne, 75008
Champs-Élysées
Tel 01 53 67 64 00
The luxury hotel Plaza Athénée is home to this elegant restaurant, which was completely refurbished in 2002. The smart art deco

dining room is filled with curios and there is a nightly piano accompaniment. Chef Philippe Marc is a disciple of maestro chef Alain Ducasse, and his gourmet menu of French dishes changes every two months.

Daily noon–2.30, 7–11.30
L €86, D €120, Wine €30
Alma-Marceau

**RITAL ET COURTS**
Map 252 off Q5
1 rue des Envierges, 75020
Belleville/Père Lachaise
Tel 01 47 97 08 41
Rital et Courts is at Belleville Gardens, one of the highest points in Paris. The restaurant and its terrace have wonderful views of the city, which you can enjoy while you dine. Alternatively, you can watch one of the short films that are regularly screened here on Thursdays, Fridays and Saturdays, when the place buzzes with cinema aficionados.

The menu is full of Italian classics, with bowls of pasta, *carpaccio* (thin slices of raw beef) and ice cream. There's nothing fancy or revolutionary about the menu, but the food is good and portions are large. Who's to argue when the view is as good as this?

Tue–Sat 10am–2am, Sun 10am–6pm
L €30, D €65, Wine €10
Pyrénées

**RIVER CAFÉ**
Map 250 off F9
146 quai de Stalingrad, 92130 Issy-les-Moulineaux
Issy-les-Moulineaux
01 40 93 50 20
www.lerivercafe.net
Dine in a big barge moored on the Seine and enjoy wonderful views of Île St-Germain. The interior is Parisian with an exotic touch: wooden floors, plants, café-de-Paris armchairs, and some rattan and neo-colonial furniture.

The menu has the same influences, with subtly spiced fine French cuisine: duck with mushrooms in a honey and lemon sauce, bay prawns with pear and pineapple chutney, and chocolate macaroon with a guava and mango cream.

Daily midday–2, 8–11. Closed Sat lunch
L €52, D €62, Wine €23
RER Issy-Plaine

**LA RÔTISSERIE DU BEAUJOLAIS**
Map 252 N8
19 quai de la Tournelle, 75005
Latin Quarter
Tel 01 43 54 17 47
You'll get lovely views of Notre-Dame from the terrace of this quayside bistro. The restaurant is under the same ownership as La Tour d'Argent, across the road (see page 276). The menu includes traditional dishes such as snails or pigs trotters, but the highlight is the roasted meat.

Tue–Sun 12–2, 7.30–10.15
L €60, D €70, Wine €18
Maubert-Mutualité

**LA RÔTISSERIE D'EN FACE**
Map 251 M8
2 rue Christine, 75006
St-Germain-des-Prés
Tel 01 43 26 40 98
www.jacques-cagna.com
This is the annexe of Jacques Cagna, the eponymous gastronomic restaurant across the street, where the celebrity chef himself rules the kitchen. Expect the same perfection here, within the relaxed setting of an elegant brasserie, with leather wall seats and lines of small square wooden tables.

On the menu, you'll find rotisserie dishes such as spit-roast chicken, suckling pig and veal kidney. Other options include meat and vegetable stew, Burgundy snails and frogs' legs in garlic and herbs.
Mon–Fri noon–2, 7–11, Sat 7–11.30
L €46, D €78, Wine €20
St-Michel

**SÉBILLON**
Map 250 off F4
20 avenue Charles de Gaulle, 92200
Neuilly
Tel 01 46 24 71 31
*Gigot d'agneau* (leg of lamb), carved and served from the trolley, and fresh seafood dominate the menu at this Parisian institution, which has been in service for over half a century. The elegant wooden bistro-style interior adds to the place's conviviality, and the humidor (for keeping your cigars just right) and valet parking service add a touch of class.
Daily noon–midnight
L €70, D €100, Wine €15
Porte Maillot

**SPICY RESTAURANT**
Map 250 J5
8 avenue Franklin Roosevelt, 75008
Champs-Élysées
Tel 01 56 59 62 59
www.spicyrestaurant.com
Be prepared for inventive cuisine which explodes with taste and looks great. Try courgettes (zucchini) marinated in olive oil and served with tomato-infused goat's milk cheese, steamed salmon served with Chinese noodles with soy sauce and fresh mint, or gingerbread pudding with caramel butter sauce and vanilla ice cream. The interior has also been spiced up with pastel woodwork and exposed bricks punctuated by bright spice pots and bouquets of dried chillies. There's also a nice terrace.
Daily noon–3, 7–midnight
L €60, D €80, Wine €16
Franklin D. Roosevelt

**SPOON FOOD AND WINE**
Map 250 H5
14 rue de Marignan, 75008
Champs-Élysées
Tel 01 40 76 34 44
www.spoon.tm.fr
The simply beautiful setting, signature of Boifils, mixes sleek lines and deep purple walls, enhanced by the pastels of the chair cushions. There's just as much creativity in the kitchen, where celebrated chef Alain Ducasse dreams up highly personalized menus—you choose the sauce and accompaniment to your meal. The menu combines French, American and Asian

influences with plenty for vegetarians. Unusually, the wine list has mostly American and New World wines, (California is particularly well represented), and some wines are available by the glass each day.
Mon–Fri noon–2, 7–11
L €100, D €130, Wine €35
Franklin D. Roosevelt

**LE STÜBLI**
Map 250 off G4
11 rue Poncelet, 75017
Ternes
Tel 01 42 27 81 86
www.stubli.com
This tea room has been an ambassador for Germany and Austria since it opened in 1956. Above the *pâtisserie*, the tea room has a Viennese setting, with lots of wood, tones of beige and green and subdued lighting. The menu includes traditional

cakes and pastries such as apple strudel and Black Forest gateau. The hot chocolate makes a perfect accompaniment. Le Stübli also runs a delicatessen shop across the street, which sells beer, cold meats and breads.
Tea room: Tue–Sat 9–6.30, Sun 9am–12.30pm
Viennese hot chocolate €4, slice of Black Forest gateau €4
Ternes

**TAILLEVENT**
Map 250 H4
15 rue Lamennais, 75008
Champs-Élysées
Tel 01 44 95 15 01
www.taillevent.com
This highly distinguished restaurant is named after a celebrated chef from the Middle Ages and is now the domain of master chef Alain Solivérès. The dining room is discreetly elegant, with wood panels and candelabra. Expect the very best of French cuisine, with rich dishes such as foie gras, lobster and truffles.

There is an exceptional wine cellar to match.
Mon–Fri noon–2, 7.30–9.30
L €220, D €300, Wine €24
Charles de Gaulle–Étoile, George V

**TANJIA**
Map 250 J5
23 rue de Ponthieu, 75008
Champs-Élysées
Tel 01 42 25 95 00

This Moroccan restaurant is owned by Cathy and David Guetta, former owners of Les Bains nightclub and still the golden couple of Parisian nightlife. The beautiful dining room, with its fountain and mezzanine, is reminiscent of a chic Moroccan palace. The lounge club in the basement is made for relaxing, with divan beds and *hookahs* (tobacco pipes). The excellent traditional cuisine, including lamb and pear *tagine* (stew) and couscous, is sometimes created by a leading Moroccan guest chef.
Mon–Fri noon–3, 8–1am, Sat–Sun 8pm–1am
L €40, D €100, Wine €30
Franklin D. Roosevelt

**LA TAVERNE**
Map 253 L5
24 boulevard des Italiens, 75009
Grands Boulevards
Tel 01 55 33 10 00
www.taverne.com
The menu here has Alsatian influences, with dishes such as sauerkraut, monkfish in beer and tarte tatin (apple

upside-down cake) with cream. The pale wood panels and candelabra give this restaurant a touch of class, while curios such as a bull's head and a massive clock are more evocative of a tavern. Dinner-and-show deals are arranged with nearby theatres.
Sun–Thu 11am–midnight, Fri–Sat 11am–1am
L €40, D €70, Wine €10
Richelieu-Drouot, Opéra

**THOUMIEUX**
Map 250 J7
79 rue St-Dominique, 75007
Invalides
Tel 01 47 05 49 75
Named after the Thoumieux family proprietors, this brasserie, which opened in 1923, is just minutes away from the Eiffel Tower. The elegant dining room has comfortable velvet wall seats and numerous mirrors. The present chef is Christian Beguet, whose menu is a top-class excursion into the cuisine of southwest France. Expect quality, hearty dishes ,

such as *cassoulet* (bean and sausage casserole) or one of the various duck dishes, including foie gras.
Daily noon–3.30, 6.30–midnight
L €40, D €60, Wine €13
Invalides

**TORAYA**
Map 251 K5
10 rue St-Florentin, 75001
Concorde
Tel 01 42 60 13 00

This is a branch of Japan's oldest *pâtisserie*, founded in the 16th century and supplier to the Japanese Imperial family. Behind the stylish façade, adorned with a tiger, the company's logo, you'll find a chic tea room with a lot of dark brown wood and white and orange leather armchairs.

The traditional pastries vary according to the seasons. An example is the leaf-shaped *Mayumi-No-Mochi,* served in autumn. Surprising in shape and taste (some use red beans), they resemble miniature works of art. The restaurant is entirely non-smoking.
Mon–Sat 10.30–7
Green tea €4, Japanese cake €4
Concorde

**LE TOTEM**
Map 250 F6
17 place du Trocadéro, 75016
Trocadéro
Tel 01 47 27 28 29
www.letotem.fr
Extend your visit to the Musée de l'Homme (see page 143) by

dining in the totem-adorned restaurant next door, with its wonderful view of the Eiffel Tower. With such an attractive setting, it's no wonder that Parisians flock here.

Other reasons to come include the bar, which is open late into the evening, the terrace, for a meal outside in fine weather, and the imaginative cuisine created by chef Christian Gaillard. Dishes include smoked salmon with green lentils and sherry and breast of guinea-fowl with Milanais rice.
Tue–Sat noon–2.30, 7.30–11.45 (bar stays open until 2am)
L €43, D €88, Wine €19
Trocadéro

SPECIAL

**LA TOUR D'ARGENT**
Map 251 N8
15–17 quai de la Tournelle, 75005
Latin Quarter
Tel 01 43 54 23 31
www.latourdargent.com
A Parisian institution since 1582, this is one of the best restaurants in France, if not the world. It sits on the sixth floor of a beautiful building overlooking the Seine, offering panoramic views of the city.

This is exquisite French cuisine at its best, with lobster quenelles and duck being a couple of the signature dishes. The wine cellar is exceptional.

Wed–Sun noon–1.30, 8–10.30, Tue 8–10.30
L €130, D €360, Wine €70
Pont Marie

**TRÉSOR**
Map 252 P7
7–9 rue du Trésor, 75004
Le Marais
Tel 01 42 71 35 17
This Italian restaurant is in a quiet no-through road in the picturesque Marais

district and has one of Paris's finest terraces.

The place had a make-over in 2002 and now has a chic white and beige interior. There are also a few quirky additions such as the goldfish-filled aquariums in the bathrooms and the shiatsu massage offered downstairs.

Food served daily 12–3, 7.30–10, but drinks available all day until 2am
L €50, D €70, Wine €18
St-Paul, Hôtel de Ville

**TSÉ**
Map 250 off F9
78 rue d'Auteuil, 75016
Tel 01 40 71 11 90
Auteuil
This bar-restaurant has been a hit with this residential area's elegant night owls since it opened in 2001. It has an extravagant interior, with Chinese lanterns and wall lamps, exotic dark wooden furniture and even an antique Tibetan four-poster bed. There is a warm and welcoming bar with a fireplace, a smoking room and a roof terrace.

The food is high quality Asian cuisine, with Japanese, Thai and Chinese influences. You'll find sushi, duck fillet in a *teriyaki* sauce (soy sauce, sake and ginger) and sesame tuna on a skewer.

Daily 10am–3am (Fri–Sat until 4am)
L €70, D €90, Wine €20
Porte d'Auteuil

**TSE YANG**
Map 250 G6
25 avenue Pierre-1er-de-Serbie, 75016
Trocadéro
Tel 01 47 20 70 22
www.tseyang.fr
Inside this elegant Chinese restaurant, in one of Paris's smartest districts, you'll find plenty of fresh flowers and some impressive murals.

Chef Yang Kui Fah brilliantly interprets the classics of Asian cuisine. Scallops in yellow rice

wine and Peking-style duck are among the house dishes. There is a comprehensive list of French wines and traditional Chinese beers.

Daily noon–2.30, 7–11.30
L €60, D €90, Wine €26
Iéna

**LE VERRE BOUTEILLE**
Map 250 off G4
85 avenue des Ternes, 75017
Ternes
Tel 01 45 74 01 02
www.leverrebouteille.com
This bistro, conveniently close to the place de l'Étoile, stays open until the small hours. Chef Patrick Ameline's ambition is to satisfy with simple food cooked to perfection, and the warm goat's cheese, country-style *croque* and chocolate cake are all to die for. There's a good selection of wines, some available by the glass if you don't fancy a whole bottle.

The interior is traditional bistro in style, with a long bar

and rectangular wooden tables with wrought-iron legs.

Daily noon–3, 7pm–5am
L €40, D €60, Wine €18
Porte Maillot

**LA VILLA MAURESQUE**
Map 250 J5
5 rue du Commandant Rivière, 75008
Champs-Élysées
Tel 01 42 25 16 69
www.villamauresque.com
Not far from the Champs-Élysées, owner Fati Abouayoub has created a stylish restaurant combining Moorish decoration with a certain French classicism. The elegant dining room is a far cry from a souk however, with square wooden tables, muted brown walls and subdued lighting. The pigeon, almond and pistachio *pastilla* (a kind of filo pastry) is the house dish, but you may also be tempted by the fig, nut and veal *tagine* (stew).

Mon–Fri noon–2.30, 8–10.30
L €60, D €90, Wine €17
St-Philippe du Roule

**VILLA MEDICI CHEZ NAPOLI**
Map 251 K8
11 bis rue St-Placide, 75006
St-Germain-des-Prés
Tel 01 42 22 51 96
www.villa-medici.com
Moustachioed Michele Napoli (see the website for a photo), has been entertaining his guests here for more than thirty years. His regular clientele keeps coming back for the tasty Italian food (choose from pizza, pasta or risotto).

The interior is splendidly faux-Italian, with a Coliseum-style main room, with pillars and a circular table arrangement. There is another room at the back where groups are entertained by the performing *pizzaiolo* (pizza chef). There is one non-smoking room.
Mon–Sat 11.30–2.30, 7–11
L €40, D €60, Wine €18
St-Placide

**VIN DES PYRÉNÉES**
Map 252 P8
25 rue Beautreillis, 75004
Le Marais
Tel 01 42 72 64 94
This restaurant takes you back to the 1930s. Gingham tablecloths, old family pictures on the walls and antique dolls in a display cabinet mark the retro look. The traditional menu includes salmon millefeuille, grilled meat (the house special dish), crème brûlée

and chocolate cake. The comprehensive wine list, as the restaurant's name suggests, includes a selection from the Pyrenees.
Sun–Fri noon–2.30, 8–11.30, Sat 8–11.30
L €26, D €40, Wine €15
St-Paul

**LE VIRAGE LEPIC**
Map 253 L2
61 rue Lepic, 75018
Montmartre
Tel 01 42 52 46 79
Book ahead for this welcoming bistro, in Montmartre's windmill-crowned rue Lepic. You'll find meat-based main courses, tasty puddings and a good wine list. In summer you can sit outside.
Wed–Mon 7pm–11.30pm
D €50, Wine €16
Blanche/Abbesses

**YUGARAJ**
Map 251 M7
14 rue Dauphine, 75006
St-Germain-des-Prés
Tel 01 43 26 44 91
www.yugaraj.com
Yugaraj is one of Paris's best Indian restaurants. The French and Indian proprietors introduced Indian cuisine to the French with their previous restaurant, which opened in 1971.

The menu contains a few surprises, with options such as crab balls among more traditional dishes. The jumbo shrimps marinated in spices are a must.
Tue–Wed and Fri–Sun noon–2, 7–10; Thu 7–10
L €60, D €90, Wine €22
Odéon

*Dining al fresco at a restaurant on the quai St-Michel (below)*

# CHAIN RESTAURANTS

Although Paris is known for some of the best—and most expensive—restaurants in the world, you can also find reasonably priced, family-friendly chains if you want a more low-key meal. The chart below shows some of the chains with restaurants in the city.

| NAME | Average in euros for 2 courses | Alcohol served | Children's menu | Take-out | Description |
|---|---|---|---|---|---|
| Bistro Romain | 18 | ✔ | ✔ | ✗ | Italian cuisine. (See page 262 for the Champs-Élysées branch.) |
| Buffalo Grill | 18 | ✔ | ✔ | ✗ | Restaurant-grills serving chicken, steaks and salads. |
| Chez Clément | 28 | ✔ | ✔ | ✗ | Comfortable, family-friendly brasserie where oysters, seafood platters and rotisserie beef and pork are on the menu. |
| Courtepaille | 14 | ✔ | ✔ | ✗ | A steak-and-chips eaterie that also has chicken dishes and salads. |
| El Rancho | 18 | ✔ | ✔ | ✗ | Tex-Mex food in a rural-Mexican interior. |
| Hippopotamus | 20 | ✔ | ✔ | ✗ | A leading chain of restaurant-grills, with 18 branches in the city. Steak is the house dish. (See page 269 for the Bastille branch.) |
| Indiana Café | 15 | ✔ | ✔ | ✗ | Expect a Tex-Mex menu, plus burgers and salads. |
| Léon de Bruxelles | 18 | ✔ | ✔ | ✗ | Belgian-style brasseries where beer, waffles, mussels and chips are included on the menu. |
| Pizza Hut | 10 | ✔ | ✔ | ✔ | A well-known chain, with pizzas big enough to share. |
| La Taverne de Maître Kanter | 18 | ✔ | ✗ | ✗ | Twelve branches serve Alsatian dishes such as sauerkraut, chicken in reisling and seafood platters. |

# CAFÉS AND FAST FOOD

| NAME | | | | | |
|---|---|---|---|---|---|
| Columbus Café | N/A | ✗ | ✗ | ✔ | Espresso bar where you can grab a tea, coffee or cookie. |
| Flunch | 6 | ✔ | ✔ | ✗ | Snacks and meals, usually in hypermarkets. |
| McDonald's | 5 | ✔ | ✔ | ✔ | The world's most famous burger-and-fries chain. |
| Pat à Pain | 8 | ✗ | ✔ | ✔ | Fresh take-out sandwiches and pastries. |
| Quick | 5 | ✔ | ✔ | ✔ | Northern Europe's equivalent to McDonald's. |

# Staying


| | |
|---|---|
| Hotel Locator Maps | **280–283** |
| Staying in Paris | **284** |
| A–Z of Hotels | **285–293** |
| Hotel Chains | **294** |

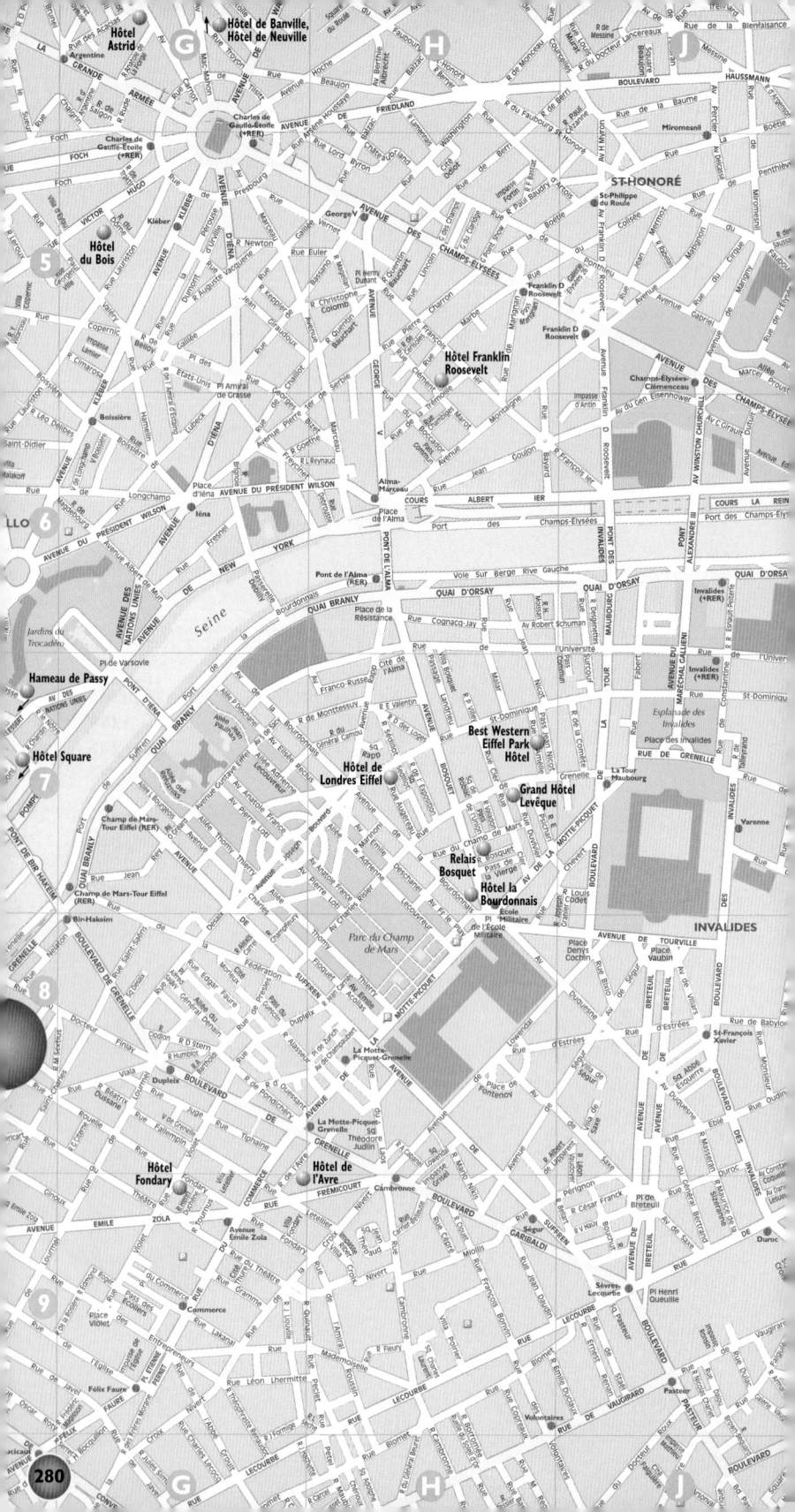
Hôtel Astrid
Hôtel de Banville, Hôtel de Neuville
Hôtel du Bois
Hôtel Franklin Roosevelt
Hameau de Passy
Hôtel Square
Hôtel de Londres Eiffel
Best Western Eiffel Park Hôtel
Grand Hôtel Levêque
Relais Bosquet
Hôtel la Bourdonnais
Hôtel Fondary
Hôtel de l'Avre
Seine
Parc du Champ de Mars
ST-HONORÉ
INVALIDES
Jardins du Trocadéro
Esplanade des Invalides
Champ de Mars-Tour Eiffel (RER)
Bir-Hakeim
Iéna
Alma-Marceau
Pont de l'Alma (RER)
Invalides (RER)
Charles de Gaulle-Étoile (RER)
Miromesnil
St-Philippe du Roule
Franklin D Roosevelt
Champs-Élysées-Clemenceau
Boissière
Place d'Iéna
Place de l'Alma
Place de la Résistance
Place des Invalides
La Tour Maubourg
Varenne
Place Vaubin
St-François Xavier
Place de Fontenoy
La Motte-Picquet-Grenelle
Dupleix
Cambronne
Ségur
Sèvres Lecourbe
Pl Henri Queuille
Pasteur
Volontaires
Cambronne
Félix Faure
Place Violet
Avenue Émile Zola
Duroc
Pl de Breteuil
Pl Jean Theodore Judlin
Pl Amiral de Grasse
Pl Adolphe Chérioux
Pont de Bir-Hakeim
Pont de Grenelle
Pont de Cambronne
Pont de Lamotte-Picquet
Pont de Sèvres

Hôtel Queen Mary
Lautrec Opéra
Ritz
Hôtel Washington Opéra
Hôtel Flor Rivoli
Hôtel St-Honoré
Hôtel Violet
Hôtel Lenox St-Germain
Hôtel Duc de St-Simon
Hôtel St-Germain
L'Hôtel
Hôtel de St-Germain
Hôtel Madison
Hôtel du Levant
Les Rives de Notre-Dame
Hôtel du Globe
Hôtel La Perle
Hôtel Atlantis St-Germain-des-Prés
Hôtel Delavigne
Grand Hôtel des Balcons
Hotel de l'Abbaye
Hôtel Claude Bernard
Hôtel du Panthéon
Relais St-Jacques
L'Atelier Montparnasse
Hôtel Delambre
Hôtel du Parc Montsouris
Hôtel Sunny
Jardin des Tuileries
Jardin du Luxembourg
Seine
ST-GERMAIN-DES-PRÉS
QUARTIER LATIN
281

GARE DE L'EST
Gare de l'Est
RUE DU HUIT MAI 1945
Canal
Hôtel de la Bretonnerie
St-Merry Hotel
Hôtel Flor Rivoli
Hôtel Violet
LE MARAIS
Hôtel de Ville
Pavillon de la Reine
Place des Vosges
Hôtel St-Paul Le Marais
St-Paul-le-Marais
Les Rives de Notre-Dame
St-Michel-Notre-Dame (RER)
Île de la Cité
Pont Marie
Hôtel des Deux Îles
Sully Morland
BASTILLE
Bastille
Le D'Artagnan
Auberge Internationale des Jeunes
Hôtel Jules César
Corail Hôtel
Grand Hôtel de France
Hôtel Prince Albert Concorde
Hôtel Claude Bernard
Minerve Hôtel
QUARTIER LATIN
Hôtel du Panthéon
Hôtel des Grandes Écoles
Jardin des Plantes
Seine
Quai de la Rapée
Gare d'Austerlitz
GARE D'AUSTERLITZ
RÉPUBLIQUE
Auberge de Jeunesse Jules Ferry
LES HALLES
Châtelet Les Halles (RER)
Étienne Marcel
Sentier
Bonne Nouvelle
Grands Boulevards
Strasbourg St-Denis
Arts et Métiers
Temple
Oberkampf
Filles du Calvaire
St-Sébastien-Froissart
St-Ambroise
Richard Lenoir
Bréguet Sabin
Chemin Vert
Parmentier
Gare de Lyon
Place Monge
Jussieu
Cardinal Lemoine
Place Valhubert
Gare d'Austerlitz
Censier-Daubenton
Place Mouffetard
Place Jussieu
Place Monge
Place Valhubert
Pont Marie
Pont Sully
Pont Morland
Pont Charles de Gaulle
Pont d'Austerlitz
Pont de la Tournelle
Pont Saint-Louis
Pont Notre-Dame
Pont Louis-Philippe
Pont Saint-Michel
Pont Neuf
Pont Alexandre III
Pont de la Concorde
Pont de Sully
Pont Morland
Pont d'Austerlitz
Pont de la Rapée
Pont Charles de Gaulle
Pont Saint-Louis
Pont Notre-Dame
Pont Louis-Philippe
Pont Saint-Michel
Pont Neuf
Pont Alexandre III
Pont de la Concorde
Pont de Sully
Pont Morland
Pont d'Austerlitz
Pont de la Rapée
Pont Charles de Gaulle
282

Auberge de Jeunesse Léo Lagrange
Terrass Hotel
Hôtel des Arts
Hôtel Prima Lepic
Hôtel Le Bouquet de Montmartre
Hôtel Regyn's Montmartre
Hôtel Batignolles Villiers
Auberge de Jeunesse Cité des Sciences
Hôtel Queen Mary
Lautrec Opéra
Ritz
Hôtel Washington Opéra
Hôtel St-Honoré
MONTMARTRE
PIGALLE
LES HALLES
Cimetière de Montmartre
Jardin des Tuileries
Seine
Porte de St-Ouen (RER)
Guy Môquet
Marcadet Poissonniers
Simplon
Jules Joffrin
Lamarck
Château Rouge
Place de Clichy
Blanche
Pigalle
Anvers
Barbès Rochechouart
Liège
St-Georges
Bellefond
Poissonière
Cadet
Trinité
Notre-Dame-de-Lorette
Le Peletier
Haussmann St-Lazare
Auber
Opéra
Richelieu Drouot
Grands Boulevards
Bonne Nouvelle
Madeleine
Quatre Septembre
Bourse
Sentier
Réaumur Sébastopol
Pyramides
Tuileries
Palais Royal-Musée du Louvre
Louvre-Rivoli
Châtelet
Les Halles
Etienne Marcel
Gare St-Lazare
Place Vendôme
Place du Marché St-Honoré
Place du Carrousel
Place des Victoires
Place des Abbesses
Place du Tertre
Place Saint-Pierre
Place Jules Joffrin
Place Dublin
Place Gabrielle
Place Pigalle
Place Cadet
Place Lamarck
Place Marcadet
Place Blanche
Place Clichy

# STAYING IN PARIS

**Paris has the whole range of accommodation options, whether you're looking for luxury at the world-famous Ritz, a comfortable three-star hotel in the Latin Quarter or a low-cost hostel. The city's hotels have had a (sometimes deserved) reputation for being dated and pokey, but recent years have seen a complete overhaul. Small designer boutique-hotels have popped up in the once-inexpensive Marais district and up river to the west, and some of the classic hotels have added health spas for some post-sightseeing pampering.**

**LUXURY**
At the top of the spectrum are the luxury hotels, some of them straight out of another era. Their prices on a one-off basis are high, but some give discounts through travel agents so it is worth enquiring back home before your trip.

**ON A BUDGET**
Paris is one of the rare European capitals where you can find a pleasant, affordable place to stay in a central part of the city. Prices often drop in July and August, when there are few business trips, and rise in May, June, September and October—the trade fair months.

Check whether the room price includes breakfast. It is often less expensive to buy your croissant and coffee in a local café rather than at the hotel. If you are bringing or renting a car, ask whether parking is available and how much it costs. Parking on the street can be expensive and frustrating.

Chain hotels on the outskirts can be less expensive, although they lack Parisian character. You'll also have to spend time taking the Métro or RER into the city heart. See page 294 for a selection of chain hotels.

**WHICH DISTRICT?**
Every district in Paris has its good and bad points and choosing which *quartier* to stay in depends on your priorities.

The 8th *arrondissement* (around the Champs-Élysées, avenue George V, avenue Montaigne and Faubourg St-Honoré) has a high concentration of luxury and four-star hotels and is handy if you want to shop for designer labels. You can also find luxury in the 1st *arrondissement* (Tuileries, Louvre, place Vendôme), although the side streets here have two- and three-star hotels.

Farther north, the 9th *arrondissement* (Opéra, *Grands Boulevards*, Faubourg Montmartre) is packed with hotels, many of them two-star. There are nightclubs and shops here.

Across the river, St-Germain-des-Prés and the Latin Quarter are less business-focused than their Right Bank counterparts and closer to the atmosphere of *vieux* Paris. There are plenty of two- and three-star hotels, as well as restaurants and cafés. Here, you are well placed for visiting the île de la Cité.

If you choose to stay in less central areas, check how close you are to a Métro or RER station.

**BEYOND PARIS**
Some farms in the Île de France have converted barns into self-catering holiday homes, providing a base for taking the RER trains into the city and for exploring the countryside around Paris.

**ALTERNATIVES TO HOTELS**
For bed-and-breakfast accommodation with host families you could try France Lodge at 2 rue Meissonier, 75017 *(tel 01 56 33 85 85)*. To rent an apartment, options include UK-based Apartment Service *(tel 020 8944 1444 from the UK; 011 44 20 8944 1444 from the US; **www.**apartment.co.uk)*; Home Rental Service at 120 avenue des Champs-Élysées *(tel 01 42 25 65 40; **www.**homerental.fr)*; or Paris Lodging *(tel 01 43 36 71 69; **www.**parislodging.fr)*.

**TIP**

- The Paris Tourist Office *(tel 0892 683 000)* has information on places to stay. You can reserve rooms if you visit in person.

**PRICES**
Prices given for the hotels on the following pages are for two people sharing a double room for one night, unless otherwise stated.

# HOTELS A–Z

**LE D'ARTAGNAN**
Map 282 off Q8
80 rue Vitruve, 75020
Ménilmontant
Tel 01 40 32 34 56
www.hostels-in.com
France's largest youth hostel occupies a seven-floor building near Père Lachaise cemetery. It has a bar (open until 2am), souvenir shop, four internet booths, electronic lockers, a free cinema, TV lounge and a laundry. Rooms are for three to eight people.
€20.60 per person, including breakfast
439 beds
Porte de Bagnolet

**L'ATELIER MONTPARNASSE**
Map 281 L9
49 rue Vavin, 75006
St-Germain-des-Prés
Tel 01 46 33 60 00
www.ateliermontparnasse.com
This three-star hotel pays tribute to 1930s Montparnasse

(then an artists' hub), with period furniture and mosaic reproductions of 1930s paintings in the bathrooms. Artists' haunts such as La Coupole (see page 266) and Le Dôme brasseries are nearby. Facilities include a laundry service, room service, cable TV, hairdryer and mini-bar. Internet connection is available in some rooms.
€107–€137, excluding breakfast
17
Vavin

**AUBERGE INTERNATIONALE DES JEUNES**
Map 282 off Q8
10 rue Trousseau, 75011
Bastille
Tel 01 47 00 62 00
www.aijparis.com
These lodgings, in the lively Bastille area, are at rock-bottom prices. Don't expect anything fancy, but the rooms are clean and the atmosphere friendly. Four-bed rooms have a separate bathroom and shower, while rooms for two or three people have a bathroom on each floor. A vending machine dispenses cold and hot drinks, and there is a safe at the front desk and internet access. Bed linen and blankets are provided.
€14 per person, including breakfast Mar–Oct; €13 Nov–Feb
200 beds
Ledru Rollin, Bastille

**AUBERGE DE JEUNESSE CITÉ DES SCIENCES**
Map 283 off N4
24 rue des Sept Arpents, 93310 Le Pré Saint-Gervais
La Villette
Tel 01 48 43 24 11
www.hostels-in.com
This youth hostel is in a modern building near the Parc de la Villette (see pages 146–147). Dormitories have four or six beds and there are electronic lockers, internet terminals, a terrace, TV room, laundry, bicycle rental and a kitchen for guests to use.
€18.50 per person, including breakfast
184 beds
Hoche

**AUBERGE DE JEUNESSE JULES FERRY**
Map 282 Q6
8 boulevard Jules Ferry, 75011
Canal St-Martin
Tel 01 43 57 55 60
www.hostels-in.com
Ideally placed for strolls along the Canal St-Martin, this youth hostel has six-bed dormitories as well as some rooms for couples. Facilities include a laundry, electronic lockers and internet terminals. Breakfast is available but there are no other cooking facilities.
€18.50 per person, including breakfast
100 beds
République

**AUBERGE DE JEUNESSE LÉO LAGRANGE**
Map 283 off K2
107 rue Martre, 92110
Clichy
Tel 01 41 27 26 90
www.hostels-in.com
This youth hostel, on the northwestern outskirts, has rooms for two to six people, as well as a TV room, laundry, electronic lockers, internet terminals and a bar/restaurant (open in summer).
€18.50 per person, including breakfast
338 beds
Mairie de Clichy

**BEST WESTERN EIFFEL PARK HÔTEL**
Map 280 H7
17 bis rue Amélie, 75007
Invalides
Tel 01 45 55 10 01
www.eiffelpark.com

The exotic decoration at this three-star hotel is thanks to the owner's trips to India and China. The bedrooms have a personal touch, such as an oriental rug or a Chinese chest of drawers, as well as minibar, modem connection, safe and hairdryer. There's a beautiful art deco bar downstairs and breakfast is served on the roof (weather permitting) or in the pleasant winter garden.
€130–185, excluding breakfast
36 rooms
Latour-Maubourg

**CORAIL HÔTEL**
Map 282 Q9
23 rue de Lyon, 75012
Gare de Lyon
Tel 01 43 43 23 54
www.corail-hotel.fr
This three-star hotel is popular with the business crowd, being close to the Gare de Lyon, with its Métro, RER and mainline train services. The lively Bastille district is also nearby. Rooms may be slightly lacking in character, but come equipped with a hairdryer, private safe, telephone and satellite TV.
€69–€73, excluding breakfast
50
In the communal areas
Gare de Lyon

**GRAND HÔTEL DES BALCONS**
Map 281 M8
3 rue Casimir-Delavigne, 75006
St-Germain-des-Prés
Tel 01 46 34 78 50
www.balcons.com
This two-star hotel is close to the Jardin du Luxembourg. Outside, there are flower-filled balconies; inside, the lobby and communal areas have an early 1900s feel, with period furniture and stained-glass windows. The bright and airy bedrooms have modem

connection, cable and satellite TV, a safe and a hairdryer. Breakfast is served in a bistro-style dining room.
€100–€150, excluding breakfast
55
Odéon

**GRAND HÔTEL DE FRANCE**
Map 282 Q9
12 rue de Lyon, 75012
Bastille
Tel 01 43 43 06 97
www.grandhoteldefrance.com
Bastille, with its bars and restaurants, is where you'll find this two-star hotel. It's good for small groups or families on a budget as rooms with three or four beds are only slightly more expensive than a double. Rooms are comfortable, if not particularly fancy, and there is parking nearby.
€72, excluding breakfast
45 rooms
Bastille, Gare de Lyon

**GRAND HÔTEL LEVÊQUE**
Map 280 H7
29 rue Cler, 75007
Eiffel Tower
Tel 01 47 05 49 15
www.hotel-leveque.com
The bedrooms at this two-star hotel have a direct line for internet access, satellite TV, safe, fan and hair dryer, and have been soundproofed to avoid disturbance from the lively fruit and vegetable market outside in the pedestrian-only street. Inside, the hotel is simple yet bright, with some nice pictures.
€84–€91, excluding breakfast
50
École-Militaire

**HAMEAU DE PASSY**
Map 280 off F7
48 rue Passy, 75016
Passy
Tel 01 42 88 47 55
www.hameaudepassy.com
In a chic residential district, this two-star hotel offers peace and quiet in a leafy cul-de-sac. The modern interior is tasteful and the bedrooms face the garden. They have a direct dial phone with modem connection and cable TV. The hotel has a fax service, individual safes at the reception and a nearby garage.
€107–€112, including breakfast
32
Passy, La Muette

**HÔTEL DE L'ABBAYE**
Map 281 L8
10 rue Cassette, 75006
St-Germain-des-Prés
Tel 01 45 44 38 11
www.hotel-abbaye.com
Calm prevails at this three-star hotel, in a former abbey. The salon and most of the rooms look out onto a terrace; four

suites have private terraces. The elegant interior has fine furniture and there is an antique fireplace in the salon. The hotel is close to the Jardin du Luxembourg. Facilities include a bar, room service, car rental and laundry service. Bedrooms have hairdryers and satellite TV.
€201–€292, including breakfast
37 and 7 suites
St-Sulpice, Sèvres-Babylone

**SPECIAL**

**L'HÔTEL**
Map 281 L7
13 rue des Beaux-Arts, 75006
St-Germain-des-Prés
Tel 01 44 41 99 00
www.l-hotel.com
This deluxe four-star hotel, in a 19th-century pavilion, was fully renovated at the turn of the millennium. The exuberantly elegant interior is by Jacques Garcia and the fully equipped rooms are named after famous

people, such as Marco Polo, Mistinguett and Oscar Wilde (who breathed his last at this hotel in 1900). The restaurant (closed Sunday, Monday and during August), has an impressive dome.
€272–€625, excluding breakfast
16 and 4 suites
Indoor
St-Germain-des-Prés

**HÔTEL DES ARTS**
Map 283 L3
5 rue de Tholozé, 75018
Montmartre
Tel 01 46 06 30 52
www.hotel-des-arts.net
This two-star hotel is close to Sacré-Cœur and the rue des Abbesses. There is some fine furniture in the warm interior. The breakfast room has

exposed brick walls and there is a collection of curios in the salon. Bedrooms have internet connection, cable and satellite

TV, a safe and a hairdryer, and there is parking nearby.
€78–€90, excluding breakfast
50
Abbesses, Blanche

**HÔTEL ASTRID**
Map 280 G4
27 avenue Carnot, 75017
Champs-Élysées
Tel 01 44 09 26 00
www.astrid-hotel.fr
This three-star hotel is in a peaceful side street close to the Champs-Élysées. No two

bedrooms are the same—Styles include romantic (think brass bedframe, chandelier and pink curtains) and country (pine furniture contrasting with blue wallpaper). Facilities include a safe, hairdryer and cable TV. There are parking spaces nearby.
€122, including breakfast
40
Charles de Gaulle-Étoile

**HÔTEL ATLANTIS ST-GERMAIN-DES-PRÉS**
Map 281 L8
4 rue du Vieux-Colombier, 75006
St-Germain-des-Prés
Tel 01 45 48 31 81
www.hotelatlantis.com
Most of the bright and airy rooms in this two-star hotel face onto pretty place St-Sulpice. All have been beautifully decorated with soft tones, fine furniture and

quilted bedspreads, and have telephone, cable and satellite TV, internet connection and a hairdryer. The communal areas are elegant and there is a grandfather clock in the breakfast room.
€115–€150, excluding breakfast
27
St-Sulpice

**HÔTEL DE L'AVRE**
Map 280 G9
21 rue de l'Avre, 75015
Champ de Mars
Tel 01 45 75 31 03
www.hoteldelavre.com
Attention has been paid to every detail at this two-star

hotel. Bedrooms have a floral design and satellite TV. In spring and summer you can have breakfast in the garden.
€70–€77, excluding breakfast
26
La-Motte-Picquet-Grenelle

**HÔTEL DE BANVILLE**
Map 280 off G4
166 boulevard Berthier, 75017
Porte de Champerret
Tel 01 42 67 70 16
www.hotelbanville.fr
The 1930s building housing this three-star hotel is decorated with objets d'art, paintings and antique furniture. The salon is the epitome of elegance and the well-equipped bedrooms have soft tones and fine furniture. The hotel is not close to the main sights, but you can take the RER or Métro into the heart of the city. The Champs-Élysées is 20 minutes' walk away.
€155–€187
38 and 1 suite
Porte de Champerret

**HÔTEL BATIGNOLLES VILLIERS**
Map 283 off K3
11bis rue des Batignolles, 75017
Clichy
Tel 01 45 22 50 58
www.parishotels.com
Most of the bedrooms at this three-star hotel are reasonably large, some with French windows. Facilities include telephone, cable and satellite TV, internet connection, minibar and hairdryer.
€69–€84, excluding breakfast
32
Rome

**HÔTEL DU BOIS**
Map 280 G5
11 rue du Dôme, 75016
Champs-Élysées
Tel 01 45 00 31 96
www.hoteldubois.com
The interior of this three-star hotel is reminiscent of an elegant English mansion. There is Georgian furniture and crimson tones in the salon, where breakfast is served, and patterned fabrics in the bedrooms. Facilities include a hairdryer, cable TV, safe and minibar. The hotel is in an elegant district.
€115–€129, excluding breakfast
41
Kléber, Charles de Gaulle-Étoile.

**HÔTEL LE BOUQUET DE MONTMARTRE**
Map 283 L3
1 rue Durantin, 75018
Montmartre
Tel 01 46 06 87 54
www.paris-montmartre-hotel.com
This two-star hotel is in the heart of *Amélie* territory (see page 309) in Montmartre.

The furnishings combine kitsch and classic Louis XVI. The bedrooms have limited facilities (phone but no TV), but have pleasing features such as little alcoves by the beds, numerous small hanging cupboards and some candelabra wall lamps. Breakfast is served in a beautiful dining room, with brocade wallpaper, period furniture, and a profusion of lamp fixtures.
€64, excluding breakfast
36
Abbesses

**HÔTEL LA BOURDONNAIS**
Map 280 H7
111–113 avenue de la Bourdonnais, 75007
Tour Eiffel
Tel 01 47 05 45 42
www.hotellabourdonnais.com
This three-star hotel is also home to the restaurant La Cantine des Gourmets, which serves exquisite French cuisine. Inside, the hotel resembles a comfortable bourgeois home, with elegant furniture and antiques. The suites and bedrooms with four beds are

perfect for families; all bedrooms have satellite TV, a safe, telephone with modem connection and a hairdryer. Breakfast is served in a pleasant winter garden.
€135–€150, excluding breakfast
57 and 3 suites
École-Militaire

**HÔTEL DE LA BRETONNERIE**
Map 282 N7
22 rue Sainte-Croix-de-la-Bretonnerie, 75004
Le Marais
Tel 01 48 87 77 63
www.labretonnerie.com
A 17th-century mansion with beamed ceilings is the refined setting for this hotel. The breakfast room has a magnificent vaulted ceiling. Bedrooms have cable and satellite TV, a safe, minibar and hairdryer; some have canopy beds. There is a laundry service.
Closed Aug
€120–€160, excluding breakfast
22 and 7 suites
Hôtel-de-Ville

**HÔTEL CLAUDE BERNARD**
Map 281 M8
43 rue des Écoles, 75005
Latin Quarter
Tel 01 43 26 32 52
www.hotelclaudebernard.com
This three-star hotel has a flamboyant, red lacquered

façade and an elegant interior. Bright tones and flowers create a warm atmosphere and there are fine fabrics and furniture in the bedrooms, which have balconies and cable and satellite TV. There is a bar, restaurant and internet booth.
€127–€171, excluding breakfast
34
Maubert-Mutualité

**HÔTEL DELAMBRE**
Map 281 K10
35 rue Delambre, 75014
Montparnasse
Tel 01 43 20 66 31
www.hoteldelambre.com
Close to Tour Montparnasse, this three-star hotel has a beautiful interior, with warm tones, wrought ironwork and period furniture covered in modern fabrics. Bedrooms have a telephone, satellite TV and a modem connection. There are two parking areas nearby.

€80–€95, excluding breakfast
31
Vavin, Edgar-Quinet, Montparnasse

**HÔTEL DELAVIGNE**
Map 281 M8
1 rue Casimir-Delavigne, 75006
St-Germain-des-Prés
Tel 01 43 29 31 50
www.hoteldelavigne.com
The bedrooms in this three-star hotel are individually decorated, using, for example, rattan, antique furniture or floral or brocade wallpaper. They have a phone, satellite TV

**SPECIAL**

**HÔTEL DUC DE ST-SIMON**
Map 281 K7
14 rue de St-Simon, 75007
Invalides
Tel 01 44 39 20 20

Antiques and fine furniture decorate this beautiful three-star hotel, in an 18th-century mansion. Although close to the animated boulevard St-Germain, rue de St-Simon is very quiet. The hotel has a bar and terrace, and a garage on boulevard Raspail.
€235–€270, excluding breakfast
29 and 5 suites
In some rooms
Rue-du-Bac

and a safe. There is a baby-sitting service. The salon is soberly classical, with period furniture. The hotel is in a great location, near the Jardin du Luxembourg.
€100–€130, excluding breakfast
34
Odéon, Cluny

**HÔTEL DES DEUX ÎLES**
Map 282 N8
59 rue St-Louis-en-l'Île, 75004
Île St-Louis
Tel 01 43 26 13 35
www.parishotels.com
A 17th-century mansion on the picturesque Île St-Louis is home to this three-star hotel. Provençal fabrics and painted rattan furniture enliven the comfortable bedrooms, which have cable TV and a

hairdryer. Paris's most famous ice cream store, Berthillon, is nearby.

€127–€150, excluding breakfast
17
Pont-Marie, St-Michel

**HÔTEL FLOR RIVOLI**
Map 281 M7
13 rue des Deux Boules, 75001
Châtelet
Tel 01 42 33 49 60
www.hotel-flor-rivoli.com
This two-star hotel is close to the Musée du Louvre and one of Paris's longest shopping streets, the rue de Rivoli,

which may take your mind off the small size of the bedrooms. It is relatively comfortable and ideal for those on a budget, prepared to sacrifice character for convenience.
€80, excluding breakfast
20
Châtelet

**HÔTEL FONDARY**
Map 280 G9
30 rue Fondary, 75015
Tour Eiffel
Tel 01 45 75 14 75
www.hotelfondary.com
This hotel is convenient if you're attending a trade fair at the Porte de Versailles. The bedrooms are small but carefully decorated with rattan furniture. Some face onto the hotel's terrace, where breakfast is served in warm weather. There is a bar, a laundry service and access to a

nearby garage. All rooms have a TV and minibar.
€68–€74, excluding breakfast
21
Émile-Zola, La-Motte-Picquet-Grenelle

**HÔTEL FRANKLIN ROOSEVELT**
Map 280 H5
18 rue Clément Marot, 75008
Champs-Élysées
Tel 01 53 57 49 50
www.hroosevelt.com
This hotel is close to the Champs-Elysées and avenue Montaigne, with its world-famous couture shops. Inside, there is subtle lighting, thick

fitted carpets, rich red fabrics and dark wood. If you're looking for a bit of luxury, the suite on the sixth floor has a king-size bed and a Jacuzzi. Facilities include a bar, reading room and winter garden.
€175–€205, excluding breakfast
48
Franklin D. Roosevelt, Alma Marceau

**HÔTEL DU GLOBE**
Map 281 L8
15 rue des Quatre-Vents, 75006
St-Germain-des-Prés
Tel 01 46 26 35 50
A two-star hotel with this much character is hard to find. There are beamed ceilings and antique furniture in the bedrooms (some even have canopy beds) and 18th-century bergère armchairs and an 18th-century mirror in the salon. Facilities for the 21st century include TV and phone. The hotel has the added bonus of being close to the Jardin du Luxembourg.
Closed Aug
€90–€150, excluding breakfast
15
Odéon

**HÔTEL DES GRANDES ÉCOLES**
Map 282 N9
75 rue Cardinal-Lemoine, 75005
Latin Quarter
Tel 01 43 26 79 23
www.hotel-grandes-ecoles.com
An oasis of peace in the lively Latin Quarter, this gem of a three-star hotel is at the end of a cul-de-sac, with its own garden. It is decorated in elegant country-house style with wicker chairs and lace tablecloths in the breakfast room and floral wallpaper and quilted bedspreads in the bedrooms. Some rooms sleep up to four people. Hotel facilities include a babysitting service and 15 covered parking spaces.

€95–€125, excluding breakfast
51
Cardinal-Lemoine, Place Monge

**HÔTEL JULES CÉSAR**
Map 282 Q8
52 avenue Ledru-Rollin, 75012
Bastille
Tel 01 43 43 15 88
www.hoteljulescesar.com
Rooms at this two-star hotel are furnished quite basically, but attention has been paid to their decoration. All have been soundproofed—a relief in the bustling Bastille area—and they have cable and satellite TV. Breakfast is served in the bistro-style dining room.
€62–€72, excluding breakfast
48
Ledru Rollin

**HÔTEL LAUTREC OPÉRA**
Map 283 M5
8–10 rue d'Amboise, 75002
Opéra
Tel 01 42 96 67 90
This three-star hotel is named after artist Henri Toulouse-Lautrec, who once lived here. It is classified as a Historic Monument and has a beautiful 18th-century façade. Inside, there's a more contemporary feel, with pale wood furniture and blue and yellow upholstery; some rooms have exposed bricks and beams and all have satellite TV.
€151–€196, excluding breakfast
60
Richelieu-Drouot

**HÔTEL LENOX ST-GERMAIN**
Map 281 L7
9 rue de l'Université, 75007
St-Germain-des-Prés
Tel 01 42 96 10 95
www.lenoxsaintgermain.com
The Lenox Club Bar at this three-star hotel has comfortable armchairs and a collection of jazz musical instruments on display. In the hotel itself, the elegant bedrooms have beautiful wall lamps and pictures, as well as a safe, telephone, modem and satellite TV. There are also

some duplex suites. Breakfast is served in a vaulted cellar.
€115–€150, excluding breakfast
34
Rue-du-Bac, St-Germain-des-Prés

**HÔTEL DU LEVANT**
Map 281 M8
18 rue de la Harpe, 75005
Latin Quarter
Tel 01 46 34 11 00
In the heart of the Latin Quarter, this three-star hotel has been around for more than two hundred years and has been run by the same family for four generations. The decoration is bright and modern, though the salon contains some antiques, together with chessboards and newspapers. The bedrooms have cable TV and internet connections, and there is a laundry service.

€107–€145, excluding breakfast
42 and 4 suites
Cluny–La Sorbonne, St-Michel

**HÔTEL DE LONDRES EIFFEL**
Map 280 H7
1 rue Augereau, 75007
Eiffel Tower
Tel 01 45 51 63 02
www.londres-eiffel.com
Comfort is a priority at this three-star hotel, with soft armchairs in the salon and king-size beds in the bedrooms. Warm yellow and raspberry tones predominate in the classically decorated interior.

€105–€115, excluding breakfast
30
École-Militaire

**HÔTEL MADISON**
Map 281 L8
143 boulevard St-Germain, 75006
St-Germain-des-Prés
Tel 01 40 51 60 00
www.hotel-madison.com
Albert Camus finished writing his novel *L'Étranger* (*The Stranger*; 1942) at this elegant three-star hotel. Les Deux-Magots café, a popular haunt of the literary and intellectual elite in the 1920s and 1930s, is opposite.
The hotel has a beautiful

18th-century style salon with bergère armchairs, tapestries and wood panels, while the bedrooms have antique furniture, satellite TV, minibar, safe and hairdryer.
€135–€255, including breakfast
53 and one suite
St-Germain-des-Prés

**HÔTEL DE NEUVILLE**
Map 280 off G4
3 rue Verniquet, 75017
Wagram
Tel 01 43 80 26 30
www.albotel.com
This three-star hotel is in a 19th-century building with a pretty terrace. The bedrooms have been carefully decorated in a contemporary style, while retaining a romantic feel. Some have canopy beds and all have cable TV and internet connection. Try to get a room with a view of Sacré-Cœur. You can park your car in the hotel's garage, although check before you arrive that there is space.
€120–€137, excluding breakfast
28
RER Pereire

**HÔTEL DU PANTHÉON**
Map 281 M9
19 place du Panthéon, 75005
Latin Quarter
Tel 01 43 54 32 95
The interior of this three-star hotel has an 18th-century feel, with gilded panels and fine fabrics. Most of the rooms look out onto the stately Panthéon, and have cable TV and a mini-

minibar. There is a laundry service and parking.
€168–€213, excluding breakfast
36
Cardinal Lemoine

**HÔTEL DU PARC MONTSOURIS**
Map 281off L10
4 rue du Parc Montsouris, 75014
Denfert-Rochereau
Tel 01 45 89 09 72
www.hotel-parc-montsouris.com
Sitting alongside the beautiful Montsouris Park in the southern part of the Left Bank, this two-star hotel is a little way from Paris's main visitor attractions. The reception area is in art deco style, while the bright and airy bedrooms are more standard. Each has a little desk, as well as cable TV, internet connection, card lock and hairdryer.
€59–€77, excluding breakfast
35
Porte d'Orléans

**HÔTEL LA PERLE**
Map 281 L8
14 rue des Canettes, 75006
St-Germain-des-Prés
Tel 01 43 29 10 10
www.hotellaperle.com
This smart three-star hotel, in a picturesque street near place

St-Sulpice, is in an 18th-century mansion with its own courtyard. Bright tones add a contemporary note to the otherwise classic interior, which has *fleur de lys* carpets and beamed ceilings. Facilities include internet connection, cable and satellite TV and a laundry service.
€153–€221, excluding breakfast
38
St-Germain-des-Prés, St-Sulpice, Mabillon

**HÔTEL PRIMA LEPIC**
Map 283 L3
29 rue Lepic, 75018
Montmartre
Tel 01 46 06 44 64
www.hotel-paris-lepic.com
This two-star hotel is close to Sacré-Cœur and place du Tertre and was renovated in 2001. The brightly painted bedrooms have been carefully

furnished, five with canopy beds. Each has a TV, hairdryer and modem connection. The hotel has three suites that can each sleep up to four people.
€96–€125, excluding breakfast
35 and 3 suites
Blanche, Abbesses

**HÔTEL PRINCE ALBERT CONCORDIA**
Map 282 off Q9
38 boulevard Diderot, 75012
Nation
Tel 01 43 43 54 92
www.hotelprincealbert.com
This hotel, part of a small chain, is within walking distance of the lively Bastille area. Behind the elegant green awning is a cosy interior. The small but beautifully decorated bedrooms have floral bed-spreads and matching curtains, as well as direct dial phone and satellite TV.
€70, excluding breakfast
25
Gare de Lyon

**HÔTEL QUEEN MARY**
Map 281 K5
9 rue Greffulhe, 75008
Opéra
Tel 01 42 66 40 50
www.hotelqueenmary.com
Elegance is the hallmark of this three-star hotel, near the Opéra Palais Garnier. The salon has moulded ceilings and printed fitted carpets, while the large dining room has a tromp-l'oeil painting. The spacious bedrooms are decorated with mahogany wood and

burgundy fabrics. There's a small terrace and the usual facilities of cable TV, safe, hairdryer and minibar in the bedrooms.
€145–€165, excluding breakfast
35 and 1 suite
Madeleine, Havre-Caumartin

**HÔTEL REGYN'S MONTMARTRE**
Map 283 M3
18 place des Abbesses, 75018
Montmartre
Tel 01 42 54 45 21
www.regynsmontmartre.com
Some of the bedrooms in this two-star hotel have views of the nearby Sacré-Cœur, while others face onto the place des Abbesses, with its lively cafes. All have been carefully decorated each with a little writing desk, as well as satellite TV and retro-style bathrooms.
€75–€110, excluding breakfast
22
Abbesses

**HÔTEL ST-GERMAIN**
Map 281 K7
88 rue du Bac, 75007
St-Germain-des-Prés
Tel 01 49 54 70 00
www.hotel-saint-germain.fr
This is hotel is in a mansion that has retained many of its original features, such as beamed ceilings and exposed stone walls. The decoration is classic, with the occasional contemporary touch. Bedrooms look out onto the garden or the terrace, and have a telephone, TV and modem. You should be aware that there is another hotel with a similar name (see page 292).
€150–€170, excluding breakfast
29
Rue-du-Bac, Sèvres-Babylone

SPECIAL

**HÔTEL SQUARE**
Map 280 off F7
3 rue de Boulainvilliers, 75016
Passy
Tel 01 44 14 91 90
www.hotelsquare.com
This four-star hotel close to the banks of the Seine is part of a larger complex. There are two restaurants, Bermuda Onion (see page 262) and Zebra Square. There's also a lounge bar with music most evenings and an art gallery with contemporary work. Sleek lines, subtle lighting, designer furniture and ethnic objets d'art create a warm, contemporary atmosphere.
€245–€390, excluding breakfast
22
Indoor
RER Kennedy-Radio-France

**HÔTEL DE ST-GERMAIN**
Map 281 L8
50 rue du Four, 75006
St-Germain-des-Prés
Tel 01 45 48 91 64
www.hotel-saint-germain.com
This two-star hotel's main selling point is its location, near the picturesque place St-Sulpice. The bedrooms are tiny but nicely decorated, with painted wooden furniture. Facilities include nearby parking and a laundry service.
€105–€120, excluding breakfast
30
St-Sulpice, Sèvres-Babylone

**HÔTEL ST-HONORÉ**
Map 281 M6
85 rue St-Honoré, 75001
Louvre
Tel 01 42 36 20 38
www.hotelsainthonore.com
This one-star hotel is on the ultrachic rue St-Honoré. Bedrooms have a telephone and cable and satellite TV, and there is parking nearby.
€74–€83, excluding breakfast
29
Châtelet

**HÔTEL ST-MERRY**
Map 282 N7
78 rue de la Verrerie, 75004
Le Marais
Tel 01 42 78 14 15
www.hotelmarais.com
If you choose room nine of this three-star hotel you'll be sleeping under a flying buttress! The hotel was built during the Renaissance as the presbytery of the Church of St-Merri. Its highly original interior also includes many late-Gothic features, including sculptures, carved woodwork and beamed ceilings.
€146–€210, excluding breakfast
11 and 1 suite
Hôtel-de-Ville, Châtelet

**HÔTEL ST-PAUL LE MARAIS**
Map 282 P7
8 rue de Sévigné, 75004
Le Marais
Tel 01 48 04 97 27
www.hotel-paris-marais.com
A former 17th-century convent houses this three-star hotel, near the Musée Carnavalet. The bar and salon have burgundy carpets and plenty of mahogany. Bedrooms have cable TV, telephone and tea and coffee-making facilities, and breakfast is served in a fine stone-vaulted room.
€130–€150, excluding breakfast
27
St-Paul

**HÔTEL SUNNY**
Map 281 M10
48 boulevard du Port-Royal, 75005
Latin Quarter
Tel 01 43 31 79 86
www.hotelsunny.com
Pastel tones predominate in the neat bedrooms of this two-star hotel. Facilities include satellite TV, hairdryers and a laundry service.
€70–€74, excluding breakfast
37
Place Monge

**HÔTEL VIOLET**
Map 281 M7
7 rue Jean-Lantier, 75001
Châtelet
Tel 01 42 33 45 38
www.franceparishotelviolet.com

This three-star hotel, within walking distance of the Louvre, Notre-Dame and Centre Georges Pompidou, has a welcoming salon, a winter garden with a fountain, and a 16th-century vaulted breakfast room.
€130, excluding breakfast
30
Châtelet

SPECIAL

**PAVILLON DE LA REINE**
Map 282 P7
28 place des Vosges, 75003
Le Marais
Tel 01 40 29 19 19
www.pavillon-de-la-reine.com
It would be hard to find a more perfect setting for a four-star hotel than this 17th-century building on the historic place des Vosges. This was the residence of Anne of Austria, Louis XIII's wife, and the exquisite interior retains

much of its period furniture, with a particularly imposing fireplace in the salon. The vaulted cellar, where you can have breakfast, has tapestries on the walls. Bedrooms have cable TV, and some have canopy beds. A more recently constructed building houses some of the bedrooms.
€365–€395, excluding breakfast
34, 14 suites and 10 duplex
Bastille, St-Paul

**HÔTEL WASHINGTON OPÉRA**
Map 281 L6
50 rue de Richelieu, 75001
Palais Royal
Tel 01 42 96 68 06
www.hotelwashingtonopera.com
Madame de Pompadour, mistress of Louis XV, once lived here. Her home is now a lavish four-star hotel. The bedrooms have *Directoire*-style furniture and marble bathrooms; some have canopy beds.
€214–€275, excluding breakfast
35 and 3 suites
Palais-Royal/Musée-du-Louvre

SPECIAL

**RITZ**
Map 281 L5
15 place Vendôme, 75001
Opéra
Tel 01 43 16 30 70
www.ritzparis.com
This world-famous hotel has been the epitome of elegance and luxury since it opened in 1898. Coco Chanel, Ernest Hemingway and Marcel Proust were regular guests here. The lavish interior is decorated

with antiques and chandeliers. The hotel has a club, several restaurants, bars and private salons, conference rooms and the gourmet cookery school, Ritz-Escoffier.
€640–€750, excluding breakfast
135 and 40 suites
Tuileries, Pyramides, Madeleine, Concorde

**MINERVE HÔTEL**
Map 282 N9
13 rue des Écoles, 75005
Latin Quarter
Tel 01 43 26 26 04
www.hotel-paris-minerve.com
Fine materials have been used throughout this three-star hotel to create an elegant but friendly atmosphere. Some of the bedrooms have

balconies and all have satellite TV. Modern, sepia frescoes depict various places in France.
€93–€125, excluding breakfast
54 (in two buildings)
Cardinal Lemoine, Jussieu

**RELAIS BOSQUET**
Map 280 H7
19 rue du Champ-de-Mars, 75007
Eiffel Tower
Tel 01 47 05 25 45
www.relaisbosquet.com
Space, elegance and comfort characterize this three-star hotel, close to the Invalides and a 10-minute walk from the Eiffel Tower. Directoire-style

furniture and soft hues set the tone. The bedrooms have cable TV, a phone, safe and minibar, as well as an iron and ironing board. The breakfast room looks out onto a pleasant terrace with flowers.
€140–€160, excluding breakfast
40
École-Militaire

**RELAIS ST-JACQUES**
Map 281 M9
3 rue de l'Abbé-de-l'Epée, 75005
Latin Quarter
Tel 01 53 73 26 00
www.relais-saint-jacques.com
This building was a stopover for pilgrims on the route to Santiago de Compostella, in northwest Spain. It's now a stylish four-star hotel with a 1920s-style bar and a Louis XV-style salon.
Bedrooms are bright, airy

and comfortable with 18th-century furniture. Some have views of the nearby Panthéon, while others have a Jacuzzi in

SPECIAL

**TERRASS HOTEL**
Map 283 L3
12 rue Joseph de Maistre, 75018
Montmartre
Tel 01 46 06 72 85
www.terrass-hotel.com
The terrace of this four-star hotel has wonderful views, as do bedrooms on the fourth floor and above. The classical decoration in the bedrooms is warmed up with blue and yellow Provençal fabrics. The hotel has its own bar and restaurant.
€225–€248, including breakfast
88 and 13 suites (2 non-smoking floors)
Place-de-Clichy

the bathroom. Courtesy transportation to the airport is provided.
€160–€250, excluding breakfast
23
RER Luxembourg

**LES RIVES DE NOTRE-DAME**
Map 281 M8
15 quai St-Michel, 75005
Latin Quarter
Tel 01 43 54 81 16
www.rivesdenotredame.com
This four-star hotel overlooks the Seine and has wonderful views of the Île de la Cité. Beamed ceilings, marble tiling, tapestries, and fine wrought-iron furniture are reminiscent of a Provençal or Tuscan villa. The bedrooms are large and two of them have sofas which can be converted into extra beds for children under 12 at no extra cost.
€183–€289, excluding breakfast
9 and 1 suite
St-Michel

# HOTEL CHAINS

| Name of Hotel Chain | Description | Number of Hotels in Paris | Telephone Numbers and Websites |
|---|---|---|---|
| Best Western | The world's largest hotel group has hotels across the city. Each shares the branding but has its own individual style. | 58 | 0800 393 130 (UK)<br>1-800/780-7234 (US)<br>0800 904 490 (France)<br>**www.**bestwestern.com |
| Campanile | This chain of hotels with restaurants has nearly 500 establishments across France. | 7 | 0825 003 003 (France)<br>**www.**campanile.fr |
| Châteaux & Hotels de France | An affiliation of hotels and chateaux providing luxury places to stay. | 16 | 0820 354 725 (France)<br>**www.**chateaux-hotels.com |
| Comfort Inn | This leading limited-service hotel chain claims 'luxury on a budget'. | 21 | 0800 444 444 (UK)<br>1-877/424-6423 (US)<br>0800 912 424 (France)<br>**www.**comfortinn.com |
| Ibis | Hotels in this budget chain usually have a restaurant, bar and 24-hour reception. | 35 | 0870 609 0963 (UK)<br>0892 686 686 (France)<br>**www.**ibishotel.com |
| Intercontinental/ Holiday Inn | The Intercontinental group includes Holiday Inn and Holiday Inn Express. | 26 | 0800 405 060 (UK)<br>1-800/465-4329 (US)<br>0800 905 999 (France)<br>**www.**ichotel.com |
| Kyriad | Comfortable, reasonably priced hotels. | 13 | 0825 003 003 (France)<br>**www.**kyriad.com |
| Marriott | The Marriotts in and around Paris include two four-star hotels, a five-star hotel and one near Roissy–Charles de Gaulle airport. | 4 | 0800 221 222 (UK)<br>1-888/236-2427 (US)<br>0800 908 333 (France)<br>**www.**marriott.com |
| Mercure | Choose from 3 grades–simple, enhanced comfort and refined. | 65 | 0870 609 0965 (UK)<br>1–800/MERCURE (US)<br>0825 883 333 (France)<br>**www.**mercure.com |
| Novotel | Comfortable hotels, usually with good-sized bedrooms. | 9 | 0870 609 0961 (UK)<br>1-800/NOVOTEL (US)<br>0825 884 444 (France) |
| Radisson | There is a Radisson at Roissy–Charles de Gaulle airport and another, with its classic Haussmann façade, on the Champs-Élysées. | 2 | 0800 374 411 (UK)<br>1-888/201-1718 (US)<br>0800 916 060 (France)<br>**www.**radisson.com |
| Relais du Silence | This is an affiliation of peaceful hotels with character and good food. | 2 | 01 44 49 90 00 (France)<br>**www.**relais-du-silence.com |
| Relais & Châteaux | A chain of smart hotels and chateaux. | 1 | 01 42 99 80 80 (France)<br>**www.**relaischateaux.fr |
| Sofitel | Comfortable hotels with restaurants. | 15 | 0870 609 0964 (UK)<br>1-800/221-4542 (US)<br>0825 885 555 (France)<br>**www.**sofitel.com |

| | |
|---|---|
| Before You Go | **296–297** |
| Practicalities | **298–299** |
| Money Matters | **300–301** |
| Health | **302–303** |
| Communication | **304–305** |
| Finding Help | **305–306** |
| Media | **306–307** |
| Opening Times and Tickets | **307–308** |
| Tourist Offices | **308–309** |
| Films and Books | **309** |
| Websites | **310** |
| Words and Phrases | **311–316** |


# Planning

### CLIMATE

- Paris's climate is generally not subject to extremes. Winters are cool, but rarely bitterly cold, while summers are warm, but not rain-free. Although the city has a reasonably low rainfall overall, be prepared for showers.
- The cliché of 'Paris in the spring' does not usually apply until well into May, when the weather finally warms up.
- Summer (June to the end of August) can be glorious. The longest days are in June and July, when you're likely to enjoy the most sunshine and comfortable temperatures. August can be hot, muggy and stormy—Parisians who haven't fled the city tend to head down to the *quais* beside the Seine for a fresher breeze.
- If you are lucky, you'll have crisp, sunny days in autumn (September to November).
- Snow is rare in winter.

**AVERAGE TEMPERATURES**

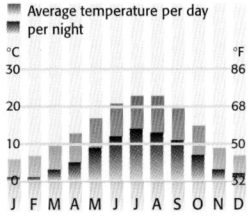


**DAYS ABOVE 18°C**

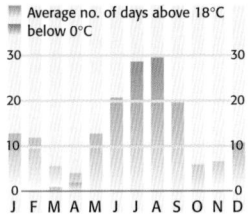


**RAINFALL**

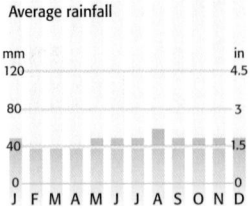


### WHEN TO GO

- Spring is a pleasant time to visit Paris, when the chestnut trees are in blossom and the weather is warming up.
- If you choose hot and sunny July you'll be battling with many other visitors, but time it right and you'll experience the Bastille Day celebrations (14 July). August is quieter, as many Parisians flee to other parts of France to escape the muggy heat. Some restaurants close for the whole month and there are fewer cultural activities.
- The weather can be pleasant in autumn but hotel rooms are harder to find as the trade fair season is in full swing. If you don't mind the cooler winter weather, December can be a magical time, with the streets sparkling with Christmas lights.
- Most monuments and museums close on 1 Jan, 1 May, 1 Nov, 11 Nov and 25 December. There are fewer buses, trains and Métro services on France's national holidays (see page 307), so try to avoid arriving on those dates.

### WHAT TO TAKE

- The key things to remember are your travel documents, money, credit cards and any medication you need. You'll also need your driving licence if you plan to rent a car while in France, and car registration and insurance documents if you are taking your own car (see pages 60–61). Apart from these essentials, there are very few things you can't buy in Paris.
- Take clothing for a range of weather conditions, even in summer. Make sure you have suitable walking shoes, an umbrella, a raincoat and sunglasses (in spring/summer). In summer you'll also need sunscreen. You may like to take some smarter clothes for going out in the evening.
- A small rucksack or shoulder bag is useful for sightseeing. But bear in mind that these are potential goldmines to pickpockets, so keep your money tucked away safely and keep an eye on your bag when you're in restaurants and other crowded places (see Finding Help, page 305).
- Take the addresses and phone numbers of emergency contacts,

**TIMES ZONES**

| City | Time difference | Time at 12 noon French time |
|---|---|---|
| Amsterdam | 0 | 12 noon |
| Berlin | 0 | 12 noon |
| Brussels | 0 | 12 noon |
| Chicago | -7 | 5am |
| Dublin | -1 | 11am |
| Johannesburg | +1* | 1pm |
| London | -1 | 11am |
| Madrid | 0 | 12 noon |
| Montréal | -6 | 6am |
| New York | -6 | 6am |
| Perth, Australia | +7* | 7pm |
| Rome | 0 | 12 noon |
| San Francisco | -9 | 3am |
| Sydney | +9* | 9pm |
| Tokyo | +8* | 8pm |

Clocks in France go forward one hour on the last Sunday in March, until the last Sunday in October.

* One hour less during French Summer Time.

**WEATHER WEBSITES AND TELEPHONE NUMBERS**

| Organization | Telephone | Notes | Website |
|---|---|---|---|
| Météo France | 0892 680 275, €0.34 per minute (within France) | Forecasts for Paris and the rest of France | www.meteo.fr/meteonet |
| The Met Office (UK) | 0900 341 1211, £0.60 per minute (within UK) | Five-day forecasts for Paris, as well as information about the UV index | www.metoffice.gov.uk |
| Paris Tourist Office | | Provides a link to the Météo France website, as well as information on air quality in Paris | www.paris-touristoffice.com |
| Weather Channel (US) | | Links to Paris forecasts from the website of the US-based Weather Channel | www.weather.com |

including the numbers to call if your credit cards are stolen.
- It is wise to take photocopies of your passport, tickets and insurance documents and keep them separately from the originals, in case of loss. Keep a separate note of your credit card numbers.
- There is a language guide on pages 311–316 of this book, but if you are keen to communicate in French you may find a separate phrase book helpful.
- A first-aid kit is a good precaution. Useful items include antiseptic cream, sticking plasters, painkillers and diarrhoea medicine.
- If you wear glasses, take a spare pair, in case of any damage, or your prescription so you can buy a replacement pair.
- There are English-language bookshops in Paris but it is generally less expensive to bring your own books.
- Camera film is widely available, but it is easier to take at least one film with you.

**CUSTOMS**

**From another EU country**

Below are the guidelines for the quantity of goods you can bring to France from another EU country, for personal use:

- 800 cigarettes
- 400 cigarillos
- 200 cigars
- 1 kg of tobacco
- 110 litres of beer
- 10 litres of spirits
- 90 litres of wine (of which only 60 litres can be sparkling wine)
- 20 litres of fortified wine (such as port or sherry)

**From a country outside the EU**

You are entitled to the allowances shown below only if you travel with the goods and do not plan to sell them.

- 200 cigarettes; or 100 cigarillos; or 50 cigars; or 250gms of tobacco
- 50cc/ml of perfume
- 250cc/ml of eau de toilette
- 2 litres of still wine
- 1 litre of spirits or strong liqueurs over 22% volume; or 2 litres of fortified wine, sparkling wine or other liqueurs
- Up to e175 of all other goods

## PASSPORTS AND VISAS

- UK, US and Canadian visitors need a passport, but not a visa, for stays of up to three months. You should have at least six months' validity remaining on your passport. Citizens of EU countries that have National Identity cards need either a passport or National Identity card.
- For more information about visa and passport requirements, look up the website of the **French tourist office** (www.franceguide.com) or the **French Embassy** (www.frenchembassy.org.uk or www.consulfrance-newyork.org).
- While in Paris, carry a photocopy of the relevant pages of your passport, so you can leave the actual passport in your hotel safe. Always keep a separate note of your passport number in case of loss or theft.
- Passport and visa rules can change at short notice so check before booking your visit.

## LONGER STAYS

- UK and other EU citizens wishing to stay longer than three months should apply for a *Carte de Séjour* from the Préfecture de Police. US and Canadian visitors need a *Carte de Séjour* and visa.
- For more information call the Immigration Department of the French Consulate in London (tel 020 7073 1248), in the US (tel 212/606 3600) or Canada (tel 514/878 4385).

## TRAVEL INSURANCE

- Make sure you have full health and travel insurance.
- EU nationals receive reduced-cost health treatment with the relevant documentation (form E111 for British citizens), but full insurance is still advised. For everyone else, full insurance is a necessity.
- Check your insurer has a 24-hour helpline.

**FRENCH EMBASSIES AND CONSULATES ABROAD**

| Country | Address | Website |
|---|---|---|
| **Australia** | 31 Market Street, St. Martin Tower, Level 26, Sydney, NSW 2000 Tel (02) 92 61 57 79 | www.consulfrance-sydney.org |
| **Canada** | 1 place Ville Marie, Bureau 2601, Montréal, Québec, H3B 4S3 Tel 514 878-4385 | www.consulfrance-montreal.org |
| **Germany** | Pariser Platz 5, 10117 Berlin. Tel 590 03 90 00 | www.botschaft-frankreich.de |
| **Ireland** | 36 Ailesbury Road, Ballsbridge, Dublin 4. Tel 01 260 1666 | www.ambafrance.ie |
| **Italy** | Via Giulia 251, 00186 Rome. Tel 06 68 60 11 | www.france-italia.it/consulat/rome |
| **New Zealand** | 34–42 Manners Street, Wellington, 12th floor, PO BOX 11-343 Tel 644 384 25 55 | www.ambafrance-nz.org |
| **Spain** | Calle Marqués de la Ensenada 10, 28004 Madrid. Tel 91 700 78 00 | www.consulfrance-madrid.org |
| **South Africa** | 3rd floor, Standard Bank Building, 191 Jan Smuts Avenue, Rosebank Tel 011 778 56 00 | www.consulfrance-jhb.org |
| **UK** | 21 Cromwell Road, London, SW7 2EN. Tel: 020 7073 1200 | www.frenchembassy.org.uk |
| **USA (Los Angeles)** | 10990 Wilshire Boulevard, suite 300, Los Angeles, CA 90024 Tel 310/235-3200 | www.consulfrance-losangeles.org |
| **USA (New York)** | 934 Fifth Avenue, New York, NY 10021. Tel 212/606-3600 | www.consulfrance-newyork.org |

# PRACTICALITIES

## ELECTRICITY

- Voltage in France is 220 volts. Sockets take plugs with two round pins. UK equipment will need an adaptor plug, which you can buy at airport and Eurostar terminals, as well *droguerie* stores.
- American appliances using 110–120 volts will need an adaptor and a transformer. Dual voltage equipment should need only an adaptor.

## LAUNDRY

- There are two options if you need a laundry service: *a laverie automatique* (laundrette) and a *pressing* (dry-cleaners).
- Dry-cleaners are more easily found but are also more expensive. Some have an economy service, but this is not recommended for your best silk jacket.

## LAVATORIES

- Every café has lavatories, although they are for customers only so you'll need to buy at least a drink. Some are coin-operated. Standards range from smelly to pristine, and you'll occasionally come across the old-fashioned squatter-style lavatories.
- It's useful to have some tissues with you, in case there's no paper. In some stores and museums you'll need to tip the attendant before using the lavatories so keep some change handy.
- Ask for *les toilettes* rather than *la toilette* (*la toilette* is what you do when you get washed and dressed in the morning). You can also use *WC*, pronounced *vay, say*.
- Coin-operated public lavatories can be found all over Paris and are usually well maintained, with automatic flushing and disinfecting.

## MEASUREMENTS

- France uses the metric system. Road distances are measured in kilometres, fuel is sold by the litre and food is weighed in grams and kilograms.

## SMOKING

- Smoking is banned in public places such as cinemas, buses and Métro stations, but is widespread in restaurants and bars.
- By law restaurants and cafés should provide a non-smoking section. Some taxis display a no-smoking sign.

## CONVERSION CHART

| From | To | Multiply by |
|---|---|---|
| Inches | Centimetres | 2.54 |
| Centimetres | Inches | 0.3937 |
| Feet | Metres | 0.3048 |
| Metres | Feet | 3.2810 |
| Yards | Metres | 0.9144 |
| Metres | Yards | 1.0940 |
| Miles | Kilometres | 1.6090 |
| Kilometres | Miles | 0.6214 |
| Acres | Hectares | 0.4047 |
| Hectares | Acres | 2.4710 |
| Gallons | Litres | 4.5460 |
| Litres | Gallons | 0.2200 |
| Ounces | Grams | 28.35 |
| Grams | Ounces | 0.0353 |
| Pounds | Grams | 453.6 |
| Grams | Pounds | 0.0022 |
| Pounds | Kilograms | 0.4536 |
| Kilograms | Pounds | 2.205 |
| Tons | Tonnes | 1.0160 |
| Tonnes | Tons | 0.9842 |

## CHILDREN

- At first glance, Paris is not a children's city, with its heavy emphasis on art and culture and its manic traffic. But there are plenty of attractions specifically aimed at younger visitors (see page 221) and many adult-focused museums offer children's worksheets and workshops. Entrance to museums is often free to children.
- Squares and parks have slides and sandpits and river trips are also a popular option. You can catch a puppet show in some of the larger parks (including the Jardin du Luxembourg) on Wednesday, Saturday and Sunday afternoons.
- Restaurants do not generally turn up their noses at the sight of a pushchair, although it is probably best to aim for family-style bistros where staff are usually more helpful. Chain restaurants (such as Bistro Romain and Hippopotamus) usually have a good-value children's menu, as do many other places.
- July and August are good times to try to get special family deals at hotels, as this is when they are less likely to be booked by people on business travel. If you need special facilities, reserve ahead.
- On the Métro and most buses, children under four travel free and children between the ages of four and nine can use half-price tickets. But bear in mind that the crowded trains can be unpleasant for children and that manoeuvring pushchairs up and down the countless stairs en route to the platforms is not easy.
- Inter-Service Parents is a free telephone advisory service that provides information (in French only) on baby-sitting agencies and children's activities (*tel 01 44 93 44 93, 9.30–12.30,*

## CLOTHING SIZES

The chart below indicates how European clothing sizes compare with those in the UK and US

| UK | Europe | USA | |
|---|---|---|---|
| 36 | 46 | 36 | SUITS |
| 38 | 48 | 38 | |
| 40 | 50 | 40 | |
| 42 | 52 | 42 | |
| 44 | 54 | 44 | |
| 46 | 56 | 46 | |
| 48 | 58 | 48 | |
| 7 | 41 | 8 | SHOES |
| 7.5 | 42 | 8.5 | |
| 8.5 | 43 | 9.5 | |
| 9.5 | 44 | 10.5 | |
| 10.5 | 45 | 11.5 | |
| 11 | 46 | 12 | |
| 14.5 | 37 | 14.5 | SHIRTS |
| 15 | 38 | 15 | |
| 15.5 | 39/40 | 15.5 | |
| 16 | 41 | 16 | |
| 16.5 | 42 | 16.5 | |
| 17 | 43 | 17 | |
| 8 | 36 | 6 | DRESSES |
| 10 | 38 | 8 | |
| 12 | 40 | 10 | |
| 14 | 42 | 12 | |
| 16 | 44 | 14 | |
| 18 | 46 | 16 | |
| 20 | 48 | 18 | |
| 4.5 | 37.5 | 6 | SHOES |
| 5 | 38 | 6.5 | |
| 5.5 | 38.5 | 7 | |
| 6 | 39 | 7.5 | |
| 6.5 | 40 | 8 | |
| 7 | 41 | 8.5 | |

*1.30–5*). Alternatively, you could try Baby Sitting Services (*tel 01 46 21 33 16, www.babysittingservices.com*).

- If you need baby-changing facilities, try the restrooms in department stores and the larger museums. You can buy baby food and other items in supermarkets and pharmacies.

### VISITORS WITH DISABILITIES

- Although Paris is not an ideal city for people with special needs, modern or refurbished hotels (space providing) offer specially adapted facilities. Major museums and sights generally have good access and staff available to assist. Information is available on their websites.
- *www.loisiretprogres.org* gives details about accessibility to La Cité des Sciences, the Louvre and seven other museums in Paris (in French only). Another useful website is *www.access-able.com*.
- A complete guide is available (in English) from the Guide Touristique des Personnes à Mobilité Réduite Paris–Île de France (*tel 01 53 80 66 66*).

### CAR RENTAL

- Driving in Paris is not recommended (see pages 60–61), but you may like to rent a car if you are venturing farther afield. It is a good idea to book in advance, especially if you want an automatic car. Make sure full insurance is included in the package. You can also arrange car rental through some travel agents when you book your travel arrangements.
- Chauffeur-driven cars include Prestige Limousines (*165 rue de la Convention, 75015, tel 01 40 43 92 92, www.prestige-limousines.fr*).

### LOCAL WAYS

- Greetings are often more formal in France, especially when they are written rather than spoken. Always offer to shake hands when you meet someone, and use *vous* rather than *tu* when addressing them.
- It is polite to use *Monsieur*, *Madame* or *Mademoiselle* when speaking to people you don't know, although think carefully about whether to choose *Madame* or *Mademoiselle* for a woman.
- The 'continental kiss' may seem strange, but it is a common form of greeting among friends. Members of the opposite sex kiss each other once on each cheek, though suburbanites and people from the provinces go through this procedure two or three times.
- Communicating in French is always the best option, even if you can manage only *bonjour*, *s'il vous plaît* and *merci*. The French are very protective about their language and the visitor who speaks loud English is much less welcome than the one who squeaks out *s'il vous plaît*, however poorly pronounced. If you can't understand the French reply, respond with *Parlez-vous anglais?* and hope the answer is *oui*.
- Churches require visitors to wear suitably modest clothes and some prefer you not to wander around during services. Don't take any photos inside without checking it is permitted.
- Waiters should be addressed as *Monsieur*, *Madame* or *Mademoiselle* when you are trying to attract their attention. Never use *garçon*.

*Blue sky and a rainbow umbrella, at the Louvre Pyramid*

**CAR RENTAL COMPANIES INCLUDE:**

| Name | Address | Telephone | Website |
|---|---|---|---|
| Avis | 5 rue Bixio, 75007 | 01 44 18 10 50 | www.avis.fr |
| Citer | 43 place Louis Armand, 75012 | 01 40 04 90 04 | www.citer.fr |
| Easyrentacar | place Vendôme, 75001 | 01 40 15 60 39 | www.easyrentacar.com |
| Europcar | Central booking | 0825 358 358 | www.europcar.fr |
| Hertz | Central booking | 01 41 91 95 25 | www.hertz.fr |
| Rent-a-Car | 79 rue de Bercy, 75012 | 01 43 45 98 99 | www.rentacar.fr |

**PLACES OF WORSHIP**

Whatever your religion, you should be able to find the appropriate church, temple, mosque or synagogue in Paris, although Catholics obviously get the biggest choice.

| | |
|---|---|
| **Catholic** | Every *arrondissement* has at least four or five Catholic churches. See pages 161–163 for details of some. There are daily services at Notre-Dame (see pages 137–141) and Sacré-Cœur (see pages 154–157). |
| **Jewish** | Synagogue: 10 rue Pavée, 75004; tel 01 48 87 21 54. Métro: St-Paul. |
| **Muslim** | Mosquée: place du Puits-de-l'Ermite, 75005; tel 01 45 35 97 33. Métro: Jussieu, Place Monge, Censier-Daubenton |
| **Protestant** | American Cathedral: 23 avenue George V, 75008; tel 01 53 23 84 00. Métro: Alma-Marceau. American Church: 65 quai d'Orsay, 75007; tel 01 40 62 05 00. Métro: Invalides. Church of Scotland: 17 rue Bayard, 75008; tel 01 40 70 09 59. Métro: Franklin D. Roosevelt. St-George's English Church: 7 rue Auguste Vacquerie, 75016; tel 01 47 20 22 51. Métro: Charles de Gaulle–Étoile. St-Michael's Church of England: 5 rue d'Aguesseau, 75008; tel 01 47 42 70 88. Métro: Madeleine. |
| **Russian Orthodox** | St-Alexandre de la Néva: 12 rue Daru, 75008; tel 01 42 27 37 34. Métro: Courcelles. |

# MONEY MATTERS

France is one of 12 European countries that have adopted the euro as their official currency. Euro notes and coins were introduced in January 2002, replacing the franc.

**BEFORE YOU GO**

- It is advisable to use a mixture of cash, traveller's cheques and credit cards, rather than relying on only one means of payment during your trip.
- Check that your credit or debit card can be used to withdraw cash from ATMs in France. Also check what fee will be charged.
- Traveller's cheques are a safer way of bringing in money as you can claim a refund if they are stolen—but commission can be high when you cash them.

**CREDIT CARDS**

Most restaurants, shops and hotels in Paris accept credit cards, but some have a minimum spending limit.

**LOST/STOLEN CREDIT CARDS**

- Before you set off, make a note of the number to ring if your credit card is stolen and keep it separately from the card itself.

**ATMS**

The city has plenty of ATMs, with instructions often given in a choice of languages. Most accept MasterCard, Visa and Diners Club. You'll need a four-digit PIN.

**BANKS**

Most banks in Paris are open Monday to Friday 10–5, but close at noon the day before a public holiday. Only banks with *change* signs change traveller's cheques or foreign currency. You'll need to take your passport.

**BUREAUX DE CHANGE**

- Bureaux de Change have longer opening hours than banks, but exchange rates can be worse.

**TIPS**

- Try to avoid using higher denomination notes when paying taxi drivers and when buying low-cost items in smaller shops.
- Never carry money or credit cards in back pockets, or other places that are easy targets for thieves.
- Keep your spare money and traveller's cheques in your hotel safe until you need them.

- You'll find them across the city, including at train stations, airports and some department stores.
- Avoid changing large amounts of traveller's cheques at hotels, where the rates may not be competitive.

**WIRING MONEY**

- In an emergency money can be wired from your home country, but this can be time-consuming and expensive, as agents charge a fee.

**BANKNOTES AND COINS**

One euro is made up of 100 cents. Euro notes come in denominations of 5, 10, 20, 50, 100, 200 and 500 euros.

Coins come in denominations of 1 and 2 euros and 1, 2, 5, 10, 20 and 50 cents.

*ATMs often give instructions in a choice of languages*

- Money can be wired from bank to bank, taking up to two working days. It is usually faster to use Travelex (*www.travelex.fr*) or Western Union (*www.westernunion.com*).
- Post offices also wire money (see Post Offices, right).

### 24-HOUR EXCHANGE SERVICES

- The Champs-Élysées has a 24-hour bureau de change: Bureaux de Change CCF Champs-Elysées, 103 avenue des Champs-Elysées (on the corner of the rue Galilée), 75008. Tel 01 40 70 27 22.
- Roissy-Charles de Gaulle and Orly Airports also have exchange services, generally open between 7am and 11.30pm

### REDUCED-PRICE TICKETS

- Students and teachers should contact the International Student Travel Confederation (*www.isic.org*) in their own country for information about the benefits available.
- Senior citizens may get reductions on transportation and admission to museums by showing a passport.
- For more information about reductions on the entry price for museums and other attractions, see Tickets, page 307.

### TAXES

- Non-EU residents can claim a VAT refund (*détaxe*) of 12 per cent on certain purchases, although you must have spent more than €175 in one shop, at one time.

**FOREIGN BANKS**

| Name | Address | Telephone |
|---|---|---|
| **American Express** | 11 rue Scribe, 75009 | 01 47 14 50 00 |
| **Barclays** | 21 boulevard de la Madeleine, 75001 | 01 44 58 32 32 |
| **Citibank** | 125 avenue des Champs-Élysées, 75008 | 01 53 23 33 60 |
| **Lloyds** | 15 avenue d'Iéna, 75016 | 01 44 43 42 41 |

- Ask the store for the relevant forms, which should be completed and stamped by the trader.
- Present the forms to Customs when you leave France, along with the receipts, and they will be stamped.
- Remember that you may have to show the goods at Customs, so keep them within easy reach.
- Post the forms back to the shop and they will either refund your credit card account or send you a cheque.
- Exempt products include food and drink, medicine, tobacco, unset gems, works of art and antiques.
- Global Refund offers a reimbursement service. For more details, tel 01 41 61 51 51 or look up the website at www.globalrefund.com.

### POST OFFICES

- Most post offices have ATMs.
- Cards accepted are listed on each dispenser and instructions are available in English.
- Money can be wired, through Western Union, via most post offices and generally takes only a few minutes to receive.
- International Money Orders can be sent from all post offices (a charge is applied).
- Most post offices offer exchange services in various currencies, including American, Australian and Canadian dollars and the British pound.

**TIPPING GUIDE**

| | |
|---|---|
| Restaurants (service included) | Change * |
| Hotels (service included) | Change * |
| Cafés (service included) | Change * |
| Taxis | 10 per cent |
| Tour Guides | €1–€1.50 |
| Porters | €1 |
| Hairdressers | €1 |
| Cloakroom attendants | 30c |
| Lavatories | Change |
| Usherettes | 30c |

* Or more if you are impressed with the level of service

*A French newspaper won't blow your budget (see chart below)*

**EVERYDAY ITEMS AND HOW MUCH THEY COST**

| | | |
|---|---|---|
| A sandwich (take-out) | | €2.20–€3.20 |
| Bottle of mineral water | (from a shop, 0.5 litres) | €0.20–€0.40 |
| Cup of coffee | (from a café, espresso) | €1–€1.85 |
| | (Crème , larger cup with milk) | €1.85–€2.25 |
| Beer | (*Un demi*–half a litre) | €1.85–€2.60 |
| Glass of house wine | | €1.85–€2.15 |
| French national newspaper | | €1–€1.20 |
| International newspaper | | €1.50–€2.30 |
| Litre of petrol | (98 unleaded) | €1.03 |
| | (diesel) | €0.81 |
| Métro ticket | (single) | €1.30 |
| | (per ticket if you buy a carnet) | €1 |
| Camera film | (36 pictures) | €7–€8 |
| 20 cigarettes | (on average) | €3.50 |

**USEFUL NUMBERS**

**General emergencies**
112
**Ambulance (emergencies)**
15
**Anti-Poison Centre**
01 40 05 48 48
**FACTS**
(Aids advice in English. Mon–Fri 11am–2pm)
01 44 93 16 69
**SOS Dentistes**
(24-hour emergency dental service)
01 43 37 51 00
**SOS Help**
(English crisis information hotline. Daily 3pm–11pm)
01 47 23 80 80
**SOS Médecins**
(24-hour emergency house calls by doctors)
01 47 07 77 77

**HEALTHY FLYING**

- If you are visiting France from the US, Australia or New Zealand you may be concerned about the effect of long-haul flights on your health. The most widely publicized concern is Deep Vein Thrombosis, or DVT. Misleadingly named economy class syndrome, DVT is the forming of a blood clot in the body's deep veins, particularly in the legs. The clot can move around the bloodstream and could be fatal.
- Those most at risk include the elderly, pregnant women and those using the contraceptive pill, smokers and the overweight. If you are at increased risk of DVT see your doctor before departing. Flying increases the likelihood of DVT because passengers are often seated in a cramped position for long periods of time and may become dehydrated.

**To minimize risk:**

- Drink water (not alcohol).
- Don't stay immobile for hours at a time.
- Stretch and exercise your legs periodically.
- Do wear elastic flight socks, which support veins and reduce the chances of a clot forming.
- A small dose of aspirin may be recommended. This thins the blood before the flight.

**EXERCISES**

1 ANKLE ROTATIONS

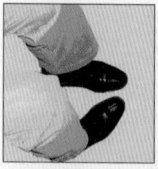

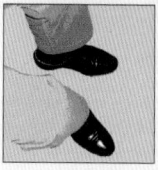

Lift feet off the floor. Draw a circle with the toes, moving one foot clockwise and the other counterclockwise.

2 CALF STRETCHES

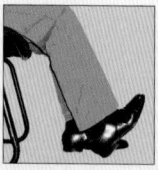

Start with heel on the floor and point foot upward as high as you can. Then lift heels high keeping balls of feet on the floor.

3 KNEE LIFTS

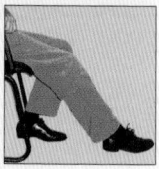

Lift leg with knee bent while contracting your thigh muscle. Then staighten leg pressing foot flat to the floor.

Other health hazards for flyers are airborne diseases and bugs spread by the plane's air-conditioning system. These are largely unavoidable but if you have a serious medical condition seek advice from a doctor before setting off.

**BEFORE YOU GO**

- EU citizens receive reduced-cost healthcare in France with the relevant documentation. For UK citizens this is the E111 form, which must be stamped by the post office before you travel. Bring a photocopy with you as well as the original, as this will be kept by the hospital or doctor if you need treatment. Full health insurance is still strongly advised.
- Full insurance is a must for citizens from non-EU countries.
- Make sure you are up to date with anti-tetanus boosters. Bring any medication you need and pack a first-aid kit. In summer, always bring sun-protection cream.

**IF YOU NEED TREATMENT**

- The French national health system is complex. Any salaried French citizen who receives treatment by a doctor or public hospital can be reimbursed by up to 70 per cent. The same is true if you are an EU citizen and have a valid E111 form. If you are relying only on E111, rather than travel insurance, make sure that the doctor you see is part of the French national health service (*a conventionné*), rather than the private system, otherwise you may face extra charges. In any case, you will have to pay up front for the consultation and treatment. To reclaim part of these costs, send the *feuille de soins* (a statement from the doctor) and your E111 to the *Caisse Primaire d'Assurance-Maladie* (the state health insurance office) before you leave the country. Call 08 20 90 41 75 to find the nearest office. Attach the labels of any medicine you have to buy.
- If you have to stay overnight in a public hospital, you will have to pay 25 per cent of the treatment costs, as well as a daily charge (*forfait journalier*). These are not refundable. It is far better to have full health insurance than to rely solely on the E111 form.
- If you are hospitalized and have insurance, ask to see the *assistante sociale* to arrange reimbursement of the costs directly through your insurers.

**FINDING A DOCTOR**

- If you need to find a doctor (*médecin*) ask at the local *pharmacie* or at your hotel. Appointments are usually made in advance, but very few doctors

| HOSPITALS WITH EMERGENCY DEPARTMENTS | | |
|---|---|---|
| **Name** | **Address** | **Telephone** |
| Hôpital Pitié Salpêtrière | 47 boulevard de l'Hôpital, 75013 | 01 42 17 72 49 |
| Hôpital St-Antoine | 184 rue du Faubourg-St-Antoine, 75012 | 01 49 28 27 08 |
| Hôpital Hôtel Dieu | 1 place du Parvis Notre-Dame, 75004 | 01 42 34 82 32 |
| Hôpital Cochin | 27 rue du Faubourg-St-Jacques, 75014 | 01 58 41 27 35 |
| Hôpital Tenon | 4 rue de Chine, 75020 | 01 56 01 64 05 |
| These hospitals are all publicly owned and belong to the Hôpitaux de Paris group (the telephone numbers are those of the emergency departments). | | |

will refuse to see an emergency case. Emergency house calls (24-hours) can be arranged by calling SOS Médecins (*tel 01 47 07 77 77*).

### FINDING A HOSPITAL

- There are plenty of hospitals in Paris—you'll find them listed in the phone book under *Hôpitaux*. Round-the-clock emergency services are called *urgences*.
- Private hospitals are a lot more expensive and treatment is not necessarily better. Check you are covered for the costs before receiving treatment.
- For ease of communication, English-speakers may prefer: The American Hospital *(63 boulevard Victor Hugo, 92200, Neuilly; tel 01 46 41 25 25)* or The Hertford British Hospital *(3 rue Barbès, 92300, Levallois-Perret; tel 01 46 39 22 22)*. Both are private hospitals.

### TAP WATER

- Tap water in Paris is drinkable, although you may prefer the taste of bottled water. In public places, you may see the sign *eau potable* (drinking water). Don't drink from anything marked *eau non potable*.

### SUMMER HAZARDS

- The sun can be strong from May to September. High-factor sun block is recommended.
- There are few biting insects as such in Paris, but if you plan to visit the surrounding region take an insect repellent.

### OPTICIANS

- Wearers of glasses and contact lenses should take their prescription in case of loss.

### DENTAL TREATMENT

- EU citizens can receive reduced-cost emergency dental treatment with form E111, but insurance is still advised. The reclaim procedure is the same as general medical treatment.
- Other visitors should check their insurance.
- It's a good idea have a dental check-up before you travel.

### PHARMACIES

- A pharmacy (*pharmacie*) is identified by an illuminated green cross. Most are open Monday to Saturday 9–7 or 8, but they usually post details on their door of another pharmacy that is open later (called the *pharmacie de garde*).
- Pharmacists are highly qualified and provide first aid, as well as supplying medication.
- They are not able to dispense prescriptions from doctors outside the French health system, so bring sufficient supplies of any prescribed drugs you need.
- Some drugs are sold by prescription, or *ordonnance*, only.
- Pharmacists sell a range of health-related items, although it is sometimes less expensive to go to the supermarket.
- In France, some commonly used medicines, such as aspirins and cold remedies, can only be bought in pharmacies.

### ALTERNATIVE MEDICAL TREATMENT

Alternative treatment is available, although certain types, such as chiropractics and reflexology are not widespread.

| OPTICIANS | |
|---|---|
| Opticiens Krys | 40 rue St-Honoré, 75001; tel 01 42 60 17 55 **www.krys.com** |
| Optic 2000 | 92 avenue des Ternes, 75017; tel 01 45 74 47 56 **www.optic2000.fr** |
| Lissac Opticien | 114 rue de Rivoli, 75001; tel 01 44 88 44 44 **www.lissac.com** |
| Alain Afflelou | 27 boulevard St-Michel, 75005; tel 01 43 54 35 01 **www.alainafflelou.com** |
| Optical Center | 123–125 rue du Faubourg-St-Martin, 75009; tel 01 42 05 40 40 **www.optical-center.com** |

**ALTERNATIVE MEDICAL TREATMENT**

Association Française de Chiropratique
**www.chiropratique.org**

Association Française d'Acupuncture
3 rue de l'Arrivée, 75015
tel 01 43 20 26 26

Association Europe Acupuncture
**www.aea-org.com**

Centre de Santé Hahnemann
*Homoeopathy, Acupuncture, Osteopathy and Herbal Treatment.*
1 rue Vergniaud, 75013
tel 01 45 80 15 03

Naturosanté
*Website about alternative medical treatments.*
**www.naturosante.com**

| LATE-NIGHT PHARMACIES | | | |
|---|---|---|---|
| **Name** | **Address** | **Telephone** | **Hours** |
| Dhéry | 84 avenue des Champs-Élysées, 75008 | 01 45 62 02 41 | 24 hours |
| Drugstore Champs-Élysées | 133 avenue des Champs-Élysées, 75008 | 01 47 20 39 25 | Mon–Fri 8.30am–1.30am, Sat noon–1.30am, Sun 10am–1.30am |
| Pharmacie des Arts | 106 boulevard du Montparnasse, 75014 | 01 43 35 44 88 | Mon–Sat 9am–midnight. Closed Sun |
| Pharmacie Européenne | 6 place de Clichy, 75009 | 01 48 74 65 18 | 24 hours |
| Pharmacie Mozart | 14 avenue Mozart, 75016 | 01 45 27 38 17 | Mon–Fri 9am–11pm, Sat 9am–8pm. Closed Sun |
| Pharmacie British Villamayor | 1 rue Auber, 75009 | 01 42 65 88 29 | Mon–Fri 8.30–8.30, Sat 10–8. Closed Sun |

# COMMUNICATION

## TELEPHONES

**French numbers** All telephone numbers in France have 10 digits. The country is divided into five regional zones, indicated by the first two digits of the phone number (see chart, below). You must dial these two digits, even if you are calling from within the zone.

**International Calls** To call France from the UK dial 00 33, then drop the first zero from the 10 digit number. To call the UK from France, dial 00 44, then drop the first zero from the area code. To call France from the US, dial 011 33, then drop the first zero from the 10 digit number. To call the US from France, dial 00 1, followed by the number.

**Call charges** For calls within France, peak period is from 8am to 7pm, Monday to Friday. You'll save money if you call outside of this time. Numbers beginning with 08 have special rates. 0800 or 0805 numbers are free. 0810 and 0811 numbers are charged at local rate. Other 08 numbers cost more than national calls—sometimes considerably more. Watch for the prefixes 0893, 0898 and 0899, which are particularly expensive.

**COUNTRY CODES FROM FRANCE**

| | |
|---|---|
| Australia | 00 61 |
| Belgium | 00 32 |
| Canada | 00 1 |
| Germany | 00 49 |
| Ireland | 00 353 |
| Italy | 00 39 |
| Netherlands | 00 31 |
| New Zealand | 00 64 |
| Spain | 00 34 |
| Sweden | 00 46 |
| UK | 00 44 |
| US | 00 1 |

**PREFIXES**

| | |
|---|---|
| 00 | International |
| 01 | Île-de-France (including Paris) |
| 02 | Northwest France |
| 03 | Northeast France |
| 04 | Southeast France |
| 05 | Southwest France |
| 06 | Mobile telephone numbers |
| 0800/0805 | Toll-free |
| 08 | Special-rate numbers |

**USEFUL TELEPHONE NUMBERS**

**Directory Inquiries**
(national)
12
(international)
3212

**TIP**

- When reserving show tickets by telephone or calling for tourist information, bear in mind that you may be calling a higher-rate telephone number. This is usually indicated by the prefix 089.

**GUIDE PRICES**

| Type of Call | Initial charge | Each further minute |
|---|---|---|
| Local, peak | €0.091 (1 min) | €0.033 |
| Local, off-peak | €0.091 (1 min) | €0.018 |
| National, peak | €0.112 (39 sec) | €0.091 |
| National, off-peak | €0.112 (39sec) | €0.061 |
| Calling the UK, off-peak | €0.11 (15 sec) | €0.12 |
| Calling the US, off-peak | €0.11 (27 sec) | €0.15 |

## PAYPHONES

- Nearly all public payphones in Paris now use a phone card (*télécarte*) rather than coins. You can buy these (with 50 or 120 units) at post offices, *tabacs*, newsagents and France Telecom shops. Some phones also accept certain credit cards, although this may make the calls more expensive.
- You do not need to pay if you're calling an emergency number.
- The phones give instructions in various languages—press the flag button to select your choice. If the phone displays the blue bell sign, you can receive incoming calls.
- Public phones in cafés and restaurants use cards, coins or have to be switched on by staff, in which case you pay after the call. They tend to be more expensive than public payphones.
- Check the rates before you use a hotel phone, as calls can be substantially higher than from a public payphone.

## MOBILE PHONES

You can usually use your own mobile, but there are a few points to check before leaving:

- Contact your Customer Service department to find out if you have any restrictions on making calls from France
- Check if you need an access code to listen to your voice mail.
- Make sure the numbers memorized in your directory are in the international format.
- Check the call charges, which can rise dramatically when you use your phone abroad.
- You can choose to rent a phone or SIM card on arrival in Paris but this can be rather an expensive solution. You could try Call'Phone (*2 avenue de la Porte de St-Cloud, 75016; tel 01 40 71 72 54; www.callphone.com;* also branches in Roissy-Charles de Gaulle and Orly airports).

## SENDING A LETTER

- Stamps (*timbres*) are sold at post offices and *tabacs*. Letters are posted in yellow mail boxes. Some have two sections, one for mail to Paris and the suburbs (*Paris–Banlieue*) and the other for national and international mail (*autres departements/étranger*).
- A letter (*lettre*) sent abroad from France should take between two and five days to arrive, although it can take longer. Write *par avion* (by air) on the envelope or postcard.
- For registered post, ask at the post office for the letter to be sent *recommandé*.
- If you are sending a parcel

**POSTAGE RATES FOR LETTERS**

| | |
|---|---|
| Within France | €0.50 |
| To Western Europe | €0.50 |
| To Eastern Europe | €0.75 |
| To America | €0.90 |
| To Africa | €0.75 |
| To Asia | €0.90 |
| To Australia | €0.90 |

*Mail boxes are yellow*

(*colis*) abroad your options are *prioritaire* (priority) or the less costly, but slower, *économique* (economy).

| CYBERCAFES | |
|---|---|
| Xs Arena | 43 boulevard de Sébastopol, 75001<br>tel 01 40 13 02 60; **www.**xsarena.com |
| Café Orbital | 3 rue de Médicis, 75006<br>tel 01 43 25 76 77; **www.**cafeorbital.com |
| Cybercafé de Paris | 15 rue des Halles, 75001<br>tel 01 42 21 11 11; **www.**cybercafeparis.com |

| INTERNET VENUES | |
|---|---|
| Cybersquare | 1 place de la République, 75003<br>tel 01 48 87 82 36; **www.**cybersquare-paris.com |
| Cyber Cube | 5 rue Mignon, 75006<br>tel 01 53 10 30 50; **www.**cybercube.fr |
| Cyber Espace Duriez | 3 rue de La Boétie, 75008<br>tel 01 47 42 91 49; **www.**duriez.fr |

### POST OFFICES

- Post offices (*bureaux de poste*) are well signposted. The postal service is known as La Poste.
- Opening hours are generally Monday to Friday 8–7, Saturday 8–noon, although some branches open later.
- Post offices tend to be busiest during lunch hours and in the late afternoon.
- Facilities usually include phones, photocopiers, fax (*télécopieur*) and access to the Minitel directory service. Poste Restante services are available, although you will have to pay a fee.
- The post office at 52 rue du Louvre is open 24 hours. Other central post offices include:
- Paris Ile de la Cité, 1 boulevard du Palais, 75004.
- Paris Archives, 67 rue des Archives, 75003.
- Paris Hôtel de Ville, 9 place de l'Hôtel de Ville, 75004.
- Paris Bastille, 12 rue Castex, 75004.
- Paris Sorbonne, 13 rue Cujas, 75005.
- Paris St-Germain-des-Prés, 53 rue de Rennes, 75006.
- Paris Pigalle, 47 boulevard de Clichy, 75009.
- Paris Champs-Elysées, 71 avenue des Champs-Élysées, 75008.
- Paris Gare de Lyon, 25 boulevard Diderot, 75012.

### LAPTOPS

- Most hotels that are two stars and above provide modem points. Telephone charges apply. You may need a modem plug adaptor.
- TGV trains have a few electrical points where you can plug your laptop in if your battery needs recharging, but you'll need a two-pin continental plug or an adaptor.

### INTERNET ACCESS

- Internet access is now fairly widespread in the capital.
- You can connect to the Net in trendy cybercafés.
- Some hotels and libraries have internet terminals.

# FINDING HELP

Most visits to Paris are trouble-free, but make sure you have adequate insurance to cover any health emergencies, thefts or legal costs that may arise. If you do become victim of crime, it is likely to be at the hands of a pickpocket, so always keep your money and mobile phone safely tucked away.

| EMERGENCY NUMBERS |
|---|
| **112**<br>General emergency number |
| **15**<br>Ambulance |
| **17**<br>Police |
| **18**<br>Fire |

### PERSONAL SECURITY

- Take a note of your traveller's cheque numbers and keep it separately from the cheques themselves, as you will need it to make a claim in case of loss.
- Don't keep wallets, purses or mobile phones in the back pockets of trousers, or anywhere else that is easily accessible to thieves. Belt bags can be particular targets as thieves know you are likely to have valuables in them. Always keep an eye on your bags in restaurants, bars and on the Métro, and hold shoulder bags close to you, fastener inwards, when you are walking in the streets.
- Thieves are especially fond of crowded Métro trains, airports, the Gare du Nord station, flea markets and tourist hotspots. Be especially vigilant if someone bumps into you—it may be a ploy to distract you while someone else snatches your money.
- If you are the victim of theft, you must report it at the local police station (*commissariat*) if you want to claim on your insurance. Keep the statement the police give you. You must also contact your credit card company as soon as possible to cancel any stolen cards.
- Paris is no more or less safe for women visitors than any other large western European city. Keep your wits about you and deal with any unwanted attention firmly and politely.
- Keep valuable items in your hotel safe.
- Outside the *périphérique*, some of Paris's suburbs can be rough. Unless you are with someone who knows the city well, it is best to stick to central areas.

### LOSS OF PASSPORT

- Always keep a separate note of your passport number and a photocopy of the page that carries your details, in case of loss or theft. If you do lose your passport, report it to the police and then contact your embassy.

### POLICE

- Each *arrondissement* has several police stations, including a main one that is open 24 hours. This is often part of the town hall. You can report crime to any of these stations. For information on driving licences and residency permits, go to the central Préfecture de Police, on the Île de la Cité.
- There are various types of police officer. The Paris police wear blue uniforms, with dark blue caps. The Seine is under the control of the river police. Demonstrations are watched over by the military-looking CRS.

### FIRE

The French fire brigade deals with a range of emergencies. They are trained to give first aid.

### HEALTH EMERGENCIES

See page 302.

### LOST PROPERTY

The Bureau des Objets Trouvés is at 36 rue des Morillons, 75015 (Monday to Thursday, 8.30–5, Friday 8.30–4.30); tel 0821 002 525 or 01 55 76 20 00.

**EMBASSIES AND CONSULATES**

| Country | Address | Website |
|---|---|---|
| Australia | 4 rue Jean-Rey, 75015; tel 01 40 59 33 00 | |
| Canada | 35 avenue Montaigne, 75008; tel 01 44 43 29 00 | www.amb-canada.fr |
| Germany | 13–15 avenue Franklin Roosevelt, 75008; tel 01 53 83 45 00 | www.amb-allemagne.fr |
| Ireland | 4 rue Rude, 75116; tel 01 44 17 67 00 | |
| Italy | 51 rue de Varenne, 75007; tel 01 49 54 03 00 | www.amb-italie.fr |
| Spain | 22 avenue Marceau, 75008; tel 01 44 43 18 00 | www.amb-espagne.fr |
| UK | 35 rue du Faubourg-St-Honoré, 75008; tel 01 44 51 31 00 | www.amb-grandebretagne.fr |
| USA | 2 avenue Gabriel, 75008; tel 01 43 12 22 22 | www.amb-usa.fr |

**LOCAL POLICE STATIONS**

| *Arrondissement* | Address | Telephone |
|---|---|---|
| 1 | place du Marché St-Honoré | 01 47 03 60 00 |
| 2 | 18 rue du Croissant | 01 44 88 18 00 |
| 3 | 5 rue Perrée | 01 53 01 93 60 |
| 4 | 2 place Baudoyer | 01 44 78 61 00 |
| 5 | 4 rue de la Montagne Ste-Geneviève | 01 44 41 51 00 |
| 6 | 78 rue Bonaparte | 01 40 46 38 30 |
| 7 | 9 rue Fabert | 01 44 18 69 07 |
| 8 | 1 avenue du Général Eisenhower | 01 53 76 60 00 |
| 9 | 14 bis rue Chauchat | 01 44 83 80 80 |
| 10 | 26 rue Louis-Blanc | 01 53 71 60 00 |
| 11 | 107 boulevard Voltaire | 01 44 93 27 30 |
| 12 | 78 avenue Daumesnil | 01 44 87 50 12 |
| 13 | 144 boulevard de l'Hôpital | 01 40 79 05 05 |
| 14 | 112–116 avenue du Maine | 01 53 74 14 06 |
| 15 | 250 rue de Vaugirard | 01 53 68 81 00 |
| 16 | 58 avenue Mozart | 01 55 74 50 00 |
| 17 | 19 rue Truffaut | 01 44 90 37 17 |
| 18 | 79 rue Clignancourt | 01 53 41 50 00 |
| 19 | 3 rue Erik Satie | 01 55 56 58 00 |
| 20 | 6 place Gambetta | 01 40 33 34 00 |

# MEDIA

### TELEVISION

- France has five non-cable television stations: the nationally owned and operated channels 2 and 3, the privately owned 1 and 6, and the Franco-German ARTE (channel 5). Almost all the shows are in French. There are adverts on all terrestrial channels except ARTE.
- **TF1** has news, recent American and French films, soaps and shows.
- **France 2** has news, recent French and foreign films, soaps, shows and documentaries.
- **France 3,** a regional and national channel, has regional and national news, regional shows, documentaries, mostly French films and, once a week, a film in its original language.
- **ARTE** is a Franco-German channel operating from 7pm every day with shows in French and German. International films are shown in their original language and there are also cultural documentaries.
- **M6** shows a lot of low budget films and past American sitcoms and soaps. There are also some interesting documentaries.
- Digital television has now taken off in France. More than 100 channels are on offer either through satellite or cable.
- If the TV listings mention *VO* (*version originale*), the show or film will be in the language in which it was made, with French subtitles (Channel 3 usually screens a good film in *VO* every Sunday at around midnight).
- Note that French television channels do not always keep exactly to schedule.
- Most hotels have at least a basic cable service, which is likely to include BBC World and CNN. Cable channels now offer multilingual versions of some shows. Ask at your hotel how to use this option as the mechanics vary. The commercial-free ARTE usually offers a choice between French and German for its cultural shows.

| CABLE TV | |
|---|---|
| Depending on what cable option your hotel has, you may have some of the following channels: | |
| BBC Prime | With a mix of BBC shows, old and new |
| Canal+ | Shows recent films (some in the original language) |
| MTV | Contemporary music channel |
| MCM | The French version of MTV |
| Eurosport or Infosport | For major sporting events |
| Planète | Nature and science documentaries |
| RAI Uno | Italian |
| TVE 1 | Spanish |
| Euronews | A European all-news channel |
| LCI | All news in French |
| Canal Jimmy | Shows some British and American shows like *Friends* and *NYPD Blue* in English or multilingual versions |
| Paris Première | A cultural channel with some films in English |
| Canal J | With children's shows until 8pm |
| Téva | A women's channel that runs some English-language shows such as *Sex in the City* |

**NEWSPAPERS**

French daily newspapers have clear political leanings.

**Le Monde**
This stately paper, left-of-centre, refuses to run photos and uses illustrations.

**Libération**
A lively paper, more clearly leftist and youth-focused.

**L'Humanité**
Left wing

**Le Figaro**
Mainstream conservative daily.

**Le Parisien**
This tabloid paper is written at a level of French that makes it fairly easy for non-native readers to understand.

**Journal du Dimanche**
Sunday newspaper.

### RADIO

- French radio stations are available mainly on FM wave lengths with a few international stations on LW. Reception in Paris is very good. All FM stations are in French.

Stations include:

- **Chérie FM:** 91.3 FM; French mainstream pop, news, reports.
- **France Infos:** 105.5 FM; news bulletins every 15 minutes.
- **France Musique:** 91.7 FM; classical and jazz music, concerts, operas, news.
- **NRJ:** 100.3 FM; French and International pop, techno, rap, R'n'B.
- **Radio Classique:** 101.1 FM; classical music.
- **Skyrock:** 96 FM; rap, hip-hop, R'n'B.
- **BBC Radio 4** 198 kHz MW; news, current affairs, drama.
- **BBC Five Live** 909 kHz MW; news and sport.
- **BBC World Service** can be heard on 648 kHz LW.

### NEWSPAPERS AND MAGAZINES

- British newspapers are available at large *kiosques* (news-stands) in tourist areas. *The International Herald Tribune* can be found at almost all news-stands, along with *The Economist, USA Today* and *The Wall Street Journal*.
- *Pariscope* is the most popular weekly listings magazine for events and films. Its competitors are the *L'Officiel du Spectacle* and the hip (and slightly more expensive) *Zurban*. All three are published on Wednesday. *Time Out* also publishes a free quarterly Paris magazine available at English-language bookshops such as W.H. Smith, where you'll also find *Paris Voice*, a free city magazine in English.
- If you're looking for a housing exchange or holiday rental in Paris, pick up a free copy of FUSAC, a handy small-ads publication published twice a month.
- *Where*, an English-language listings magazine, is distributed free in hotels.
- Weekly news magazines include *Le Nouvel Observateur*, *Le Point* and *L'Express*.
- For women's fashions, options include *Elle*, *Vogue* or *Marie Claire*.
- For celebrity gossip and lots of photos, try *Paris Match*, *Voici* or *Gala*.

# OPENING TIMES AND TICKETS

### TICKETS

- If you want to see as many museums and other sights as possible, it may be worth buying a *Carte Musées-Monuments* (*www.intermusees.com*). This gives free entry to around 40 museums and monuments in the city, and another 22 in the rest of the Île-de-France. A one-day pass costs €15, a three-day pass €30 and a five-day pass €45. You can buy them from participating museums, the Paris Tourist Office, major Métro

**NATIONAL HOLIDAYS**

France has 11 national holidays (*jours fériés*), when Métro, bus and RER services are reduced and banks and many museums and shops close. The most steadfastly respected are 1 January, 1 May, 1 November, 11 November and 25 December. If you're in Paris during a national holiday, it's a good idea to ring ahead to see if the sight you want to visit is open.

| | |
|---|---|
| 1 Jan | New Year's Day |
| March/April | Easter Monday |
| 1 May | Labour Day |
| 8 May | VE Day |
| A Thursday in May | Ascension Day |
| May/June | Whit Monday |
| 14 July | Bastille Day |
| 15 August | Assumption Day |
| 1 November | All Saints' Day |
| 11 November | Remembrance Day |
| 25 December | Christmas Day |

| OPENING TIMES | | |
|---|---|---|
| **Banks** | Monday to Friday 10–5. | Smaller branches may close for lunch. Others are open on Saturday but closed Monday. Banks close at noon on the day before a national holiday, as well as on the holiday itself. |
| **Shops** | Monday to Saturday 9am–7pm. | Some boutiques have a later start. Lunchtime closures are rare in the city, although small specialist traders may take a one- or two-hour break. Saturday is the busiest shopping day, while on Sunday most shops remain closed. |
| **Museums** | Most national museums close on Tuesday (the Musée d'Orsay is a notable exception, closing on Monday). Municipal museums (including the Musée Carnavalet and the Musée Cognacq-Jay) close on Monday. | Entrance is often free on the first Sunday of the month, although this can lead to uncomfortable crowds. The key museums usually have a late-night opening (*nocturne*), when there are fewer crowds. If you are trekking to the other side of the city to see one of the smaller museums, ring in advance—opening hours can be idiosyncratic and the renovation craze has not helped. |
| **Restaurants** | Lunch is generally served from 12–2 or 2.30 and dinner from 7.30–10 or 11. | Most Parisians wait until around 9pm to dine out. Brasseries usually serve food all day. Some restaurants close for the whole of August |
| **Nightlife** | Club action starts well after midnight and continues to around 5am. | |
| **Post offices** | Monday to Friday 8–7, Saturday 8–noon. | Some branches open later. |
| **Pharmacies** | Mon–Sat 9–7 or 8. | All display a list of local pharmacies that open later and on Sunday. |

stations and FNAC ticket counters. Passes do not cover temporary exhibitions.

- Students with an International Student Identity Card and senior citizens receive reduced-price entry at some museums.
- For information on theatre and concert tickets, see page 193.
- For information on Métro, bus and RER tickets, see pages 48.
- Most cinemas offer reduced-price tickets for all on Mondays. Reductions are available for students on certain days (with a valid International Student Identity Card) and for senior citizens (valid identity required).
- Theatres also offer special-priced tickets with varying conditions.
- Most museums are free for under 18s and offer reduced prices to young people aged between 18 and 25.
- Season tickets are available for people wishing to visit a particular sight or museum many times during a longer stay in Paris. Apply to each museum or sight.
- Most shows, including drama, opera, concerts and sporting events, can be booked through the FNAC shops (*www.fnac.com*) for a small fee.

# TOURIST OFFICES

- Paris's main tourist office, due to move to rue des Pyramides in May 2004, is a handy source of information on anything from sightseeing and accommodation to exhibitions and children's activities. You can also buy the *Carte Musées-Monuments* pass and the *Paris Visite* bus and Métro pass. There are other branches around the city.
- The regional tourist office, the Comité Régional du Tourisme—Paris Île-de-France, has offices at the Carrousel du Louvre and Disneyland Resort Paris. It covers the whole of the Île de France, including Versailles.
- In the summer there are also information kiosks at various sites around the city.

**TOURIST OFFICES**

**Paris Tourist Office**
**(Paris Convention and Visitors Bureau)**
25–27 rue des Pyramides, 75001
Tel 0892 683 000 (€0.34 per minute)
Open daily 9–8, May–Oct; 10–7 rest of year. Closed 1 May, 25 Dec.
Métro: Pyramides
**www.**paris-touristoffice.com

The headquarters of the Paris Tourist Office is due to move to rue des Pyramides in May 2004, after leaving its former site on the Champs-Élysées. Other branches are at the Eiffel Tower (May–Nov), Gare de Lyon, Gare du Nord, Opéra (11 rue Scribe) and Montmartre (21 place du Tertre).

**Maison de la France**
The French Tourist Office.
(No public access to its Paris office.)
**www.**franceguide.com

**Paris Ile-de-France**
Carrousel du Louvre (lower level)
Tel 01 44 50 19 98/0826 166 666
Open Wed–Mon 9–7
Métro: Tuileries
**www.**Paris-ile-de-france.com

There is also an office at Disneyland Resort Paris (Place des Passagers-du-Vent; tel 01 60 43 33 33).

**FRENCH TOURIST OFFICES**

The French Tourist Office has a useful website–**www.**franceguide.com–but its head office in Paris is not open to the public. Some of its offices abroad are listed below.

**Australia**
Level 20, 25 Bligh Street, Sydney, NSW 2000; tel (02) 9231 5244;
email: info.au@franceguide.com

**Canada**
1981 avenue McGill College, Suite 490, Montréal, H3A 2W9
tel (514) 876 9881;
email: mfrance@attcanada.net

**Germany**
Westendstrasse 47, 60325, Frankfurt;
tel 0190 57 00 25 (€0.62 per min);
email: info.de@franceguide.com

**Ireland**
30 Merrion Street Upper, Dublin;
tel 15 60 235 235;
email: info.ie@franceguide.com

**Italy**
Via Larga 7, 20122, Milan; tel 166 116 216 (€1.31 per min +IVA);
email: info.it@franceguide.com

**Spain**
Plaza de España 18, Torre de Madrid 8a Pl. Of. 5, 28008, Madrid;
tel 906 34 36 38 (€0.35 per min);
email: info.es@franceguide.com

**UK**
178 Piccadilly, London, W1V 0AL;
tel 09068 244 123 (60 pence per min);
email: info.uk@franceguide.com

**USA** (New York)
444 Madison Avenue, 16th floor, New York, NY10022; tel 212/838–7800;
email: info@francetourism.com

**USA** (Los Angeles)
9454 Wilshire boulevard, Suite 715, 90212, Beverly Hills, California;
tel 310/271–6665;
email: info@francetourism.com

# FILMS AND BOOKS

## FILMS

- It's always a good idea to get in the mood of a destination before visiting. The ultimate Paris atmosphere-steeped film is, of course, *Le Fabuleux Destin d'Amélie Poulain* (2001). Although it depicts an idealized vision of Montmartre's charm, much of that quaintness still exists in this Paris 'village' (see page 108–109), and it is drawing new flocks of visitors to the area around rue des Abbesses and rue Lepic.
- For a more realistic view of everyday life today in another Paris district, the Bastille, see *When the Cat's Away* (1997), a charming small-budget film by Cédric Klapisch.
- Other fairly recent films set primarily in Paris include *French Kiss* (1995), in which Meg Ryan overdoses on French cheese; Woody Allen's romantic musical *Everybody Says I Love You* (1996); *Prêt-à-Porter* (*Ready to Wear*; 1994), Robert Altman's acidic look at the city's fashion world, featuring a whole roster of stars; and *Jefferson in Paris* (1995), in which James Ivory depicts late 18th-century Paris, just before the Revolution, during Thomas Jefferson's tenure as ambassador to France.
- No one has better expressed the romance of the City of Light than Audrey Hepburn in such delightful films as *Sabrina* (1954; remade in 1995 with Julia Ormond) and *Funny Face* (1957), in which she falls in love with Paris and almost upstages co-star Fred Astaire with her jazzy dance in a basement nightclub. In *Love in the Afternoon* (1957) Hepburn cavorts illicitly with Gary Cooper at the Ritz Hotel; she is paired with Cary Grant in *Charade* (1963), a sophisticated crime comedy.
- For tap dances around Paris monuments, see *An American in Paris* (1951), starring Gene Kelly, Leslie Caron and a Gershwin score.

## BOOKS

- For those who prefer to find their atmosphere on the page, Adam Gopnik's essays in *Paris to the Moon* (2000) provide one American's view of life in the French capital today.
- Ernest Hemingway's *A Moveable Feast* (published in 1964) and Gertrude Stein's *The Autobiography of Alice B. Toklas* (1933) describe a more romantic era in the early 20th century, when a young couple could live on $5 a day and an art collector could snap up works by Pablo Picasso and Henri Matisse for a song.
- A less flattering portrait of Paris can be found in *Down and Out in Paris and London* (1933), in which George Orwell describes the horrors of trying to survive in the city in the 1930s without a *sou*.
- The classics are always reliable for a vivid historic vision of Parisian life. Read Victor Hugo's *The Hunchback of Notre-Dame* (1831) or *Les Miserables* (1862), or Charles Dickens' take on the French Revolution in *A Tale of Two Cities* (1859).
- Mystery lovers will get into the atmosphere of the City of Light from George Simenon's *Inspector Maigret* series.

*Why not try a show to give you a taste of Paris?*

# USEFUL WEBSITES

**www.fodors.com**
A comprehensive travel-planning site that lets you research prices, reserve air tickets and ask questions to fellow visitors. (English)

**www.franceguide.com**
You'll find practical advice on everything from arriving in France to buying a property on this site, belonging to the French Tourist Office. There are also features on holidays in other parts of France. (French, English, German, Italian, Spanish, Dutch, Portuguese)

**www.intermusees.com**
The organization that runs the *Carte Musées-Monuments* pass. (French, English)

**www.lemonde.fr**
Catch up on current events on the site of *Le Monde* newspaper. (French)

**www.meteo.fr/meteonet**
Weather forecasts for Paris and the rest of France. (French, English, Spanish)

**www.monum.fr**
Learn more about some of Paris's most historic monuments, including the Arc de Triomphe, Panthéon and Notre-Dame, on the site of the Centre des Monuments Nationaux. (French, English)

**www.pagesjaunes.fr**
France's phone directory, online. (French, English)

**www.paris.fr**
The information on the city council's website ranges from current events to exploring Paris's bicycle ways. There is also news about the running of the city, aimed at residents. (French, English)

**www.parisdigest.com**
An independent site that guides you to the best the city has to offer, whether you want to sightsee, shop or eat out. (English)

**www.parisfranceguide.com**
A site aimed at English-speakers living in or visiting Paris, with information ranging from fashion to visiting the dentist. (English)

**www.paris-ile-de-france.com or www.pidf.com**
Special offers, plus information on events, hotels, the Métro and the weather, on the site of the Île de France regional tourist office. (French, English)

**www.paris-touristoffice.com**
The website of the Paris Tourist Office is packed with information on sights, restaurants, shops, hotels, events and the Métro. It also has useful links to other sites. (French, English)

**www.parisvoice.com**
An insider's view of Paris, aimed at English-speaking Parisians. Includes book reviews, an entertainment calendar and even an agony aunt. (English)

**www.ratp.fr**
The site of Paris's Métro and bus operator, with information about getting around. (French, English)

**www.rmn.fr**
Site of the Réunion des Musées Nationaux. (French, English)

**www.theAA.com**
The Automobile Association website contains a helpful route planner if you are planning excursions further afield. You can also buy maps of France. (English)

Other websites are listed alongside the relevant sights, or in the On the Move and Planning pages.

*Surf the Net to get the latest on events in Paris*

**KEY SIGHTS QUICK WEBSITE FINDER**

| Sight | Website | Page |
|---|---|---|
| Arc de Triomphe | www.monum.fr | 76–79 |
| Centre Georges Pompidou | www.centrepompidou.fr | 82–86 |
| Conciergerie | www.monum.fr | 89–91 |
| Grande Arche | www.grandearche.com | 94 |
| Institute du Monde Arabe | www.imarabe.org | 98 |
| Invalides | www.invalides.org | 99–101 |
| Jardin du Luxembourg | www.senat.fr | 102–103 |
| Montmartre | www.montmartrenet.com | 108–109 |
| La Mosquée | www.la-mosquee.com | 110 |
| Musée des Arts Décoratif | www.ucad.fr | 111 |
| Musée Carnavalet | www.paris.fr/musees/musee_carnavalet | 114–115 |
| Musée du Louvre | www.louvre.fr | 118–123 |
| Musée Marmottan–Monet | www.marmottan.com | 124–125 |
| Muséum National d'Histoire Naturelle | www.mnhn.fr | 127 |
| Musée National du Moyen Âge–Thermes de Cluny | www.musee-moyenage.fr | 128–129 |
| Musée d'Orsay | www.musee-orsay.fr | 130–134 |
| Musée Picasso | www.musee-picasso.fr | 135 |
| Musée Rodin | www.musee-rodin.fr | 136 |
| Notre-Dame | www.monum.fr | 137–141 |
| Opéra Palais Garnier | www.opera-de-paris.fr | 142 |
| Panthéon | www.monum.fr | 144 |
| Parc de la Villette and www.cite-musique.fr | www.cite-sciences.fr 146–147 | |
| Sacré-Cœur | www.sacre-coeur-montmartre.com | 154–157 |
| Sainte-Chapelle | www.monum.fr | 158–160 |
| Tour Eiffel | www.eiffel-tower.com | 164–169 |
| Tour Montparnasse | www.tourmontparnasse56.com | 170 |

# WORDS AND PHRASES

**Even if you're far from fluent, it is always a good idea to try to speak a few words of French while in Paris. The words and phrases on the following pages should help you with the basics, from ordering a meal to dealing with emergencies.**


- Conversation see page 311
- Useful Words see page 311
- Shopping see page 312
- Numbers see page 312
- Post and Telephones see page 312
- Days, Months, Holidays, Times see page 313
- Hotels see page 313
- Getting Around see page 314
- Money see page 314
- Colours see page 314
- Restaurants see pages 314–315
- Food and Drink see page 315
- Tourist Information see page 316
- Illness and Emergencies see page 316


## CONVERSATION

What is the time?
**Quelle heure est-il?**

When do you open/close?
**A quelle heure ouvrez/fermez-vous?**

I don't speak French.
**Je ne parle pas français.**

Do you speak English?
**Parlez-vous anglais?**

I don't understand.
**Je ne comprends pas.**

Please repeat that.
**Pouvez-vous répéter (s'il vous plaît)?**

Please speak more slowly.
**Pouvez-vous parler plus lentement?**

What does this mean?
**Qu'est-ce que ça veut dire?**

Write that down for me please.
**Pouvez-vous me l'écrire, s'il vous plaît?**

Please spell that.
**Pouvez-vous me l'épeler, s'il vous plaît?**

I'll look that up (in the dictionary).
**Je vais le chercher (dans le dictionnaire).**

My name is...
**Je m'appelle...**

What's your name?
**Comment vous appelez-vous?**

This is my wife/husband.
**Voici ma femme/mon mari.**

**Voici ma fille/mon fils.**
This is my daughter/son.

This is my friend.
**Voici mon ami(e).**

Hello, pleased to meet you.
**Bonjour, enchanté(e).**

I'm from ...
**Je viens de ...**

I'm on holiday.
**Je suis en vacances.**

I live in ...
**J'habite à ...**

Where do you live?
**Où habitez-vous?**

Good morning.
**Bonjour.**

Good evening.
**Bonsoir.**

Goodnight.
**Bonne nuit.**

Goodbye.
**Au revoir.**

See you later.
**A plus tard.**

How much is that?
**C'est combien?**

May I/Can I?
**Est-ce que je peux?**

I don't know.
**Je ne sais pas.**

You're welcome.
**Je vous en prie.**

How are you?
**Comment allez-vous?**

I'm sorry.
**Je suis désolé(e).**

Excuse me.
**Excusez-moi.**

That's all right.
**De rien.**

## USEFUL WORDS

| Yes | There | Who | How | Open | Please |
|---|---|---|---|---|---|
| **Oui** | **Là-bas** | **Qui** | **Comment** | **Ouvert** | **S'il vous plaît** |
| No | Here | When | Later | Closed | Thank you |
| **Non** | **Ici** | **Quand** | **Plus tard** | **Fermé** | **Merci** |
| | Where | Why | Now | | |
| | **Où** | **Pourquoi** | **Maintenant** | | |

## SHOPPING

Could you help me, please?
**(Est-ce que) vous pouvez m'aider, s'il vous plaît?**

How much is this?
**C'est combien?/Ça coûte combien?**

I'm looking for ...
**Je cherche ...**

When does the shop open/close?
**A quelle heure ouvre/ferme le magasin?**

I'm just looking, thank you.
**Je regarde, merci.**

This isn't what I want.
**Ce n'est pas ce que je veux.**

This is the right size.
**C'est la bonne taille.**

Do you have anything less expensive/smaller/larger?
**(Est-ce que) vous avez quelque chose de moins cher/plus petit/plus grand?**

I'll take this.
**Je prends ça.**

Do you have a bag for this, please?
**(Est-ce que) je peux avoir un sac, s'il vous plaît?**

Do you accept credit cards?
**(Est-ce que) vous acceptez les cartes de crédit?**

I'd like ....grams please.
**Je voudrais ...grammes, s'il vous plaît.**

I'd like a kilo of ...
**Je voudrais un kilo de ...**

What does this contain?
**Quels sont les ingrédients?/ Qu'est-ce qu'il y a dedans?**

I'd like ... slices of that.
**J'en voudrais ... tranches.**

Bakery
**Boulangerie**

Bookshop
**Librairie**

Chemist
**Pharmacie**

Supermarket
**Supermarché**

Market
**Marché**

Sale
**Soldes**

## NUMBERS

| | | | | | |
|---|---|---|---|---|---|
| 1<br>**un** | 6<br>**six** | 11<br>**onze** | 16<br>**seize** | 21<br>**vingt et un** | 70<br>**soixante-dix** |
| 2<br>**deux** | 7<br>**sept** | 12<br>**douze** | 17<br>**dix-sept** | 30<br>**trente** | 80<br>**quatre-vingts** |
| 3<br>**trois** | 8<br>**huit** | 13<br>**treize** | 18<br>**dix-huit** | 40<br>**quarante** | 90<br>**quatre-vingt dix** |
| 4<br>**quatre** | 9<br>**neuf** | 14<br>**quatorze** | 19<br>**dix-neuf** | 50<br>**cinquante** | 100<br>**cent** |
| 5<br>**cinq** | 10<br>**dix** | 15<br>**quinze** | 20<br>**vingt** | 60<br>**soixante** | 1000<br>**mille** |

## POST AND TELEPHONES

Where is the nearest post office/mail box?
**Où se trouve la poste/la boîte aux lettres la plus proche?**

How much is the postage to...?
**A combien faut-il affranchir pour ...?**

I'd like to send this by air mail/ registered mail.
**Je voudrais envoyer ceci par avion/en recommandé.**

Can you direct me to a public phone?
**Pouvez-vous m'indiquer la cabine téléphonique la plus proche?**

What is the number for directory enquiries?
**Quel est le numéro pour les renseignements?**

Where can I find a telephone directory?
**Où est-ce que je peux trouver un annuaire?**

Where can I buy a phone card?
**Où est-ce que je peux acheter une télécarte?**

Please put me through to...
**Pouvez-vous me passer ..., s'il vous plaît?**

Can I dial direct to ...?
**Est-ce que je peux appeler directement en ...?**

Do I need to dial 0 first?
**Est-ce qu'il faut composer le zéro (d'abord)?**

What is the charge per minute?
**Quel est le tarif à la minute?**

Have there been any calls for me?
**Est-ce que j'ai eu des appels téléphoniques?**

Hello, this is ...
**Allô, c'est ... (à l'appareil)?**

Who is speaking please ...?
**Qui est à l'appareil, s'il vous plaît?**

I would like to speak to ...
**Je voudrais parler à ...**

## DAYS/MONTHS/HOLIDAYS/TIMES

| | | | | | |
|---|---|---|---|---|---|
| Monday<br>**lundi** | January<br>**janvier** | August<br>**août** | spring<br>**printemps** | morning<br>**matin** | day<br>**le jour** |
| Tuesday<br>**mardi** | February<br>**février** | September<br>**septembre** | summer<br>**été** | afternoon<br>**après-midi** | month<br>**le mois** |
| Wednesday<br>**mercredi** | March<br>**mars** | October<br>**octobre** | autumn<br>**automne** | evening<br>**soir** | year<br>**l'année** |
| Thursday<br>**jeudi** | April<br>**avril** | November<br>**novembre** | winter<br>**hiver** | night<br>**nuit** | |
| Friday<br>**vendredi** | May<br>**mai** | December<br>**décembre** | holiday<br>**vacances** | today<br>**aujourd'hui** | |
| Saturday<br>**samedi** | June<br>**juin** | | Easter<br>**Pâques** | yesterday<br>**hier** | |
| Sunday<br>**dimanche** | July<br>**juillet** | | Christmas<br>**Noël** | tomorrow<br>**demain** | |

## HOTELS

Do you have a room?
**(Est-ce que) vous avez une chambre?**

I have a reservation for … nights.
**J'ai réservé pour … nuits.**

How much each night?
**C'est combien par nuit?**

Double room.
**Une chambre pour deux personnes/double.**

Twin room.
**Une chambre à deux lits/ avec lits jumeaux.**

Single room.
**Une chambre à un lit/pour une personne.**

With bath/shower/lavatory.
**Avec salle de bain/ douche/WC.**

Is the room air-conditioned/ heated?
**(Est-ce que) la chambre est climatisée/chauffée?**

Is breakfast/lunch/dinner included in the cost?
**(Est-ce que) le petit déjeuner/le déjeuner/le dîner est compris dans le prix?**

Is there a lift in the hotel?
**(Est-ce qu')il y a un ascenseur à l'hôtel?**

Is room service available?
**(Est-ce qu')il y a le service en chambre?**

When do you serve breakfast?
**À quelle heure servez-vous le petit déjeuner?**

May I have breakfast in my room?
**(Est-ce que) je peux prendre le petit déjeuner dans ma chambre?**

Do you serve evening meals?
**(Est-ce que) vous servez le repas du soir/le dîner?**

I need an alarm call at…
**Je voudrais être réveillé(e) à… heures.**

I'd like an extra blanket/pillow.
**Je voudrais une couverture/ un oreiller supplémentaire, s'il vous plaît.**

May I have my room key?
**(Est-ce que) je peux avoir la clé de ma chambre?**

Will you look after my luggage until I leave?
**Pouvez-vous garder mes bagages jusqu'à mon départ?**

Is there parking?
**(Est-ce qu') il y a un parking?**

Where can I park my car?
**Où est-ce que je peux garer ma voiture?**

Do you have babysitters?
**(Est-ce que) vous avez un service de babysitting/garde d'enfants?**

When are the sheets changed?
**Quand changez-vous les draps?**

The room is too hot/cold.
**Il fait trop chaud/froid dans la chambre.**

Could I have another room?
**(Est-ce que) je pourrais avoir une autre chambre?**

I am leaving this morning.
**Je pars ce matin.**

What time should we leave our room?
**A quelle heure devons-nous libérer la chambre?**

Can I pay my bill?
**(Est-ce que) je peux régler ma note, s'il vous plaît?**

May I see the room?
**(Est-ce que) je peux voir la chambre?**

Thank you for your hospitality.
**Merci pour votre hospitalité.**

Swimming pool.
**Piscine.**

No smoking.
**Non fumeur.**

## GETTING AROUND

Where is the information desk?
**Où est le bureau des renseignements?**

Where is the timetable?
**Où sont les horaires?**

Does this train/bus go to...?
**Ce train/bus va à...?**

Do you have a Métro/bus map?
**Avez-vous un plan du Métro/des lignes de bus?**

Please can I have a single/return ticket to...?
**Je voudrais un aller simple/un aller-retour pour..., s'il vous plaît.**

I'd like to rent a car.
**Je voudrais louer une voiture.**

Where are we?
**Où sommes-nous?**

I'm lost.
**Je me suis perdu(e).**

Is this the way to...?
**C'est bien par ici pour aller à...?**

I am in a hurry.
**Je suis pressé(e).**

Where can I find a taxi?
**Où est-ce que je peux trouver un taxi?**

How much is the journey?
**Combien coûte la course?**

Go straight on.
**Allez tout droit.**

Turn left.
**Tournez à gauche.**

Turn right.
**Tournez à droite.**

Cross over.
**Traversez.**

Traffic lights.
**Les feux.**

Intersection.
**Carrefour.**

Corner.
**Coin.**

No parking
**Interdiction de stationner**

Train/bus/Métro station
**La gare SNCF/routière/la station de Métro.**

Do you sell travel cards?
**Avez-vous des cartes d'abonnement?**

Do I need to get off here?
**(Est-ce qu') il faut que je descende ici?**

Where can I buy a ticket?
**Où est-ce que je peux acheter un billet/ticket?**

Where can I reserve a seat?
**Où est-ce que je peux réserver une place?**

Is this seat free?
**(Est-ce que) cette place est libre?**

Where can I find a taxi?
**Où est-ce que je peux trouver un taxi?**

## MONEY

Is there a bank/currency exchange office nearby?
**(Est-ce qu') il y a une banque/un bureau de change près d'ici?**

Can I cash this here?
**(Est-ce que) je peux encaisser ça ici?**

I'd like to change sterling/dollars into euros.
**Je voudrais changer des livres sterling/dollars en euros.**

Can I use my credit card to withdraw cash?
**(Est-ce que) je peux utiliser ma carte de crédit pour retirer de l'argent?**

What is the exchange rate today?
**Quel est le taux de change aujourd'hui?**

## COLOURS

| | |
|---|---|
| brown<br>**marron/brun** | blue<br>**bleu(e)** |
| black<br>**noir(e)** | green<br>**vert(e)** |
| red<br>**rouge** | yellow<br>**jaune** |

I'd like to reserve a table for ... people at ...
**Je voudrais réserver une table pour ... personnes à ...heures, s'il vous plaît.**

A table for ..., please.
**Une table pour ..., s'il vous plaît.**

We have/haven't booked.
**Nous avons/n'avons pas réservé.**

What time does the restaurant open?
**A quelle heure ouvre le restaurant?**

We'd like to wait for a table.
**Nous aimerions attendre qu'une table se libère.**

Could we sit there?
**(Est-ce que) nous pouvons nous asseoir ici?**

Is this table taken?
**(Est-ce que) cette table est libre?**

Are there tables outside?
**(Est-ce qu') il y a des tables dehors/à la terrasse?**

Where are the lavatories?
**Où sont les toilettes?**

Could you warm this up for me?
**(Est-ce que) vous pouvez me faire réchauffer ceci/ça, s'il vous plaît?**

Do you have nappy-changing facilities?
**(Est-ce qu') il y a une pièce pour changer les bébés?**

We'd like something to drink.
**Nous voudrions quelque chose à boire.**

Could we see the menu/wine list?
**(Est-ce que) nous pouvons voir le menu/la carte des vins, s'il vous plaît?**

Is there a dish of the day?
**(Est-ce qu') il y a un plat du jour?**

What do you recommend?
**Qu'est-ce que vous nous conseillez?**

## RESTAURANTS

This is not what I ordered.
**Ce n'est pas ce que j'ai commandé.**

I can't eat wheat/sugar/salt/pork/beef/dairy.
**Je ne peux pas manger de blé/sucre/sel/porc/bœuf/produits laitiers.**

I am a vegetarian.
**Je suis végétarien(ne).**

I'd like…
**Je voudrais …**

Could we have some more bread?
**(Est-ce que) vous pouvez nous apporter un peu plus de pain, s'il vous plaît?**

How much is this dish?
**Combien coûte ce plat?**

Is service included?
**(Est-ce que) le service est compris?**

Could we have some salt and pepper?
**(Est-ce que) vous pouvez nous apporter du sel et du poivre, s'il vous plaît?**

May I have an ashtray?
**(Est-ce que) je peux avoir un cendrier, s'il vous plaît?**

Could I have bottled still/sparkling water?
**(Est-ce que) je peux avoir une bouteille d'eau minérale/gazeuse, s'il vous plaît?**

The meat is too rare/overcooked.
**La viande est trop saignante/trop cuite.**

The food is cold.
**La nourriture est froide.**

Can I have the bill, please?
**(Est-ce que) je peux avoir l'addition, s'il vous plaît?**

The bill is not right.
**Il y a une erreur sur l'addition.**

We didn't order this.
**Nous n'avons pas commandé ça.**

I'd like to speak to the manager, please.
**Je voudrais parler au directeur, s'il vous plaît.**

The food was excellent.
**La nourriture était excellente.**

## FOOD AND DRINK

Breakfast
**Petit déjeuner**

Lunch
**Déjeuner**

Dinner
**Dîner**

Coffee
**Café**

Tea
**Thé**

Orange juice
**Jus d'orange**

Apple juice
**Jus de pomme**

Milk
**Lait**

Beer
**Bière**

Red wine
**Vin rouge**

White wine
**Vin blanc**

Bread roll
**Petit pain**

Bread
**Pain**

Sugar
**Sucre**

Wine list
**Carte/liste des vins**

Main course
**Le plat principal**

Dessert
**Dessert**

Salt/pepper
**Sel/poivre**

Cheese
**Fromage**

Knife/fork/spoon
**Couteau/Fourchette/Cuillère**

Soups
**Soupes/potages**

Vegetable soup
**Soupe de légumes**

Chicken soup
**Soupe au poulet**

Lentil soup
**Soupe aux lentilles**

Mushroom soup
**Soupe aux champignons**

Sandwiches
**Sandwichs**

Ham sandwich
**Sandwich du jambon**

Dish of the day
**Plat du jour**

Fish dishes
**Les poissons**

Prawns
**Crevettes roses/bouquet**

Oysters
**Huîtres**

Salmon
**Saumon**

Haddock
**Aiglefin**

Squid
**Calmar**

Meat dishes
**Viandes**

Roast chicken
**Poulet rotî**

Casserole
**Plat en cocotte**

Roast lamb
**Gigot**

Mixed cold meat
**L'assiette de charcuterie**

Potatoes
**Pommes de terre**

Cauliflower
**Chou-fleur**

Green beans
**Haricots verts**

Peas
**Petits pois**

Carrots
**Carottes**

Spinach
**Épinards**

Onions
**Oignons**

Lettuce
**Laitue**

Cucumber
**Concombre**

Tomatoes
**Tomates**

Fruit
**Les fruits**

Apples
**Pommes**

Strawberries
**Fraises**

Peaches
**Pêches**

Pears
**Poires**

Fruit tart
**Tarte aux fruits**

Pastry
**Pâtisserie**

Chocolate cake
**Gâteau au chocolat**

Cream
**Crème**

Ice cream
**Glace**

Chocolate mousse
**Mousse au chocolat**

## TOURIST INFORMATION

Where is the tourist information office, please?
**Où se trouve l'office du tourisme, s'il vous plaît?**

Do you have a city map?
**Avez-vous un plan de la ville?**

Where is the museum?
**Où est le musée?**

Can you give me some information about...?
**Pouvez-vous me donner des renseignements sur ...?**

What are the main places of interest here?
**Quels sont les principaux sites touristiques ici?**

Please could you point them out on the map?
**Pouvez-vous me les indiquer sur la carte, s'il vous plaît?**

What sights/hotels/restaurants can you recommend?
**Quels sites/hôtels/restaurants nous recommandez-vous?**

We are staying here for a day.
**Nous sommes ici pour une journée.**

I am interested in...
**Je suis intéressé(e) par...**

Does the guide speak English?
**Est-ce qu'il y a un guide qui parle anglais?**

Do you have any suggested walks?
**Avez-vous des suggestions de promenades?**

Are there guided tours?
**Est-ce qu'il y a des visites guidées?**

Are there organised excursions?
**Est-ce qu'il y a des excursions organisées?**

Can we make reservations here?
**Est-ce que nous pouvons réserver ici?**

What time does it open/close?
**Ça ouvre/ferme à quelle heure?**

What is the admission price?
**Quel est le prix d'entrée?**

Is there a discount for senior citizens/students?
**Est-ce qu'il y a des réductions pour les personnes âgées/ les étudiants?**

Do you have a brochure in English?
**Avez-vous un dépliant en anglais?**

What's on at the cinema?
**Qu'est-ce qu'il y a au cinéma?**

Where can I find a good nightclub?
**Où est-ce que je peux trouver une bonne boîte de nuit?**

Do you have a schedule for the theatre/opera?
**Est-ce que vous avez un programme de théâtre/ d'opéra?**

Should we dress smartly?
**Est-ce qu'il faut mettre une tenue de soirée?**

What time does the show start?
**A quelle heure commence le spectacle?**

How do I reserve a seat?
**Comment fait-on pour réserver une place?**

Could you reserve tickets for me?
**Pouvez-vous me réserver des billets?**

## ILLNESS AND EMERGENCIES

I don't feel well.
**Je ne me sens pas bien.**

Could you call a doctor?
**(Est-ce que) vous pouvez appeler un médecin/un docteur, s'il vous plaît?**

Is there a doctor/pharmacist on duty?
**(Est-ce qu') il y a un médecin/docteur/une pharmacie de garde?**

I feel sick.
**J'ai envie de vomir.**

I need to see a doctor/dentist.
**Il faut que je voie un médecin/docteur/ un dentiste.**

Please direct me to the hospital.
**(Est-ce que) vous pouvez m'indiquer le chemin pour aller à l'hôpital, s'il vous plaît?**

I have a headache.
**J'ai mal à la tête.**

I've been stung by a wasp/bee.
**J'ai été piqué(e) par une guêpe/abeille.**

I have a heart condition.
**J'ai un problème cardiaque.**

I am diabetic.
**Je suis diabétique.**

I'm asthmatic.
**Je suis asmathique.**

I'm on a special diet.
**Je suis un régime spécial.**

I am on medication.
**Je prends des médicaments.**

I have left my medicine at home.
**J'ai laissé mes médicaments chez moi.**

I need to make an emergency appointment.
**Je dois prendre rendez-vous d'urgence.**

I have bad toothache.
**J'ai mal aux dents.**

I don't want an injection.
**Je ne veux pas de piqûre.**

Help!
**Au secours!**

I have lost my passport/ wallet/purse/handbag.
**J'ai perdu mon passeport/ portefeuille/porte-monnaie/sac à main.**

I have had an accident.
**J'ai eu un accident.**

My car has been stolen.
**On m'a volé ma voiture.**

I have been robbed.
**J'ai été volé(e).**

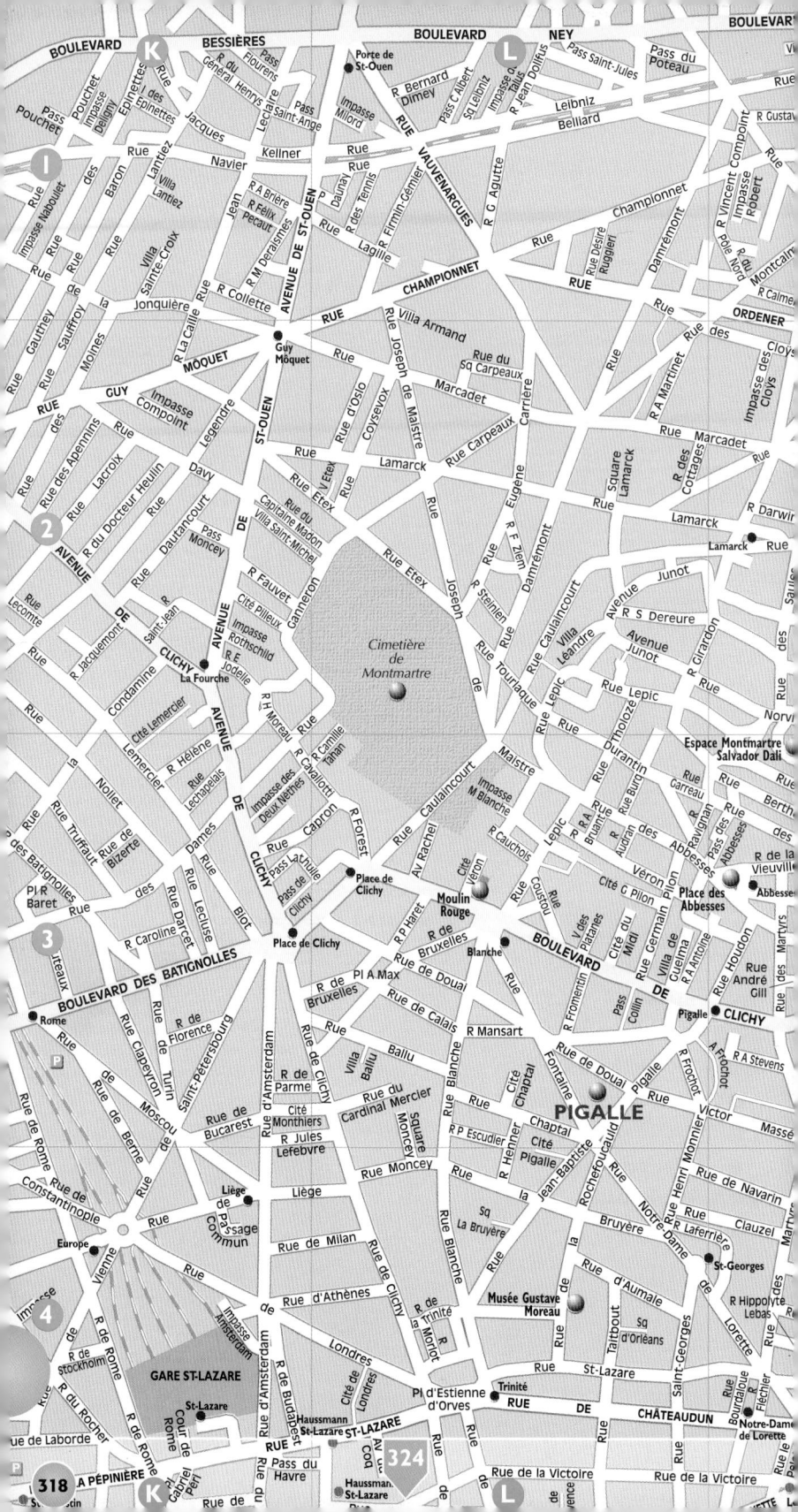
BOULEVARD
BESSIÈRES
BOULEVARD
NEY
Porte de St-Ouen
Pass Saint-Jules
Pass du Poteau
Pass Pouchet
Pouchet
Impasse Deligny
Epinettes
Rue des Epinettes
R du Général Henris
Pass Fleurons
Leclaire
Pass Saint-Ange
Jacques
Impasse Milord
R Bernard Dimey
Pass C Albert
Sq Leibniz
Impasse du Tilleul
R Jean Dolifus
Leibniz
Belliard
Rue
Kellner
Navier
Rue
Dauvat
Rue des Tennis
R Firmin-Gémier
R G Aguette
Rue VAUVENARGUES
Villa Lantiez
Baron
Lantiez
Impasse Nabouliet
R A Brière
R Félix Pecqueur
Jean
R M Derainsmes
Villa Sainte-Croix
Rue
Lagille
Championnet
Rue Désiré Ruggieri
Damrémont
R Vincent Compoint
Impasse Robert
R du Pôle Nord
Montcalm
R Calmel
CHAMPIONNET
RUE
AVENUE DE ST-OUEN
R Collette
Jonquière
Rue
Villa Armand
Rue Joseph de Maistre
Rue du Sq Carpeaux
Marcadet
Carrière
R A Martinet
Rue des Cloys
Impasse des Cloys
ORDENER
Cauthey
Sauffroy
Moines
R La Caille
MOQUET
Guy Moquet
GUY
Impasse Compoint
Legendre
ST-OUEN
Rue d'Osio
Coysevox
Rue Carpeaux
Rue Marcadet
Rue des Apennins
Lacroix
Davy
Rue V Etex
Rue Etex
Rue du Capitaine Madon
Villa Saint-Michel
Square Lamarck
R des Cottages
Lamarck
R Darwin
Rue du Docteur Heulin
Dautancourt
Pass Moncey
Rue Etex
Rue Eugène
R F Ziem
Damrémont
Lamarck
Rue Lecomte
R Jacquemont
R Saint-Jean
Cité Pilleux
Impasse Rothschild
R E Lodelle
R Fauvet
Canneron
Cimetière de Montmartre
Rue Joseph
R Steinlen
Rue Caulaincourt
Villa Léandre
Avenue Junot
R S Dereure
Avenue Junot
R Girardon
Condamine
CLICHY
La Fourche
Cité Lemercier
R H Moreau
R Camille Tahan
Rue Tourlaque
Rue Lepic
Rue Lepic
Rue Ornoloz
Rue Durantin
Espace Montmartre Salvador Dali
Lemercier
R Hélène
Rue Lachapelais
Impasse des Deux Nèches
R Cavaliotti
Maistre
Impasse M Blanche
Rue Garreau
Rue Berthe
Noliet
Rue Truffaut
Rue de Bizerte
Dames
Capron
R Forest
Rue Caulaincourt
AV Rachel
R Cauchois
Lepic
R R A Briant
Rue Burq
R Audran
R Ravignan
Pass des Abbesses
R de la Vieuville
Abbesses
Pl R Baret
Rue Lecluse
Rue Parcet
Rue Biot
Pass Latrille
Pass de Clichy
Place de Clichy
Cité Véron
Moulin Rouge
Rue Coustou
Véron
Cité G Pilon
Place des Abbesses
Place de Clichy
R Caroline
R P Haret
R de Bruxelles
Blanche
BOULEVARD DE CLICHY
Cité du Midi
Villa de Guelma
R A Antoine
Rue Houdon
Rue André Gill
Rue des Martyrs
BOULEVARD DES BATIGNOLLES
Pl A Max
Rue de Douai
R de Bruxelles
Rue de Calais
R Mansart
R Fromentin
Pass Collin
Pigalle
CLICHY
Rue de Florence
Rue Clapeyron
Rue de Turin
Saint-Petersbourg
Rome
Villa Ballu
Ballu
Rue de Clichy
R de Parme
Rue d'Amsterdam
Rue Blanche
Cité Chaptal
Fontaine
Rue de Douai
Pigalle
R Frochot
R A Stevens
Rue de Berne
Rue de Moscou
Rue de Bucarest
Cité Monthiers
R Jules Lefebvre
Rue du Cardinal Mercier
Square Moncey
R P Escudier
Chaptal
Cité Pigalle
PIGALLE
Victor Massé
Rue de Rome
Rue de Constantinople
Liège
Rue Moncey
Rue Henner
Rue Jean-Baptiste Rousseau
Rue Henri Monnier
Rue de Navarin
Passage Commun
Europe
Vienne
Rue de Milan
Sq La Bruyère
Bruyère
R Laferrière
Clauzel
St-Georges
Rue d'Athènes
Rue de Clichy
R de la Trinité
Musée Gustave Moreau
Rue d'Aumale
R Hippolyte Lebas
Impasse Amsterdam
R de Rome
R de Stockholm
GARE ST-LAZARE
Londres
Cité de Londres
Taitbout
Sq d'Orléans
Rue St-Georges
Rue Lorette
St-Lazare
Pl d'Estienne d'Orves
Trinité
RUE DE CHÂTEAUDUN
Rue Bourdaloue
R Fléchier
Notre-Dame de Lorette
Rue de Laborde
Cour de Rome
Haussmann St-Lazare
ST-LAZARE
RUE
Rue de Budapest
Rue d'Amsterdam
Pass du Havre
Haussmann St-Lazare
Rue de la Victoire
Rue de la Victoire
Rue de Prony
R Gabriel Péri
Rue de
318
LA PÉPINIÈRE
324
K
L
I
2
3
4

Main road

Other road

Minor road/path

Railway

Park

Important building

Featured place of interest

Tourist Information Office

Métro station

Railway station

Parking area

318-333

0 250 m

0 250 yds

# Maps

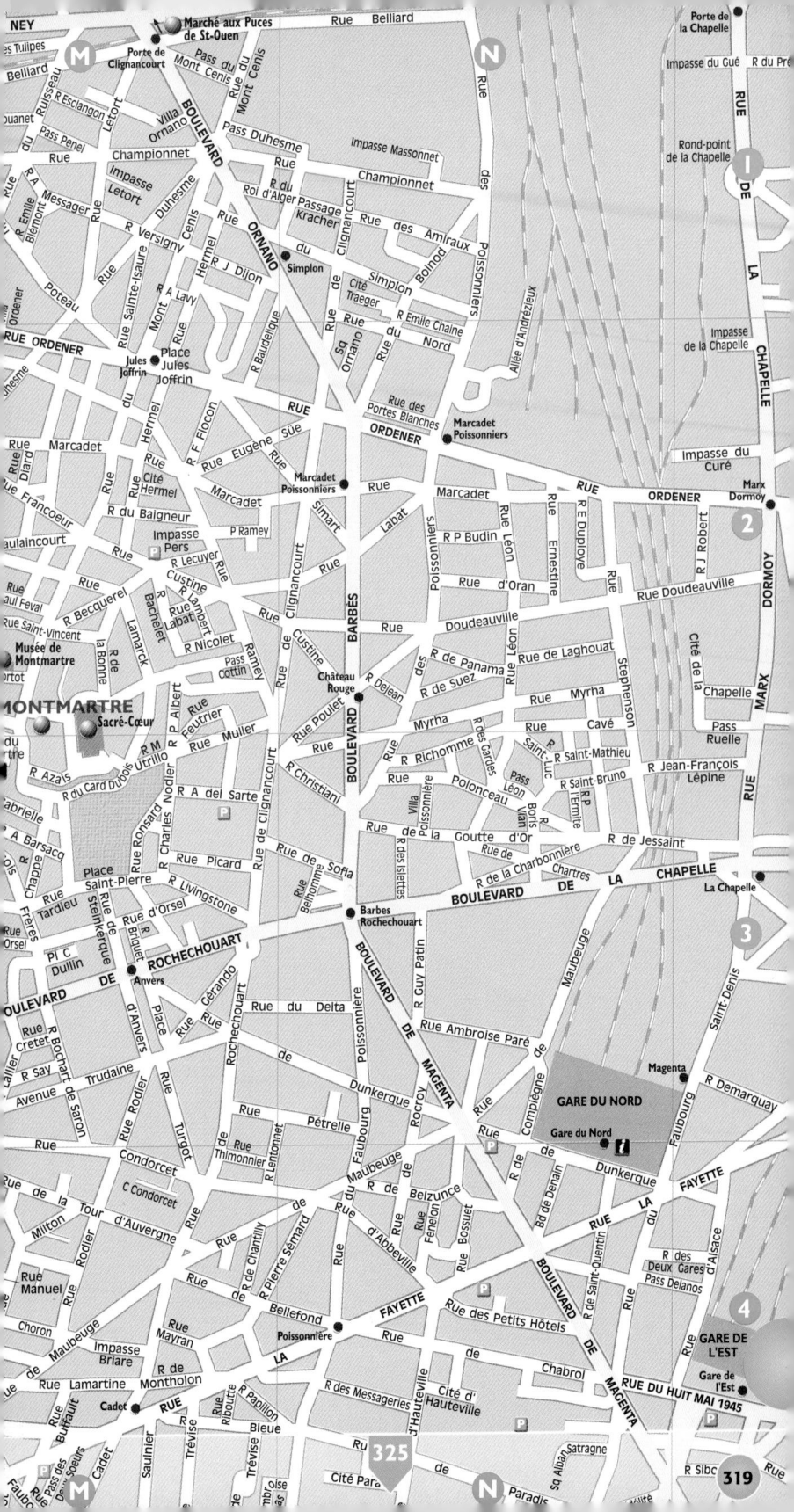
Marché aux Puces de St-Ouen
Porte de Clignancourt
Porte de la Chapelle
Rond-point de la Chapelle
Impasse du Curé
Marx Dormoy
Marcadet Poissonniers
Place Jules Joffrin
Jules Joffrin
Simplon
Musée de Montmartre
MONTMARTRE
Sacré-Cœur
Château Rouge
Barbès Rochechouart
Anvers
Poissonnière
Cadet
GARE DU NORD
Gare du Nord
Magenta
GARE DE L'EST
Gare de l'Est
La Chapelle
BOULEVARD DE LA CHAPELLE
BOULEVARD DE MAGENTA
BOULEVARD DE LA FAYETTE
RUE ORDENER
RUE DE LA CHAPELLE
RUE DU HUIT MAI 1945
BOULEVARD ORNANO
BOULEVARD BARBÈS
RUE DORMOY
RUE MARX
1
2
3
4
325
319

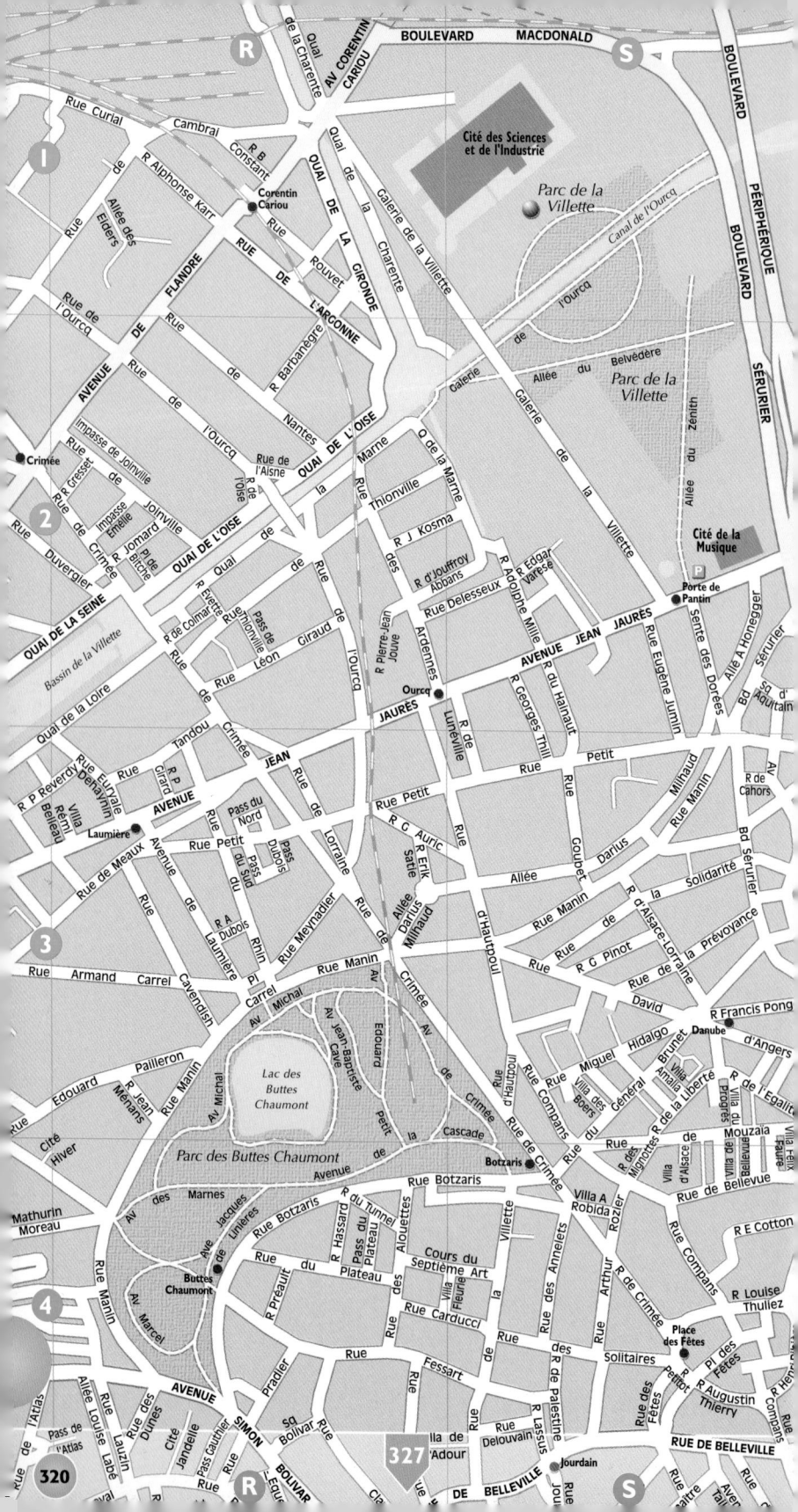
BOULEVARD MACDONALD
BOULEVARD PÉRIPHÉRIQUE SÉRURIER
Cité des Sciences et de l'Industrie
Parc de la Villette
Canal de l'Ourcq
Cité de la Musique
Porte de Pantin
Corentin Cariou
Crimée
Laumière
Ourcq
Jaurès
Botzaris
Buttes Chaumont
Place des Fêtes
Jourdain
Danube
Bassin de la Villette
Lac des Buttes Chaumont
Parc des Buttes Chaumont
QUAI DE LA GIRONDE
RUE DE FLANDRE
AVENUE DE L'ARCONNE
QUAI DE L'OISE
QUAI DE LA SEINE
AVENUE JEAN JAURÈS
RUE DE BELLEVILLE
AVENUE SIMON BOLIVAR
Rue de Crimée
Rue de Belleville
Rue de Meaux
Rue Manin
Rue Petit
Rue Botzaris
Rue Curial
Rue Duvergier
Rue de l'Ourcq
Rue de la Vilette
Rue Eugène Jumin
Rue Delesseux
Rue Armand Carrel
Rue Meynadier
Rue Lorraine
Rue Cavendish
Rue Pailleron
Rue Mathurin Moreau
Rue Louise Thuliez
Rue Augustin Thierry
Rue Cardinet
Rue Fessart
Rue Pradier
Rue Delouvain
Rue Lassus
Rue Petit
Rue Milnaud
Rue Darius
Rue Coubet
Rue Manin
Rue Miguel Hidalgo
Rue Compans
Rue Arthur Rozier
Rue des Annelets
Rue Cardinet
Rue Fessart
Rue Delouvain
Rue Lassus
Rue Louise Thuliez
Rue Augustin Thierry
Rue des Fêtes

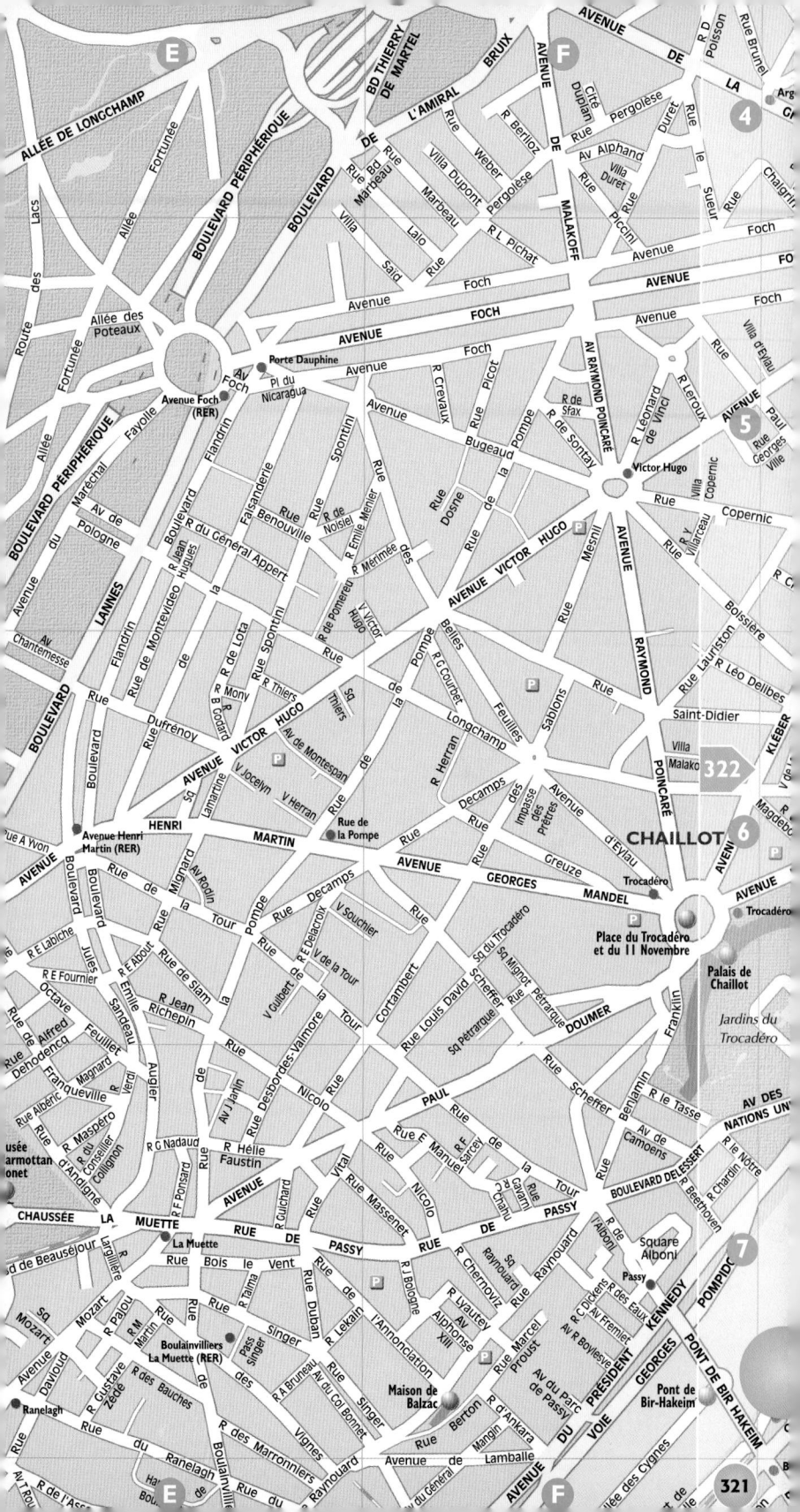
E
F
4
5
6
7
322
321
ALLÉE DE LONGCHAMP
BOULEVARD PÉRIPHÉRIQUE
BOULEVARD DE L'AMIRAL
BD THIERRY DE MARTEL
AVENUE DE LA BRUIX
AVENUE FOCH
AVENUE DU PRÉSIDENT KENNEDY
AVENUE DU VOIE
AVENUE VICTOR HUGO
AVENUE HENRI MARTIN
AVENUE GEORGES MANDEL
AVENUE DES NATIONS UN
BOULEVARD DE LA MUETTE
RUE DE PASSY
RUE DE PAUL DOUMER
RUE DE LA POMPE
RUE DE LA TOUR
RUE DE LA PAIX

F
G
H
4
5
6
7
321
322
328
AVENUE DE LA GRANDE ARMÉE
AVENUE DE WAGRAM
AVENUE DE FRIEDLAND
AVENUE FOCH
AVENUE HOCHE
AVENUE VICTOR HUGO
AVENUE KLÉBER
AVENUE D'IÉNA
AVENUE GEORGE V
AVENUE RAYMOND POINCARÉ
AVENUE DU PRÉSIDENT WILSON
AVENUE DES NATIONS UNIES
AVENUE DE NEW YORK
QUAI BRANLY
PONT D'IÉNA
PONT DE BIR-HAKEIM
PONT DE L'ALMA
BOULEVARD DE LESSERT
Argentine
Charles de Gaulle-Étoile (+RER)
Arc de Triomphe
Kléber
George V
Victor Hugo
Boissière
Musée Baccarat
Musée National des Arts Asiatiques-Guimet
Place d'Iéna
Iéna
Musée d'Art Moderne de la Ville de Paris
Musée Galliéra
Alma-Marceau
Place de l'Alma
Pont de l'Alma
Pont de l'Alma (RER)
Les Égouts
Trocadéro
Place du Trocadéro et du 11 Novembre
Palais de Chaillot
Jardins du Trocadéro
Seine
Place de la Résistance
Musée du Quai Branly
Pl de Varsovie
Tour Eiffel
Champ de Mars-Tour Eiffel (RER)
Pont de Bir-Hakeim
Bir-Hakeim
Passy
Parc du Champ

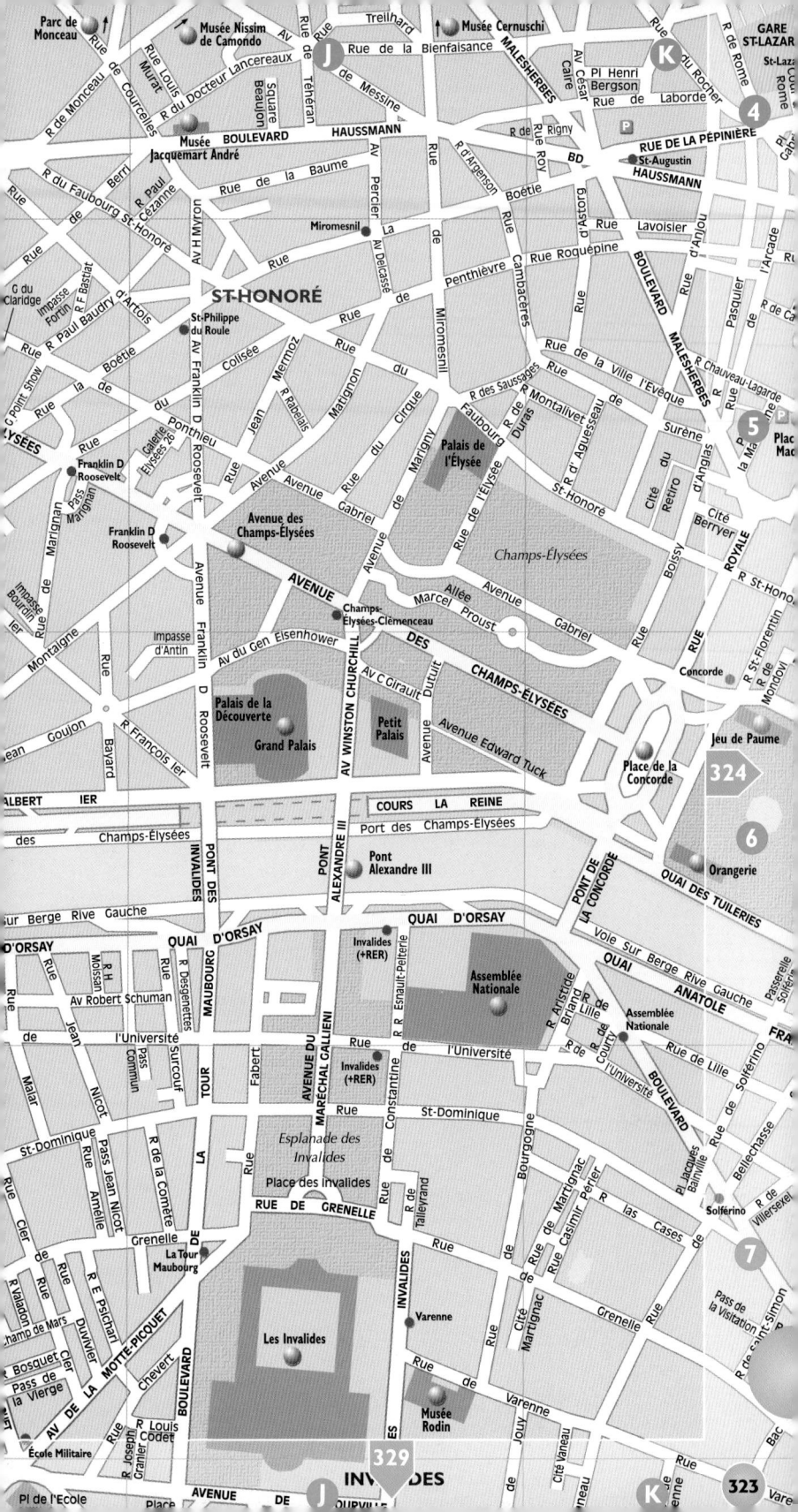
Parc de Monceau
Musée Nissim de Camondo
Musée Cernuschi
GARE ST-LAZAR
Rue de la Bienfaisance
Rue de Monceau
Rue de Courcelles
Rue Louis Murat
R du Docteur Lancereaux
Square Beaujon
Rue de Téhéran
Rue de Messine
Av Malesherbes
Av César Caire
Pl Henri Bergson
Rue de Laborde
R de Rome
Musée Jacquemart André
BOULEVARD HAUSSMANN
R de Rigny
Rue Roy
BD HAUSSMANN
RUE DE LA PÉPINIÈRE
St-Augustin
R du Faubourg St-Honoré
R Paul Cézanne
Rue de la Baume
R d'Argenson
Boétie
Miromesnil
Av Delassé
Rue Lavoisier
Rue Roquépine
Rue Penthièvre
Rue Cambacères
Av d'Antin
Rue d'Anjou
Rue Pasquier
Rue de l'Arcade
ST-HONORÉ
St-Philippe du Roule
Impasse Fortin
R F Bastiat
R Paul Baudry
R d'Artois
Rue Boétie
Av Franklin D Roosevelt
Colisée
Rue Mermoz
Rue Jean Mermoz
R Rabelais
Rue Matignon
Rue du Cirque
Rue Miromesnil
Rue de la Ville l'Évêque
R des Saussaies
R Montaliver
R d'Aguesseau
Faubourg St-Honoré
R de Duras
Palais de l'Élysée
Rue de l'Élysée
Surène
Cité du Retiro
Cité d'Anglas
Cité Berryer
Rue Boissy
Rue Royale
R St-Honoré
Plac Mac
Galerie Élysées 26
Franklin D Roosevelt
Pass Marignan
Rue de Marignan
Avenue des Champs-Élysées
Champs-Élysées
Avenue Gabriel
Avenue Marcel Proust
Allée
Champs-Élysées-Clémenceau
Impasse Bourdin
Impasse d'Antin
Av du Gén Eisenhower
AVENUE DES CHAMPS-ÉLYSÉES
Av C Girault
Rue Dutuit
Concorde
R St-Florentin
R de Mondovi
Palais de la Découverte
Grand Palais
Petit Palais
Avenue Edward Tuck
Jeu de Paume
Place de la Concorde
324
R Goujon
R Bayard
R François Ier
Av Winston Churchill
COURS LA REINE
Port des Champs-Élysées
Pont des Invalides
Pont Alexandre III
Pont de la Concorde
Orangerie
QUAI DES TUILERIES
Rive Gauche
QUAI D'ORSAY
Invalides (+RER)
Assemblée Nationale
Voie Sur Berge Rive Gauche
QUAI ANATOLE FRANCE
R H Moissan
R Desgenettes
Av Robert Schuman
Rue de l'Université
Pass Commun
Rue Surcouf
Rue Fabert
Av du Maréchal Gallieni
R R Esnault-Pelterie
R Aristide Briand
R de Lille
R de Courty
Rue de Lille
Rue de Solférino
Rue Malar
Rue Nicot
Rue St-Dominique
Esplanade des Invalides
Place des invalides
Rue de Constantine
Rue de Bourgogne
R de Talleyrand
Pl Jacques Bainville
Solférino
R de Villersexel
Rue Amélie
Pass Jean Nicot
R de la Comète
Rue de Grenelle
R de Martignac
R Casimir Perier
R las Cases
Bellechasse
La Tour Maubourg
Rue de Varenne
Cité Martignac
Pass de la Visitation
R de Saint-Simon
Les Invalides
Varenne
Musée Rodin
Rue Duvivier
R E Psichari
Av de la Motte-Picquet
Boulevard Chevert
R Louis Codet
R Joseph Granier
École Militaire
329
323
Pl de l'École
Place de l'Université
Cité Vaneau

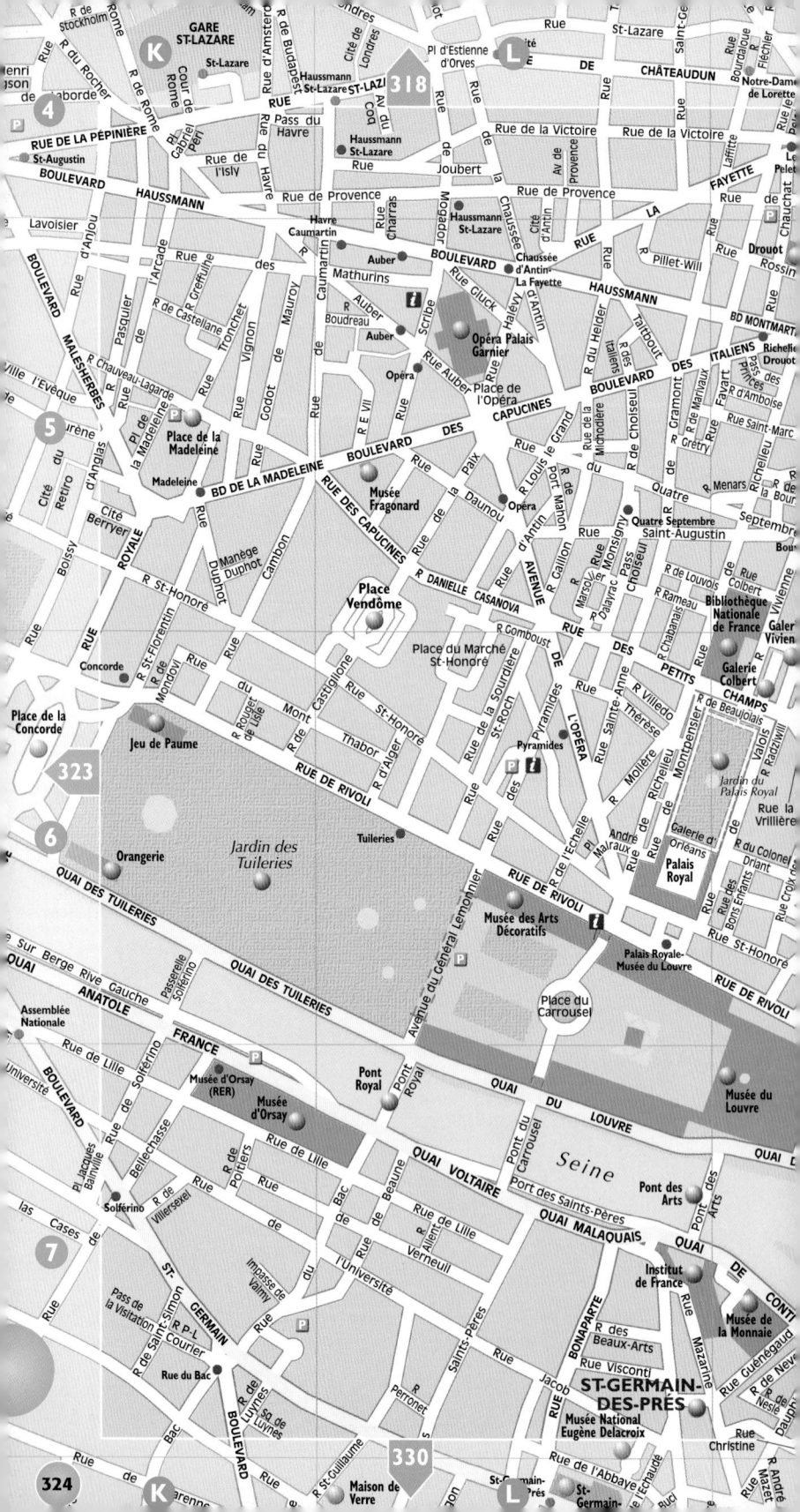
GARE ST-LAZARE
St-Lazare
Haussmann St-Lazare
ST-LAZARE
318
Pl d'Estienne d'Orves
RUE DE CHÂTEAUDUN
Notre-Dame de Lorette
Pass du Havre
RUE DE LA PÉPINIÈRE
St-Augustin
Haussmann St-Lazare
Rue de la Victoire
Rue de l'Isly
BOULEVARD HAUSSMANN
Rue de Provence
Havre Caumartin
Haussmann St-Lazare
Auber
BOULEVARD HAUSSMANN
Chaussée d'Antin La Fayette
Drouot
Mathurins
Opéra Palais Garnier
Opéra
Place de l'Opéra
BOULEVARD DES CAPUCINES
BD MONTMARTRE
BOULEVARD DES ITALIENS
Richelieu Drouot
Place de la Madeleine
Madeleine
BD DE LA MADELEINE
Musée Fragonard
Opéra
Quatre Septembre
Saint-Augustin
RUE DES CAPUCINES
Place Vendôme
Place du Marché St-Honoré
Bibliothèque Nationale de France
Galerie Vivienne
Galerie Colbert
Concorde
Place de la Concorde
Jeu de Paume
323
RUE DE RIVOLI
Pyramides
Jardin du Palais Royal
Tuileries
Jardin des Tuileries
Orangerie
Galerie d'Orléans
Palais Royal
QUAI DES TUILERIES
Musée des Arts Décoratifs
Palais Royale-Musée du Louvre
Place du Carrousel
Assemblée Nationale
QUAI ANATOLE FRANCE
Musée d'Orsay (RER)
Musée d'Orsay
Pont Royal
QUAI DU LOUVRE
Musée du Louvre
Seine
QUAI VOLTAIRE
Pont du Carrousel
Pont des Arts
QUAI MALAQUAIS
Solférino
Rue du Bac
Institut de France
Musée de la Monnaie
ST-GERMAIN-DES-PRÉS
Musée National Eugène Delacroix
330
324
Maison de Verre
St-Germain-des-Prés

GARE DE L'EST
Gare de l'Est
RUE DU HUIT MAI 1945
BOULEVARD DE STRASBOURG
MAGENTA
Passage Verdeau
Passage Jouffroy
Musée Grévin
Passage des Panoramas
Grands Boulevards
BOULEVARD POISSONNIÈRE
Bonne Nouvelle
BD DE BONNE NOUVELLE
Strasbourg St-Denis
BD ST-DENIS
BOULEVARD ST-MARTIN
La Bourse
Place des Victoires
Sentier
Réaumur Sébastopol
Musée des Arts et Métiers
Arts et Métiers
LES HALLES
Etienne Marcel
St-Eustache
Les Halles
Galerie Véro-Dodat
Jardin du Forum des Halles
Fontaine des Innocents
Châtelet Les Halles (+RER)
Rambuteau
Musée d'Art et d'Histoire du Judaïsme
Centre Georges Pompidou
Musée de l'Histoire de France
Châtelet
St-Merri
IRCAM
LE MARAIS
St-Germain-l'Auxerrois
Pont Neuf-La Monnaie
Hôtel de Ville
Palais de Justice
Conciergerie
Sainte-Chapelle
Pont Neuf
Cité
Pl. Louis Lépine
Île de la Cité
St-Michel-Notre-Dame (RER)
Maison Européenne de la Photographie
BD DU PALAIS
QUAI DE L'HOTEL DE VILLE
QUAI DES GRANDS AUGUSTINS
RUE DE RIVOLI
AVENUE VICTORIA
QUAI DE GESVRES
PONT NOTRE-DAME
PONT AU CHANGE
RUE DE LA CITÉ
BOULEVARD SÉBASTOPOL
BOULEVARD DU TEMPLE
BOULEVARD RENARD
RUE ETIENNE MARCEL
RUE DE RIVOLI
RUE DE LA MÉGISSERIE
QUAI DE LA MONNAIE
RUE DE RIVOLI
RUE DE RENARD
RUE DE BEAUBOURG
RUE DE MONTMORENCY
RUE DE MONTMORENCY
RUE DE LA FERRONNERIE
RUE DE RIVOLI
RUE DE RENARD
RUE DE BEAUBOURG

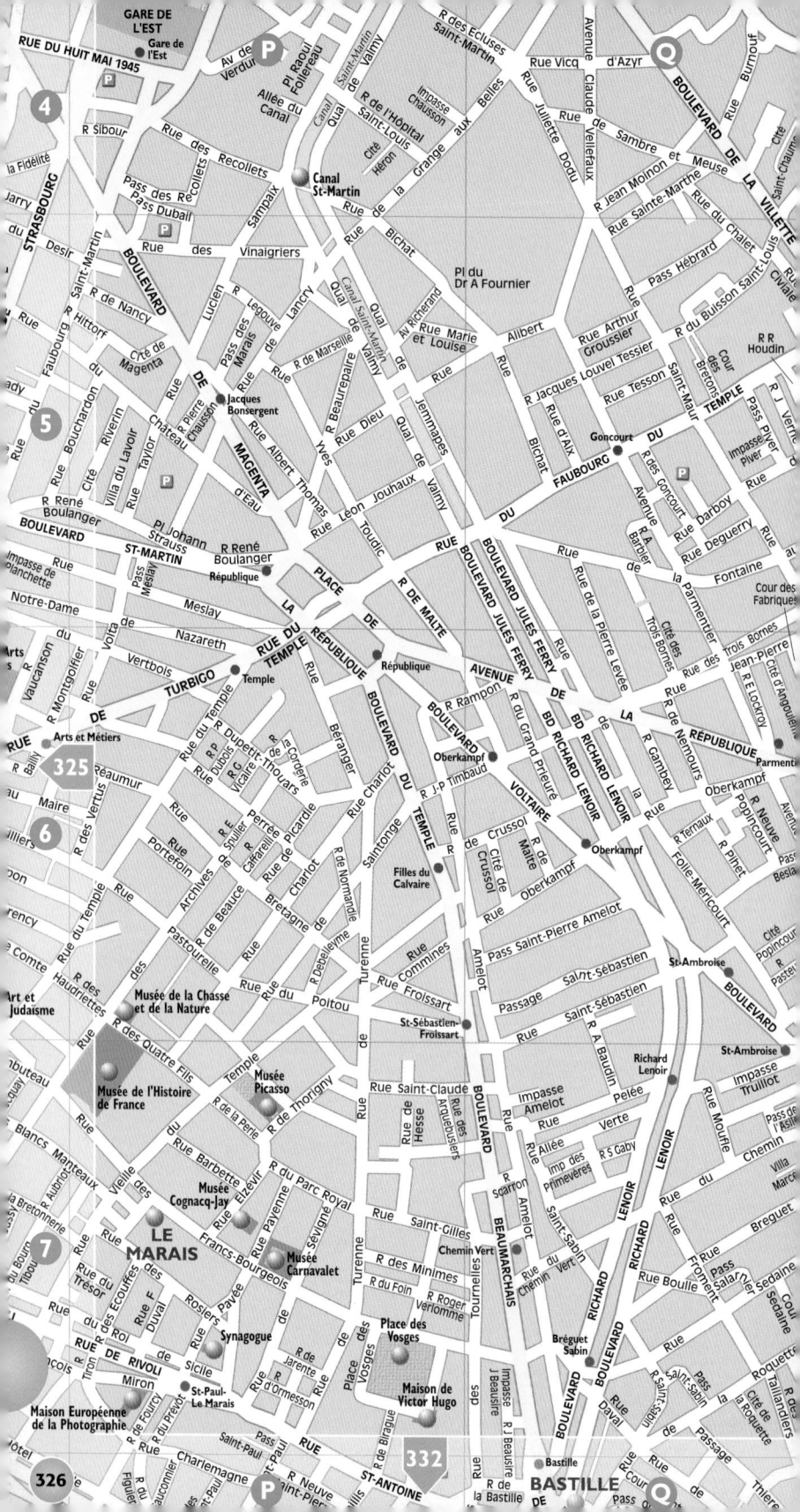
GARE DE L'EST
Gare de l'Est
RUE DU HUIT MAI 1945
Av de Verdun
Pl Raoul Follereau
Allée du Canal
Canal St-Martin
R Sibour
Rue des Recollets
Pass des Recollets
Pass Dubail
Rue des Vinaigriers
Rue de la Grange aux Belles
R de l'Hôpital Saint-Louis
Impasse Chausson
Cité Héron
R des Ecluses Saint-Martin
Rue Vicq d'Azyr
Avenue Claude Vellefaux
Rue Juliette Dodu
BOULEVARD DE LA VILLETTE
R Jean Moinon
Rue Sainte-Marthe
Rue du Chalet
Rue de Sambre et Meuse
Rue Bichat
Pl du Dr A Fournier
Av Richerand
Rue Marie et Louise
Alibert
Rue Arthur Groussier
R du Buisson Saint-Louis
Pass Hébrard
R R Houdin
Cour des Bretons
Rue Tesson
Saint-Maur
TEMPLE
R J Verne
Pass Pivet
Impasse Pivet
Rue Darboy
Rue Deguerry
Rue de la Fontaine
Cour des Fabriques
Cité des Trois Bornes
Rue des Trois Bornes
Jean-Pierre
Cité d'Angoulême
R E Lockroy
Parmentier
R de la Parmentier
Rue de la Pierre Levée
Goncourt
R des Goncourt
Avenue R A Barbier
Rue d'Alix
Rue Louvel Tessier
Jacques
Bichat
DU FAUBOURG
Rue Jemmapes
Quai de Valmy
Canal Saint-Martin
Quai de Jemmapes
Rue Beaurepaire
R de Marseille
Rue Dieu
Rue Léon Jouhaux
Rue Toudic
Rue Albert Thomas
Rue Lucien Lefèvre
Rue Legouve
Rue Lancry
Pass des Marais
Rue de Nancy
R Hittorf
Faubourg du Temple
Cité de Magenta
Rue Bouchardon
Rue Riverin
Villa du Lavoir
Rue Taylor
R Pierre Chausson
Rue Château d'Eau
Jacques Bonsergent
BOULEVARD DE MAGENTA
Pl Johann Strauss
R René Boulanger
ST-MARTIN
Impasse de la Planchette
Pass Mesdan
République
Notre-Dame
Meslay
Nazareth
Vertbois
Voltaire
R Montgolfier
Vaucanson
Arts et Métiers
Temple
TURBIGO
RUE DU TEMPLE
PLACE DE LA RÉPUBLIQUE
R DE MALTE
BOULEVARD JULES FERRY
AVENUE DE LA RÉPUBLIQUE
BD RICHARD LENOIR
R du Grand Prieuré
R Rampon
R J-P Timbaud
Oberkampf
R Gambey
R de Nemours
R Popincourt
R Neuve Popincourt
R Pinel
R Fenaux
Folie-Méricourt
Cité Popincourt
Rue Béranger
Rue Charlot
Rue du Temple
R Dupetit-Thouars
R Dubois
R Vicaire
R Perrée
R Caffarelli
R Sujier
Rue de Picardie
Rue Portefoin
Rue Archives
R de Beauce
Rue de Bretagne
Rue Pastourelle
R des Haudriettes
Rue du Temple
Rue Saintonge
Rue de Normandie
Rue Debelleyme
Rue Turenne
Rue de Crussol
Cité de Crussol
R de Malte
Oberkampf
Filles du Calvaire
Rue Oberkampf
Rue Commines
Rue Froissart
Pass Saint-Pierre Amelot
Passage Saint-Sébastien
Rue Saint-Sébastien
St-Sébastien-Froissart
St-Ambroise
BOULEVARD
R A Baudin
Richard Lenoir
Impasse Truillot
Rue Moufle
Rue Pelée
Impasse Amelot
Rue Verte
Rue Alibert
Imp des Primevères
R S Gaby
Rue du Chemin Vert
Rue Saint-Sabin
Rue Bouillé
Rue Sedaine
Cour Sedaine
Pass Salamandre
Rue Breguet
Villa Marcel
Rue Saint-Gilles
Rue des Minimes
R du Foin
R Roger Verlomme
Chemin Vert
BEAUMARCHAIS
Tournelles
Place des Vosges
Maison de Victor Hugo
Impasse J Beausire
R J Beausire
Bréguet Sabin
BOULEVARD RICHARD LENOIR
Rue Daval
Rue Saint-Sabin
Rue de la Roquette
Cité de la Roquette
Passage de la Roquette
Rue Tailandiers
Rue Roquette
Rue Cour des Trois Bornes
Rue Thiers
Bastille
BASTILLE
R de la Bastille
Rue Charlemagne
Rue Saint-Paul
Rue Neuve Saint-Pierre
Rue Figuier
R du Pelleur
R du Prévôt
Rue Miron
Rue Fourcy
Rue Rosiers
Rue Pavée
Rue Duval
Rue Roi de Sicile
Rue d'Ormesson
Rue de Jarente
Rue de Sévigné
Rue Payenne
Rue Elzévir
Rue Barbette
Rue Vieille du Temple
Rue Blancs Manteaux
Rue Aubriot
Rue Tresor
Rue des Ecouffes
Rue de Rivoli
Rue de Sévigné
Rue Francs-Bourgeois
Rue du Parc Royal
Rue Saint-Claude
Rue de Thorigny
Rue de la Perle
Rue de Poitou
Rue du Temple
Rue de Hesse
Rue des Arquebusiers
Rue Barbette
Rue Elzévir
Rue Payenne
Rue

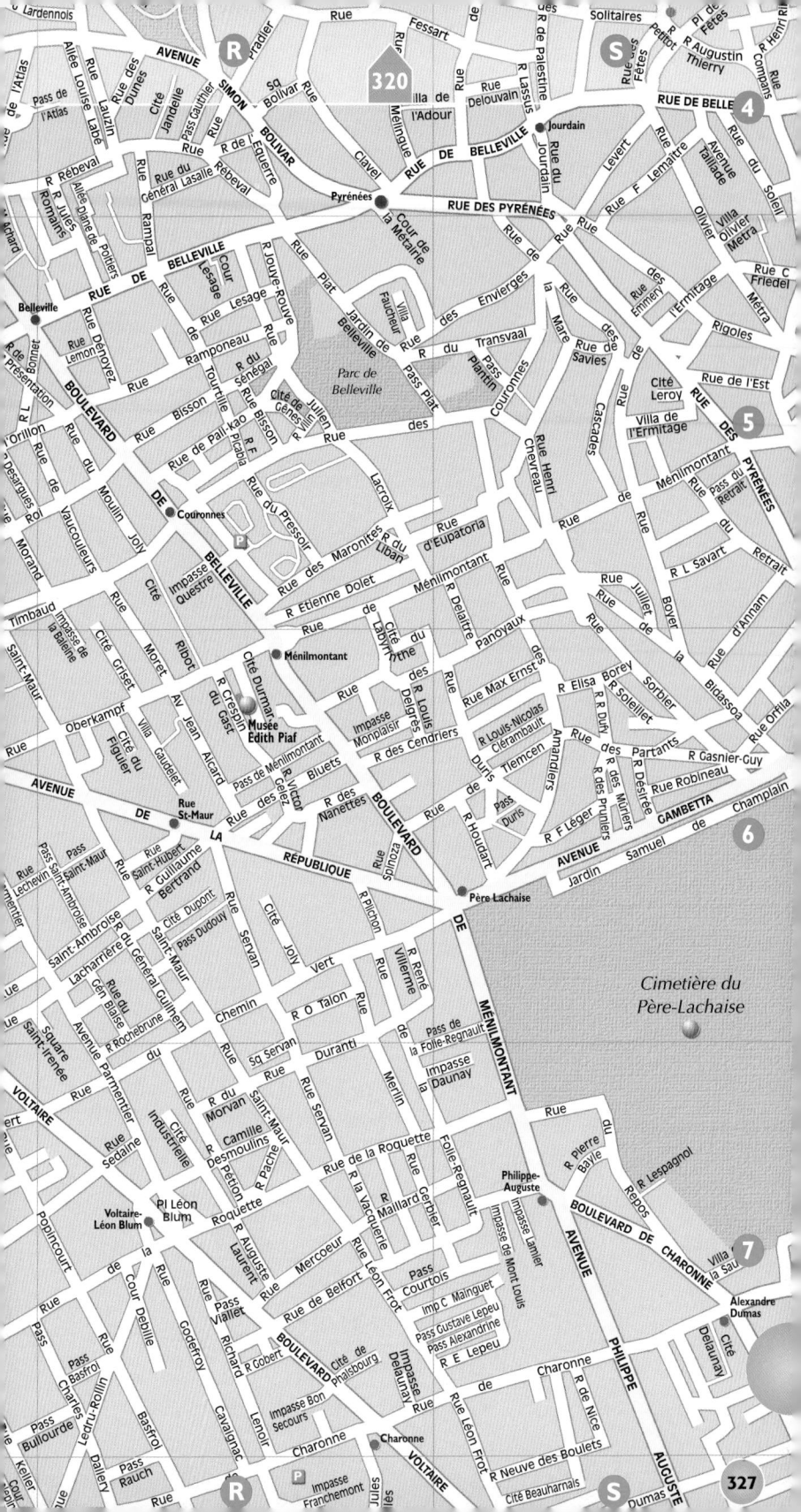
Parc de Belleville
Cimetière du Père-Lachaise
Belleville
Couronnes
Ménilmontant
Pyrénées
Jourdain
Place de l'Adour
Place Colonel Fabien
Place Léon Blum
Voltaire-Léon Blum
Philippe-Auguste
Alexandre Dumas
Père Lachaise
Charonne
Rue Oberkampf
Rue Saint-Maur
Rue de Belleville
Rue des Pyrénées
Rue de la Roquette
Rue Vieille du Temple
Rue Ménilmontant
Rue Oberkampf
Rue Saint-Maur
Rue de la République
Rue Voltaire
Rue Philippe-Auguste
Rue Gambetta
Rue Ménilmontant
Rue Vieille du Temple

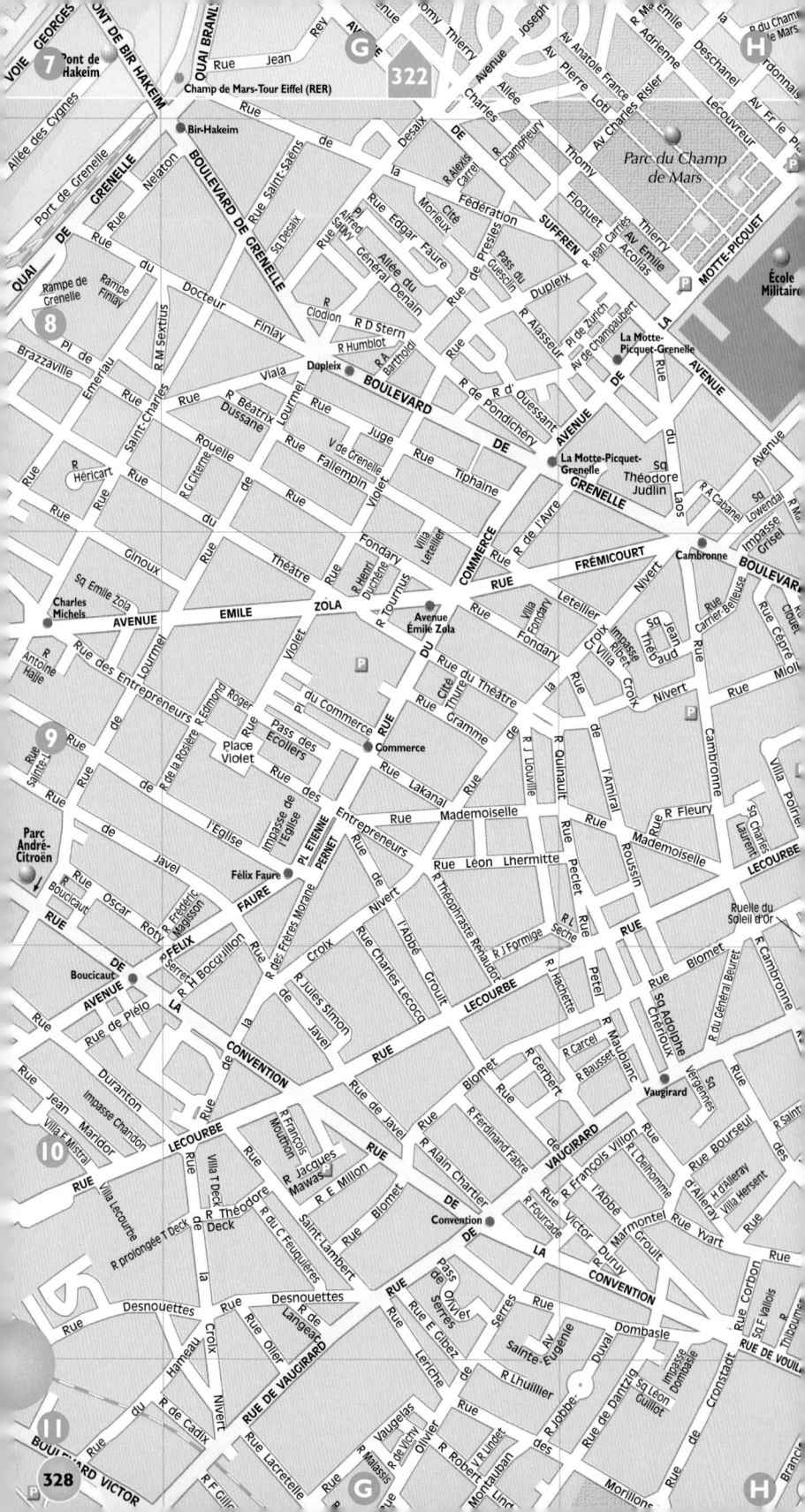
Pont de Bir-Hakeim
Champ de Mars-Tour Eiffel (RER)
Bir-Hakeim
Parc du Champ de Mars
École Militaire
La Motte-Picquet-Grenelle
Dupleix
Cambronne
Commerce
Convention
Vaugirard
Félix Faure
Boucicaut
Charles Michels
Avenue Émile Zola
Parc André-Citroën
Place Violet
Théodore Judlin
Rampe de Grenelle
Ruelle du Soleil d'Or
Impasse Griset
Impasse Dombasle
Villa Letellier
Villa Lecourbe
Villa Hersent
Villa Poirier
Villa Lowenda
Villa Croix
Villa Fondary
Villa Thure
Villa Emile Zola
Villa Dupleix
Villa Dupleix
Villa Lowenda
Villa Croix
Villa Fondary
Villa Thure
Villa Emile Zola
Villa Dupleix

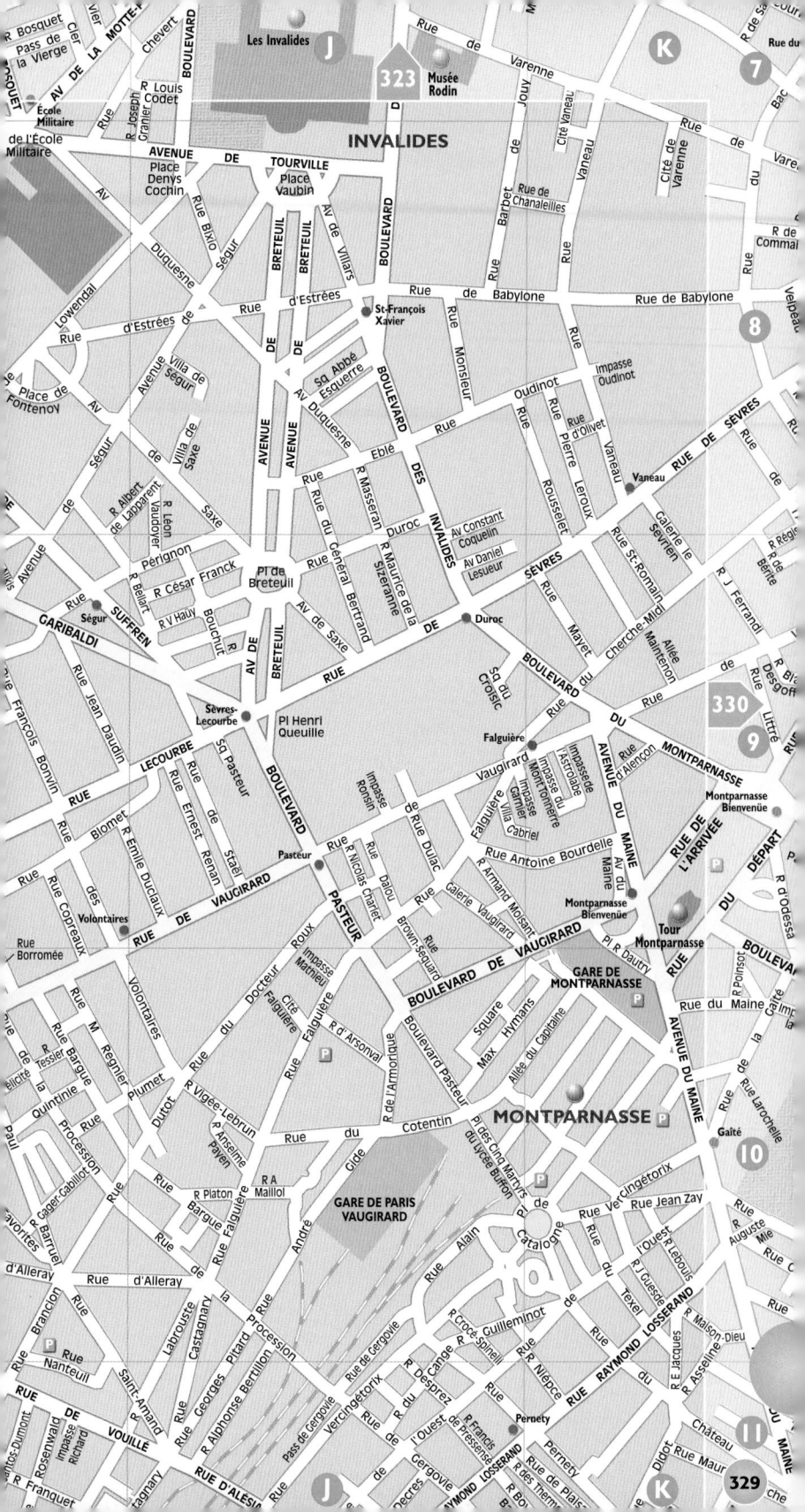
Les Invalides
Musée Rodin
INVALIDES
AVENUE DE TOURVILLE
Place Denys Cochin
Place Vauban
École Militaire
de l'École Militaire
R Bosquet
Pass de la Vierge
R Louis Codet
R Joseph Cramier
BOULEVARD DE LA MOTTE-PICQUET
BOULEVARD DES INVALIDES
BOULEVARD DE VAUGIRARD
BOULEVARD DE MONTPARNASSE
BOULEVARD DU MONTPARNASSE
BOULEVARD DE LA RUE DE SÈVRES
AVENUE DE SÉGUR
AVENUE DE SAXE
AVENUE DU MAINE
AVENUE DU RUE DE L'ARRIVÉE
RUE DE VAUGIRARD
RUE DE SUFFREN
RUE DE VOUILLÉ
RUE D'ALÉSIA
RUE RAYMOND LOSSERAND
RUE DU DÉPART
RUE DE SÈVRES
RUE DE GARIBALDI
RUE DE LECOURBE
RUE DE PASTEUR
RUE DE BABYLONE
RUE DE VARENNE
RUE DE CHANALEILLES
RUE DE CHERCHE-MIDI
RUE DE MAYET
RUE DE MONTPARNASSE
RUE DE VANEAU
RUE DE BRETEUIL
RUE DE SAXE
RUE DE SÉGUR
RUE DE VOLONTAIRES
RUE DE DUROC
RUE DE GERGOVIE
RUE DE CERGOVIE
RUE DE PERNETY
RUE DE PLAISANCE
RUE DE CATALOGNE
RUE DE VERCINGÉTORIX
RUE DE LA CROIX-NIVERT
RUE DE LA PROCESSION
RUE DE LA FALGUIÈRE
RUE DE LA CITÉ FALGUIÈRE
RUE DE LA CITÉ VANEAU
RUE DE LA CITÉ DE VARENNE
RUE DE LA MAISON-DIEU
RUE DE LA GAITÉ
RUE DE LA LAROCHELLE
RUE DE LA CHÂTEAU
RUE DE LA MAURIC
RUE DE LA BERTE
RUE DE LA BOURDELLE
RUE DE LA BOURDONNAIS
RUE DE LA BOURDONNAIS
RUE DE LA BOURDONNAIS

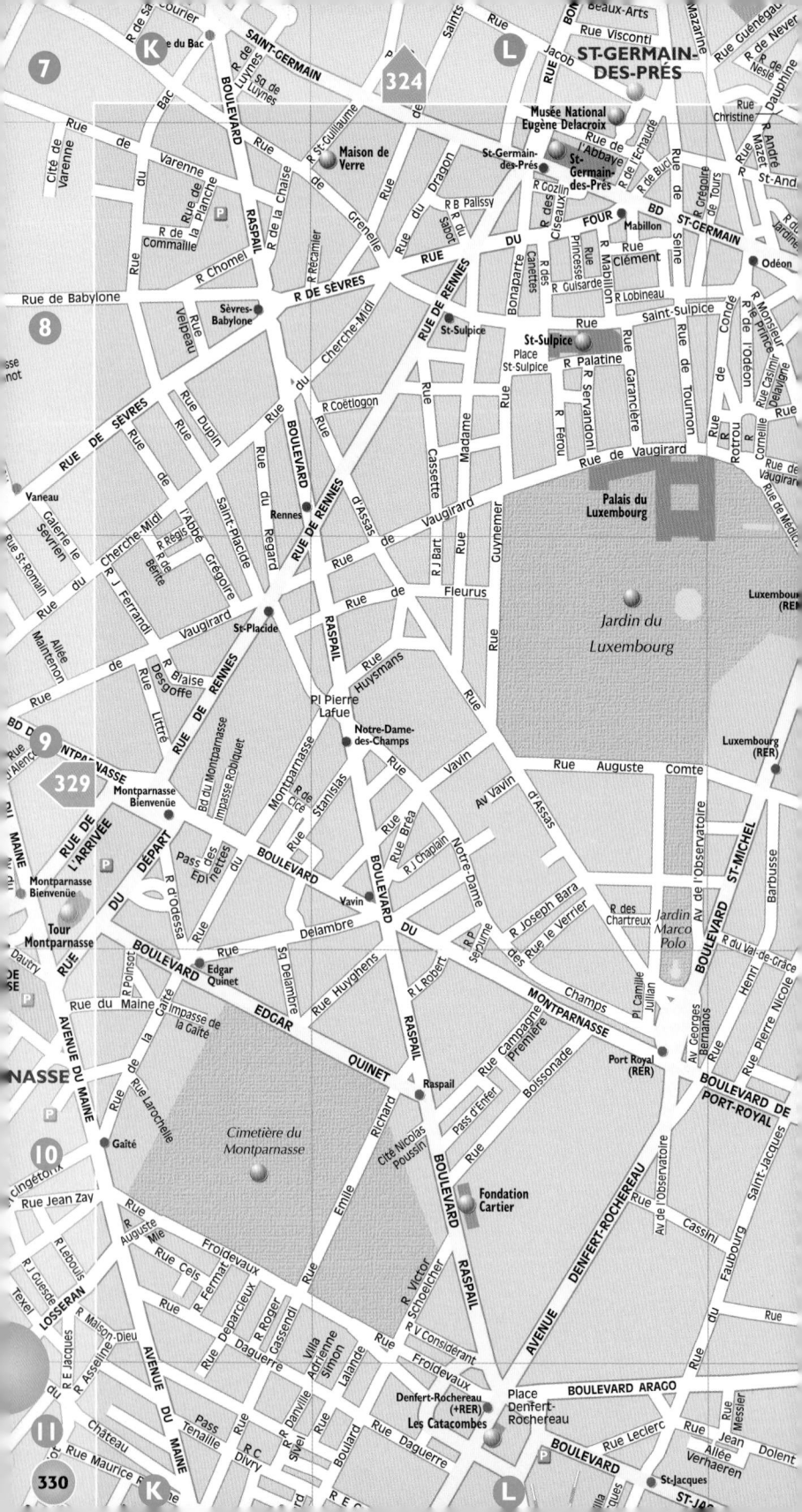
ST-GERMAIN-DES-PRÉS
Musée National Eugène Delacroix
Maison de Verre
St-Germain-des-Prés
Mabillon
Odéon
Sèvres-Babylone
St-Sulpice
Place St-Sulpice
Palais du Luxembourg
Jardin du Luxembourg
Rennes
St-Placide
Notre-Dame-des-Champs
Montparnasse Bienvenüe
Tour Montparnasse
Edgar Quinet
Vavin
Raspail
Port Royal (RER)
Cimetière du Montparnasse
Gaîté
Fondation Cartier
Denfert-Rochereau (+RER)
Les Catacombes
Place Denfert-Rochereau
St-Jacques
Luxembourg (RER)
Jardin Marco Polo
BOULEVARD ST-GERMAIN
RUE DE RENNES
RUE DE SÈVRES
BOULEVARD MONTPARNASSE
BOULEVARD ST-MICHEL
BOULEVARD DE PORT-ROYAL
AVENUE DENFERT-ROCHEREAU
AVENUE DU MAINE
RUE DE L'ARRIVÉE
BOULEVARD ARAGO
BOULEVARD EDGAR QUINET
BOULEVARD RASPAIL
BOULEVARD DU MONTPARNASSE
RUE DU BAC
RUE DE VAUGIRARD
RUE DE FLEURUS
RUE DE VAVIN
RUE DE BABYLONE
RUE DE LA CHAISE
RUE DU DRAGON
RUE DE GRENELLE
RUE DE VARENNE
RUE DE LA PLANCHE
RUE DE COMMAILLE
RUE DE CHOMEL
RUE DE BONAPARTE
RUE DE GUISARDE
RUE DE LOBINEAU
RUE DE SAINT-SULPICE
RUE DE PALATINE
RUE DE VERNEUIL
RUE DE LA CHAISE
RUE DE CHERCHE-MIDI
RUE DE CASSETTE
RUE DE MADAME
RUE DE GARANCIÈRE
RUE DE TOURNON
RUE DE L'ODÉON
RUE DE VANEAU
RUE DE SEVRES
RUE DE GRENELLE
RUE DE VAUGIRARD
RUE DE FLEURUS
RUE DE VAVIN
RUE DE MONTPARNASSE
RUE DE DEPART
RUE DE L'ARRIVÉE
RUE DU MAINE
RUE DE LA GAÎTÉ
RUE DE LA CHAISE
RUE DE LA PLANCHE
RUE DE COMMAILLE
RUE DE CHOMEL
RUE DE BABYLONE
RUE DE SÈVRES
RUE DE VAUGIRARD
RUE DE FLEURUS
RUE DE VAVIN
RUE DE MONTPARNASSE
RUE DE DEPART

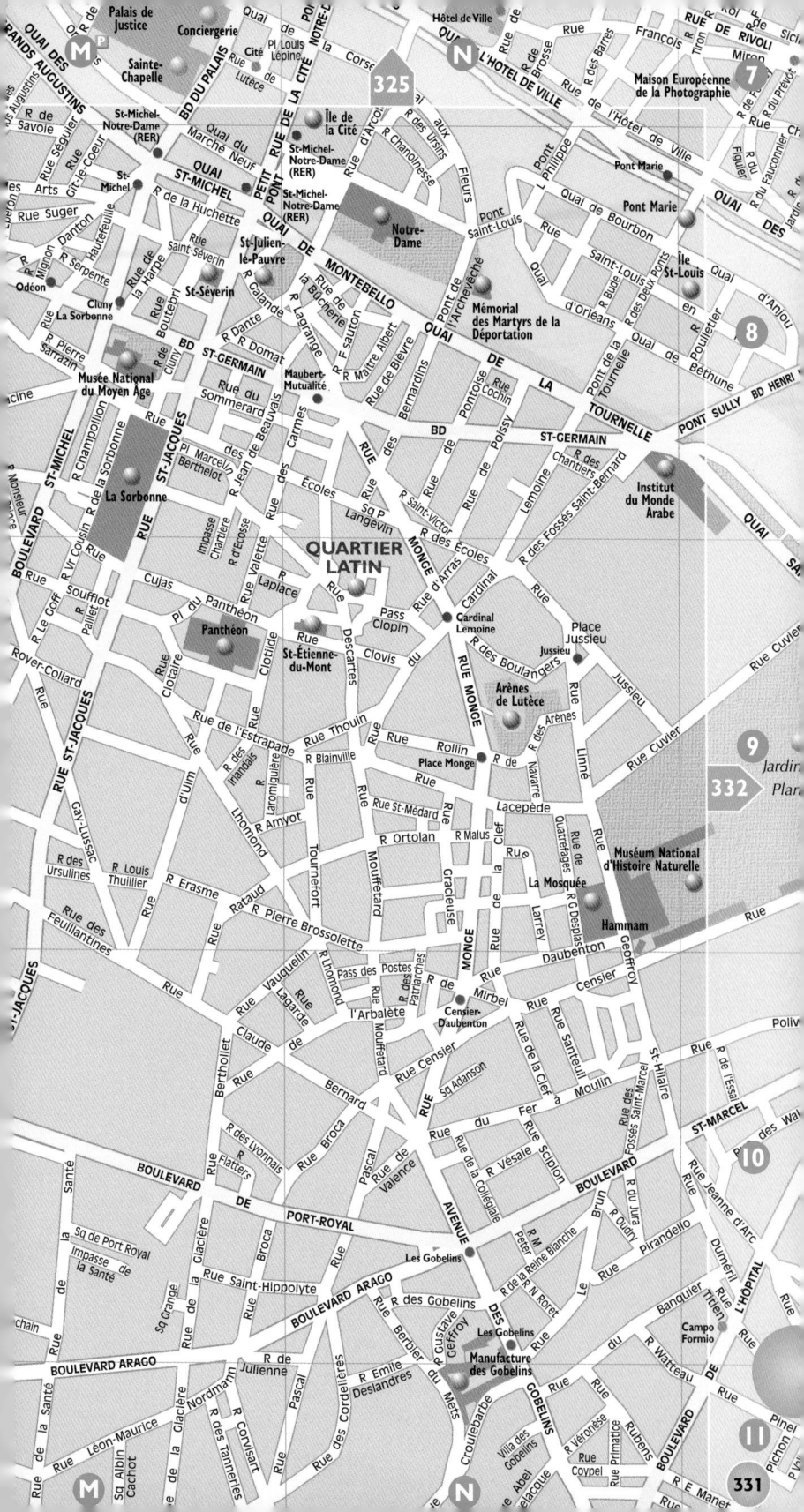
Palais de Justice
Conciergerie
Sainte-Chapelle
Cité
Pl. Louis Lépine
Hôtel de Ville
Maison Européenne de la Photographie
Île de la Cité
St-Michel-Notre-Dame (RER)
Pont Marie
Pont Saint-Louis
Notre-Dame
St-Michel
St-Julien-le-Pauvre
St-Séverin
Odéon
Cluny
La Sorbonne
Mémorial des Martyrs de la Déportation
Île St-Louis
Musée National du Moyen Age
Maubert-Mutualité
Institut du Monde Arabe
QUARTIER LATIN
Panthéon
St-Étienne-du-Mont
Cardinal Lemoine
Place Jussieu
Arènes de Lutèce
Place Monge
Muséum National d'Histoire Naturelle
La Mosquée
Hammam
Censier-Daubenton
Les Gobelins
Manufacture des Gobelins
Campo Formio
QUAI DES GRANDS AUGUSTINS
BD DU PALAIS
RUE DE LA CITÉ
PETIT PONT
QUAI ST-MICHEL
QUAI DE MONTEBELLO
QUAI DE LA TOURNELLE
PONT SULLY
BD HENRI IV
BD ST-GERMAIN
RUE ST-JACQUES
BOULEVARD ST-MICHEL
RUE MONGE
BOULEVARD DE PORT-ROYAL
BOULEVARD ARAGO
AVENUE DES GOBELINS
BOULEVARD DE L'HÔPITAL
ST-MARCEL
QUAI DES ORFÈVRES
RUE DE RIVOLI
RUE DE L'HÔTEL DE VILLE
325
332
331
7
8
9
10
11
M
N

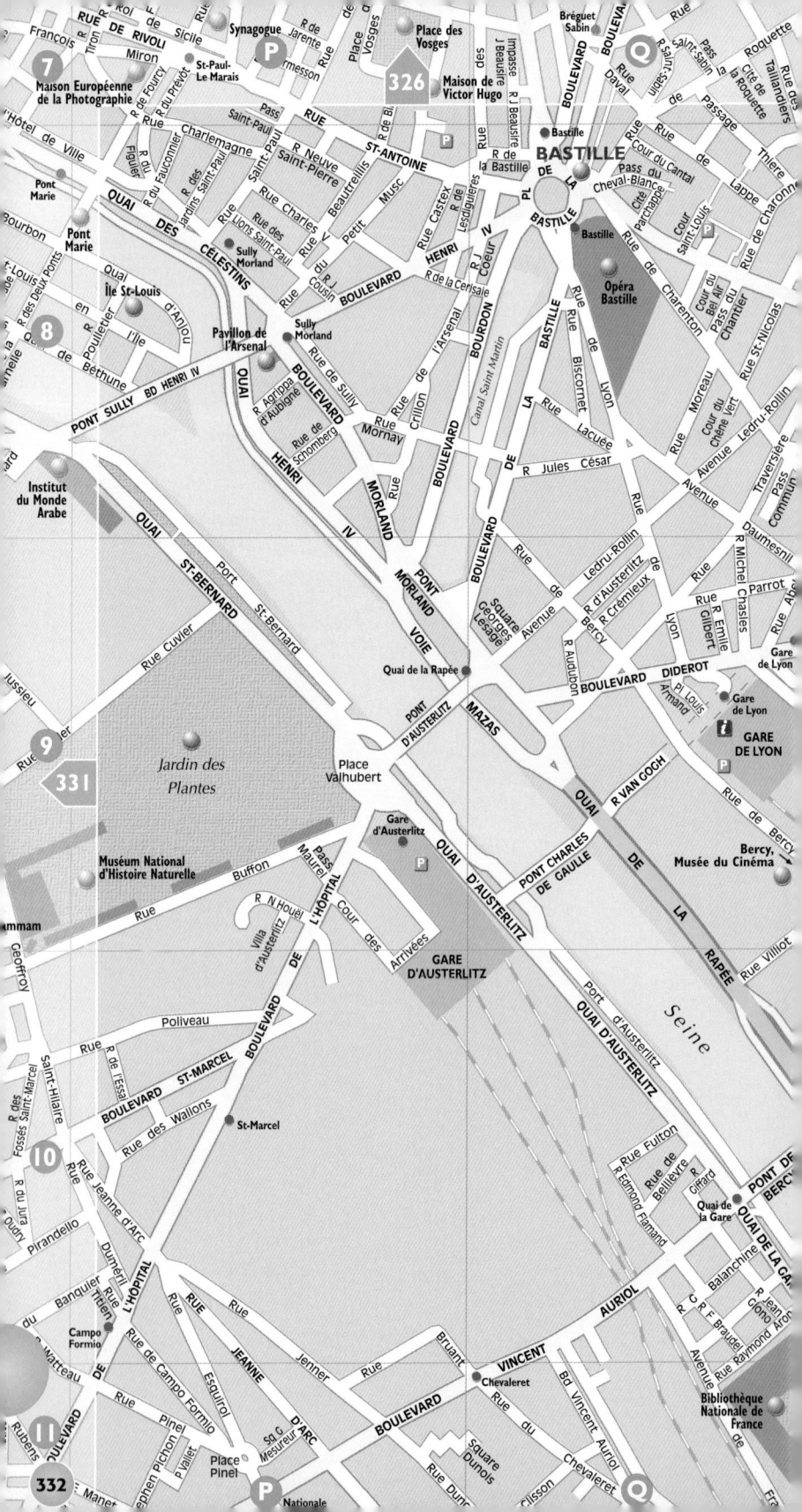
RUE DE RIVOLI
Synagogue
Place des Vosges
Bréguet Sabin
7
Maison Européenne de la Photographie
St-Paul-Le Marais
326
Maison de Victor Hugo
BOULEVARD
Bastille
BASTILLE
RUE ST-ANTOINE
PL. DE LA BASTILLE
Pont Marie
QUAI DES CELESTINS
Sully Morland
Opéra Bastille
Île St-Louis
8
Pavillon de l'Arsenal
BOULEVARD HENRI IV
PONT SULLY
Canal Saint-Martin
Institut du Monde Arabe
QUAI ST-BERNARD
PONT MORLAND
VOIE MAZAS
Quai de la Rapée
PONT D'AUSTERLITZ
Gare de Lyon
GARE DE LYON
9
331
Jardin des Plantes
Place Valhubert
Gare d'Austerlitz
Muséum National d'Histoire Naturelle
QUAI D'AUSTERLITZ
PONT CHARLES DE GAULLE
QUAI DE LA RAPÉE
Bercy, Musée du Cinéma
GARE D'AUSTERLITZ
Seine
BOULEVARD ST-MARCEL
St-Marcel
10
Quai de la Gare
Campo Formio
Chevaleret
11
332
Bibliothèque Nationale de France
Place Pinel

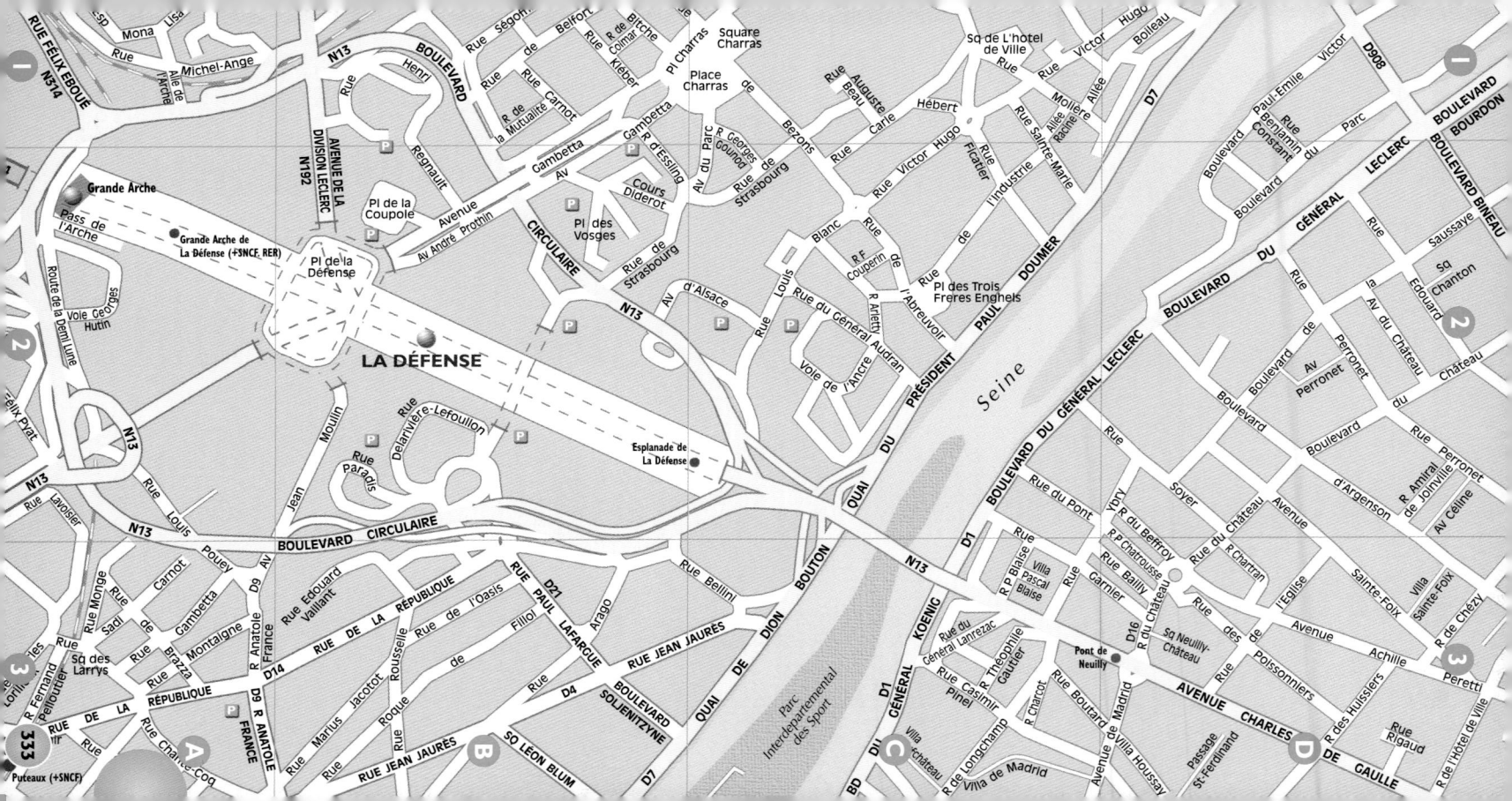
Grande Arche
Grande Arche de La Défense (+SNCF, RER)
Pass de l'Arche
Route de la Demi Lune
Voie Georges Hutin
LA DÉFENSE
Esplanade de La Défense
Pl de la Défense
Pl de la Coupole
Pl des Vosges
Cours Diderot
Square Charras
Place Charras
Pl des Trois Frères Enghels
Seine
Parc Interdépartemental des Sport
Pont de Neuilly
Sq des Larrys
Sq de L'hôtel de Ville
Sq Neuilly-Château
Villa Pascal Blaise
Villa Sainte-Foix
Villa de Madrid
Passage St-Ferdinand
Puteaux (+SNCF)
RUE FÉLIX EBOUÉ
N314
BOULEVARD
N13
AVENUE DE LA DIVISION LECLERC
N192
CIRCULAIRE
BOULEVARD CIRCULAIRE
RUE DE LA RÉPUBLIQUE
D14
D9 R ANATOLE FRANCE
RUE PAUL LAFARGUE
D21
RUE JEAN JAURÈS
D4
BOULEVARD SOLIENITZYNE
SQ LÉON BLUM
D7
QUAI DE DION BOUTON
QUAI DU PRÉSIDENT PAUL DOUMER
BOULEVARD DU GÉNÉRAL LECLERC
D1
D16
AVENUE CHARLES DE GAULLE
D908
BOULEVARD BOURDON
BOULEVARD BINEAU
333

Acacias, Rue des 322 G4
Aguesseau, Rue d' 323 K5
Alger, Rue d' 324 L6
Abbaye, Rue de l' 330 L8
Abbé Esquerre, Square 329 J8
Abbé Grégoire, Rue de l' 330 K8
Abbesses, Passage des 318 M3
Abbesses, Rue des 318 L3
Abbeville, Rue d' 319 N4
Abel Hovelacque, Rue 331 N11
Abel, Rue 332 Q9
Adanson, Square 331 N10
Adrienne Lecouvreur, Allée 322 H7
Agrippa d'Aubigné, Rue 332 P8
Alain, Rue 329 J10
Alasseur, Rue 328 G8
Alban Satragne, Square 325 N4
Albéric Magnard, Rue 321 E7
Albert 1er, Cours 323 H6
Albert de Lapparent, Rue 329 J8
Albert de Mun, Avenue de 322 G6
Albert Thomas, Rue 326 P5
Albert, Rue P 319 M2
Alboni, Rue de l' 321 F7
Alboni, Square 321 F7
Alençon, Rue d' 329 K9
Alexandre III, Pont 323 J6
Alexandrie, Rue d' 325 N5
Alexandrine, Pass 327 S7
Alexis Carrel, Rue 328 G8
Alfred Dehodencq, Rue 321 E7
Alfred Sauvy, Place 328 G8
Allent, Rue 324 L7
Alma, Cité de l' 322 H7
Alma, Place de l' 322 H6
Alma, Pont de l' 322 H6
Alphonse XIII, Avenue 321 F7
Alsace, Rue d' 319 P4
Amandiers, Rue des 327 S6
Amboise, Rue d' 324 M5
Ambroise Paré, Rue 319 N3
Ambroise Thomas, Rue 325 M4
Amélie, Rue 323 H7
Amelot, Impasse 326 Q7
Amelot, Rue 326 Q7
Amiral d'Estaing, Rue de l' 322 G5
Amiral de Grasse, Place 322 G5
Amsterdam, Impasse 318 K4
Amsterdam, Rue d' 318 K3
Amyot, Rue 331 M9
Anatole de la Forge, Rue 322 G4
Anatole France, Avenue 322 G7
Anatole France, Quai 323 K6
Andigné, Rue d' 321 E7
André Gide, Rue 329 J10
André Gill, Rue 318 M3
André Malraux, Place 324 L6
André Mazet, Rue 330 M8
André Prothin, Avenue 333 B2
Angoulème, Cité d' 326 Q6
Anjou, Quai d' 332 P8
Anjou, Rue d' 323 K5
Ankara, Rue d' 321 F7
Annam, Rue d' 327 S6
Annonciation, Rue de l' 321 F7
Anselme Payen, Rue 329 J10
Antin, Cité d' 324 L4
Antin, Impasse d' 323 J6
Antin, Rue d' 324 L5
Antoine Bourdelle, Rue 329 J9
Antoine Hajje, Rue 328 F9
Antoine, Rue A 318 L3
Anvers, Place d' 319 M3
Apennins, Rue des 318 K2
Arago, Boulevard 330 L11
Arcade, Rue de l' 324 K5
Arche, Pass de l' 333 A2
Archevêché, Pont de l' 331 N8
Archives, Rue des 326 P6
Arcole, Rue d' 331 N8
Arènes, Rue des 331 N9
Argenson, Rue d' 323 J4
Argentine, Rue d' 322 G4
Argout, Rue d' 325 M6
Aristide Briand, Rue 323 K6
Armand Moisant, Rue 329 J9
Armorique, Rue de l' 329 J10
Arquebusiers, Rue des 326 P7
Arras, Rue d' 331 N9
Arrivée, Rue de l' 329 K9
Arrivées, Cour des 332 P9
Arsenal, Rue de l' 332 P8
Arsène Houssaye, Rue 322 H4
Arsonval, Rue d' 329 J10
Artois, Rue d' 323 H5
Arts, Pont des 324 L7
Asile, Passage de l' 326 Q7
Assas, Rue d' 330 L9
Assomption, Rue de l' 321 E8
Astorg Rue d' 323 K4
Astrolabe, Impasse de l' 329 K9
Athènes, Rue d' 318 L4
Atlas, Rue de l' 327 Q4
Auber, Rue 324 L5
Aubriot, Rue 325 N7
Audran, Rue 318 L3
Audubon, Rue 332 Q9
Augereau, Rue 322 H7
Auguste Comte, Rue 330 L9
Auguste Laurent, Rue 327 R7
Auguste Mie, Rue 330 K10
Auguste Vacquerie, Rue 322 G5
Aumale, Rue d' 318 L4
Austerlitz, Pont d' 332 P9
Austerlitz, Rue d' 332 Q9
Aux Ours, Rue 325 N6
Avenue Gabriel 323 K5
Azais, Rue 319 M3

Babylone, Rue de 329 J8
Bac, Rue du 330 K8
Bachaumont, Rue 325 M6
Bachelet, Rue 319 M2
Baigneur, Rue du 319 M2
Bailleul, Rue 325 M6
Bailly, Rue 325 N6
Baleine, Impasse de la 327 R5
Ballu, Rue 318 L3
Balzac, Rue 322 H4
Banque, Rue de la 325 M5
Banquier, Rue du 331 N10
Barbet de Jouy, Rue 329 J8
Barbette, Rue 326 P7
Baret, Place R 318 K3
Barres, Rue des 325 N7
Barsacq, Rue A 319 M3
Bart, Rue J 330 L9
Bartholdi, Rue A 328 G8
Basfour, Passage 325 N6
Basfroi, Pass 327 R7
Basfroi, Rue 327 R7
Bassano, Rue de 322 G5
Bastiat, Rue F 323 H5
Bastille, Boulevard de la 332 Q8
Bastille, Place de la 332 Q8
Bastille, Rue de la 332 Q8
Batignolles, Boulevard des 318 K3
Batignolles, Rue des 318 K3
Bauches, Rue des 321 E7
Baudelique, Rue 319 M2
Baudin, Rue A 326 Q6
Bayard, Rue 323 H6
Béatrix Dussane, Rue 328 G8
Beaubourg, Rue 325 N6
Beauce, Rue de 326 P6
Beaujolais, Rue de 324 M6
Beaujon, Rue 322 H4
Beaumarchais, Boulevard 326 Q7
Beaune, Rue de 324 L7
Beauregard, Rue 325 N5
Beaurepaire, Rue 326 P5
Beausejour, Boulevard de 321 E7
Beausire, Impasse J 326 Q7
Beausire, Rue J 326 Q7
Beautreillis, Rue 332 P8
Beaux-Arts, Rue des 324 L7
Becquerel, Rue 319 M2
Beethoven, Rue 322 F7
Bel Air, Cour du 332 Q8
Belfort, Rue de 327 R7
Belhomme, Rue 319 N3
Bellart, Rue 329 J9
Bellechasse, Rue de 324 K7
Bellefond, Rue de 319 N4
Belloy, Rue de 322 G5
Belzunce, Rue de 319 N4
Béranger, Rue 326 P6
Berbier du Mets, Rue 331 N10
Bercy, Rue de 332 Q9
Berger, Rue 325 M6
Bergère, Cité 325 M5
Bergère, Rue 325 M5
Bérite, Rue de 330 K9
Bernardins, Rue des 331 N8
Berne, Rue de 318 K3
Berri, Rue de 322 H5
Berryer, Cité 324 K5
Berryer, Rue 322 H4
Berthaud, Impasse 325 N6
Berthe, Rue 318 M3
Berthie Albrecht, Avenue 322 H4
Berthollet, Rue 331 M10
Berton, Rue 321 F7
Beslay, Passage 326 Q6
Béthune, Quai de 331 N8
Bidassoa, Rue de la 327 S6
Bienfaisance, Rue de la 323 J4
Bièvre, Rue de 331 N8
Biot, Rue 318 K3
Bir Hakeim, Pont de 322 F7
Birague, Rue de 326 P8
Biscornet, Rue 332 Q8
Bixio, Rue 329 J8
Bizerte, Rue de 318 K3
Blainville, Rue 331 N9
Blaise Desgoffe, Rue 330 K9
Blanche, Impasse M 318 L3
Blanche, Rue 318 L4
Blancs Manteaux, Rue des 325 N7
Bleue, Rue 319 M4
Blondel, Rue 325 N5
Bluets, Rue des 327 R6
Boccador, Rue du 322 H6
Bochart de Saron, Rue 319 M3
Bois le Vent, Rue 321 E7
Boissonade, Rue 330 L10
Boissy d'Anglas, Rue 323 K5
Bologne, Rue J 321 F7
Bon Secours, Impasse 327 R7
Bonaparte, Rue 324 L7
Bonne Nouvelle, Boulevard de 325 N5
Bonne Nouvelle, Impasse de 325 N5
Bonne, Rue de la 319 M2
Bons Enfants, Rue des 324 M6
Boris Vian, Rue 319 N3
Bosquet, Avenue 322 H7
Bosquet, Rue 323 H7
Bossuet, Rue 319 N4
Bouchardon, Rue 325 N5
Bouchut, Rue 329 J9
Boucicaut, Rue 328 F9
Boudreau, Rue 324 L5
Boulainvilliers, Hameau de 321 E8
Boulainvilliers, Rue de 321 E8
Boulangers, Rue des 331 N9
Boulard, Rue 330 L11
Boulle, Rue 326 Q7
Bouloi, Rue 325 M6
Bourbon, Quai de 331 N8
Bourdaloue, Rue 318 M4
Bourdin, Impasse 323 H5
Bourdon, Boulevard 332 P8
Bourdonnais, Avenue de la 322 H7
Bourdonnais, Port de la 322 G6
Bourdonnais, Rue des 325 M7
Bourg Tibourg, Rue du 325 N7
Bourgeois, Allée L 322 G7
Bourgogne, Rue de 323 J7
Bourse, Place de la 325 M5
Bourse, Rue de la 324 M5
Boutebrie, Rue 331 M8
Boylesve, Avenue R 321 F7
Brady, Passage 325 N5
Branly, Quai 322 G7
Brantôme, Rue 325 N6
Brazzaville, Place de 328 F8
Bréa, Rue 330 L9

Breguet, Rue 326 Q7
Bretagne, Rue de 326 P6
Breteuil, Avenue de 329 J8
Breteuil, Place de 329 J9
Brey, Rue 322 G4
Briare, Impasse 319 M4
Brignole, Rue 322 G6
Briquet, Rue 319 M3
Brisemiche, Rue 325 N7
Broca, Rue 331 M10
Brosse, Rue de 325 N7
Brown-Sequard, Rue 329 J10
Bruant, Rue A 318 L3
Brun, Rue le 331 N10
Bruneau, Rue A 321 E7
Bruxelles, Rue de 318 L3
Bucarest, Rue de 318 K3
Bûcherie, Rue de la 331 N8
Buci, Rue de 330 L8
Budapest, Rue de 318 K4
Bude, Rue 331 N8
Buffault, Rue 319 M4
Buffon, Rue 332 P9
Bullourde, Passage 327 R7
Burnouf, Rue 326 Q4
Burq, Rue 318 L3

Cabanel, Rue A 328 H8
Cadet, Rue 325 M4
Caffarelli, Rue 326 P6
Caille, Rue la 318 K2
Caire, Rue du 325 N5
Calais, Rue de 318 L3
Cambacères, Rue 323 J5
Cambon, Rue 324 K5
Cambronne, Rue 328 H9
Camille Desmoulins, Rue 327 R7
Camille Jullian, Place 330 L10
Camille Tahan, Rue 318 L3
Camoens, Avenue de 321 F7
Campagne Première, Rue 330 L10
Canal, Allée du 326 P4
Canettes, Rue des 330 L8
Cantal, Cour du 332 Q8
Capitaine Madon, Rue du 318 K2
Capitaine, Allée du 329 J10
Capron, Rue 318 K3
Capucines, Boulevard des 324 L5
Capucines, Rue des 324 L5
Card Dubois, Rue du 319 M3
Cardinal Lemoine, Rue du 331 N8
Cardinal Mercier, Rue du 318 L3
Carmes, Rue des 331 N8
Carnot, Avenue 322 G4
Caroline, Rue 318 K3
Carpeaux, Rue du Square 318 L2
Carpeaux, Rue 318 L2
Carrousel, Place du 324 L6
Carrousel, Pont du 324 L7
Casimir Delavigne, Rue 330 M8
Casimir Périer, Rue 323 K7
Cassette, Rue 330 L8
Cassini, Rue 330 L10
Castellane, Rue de 324 K5
Castex, Rue 332 P8
Castiglione, Rue de 324 L6
Catalogne, Pl de 329 K10
Cauchois, Rue 318 L3
Caulaincourt, Rue 318 L2
Caumartin, Rue de 324 L5
Cavallotti, Rue 318 K3
Célestins, Quai des 332 P8
Cels, Rue 330 K10
Cendriers, Rue des 327 R6
Cerisaie, Rue de la 332 P8
Cerisoles, Rue de 322 H5
César Caire, Avenue 323 K4
César Franck, Rue 329 J9
Chabanais, Rue 324 L5
Chabrol, Rue de 319 N4
Chahu, Rue C 321 F7
Chaillot, Rue de 322 G5
Chaise, Rue de la 330 K8
Chalet, Rue du 326 Q4
Chalgrin, Rue 322 G4
Chambiges, Rue 322 H6
Champ de Mars, Rue du 323 H7
Champaubert, Avenue de 328 H8
Champfleury, Rue 328 G8
Champollion, Rue 331 M8
Champs, Galerie des 322 H5
Champs-Élysées, Avenue des 322 H5
Champs-Élysées, Port des 323 J6
Chanaleilles, Rue de 329 K8
Chandon, Impasse 328 F10
Change, Pont au 325 M7
Chanoinesse, Rue 331 N8
Chantier, Passage du 332 Q8
Chantiers, Rue des 331 N8
Chantilly, Rue de 319 M4
Chapelle, Boulevard de la 319 N3
Chapelle, Cité de la 319 P2
Chapelle, Impasse de la 319 P2
Chapelle, Rond-Point de la 319 P1
Chapelle, Rue de la 319 P1
Chaplain, Rue J 330 L9
Chapon, Rue 325 N6
Chappe, Rue 319 M3
Chaptal, Cité 318 L3
Chaptal, Rue 318 L3
Charbonnière, Rue de la 319 N3
Chardin, Rue 322 F7
Charenton, Rue de 332 Q8
Charlemagne, Rue 332 P8
Charles Dallery, Passage 327 R7
Charles de Gaulle, Avenue 333 D3
Charles de Gaulle, Pont 332 Q9
Charles Floquet, Avenue 328 H8
Charles Nodier, Rue 319 M3
Charles Risler, Avenue 328 H7
Charles V, Rue 332 P8
Charlot, Rue 326 P6
Charonne, Boulevard de 327 S7
Charonne, Rue de 332 Q8
Charras, Rue 324 L4
Chartière, Impasse 331 M8
Chartres, Rue de 319 N3
Chartreux, Rue des 330 L9
Château d'Eau, Rue du 326 P5
Châteaubriand, Rue 322 H5
Châteaudun, Rue de 318 L4
Chauchat, Rue 324 M4
Chaussée d'Antin, Rue de la 324 L4
Chausson, Impasse 326 P4
Chauveau-Lagarde, Rue 324 K5
Chemin Vert, Rue du 326 Q7
Chêne Vert, Cour du 332 Q8
Chénier, Rue 325 N5
Cherche-Midi, Rue du 329 K9
Chernoviz, Rue 321 F7
Cheval-Blanc, Passage du 332 Q8
Chevert, Rue 323 J7
Choiseul, Passage 324 L5
Choiseul, Rue de 324 L5
Chomel, Rue 330 K8
Choron, Rue 319 M4
Christiani, Rue 319 N3
Christophe Colomb, Rue 322 H5
Cimarosa, Rue 322 G5
Cinq Martyrs du Lycée Buffon, Place des 329 J10
Circulaire, Boulevard 333 B2
Cirque, Rue du 323 J5
Ciseaux, Rue Des 330 L8
Cité Paradis 319 N4
Cité, Rue de la 325 N7
Citerne, Rue G 328 G8
Cladel, Rue L 325 M5
Clapeyron, Rue 318 K3
Claridge, Galerie du 323 H5
Claude Bernard, Rue 331 M10
Claude Vellefaux, Avenue 326 Q4
Clauzel, Rue 318 M4
Clef, Rue de la 331 N9
Clément Marot, Rue 322 H5
Clément, Rue 330 L8
Cler, Rue 323 H7
Cléry Rue de 325 N5
Clichy, Avenue de 318 K2
Clichy, Boulevard de 318 L3
Clichy, Passage de 318 K3
Clichy, Rue de 318 L4
Clodion, Rue 328 G8
Clopin, Pass 331 N9
Clotaire, Rue 331 M9
Clotilde, Rue 331 M9
Clovis, Rue 331 N9
Cloÿs, Impasse des 318 M2
Cloÿs, Rue des 318 M2
Cluny, Rue de 331 M8
Cochin, Rue 331 N8
Coëtlogon, Rue 330 L8
Cognacq-Jay, Rue 322 H6
Col Bonnet, Avenue du 321 E7
Colbert, Rue 324 M5
Colisée, Rue du 323 J5
Collégiale, Rue de la 331 N10
Collin, Pass 318 L3
Colonel Driant, Rue du 324 M6
Comète, Rue de la 323 J7
Commaille, Rue de 330 K8
Commines, Rue 326 P6
Commun, Passage 318 K4
Commun, Passage 323 J7
Commun, Passage 332 Q8
Compiègne, Rue de 319 N3
Compoint, Impasse 318 K2
Concorde, Pont de la 323 K6
Condamine, Rue la 318 K2
Condé, Rue de 330 M8
Condorcet, Cours 319 M4
Condorcet, Rue 319 M4
Conseiller Collignon, Rue du 321 E7
Conservatoire, Rue du 325 M5
Constantine, Rue de 323 J7
Constantinople, Rue de 318 K4
Conti, Quai de 324 M7
Coq Héron, Rue 325 M6
Coq, Avenue du 324 L4
Cordelières, Rue des 331 N11
Corderie, Rue de la 326 P6
Corneille, Rue 330 M8
Corse, Quai de la 325 M7
Cortot, Rue 319 M2
Cotentin, Rue du 329 J10
Cottages, Rue des 318 L2
Cottin, Passage 319 M2
Coupole, Place de la 333 B2
Courcelles, Rue de 323 H4
Courier, Rue P-L 324 K7
Courtois, Passage 327 R7
Courty, Rue de 323 K6
Cousin, Rue Victor 331 M9
Coustou, Rue 318 L3
Coypel, Rue 331 N11
Coysevox, Rue 318 L2
Crémieux, Rue 332 Q9
Crespin du Gast, Rue 327 R6
Cretet, Rue 319 M3
Crillon, Rue 332 P8
Crocé-Spinelli, Rue 329 J10
Croisic, Square du 329 J9
Croissant, Rue du 325 M5
Croix des Petits Champs, Rue 324 M6
Croulebarbe, Rue 331 N11
Crussol, Cité de 326 Q6
Crussol, Rue de 326 Q6
Cujas, Rue 331 M9
Curé, Impasse du 319 P2
Custine, Rue 319 M2
Cuvier, Rue 331 N9
Cygnes, Allée des 321 F8

Daguerre, Rue 330 K10
Dalayrac, Rue 324 L5
Dalou, Rue 329 J9
Dames, Rue des 318 K3
Damiette, Rue de 325 N5
Damrémont, Rue 318 L2
Daniel Lesueur, Avenue 329 J9
Daniel Stern, Rue 328 G8
Danielle Casanova, Rue 324 L5
Dante, Rue 331 M8
Danton, Rue 331 M8
Dany, Impasse 318 K4
Darcet, Rue 318 K3
Darwin, Rue 318 M2
Daubenton, Rue 331 N10
Daumesnil, Avenue 332 Q8
Daunay, Impasse 327 S7
Daunou, Rue 324 L5

Dauphiné, Place 325 M7
Dauphine, Rue 324 M7
Dautancourt, Rue 318 K2
Dautry, Place R 329 K10
Daval, Rue 326 Q7
Davioud, Rue 321 E7
Davy, Rue 318 K2
De Tournon, Rue 330 L8
De Vaugirard, Rue 330 L8
Debelleyme, Rue 326 P6
Debille, Cour 327 R7
Debilly, Passerelle 322 G6
Debrousse, Rue 322 H6
Défense, Place de la 333 B2
Delambre, Rue 330 L9
Delambre, Square 330 K10
Delanos, Passage 319 P4
Delarivière-Lefoullon, Rue 333 B2
Delaunay, Cité 327 S7
Delaunay, Impasse 327 R7
Delcassé, Avenue 323 J5
Delepine, Cour 327 Q8
Delessert, Boulevard 321 F7
Delta, Rue du 319 N3
Demarquay, Rue 319 P3
Demi Lune, Route de la 333 A2
Denain, Boulevard de 319 N4
Denfert-Rochereau, Avenue 330 L10
Denfert-Rochereau, Place 330 L11
Denys Cochin, Place 329 J8
Deparcieux, Rue 330 K10
Départ, Rue du 329 K9
Dereure, Rue S 318 L2
Desaix, Rue 328 G8
Desaix, Square 328 G8
Desbordes-Valmore, Rue 321 E7
Descartes, Rue 331 N9
Deschanel, Allée P 322 G7
Desgenettes, Rue 323 J6
Desir, Passage du 325 N5
Désirée, Rue 327 S6
Deux Gares, Rue des 319 P4
Deux Nèthes, Impasse des 318 K3
Deux Ponts, Rue des 331 N8
Deux Soeurs, Passage des 325 M4
Diard, Rue 319 M2
Dickens, Rue C 321 F7
Diderot, Boulevard 332 Q9
Diderot, Cours 333 B2
Dieu, Rue 326 P5
Division Leclerc, Avenue de la 333 B2
Docteur A Fournier, Place du 326 P5
Docteur Finlay, Rue du 328 G8
Docteur Heulin, Rue du 318 K2
Docteur Lancereaux, Rue du 323 J4
Docteur Roux, Rue du 329 J10
Domat, Rue 331 M8
Dôme, Rue du 322 G5
Douai, Rue de 318 L3
Dragon, Rue du 330 L8
Drouot, Rue 325 M4
Dubail, Passage 326 P4
Duban, Rue 321 E7
Dubois, Rue P 326 P6
Dudouy, Passage 327 R6
Dufy, Rue R 327 S6
Dulac, Rue 329 J9
Dullin, Place C 319 M3
Dumont d'Urville, Rue 322 G5
Dunkerque, Rue de 319 N3
Dupetit-Thouars, Rue 326 P6
Duphot, Manège 324 K5
Duphot, Rue 324 K5
Dupin, Rue 330 K8
Dupleix, Rue 328 G8
Dupont, Cité 327 R6
Duquesne, Avenue 329 J8
Duranti, Rue 327 R7
Durantin, Rue 318 L3
Duranton, Rue 328 F10
Duras, Rue de 323 J5
Duris, Passage 327 S6
Duris, Rue 327 S6
Durmar, Cité 327 R6
Duroc, Rue 329 J9
Dussoubs, Rue 325 N5
Dutot, Rue 329 J10
Dutuit, Avenue 323 J6
Duval, Rue F 326 P7
Duvivier, Rue 323 H7

Eaux, Rue des 321 F7
Eblé, Rue 329 J8
Echaudé, Rue de l' 330 L8
Echelle, Rue de l' 324 L6
Echiquier, Rue de l' 325 N5
Ecluses Saint-Martin, Rue des 326 P4
École Militaire, Place de l' 329 H8
Écoles, Rue des 331 M8
Ecosse, Rue d' 331 M8
Ecouffes, Rue des 326 P7
Edgar Faure, Rue 328 G8
Edgar Poe, Rue 327 Q4
Edgar Quinet, Boulevard 330 K10
Edouard Manet, Rue 331 N11
Edouard VII, Rue 324 L5
Edward Tuck, Avenue 323 J6
Elisa Borey, Rue 327 S6
Elisée Reclus, Avenue 322 G7
Élysée, Rue de l' 323 J5
Elysées 26, Galerie 323 J5
Elzévir, Rue 326 P7
Emeriau, Rue 328 F8
Emile Acollas, Avenue 328 H8
Emile Deschanel, Avenue 322 H7
Emile Deslandres, Rue 331 N11
Emile Duclaux, Rue 329 J9
Emile Gilbert, Rue 332 Q9
Emile Richard, Rue 330 L10
Emile Zola, Square 328 F9
Enfer, Passage d' 330 L10
Enghien, Rue d' 325 N5
Eperon, Rue de l' 331 M8
Erasme, Rue 331 M9
Ermite, Rue P l' 319 N3
Ernest Cresson, Rue 330 L11
Ernest Renan, Rue 329 J9
Escudier, Rue P 318 L3
Esnault-Pelterie, Rue Robert 323 J6
Essling, Rue d' 333 B2
Estienne d'Orves, Place d' 318 L4
Estrapade, Rue de l' 331 M9
Estrées, Rue d' 329 J8
Etats-Unis, Place des 322 G5
Etex, Rue 318 L2
Étienne Marcel, Rue 325 M6
Etoile, Rue de l' 322 G4
Eugène Carrière, Rue 318 L2
Eugène Süe, Rue 319 M2
Euler, Rue 322 G5
Exposition, Rue de l' 322 H7

Fabert, Rue 323 J7
Fabriques, Cour des 326 Q6
Fagon, Rue 331 N11
Falguière, Cité 329 J10
Falguière, Rue 329 J10
Fallempin, Rue 328 G8
Faubourg Montmartre, Rue du 325 M4
Faubourg Poissonnière, Rue du 325 N4
Faubourg Saint-Denis, Rue du 325 N5
Faubourg Saint-Jacques, Rue du 330 M10
Faubourg Saint-Martin, Rue du 325 N5
Faubourg St-Honoré, Rue du 323 J5
Fauconnier, Rue du 332 P8
Fauvet, Rue 318 K2
Favart, Rue 324 M5
Fédération, Rue de la 328 G8
Félix Faure, Avenue 328 F10
Félix Pyat, Rue 333 A2
Fénelon, Rue 319 N4
Fer À Moulin, Rue du 331 N10
Fermat, Rue 330 K10
Fermes, Cour des 325 M6
Férou, Rue 330 L8
Ferrandi, Rue J 330 K9
Ferronnerie, Rue de la 325 N7
Feuillantines, Rue des 331 M9
Feutrier, Rue 319 M2
Feydeau, Rue 324 M5
Fidélité, Rue de la 325 N4
Figuier, Cité du 327 R6
Figuier, Rue du 332 P8
Finlay, Rampe 328 F8
Flatters, Rue 331 M10
Fléchier, Rue 318 M4
Fleurs, Quai aux 331 N8
Fleurus, Rue de 330 L9
Flocon, Rue F 319 M2
Florence, Rue de 318 K3
Foin, Rue du 326 P7
Folie-Méricourt, Rue de la 326 Q6
Folie-Regnault, Pass de la 327 S7
Fontaine, Rue 318 L3
Fontenoy, Place de 329 H8
Forest, Rue 318 L3
Fortin, Impasse 323 H5
Fossés Saint-Bernard, Rue des 331 N8
Fossés Saint-Marcel, Rue des 331 N10
Four, Rue du 330 L8
Fourcy, Rue de 326 P7
Fr le Play, Avenue 328 H8
Franchemont, Impasse 327 R8
Francoeur, Rue 319 M2
François Ier, Rue 323 J6
François Miron, Rue 326 P7
François, Rue 325 N7
Franco-Russe, Avenue 322 H7
Francs-Bourgeois, Rue des 326 P7
Franklin D Roosevelt, Avenue 323 J5
Fremiet, Avenue 321 F7
Fresnel, Rue 322 G6
Freycinet, Rue 322 G6
Friedland, Avenue de 322 H4
Frochot, Allée 318 M3
Frochot, Rue 318 L3
Froidevaux, Rue 330 K10
Froissart, Rue 326 P6
Froment, Rue 326 Q7
Fromentin, Rue 318 L3

Gabriel Péri, Place 324 K4
Gabriel, Avenue 323 J5
Gabrielle, Rue 319 M3
Gaby, Rue S 326 Q7
Gaillon, Rue 324 L5
Gaîté, Impasse de la 330 K10
Gaîté, Rue de la 330 K10
Galande, Rue 331 M8
Galilée, Rue 322 G5
Gambetta, Avenue 327 S6
Gambetta, Avenue 333 B2
Gambey, Rue 326 Q6
Ganneron, Rue 318 K2
Garancière, Rue 330 L8
Gardes, Rue des 319 N3
Garnier, Impasse 329 J9
Garreau, Rue 318 L3
Gasnier-Guy, Rue 327 S6
Gauthey, Rue 318 K2
Gavarni, Rue 321 F7
Gay-Lussac, Rue 331 M9
Général Bertrand, Rue du 329 J8
Général Blais, Rue du 327 R6
Général Camou, Rue du 322 H7
Général Denain, Allée du 328 G8
Général Eisenhower, Avenue du 323 J6
Général Guilhem, Rue du 327 R6
Général Lemonnier, Avenue du 324 L6
Général Mangin, Avenue du 321 F7
Geoffroy St-Hilaire, Rue 331 N9
George V, Avenue 322 H5
Georges Pompidou, Voie 321 F7
Georges Bernanos, Avenue 330

L10
Georges Bizet, Rue 322 G6
Georges Desplas, Rue 331 N9
Georges Hutin, Voie 333 A2
Georges Lesage, Square 332 Q9
Georges Pompidou, Voie 328 F7
Georges Ville, Rue 322 G5
Gérando, Rue 319 M3
Gerbier, Rue 327 R7
Gergovie, Rue de 329 J10
Germain Pilon, Rue 318 L3
Gesvres, Quai de 325 N7
Ginoux, Rue 328 F9
Girardon, Rue 318 L2
Girault, Avenue C 323 J6
Gît-Le-Coeur, Rue 331 M8
Gluck, Rue 324 L5
Gobelins, Avenue des 331 N10
Gobelins, Rue des 331 N10
Gobert, Rue 327 R7
Godefroy Cavaignac, Rue 327 R7
Godot de Mauroy, Rue 324 K5
Goethe, Rue 322 G6
Goff, Rue le 331 M9
Gomboust, Rue 324 L6
Goutte d'Or, Rue de la 319 N3
Gozlin, Rue 330 L8
Gracieuse, Rue 331 N9
Gramont, Rue de 324 L5
Grand Cerf, Passage du 325 N6
Grand Prieuré, Rue du 326 Q6
Grande Armée, Avenue de la 322 G4
Grands Augustins, Quai des 325 M7
Grands Augustins, Rue des 325 M7
Grange aux Belles, Rue de la 326 P4
Grangé, Square 331 M10
Gravilliers, Rue des 325 N6
Grèard, Avenue O 322 G7
Greffulhe, Rue 324 K5
Grégoire de Tours, Rue 330 L8
Grenelle, Boulevard de 328 G8
Grenelle, Port de 328 F8
Grenelle, Quai de 328 F8
Grenelle, Rampe de 328 F8
Grenelle, Rue de 323 K7
Grenelle, Voie de 328 G8
Greneta, Rue 325 N6
Grétry, Rue 324 L5
Grisel, Impasse 328 H8
Griset, Cité 327 R6
Gué, Impasse du 319 P1
Guénégaud, Rue 324 M7
Guesclin, Passage du 328 G8
Guesde, Rue J 329 K10
Guichard, Rue 321 E7
Guillaume Bertrand, Rue 327 R6
Guilleminot, Rue 329 J10
Guisarde, Rue 330 L8
Gustave Eiffel, Avenue 322 G7
Gustave Geffroy, Rue 331 N10
Gustave Lepeu, Passage 327 S7
Gustave Zédé, Rue 321 E7
Guy Môquet, Rue 318 K2
Guy Patin, Rue 319 N3
Guynemer, Rue 330 L9

Halévy, Rue 324 L5
Halles, Rue des 325 M7
Hameau, Rue du 328 F11
Hamelin, Rue 322 G6
Haret, Rue P 318 L3
Harlay, Rue de 325 M7
Harpe, Rue de la 331 M8
Haudriettes, Rue des 325 N6
Haussmann, Boulevard 324 L5
Hautefeuille, Rue 331 M8
Hauteville, Cité d' 319 N4
Hauteville, Rue d' 325 N5
Haüy, Rue V 329 J9
Havre, Passage du 324 K4
Havre, Rue du 324 K4
Helder, Rue du 324 L5
Hélène, Rue 318 K3
Hélie Faustin, Rue 321 E7
Henner, Rue 318 L3
Henri Barbusse, Rue 330 M9
Henri Bergson, Place 323 K4
Henri IV, Boulevard 332 P8
Henri IV, Quai 332 P8
Henri Monnier, Rue 318 L4
Henri Queuill, Place 329 J9
Henry Dunant, Place 322 H5
Héricart, Rue 328 F8
Hermel, Cité 319 M2
Hermel, Rue 319 M2
Hérold, Rue 325 M6
Héron, Cité 326 P4
Hesse, Rue de 326 P7
Hippolyte Lebas, Rue 318 M4
Hittorf, Rue 325 N5
Hoche, Avenue 322 H4
Hôpital Saint-Louis, Rue de l' 326 P4
Horloge, Quai de l' 325 M7
Hotel de Ville, Quai de l' 325 N7
Hôtel de Ville, Rue de l' 325 N7
Houdart, Rue 327 S6
Houdon, Rue 318 M3
Huchette, Rue de la 331 M8
Huit Mai 1945, Rue du 319 N4
Humblot, Rue 328 G8
Huyghens, Rue 330 L10
Huysmans, Rue 330 L9

Iéna, Avenue d' 322 G5
Iéna, Place d' 322 G6
Iéna, Pont d' 322 G7
Industrie, Passage de l' 325 N5
Industrielle, Cité 327 R7
Innocents, Rue des 325 M7
Invalides, Boulevard des 323 J7
Invalides, Place des 323 J7
Invalides, Pont des 323 J6
Irlandais, Rue des 331 M9
Islettes, Rue des 319 N3
Isly, Rue de l' 324 K4
Italiens, Boulevard des 324 L5
Italiens, Rue des 324 L5

Jacob, Rue 324 L7
Jacquemont, Rue 318 K2
Jacques Bainville, Place 323 K7
Jacques Coeur, Rue 332 Q8
Jacques, Rue E 329 K10
Janin, Avenue J 321 E7
Jardinet, Rue du 330 M8
Jardins St-Paul, Rue des 332 P8
Jarente, Rue de 326 P7
Jarry, Rue 325 N4
Jean Aicard, Avenue 327 R6
Jean Beausire, Rue 332 Q8
Jean Carriès, Rue 328 H8
Jean de Beauvais, Rue 331 M8
Jean Giraudoux, Rue 322 G5
Jean Goujon, Rue 323 H6
Jean Lantier, Rue 325 M7
Jean Maridor, Rue 328 F10
Jean Mermoz, Rue 323 J5
Jean Moulin, Avenue 333 B2
Jean Nicot, Passage 323 H7
Jean Nicot, Rue 323 H6
Jean Paulhan, Allée 322 G7
Jean Rey, Rue 322 G7
Jean Zay, Rue 329 K10
Jean-Baptiste Pigalle, Rue 318 L3
Jean-François Lépine, Rue 319 P3
Jean-Jacques Rousseau, Rue 325 M6
Jean-Pierre Timbaud, Rue 326 Q6
Jemmapes, Quai de 326 P5
Jessaint, Rue de 319 N3
Jeûneurs, Rue des 325 M5
JJodelle, Rue E 318 K2
Johann Strauss, Place 326 P5
Joly, Cité 327 R6
Joseph Bara, Rue 330 L9
Joseph Bouvard, Avenue 322 G7
Joseph de Maistre, Rue 318 L2
Joseph Granier, Rue 329 J7
Joubert, Rue 324 L4
Jouffroy, Passage 325 M5
Jour, Rue du 325 M6
Juge, Rue 328 G8
Jules César, Rue 332 Q8
Jules Cousin, Rue 332 P8
Jules Joffrin, Place 319 M2
Jules Lefebvre, Rue 318 K3
Jules Vallès, Rue 327 R8
Julienne, Rue de 331 M10
Juliette Dodu, Rue 326 Q4
Junot, Avenue 318 L2
Jura, Rue du 331 N10
Jussieu, Rue 331 N9

Keller, Rue 327 Q7
Keppler, Rue 322 G5
Kléber, Avenue 322 G5

La Baume, Rue de 323 J4
La Boétie, Rue 323 H5
La Bruyère, Rue 318 L4
La Bruyère, Square 318 L4
La Fayette, Rue 319 N4
La Motte-Picquet, Avenue de 323 H7
La Pérouse, Rue 322 G5
La Planche, Rue de 330 K8
La Rochefoucauld, Rue de 318 L4
La Sourdière, Rue de 324 L6
La Tour d'Auvergne, Rue de 319 M4
La Tour Maubourg, Boulevard de 323 J6
La Trémoille, Rue de 322 H6
La Vrillière, Rue 324 M6
Laborde, Rue de 323 K4
Labrouste, Rue 329 J10
Labyrinthe, Cité du 327 R6
Lacepède, Rue 331 N9
Lacharrière, Rue 327 R6
Lacroix, Rue 318 K2
Lacuée, Rue 332 Q8
Laferrière, Rue 318 L4
Laffitte, Rue 324 M4
Lagarde, Rue 331 N10
Lagrange, Rue 331 N8
Lalande, Rue 330 L11
Lallier, Rue 319 M3
Lamarck, Rue 318 L2
Lamarck, Square 318 L2
Lamartine, Rue 319 M4
Lamballe, Avenue de 321 F8
Lambert, Rue 319 M2
Lamennais, Rue 322 H4
Lamier, Impasse 322 G5
Lamier, Impasse 327 S7
Lancry, Rue de 326 P5
Landrieu, Passage 322 H7
Langevin, Rue G 325 N7
Langevin, Square Paul 331 N8
Laos, Rue du 328 H8
Laplace, Rue 331 M9
Lappe, Rue de 332 Q8
Lardennois, Rue G 327 Q4
Largillière, Rue 321 E7
Larochelle, Rue 330 K10
Laromiguière, Rue 331 M9
Larrey, Rue 331 N9
Las Cases, Rue 323 K7
Lathuile, Passage 318 K3
Laumain, Rue G 325 N5
Lavoisier, Rue 323 K5
Lavoisier, Rue 333 A2
Le Franc, Rue S 325 N7
Le Nôtre, Rue 322 F7
Le Peletier, Rue 324 M4
Le Sevrien, Galerie 329 K8
Le Tasse, Rue 321 F7
Lebouis, Rue 329 K10
Lechapelais, Rue 318 K3
Lechevin, Rue 327 Q6
Leclerc, Rue 330 L11
Lecluse, Rue 318 K3
Lecomte, Rue 318 K2
Lecuyer, Rue 319 M2
Ledru-Rollin, Avenue 332 Q9
Legendre, Rue 318 K2
Léger, Rue F 327 S6
Legouve, Rue 326 P5
Lekain, Rue 321 E7
Lemercier, Cité 318 K2
Lemercier, Rue 318 K3
Lemoine, Passage 325 N5
Lentonnet, Rue 319 N3
Léon Blum, Place 327 R7
Léon Frot, Rue 327 R7
Léon Jouhaux, Rue 326 P5
Léon Vaudoyer, Rue 329 J8

Léon, Passage 319 N3
Léopold Bellan, Rue 325 M6
Lepeu, Rue E 327 S7
Lepic, Rue 318 L2
Lesdiguieres, Rue de 332 P8
Lespagnol, Rue 327 S7
Lhomond, Rue 331 M9
Liège, Rue de 318 K4
Lille, Rue de 323 K6
Lincoln, Rue 322 H5
Linné, Rue 331 N9
Lions Saint-Paul, Rue des 332 P8
Littré, Rue 330 K9
Livingstone, Rue 319 M3
Lobau, Rue de 325 N7
Lobineau, Rue 330 L8
Lockroy, Rue E 326 Q6
Loges, Rue Dupont des 322 H7
Lombards, Rue des 325 N7
Londres, Cité de 318 L4
Londres, Rue de 318 L4
Longchamp, Rue de 322 G6
Lord Byron, Rue 322 H5
Louis Armand, Place 332 Q9
Louis Codet, Rue 323 J7
Louis Delgrès, Rue 327 R6
Louis le Grand, Rue 324 L5
Louis Lépine, Place 325 M7
Louis Murat, Rue 323 J4
Louis Pouey, Rue 333 A2
Louis Thuillier, Rue 331 M9
Louis-Nicolas Clérambault, Rue 327 S6
Lourmel, Rue de 328 G8
Louvois, Rue de 324 L5
Louvre, Place du 325 M7
Louvre, Quai du 324 L7
Louvre, Rue du 325 M6
Lowendal, Avenue de 329 H8
Lowendal, Square 328 H8
Lubeck, Rue de 322 G6
Lucien Sampaix, Rue 326 P4
Lune, Rue de la 325 N5
Lutèce, Rue de 325 M7
Luynes, Rue de 324 K7
Luynes, Square de 324 K7
Lyautey, Rue 321 F7
Lyon, Rue de 332 Q8
Lyonnais, Rue des 331 M10

Mabillon, Rue 330 L8
Macdonald, Boulevard 320 S1
Mac-Mahon, Avenue 322 G4
Madame, Rue 330 L8
Madeleine, Boulevard de la 324 K5
Madeleine, Place de la 324 K5
Magdebourg, Rue de 322 G6
Magellan, Rue 322 H5
Magenta, Boulevard de 319 N4
Magenta, Cité de 326 P5
Mail, Rue du 325 M6
Maillard, Rue 327 R7
Maillol, Rue A 329 J10
Maine, Avenue du 330 K10
Maine, Rue du 330 K10
Mainguet, Impasse C 327 S7
Maintenon, Allée 329 K9
Maire, Rue au 325 N6
Maison-Dieu, Rue 330 K10
Maître Albert, Rue 331 N8
Malaquais, Quai 324 L7
Malar, Rue 323 H7
Malesherbes, Boulevard 323 K5
Malte, Rue de 326 Q6
Malus, Rue 331 N9
Mandar, Rue 325 M6
Mansart, Rue 318 L3
Manuel, Rue E 321 F7
Manuel, Rue 319 M4
Marais, Passage des 326 P5
Marbeuf, Rue 322 H5
Marcadet, Rue 319 M2
Marceau, Avenue 322 G5
Marcel Proust, Allée 323 J5
Marcel Proust, Rue 321 F7
Marcelin Berthelot, Place 331 M8
Marché Neuf, Quai du 331 M8
Marché St-Honoré, Place du 324 L6
Maréchal Gallieni, Avenue du 323 J7
Marie et Louise, Rue 326 P5
Marie Stuart, Rue 325 N6
Marie, Rue G 325 M5
Marignan, Passage 323 H5
Marignan, Rue de 323 H5
Marigny, Avenue de 323 J5
Marinoni, Rue 322 H7
Mario Nikis, Rue 328 H8
Marivaux, Rue de 324 L5
Marronniers, Rue des 321 E8
Marseille, R de 326 P5
Marsollier, Rue 324 L5
Martel, Rue 325 N4
Martignac, Cité 323 K7
Martignac, Rue de 323 K7
Martin, Rue M 321 E7
Martinet, Rue A 318 L2
Martini, Impasse 325 N5
Martyrs, Rue des 318 M4
Marx Dormoy, Rue 319 P2
Maspéro, Rue 321 E7
Massenet, Rue 321 F7
Masseran, Rue 329 J8
Mathieu, Impasse 329 J10
Mathurins, Rue des 324 K5
Matignon, Avenue 323 J5
Maubeuge, Rue de 319 M4
Maurel, Passage 332 P9
Maurice de la Sizeranne, Rue 329 J9
Max Ernst, Rue 327 S6
Max Hymans, Square 329 J10
Max, Place A 318 L3
Mayet, Rue 329 K9
Mayran, Rue 319 M4
Mazagran, Rue de 325 N5
Mazarine, Rue 324 L7
Mazas, Voie 332 P9
Mechain, Rue 331 M10
Médicis, Rue de 330 M8
Mégisserie, Quai de la 325 M7
Menars, Rue 324 M5
Menilmontant, Boulevard de 327 R6
Ménilmontant, Pass de 327 R6
Mercoeur, Rue 327 R7
Merlin, Rue 327 R6
Meslay, Passage 326 P5
Meslay, Rue 325 N5
Messageries, Rue des 319 N4
Messine, Avenue de 323 J4
Metz, Rue de 325 N5
Michel Chasles, Rue 332 Q9
Michel Le Comte, Rue 325 N6
Michel Peter, Rue 331 N10
Michel Sextius, Rue 328 F8
Michodière, Rue de la 324 L5
Midi, Cité du 318 L3
Mignon, Rue 331 M8
Milan, Rue de 318 L4
Milton, Rue 319 M4
Minimes, Rue des 326 P7
Mirbel, Rue de 331 N10
Miromesnil, Rue de 323 J5
Mogador, Rue de 324 L4
Moines, Rue des 318 K2
Moissan, Rue H 323 H6
Molière, Rue 324 L6
Monceau, Rue de 323 H4
Moncey, Passage 318 K2
Moncey, Rue 318 L4
Moncey, Square 318 L3
Mondovi, Rue de 324 K6
Monge, Rue 331 N9
Monnaie, Rue du la 325 M7
Monplaisir, Impasse 327 R6
Monsieur le Prince, Rue 330 M8
Monsieur, Rue 329 J8
Monsigny, Rue 324 L5
Mont Louis, Impasse de 327 S7
Mont Thabor, Rue du 324 K6
Mont Tonnerre, Impasse du 329 K9
Montaigne, Avenue 323 H6
Montalivet, Rue 323 K5
Montebello, Quai de 331 N8
Montgolfier, Rue 325 N6
Monthiers, Cité 318 K3
Montholon, Rue de 319 M4
Montmartre, Boulevard 324 M5
Montmartre, Rue 325 M5
Montmorency, Rue de 325 N6
Montorgueil, Rue 325 M6
Montparnasse, Rue du 330 K9
Montparnasse,Boulevard du 329 K9
Montpensier, Rue de 324 L6
Monttessuy, Rue de 322 H7
Montyon, Rue de 325 M5
Moreau, Rue H 318 K2
Moreau, Rue 332 Q8
Moret, Rue 327 R6
Morieux, Cité 328 G8
Morland, Boulevard 332 P8
Morland, Pont 332 P9
Morlot, Rue 318 L4
Mornay, Rue 332 P8
Morvan, Rue du 327 R7
Moscou, Rue de 318 K3
Motte-Picquet, Avenue de la 328 H8
Mouffetard, Rue 331 N9
Moufle, Rue 326 Q7
Moulin Joly, Rue du 327 R5
Moussy, Rue de 325 N7
Mozart, Avenue 321 E7
Mozart, Square 321 E7
Muette, Chaussée la 321 E7
Muller, Rue 319 M3
Mûriers, Rue des 327 S6
Myron, Avenue H 323 J4

Nadaud, Rue G 321 E7
Nancy, R de 326 P5
Nancy, Rue de 325 N5
Nanettes, Rue des 327 R6
Nations Unies, Avenue des 322 G6
Navarin, Rue de 318 M4
Navarre, Rue des 331 N9
Nelaton, Rue 328 F8
Nemours, Rue de 326 Q6
Neslé, Rue de 324 M7
Neuf, Pont 325 M7
Neuve Popincourt, Rue 326 Q6
Neuve Saint-Pierre, Rue 332 P8
Nevers, Rue de 324 M7
New York, Avenue de 322 G6
Newton, Rue 322 G5
Nice, Rue de 327 S7
Nicolas Charlet, Rue 329 J9
Nicolas Houël, Rue 332 P9
Nicolas Poussin, Cité 330 L10
Nicolas Roret, Rue 331 N10
Nicolet, Rue 319 M2
Nicolo, Rue 321 E7
Nollet, Rue 318 K3
Normandie, Rue de 326 P6
Norvins, Rue 318 M2
Notre-Dame de Lorette, Rue 318 L4
Notre-Dame de Nazareth, Rue 325 N5
Notre-Dame des Champs, Rue 330 L9
Notre-Dame des Victoires, Rue 325 M5
Notre-Dame, Pont 325 N7

Oberkampf, Rue 326 Q6
Observatoire, Avenue de l' 330 L9
Odéon, Rue de l' 330 M8
Odessa, Rue d' 329 K9
Odiot, Cité 322 H5
Olivet, Rue d' 329 K8
Opéra, Avenue de l' 324 L5
Opéra, Place de l' 324 L5
Ordener, Rue 319 M2
Orfèvres, Quai des 325 M7
Orfèvres, Rue des 325 M7
Orfila, Rue 327 S6
Orléans, Galerie d' 324 L6
Orléans, Quai d' 331 N8
Orléans, Square d' 318 L4
Ormesson, Rue d' 326 P7
Orsay, Quai d' 323 J6
Orsel, Rue d' 319 M3
Ortolan, Rue 331 N9
Oscar Roty, Rue 328 F9
Oslo, Rue d' 318 L2
Oudinot , Impasse 329 K8
Oudinot, Rue 329 J8

Oudry, Rue 331 N10
Ouessant, Rue d' 328 G8
Ourcq, Galerie de l' 320 S1

Pache, Rue 327 R7
Paillet, Rue 331 M9
Paix, Rue de la 324 L5
Pajou, Rue 321 E7
Palais, Boulevard du 325 M7
Palatine, Rue 330 L8
Palestro, Rue de 325 N6
Palissy, Rue B 330 L8
Panoramas, Passage des 325 M5
Panoyaux, Rue des 327 R6
Panthéon, Place du 331 M9
Papillon, Rue 319 M4
Papin, Rue 325 N6
Paradis, Cité 325 N4
Paradis, Rue de 325 N4
Paradis, Rue 333 B2
Parc de Passy, Avenue du 321 F7
Parc Royal, Rue du 326 P7
Parchappe, Cité 332 Q8
Parme, Rue de 318 K3
Parrot, Rue 332 Q9
Partants, Rue des 327 S6
Pascal, Rue 331 N10
Pasquier, Rue 324 K5
Passy, Rue de 321 F7
Pasteur, Boulevard 329 J9
Pasteur, Rue 326 Q6
Pasteur, Square 329 J9
Pastourelle, Rue 326 P6
Patriarches, Rue des 331 N10
Paul Baudry, Rue 323 H5
Paul Cézanne, Rue 323 J4
Paul Feval, Rue 319 M2
Paul Lelong, Rue 325 M5
Paul Valéry, Rue 322 G5
Pavée, Rue 326 P7
Payenne, Rue 326 P7
Pecquay, Rue 325 N7
Pelée, Rue 326 Q7
Penthièvre, Rue de 323 J5
Pépinière, Rue de la 324 K4
Percier, Avenue 323 J4
Perle, Rue de la 326 P7
Pernelle, Rue 325 N7
Perrault, Rue 325 M7
Perrée, Rue 326 P6
Perronet, Rue 324 L7
Pers, Impasse 319 M2
Pétion, Rue 327 R7
Petit Musc, Rue du 332 P8
Petit Pont 331 M8
Petites Ecuries, Cour des 325 N5
Petites Ecuries, Rue des 325 N5
Petits Carreaux, Rue des 325 M5
Petits Champs, Rue des 324 L6
Petits Hôtels, Rue des 319 N4
Pétrelle, Rue 319 N3
Phalsbourg, Cité de 327 R7
Philippe Auguste, Avenue 327 S7
Philippe, Pont L 331 N8
Picard, Rue 319 M3
Picardie, Rue de 326 P6
Pierre 1er de Serbie, Avenue 322 G6
Pierre Bayle, Rue 327 S7
Pierre Brossolette, Rue 331 M9
Pierre Charron, Rue 322 H5
Pierre Chausson, Rue 326 P5
Pierre Lafue, Place 330 L9
Pierre Leroux, Rue 329 K8
Pierre Loti, Avenue 322 G7
Pierre Nicole, Rue 330 M10
Pierre Sarrazin, Rue 331 M8
Pierre Sémard, Rue 319 N4
Pigalle, Cité 318 L4
Pihet, Rue 326 Q6
Pirandello, Rue 331 N10
Planche, Rue de la 330 K8
Planchette, Impasse de la 325 N5
Platon, Rue 329 J10
Plâtre, Rue du 325 N7
Plélo, Rue de 328 F10
Plichon, Rue 327 R6
Poinsot, Rue 330 K10
Point Show, Galerie 323 H5
Poirée, Rue B 325 M7
Poissonnière, Boulevard 325 M5
Poissonnière, Rue 325 N5
Poissy, Rue de 331 N8
Poitiers, Rue de 324 K7
Poitou, Rue du 326 P6
Polonceau, Rue 319 N3
Ponceau, Passage du 325 N5
Pondichéry, Rue de 328 G8
Ponsard, Rue F 321 E7
Pont Neuf, Rue du 325 M7
Pont, Rue du 333 C2
Ponthieu, Rue de 323 J5
Pontoise, Rue de 331 N8
Popincourt, Cité 326 Q6
Popincourt, Rue 327 Q7
Port Mahon, Rue de 324 L5
Port Royal, Square de 331 M10
Portefoin, Rue 326 P6
Port-Royal, Boulevard de 331 M10
Postes, Pass des 331 N10
Poulletier, Rue 332 P8
Prado, Passage du 325 N5
Pré, Rue du 319 P1
Presbourg, Rue de 322 G5
Président Kennedy, Avenue du 321 F7
Président Paul Doumer, Quai du 333 C2
Président Wilson, Avenue du 322 G6
Presles, Rue de 328 G8
Prévôt, Rue du 326 P7
Primatice, Rue 331 N11
Primevères, Impasse des 326 Q7
Princes, Passage des 324 M5
Princesse, Rue 330 L8
Prony, Rue de 333 A2
Provence, Avenue de 324 L4
Provence, Rue de 324 L4
Pruniers, Rue des 327 S6
Psichari, Rue E 323 H7
Puteaux, Rue 318 K3
Pyramides, Rue des 324 L6
Quatre Fils, Rue des 326 P6
Quatre Septembre, Rue du 324 L5
Quatrefages, Rue de 331 N9
Quentin Bauchart, Rue 322 H5
Quincampoix, Rue 325 N7

Rabelais, Rue 323 J5
Rachel, Avenue 318 L3
Racine, Rue 331 M8
Radziwill, Rue 324 M6
Rambuteau, Rue 325 N6
Rameau, Rue 324 L5
Ramey, Passage 319 M2
Ramey, Rue 319 M2
Rampon, Rue 326 P6
Ranelagh, Rue du 321 E8
Raoul Follereau, Place 326 P4
Rapée, Quai de la 332 Q9
Rapp, Avenue 322 H7
Rapp, Square 322 H7
Raspail, Boulevard 324 K7
Raspail, Boulevard 330 K8
Rataud, Rue 331 M9
Rauch, Passage 327 R8
Ravignan, Rue 318 L3
Raynouard, Rue 321 F7
Raynouard, Square 321 F7
Réaumur, Rue 326 P6
Récamier, Rue330 L8
Recollets, Passage des 326 P4
Recollets, Rue des 326 P4
Refuzniks, Allée des 322 G7
Regard, Rue du 330 K8
Régis, Rue 330 K9
Reilhac, Passage 325 N5
Reine Blanche, Rue de la 331 N10
Reine, Cours la 323 J6
Renard, Rue du 325 N7
René Boulanger, Rue 325 N5
René Villerme, Rue 327 R6
Rennes, Rue de 330 L8
Repos, Rue du 327 S7
République, Avenue de la 326 Q6
République, Place de la 326 P6
Résistance, Place de la 322 H6
Retiro, Cité du 323 K5
Reynaud, Rue L 322 H6
Riboutte, Rue 319 M4
Richard Lenoir, Boulevard 326 Q7
Richard Lenoir, Rue 327 R7
Richelieu, Rue de 324 L6
Richer, Rue 325 M4
Richerand, Avenue 326 P5
Richomme, Rue R 319 N3
Rigny, Rue de 323 K4
Rive Gauche, Voie Sur Berge 323 H6
Riverin, Cité 326 P5
Rivoli, Rue de 325 M7
Robert Schuman, Avenue 323 H6
Robert, Rue J 319 P2
Robert, Rue L 330 L10
Robineau, Rue 327 S6
Rochebrune, Rue 327 R6
Rochechouart, Boulevard de 319 M3
Rochechouart, Rue de 319 M3
Rocher, Rue du 318 K4
Rocroy, Rue de 319 N3
Rodier, Rue 319 M4
Roger Verlomme, Rue 326 P7
Roger, Rue 330 K10
Roi de Sicile, Rue du 326 P7
Rollin, Rue 331 N9
Rome, Cour de 318 K4
Rome, Rue de 318 K4
Ronsard, Rue 319 M3
Ronsin, Impasse 329 J9
Roquépine, Rue 323 K5
Roquette, Cité de la 326 Q7
Roquette, Rue de la 327 R7
Rosiers, Rue des 326 P7
Rossini, Rue 324 M5
Rothschild, Impasse 318 K2
Rotrou, Rue 330 M8
Rouelle, Rue 328 F8
Rougemont, Rue 325 M5
Rouget de Lisle, Rue 324 K6
Roulé, Rue du 325 M6
Roulé, Square du 322 H4
Rousseau, Avenue T 321 E8
Rousselet, Rue329 K8
Roy, Rue 323 K4
Royal, Pont 324 L7
Royale, Rue 324 K5
Royer-Collard, Rue 331 M9
Rubens, Rue 331 N11
Rude, Rue 322 G4
Rue De Sèvres 329 J9
Rue Larochelle330 K10
Ruelle, Passage 319 P2

Sabot, Rue du 330 L8
Sacy, Avenue S de 322 G7
Saigon, Rue de 322 G4
St-André des Arts, Rue 330 M8
St-Antoine, Rue 332 P8
St-Bernard, Port 332 P9
St-Bernard, Quai 332 P9
St-Denis, Boulevard 325 N5
St-Dominique, Rue 323 J7
St-Florentin, Rue 324 K5
St-Germain, Boulevard 330 L8
St-Germain-L'auxerrois, Rue 325 M7
St-Guillaume, Rue 330 L8
St-Honoré, Rue 324 M6
St-Jacques, Boulevard 330 L11
St-Jacques, Rue 331 M9
St-Lazare, Rue 318 L4
St-Martin, Boulevard 326 P5
St-Médard, Rue 331 N9
St-Michel, Boulevard 330 M9
St-Michel, Quai 331 M8
St-Nicolas, Rue 332 Q8
St-Ouen, Avenue de 318 K2
St-Roch, Rue 324 L6
St-Romain, Rue 329 K9
St-Sulpice, Place 330 L8
St-Ambroise, Passage 327 R6
St-Ambroise, Rue 327 R6
St-Augustin, Rue 324 L5

St-Bruno, Rue 319 N3
St-Charles, Rue 328 F8
St-Chaumont, Cité 326 Q4
St-Claude, Rue 326 P7
St-Denis, Rue 325 N6
Sainte-Anne, Rue 324 L6
Sainte-Apolline, Rue 325 N5
Sainte-Croix de la Bretonnerie, Rue 325 N7
Sainte-Foy, Passage 325 N5
Sainte-Foy, Rue 325 N5
Sainte-Lucie, Rue 328 F9
Sainte-Marie, Rue 333 C2
Sainte-Marthe, Rue 326 Q4
St-Fiacre, Rue 325 M5
St-Georges, Rue 318 L4
St-Gilles, Rue 326 P7
St-Hippolyte, Rue 331 M10
St-Hubert, Rue 327 R6
St-Irenée, Square 327 R6
St-Jean, Rue 318 K2
St-Joseph, Rue 325 M5
St-Louis, Cour 332 Q8
St-Louis, Pont 331 N8
St-Louis, Rue en l'Île 331 N8
St-Luc, Rue 319 N3
St-Marc, Rue 324 M5
St-Martin, Rue 325 N6
St-Mathieu, Rue 319 N3
St-Maur, Passage 327 R6
St-Maur, Rue 327 R6
St-Merri, Rue 325 N7
Saintonge, Rue de 326 P6
St-Paul, Passage 332 P7
St-Paul, Rue 332 P8
St-Pétersbourg, Rue de 318 K3
St-Pierre Amelot, Passage 326 Q6
St-Pierre, Place 319 M3
St-Placide, Rue 330 K8
St-Quentin, Rue de 319 N4
St-Sabin, Passage 326 Q7
St-Sabin, Rue 326 Q7
St-Saëns, Rue 328 G8
St-Sauveur, Rue 325 N6
St-Sébastien, Passage 326 Q6
St-Sébastien, Rue 326 Q6
St-Séverin, Rue 331 M8
St-Simon, Rue de 324 K7
Saints-Pères, Port des 324 L7
Sints-Pères, Rue des 324 L7
St-Sulpice, Rue 330 L8
St-Victor, Rue 331 N8
St-Vincent, Rue 319 M2
Salarnier, Passage 326 Q7
Sambre et Meuse, Rue de 326 Q4
Samuel de Champlain, Jardin 327 S6
Santé, Impasse de la 331 M10
Santé, Rue de la 331 M10
Santeuil, Rue 331 N10
Sarcey, Rue F 321 F7
Sarte, Rue A del 319 M3
Sauffroy, Rue 318 K2
Saules, Rue des 318 M2
Saulnier, Rue 325 M4
Saussages, Rue des 323 J5
Sauton, Rue Frédéric 331 N8
Savoie, Rue de 331 M8
Saxe, Avenue de 329 J8
Say, Rue 319 M3
Scarron, Rue 326 Q7
Schomberg, Rue de 332 P8
Scipion, Rue 331 N10
Scribe, Rue 324 L5
Sébastopol, Boulevard de 325 N6
Sedaine, Cour 326 Q7
Sedaine, Rue 326 Q7
Sédillot, Rue 322 H7
Sedillot, Square 322 H7
Séguier Hautefeuille, Rue 331 M8
Séguier, Rue 331 M8
Ségur, Avenue de 329 H8
Seine, Rue de 330 L8
Sejourne, Rue P 330 L9
Sentier, Rue du 325 M5
Serpente, Rue 331 M8
Servan, Rue 327 R6
Servan, Square 327 R7
Servandoni, Rue 330 L8
Sévigné, Rue de 326 P7
Sèvres, Rue de 329 J9
Sevrien, Galerie le 330 K8
Sibour, Rue 326 P4
Singer, Passage 321 E7
Singer, Rue 321 E7
Sofia, Rue de 319 N3
Soleillet, Rue 327 S6
Solférino, Passerelle 324 K6
Solférino, Rue de 324 K7
Sommerard, Rue du 331 M8
Sorbier, Rue 327 S6
Sorbonne, Rue de la 331 M8
Soufflot, Rue 331 M9
Spinoza, Rue 327 R6
Spuller, Rue E 326 P6
Staël, Rue de 329 J9
Stanislas, Rue 330 L9
Steinkerque, Rue de 319 M3
Steinlen, Rue 318 L2
Stevens, Rue A 318 M3
Stockholm, Rue de 318 K4
Strasbourg, Boulevard de 325 N5
Strasbourg, Rue de 333 B2
Suffren, Avenue de 328 H8
Suffren, Port de 322 G7
Suger, Rue 331 M8
Sully, Pont 332 P8
Sully, Rue de 332 P8
Surcouf, Rue 323 J7
Surène, Rue de 323 K5

Taillandiers, Rue des 326 Q7
Taitbout, Rue 324 L5
Talleyrand, Rue de 323 J7
Talma, Rue 321 E7
Talon, Rue O 327 R6
Tanneries, Rue des 331 M11
Tardieu, Rue 319 M3
Taylor, Rue 326 P5
Téhéran, Rue de 323 J4
Temple, Boulevard du 326 P6
Temple, Rue du 326 P6
Ternaux, Rue 326 Q6
Tertre, Place du 319 M3
Texel, Rue du 329 K10
Théâtre, Rue du 328 G8
Théodore Judlin, Square 328 H8
Thérèse, Rue 324 L6
Thiere, Passage 332 Q8
Thimonnier, Rue 319 M4
Tholozé, Rue 318 L2
Thomy Thierry, Allée 322 G7
Thorel, Rue 325 N5
Thorigny, Rue de 326 P7
Thouin, Rue 331 N9
Tilsitt, Rue de 322 G4
Timbaud, Rue J-P 326 P6
Tiphaine, Rue 328 G8
Tiquetonne, Rue 325 N6
Tiron, Rue 325 N7
Tlemcen, Rue de 327 S6
Tourlaque, Rue 318 L2
Tournefort, Rue 331 N9
Tournelle, Pont de la 331 N8
Tournelle, Quai de la 331 N8
Tournelles, Rue des 326 Q7
Tourville, Avenue de 329 J8
Tracy, Rue de 325 N5
Traktir, Rue de 322 G5
Traversière, Rue 332 Q8
Treilhard, Rue 323 J4
Trésor, Rue du 325 N7
Trévise, Cité de 319 M4
Trévise, Cité 325 M4
Trévise, Rue de 325 M4
Trinité, Rue de la 318 L4
Trois Bornes, Cité des 326 Q6
Trois Bornes, Rue des 326 Q6
Trois Freres Enghels, Place des 333 C2
Trois Frères, Rue des 319 M3
Tronchet, Rue 324 K5
Troyon, Rue 322 G4
Trudaine, Avenue 319 M3
Truffaut, Rue 318 K3
Truillot, Impasse 326 Q7
Tuileries, Quai des 324 K6
Turbigo, Rue de 326 P6
Turenne, Rue de 326 P6
Turgot, Rue 319 M3
Turin, Rue de 318 K3

Ulm, Rue d' 331 M9
Union, Passage de l' 323 H7
Université, Rue de l' 323 J7
Ursins, Rue des 331 N8
Ursulines, Rue des 331 M9
Utrillo, Rue M 319 M3
Uzes, Rue d' 325 M5

Vacquerie, Rue la 327 R7
Valadon, Rue 323 H7
Val-de-Grâce, Rue du 330 M9
Valence, Rue de 331 N10
Valentin, Rue E 322 H7
Valette, Rue 331 M9
Valhubert, Place 332 P9
Valmy, Impasse de 324 K7
Valmy, Quai de 326 P5
Valois, Rue de 324 M6
Van Gogh, Rue 332 Q9
Vaneau, Cité 329 K8
Vaneau, Rue 329 K8
Varenne, Cité de 329 K8
Varenne, Rue de 323 J7
Varsovie, Place de 322 G7
Vaubin, Place 329 J8
Vaucanson, Rue 325 N6
Vaugirard, Boulevard de 329 J10
Vaugirard, Galerie 329 J9
Vaugirard, Rue de 329 J9
Vauquelin, Rue 331 M10
Vavin, Avenue 330 L9
Vavin, Rue 330 L9
Velpeau, Rue 330 K8
Verdeau, Passage 325 M5
Verdi, Rue 321 E7
Verdun, Avenue de 326 P4
Verhaeren, Allée 330 M11
Vernet, Rue 322 H5
Verneuil, Rue de 324 L7
Véron, Cité 318 L3
Véron, Rue 318 L3
Véronèse, Rue 331 N11
Verrerie, Rue de la 325 N7
Verrier, Rue le 330 L9
Vertbois, Rue du 325 N6
Verte, Allée 326 Q7
Vertus, Rue des 326 P6
Vésale, Rue 331 N10
Viala, Rue 328 G8
Viallet, Passage 327 R7
Vicaire, Rue G 326 P6
Victoire, Rue de la 324 L4
Victor Considérant, Rue 330 L10
Victor Gelez, Rue 327 R6
Victor Massé, Rue 318 M3
Victor Schoelcher, Rue 330 L10
Vieille du Temple, Rue 326 P7
Vienne, Rue de 318 K4
Vierge, Passage de la 323 H7
Vieuville, Rue de la 318 M3
Vigée-Lebrun, Rue 329 J10
Vignes, Rue des 321 E7
Vignon, Rue 324 K5
Villaret de Joyeuse, Square 322 G4
Villars, Avenue de 329 J8
Ville l'Evêque, Rue de la 323 K5
Villedo, Rue 324 L6
Villersexel, Rue de 324 K7
Vinaigriers, Rue des 326 P5
Visconti, Rue 324 L7
Visitation, Passage de la 324 K7
Vital, Rue 321 E7
Vivienne, Rue 324 M5
Volta, Rue 326 P6
Voltaire, Boulevard 326 Q6
Voltaire, Quai 324 L7
Vosges, Place des 326 P7
Vosges, Place des 333 B2

Wagram, Avenue de 322 G4
Washington, Rue 322 H5
Winston Churchill, Avenue 323 J6

Ybry, Rue 333 D2
Yves Toudic, Rue 326 P5

Ziem, Rue F 318 L2

# INDEX

**The sights featured on pages 76 to 170 have been entered in bold here.**


**A**

Abélard and Héloïse 27, 88
Académie Française 29, 98
ACCOMMODATION 284–294
apartment rental 284
bed-and-breakfast 284
hotels 9, 284–294
self-catering 284
youth hostels 284–285
Agnès B 9, 185
AIRPORTS AND AIR SERVICES 42–43
Beauvais Tillé 42, 43
health hazards for flyers 302
Orly 42, 43
Roissy-Charles de Gaulle 42, 43
transportation to city 42–43
visitors with disabilities 62
Allée des Cygnes 21, 151
alternative medicine 303
American Cultural Center 81, 113
**André-Citroën, Parc 145**
Antik Batik 9, 185
antiques 14, 176, 183
apartment rental 284
Apollinaire, Guillaume 169
Aquaboulevard 216
aquapark 216
aquatherapy 220
**Arab World Institute** 39, **98**
**Arc de Triomphe** 8, 10, 34–35, 72, **76-78**
Arc du Carrousel 79, 105
**Arènes de Lutèce 80**
*Argonaute* 146
Armée, Musée de l' 99, 100
*arrondissements* 4
**Art et d'Histoire du Judaïsme, Musée d'** 70, 107, **112**
art galleries *see* museums and galleries
**Art Moderne de la Ville de Paris, Musée d'** 75, **112**
**Art Moderne, Musée National d' 82, 84, 86**
**Arts Asiatiques-Guimet, Musée National des** 75, **126**
arts venues 198
**Arts Décoratifs, Musée des** 73, **111**
**Arts et Métiers, Musée des 111**
**Assemblée Nationale 80**
Atelier Brancusi 84, 85
ATMs 300
Au Bon Marché 19, 161, 191
Au Lapin Agile 19, 108, 199
Auditorium du Louvre 201
Avenue des Champs-Élysées *see* Champs-Élysées
avenue Montaigne 177

**B**

baby-changing facilities 299
baby-sitting services 298–299
**Baccarat, Musée 112**
Bacon, Francis 150
Les Bains 214
Balabus 20, 55
ballet 193
Balzac, Honoré de 88, 106
**Balzac, Maison de 106**
banks 300, 301, 308
Banque de France 73, 149
bars 209–213, 254
Bartholdi, Auguste 21
**La Bastille** 5, **80**
Bastille Day 78, 222, 296
Bastille, storming of 33
Bateau-Lavoir 71, 109, 226
*bateaux mouches* 20, 248
Batobus 58
Baudelaire, Charles 87
Beaubourg 86
*see also* **Centre Georges Pompidou**
Beaujolais Nouveau 222
beauty salons and treatments 220
Beauvais Tillé 42, 43
Beaux-Arts de la Ville, Musée des 72, 95
Beckett, Samuel 87
bed-and-breakfast 284
begging 50
**Bercy 81**
Bercy, Parc de 81
Berlioz, Hector 87, 161, 226
Bernhardt, Sarah 88
**Bibliothèque Nationale de France–Site François Mitterrand** 39, 81, 153
**Bibliothèque Nationale de France–Site Richelieu** 81, 230
bicycles *see* cycling
billiards 216
Binoche, Juliette 18
Bizet, Georges 88
boat trips 10, 234–235, 248
**Bois de Boulogne** 10, **236**
**Bois de Vincennes** 10, **237**
Boltanski, Christian 112
BOOKS
*les bouquinistes* 161, 232
reading list 309
Shakespeare and Company 9, 20, 21, 152, 182
shops 176, 182
boulevard Haussmann 179
boulevard St-Michel 152, 228
Boulogne, Daniel 22
*les bouquinistes* 161, 232
Bourbon, Palais 80
Bourdelle, Émile-Antoine 110
Bourdelle, Musée 110
**La Bourse 81**
bowling 216–217
Braille, Louis 144
Brancusi, Constantin 84, 87
Braque, Georges 39, 71, 109, 145
brasseries and bistros 12, 35, 108, 254, 278
BRIDGES
Passerelle de Solférino 234
Passerelle Debilly 234
Petit Pont 235
**Pont Alexandre III 151**, 234
**Pont de l'Alma 151**, 234
**Pont des Arts** 22, 73, **151**, 153, 232, 234
**Pont de Bir-Hakeim 151**
Pont du Carrousel 234
Pont de la Concorde 234
Pont de Grenelle 21
Pont d'Iena 234
Pont des Invalides 234
**Pont Marie** 234, **151**
**Pont Neuf** 19, 73, **151**, 232, 235
**Pont Royal 151**, 234
Pont St-Michel 235
bureaux de change 300–301
Buren, Daniel 104, 180
BUSES
airport 43
Balabus 55
bus stops 54
bus tours 248
information 55
long-distance 46
night buses 55
sightseeing routes 54
tickets 54
visitors with disabilities 62
La Butte 109
Buttes-Chaumont, Parc des 22

**C**

cabaret 19, 193, 198–9
Café Beaubourg 9, 213
Café Les Deux Magots 9, 161, 211, 233
Café de Flore 9, 161, 181, 213, 233
Café de l'Industrie 212
cafés 9, 12, 213–214, 254
cafés psycho 13
Callas, Maria 88
**Canal St-Martin 81**, 248
Canaletto 113
cancan 19, 37, 111
Capucines, Musée des 116
car rental 299
**Carnavalet, Musée** 8, 70, 107, **114–115**, 224
*Carte Musée-Monuments* 307–308
**Les Catacombes 81**
Catherine de Medici 29, 105, 150
celebrity spotting 19
CEMETERIES
**Les Catacombes 81**
**Cimetière de Montmartre** 71, **87**, 226
**Cimetière du Montparnasse 87**, 110
**Cimetière du Père-Lachaise 88**, 113
**Centre Georges Pompidou** 8, 16, 70, **82–86**, 193, 205
Centre National de la Photographie 106
**Cernuschi, Musée 113**
Chagall, Marc 39, 110, 142
**Chaillot, Palais de** 8, 75, **143**
chain stores 190–191
Chalgrin, Jean-François 163
**Champ-de-Mars** 75, **87**
**CHAMPS-ÉLYSÉES** 5, 10, 15, **72, 77, 78–79**, 177
eating out 72, 258
sights 72
Chanel 186
Chanel, Coco 149, 186
channel tunnel rail link 44–45
**Chantilly 238-239**
Chareau, Pierre 106
Charlemagne 25, 117
Charles VII 26, 27
**Chasse et de la Nature, Musée de la** 70, **113**
**Château de Chantilly 238–239**
**Château de Fontainebleau** 28, **242–243**
**Château de Vincennes 237**
CHILDREN'S PARIS 221, 298–299
baby-changing facilities 299

baby-sitting services 298–299
eating out 298
farms and wildlife parks 221
Jardin du Luxembourg 103
museums 221
parks and gardens 221
public transportation 47, 298
puppet shows 103, 207, 298
theatre 207
theme parks 221
Chinese New Year 222
Chirac, Jacques 5, 39
Chopin, Frédéric 88, 149
Christo 151
CHURCHES AND CATHEDRALS
Église du Dôme 101
La Madeleine 149, 201
**Notre-Dame** 8, 10, 26, 74, 96, **137-141**, 235
places of worship 299
**Sacré-Cœur** 8, 71, 108, **154–157**, 226
**Sainte-Chapelle** 26, 27, 74, 91, 96, **158–160**
**St-Étienne-du-Mont** 74, **161**
**St-Eustache** 73, **161**
**St-Germain-l'Auxerrois** 73, **162**
**St-Germain-des-Prés** 161, **162**, 232
St-Jean-l'Évangeliste 145, 227
**St-Julien-le-Pauvre** 74, **162**, 228
St-Louis-des-Invalides 101
**St-Merri** 86, **162**
St-Paul-St-Louis 224
St-Pierre-de-Montmartre 71, 226
**St-Séverin** 74, **162-163**, 228
**St-Sulpice 163**, 232
visiting 299
Churchill, Winston 237
**Cimetière de Montmartre** 71, **87**, 226
**Cimetière du Montparnasse 87**, 110
**Cimetière du Père-Lachaise 88**, 113
Cinaxe 146
cinema 16, 17, 18, 193, 199–201, 308, 309
Cinéma en Plein Air 17
**Cinéma, Musée du 113**, 143
Cinématique Française 113, 143
Cinq Jours de l'Objet Extraordinaire 14
circus 201
**Cité de la Musique 146-147**, 201
**Cité des Sciences et de l'Industrie 146**, 147
Citroën, André 87
CITY TOURS 248
bicycle tours 59
boat trips 10, 234–235, 248
bus tours 248
walking tours 248
classical music 193, 201–203
climate 296
CLOCKS
*Le Défenseur du Temps* 85
Tour de l'Horloge 91
clothing sizes 298
Clovis 25
Club Med World 18, 20, 221
clubs 9, 214–215, 308
**Cluny Museum** 8, 74, **128–129**, 203
Cocteau, Jean 104, 136
**Cognacq-Jay, Musée** 70, **113**
coin and medal museum 117, 232
Colbert, Jean-Baptiste 31, 107
Colette 104, 180
Colonne de Juillet 80
Comédie Française 104, 193, 206
comedy venues 203
Communards 36, 37, 88
COMMUNICATION 304–305
cyber cafés 305
Internet access 305
laptops 305
post offices and postal services 301, 304–305, 308
telephones 304
CONCERTS 201–203
Auditorium du Louvre 201
Cité de la Musique 146–147, 201
Hôtel de Soubise 117
La Madeleine 201
Maison de Radio France 201
Musée National du Moyen Âge–Thermes de Cluny 203
Parc de la Villette 147
St-Eustache 161
St-Julien-le-Pauvre 162
St-Merri 86, 162
Théâtre Musical Paris Châtelet 203
Zénith 147
**Conciergerie** 74, **89–91**, 96, 235
Condé, Musée 238, 239
contemporary live music 203–205
'continental kiss' 299
conversion chart 298
La Coupole 110, 266
cour du Commerce St-André 232
CREDIT CARDS 176, 300
lost/stolen 300
crime and personal safety 5, 305
Crown of Thorns 27, 140, 160
Cubism 39, 86, 226
cultural life 16–17
*see also* performing arts
Curie, Marie and Pierre 144
customs regulations 297
cyber cafés 305
cycling 59, 217


## D


Dalí, Salvador 71, 92, 145
dance 193, 201–203, 217
Danton, Georges 232
de Beauvoir, Simone 87
de Gaulle, Charles 39, 78, 133
Découverte, Palais de la 72, 95
**La Défense 92**, 94
*Le Défenseur du Temps* 85
Degas, Edgar 87
Delacroix, Eugène 80, 88, 120, 126, 163, 232
Delanoë, Bertrand 5, 40
Deneuve, Catherine 19
dental treatment 303
department stores 191–192
Descartes, René 162
Desmoulins, Camille 104
Les Deux Magots 9, 161, 211, 233
Diana, Princess of Wales 149, 151
Diderot, Denis 31
Dietrich, Marlene 149
*Directoire* 34
disabilities, visitors with 62, 299
**Disneyland Resort Paris 240–241**
districts of Paris 5
doctors 302–303
donkey rides 102, 103
drag revues 19
Dreyfus Affair 112
drinking water 303
DRIVING 60–61
breakdown 61
car rental 299
drinking and 61
driving customs 60
fuel 61
hints 60, 61
insurance 61
in Paris 60–61
parking 60
regulations 60, 61
road signs 61
road systems 61
seatbelts 61
speed limits 60, 61
to Paris 46
**Drouot 92**
Dufy, Raoul 169
Duncan, Isadora 88, 136


## E


EATING OUT 12–13, 254–278
brasseries and bistros 12, 35, 108, 254, 278
on a budget 254
cafés and bars 254
with children 298
etiquette 254
fast food 13, 278
ice cream 13
map 250–253
menu reader 256–257
opening times 254
regional and international cuisine 255, 259
salons de thé 9, 254
vegetarian food 255, 259
*see also* restaurants
**École Militaire** 75, **87**
Ecole Nationale Supérieure des Beaux-Arts 161, 232
the economy 4
Edison, Thomas 111
**Edith Piaf, Musée 113**
Église du Dôme 101
**Les Égouts** 75, **92**
Egyptian obelisk 148, 230
Eiffel, Gustave 21, 167, 169
**EIFFEL TOWER** 8, 10, 22, 36, **75, 164–169**, 234
eating out 75
sights 75
electricity 298
Élysée Palace 72
embassies and consulates 297, 306
emergencies 302, 303, 305
emergency telephone numbers 302, 305
entertainment 18–19
*see also* nightlife; performing arts

**Espace Montmartre–Salvador Dalí** 71, **92**, 109
etiquette 254, 299
*Étoile* 36, 79
**Eugène Delacroix, Musée National 126**, 232
euro 300
Eurostar 44, 45
Eurotunnel 45, 46
EXCURSIONS 236–247
**Bois de Boulogne** 10, 236
**Bois de Vincennes** 10, **237**
**Chantilly 238–239**
**Disneyland Resort Paris 240-241**
**Fontainebleau** 28, **242–243**
map 236
**Versailles** 30-31, **244–247**

## F

farms and wildlife parks 221
fashion 14–15
fashion shopping 176, 185–187
fast food 13, 278
Faubourg Montmartre 92
Faubourg St-Antoine 92
Faubourg St-Germain 92
Faubourg St-Honoré 5, 92, 177
**Les Faubourgs 92**
Fauchon 9, 149, 179, 184
Ferme Ouverte de Gally 221
ferry services 46
Festival d'Automne 222
Festival de Cinéma en Plein Air 222
festivals and events 222
Fête de la Musique 18, 222
Fête des Rois 222
FIAC (Foire International d'Art Contemporain) 222
film festival 17, 222
fire services 306
flea market 9, 109
Floral de Paris, Parc 205, 237
florists 190–191
flower market 96–97, 192
flying lessons 217
Foire de Paris 222
Foire St-Germain 222
Foire du Trône 18
Folies-Bergère 199
**Fondation Cartier 93**, 95
**Fontaine des Innocents 93**
Fontaine Médicis 103
Fontaine St-Michel 152, 228
**Fontainebleau** 28, **242–243**
FOOD AND DRINK
shopping for 176, 184–185
*see also* eating out
Forum des Halles 73, 95, 180
Foucault 144
FOUNTAINS
**Fontaine des Innocents 93**, 95
Fontaine Médicis 103
Fontaine St-Michel 152, 228
Jardins du Trocadéro 149
Stravinsky Fountain 17, 70, 84, 85
Versailles 246
Fourmi 211
**Fragonard, Musée 116**
Franco-Prussian War (1870–1871) 37, 157
François I 28, 29, 242
funicular 108, 155

## G

Galerie Colbert 73, 93
Galerie Mansart 81
Galerie Mazarine 81
Galerie Véro-Dodat 93
Galerie Vivienne 73, 93, 180
**Les Galeries** 10, **93**
Galeries Lafayette 179
Galliera, Palais 116
GALLO-ROMAN REMAINS
**Arènes de Lutèce 80**
baths 24, 129, 153
GARDENS AND PARKS
Jardin d'Acclimatation 221
**Jardin du Luxembourg** 10, 74, **102–103**, 153, 232
**Jardin du Palais Royal** 73, **104**, 230
**Jardin des Plantes 127**
**Jardin des Tuileries** 10, 72, 73, **105**, 230
Jardins du Ranelagh 124
Jardins du Trocadéro 75, 149
Jean Rictus garden 22
Maison du Jardinage 221
**Parc André-Citroën 145**
Parc de Bercy 81
Parc des Buttes-Chaumont 22
Parc Floral de Paris 205, 237
**Parc de Monceau 145**
**Parc Montsouris 145**
Parc de la Turlure 8, 226
**Parc de la Villette 146–147**
Gare de Lyon 40, 243
Gare Montparnasse 110
Gare du Nord 44–45
Gaultier, Jean-Paul 16, 116
gay and lesbian Paris 215
Gehry, Frank 81, 113
**La Géode 146**, 200
Georges restaurant 268
gifts 183–184
**Gobelin tapestry workshops 107**
golf 217
*Grand Axis* 79, 94, 105
**Grand Palais** 72, **95**
Grand and Petit Trianon 245, 247
Le Grand Rex 17, 200
**Grande Arche** 8, 39, 79, 92, **94**
**Grévin, Musée 116**
guillotine 32, 148, 232
Guimard, Hector 50, 163
**Gustave Moreau, Musée 116**

## H

**Les Halles** 5, 73, **95**, 180
Hammam (Turkish baths) 110
Hardouin-Mansart, Jules 101, 149, 151, 246, 247
Haussmann, Baron 36, 88, 92, 153, 237
haute couture 14, 15
HEALTH 302–303
alternative medical treatment 303
dental treatment 303
doctors 302–303
drinking water 303
emergency telephone numbers 302
health hazards for flyers 302
hospital emergency departments 303
medical treatment 297, 302, 303
opticians 303
pharmacies 303
summer hazards 303
HEALTH AND BEAUTY 220
aquatherapy 220
beauty salons 220
beauty treatments 220
shopping for beauty products 188–189
thalassotherapy 220
Turkish baths 110
health insurance 297, 302
heatwave (2003) 40
helicopter tours 217
Hemingway, Ernest 39, 103, 110, 149, 161, 209, 211
Henri IV 28, 29, 145, 150, 151, 224
Henri Langlois Cinema Museum 113, 143
Henry VI of England 27
**Histoire de France, Musée de l' 116–117**
**Histoire Naturelle, Muséum National d' 127**
HISTORY OF PARIS 24–40
Communards 36, 37, 88
Franco-Prussian War (1870–1871) 37, 157
Franks 24, 25
Louis XIV 30, 31, 101, 104, 117, 149, 151, 161
medieval Paris 26–27
Napoleon Bonaparte 34–35, 75, 77, 78, 79, 87, 99, 101, 115, 117, 123, 242–243
rebuilding of Paris 36
Renaissance 28
Revolution 32–33, 80, 90, 91, 114, 148
Romans 24
student riots (1968) 39, 153
twenty-first century Paris 40
Wars of Religion 29
World Wars 38, 39, 99, 107, 237
home and garden stores 189–190
**Homme, Musée de l' 143**
horse-racing 238
horse-riding 217
hospital emergency departments 303
hot-air balloon tours 217–218
L'Hotel 9, 286
Hôtel Biron 136
Hôtel de Cluny 129
Hôtel-Dieu 235
Hôtel Duc de St-Simon 9, 292
Hôtel de Guénégaud 113
Hôtel de la Monnaie 117, 232
Hôtel de Rohan 107
Hôtel Salé 135, 224
Hôtel de Soubise 107, 116–117, 224
Hôtel Square 9, 292
Hôtel de Sully 107, 224
**Hôtel de Ville** 70, **95**
HOTELS 9, 284–294
chains 294
map 280–283
Hugues Capet 24, 25
Hugo, Victor 26, 37, 78, 103, 106, 140, 144, 150

**Hunting and Nature, Museum of** 70, **113**

## I

ice cream 13, 98
**Île de la Cité** 5, 24, 74, **96–97**
Île-de-France 4
**Île St-Louis** 5, 74, **98**
Impressionism 124, 125, 130
in-line skating 15, 59, 218–219
**Institut de France 98**, 232
**Institut du Monde Arabe** 16, 39, **98**
INSURANCE
driving 61
health 297, 302
travel 297
Internet access 305
**Les Invalides** 35, 75, **99–101**, 234
IRCAM (Institute de Recherche et Coordination de l'Acoustique et de la Musique) 84, 85

## J

**Jacquemart André, Musée 117**
Jardin d'Acclimatation 221
**Jardin du Luxembourg** 10, 19, 74, **102–103**, 153, 232
**Jardin du Palais Royal** 73, **104**, 230
**Jardin du Plantes 127**
**Jardin des Tuileries** 10, 72, 73, **105**, 230
Jardins du Ranelagh 124
Jardins du Trocadéro 75, 149
jazz 193, 204, 205, 222
Jean Rictus garden 22
**Jeu de Paume** 73, 105, **106**
jewellery 188
Jewish culture 112
Jewish quarter 70, 107, 163, 178, 224
Joan of Arc 27, 117
Joinville-le-Pont 21
Julius Caesar 24
July Column 80

## K

karting 218
*The Kiss* (Brancusi) 87
*The Kiss* (Rodin) 22, 136

## L

la Fontaine, Jean de 88
Labour Day 222
Laboure, Catherine 37
LANGUAGE 5, 299
language guide 311–316
menu reader 256–257
Lapin Agile 199
laptops 305
**LATIN QUARTER** (Quartier Latin) 5, **74**, **152–153**
eating out 74, 229, 258
sights 74
walk 228–229
laundry and dry-cleaning 298
Laval, Pierre 87
lavatories 298
Lavoisier, Antoine 33
Le Brun, Charles 30, 246
Le Nôtre, André 30, 72, 78–79, 105, 238, 242, 246
Le Train Bleu 12, 13
Le Vau, Louis 30, 98, 247
Left Bank (Rive Gauche) 14, **153**
Leonardo da Vinci 28, 29, 119
Liberty Flame 151
Lion of Belfort 21
Liszt, Franz 161
Living Horse Museum 238, 239
long stays in Paris 297
lost property 306
Louis IX (St. Louis) 27, 160
Louis XIII 30, 242, 246
Louis XIV (Sun King) 30, 31, 101, 104, 117, 149, 151, 161
Louis XV 31, 87, 144, 148
Louis XVI 33, 148, 247
Louis XVII (the Dauphin) 33
Louis XVIII 35
**Louvre, Musée du** 8, 10, 16, 29, 39, 73, **118–123**, 230, 234
LUGGAGE
left luggage 64
lost luggage 45
Lutetia 24
Luxembourg, Musée du 102
Luxembourg, Palais du 102, 232

## M

Mackintosh, Charles Rennie 133
La Madeleine 149, 201
**Maison de Balzac 106**
Maison Berthillon 13, 98
Maison de la Culture du Japon à Paris 201
**Maison Européenne de la Photographie 106**
Maison du Jardinage 221
Maison de Jean Hérouët 224
Maison de Radio France 201
**Maison de Verre 106**
**Maison de Victor Hugo** 70, **106**
Malmaison, Château de 34
Malraux, André 107, 113
**Manufacture des Gobelins 107**
MAPS
airport locator 42
Champs-Élysées 79
city locator 4
eating out locator 250–253
excursions 236
Greater Paris 6–7
hotels locator 280–283
Métro 52–53
performing arts locator 194–197
Seine river trip 235
shopping areas 177–181
shopping locator 172–175
sightseeing areas 70–75
sights locator 66–69
train station locator 57
Versailles 247
walks 224–233
**LE MARAIS** 5, **70**, **107**
eating out 70, 178, 225, 258
shopping 178
sights 70
walk 224–225
Marat, Jean-Paul 232
Marathon International de Paris 222
Marché d'Aligre 192
Marché du Boulevard Raspail 192
Marché aux Fleurs 96–97, 192
**Marché aux Puces de St-Ouen** 9, **107**
Marché Réunion 192
Marie de Medici 29, 78, 102, 103
Marie-Antoinette 31, 33, 90, 111, 117, 148, 242, 246
Marine, Musée National de la 143
MARKETS 10, 192
Marché d'Aligre 192
Marché du Boulevard Raspail 192
Marché aux Fleurs 96–97, 192
**Marché aux Puces de St-Ouen** 9, **107**
Marché Réunion 192
Marly Horses 77, 122
**Marmottan Monet, Musée 124–125**
*La Marseillaise* (sculpture) 78, 79
martial arts venues 218
Massouiter, Brigitte 22
Matisse, Henri 112, 136
Maupassant, Guy de 87, 169
Mazarin, Cardinal 30, 31, 81, 98
measurements and weights 298
MEDIA 306–307
newspapers and magazines 307
radio 307
television 306–307
medical treatment 297, 302, 303
**Mémorial des Martyrs de la Déportation** 96, **107**
menu reader 256–257
Merson, Olivier 156
Mesmer, Anton 149
MÉTRO 47–53
lines 49, 50–51
map and symbols 49, 52–53
tickets 47–48
travel information 47, 51
user tips 47, 50, 51
visitors with disabilities 62
**Military Academy** 75, **87**
Miller, Henry 39, 145
mime artists 18
Mitterrand, François 39, 44, 133, 142
mobile phones 304
**Mode de la Ville de Paris, Musée de la** 75, **116**
Modern Art movements 86
Modigliani, Amedeo 88, 110
Molière, Jean-Baptiste 88, 104
*Mona Lisa* 28, 119
**Monceau, Parc de 145**
Monet, Claude 124, 125, 130, 142
MONEY 300–301
ATMs 300
banknotes and coins 300
banks 300, 301
bureaux de change 300–301
credit cards 176, 300
euro 300
everyday items and prices 301
post offices 301
taxes 301
ticket concessions 301, 307–308
tipping 301

traveller's cheques 300, 305
wiring money 301
**Monnaie, Musée de la 117**, 232
Montand, Yves 88
MONTMARTRE 5, 10, **71**, **108–109**
eating out 71, 227, 258
sights 71
walk 226–227
**Montmartre Cemetery** 71, **87**, 226
**Montmartre, Musée de** 71, 108, **126**
Montmartrobus 108
**Montparnasse** 5, **110**
**Montparnasse Cemetery 87**
**Montsouris, Parc 145**
Monuments Français, Musée des 143
Moore, Henry 105
Moreau, Gustave 87, 116
Morrison, Jim 88
**La Mosquée 110**
Moulin, Jean 144
Moulin de la Galette 108, 109, 226
Moulin Radet 108, 226, 227
**Moulin Rouge** 10, 19, 37, 71, 109, **111**, 199, 226
**Moyen Âge, Musée National du, Thermes de Cluny** 8, 74, **128–129**, 203, 228
Mur des Fédérés 88
Le Mur des Je t'Aime 22
MUSEUMS AND MONUMENTS
annual closures 296, 308
*Carte Musée-Monuments* 307–308
concessions 301, 307
opening times 308
MUSEUMS AND GALLERIES
**Espace Montmartre–Salvador Dalí** 71, **92**, 109
**Fondation Cartier 93**
**Institut du Monde Arabe** 39, **98**
**Jeu de Paume** 73, 105, **106**
**Maison de Balzac 106**
**Maison de Victor Hugo** 70, **106**
**Maison Européenne de la Photographie 106**
Musée de l'Armée 99, 100
**Musée d'Art et d'Histoire du Judaïsme** 70, 107, **112**
**Musée d'Art Moderne de la Ville de Paris** 75, **112**
**Musée des Arts Décoratifs** 73, **111**
**Musée des Arts et Métiers 111**
**Musée Baccarat 112**
Musée des Beaux-Arts de la Ville 72, 95
Musée Bourdelle 110
**Musée Carnavalet** 8, 70, 107, **114–115**, 224
**Musée Cernuschi 113**
**Musée de la Chasse et de la Nature** 70, **113**
**Musée du Cinéma 113**, 143
Musée du Cinéma Henri-Langlois 143
**Musée Cognacq-Jay** 70, **113**
Musée Condé 238, 239
**Musée Edith Piaf 113**
**Musée Fragonard 116**
**Musée Galliéra–Musée de la Mode de la Ville de Paris** 75, **116**
**Musée Grévin 116**
**Musée Gustave Moreau 116**
**Musée de l'Histoire de France 116–117**
**Musée de l'Homme 143**
**Musée Jacquemart André 117**
**Musée du Louvre** 8, 10, 16, 29, 39, 73, **118–123**, 230, 234
Musée du Luxembourg 102
**Musée Marmottan Monet 124–125**
**Musée de la Monnaie 117**, 232
**Musée de Montmartre** 71, 108, **126**
Musée des Monuments Français 143
Musée de la Musique 146–147
**Musée National d'Art Moderne 82**, **84**, 86
**Musée National des Arts Asiatiques-Guimet** 75, **126**
**Musée National Eugène Delacroix 126**, 232
**Musée National de la Marine 143**
**Musée National du Moyen Âge–Thermes de Cluny** 8, 74, **128–129**, 203, 228
**Musée Nissim de Camondo 126**
**Musée d'Orsay** 8, 16, **130–134**, 234
**Musée Picasso** 8, 70, 107, **135**, 224
Musée des Plans-Reliefs 99
**Musée du Quai Branly** 75, **126**
**Musée Rodin** 8, 22, **136**
Musée de la Sculpture en Plein Air 136
Musée Vivant du Cheval 238, 239
**Muséum National d'Histoire Naturelle 127**
**Orangerie** 73, 105, **142**
Palais de la Découverte 72, 95
MUSIC
classical music 193, 201–203
contemporary live music 203–205
festivals 222
jazz 193, 204, 205, 222
music store 182–183
opera 193, 201–203
*see also* concerts
Musique, Musée de la 146–147


## N


Napoleon Bonaparte 34–35, 75, 77, 78, 79, 87, 99, 101, 115, 117, 123, 242–243
Napoleon III 36, 37, 106, 142
National Archives 117, 224
National Assembly **80**
national holidays 307
National Library **81**
**Natural History Museum 127**
newspapers and magazines 307
Nicholas II, Tsar 151
NIGHTLIFE 209–215
bars 209–213, 254
cafés 9, 13, 213–214, 254
clubs 9, 214–215, 308
gay and lesbian nightlife 215
Nijinsky, Vaslav 38
**Nissim de Camondo, Musée 126**
Noir, Victor 88
**Notre-Dame** 8, 10, 20, 26, 74, 96, **137–141**, 235
Nuit Blanche 222


## O


Odéon Théâtre de l'Europe 193, 232
Offenbach, Jacques 87
OPENING TIMES
banks 308
museums and monuments 308
nightlife 308
pharmacies 308
post offices 308
restaurants 254, 308
shops 176, 308
opera 193, 201–203
Opéra (area) 179
**Opéra Bastille** 10, 39, **142**, 193, 202
Opéra du Château de Versailles 202
**Opéra Palais Garnier** 10, 19 **142**, 179, 193, 202, 230
opticians 303
**Orangerie** 73, 105, **142**
Orly Airport 42, 43
**Orsay, Musée d'** 8, 16, **130–134**, 234


## P


packing advice 296–297
paintball 218
Palais Bourbon 80
**Palais de Chaillot** 8, 75, **143**
Palais de la Découverte 72, 95
Palais de l'Élysée 72
Palais Galliéra 116
Palais de Justice 20, 89, 91, 97
Palais du Luxembourg 102, 232
Palais Omnisports 81
Palais Royal 17, 73, 180
Palais de Tokyo 112, 198
**Panthéon** 8, 74, **144**
**Parc André-Citroën 145**
Parc Astérix 221
Parc de Bercy 81
Parc des Buttes-Chaumont 22
Parc Floral de Paris 205, 237
**Parc de Monceau 145**
**Parc Montsouris 145**
Parc de la Turlure 8, 226
**Parc de la Villette 146–147**
Parc Zoologique de Paris 237
Parc Zoologique de Thoiry 221
Parfum, Musée 116
PARIS
*arrondissements* 5

best of Paris 8–10
cultural life 16–17
districts 5
economy 4
history 24–40
multiculturalism 5
Parisian style 14–15
politics 4, 40
population 4, 40
Paris Jazz 222
Paris Mint 117, 232
**Paris Mosque 110**
Paris Plage 21, 40
Paris Quartier d'Été 222
Parissi 24, 97
parking 60
parks *see* gardens and parks
Pascal, Blaise 111
Passage Jouffroy 93
Passage des Panoramas 93
Passage Verdeau 93
Passerelle Debilly 234
Passerelle de Solférino 234
PASSPORTS AND VISAS 297
lost passport 306
Pasteur, Louis 36
patron saints 25
**Pavillon de l'Arsenal 145**
Pavillon de la Reine 9, 150, 292
Pavillon du Roi 150
Pei, I.M. 16, 119, 123
pelota 218
**Père-Lachaise, Cimetière du 88**, 113
PERFORMING ARTS 193–208
arts venues 198
ballet 193
cabaret 193, 198–199
cinemas 193, 199–201
circus 201
classical music 193, 201–203
comedy 203
contemporary live music 203–205
dance 193, 201–203
dress code 193
jazz 193, 204, 205, 222
locator maps 194–197
opera 193, 201–203
theatre 193, 205–208
tickets 193
perfume 116, 176, 188–189
Petit Palais 72, 95
Petit Pont 235
Le Petit Train de Montmartre 71, 108
pharmacies 303, 308
Piaf, Edith 88, 113
Picasso, Pablo 39, 71, 109, 135
**Picasso, Musée** 8, 70, 107, **135**, 224
**Pigalle** 5, **145**
Piscine Deligny 21
Pissarro, Camille 169, 226
**place des Abbesses** 71, **145**
place de la Bastille 32, 80
**place de la Concorde** 8, 72, **148**, 230, 234
place Emile Goudeau 226
place de l'Hôtel de Ville 95
**place de la Madeleine 149**, 179
place St-Michel 152
place du Tertre 108, 226
**place du Trocadéro et du 11 Novembre 149**
**place Vendôme 149**, 230
**place des Victoires** 73, **149**, 180
**place des Vosges** 10, 70, **150**, 224
places of worship 299
*see also* churches and cathedrals
Plans-Reliefs, Musée des 99
police 306
politics 4, 40
Pompadour, Marquise de 31, 87
Pompidou, Georges 85, 170
**Pompidou Centre** 8, 16, 70, **82–86**, 193, 204
**Pont Alexandre III** 21, **151**, 234
**Pont de l'Alma 151**
**Pont des Arts** 22, 73, **151**, 153, 232, 234
**Pont de Bir-Hakeim 151**
Pont du Carrousel 234
Pont de la Concorde 234
Pont de Grenelle 21
Pont d'Iena 234
Pont des Invalides 234
**Pont Marie 151**, 234
**Pont Neuf** 19, 73, **151**, 235
**Pont Royal 151**
Pont St-Michel 235
population 4, 40
post offices and postal services 301, 304–305, 308
Pound, Ezra 39
Printemps 179, 192
Printemps des Rues 222
Le Procope 228, 273
Proust, Marcel 88, 115, 149
PUBLIC TRANSPORTATION 47–58
Batobus 58
buses 54–55
children 47, 298
Métro 47–53
taxis 42, 58
trains 56–57
visitors with disabilities 62
*see also* travel
puppet shows 103, 207, 298

## Q

**Quai Branly, Musée du** 75, **126**
Quartier Latin *see* **Latin Quarter**

## R

radio 307
rail services *see* train services
*Reclining Figure* (Moore) 105
Red Light district 145
Regine 215
Renoir, Pierre-Auguste 109, 125, 126, 130, 132, 145, 226
RER train network 42, 51, 56–57
RESTAURANTS 9, 254, 258–277
alphabetical listing 260–277
by area 258
by cuisine 259
chain restaurants 278
dress code 254
menu reader 256–257
opening times 254, 308
service charge 254
Revolution 32–33, 80, 90, 91, 114, 148
Richelieu, Cardinal 29, 104, 150, 161, 163
**RIGHT BANK (Rive Droite) 73, 153**, 180
eating out 73, 180, 231
sights 73
walk 230-231
*Rite of Spring* premiere 38
Ritz 9, 149, 293
Rive Droite *see* Right Bank
Rive Gauche *see* Left Bank
river trip 10, 234–235, 248
Robespierre, Maximilien 33
Rodin, Auguste 22, 133, 136
**Rodin, Musée** 8, 22, **136**
Rogers, Richard 150
Roissy-Charles de Gaulle 42, 43
Roland-Garros 222
roller-blading 15, 59, 218–219
romance 22
Royal, Palais 73, 180
Rude, François 78, 79, 132
rue Bonaparte 181
rue du Cherche-Midi 181
rue des Francs-Bourgeois 178. 224
rue de Grenelle 181
rue Monsieur le Prince 228
rue du Roi de Sicile 178
rue des Rosiers 178, 224
rue Tronchet 179
rue Vieille-du-Temple 178, 224

## S

**Sacré-Cœur** 8, 71, 108, **154–157**, 226
St. Bartholomew's Eve massacre 29
**Sainte-Chapelle** 26, 27, 74, 91, 96, **158–160**
St. Denis 25, 109, 226
**St-Étienne-du-Mont** 74, **161**
**St-Eustache** 73, **161**
St. Geneviève 25
**St-Germain-l'Auxerrois** 73, **162**
**St-Germain-des-Prés** 5, 10, **161**, **162**, 181
eating out 181, 233, 258
walk 232–233
**St-Germain-des-Prés** (church) 161, **162**, 232
St-Jean-l'Évangeliste 145, 227
St-Julien-le-Pauvre 74, **162**, 228
St-Louis-des-Invalides 101
**St-Merri** 86, **162**
St-Paul-St-Louis 224
St-Pierre-de-Montmartre 71, 226
Saint-Saëns, Camille 87, 162
St-Séverin 74, **162–163**, 228
**St-Sulpice 163**, 232
sales tax 301
*Salon du Chocolat* 15
salons de thé 9, 254
La Samaritaine 8, 192, 234
Sartre, Jean-Paul 87, 103, 152, 161, 213
Sax, Adolphe 87
seasons 296
Seine 20–21
Seine cruise 10, 234–235
senior citizens 63, 301, 308
Sévigné, Madame de 31, 114, 115
sewers 75, **92**
Shakespeare and Company 9, 20, 21, 152, 182
Shakespeare performances 17
shoes and accessories 176, 187–188
SHOPPING 9, 176–192
antiques 176, 183

books 176, 182
chain stores 190–191
credit cards 176
department stores 191–192
designer discount clothing 176
fashion 176, 185–187
florists 190–191
food and drink 176, 184–185
gifts 183–184
health and beauty 188–189
home and garden 189–190
jewellery 188
locator map 172–175
markets 192
music 182–183
opening times 176, 308
perfume 176, 188–189
shoes and accessories 176, 187–188
shopping areas 177–181
sporting goods 189
taxes 301
VAT refunds 301
Signoret, Simone 88
smoking etiquette 298
soccer 216
**La Sorbonne** 27, 74, 153, **163**
SPORTS AND ACTIVITIES 216–220
aquapark 216
bicycling 59, 217
billiards 216
bowling 216–217
dance 217
flying 217
golf 217
health and beauty 220
helicopter tours 217
horse-riding 217
hot-air balloon tours 217–218
in-line skating 15, 59, 218–219
karting 218
martial arts 218
paintball 218
pelota 218
roller-blading 15, 59, 218–219
soccer 216
sports venue 219
sports clubs 219
sports park 219
sports shops 189
squash 219
stadiums 216
swimming 216, 219
tennis 219, 222
yoga 219-220
square de l'Île de France 96
square Jean XXIII 96
square René Viviani 74, 152, 228
square Suzanne-Buisson 226
squash 219
stamps 304
Starck, Philippe 17, 45
Statue of Liberty 21, 103
Stein, Gertrude 39
stock exchange **81**
Stravinsky, Igor 38
Stravinsky Fountain 17, 70, 84, 85
student riots (1968) 39, 153
student visitors 301, 308
style, Parisian 14–15
sun safety 303
swimming 216, 219
**synagogue 163**


## T


tap water 303
tapestries 107, 128
taxes 301
taxis 42, 58
telephones 304
television 306, 307
tennis 219, 222
Terrass Hotel 293
thalassotherapy 220
theatre 193, 205–208, 308
Théâtre des Champs-Élysées 17, 202
Théâtre-Musée des Capucines 116
theme parks 221
time zones 296
tipping 301
Tokyo, Palais de 112, 198
Tomb of the Unknown Soldier 78
Toulouse-Lautrec, Henri 37, 109, 145
La Tour d'Argent 276
**La Tour Eiffel** 8, 10, 36, 75, **164–169**, 234
Tour de France 78, 222
Tour de l'Horloge 91
**Tour Montparnasse** 8, 110, **170**
tourist offices 308–309
**Town Hall** 70, **95**
TRAIN SERVICES 44–45, 56–57, 63–64
concessions 63
cross-Channel 44–45
from Paris 63–64
information 56, 57
left luggage 64
mainline stations 64
Métro 47–53
overnight trains 63–64
RER lines 42, 51, 56–57
timetables 64
Transilien network 57
visitors with disabilities 62
Transilien train network 57
TRAVEL
air 42–43
cross-Channel 44–45
ferry services 46
long-distance buses 46
lost luggage 45
trains 42, 44–45, 51, 56–57, 63–64
*see also* public transportation
travel insurance 297
travellers' cheques 300, 305
Trintignant, Marie 88
Trocadéro 5
Turkish baths 110
Turlure, Parc de la 8, 226


## U


unemployment rate 4
Union Centrale des Arts Décoratifs (UCAD) 111
universities 39, 163
*see also* **La Sorbonne**
Utrillo, Maurice 169


## V


Van Gogh, Vincent 132, 226
Vanessa Bruno 9, 187
vegetarian food 255
*Venus de Milo* 120
Vercingetorix 24, 25
Verlaine, Paul 152, 169
Verne, Jules 37
**Verre, Maison de 106**
**Versailles** 30–31, **244–247**
**Victor Hugo, Maison de** 70, **106**
views over Paris 8
Villon, François 28
**Vincennes, Château de 237**
vineyard, Montmartre 71, 108
Viollet-le-Duc, Eugène 139, 140, 143, 162
VIP Room 215
Visitors with Disabilities 62, 299
Vivant du Cheval, Musée 238, 239
Voltaire, François Marie Arouet de 31, 144


## W


WALKING IN PARIS 59
guided walking tours 248
Latin Quarter 228–229
Le Marais 224–225
Montmartre 226–227
Right Bank 230–231
St-Germain-des-Prés 232–233
Wars of Religion 29
**waxwork museum 116**
WEATHER
rainfall and temperature 296
websites 296
Weber, Louise (La Goulue) 37, 87
website information 296, 310
Welles, Orson 16
Wilde, Oscar 88
windmills 108, 226, 227
*Winged Victory of Samothrace* 120
women visitors 305
Words and Phrases 311–316
World War II 39, 99, 107, 237


## Y


yoga 219–220
youth hostels 284, 285


## Z


Zadkine, Ossip 87
Zénith 147
Zola, Émile 87, 144, 169
Zoologique de Paris, Parc 237
Zoologique de Thoiry, Parc 221

# ACKNOWLEDGEMENTS

Abbreviations for the picture credits are as follows:
AA = AA World Travel Library, t (top), b (bottom), c (centre), l (left), r (right)

### UNDERSTANDING PARIS

**5l** AA/C Sawyer; **5c** AA/M Jourdan; **5r** AA/M Jourdan; **8l** AA/W Voysey; **8tr** AA/C Sawyer; **8ctr** AA/W Voysey; **8cbr** AA/C Sawyer; **8br** AA/C Sawyer; **9t** AA/C Sawyer; **9lt** AA/C Sawyer; **9ct** AA/C Sawyer; **9cb** Brasserie Lorraine; **9ub** AA/M Jourdan; **9b** Brand X Pictures; **9r** AA/M Jourdan; **10tl** AA/M Jourdan; **10tc** AA/J. Tims; **10tr** AA/M Jourdan; **10cl** AA/M Jourdan; **10bl** AA/T. Souter; **10ltr** AA/M. Chaplow; **10ucr** AA/C Sawyer; **10lcr** AA/P Kenward; **10ubr** AA/T. Souter; **10br** AA/M. Jourdan

### LIVING PARIS

**11** AA/K Paterson; **12/13b/g** AA/M Jourdan; **12tl** AA/M Jourdan; **12tc** AA/M Jourdan; **12tr** AA/C Sawyer; **12ctl** AA/M Jourdan; **12c** AA/B Rieger; **12cr** © "BE", Boulangepicier/Alain Ducasse. Photo: M. de L'Ecotais; **12cl** AA/B. Smith; **12bl** AA/C Sawyer; **13tl** AA/M Jourdan; **13tc** AA/M Jourdan; **13tr** AA/C Sawyer; **13cl** AA/T. Souter; **13cr** Courtesy Le Train Bleu; **13bl** Rex Features Ltd; **14/15** AA/K Paterson; **14tl** AA/M Jourdan; **14tc** AA/M Jourdan; **14tr** AA/B Rieger; **14ctl** AA/M Jourdan; **14c** AA/C Sawyer; **14cr** AA/M Jourdan; **14l** AA/B Rieger; **15tl** AA/M Jourdan; **15tr** AA/M Jourdan; **15cl** AA/P Kenward; **15c** AA/M Jourdan; **15cr** AA/M Jourdan; **15bl** AA/M Jourdan; **15r** Rex Features Ltd; **15b** Rex Features Ltd; **16/17b/g** AA/K Paterson; **16t** AA/J Tims; **16cl** AA/C Sawyer; **16c** AA/M Jourdan; **16cr** AA/J Tims; **16r** Rex Features Ltd; **16cl** AA/M Jourdan; **16bl** AA/M Jourdan; **17tl** AA/T. Souter; **17tc** AA/B Rieger; **17tr** AA/M Jourdan; **16/17** AA/J Tims; **17c** Courtesy Modus Publicity; **17cr** AA/M Jourdan; **18/19b/g** AA/M Jourdan; **18tl** Paramount/Kobal; **18tc** AA/K Paterson; **18tr** AA/T. Souter; **18cl** Rex Features Ltd; **18cr** AA; **18b** AA/M Jourdan; **19tl** Courtesy Club Med; **19c** AA/T. Souter; **19tr** AA/K Paterson; **19cr** AA/M Jourdan; **20/1b/g** AA/M Jourdan; **20tl** AA/M Jourdan; **20tr** AA/M Jourdan; **20cl** AA/K Paterson; **20cl** AA/K Paterson; **20cr** Courtesy Club Med; **21tl** AA/M Jourdan; **21tr** AA/C Sawyer; **21cl** AA/T. Souter; **21ctr** AA/M Jourdan; **21cr** AA/T. Souter; **21b** AA/M Jourdan; **22b/g** AA/C Sawyer; **22tl** AA; **22tr** AA/T. Souter; **22c** AA/M Jourdan; **22ctr** AA/M Jourdan; **22cr** AA/M Jourdan

### THE STORY OF PARIS

**23** AA; **24/5** AA; **24cl** AA/K Paterson; **24cr** AA; **24bl** AA; **25cl** AA/B Rieger; **25cr** AA; **25bl** Mary Evans Picture Library; **25br** AA; **26/7** AA/P Enticknap; **26cl** AA; **26cr** AA/P Enticknap; **26bl** AA; **26br** AA/J Tims; **27cl** Mary Evans Picture Library; **27cr** AA; **27bl** AA; **27bc** M. Jourdan; **27br** AA; **28cl** AA/D Noble; **28cr** Mary Evans Picture Library; **28bl** AA/D Noble; **28/9** Mary Evans Picture Library; **28/9b/g** AA/R Moore; **29cl** AA; **29cr** AA; **29bl** AA; **29c** AA; **29br** AA; **30/1** AA/D Noble; **30cl** AA/P Kenward; **30bl** AA/M Jourdan; **31cl** AA; **31c** AA; **31cr** AA; **31bc** AA; **31br** AA/M Jourdan; **32/3** AA; **32c** AA; **32bl** AA/P Kenward; **32/3** Mary Evans Picture Library; **33cl** AA; **33c** AA; **33cl** AA; **33bc** AA/K Paterson; **33br** Mary Evans Picture Library; **34/5** AA/M Jourdan; **34cl** AA; **34c** AA/J Tims; **34bl** AA; **35cl** AA; **35c** Mary Evans Picture Library; **35cr** AA; **35b** Mary Evans Picture Library; **36/7** AA; **36cl** AA/M Jourdan; **36bl** Illustrated London News; **36bc** AA/M Short; **36br** AA; **37cl** AA; **37c** Illustrated London News; **37cr** Illustrated London News; **37bl** AA; **37bc** AA/C Sawyer; **37br** Mary Evans Picture Library; **38/9** AA/C Sawyer; **38cl** AA; **38cr** Rex Features Ltd; **38bl** Illustrated London News; **38br** Hulton Archive/Getty Images; **38bc** *L'Apres Midi d'un Faune* by Debussy, Nijinsky's Faune costume, 1912 by Leon Bakst, Bibliotheque Nationale/Bridgeman Art Library; **39cl** Illustrated London News; **39c** Rex Features Ltd; **39tr** Rex Features Ltd; **39b** AA/C Sawyer; **39br** AA/K Paterson; **40b/g** AA/M Jourdan; **40cl** AA; **40cr** Rex Features Ltd; **40ubl** Rex Features Ltd; **40bl** AA/M Jourdan; **40br** Jean-Louis Margoche for www.parisrama.com, the Paris lover's website

### ON THE MOVE

**41** AA/K Paterson; **42/3** Digital Vision; **43** AA/C Sawyer; **44/45** Digital Vision; **44** AA/C Sawyer ; **45tl** AA/C Sawyer; **45b** AA/C Sawyer; **46t** Digital Vision; **46b** Digital Vision; **47t** AA/B Rieger; **47c** AA/C Sawyer; **48t** AA/B Rieger; **48b** AA/C Sawyer; **49t** AA/C Sawyer; **49r** AA/T Souter; **50/1t** AA/C Sawyer; **51** AA/C Sawyer; **52/3** AA/C Sawyer; **54/5** AA/M Jourdan; **54** AA/M Jourdan; **55** AA/M Jourdan; **56/7** Digital Vision; **56** AA/C Sawyer; **57cl** AA/C Sawyer; **57br** AA/C Sawyer; **58t** Digital Vision; **58cr** AA/K Paterson; **58br** AA; **59t** AA/M Jourdan; **59r** AA/M Jourdan; **60/1** Digital Vision; **60** AA/T Souter; **61** AA; **62** AA/S McBride; **63t** Digital Vision; **63b** AA/M Adelman; **64t** Digital Vision; **64r** AA/C Sawyer

### THE SIGHTS

**65** AA/J A Tims; **70l** AA/C Sawyer; **70r** AA/C Sawyer; **71l** AA/C Sawyer; **71r** AA/C Sawyer; **72l** AA/M Jourdan; **72r** AA/J Tims; **73l** AA/C Sawyer; **73r** AA/M Jourdan; **74l** AA/C Sawyer; **74r** AA/M Jourdan; **75l** AA/B Rieger; **75r** AA/C Sawyer; **76** AA/M Jourdan; **77t** AA/J Tims; **77cl** AA/K Paterson; **77cr** AA/M Jourdan; **77b** AA/P Kenward; **78cl** AA/K. Glendenning; **78c** AA/M Jourdan; **78cr** AA/J Tims; **78b** AA/M Jourdan; **79l** AA/M Jourdan; **79r** AA/M Jourdan; **80t** AA/M Jourdan; **80b** AA/P Kenward; **81tl** AA/M Jourdan; **81tr** AA/J Tims; **82t** AA/M Jourdan; **82cl** AA/M Jourdan; **82c** AA/M Jourdan; **82cr** AA/M Jourdan; **82b** AA/J Tims; **83** AA/T Souter; **84/5** AA/M Jourdan; **86** AA/M Jourdan; **87tl** AA/T Souter; **87tr** AA/C Sawyer; **87b** AA/C Sawyer; **88tr** AA/M Jourdan; **88l** AA/J Tims; **89t** AA/J Tims; **89c** AA/T Souter; **90/1** AA/T Souter; **90** AA/M Jourdan; **92l** AA/J Tims; **92c** AA/C Sawyer; **92r** AA/C Sawyer; **93l** AA/C Hatley with kind permission of the Fondation Cartier; **93r** AA/J Tims; **94t** AA/J Tims; **94l** AA/J Tims; **95t** AA; **95b** AA/M Jourdan; **96t** AA/B Rieger; **96c** AA/K Paterson; **96b** AA/M Jourdan; **97** AA/C Sawyer; **98t** AA/M Jourdan; **98b** AA/M Jourdan; **99t** AA/K Paterson; **99cl** AA/K Paterson; **99cr** AA/M Jourdan; **100l** AA; **100r** AA/B Rieger; **101t** AA/B Rieger; **102t** AA/P Enticknap; **102cl** AA/C Sawyer; **102c** AA/C Sawyer; **102cr** AA/M Jourdan; **102b** AA/M Jourdan; **103** AA/M Jourdan; **104t** AA/K Glendenning; **104l** AA/T Souter; **104b** AA/M Jourdan; **105t** AA/M Jourdan; **105r** AA/M Jourdan; **106l** AA/K Paterson; **106c** Gobelins tapestry, *Fin de Siecle de cinq a sept*, after Eduardo Arroyo (GOBT1336), Courtesy Collection du Mobilier National, cliché Mobilier National. Photo: Mobilier National – Isabelle Bideau; **106r** AA/J Tims; **107l** AA/K Paterson; **107r** AA/K Glendenning; **108t** AA/M Jourdan; **108l** AA/M Jourdan; **108r** AA/M Jourdan; **109l** AA/M Jourdan; **109r** AA/M Jourdan; **110t** AA/C Sawyer; **110b** AA/C Hatley; **111l** AA/P Enticknap; **111r** Courtesy Union Central des Arts Decoratifs. Photo: L. Sully Jaulmes; **112t** AA/M Jourdan; **112b** AA/M Jourdan; **113l** AA/K Glendenning; **113r** *View of the Canal of Santa Chiara, Venice* (oil on canvas) by Canaletto, Musee Cognacq-Jay, Paris/Bridgeman Art Library; **114t** AA/K Paterson; **114l** AA/M Jourdan; **114l** AA/J Tims; **115l** AA/M Jourdan; **115r** AA/K Paterson; **116l** AA/J Tims; **116r** Courtesy GREVIN Paris Wax Museum; **117l** AA/K Glendenning; **117r** AA/B Rieger; **117b** AA/P Kenward; **118** AA/M Jourdan; **119t** *Mona Lisa*, c.1503-6 (oil on panel) by Leonardo da Vinci, Louvre, Paris/Bridgeman Art Library; **119c** Egyptian papyrus, Louvre, Paris/Bridgeman Art Library; **119l** AA/T. Souter; **119r** AA/M Jourdan; **120** AA/J Tims; **121** AA/M Jourdan; **122/3t** AA/M Jourdan; **124t** *Promenade near Argenteuil*, 1873 (oil on canvas) by Claude Monet, Musee Marmottan, Paris, Bridgeman Art Library © ADAGP, Paris and DACS, London, 2004; **124c** *Impression: Sunrise, Le Havre*, 1872 (oil on canvas) by Claude Monet, Musee Marmottan, Paris, Bridgeman Art Library © ADAGP, Paris and DACS, London, 2004; **124b** Illuminated initial 'R', depicting St Catherine of Alexandria, c. 15th century by Luchino Belbello, Musee Marmottan, Paris, Giraudon/Bridgeman Art Library; **125** AA/J Tims, **126r** AA/J Tims, **126l** *Two Cranes on the edge of a Pond*, 17th century (w/c on paper) by Indian School, Musee Guimet, Paris/Bridgeman Art Library; **127l** AA/C Hatley; **127r** AA/J Tims; **127b** AA/C Hatley; **128t** AA/J Tims; **128l** *The Lady and the Unicorn: "Sight"*, 15th century (tapestry) by French School, Musee National du Moyen Age et des Thermes de Cluny, Paris/Bridgeman Art Library; **128c** Scene from the Old Testament, mid-13th century (stained glass) by French School, Musee National du Moyen Age et

des Thermes de Cluny, Paris/J.P.Zenobel/Bridgeman Art Library; **128r** AA/M Jourdan; **129** AA/K Paterson; **130t** *Ball at the Moulin de la Galette*, 1876 (oil on canvas) by Pierre Auguste Renoir, Musee d'Orsay, Paris/Giraudon/Bridgeman Art Library; **130l** AA/P Enticknap; **130c** *End of an Arabesque,* 1877 (oil & pastel on canvas) by Edgar Degas, Musee d'Orsay, Paris/Bridgeman Art Library; **130r** AA/J Tims; **131** AA/M Jourdan; **132t** AA/M Jourdan; **132b** AA/T Souter; **132/3** AA/M Jourdan; **133r** AA/M Jourdan; **133b** AA/M Jourdan; **133c** Dining room belonging to Adrien Benard at Champrosay, 1900-01 (photo) by Alexandre Charpentier, Musee d'Orsay, Paris/Bridgeman Art Library; **134b** AA/J A Tims; **135l** AA/M Jourdan; **135r** AA/M Jourdan © Succession Picasso/DACS 2004; **136** AA/M Jourdan; **137t** AA/K Paterson; **137l** AA/C Hatley; **137c** AA/M Jourdan; **137r** AA/P Enticknap; **138** AA/C Sawyer; **139l** AA/P Enticknap; **139c** AA/C Sawyer; **139r** AA/C Sawyer; **140/1** AA/C Sawyer; **141tr** AA/P Enticknap; **142t** AA; **142b** AA/M Jourdan; **143** AA/K Paterson; **144tl** AA/M Jourdan; **144tr** AA/J Tims; **144b** AA/M Jourdan; **145l** AA/K Paterson; **145r** AA/C Sawyer; **146** AA/M Jourdan; **147l** AA/T. Souter; **147c** AA/K Paterson; **147r** AA/M Jourdan; **148t** AA/M Jourdan; **148cl** AA/M Jourdan; **149tl** AA/M Jourdan; **149tc** AA/B Rieger; **149tr** AA/M Jourdan; **149b** AA/M Jourdan; **150t** AA/M Jourdan; **150cl** AA/B Rieger; **151tl** AA/M Jourdan; **151c** AA/M Jourdan; **151r** AA/T Souter; **152t** AA/C Sawyer; **152cl** AA/M Jourdan; **152c** AA/C Sawyer; **152cr** AA/C Sawyer; **153l** AA/M Jourdan; **153r** AA/M Jourdan; **154** Courtesy Sacre-Coeur de Montmartre; **155t** AA/B Rieger; **155cl** AA/K Paterson; **155c** AA/K Paterson; **155cr** AA/J Tims; **155b** AA/K Glendenning; **156/7** AA/K Paterson; **158** AA/J Tims; **159cl** AA/J Tims; **159t** Courtesy Centre des Monuments Nationaux; **159c** Courtesy Centre des Monuments Nationaux; **159cr** Courtesy Centre des Monuments Nationaux; **161l** AA/M Jourdan; **161r** AA/K Paterson; **162l** AA/K Glendenning; **162c** AA/K Glendenning; **162r** AA/C Sawyer; **163l** AA/C Sawyer; **163c** AA/M Jourdan; **163r** AA/T Souter; **164t** AA/M Jourdan; **164l** AA/M Jourdan; **164c** AA/B Rieger; **164r** AA/J Tims; **165** AA/J Tims; **166/7** AA/K Paterson; **168** AA/T Souter; **169** AA/M. Jourdan; **170t** AA/C Sawyer; **170cl** AA/C. Sawyer

### WHAT TO DO

**171** AA M Jourdan; **176t** AA/C Sawyer; **176c** AA/C Sawyer; **176l** AA/C Sawyer; **176r** AA/C Sawyer; **177l** AA/C Sawyer;**177r** AA/C Sawyer; **178l** AA/T Souter; **178r** AA/C Sawyer; **179l** AA/K Paterson; **179r** AA/M Jourdan; **180l** AA/C Sawyer; **180r** AA M Jourdan; **181l** AA/C Sawyer; **181r** AA/T Souter; **182/3t** AA/C Sawyer; **182c** AA/C Sawyer; **182c** Librairie Ulysse; **182b** AA/C Sawyer; **183cl** Bruno Synave/Virgin Stores; **183c** AA/C Sawyer; **183br** AA/C Sawyer; **184/5t** AA/C Sawyer; **184c** AA/B Rieger; **184br** AA/C Sawyer; **185c** AA/C Sawyer; **185cr** AA/C Sawyer; **186/7t** AA C/Sawyer; **186l** AA/C Sawyer; **187l** AA/C Sawyer; **187c** AA/C Sawyer; **187tr** AA/C Sawyer; **187b** AA/C Sawyer; **188/9t** AA/C Sawyer; **188l** AA/C Sawyer; **188tr** AA/C Sawyer; **188br** AA/C Sawyer; **189bl** AA/C Sawyer; **189ct** AA/C Sawyer; **189cb** AA/C Sawyer; **189br** AA/C Sawyer; **190/1t** AA/C Sawyer; **190** AA/C Sawyer; **192t** AA/C Sawyer; **192cl** Galeries Lafayette; **192c** AA/J A Tims; **192cr** AA/W Voysey; **193ct** Digital Vision; **193cb** AA/M Jourdan; **198/9t** AA/P Enticknap; **198c** AA/M Jourdan; **199bl** AA/K Paterson; **199c** AA/W Voysey; **199bc** AA/M Jourdan; **200/1t** Opera Comique; **200bl** AA/C Sawyer; **200bc** AA/B Rieger; **200br** AA/B Rieger; **201** AA/M Jourdan; **202/3t** Opera Comique;**202l** Opera Bastille; **202ct** Opera Comique; **202cb** AA/M Jourdan; **203** La Balle Au Bond; **204/5t** Elysee Monmartre; **204** Elysee Monmartre; **205cl** AA/W Voysey; **205b** Satellit Café; **206/7t** AA/K Paterson; **206bl** AA/P Kenward; **207** AA/B Rieger; **208t** AA/K Paterson; **208c** AA/T Souter; **209t** AA/T Souter; **209cl** Brand X Pics; **210/1t** AA/T Souter; **211cl** AA/C Sawyer; **211c** Favela Chic; **211cr** AA/K Paterson; **212/3t** AA T Souter; **212tl** Klein Holland; **212bl** Lizard Lounge; **213** AA/B Rieger; **214/5t** Brand X Pics; **215** Le Nouveau Casino/Luc Boegly; **216/7t** AA/K Paterson; **216b** Photodisc; **217r** France Montgolfières/R Short; **218/9t** AA/K Paterson; **218cl** Kart'in; **218cr** Atomik Paintball; **220** Printemps; **220cl** Printemps; **221t** AA/K Paterson; **221br** Parc Astérix; **222t** AA/M Lynch; **222c** AA/M Lynch

### OUT AND ABOUT

**223** AA M Jourdan; **224** AA/J Tims; **225t** AA/M Jourdan; **225bl** AA/B Rieger; **225br** AA/M Jourdan; **227t** AA/M Jourdan; **227bl** AA/M Jourdan; **227br** M. Jourdan; **228/9** AA/C Sawyer; **229tl** AA/C Sawyer; **229tr** AA/C Sawyer; **229br** AA/M Jourdan; **230b** AA/M Jourdan; **231tl** AA/K Paterson; **231tr** AA; **231bl** AA/M Jourdan; **231br** AA/M Jourdan; **233tl** AA/M Jourdan; **233tr** AA/M Jourdan; **233bl** AA/M Jourdan; **233cr** AA/M Jourdan; **234c** AA/M Jourdan; **234b** AA/B Rieger; **235** AA/M Jourdan; **236** AA/K Paterson; **237** AA/K Paterson; **238** AA/D. Noble; **239** AA/C Hatley; **240c** © Disney; **240cb** © Disney; **240/1** © Disney; **241** © Disney; **242** AA/M Jourdan; **243t** AA/M Jourdan; **243b** AA/M Jourdan; **244/5** AA/M Jourdan; **245** AA/M Jourdan; **246** AA/M Jourdan; **247** AA/M Jourdan; **248tl** AA/M Jourdan; **248tc** AA/M Jourdan; **248tr** AA/M Jourdan

### EATING

**249** AA/C Sawyer; **254cl** AA/C Sawyer; **254c** AA; **254cr** AA/C Sawyer; **255t** AA/e Meacher; **255b** AA B Smith; **256cl** AA/T Souter; **256c** AA M Jourdan; **256r** AA/M Jourdan; **257cl** AA/M Jourdan; **257c** AA/B Rieger; **257cr** AA/B Smith; **257br** Rex Features Ltd; **258cl** AA/E Meacher; **258c** AA/C Sawyer; **258r** AA/B Smith; **259cl** AA/C Sawyer; **259c** AA/T Souter; **259cr** AA/B Rieger; **260cl** AA/C Sawyer; **261bl** AA/C Sawyer; **261c** AA/C Sawyer; **261cr** AA/C Sawyer; **262cl** AA/C Sawyer; **263tc** AA/C Sawyer; **264cl** AA/C Sawyer; **264cc** AA/C Sawyer; **264tr** AA/C Sawyer; **264cr** AA/C Sawyer; **265bl** AA/C Sawyer; **265cr** AA/C Sawyer; **265br** AA/C Sawyer; **266cl** AA/C Sawyer; **266cc** AA/C Sawyer; **266br** AA/C Sawyer; **267cc** AA/C Sawyer; **267tr** AA/C Sawyer; **268tl** AA/C Sawyer; **268br** AA/C Sawyer; **269bl** AA; **269ctr** AA/C Sawyer; **269cbr** AA/C Sawyer; **270cl** AA/C Sawyer; **270c** AA/C Sawyer; **270ctl** AA/C Sawyer; **271cbl** AA/C Sawyer; **271c** AA/C Sawyer; **272cl** AA/C Sawyer; **272bl** AA; **272c** AA/C Sawyer; **272br** AA/C Sawyer; **273cl** AA/C Sawyer; **273bl** AA/C Sawyer; **273c** AA/C Sawyer; **274c** AA/C Sawyer; **274tr** AA/C Sawyer; **274br** AA/C Sawyer; **275tl** AA/C Sawyer; **275bl** AA/C Sawyer; **275c** AA/C Sawyer; 275bc AA/C Sawyer; **275cr** AA/C Sawyer; **276cl** AA/C Sawyer; **276bl** AA/C Sawyer; **276bc** AA/C Sawyer; **276cr** AA/C Sawyer; **277tc** AA/C Sawyer; **277b** AA/C Sawyer; **278cr** AA/C Sawyer; **278bl** AA/B Rieger; **278cbt** AA/C Sawyer; **278cbb** AA/C Sawyer; **278br** AA/T Souter

### STAYING

**279** AA/C Sawyer; **284cl** AA/C Sawyer; **284c** AA; **284cr** AA/C Sawyer; **285cl** AA/C Sawyer; **285cr** AA/C Sawyer; **286tl** AA/C Sawyer; **286c** AA/C Sawyer; **286cr** AA/C Sawyer; **286br** AA/C Sawyer; **287cl** AA/C Sawyer; **287bl** AA/C Sawyer; **287c** AA/C Sawyer; **287cr** AA/C Sawyer; **288cl** AA/C Sawyer; **288tc** AA/C Sawyer; **288tr** AA/C Sawyer; **288cr** AA/C Sawyer; **288c** AA/C Sawyer; **289tl** AA/C Sawyer; **289tc** AA/C Sawyer; **289cl** AA/C Sawyer; **289c** AA/C Sawyer; **289cr** AA/C Sawyer; **290cl** AA/C Sawyer; **290tc** AA/C Sawyer; **290tr** AA/C Sawyer; **290c** AA/C Sawyer; **290br** AA/C Sawyer; **291cl** AA/C Sawyer; **291c** AA/C Sawyer; **292bc** AA/C Sawyer; **292cr** AA/C Sawyer; **293tcl** AA/C Sawyer; **293bcl** AA/C Sawyer; **293tcc** AA/C Sawyer; **293bc** AA/C Sawyer; 293bl AA/C Sawyer

### PLANNING

**295** AA/C Sawyer; **299** AA/C Sawyer; **301l** AA/C Sawyer; **301r** AA/B Rieger; **305** AA/C Sawyer; **309** AA/M. Jourdan; **310** AA M Jourdan

The editors would like to thank Eurostar and the Paris Tourist Office for their assistance during the research for this book and acknowledge the contribution of Fiona Dunlop.

**Project editors**
Kathryn Glendenning, Cathy Hatley

**AA Travel Guides design team**
David Austin, Glyn Barlow, Alan Gooch, Kate Harling, Bob Johnson, Nick Otway, Carole Philp, Keith Russell

**Additional design work**
Nautilus Design, Jo Tapper

**Picture research**
Kathy Lockley, Carol Walker

**Internal repro work**
Michael Moody, Ian Little, Susan Crowhurst

**Production**
Lyn Kirby, Helen Sweeney

**Mapping**
Maps produced by the Cartography Department of AA Publishing

**Main contributors**
Lindsay Bennett, Heidi Ellison, Colin Follett, Kathryn Glendenning, Cathy Hatley, Elisabeth Morris, Michael Nation, Josephine Perry, Laurence Phillips, Andrew Sanger, The Content Works

**Copy editor**
Philippa Richmond

Published by AA Publishing, a trading name of Automobile Association Developments Limited, whose registered office is Southwood East, Apollo Rise, Farnborough, Hampshire, GU14 0JW. Registered number 1878835.

A CIP catalogue record for this book is available from the British Library.

ISBN 10: 0-7495-40087
ISBN 13: 978-0-7495-4008-1

All rights reserved. No part of this publication may be reproduced, stored in a retrieval system, or transmitted in any form or by any means, electronic, mechanical, photocopying, recording or otherwise, without the prior permission of the copyright owner.

**© Automobile Association Developments Limited 2004**
Reprinted June 2004, Jan 2005

Key Guide is a registered trademark in Australia and is used under license.
Binding style with plastic section dividers by permission of AA Publishing.

Colour separation by Keenes
Printed and bound by Leo, China

Find out more about AA Publishing and the wide range of travel publications and services the AA provides by visiting our website at www.theAA.com

A02508
Mapping in this title produced from Paris data © Tele Atlas N.V. 2003
& mapping © GEOnext (Gruppo De Agostini) Novara
Relief map images supplied by Mountain High Maps ® Copyright © 1993 Digital Wisdom, Inc
Weather chart statistics supplied by Weatherbase © Copyright 2003 Canty and Associates, LLC

**We believe the contents of this book are correct at the time of printing. However, some details, particularly prices, opening times and telephone numbers do change. We do not accept responsibility for any consequences arising from the use of this book. This does not affect your statutory rights. We would be grateful if readers would advise us of any inaccuracies they may encounter, or any suggestions they might like to make to improve the book. There is a form provided at the back of the book for this purpose, or you can email us at Keyguides@theaa.com/bookshop**

**COVER PICTURE CREDITS**

**Front Cover:** AA/P. Kenward
**Back Cover, top to bottom:** AA; AA/M. Jourdan; AA/B. Rieger; AA/C. Sawyer
**Spine** AA/P, Kenward

# Dear Key Guide Reader

**Thank you for buying Key Guide Paris.**
**Your comments and opinions are very important to us, so please help us to improve our travel guides by taking a few minutes to complete this questionnaire.**

*You do not need a stamp (unless posted outside the UK). If you do not want to cut this page from your guide, then photocopy it or write your answers on a plain sheet of paper.*

*Send to:* Key Guide Editor, AA World Travel Guides
FREEPOST SCE 4598, Basingstoke RG21 4GY

**ABOUT THIS GUIDE** Where did you buy it?_____

_____

When? _ _ month/ _ _ year

Why did you choose AA Key Guide Paris?

- ❑ Price
- ❑ AA Publication
- ❑ Used this series before; title_____
- ❑ Cover
- ❑ Other_____

_____

Please rate how helpful the following features of the guide are to you: very helpful (**VH**), helpful (**H**) or little help (**LH**)

| | | | |
|---|---|---|---|
| Size | **VH** | **H** | **LH** |
| Layout | **VH** | **H** | **LH** |
| Photos | **VH** | **H** | **LH** |
| Excursions | **VH** | **H** | **LH** |
| Entertainment | **VH** | **H** | **LH** |
| Hotels | **VH** | **H** | **LH** |
| Maps | **VH** | **H** | **LH** |
| Practical info | **VH** | **H** | **LH** |
| Restaurants | **VH** | **H** | **LH** |
| Shopping | **VH** | **H** | **LH** |
| Walks | **VH** | **H** | **LH** |
| Sights | **VH** | **H** | **LH** |
| Transport info | **VH** | **H** | **LH** |

*continued on next page*

What was your favourite sight, attraction or feature listed in the guide?

Page _____

Please give your reason _____

_____

Which features in the guide could be changed or improved, or any other comment you would like to make:

_____

_____

**ABOUT YOU**

Name (*Mr/Mrs/Ms*) _____

Address _____

_____

_____ Postcode _____

Daytime tel nos _____

Which age group are you in?

Under 25 ❑ 25–34 ❑ 35–44 ❑ 45–54 ❑ 55+ ❑

How many trips do you make a year?

Less than one ❑ One ❑ Two ❑ Three or more ❑

Are you an AA member? Yes ❑ No ❑

**ABOUT YOUR TRIP**

When did you book? _ _ month/_ _ year

When did you travel? _ _ month/_ _ year

Were you travelling for business or leisure? _____

How many nights did you stay? _____

How did you travel?

Individual ❑ Couple ❑ Family ❑ Group ❑

Did you buy any other travel guides for your trip? _____

If yes, which ones? _____

_____

_____

Thank you for taking the time to complete this questionnaire. Please send it to us as soon as possible, and remember, you do not need a stamp (*unless posted outside the UK*).

The AA and the Automobile Association Limited, their subsidiaries and any other companies or bodies in which either has an interest ('the AA Group') may use information about you to provide you with details of other products and services, by telephone or in writing. The AA Group as a matter of policy does not release its lists to third parties.

If you do not wish to receive further information please tick the box ❑

FRIDAY